THEORY OF NETS:
FLOWS IN NETWORKS

THEORY OF NETS: FLOWS IN NETWORKS

Wai-Kai Chen
Professor

*Department of Electrical Engineering
and Computer Science
University of Illinois at Chicago
Chicago, Illinois*

WILEY

A Wiley-Interscience Publication

JOHN WILEY & SONS

New York / Chichester / Brisbane / Toronto / Singapore

Library of Congress Cataloging-in-Publication Data:

Chen, Wai-Kai, 1936–
    Theory of nets: flows in networks/Wai-Kai Chen.
        p.   cm.
    "A Wiley-Interscience publication."
    Includes bibliographical references.
    1. Networks analysis (Planning) 2. Graph theory. I. Title.
    T57.85.C44   1990
    658.4'032—dc20   89-16721
                                                          CIP

ISBN 0-471-85148-5

Printed in the United States of America

10 9 8 7 6 5 4 3 2 1

CONTENTS

Preface   ix

1 Graphs and Networks   1

   1.1 Basic Definitions of Abstract Graphs, 1
   1.2 Operations on Graphs, 10
   1.3 Nonseparable Graphs and Bipartite Graphs, 14
   1.4 Planar Graphs, 18
   1.5 Dual Graphs, 36
   1.6 2-Isomorphism, 48
   1.7 Matrices Associated with a Graph, 52
      1.7.1 Incidence Matrix, 53
      1.7.2 Circuit Matrix, 57
      1.7.3 Cut Matrix, 63
      1.7.4 Interrelationships Among the Matrices $\mathbf{A}$, $\mathbf{B}_f$ and $\mathbf{Q}_f$, 70
      1.7.5 Node-to-Datum Path Matrix, 71
   1.8 Directed Graphs, 74
      1.8.1 Matrices Associated with a Directed Graph, 81
      1.8.2 Interrelationships Among the Matrices, 89
      1.8.3 Some Important Classes of Directed Graphs, 91
   1.9 The Circuit Matrix Associated with a Planar Graph or Directed Graph, 93
   1.10 Summary and Suggested Reading, 96
   References, 97

v

2   The Shortest Directed Path Problem   **99**

2.1   Shortest Directed Paths, 100
2.2   Shortest Directed Path Algorithms, 103
    2.2.1   Dijkstra Algorithm, 103
    2.2.2   Ford–Moore–Bellman Algorithm, 113
    2.2.3   Yen Algorithm, 122
    2.2.4   Ford–Fulkerson Algorithm, 130
2.3   Multiterminal Shortest Directed Paths, 139
    2.3.1   Matrix Algorithm, 139
    2.3.2   Floyd–Warshall Algorithm, 146
2.4   Enumeration of the Shortest Directed Paths by Decomposition, 153
2.5   Summary and Suggested Reading, 160
References, 162

3   Maximum Flows in Networks   **167**

3.1   Flows, 167
3.2 s–t Cuts, 170
3.3   Maximum Flow, 177
3.4   Ford–Fulkerson Algorithm, 184
    3.4.1   Integrity Theorem, 191
    3.4.2   Irrational Arc Capacities, 192
3.5   Layered Nets, 197
3.6   A Blocking Flow Algorithm, 205
3.7   Variants of the Ford–Fulkerson Algorithm, 215
    3.7.1   Edmonds–Karp Algorithm, 216
    3.7.2   Dinic Algorithm, 220
    3.7.3   Other Variations, 221
3.8   Karzanov Algorithm, 223
3.9   Flows in Undirected and Mixed Nets, 229
3.10 Flows in Node-and-Arc Capacitated Nets, 231
3.11 Summary and Suggested Reading, 233
References, 236

4   Minimum Trees and Communication Nets   **240**

4.1   Forests, Subtrees and Trees, 241
4.2   Minimum and Maximum Trees, 246
4.3   Minimum and Maximum Tree Algorithms, 252
    4.3.1   Borůvka Algorithm, 254
    4.3.2   Kruskal Algorithm, 259
    4.3.3   Prim Algorithm, 261
    4.3.4   General Remarks, 265
4.4   Terminal Capacity Matrix, 266

4.5   Synthesis of a Flow-Equivalent Tree, 275
    4.5.1   Gomory–Hu Algorithm, 280
    4.5.2   Proof of the Gomory–Hu Algorithm, 290
4.6   Synthesis of Optimum Undirected Communication Nets, 293
    4.6.1   Gomory–Hu Procedure, 297
    4.6.2   Dominant Flow Realization, 303
4.7   Oriented Communication Nets, 308
4.8   Summary and Suggested Reading, 314
References, 315

5   Feasibility Theorems and Their Applications   **318**

5.1   A Supply–Demand Theorem, 318
5.2   An Extended Supply–Demand Theorem, 335
5.3   Circulation Theorem, 345
5.4   Feasible Circulation Algorithm, 357
5.5   Flows in Nets with Lower Bounds on Arcs, 366
5.6   Feasible Flows in Node-and-Arc Capacitated Nets, 372
5.7   Summary and Suggested Reading, 383
References, 385

6   Applications of Flow Theorems to Subgraph Problems   **386**

6.1   The Subgraph Problem of a Directed Graph, 386
6.2   Digraphic Sequences, 413
6.3   The Subgraph Problem of a Graph, 432
6.4   Graphical Sequences, 441
6.5   The (p, s)-Matrix, 449
6.6   Realization of the 1-Matrix and the $(1, 0)$-Matrix, 463
6.7   Minimal Transformations, 469
6.8   Summary and Suggested Reading, 480
References, 482

Index   **485**

PREFACE

Flow net theory has developed considerably since beginnings in the 1950's. It has been used widely in electrical engineering, computer science, social science, and in the solution of economic problems. The fact is that any system involving a binary relation can be represented by a network. The book presents a unified treatment of the fundamental theory of networks such as the telephone network, the pipeline network, the power grid, and the airline network involving the communication, transmission, transportation, flow, or movement of commodities through a network. It discusses the underlying problems, properties common to all these networks, and techniques for their solution. The guiding principle throughout the book has been mathematical precision. Thus, nearly all the assertions are rigorously proved; many of these proofs are believed to be new and novel. Furthermore, algorithms that are computationally efficient are included. All basic concepts are defined and many examples are included to illustrate them. Hence, no prior background in networks is required.

There are six chapters in the book. Chapter 1 establishes the basic vocabulary for describing graphs and networks and provides a number of results that are needed in the subsequent analysis. Thus, the reader is urged to study the convention of this chapter carefully before proceeding to the other chapters. Chapter 2 gives a fairly complete exposition of the shortest directed path problem. Chapter 3 studies the problem of maximizing flow from one point to another in a capacity-constrained network. From our viewpoint, this is the most fundamental problem dealt with in the book. Its solution provides answers to many other feasibility and combinatorial questions. Chapter 4 considers the minimum tree problem and extends the terminal pair flow to multiterminal flow. The applications of the flow theorems to feasibility and subgraph problems are taken up in Chapters 5 and 6.

The material presented in the book has been classroom-tested at the University of Illinois at Chicago for the past several years. There is little difficulty in fitting the book into a one-semester or one-quarter course. For example, the first five chapters contain material suitable for a one-semester course, whereas the first four chapters are suitable for a one-quarter course. The presentation and organization of the book are such that it is also suitable for individual study by practicing engineers and computer scientists.

I am indebted to many of my students over the years who participated in testing the material of this book. Special thanks are due to my doctoral students Hui Tang and Yang Liu and visiting scholar Hui-Yun Wang of Tianjin University, who gave the manuscript a careful and critical reading. Ms. Tang also assisted me in preparing the index and proofread the entire manuscript with the help of Mr. Yang Liu. Finally, I express my appreciation to my wife, Shiao-Ling and children, Jerome and Melissa, for their patience and understanding during the preparation of the book.

WAI-KAI CHEN

Chicago, Illinois

THEORY OF NETS:
FLOWS IN NETWORKS

1

GRAPHS AND NETWORKS

Many physical networks such as the telephone network, the pipeline network, the power grid, and the airline network involving the communication, transmission, transportation, flow, or the movement of commodities through a network can be modeled by an intuitive diagrammatic representation called a *graph*. The graphs that we are about to discuss are simple geometrical figures consisting of nodes or points and edges or lines that connect some of these nodes. They are sometimes called *linear graphs*. The purpose of this chapter is to establish the basic vocabulary for describing graphs and provide a number of basic results that are needed in the subsequent analysis.

1.1 BASIC DEFINITIONS OF ABSTRACT GRAPHS

An *abstract graph* $G(V, E)$ or simply a *graph* G consists of a set V of elements called *nodes* and a set E of *unordered* pairs of the form (i, j) or (j, i), $i, j \in V$, called *edges*. Other names commonly used for a node are *vertex, point, junction, 0-simplex, 0-cell,* and *element*; and for an edge *line, branch, arc, 1-simplex,* and *element*. We say that the edge (i, j) is *connected* between the nodes i and j, and that (i, j) is *incident* with the nodes i and j, or conversely that i and j are *incident* with (i, j). In applications, a graph is usually represented equivalently by a *geometric diagram* in which the nodes are indicated by small circles or dots, while any two of them, i and j, are joined by a continuous curve, or even a straight line, between i and j, if and only if (i, j) is in E.

In many situations, it is convenient to permit a pair of nodes to be connected by several distinct edges called *parallel edges*. The parallel edges between the nodes i and j are denoted by the symbols $(i, j)_1, (i, j)_2, \ldots, (i, j)_k, k \geqq 2$. If no particular edge is specified, the symbol (i, j) is used to denote any one of them connected between i and j. Nodes i and j are called the *endpoints* of (i, j). We also admit edges for which the two endpoints are identical. Such an edge (i, i) is called a *self-loop*. If there are two or more self-loops at a node, they are also referred to as the *parallel edges*. In a geometric diagram, the parallel edges may be represented by continuous lines connected between the same pair of nodes, and a self-loop (i, i) may be introduced as a circular arc returning to the node i and passing through no other nodes.

As an example, consider the graph $G(V, E)$ in which

$$V = \{1, 2, 3, 4, 5, 6, 7, 8\} \tag{1.1}$$

$$E = \{(1, 2), (3, 4), (3, 5), (3, 6), (4, 5), (4, 6)_1, (4, 6)_2,$$
$$(3, 3)_1, (3, 3)_2, (6, 6), (7, 8)_1, (7, 8)_2, (7, 8)_3\} \tag{1.2}$$

The corresponding geometric graph is shown in Fig. 1.1, in which there is a self-loop at node 6, two self-loops at node 3, two parallel edges between nodes 4 and 6, and three parallel edges between nodes 7 and 8. We emphasize that in a graph the order of the nodes i and j in (i, j) is immaterial. We consider $(i, j) = (j, i)$, e.g. $(1, 2) = (2, 1)$ and $(7, 8)_1 = (8, 7)_1$.

A graph $G(V, E)$ is said to be *finite* if both V and E are finite sets. In this book, we deal only with finite graphs. Infinite graphs have some very interesting properties. For interested readers, we refer to König (1950) and Ore (1962).

A *subgraph* of a graph $G(V, E)$ is a graph $G_s(V_s, E_s)$ in which V_s and E_s are subsets of V and E, respectively. If V_s or E_s is a proper subset, the subgraph is called a *proper subgraph*. If $V_s = V$, the subgraph is said to be a

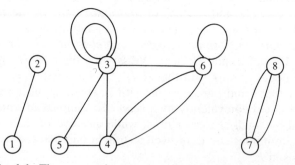

Fig. 1.1. The geometric representation of an abstract graph.

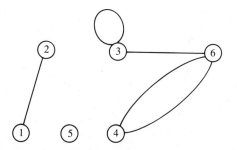

Fig. 1.2(a). A subgraph of the graph in Fig. 1.1 containing an isolated node, node 5.

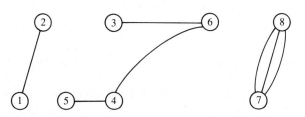

Fig. 1.2(b). A spanning subgraph of the graph of Fig. 1.1.

spanning subgraph of G. If V_s or E_s is empty, the subgraph is the *null graph* and is denoted by the symbol ∅. The null graph is considered as a subgraph of every graph. An *isolated node* is a node not incident with any edge.

Some examples of subgraphs of the graph of Fig. 1.1 are presented in Fig. 1.2. Fig. 1.2(a) is a subgraph containing an isolated node 5, and Fig. 1.2(b) is a spanning subgraph since it contains all the nodes of the given graph. Both subgraphs in Fig. 1.2 are examples of proper subgraphs.

We say that two subgraphs are *edge-disjoint* if they have no edges in common, and *node-disjoint* if they have no nodes in common. Thus, two subgraphs are node-disjoint only if they are edge-disjoint, but the converse is not always true. For our purposes, a subgraph will be represented by the juxtaposition of its edges if it does not contain any isolated nodes. For example, in Fig. 1.1 the subgraphs

$$G_1 = (1, 2)(3, 3)_1(3, 6)(6, 6) \qquad (1.3a)$$

$$G_2 = (4, 5)(7, 8)_1(7, 8)_2 \qquad (1.3b)$$

as shown in Fig. 1.3 are node-disjoint, and thus they are also edge-disjoint. On the other hand, the subgraphs of Figs. 1.2(a) and 1.3(b) are edge-disjoint but they are not node-disjoint.

In a graph G we say that the nodes i and j are *adjacent* if (i, j) is an edge of G. All the nodes adjacent to a node i are the *neighboring nodes* of i. If G_s

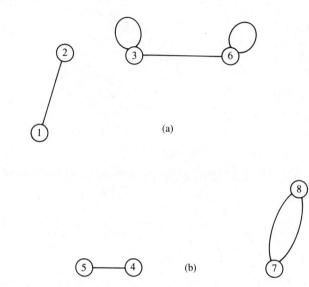

Fig. 1.3. Two node-disjoint subgraphs of the graph of Fig. 1.1: (a) G_1; (b) G_2.

is a subgraph of G, by the *complement* $\bar{G}_s$ of G_s in G we mean the subgraph of G consisting of all the edges $\bar{E}_s$ that do not belong to G_s and all the nodes of G except those that are in G_s but not in $\bar{E}_s$. Clearly, G_s and $\bar{G}_s$ are edge-disjoint but not necessarily node-disjoint, and their node sets may not be complementary. Thus, the complement of the null graph in G is the graph G itself, and the complement of G in G is the null graph. We say that G_s and $\bar{G}_s$ are the *complementary subgraphs* of G. For example, the subgraphs shown in Fig. 1.4 are complementary subgraphs of the graph of Fig. 1.1.

In the above discussion, we indicated that a graph can be represented by a geometric diagram. However, in drawing the diagram, we have a great deal of freedom in the choice of the location of the nodes and in the form of the lines joining them. This may make the diagrams of the same graph look entirely different. In such situations we would like to have a precise way of saying that two graph diagrams are really the same even though they are drawn or labeled differently. The following term provides the necessary terminology for this purpose.

DEFINITION 1.1

Isomorphism. Two graphs G_1 and G_2 are said to be *isomorphic*, written as $G_1 = G_2$, if there exists a one-to-one correspondence between the elements of their node sets and a one-to-one correspondence between the elements of their edge sets and such that the corresponding edges are incident with the corresponding nodes.

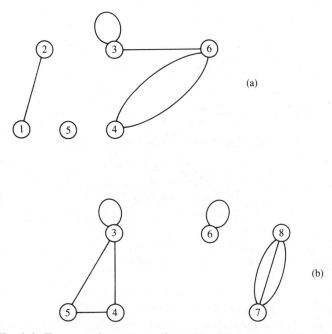

Fig. 1.4. Two complementary subgraphs of the graph of Fig. 1.1.

Thus, in two isomorphic graphs the corresponding nodes are connected by the edges in one if and only if they are also connected by the same number of edges in the other. The definition places two requirements on isomorphism of two graphs. First, they must have the same number of nodes and edges. Second, the incidence relationships must be preserved. The latter is usually difficult to establish.

The two graphs $G_1(V_1, E_1)$ and $G_2(V_2, E_2)$ shown in Fig. 1.5 look quite different, but they are isomorphic. The isomorphism of these two graphs

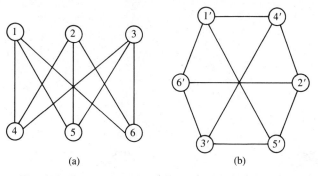

Fig. 1.5. Two isomorphic graphs G_1 (a) and G_2 (b).

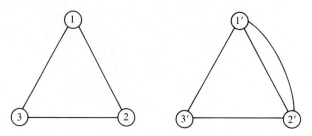

Fig. 1.6. Two nonisomorphic graphs.

can be established by considering the nodes $i \in V_1$ and $i' \in V_2$ ($i = 1, 2, 3, 4, 5, 6$) to be the corresponding elements of their node sets. It is straightforward to verify that the corresponding edges are incident with the corresponding nodes. In other words, the incidence relationships are preserved. However, the two graphs of Fig. 1.6 are not isomorphic even though there exists a one-to-one correspondence between their node sets which preserves adjacency.

A *labeled graph* is a graph in which the nodes or edges of the graph are properly labeled. In this book, the terms *graph* and *labeled graph* are used as synonyms. The graphs that we have witnessed so far are all labeled graphs, the nodes being labeled by the integers $1, 2, \ldots,$ or $1', 2', \ldots$. A *weighted graph* is a graph in which either the edges or the nodes or both are assigned weights. The graph of Fig. 1.7 is an example of a labeled weighted graph, where the nodes are labeled by the integers $1, 2, 3, 4, 5$ and the edges are assigned weights which may represent, for example, distances between the nodes.

DEFINITION 1.2

Edge Sequence. An *edge sequence of length $k - 1$* in a graph G is a finite
   sequence of edges of the form

$$(i_1, i_2), (i_2, i_3), \ldots, (i_{k-1}, i_k) \tag{1.4}$$

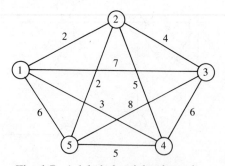

Fig. 1.7. A labeled weighted graph.

$k \geqq 2$, in G. The edge sequence is said to be *closed* if $i_1 = i_k$, and *open* otherwise. In an open edge sequence, the node i_1 is called the *initial node*, and the node i_k is the *terminal node*; together they are called the *endpoints*. All the other nodes are the *internal nodes*.

In an edge sequence, not all the nodes are necessarily distinct and the same edge may appear several times. In Fig. 1.7, for example, the sequence of edges

$$(1, 2), (2, 4), (4, 2), (2, 3), (3, 5), (5, 3), (3, 4) \tag{1.5}$$

is an open edge sequence of length 7. Node 1 is the initial node and node 4 is the terminal node of the edge sequence. Likewise, the edge sequence

$$(5, 2), (2, 4), (4, 3), (3, 4), (4, 1), (1, 5) \tag{1.6}$$

is a closed edge sequence of length 6.

We say that the edge sequence (1.4) is *connected* between its initial and terminal nodes or between the nodes i_1 and i_k, and that for $k > 2$, (i_{x-1}, i_x) and (i_x, i_{x+1}), $1 < x < k$, are *successive edges* in the sequence. An isolated node is considered to be an edge sequence of zero length.

DEFINITION 1.3

Edge Train. If all the edges appearing in an edge sequence are distinct, the edge sequence is called an *edge train*.

Thus, an edge train can go through a node more than once but cannot retrace parts of itself, as an edge sequence can. An example of an edge train in Fig. 1.7 is given by

$$(1, 2), (2, 4), (4, 3), (3, 5), (5, 4) \tag{1.7}$$

The edge train is open and is of length 5. If, in addition, all the nodes in an edge train are distinct except the initial and the terminal nodes, we have the usual concepts of a path and a circuit.

DEFINITION 1.4

Path. An open edge train as shown in (1.4) is called a *path of length $k - 1$* if all the nodes $i_1, i_2, \ldots, i_k$ are distinct. An isolated node is considered as a path of zero length.

DEFINITION 1.5

Circuit. A closed edge train as shown in (1.4) is called a *circuit of length $k - 1$* if $i_1 = i_k$ and all the nodes $i_1, i_2, \ldots, i_{k-1}$ are distinct.

Therefore, a self-loop is a circuit of length 1. In the literature, the term *circuit* is also frequently referred to as a *cycle* or *loop*. In Fig. 1.7, the open edge train

$$(1, 2), (2, 4), (4, 5), (5, 3) \qquad (1.8)$$

is a path of length 4, and the closed edge train

$$(1, 2), (2, 4), (4, 5), (5, 3), (3, 1) \qquad (1.9)$$

is a circuit of length 5.

DEFINITION 1.6
Connectedness. A graph is said to be *connected* if there is a path between every pair of its nodes.

Intuitively speaking, a graph is connected if it has only one piece. The graphs in Figs. 1.5(a), 1.5(b) and 1.7 are examples of connected graphs, and the one shown in Fig. 1.1 is not connected.

DEFINITION 1.7
Component. A *component* of a graph is a connected subgraph containing the maximal number of edges. An isolated node is a component.

As a result, if a graph is not connected it must contain a number of components. One or many of these components may each consist of an isolated node. For example, in Fig. 1.2(a) the graph has three components, one of which is an isolated node.

DEFINITION 1.8
Rank. The *rank r* of a graph with n nodes and c components is defined as the number $r = n - c$. The rank of the null graph is zero.

DEFINITION 1.9
Nullity. The *nullity m* of a graph with b edges, n nodes, and c components is defined as the number $m = b - n + c$ ($= b - r$). The nullity of the null graph is zero.

Rank and nullity are two numbers that are frequently encountered in graph theory. The term *nullity* is also known by the names of *circuit rank*, *cyclomatic number, cycle rank, connectivity,* and *first Betti number.* We notice that all these numbers are nonnegative, as can be seen from the following theorem.

THEOREM 1.1

The rank and nullity of a graph are both nonnegative. A graph is of nullity 0 if and only if it contains no circuits, and is of nullity 1 if and only if it contains a single circuit.

It is straightforward to verify that the rank and nullity of an unconnected graph are simply the sums of the ranks and nullities of its components, respectively.

DEFINITION 1.10
Degree. The *degree* of a node i of a graph, denoted by $d(i)$, is the number of edges incident with the node i.

Thus, an isolated node is a node of zero degree. Because each edge is incident with two nodes, it contributes 2 to the sum of the degrees of the nodes, giving

$$\sum_{i=1}^{n} d(i) = 2b \tag{1.10}$$

THEOREM 1.2

The sum of the degrees of the nodes of a graph is twice the number of its edges.

If V_1 and V_2 are the sets of nodes having odd and even degrees of a graph, then the left-hand side of the equation

$$\sum_{i=1}^{n} d(i) - \sum_{j\in V_2} d(j) = \sum_{k\in V_1} d(k) \tag{1.11}$$

is always even. This establishes the following result.

COROLLARY 1.1

The number of nodes of odd degree of a graph is always even.

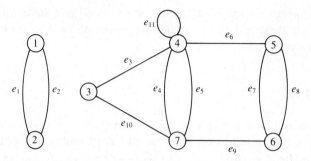

Fig. 1.8. A graph used to illustrate rank, nullity, and degree.

The graph G of Fig. 1.8 is of rank 5 $(=7-2)$ and of nullity 6 $(=11-7+2)$. The degrees of its nodes are given as follows:

$$d(1) = 2, \qquad d(2) = 2, \qquad d(3) = 2, \qquad d(4) = 6,$$
$$d(5) = 3, \qquad d(6) = 3, \qquad d(7) = 4 \tag{1.12}$$

showing that

$$\sum_{i=1}^{7} d(i) = 2+2+2+6+3+3+4 = 22 = 2 \times 11 \tag{1.13}$$

The nodes of odd degree are nodes 5 and 6, confirming that the number of nodes of odd degree is even, being 2.

1.2 OPERATIONS ON GRAPHS

In this section, we define a number of operations on graphs that are useful in expressing the structure of a given graph in terms of smaller or simpler graphs. We already have introduced the notion of the complement of a subgraph.

By the *removal of a node i* from a graph G we mean the operation that results in the subgraph consisting of all the nodes of G except i and all the edges not incident with i. In other words, it is the subgraph containing all the nodes and edges not incident with i. Likewise, the *removal of an edge* (i, j) from G yields the subgraph containing all the nodes and edges of G except the edge (i, j). The removal of a set of nodes or edges is a series of operations that remove the single elements of the set in succession.

Four set-theoretic binary operations *union, intersection, difference,* and *ring sum* represented by $\cup$, $\cap$, $-$, and $\oplus$, respectively, will be defined. They are used in two slightly different contexts. For example, if S_1 and S_2 are two sets, then $S_1 \cup S_2$ denotes the set consisting of all the elements which

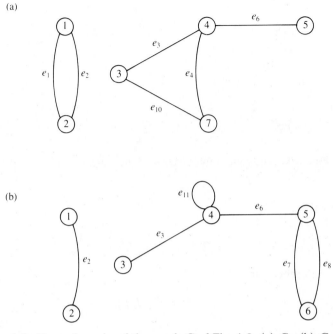

Fig. 1.9. Two subgraphs of the graph G of Fig. 1.8: (a) G_1; (b) G_2.

are either in S_1 or in S_2 or in both. If $G_1(V_1, E_1)$ and $G_2(V_2, E_2)$ are two subgraphs of a graph $G(V, E)$, then $G_1 \cup G_2$ represents the subgraph of G with node set $V_1 \cup V_2$ and edge set $E_1 \cup E_2$. The set $S_1 \cup S_2$ is the *set union* of S_1 and S_2, whereas $G_1 \cup G_2$ is called the *sum graph* of G_1 and G_2. Likewise, the *intersection* $S_1 \cap S_2$ of S_1 and S_2 is the set consisting of all the elements which are in both S_1 and S_2. The *intersection graph* $G_1 \cap G_2$ of G_1 and G_2 is the subgraph of G with the node set $V_1 \cap V_2$ and the edge set $E_1 \cap E_2$. Clearly, these operations can be extended to an arbitrary family of subgraphs.

Two subgraphs G_1 and G_2 of the graph G of Fig. 1.8 are shown in Fig. 1.9. The sum graph $G_1 \cup G_2$ of G_1 and G_2 is presented in Fig. 1.10, whereas the intersection graph $G_1 \cap G_2$ is as indicated in Fig. 1.11.

The *difference* $S_1 - S_2$ of the sets S_1 and S_2 is the set consisting of all the elements that are in S_1 but not in S_2. The *ring sum* $S_1 \oplus S_2$ of the sets S_1 and S_2 is the set consisting of all the elements that are either in S_1 or in S_2 but not in both. The ring sum is also known as the *symmetric difference*, because it is the difference between the union and intersection of S_1 and S_2:

$$S_1 \oplus S_2 = (S_1 \cup S_2) - (S_1 \cap S_2) \qquad (1.14)$$

For example, the ring sum of the sets $S_1 = \{a, b, c, d, e, f\}$ and $S_2 =$

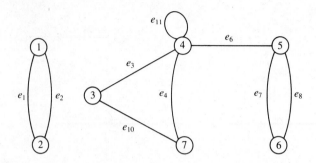

Fig. 1.10. The sum graph $G_1 \cup G_2$ of the subgraphs of Fig. 1.9.

$\{a, c, e, h\}$ is given by

$$S_1 \oplus S_2 = \{b, d, f, h\} \tag{1.15}$$

and their differences are

$$S_1 - S_2 = \{b, d, f\} \tag{1.16a}$$

$$S_2 - S_1 = \{h\} \tag{1.16b}$$

Observe that the order in performing the difference operation is important.

Likewise, if G_1 and G_2 are two subgraphs of G not containing any isolated nodes, then by $G_1 - G_2$ we mean the subgraph consisting of all the edges of G_1 that are not in G_2, and $G_1 \oplus G_2$ is the subgraph consisting of all the edges that are either in G_1 or in G_2 but not in both. In particular, we have

$$G_1 \oplus \varnothing = \varnothing \oplus G_1 = G_1 \tag{1.17}$$

Consider, for example, two subgraphs G_1 and G_2 of the labeled graph G of Fig. 1.8. The subgraphs are denoted by the juxtaposition of their edge labels

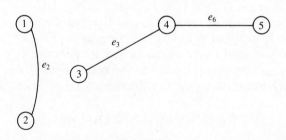

Fig. 1.11. The intersection graph $G_1 \cap G_2$ of the subgraphs of Fig. 1.9.

as

$$G_1 = e_1 e_2 e_3 e_4 e_6 e_{10} \qquad (1.18a)$$

$$G_2 = e_2 e_3 e_6 e_7 e_8 e_{11} \qquad (1.18b)$$

giving

$$G_1 - G_2 = e_1 e_2 e_3 e_4 e_6 e_{10} - e_2 e_3 e_6 e_7 e_8 e_{11} = e_1 e_4 e_{10} \qquad (1.19a)$$

$$G_2 - G_1 = e_2 e_3 e_6 e_7 e_8 e_{11} - e_1 e_2 e_3 e_4 e_6 e_{10} = e_7 e_8 e_{11} \qquad (1.19b)$$

$$G_1 \oplus G_2 = G_2 \oplus G_1 = e_1 e_4 e_7 e_8 e_{10} e_{11} \qquad (1.19c)$$

We emphasize that the difference and ring-sum operations of two subgraphs are defined only for those subgraphs containing no isolated nodes. In terms of the difference operation, the removal of an edge e_i from a graph G is equivalent to the operation $G - e_i$, which may involve an ambiguity of an isolated node.

THEOREM 1.3

The ring sum of two circuits is a circuit or an edge-disjoint union of circuits.

THEOREM 1.4

The set of circuits and edge-disjoint unions of circuits of a graph is an abelian group under the ring-sum operation.

The proofs of these two theorems are straightforward, and are omitted.

Let (i, j) be an edge of a graph G. By *shorting the edge* (i, j) of G we mean the operation that first removes the edge (i, j) and then identifies the nodes i and j in the resulting graph. The operation may result in additional self-loops. In particular, the removal of a self-loop from G is equivalent to the operation of shorting the self-loop. In Fig. 1.8 the shorting of the edge $e_4 = (4, 7)_1$ results in the graph shown in Fig. 1.12 containing two self-loops.

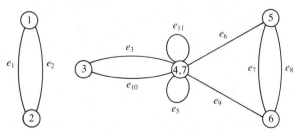

Fig. 1.12. The resulting graph after shorting the edge $(4, 7)_1$ in the graph of Fig. 1.8.

DEFINITION 1.11

Sectional Subgraph. The *sectional subgraph* induced by a subset V_s of the node set of a graph, denoted by $G[V_s]$, is the subgraph whose node set is V_s and whose edge set consists of all those edges of G connecting two nodes of V_s.

The term *sectional subgraph* is frequently referred to as the *induced subgraph*. It is the maximal subgraph of G with the node set V_s, and can be obtained from G by the removal of all the nodes that are not in V_s. Thus, two nodes of V_s in $G[V_s]$ are adjacent if and only if they are adjacent in G. When $V_s = V$, the node set of G, the sectional subgraph is G itself, i.e. $G[V] = G$. For a single node $V_s = \{i\}$, $G[V_s]$ is either the null graph or the subgraph consisting of all the self-loops at node i.

For the graph G of Fig. 1.8, the sectional subgraph $G[V_s]$ induced by the subset $V_s = \{1, 2, 3, 4, 7\}$ is presented in Fig. 1.13. In terms of edge-designation symbols, we have

$$G[V_s] = e_1 e_2 e_3 e_4 e_5 e_{10} e_{11} \tag{1.20}$$

On the other hand, the subgraph G_1 of Fig. 1.9(a) is not the sectional subgraph induced by $V_s = \{1, 2, 3, 4, 5, 7\}$ because it is not the maximal subgraph with node set V_s.

1.3   NONSEPARABLE GRAPHS AND BIPARTITE GRAPHS

Graphs can be classified in many different ways depending upon their structures. For example, we have already classified graphs on the basis of their connectivity. In this section, we introduce two important classes of graphs.

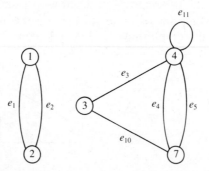

Fig. 1.13. The sectional subgraph $G[\{1, 2, 3, 4, 7\}]$ induced by the subset $\{1, 2, 3, 4, 7\}$ of the node set of the graph of Fig. 1.8.

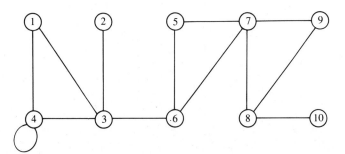

Fig. 1.14. A separable graph with cutpoints 3, 4, 6, 7 and 8.

DEFINITION 1.12

Cutpoint. In a connected graph G, if there is a proper nonnull subgraph G_s such that G_s and its complement have only node i in common, then the node i is called a *cutpoint* of G. A node of an unconnected graph is a cutpoint if the node is a cutpoint in one of its components.

The term *cutpoint* is sometimes referred to as an *articulation point*. In the graph G of Fig. 1.14, the nodes 3, 4, 6, 7 and 8 are cutpoints, but the nodes 2 and 5 are not. If G has no self-loops, a cutpoint may also be defined as a node whose removal will increase the number of components at least by one. If G has self-loops, the statement, however, is not generally true. For example, node 4 in the graph of Fig. 1.14 is a cutpoint, but its removal will not increase the number of components at least by one.

THEOREM 1.5

A node j of a graph that contains no self-loops is a cutpoint if and only if there are two nodes i and k distinct from j such that every path connecting the nodes i and k contains the node j.

The theorem is intuitively true. Its proof is straightforward and is omitted.

DEFINITION 1.13

Nonseparable Graph. A connected nonnull graph is said to be *nonseparable* if it contains no cutpoints. All other nonnull graphs are considered as *separable*.

Thus, an unconnected nonnull graph is a trivial example of a separable graph. The graphs of Figs. 1.12–1.14 are other examples of separable

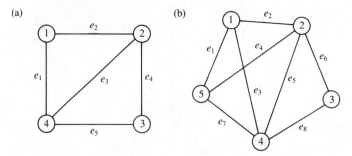

Fig. 1.15. Examples of nonseparable graphs.

graphs. Examples of nonseparable graphs are presented in Fig. 1.15. It follows from the definition that a connected separable graph must contain a cutpoint, and such a graph must contain at least one nonnull subgraph which has only one node in common with its complement. This gives the following result.

THEOREM 1.6

A necessary and sufficient condition that a graph containing at least two edges be nonseparable is that every proper nonnull subgraph of the graph have at least two nodes in common with its complement.

In the graph of Fig. 1.14, node 6 is a cutpoint because there exist two nodes, say, 1 and 10 such that every path connecting these two nodes contains node 6. In Fig. 1.15(a), the graph is nonseparable because for each proper nonnull subgraph, say, $e_1 e_2 e_3$ it has at least two nodes in common with its complement $e_4 e_5$. A graph containing at least two edges, one of them being a self-loop, is separable. A single edge is a nonseparable graph.

DEFINITION 1.14

Block. A *block* of a graph is a nonseparable subgraph containing the maximal number of edges.

If a connected graph G is separable, we can separate G into blocks by splitting off the cutpoints. This process is called the *decomposition* of a separable graph into blocks. For example, the decomposition of the graph of Fig. 1.14 is presented in Fig. 1.16. Clearly, the decomposition is unique.

In addition to nonseparable graphs, there is another class of graphs occurring frequently in matching theorems. They are defined below.

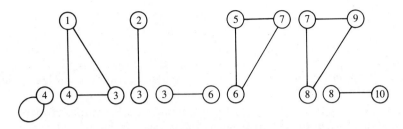

Fig. 1.16. The unique decomposition of the graph of Fig. 1.14.

DEFINITION 1.15

Bipartite Graph. A graph $G(V, E)$ is said to be *bipartite* if its node set V can be partitioned into two disjoint subsets V_1 and V_2 such that each of its edges has one endpoint in V_1 and the other in V_2.

As a result, a nonnull subgraph of a bipartite graph is bipartite. All the paths connecting two nodes of V_1 or V_2 are of even length, and all paths are of odd length if one of the endpoints is in V_1 and the other in V_2. The graph of Fig. 1.17 is an example of a bipartite graph with node sets $V_1 = \{1, 2, 3, 4, 5\}$ and $V_2 = \{6, 7, 8, 9\}$. All the paths connecting the nodes, say, 2 and 4 are of even length, and all paths connecting nodes 1 and 8 are of odd length.

A complete characterization of a bipartite graph is given below.

THEOREM 1.7

A nonnull graph is bipartite if and only if either it has no circuits or each of its circuits is of even length.

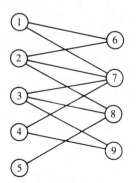

Fig. 1.17. An example of a bipartite graph $K_{5,4}$.

Proof. The necessary part is obvious. To prove sufficiency, assume that a graph $G(V, E)$ has this property. Without loss of generality, we may further assume that G is connected; for if not we can consider the components of G separately. Also, we can assume that G has no self-loops.

Let i be a node of G, and let V_2 be the set consisting of all the nodes j such that the length of a shortest path from i to j is even with i being included in V_2. Let $V_1 = V - V_2$. Then each node $k \in V_1$ has the property that the length of a shortest path from i to k is odd. To show that every edge (u, v) of G is connected between a node $u \in V_1$ and a node $v \in V_2$, we first assume that both u and v are in V_2. Let P_{iu} and P_{iv}^* be the shortest paths of even lengths from i to u and v, respectively. Starting from the nodes u and v, let j be the first common node in P_{iu} and P_{iv}^*. Then the shortest paths from j to u and from j to v are either both even or both odd. This would imply that the sum graph, formed by the edge (u, v) and the shortest paths from j to u and j to v, is a circuit of odd length, which would contradict the assumption that every circuit of G is of even length.

In a similar manner, we can show that no two nodes in V_1 are connected by an edge. Thus, G is bipartite and the proof is completed.

1.4 PLANAR GRAPHS

Our discussions so far have been entirely in terms of the abstract graph. The geometric diagram has served only for illustrative purposes. On the other hand, planar graphs can be defined in terms of their geometric diagrams.

DEFINITION 1.16

Planar Graph. A graph is said to be *planar* if its geometric diagram can be drawn on a plane such that no two edges have an intersection that is not a node.

We recognize that the geometric diagram of a graph can be drawn on a plane without intersections if and only if it can be drawn on a sphere without intersections. As a matter of fact, using stereographic projection, we can establish a one-to-one correspondence between these two drawings as follows: Let a sphere be kept on a plane such that the point of contact (south pole) is the origin of the coordinate system in the plane. Let z be the intersection (north pole) of the sphere and the line which is perpendicular to the plane and passes through the origin of the plane. Joining z to any point p of the sphere by a straight line and extending the line to meet the plane at p', we establish a one-to-one correspondence between points on the plane and points on the sphere. This procedure is referred to as a *mapping* between the sphere and the plane. Thus, the geometric diagram of a graph on a plane can always be mapped onto a sphere and vice versa, provided that z is chosen not on the diagram.

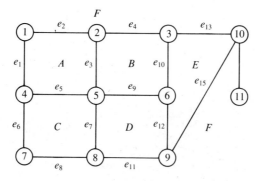

Fig. 1.18. A planar graph with its six regions.

DEFINITION 1.17

Region (Window). The areas into which the geometric diagram of a planar graph divides the plane, when it is drawn on a plane without intersections, are called the *regions* (*windows*) of the planar graph. The unbounded region is called the *outside region*.

A region is characterized by the edges on its boundary. In electrical network theory, the circuit formed by the boundary edges of a region is known as a *mesh* because it has the appearance of mesh of a fishing net. We remark that the graph corresponding to an electrical network usually does not contain any self-loops, so there is no ambiguity in defining the mesh of a region.

In Fig. 1.18 the graph is planar and it has six regions A, B, C, D, E and F, the outside region being F. These regions are bounded by the meshes $e_1e_2e_3e_5$, $e_3e_4e_9e_{10}$, $e_5e_6e_7e_8$, $e_7e_9e_{11}e_{12}$, $e_{10}e_{12}e_{13}e_{15}$ and $e_1e_2e_4e_6e_8e_{11}e_{13}e_{15}$, respectively. The graphs of Figs. 1.5 and 1.7 are examples of nonplanar graphs.

THEOREM 1.8

Any region of a planar graph can be the outside region of the planar graph.

Proof. First draw the geometric diagram of a planar graph on a sphere without intersections. Rotate the sphere so that the point z discussed above is inside the given region. Map the geometric diagram back onto the plane, and we obtain the desired result.

For example, the region D bounded by the mesh $e_7e_9e_{11}e_{12}$ of the planar graph of Fig. 1.18 can be made the outside region as shown in Fig. 1.19.

Planar graphs are useful in practical applications. For example, in printed circuits an electrical network can be printed on a single plane surface if and

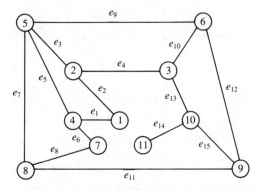

Fig. 1.19. The interior region D of the planar graph of Fig. 1.18 being made the outside region.

only if it corresponds to a planar graph. The notion of duality in electrical network theory is also closely related to planar graphs. The classical Euler formula for polyhedra relates the number of regions of a planar graph to the numbers of edges and nodes.

THEOREM 1.9

For an n-node connected planar graph with b edges and q regions (including the outside region)

$$n - b + q = 2 \tag{1.21}$$

Proof. We prove this theorem by induction over the number b of edges of a connected planar graph G. For $b = 1$, the theorem is seen to be true. Assume that the assertion is true for any $b - 1$, $b \geqq 2$. We show that it is also true for any b. If G has no circuit, then G has $n - 1$ edges, and equality (1.21) is satisfied. So let us assume that G has at least one circuit. If G' is the graph obtained from G by the removal of a boundary edge e of the outside region of G, then G' has n nodes, $b - 1$ edges, and $q - 1$ regions. By induction hypothesis, we have

$$n - (b - 1) + (q - 1) = 2 \tag{1.22}$$

and the theorem follows.

An easy consequence of Euler's formula is the following that establishes an upper bound for the number of edges in a planar graph not containing parallel edges and self-loops.

COROLLARY 1.2

The number b of edges in an n-node planar graph, $n \geqq 3$, that does not contain any parallel edges and self-loops is bounded above by $3n - 6$, or

$$b \leqq 3n - 6 \tag{1.23}$$

Proof. The maximum number of edges that can occur in an n-node planar graph G' is when every edge of G' is contained in at least one of the circuits formed by the boundary edges of the regions of G' and when each of these circuits is of length 3. If b' and q' are the numbers of edges and regions of G', respectively, then $2b' = 3q'$ because each edge of G' is contained in exactly two such circuits. Using this in conjunction with (1.21) gives $b' = 3n - 6$. This establishes an upper bound for the number of edges in any planar graph that does not contain any parallel edges and self-loops. So the corollary is proved.

Using this result, it is easy to confirm that the graph of Fig. 1.7 is nonplanar because $b = 10 > 9 = 3n - 6$, a violation of (1.23). A similar result for a planar graph not containing any circuits of length 3 is given below.

COROLLARY 1.3

The number b of edges in an n-node nonseparable planar graph, $n \geqq 3$, that does not contain any parallel edges, self-loops, and circuits of length 3, is bounded above by $2n - 4$, or

$$b \leqq 2n - 4 \tag{1.24}$$

The bipartite graph G_1 of Fig. 1.5(a) is not planar, because it violates condition (1.24): $b = 9 \nleqq 2n - 4 = 2 \times 6 - 4 = 8$.

COROLLARY 1.4

Every planar graph that contains at least four nodes and that does not contain any parallel edges and self-loops has at least four nodes of degree not exceeding 5.

Proof. Let G be an n-node planar graph containing no parallel edges and self-loops. Without loss of generality, assume that in G there is no node of degree 1; for otherwise the corollary follows by induction over the number of nodes of G.

Let the nodes of G be labeled such that if $i < j$ then $d(i) \leqq d(j)$. If G

contains at most three nodes of degree not exceeding 5, from (1.10) we have

$$2b = d(1) + d(2) + d(3) + \sum_{i=4}^{n} d(i)$$

$$\geqq d(1) + d(2) + d(3) + 6(n-3) \tag{1.25}$$

or

$$b \geqq \frac{d(1) + d(2) + d(3) - 6}{2} + 3n - 6 \geqq 3n - 6 \tag{1.26}$$

Combining this with (1.23) shows that (1.26) must hold with the equality sign. This is possible only if nodes 1, 2, and 3 are of degree 2. If nodes 1, 2 and 3 are of degree 2, then not every circuit formed by the boundary edges of a region is of length 3 and (1.23) holds only for the strict inequality:

$$b < 3n - 6 \tag{1.27}$$

showing that (1.26) is not possible. The corollary follows.

It is quite obvious that a graph is planar if and only if each of its components is planar. It is less obvious that a graph is planar if and only if each of its blocks is planar. It was shown by Whitney (1932) that in studying planarity, it is sufficient to consider only nonseparable graphs.

THEOREM 1.10

A graph is planar if and only if each of its blocks is planar.

The theorem follows directly from the fact that a separable graph can be decomposed into blocks and that the decomposition is unique. Thus, if each block is planar, the reconnection of these blocks at the cutpoints results in a planar graph.

A planar graph is a graph that can be drawn on a plane without intersection. Very often the question arises as to whether or not a planar graph can be drawn on a plane with straight lines. One obvious restriction is that the graph cannot have any parallel edges or self-loops. It was shown by Wagner (1936), Fáry (1948) and Stein (1951) independently that every planar graph containing no parallel edges and self-loops can be embedded in the plane with straight line edges.

THEOREM 1.11

Every planar graph that does not contain any parallel edges and self-loops can be drawn on a plane without intersection using only straight lines as edges.

Proof. Let G be a planar graph that does not contain any parallel edges and self-loops. Let G^* be the graph obtained from G by adding as many edges as possible between any two nonadjacent nodes of a mesh without introducing any parallel edges and self-loops. The added edges lie interior to the regions. Clearly, G is a subgraph of G^* and each mesh of G^* is of length 3; for, otherwise, additional edges can be inserted. It is sufficient to show that G^* can be drawn on a plane without intersection using only straight lines as edges, or to show that G^* has a straight-line representation.

We prove the theorem by induction over the number of nodes of G^*. Certainly, if G^* has less than four nodes, it has a straight-line representation. Assume that the assertion is true for any G^* with k nodes, $3 \leqq k \leqq n$. We show that it is also true for any G^* with $n + 1$ nodes. If all the nodes of G^* lie on the circuit formed by the boundary edges of the outside region called the *outside mesh*, G^* has a straight-line representation. Thus, we assume that there is a node i of G^* lying interior to the outside mesh.

Let G' be the graph obtained from G^* by the removal of the node i and all edges $(i, j_1), (i, j_2), \ldots, (i, j_u)$ incident on i and by adding edges $(j_1, j_3), (j_1, j_4), \ldots, (j_1, j_{u-1})$, $u \geqq 4$. For $u = 3$, no additional edges will be inserted. Clearly, the edges $(j_1, j_2), (j_2, j_3), \ldots, (j_u, j_1)$ are in G' and G^*, and form a circuit L_1 that separates i from the other nodes of G^*. The graph G' is identical with G^* outside the circuit L_1. If G' does not contain any parallel edges, by induction hypothesis G' possesses a straight-line representation. Now, we remove the edges $(j_1, j_3), (j_1, j_4), \ldots, (j_1, j_{u-1})$ from G' and then insert a node i inside the circuit L_1 and connect it to each of the nodes $j_1, j_2, \ldots, j_u$ with edges. The resulting graph is a straight-line representation of G^*.

If G' contains parallel edges, they are introduced when new edges $(j_1, j_3), (j_1, j_4), \ldots, (j_1, j_{u-1})$ are added and when there are edges lying exterior to L_1 connecting j_1 and some of the nodes $j_3, j_4, \ldots, j_{u-1}$ in G^*. Let one of these exterior edges be (j_1, j_v), $3 \leqq v \leqq u - 1$. Then the circuit L_2 formed by the edges (j_1, i), (i, j_v) and (j_v, j_1) separates j_2 from j_u in G^*. Let the circuit L_2 and that part of G^* which is exterior to L_2 form a graph G_1, and let L_2 and its interior in G^* form a graph G_2. Since G_1 and G_2 have at most n nodes, by induction hypothesis, they have straight-line representations. Putting these straight-line representations together shows that G^* possesses a straight-line representation, so does its subgraph G. This completes the proof of the theorem.

The planar graph of Fig. 1.20(a) can be drawn on a plane without intersection using only straight lines as edges as shown in Fig. 1.20(b). A more complicated planar graph is presented in Fig. 1.21. This graph possesses a straight-line representation as illustrated in Fig. 1.22.

We now proceed to the characterization of a planar graph in terms of certain forbidden subgraphs. These subgraphs are special kinds of graphs defined below.

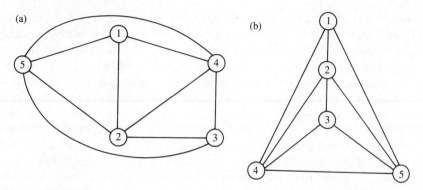

Fig. 1.20. A planar graph (a) and its straight-line representation (b).

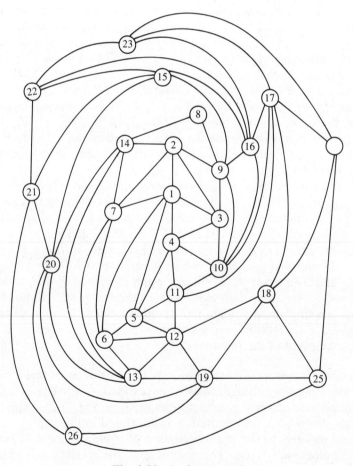

Fig. 1.21. A planar graph.

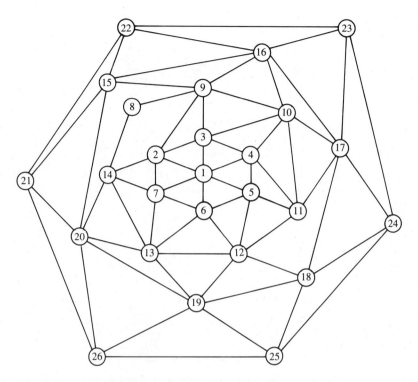

Fig. 1.22. A straight-line representation of the planar graph of Fig. 1.21.

DEFINITION 1.18

Complete Graph. A self-loopless graph is said to be *complete* and of *order* k if for every pair of nodes there are k and only k edges connected between them. A complete graph of order 1 is simply called a *complete graph*. The n-node complete graph of order 1 is denoted by K_n.

The 5-node complete graph of order 2 is shown in Fig. 1.23. Fig. 1.24(a) is the 5-node complete graph K_5 and Fig. 1.24(b) is the 6-node complete graph K_6.

DEFINITION 1.19

Complete Bipartite Graph. A bipartite graph whose node set is partitioned into the subsets V_1 and V_2 is said to be *complete* and of *order* k if for every pair of nodes i and j, $i \in V_1$ and $j \in V_2$, there are k and only k edges connected between them. A complete bipartite graph of order 1 is simply called a *complete bipartite graph*. If V_1 and V_2 have m and n nodes, the complete bipartite graph of order 1 is denoted by $K_{m,n}$.

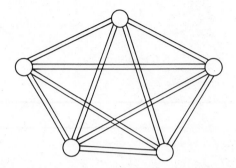

Fig. 1.23. The 5-node complete graph of order 2.

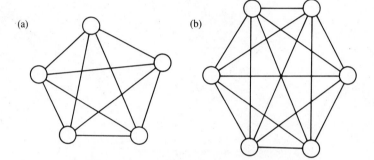

Fig. 1.24. The complete graphs K_5 (a) and K_6 (b).

The graph of Fig. 1.25 is a complete bipartite graph of order 2. The complete bipartite graphs $K_{3,3}$ and $K_{3,4}$ are shown in Fig. 1.26.

An edge of a graph is said to be *subdivided* if it is replaced by a path of length at least 2 as shown in Fig. 1.27. The forbidden subgraphs used to characterize a planar graph are $K_{3,3}$ and K_5 of Fig. 1.28 and their variants. The variants of $K_{3,3}$ and K_5 are defined below.

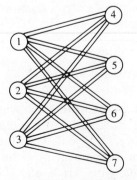

Fig. 1.25. A complete bipartite graph of order 2.

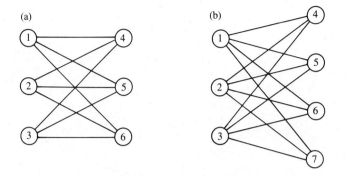

Fig. 1.26. The complete bipartite graphs $K_{3,3}$ (a) and $K_{3,4}$ (b).

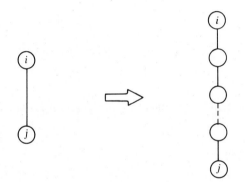

Fig. 1.27. The replacement of an edge by a path of length at least 2.

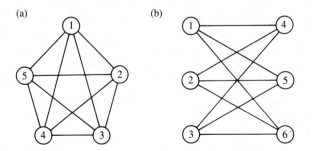

Fig. 1.28. The forbidden subgraphs K_5 (a) and $K_{3,3}$ (b) used to characterize a planar graph.

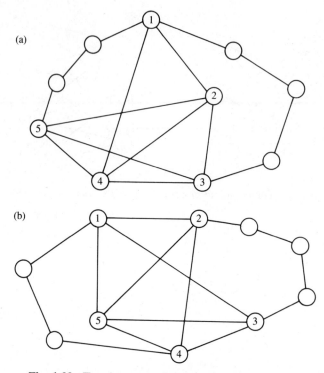

(a)

(b)

Fig. 1.29. Two homeomorphic graphs: (a) G_1; (b) G_2.

DEFINITION 1.20

Homeomorphism. Two graphs are said to be *homeomorphic* if both can be
obtained from the same graph by a sequence of subdivisions of the edges.

The graphs G_1 and G_2 of Fig. 1.29 are homeomorphic because both can
be obtained from the graph K_5 of Fig. 1.28(a) by a sequence of subdivisions
of edges. For example, if we subdivide the edges $(1, 5)$ and $(1, 3)$ of K_5
twice and three times, respectively, we obtain G_1. Likewise, if we subdivide
$(1, 4)$ and $(2, 3)$ of K_5, we obtain G_2. Two circuits of different lengths are
homeomorphic because the longer circuit can be obtained from the shorter
one by a sequence of subdivisions.

An alternative way to describe homeomorphism of two graphs is to use
the operation of shorting an edge. Two graphs are homeomorphic if both
can be reduced to the same graph by a sequence of operations that short
edges incident to nodes of degree 2. The forbidden subgraphs used to
characterize a planar graph are those homeomorphic to $K_{3,3}$ or K_5. The
following basic theorem on planar graphs is due to Kuratowski (1930), the
proof of which depends on many point–set topological ideas that have not
been developed here. We follow the proof of Dirac and Schuster (1954).

THEOREM 1.12

A graph is planar if and only if it has no subgraph homeomorphic to K_5 or $K_{3,3}$.

Proof. Necessity. The necessity follows from Corollaries 1.2 and 1.3 in that since K_5 and $K_{3,3}$ are nonplanar, a graph containing a subgraph homeomorphic to either of these is also nonplanar.

Sufficiency. We prove the theorem by induction over the number of edges. The theorem is certainly true for any graph having less than four edges. Assume that the condition is sufficient for any graph having less than b edges. We show that the assertion is valid for any graph G having b edges. Since by Theorem 1.10 a graph is planar if and only if each of its blocks is planar, without loss of generality it is sufficient to consider only non-separable graphs G. To complete the proof, assume that the assertion is false, i.e. G is a b-edge nonseparable nonplanar graph that does not contain a subgraph homeomorphic to either K_5 or $K_{3,3}$.

Let (x, y) be an arbitrary edge of G. Let G' be the graph obtained from G by the removal of (x, y). We first show that there is a circuit in G' containing the nodes x and y. Since G is nonseparable, G' is connected. Moreover, since G' contains $b - 1$ edges, it is also planar. Assume that there is no circuit in G' containing the nodes x and y. Then x and y must lie in different blocks of G'. Hence, by Theorem 1.5 there exists a cutpoint z such that every path connecting the nodes x and y contains the node z. We construct the graph G'' by adding to G' the edges (x, z) and (y, z) if they are not already present in G'. Observe that in G'' the nodes x and y still lie in different blocks. Let G'' be decomposed into the subgraphs G_1'' and G_2'' by splitting off the cutpoint z. Certainly, G_1'' and G_2'' each contain at most $b - 1$ edges. By induction hypothesis, G_1'' and G_2'' are planar graphs. According to Theorem 1.8, both G_1'' and G_2'' can be drawn in the plane so that the edges (x, z) and (y, z) appear in the circuits formed by the boundary edges of the outside regions. Connecting G_1'' and G_2'' back at z to form G'' and inserting the edge (x, y) to G'' results in a planar graph, for which G is a subgraph. This requires that G be planar, contradicting the assumption. Therefore, there is a circuit in G' containing x and y.

There may be many circuits containing x and y in G'. Let L be a circuit of G' containing x and y such that it encloses the maximum number of regions interior to it. Orient the edges of L in a cyclic fashion, so that L_{uv} denotes the path from u to v along L. If v does not immediately follow u on L, we use the symbol $L(u, v)$ to denote the subpath of L_{uv} obtained by the removal of u and v. The circuit L also serves to specify a node, an edge, or a region which is inside L and one which is outside. By the *exterior* of L, we mean the subgraph of G' induced by the nodes lying outside L, and the components of this subgraph are called the *exterior components* of L. By an *outer piece* of L, we mean an exterior component together with all the edges incident with it or an edge exterior to L meeting two nodes of L. Likewise, we define the *interior* of L, an *interior component*, and an *inner piece*. An outer or inner piece is said to be u–v *separating* if it meets $L(u, v)$ and $L(v, u)$. Clearly, if u and v are adjacent on L, an outer or inner piece cannot be u–v separating.

Since G' is connected, each outer piece must meet L. Furthermore, G' has no cutpoints, for otherwise $G = G' \cup (x, y)$ would contain a cutpoint. By splitting off the cutpoint and by induction hypothesis, this would imply that G is planar, a contradiction. Thus, G' has no cutpoints. By Theorem 1.6, we conclude that each outer piece must have at least two nodes in common with L. An outer piece cannot meet $L(x, y)$ or $L(y, x)$ in more than one node. If it did so we could find another circuit enclosing more regions than L. For the same reason, no outer piece can meet x or y. Therefore, every outer piece meets L in exactly two nodes and is x–y separating. In addition, there is at least one inner piece that is x–y separating. If this were not so we could introduce the edge (x, y) in such a way that G would be planar, contrary to the assumption.

Let I_1 be an x–y separating inner piece that is nearest to x in the sense of encountering nodes of this inner piece on moving along L from x. Continuing out from x along L, we can index the other x–y separating inner pieces as I_2, I_3, and so forth. We order these inner pieces for the purpose of relocating them in the plane later.

Let x_2 and x_3 be the first and last nodes of I_1 meeting $L(x, y)$, and y_2 and y_3 be the first and last nodes of I_1 meeting $L(y, x)$, as indicated in Fig. 1.30. We show that there exists an x–y separating outer piece Q meeting $L(x, y)$, say, at x_1, and $L(y, x)$, say, at y_1, such that there is an inner piece that is

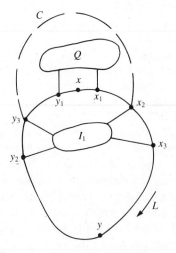

Fig. 1.30. Figure used to prove sufficiency of Theorem 1.12.

both $x-y$ separating and x_1-y_1 separating. Suppose that the assertion is false. Then every $x-y$ separating outer piece, which has exactly two nodes in common with L, must have these common nodes on either $L(y_3, x_2)$ or $L(x_3, y_2)$, for otherwise the assertion is true. Without loss of generality, assume that x_1 and y_1 lie on $L(y_3, x_2)$, as shown in Fig. 1.30. As a result, we can draw a curve C connecting y_3 and x_2 in the exterior of L so that it does not meet any edges of G', as depicted in Fig. 1.30. Now, the inner piece I_1 can be transferred outside of C in a planar manner. If the remaining $x-y$ separating inner pieces I_2, I_3, and so forth could all be so transferred, in order, the resulting graph is such that we can draw a line from x to y without meeting any edges of G'. Since G' contains $b-1$ edges, by induction hypothesis G' is planar. The above argument shows that G, which can be obtained from G' by connecting an edge between x and y inside L, is also planar, a contradiction. Thus, there is an $x-y$ separating outer piece Q meeting $L(x, y)$ at x_1 and $L(y, x)$ at y_1 such that there exists an inner piece I which is both $x-y$ separating and x_1-y_1 separating.

For this choice of outer piece Q and inner piece I, there are four potential nodes at which I meets L that are of particular interest. We denote by w_0, w_0', w_1 and w_1' the nodes at which I meets $L(x, y)$, $L(y, x)$, $L(x_1, y_1)$, and $L(y_1, x_1)$, respectively. Four cases are distinguished, depending on the relative position on L of these four nodes.

Case 1

w_1 or w_1' is on $L(x, y)$ and the other is on $L(y, x)$. Then we can take, say, $w_0 = w_1$ and $w_0' = w_1'$, as indicated in Fig. 1.31. In this case, G contains a subgraph homeomorphic to $K_{3,3}$ with the two sets of nodes identified in Fig. 1.31 by the solid and open dots.

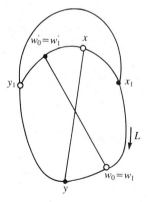

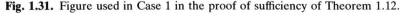

Fig. 1.31. Figure used in Case 1 in the proof of sufficiency of Theorem 1.12.

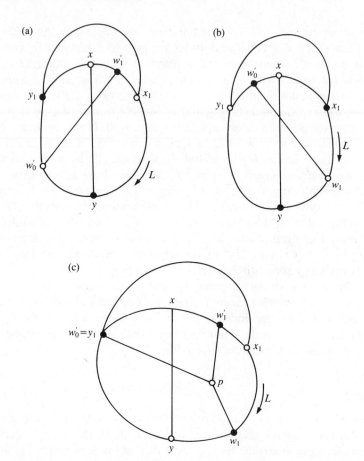

Fig. 1.32. Figures used in Case 2 in the proof of sufficiency of Theorem 1.12.

Case 2

Both w_1 and w_1' are on either $L(x, y)$ or $L(y, x)$. Without loss of generality, assume that both lie on $L(x, y)$. If $w_0' \neq y_1$, then G contains a subgraph homeomorphic to $K_{3,3}$, as shown in Fig. 1.32(a) or (b), depending on whether w_0' lies on $L(x_1, y_1)$ or $L(y_1, x_1)$, respectively. On the other hand, if $w_0' = y_1$, then there is a node p in I from which there are disjoint paths to w_1, w_1' and y_1, all of whose nodes except w_1, w_1' and y_1 belong to I. Again, in this case G contains a subgraph homeomorphic to $K_{3,3}$, as depicted in Fig. 1.32(c).

Case 3

$w_1 = y$ and $w_1' \neq x$. Without loss of generality, assume that w_1' lies on $L(x, y)$. If w_0' is on $L(y, y_1)$, then G contains a subgraph homeomorphic

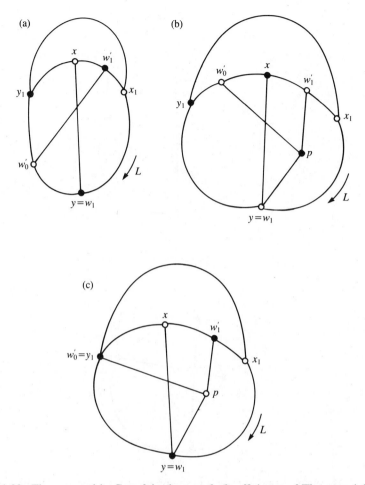

Fig. 1.33. Figures used in Case 3 in the proof of sufficiency of Theorem 1.12.

to $K_{3,3}$, as shown in Fig. 1.33(a). If w_0' is on $L(y_1, x)$, there exists a node p in I from which there are disjoint paths to $w_1 = y$, w_1' and w_0', all of whose nodes except w_1, w_1' and w_0' belong to I. In this case, G contains a subgraph homeomorphic to $K_{3,3}$, as depicted in Fig. 1.33(b). Finally, if $w_0' = y_1$, we have the situation shown in Fig. 1.33(c), and G again contains a subgraph homeomorphic to $K_{3,3}$.

Case 4

$w_1 = y$ and $w_1' = x$. In the present situation, we assume that $w_0 = x_1$ and $w_0' = y_1$, for otherwise we are in one of the situations covered in Case 1, 2 or 3 above. To facilitate our discussion, two subcases are distinguished. If P_{xy} and $P_{x_1y_1}$ denote the shortest paths in I between x and y and x_1 and y_1,

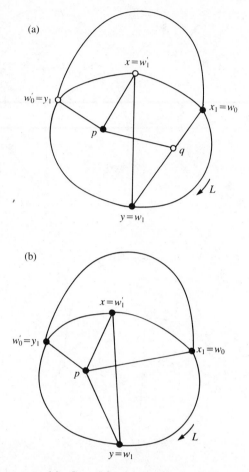

Fig. 1.34. Figures used in Case 4 in the proof of sufficiency of Theorem 1.12.

respectively, then they must intersect since I is planar. If they have more than one node in common, as depicted in Fig. 1.34(a), then G contains a subgraph homeomorphic to $K_{3,3}$. Otherwise, G contains a subgraph homeomorphic to K_5, as shown in Fig. 1.34(b).

Since these are all the possibilities, it follows that G must be a planar graph. This completes the proof of the theorem.

As an illustration, consider the *Petersen graph* of Fig. 1.35. The graph is nonplanar because it contains a subgraph as shown in Fig. 1.36(a) which is homeomorphic to $K_{3,3}$ of Fig. 1.36(b). Observe that since every node of the Petersen graph is of degree 3, none of its subgraphs can be homeomorphic to K_5.

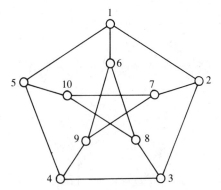

Fig. 1.35. The Petersen graph.

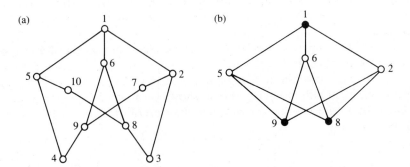

Fig. 1.36. A subgraph of the Petersen graph which is homeomorphic to $K_{3,3}$.

In addition to the above characterization of a planar graph, a dual form of Kuratowski's theorem in terms of graph contractions was independently given by Wagner (1937) and Harary and Tutte (1965).

DEFINITION 1.21

Graph Contraction. A graph G_1 is said to be *contractible* to a graph G_2 if G_2 can be obtained from G_1 by a sequence of edge shorting operations.

For example, the Petersen graph is contractible to K_5 of Fig. 1.37 by shorting the edges $(1, 6), (2, 7), (3, 8), (4, 9)$, and $(5, 10)$. An alternative form to Kuratowski's result is stated below.

THEOREM 1.13

A graph is planar if and only if it does not contain a subgraph contractible to K_5 or $K_{3,3}$.

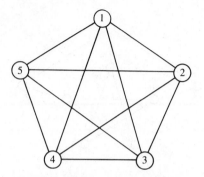

Fig. 1.37. The complete graph K_5.

Since the Petersen graph is contractible to K_5, it satisfies the condition of Theorem 1.13, confirming an earlier assertion that the Petersen graph is nonplanar.

In a related paper, Tutte (1963) gives an algorithm on the drawing of a graph in the plane, so that whenever his procedure fails to draw the entire graph, it must contain a subgraph homeomorphic to K_5 or $K_{3,3}$. The algorithm, in addition to being able to show how to draw a planar graph in a plane without intersection, provides another proof of Kuratowski's theorem (Theorem 1.12).

1.5 DUAL GRAPHS

In the preceding section, we showed that a planar graph can be characterized in terms of certain forbidden subgraphs. In this section, we demonstrate that planarity can also be expressed in terms of the existence of dual graphs. We first review the notion of a geometric dual of a planar graph, give an algebraic definition of duality due to Whitney (1932, 1933*a*), and then show that these two concepts are consistent and coincide.

DEFINITION 1.22

Geometric Dual. Given a planar graph, its *geometric dual* is constructed as follows: Place a node in each region of the planar graph including the outside region, and, if two regions have an edge e in common, connect the nodes inside the two adjacent regions by an edge e' crossing only e.

Consider, for example, the planar graph G of Fig. 1.38. Its geometric dual G' is constructed as shown in Fig. 1.39, and is redrawn in Fig. 1.40. Suppose that we construct the geometric dual G'' of G' again as depicted in Fig. 1.41. We find that G'' is isomorphic to the original graph G. Thus, the dual of the dual of the planar graph G of Fig. 1.38 is the original graph G.

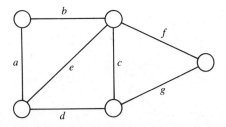

Fig. 1.38. A planar graph used to construct its geometric dual.

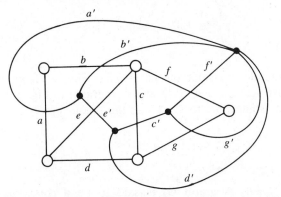

Fig. 1.39. The construction of a geometric dual graph.

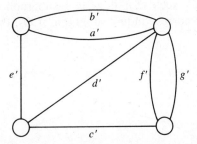

Fig. 1.40. A geometric dual of the graph of Fig. 1.38.

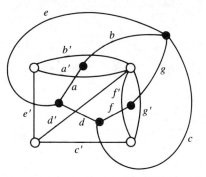

Fig. 1.41. A dual of a dual of the graph of Fig. 1.38.

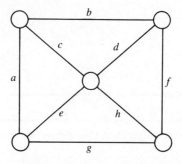

Fig. 1.42. A planar graph.

As another example, consider the graph G of Fig. 1.42, whose geometric dual G' is constructed in Fig. 1.43 and is redrawn in Fig. 1.44, for clarity. This dual G' is isomorphic to G. Thus, the planar graph G of Fig. 1.42 is self-dual.

DEFINITION 1.23

Combinatorial Dual. A graph G_2 is said to be a *combinatorial dual* of another graph G_1 if there exists a one-to-one correspondence between the edges of G_1 and G_2 such that if g_1 is a subgraph of G_1 and g_2 is the complement of the corresponding subgraph of G_2, then

$$r_2 = R_2 - m_1 \tag{1.28}$$

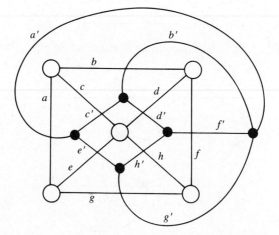

Fig. 1.43. The construction of a geometric dual of the planar graph of Fig. 1.42.

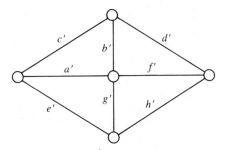

Fig. 1.44. The dual graph of the planar graph of Fig. 1.42.

where r_2 and R_2 are the ranks of g_2 and G_2, respectively, and m_1 is the nullity of g_1.

In the late part of this section, we shall demonstrate that the two concepts are consistent and one implies the other. For illustrative purposes, we use the graph G_1 of Fig. 1.45(a) and its geometric dual G_2 of Fig. 1.45(b) to clarify the notion of combinatorial dual. First, the edges are labeled as in Fig. 1.45 such that a corresponds to a', b to b', etc. Let $g_1 = abeg$. Then the corresponding subgraph of g_1 in G_2 is $a'b'e'g'$, so that its complement is $g_2 = c'd'f'$. These two subgraphs g_1 and g_2 are presented in Fig. 1.46. Then from Fig. 1.45(b) and Fig. 1.46 we have

$$r_2 = 2, \qquad R_2 = 3, \qquad m_1 = 1 \tag{1.29}$$

giving

$$r_2 = 2 = R_2 - m_1 = 3 - 1 = 2 \tag{1.30}$$

For another example, choose $g_1 = defg$, so that $m_1 = 1$. Then $g_2 = a'b'c'$ with $r_2 = 2$. Again, this gives

$$r_2 = 2 = R_2 - m_1 = 3 - 1 = 2 \tag{1.31}$$

(a)

(b)

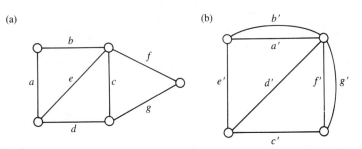

Fig. 1.45. A planar graph G_1 (a) and its geometric dual G_2 (b).

(a)   (b)

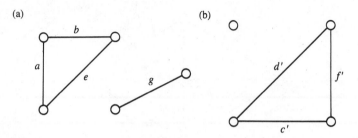

Fig. 1.46. The subgraphs g_1 (a) and g_2 (b) of the graphs G_1 and G_2 of Fig. 1.45.

THEOREM 1.14

If G_2 is a combinatorial dual of a graph G_1, then the rank of G_2 equals the nullity of G_1 and the rank of G_1 equals the nullity of G_2.

Proof. Let $g_1 = G_1$ be the improper subgraph of G_1. Then the corresponding subgraph of $g_1 = G_1$ in G_2 is G_2 itself, so that its complement g_2 is the null graph $\varnothing$. Hence, the rank r_2 of g_2 is 0 and the nullity m_1 of g_1 equals that of G_1 or $m_1 = M_1$. Since G_2 is a combinatorial dual of G_1, from (1.28) we have

$$r_2 = 0 = R_2 - m_1 = R_2 - M_1 \tag{1.32}$$

where R_2 is the rank of G_2, or

$$R_2 = M_1 \tag{1.33}$$

This shows that the rank of G_2 equals the nullity of G_1. The second part of the theorem follows immediately from the facts that since G_1 and G_2 contain the same number of edges and since the sum of rank and nullity equals the number of edges, we have from (1.33)

$$R_1 + M_1 = R_2 + M_2 = M_1 + M_2 \tag{1.34}$$

where R_1 and M_2 denote the rank and nullity of G_1 and G_2, respectively, or

$$R_1 = M_2 \tag{1.35}$$

THEOREM 1.15

If G_2 is a combinatorial dual of a graph G_1, then G_1 is a combinatorial dual of G_2.

Proof. Let g_2 be a subgraph of G_2 and let g_1 be the complement of the corresponding subgraph of g_2 in G_1. As before, denote by r_i, R_i, m_i and M_i the ranks and nullities of g_i and G_i, respectively. Then since G_2 is a combinatorial dual of G_1,

$$r_2 = R_2 - m_1 \tag{1.36}$$

If b_1, b_2 and B denote the numbers of edges in g_1, g_2 and G_1 (or G_2), respectively, we have

$$b_1 + b_2 = B \tag{1.37}$$

From Theorem 1.14, $R_2 = M_1$, giving from (1.36) and (1.37)

$$r_1 = b_1 - m_1 = b_1 - (R_2 - r_2) = b_1 - M_1 + (b_2 - m_2)$$
$$= B - M_1 - m_2 = R_1 - m_2 \tag{1.38}$$

This shows that G_1 is a combinatorial dual of G_2, and the proof of the theorem is completed.

As a result, it is not necessary to say that G_1 is a dual of G_2 or G_2 is a dual of G_1. It is meaningful and sufficient to state that G_1 and G_2 are dual graphs. Before we prove the main results of this section, we need the following two theorems of Whitney (1932).

THEOREM 1.16

The combinatorial dual of a nonseparable graph is nonseparable.

THEOREM 1.17

Let G_1 and G_2 be the combinatorial dual graphs, and let (α_1, α_2) and (β_1, β_2) be their corresponding edges. If $G_1' = G_1 - (\alpha_1, \alpha_2)$ and G_2' is the graph obtained from G_2 by shorting the edge (β_1, β_2), then G_1' and G_2' are duals having the same corresponding edges as in G_1 and G_2.

Proof. To show that G_1' and G_2' are duals, let g_1' be any subgraph of G_1' and let g_2' be the complement of the corresponding subgraph of g_1' in G_2'. If g_1 is the subgraph of G_1 corresponding to g_1' in G_1', then the nullities m_1 and m_1' of g_1 and g_1' are equal or

$$m_1 = m_1' \tag{1.39}$$

Furthermore, if g_2 is the complement of the subgraph corresponding to g_1 in G_2, then since G_1 and G_2 are duals,

$$r_2 = R_2 - m_1 \qquad (1.40)$$

where r_2 and R_2 are the ranks of g_2 and G_2, respectively. Observe that g_2' can be obtained from g_2 by shorting the edge (β_1, β_2). In doing so, the number of components remains unaltered, whereas the number of nodes is reduced by one if $\beta_1 \neq \beta_2$ and remains the same if $\beta_1 = \beta_2$:

$$r_2' = r_2 - 1, \quad \text{if } \beta_1 \neq \beta_2 \qquad (1.41a)$$

$$r_2' = r_2, \qquad \text{if } \beta_1 = \beta_2 \qquad (1.41b)$$

and, in particular, if $g_2 = G_2$

$$R_2' = R_2 - 1, \quad \text{if } \beta_1 \neq \beta_2 \qquad (1.42a)$$

$$R_2' = R_2, \qquad \text{if } \beta_1 = \beta_2 \qquad (1.42b)$$

where r_2' and R_2' are the ranks of g_2' and G_2', respectively. Combining these equations (1.39)–(1.42) yields

$$r_2' = R_2' - m_1' \qquad (1.43)$$

showing that G_2' is a dual of G_1'. This completes the proof of the theorem.

Instead of characterizing a planar graph in terms of certain forbidden subgraphs, Whitney (1932, 1933a) showed that planarity can be stated in terms of combinatorial duals.

THEOREM 1.18

A graph is planar if and only if it has a combinatorial dual.

Proof. Necessity. Let G_1 be a planar graph. Without loss of generality, assume that G_1 is connected. Since G_1 is planar, it can be mapped onto a sphere. Then by Theorem 1.9, G_1 divides the sphere into $M_1 + 1$ regions, where M_1 is the nullity of G_1. Let G_2 be the geometric dual of G_1 constructed in accordance with Definition 1.22. Then G_2 contains $M_1 + 1$ nodes. It remains to be shown that G_2 is a combinatorial dual of G_1.

Let g_1 be a subgraph of G_1, and let g_2 be the complement of the corresponding subgraph of g_1 in G_2. To establish necessity, we show that

$$r_2 = R_2 - m_1 \qquad (1.44)$$

where r_2 and R_2 are the ranks of g_2 and G_2, respectively, and m_1 the nullity of g_1. To this end, we present a scheme for simultaneously constructing g_1 and g_2, as follows: Draw G_2 on the sphere and put all the nodes of G_1 inside the appropriate regions of G_2. Each time an edge of g_1 is inserted, delete the corresponding edge of G_2 but leave the endpoints behind. Thus, when g_1 is constructed, g_2 is also formed.

We next demonstrate that in the above construction process, each time the nullity of the subgraph of G_1 is increased by one after adding an edge, the number of components in the subgraph of G_2 is also increased by one after deleting the corresponding edge of G_2. Furthermore, if the nullity of the subgraph of G_1 is unaltered, the number of components in the subgraph of G_2 remains unaltered. We remark that some of the components may consist of isolated nodes. Observe that the nullity of the G_1-subgraph is increased only when an edge is inserted between two nodes in the same component. Let (α_1, α_2) be such an edge, and let (β_1, β_2) be its corresponding edge in G_2. Since α_1 and α_2 belong to the same component, there is a path connecting α_1 and α_2 in the constructed subgraph of G_1. This path together with (α_1, α_2) forms a circuit L. When (β_1, β_2) is removed, the nodes β_1 and β_2 cannot be in the same component; for, otherwise, there is a path $P_{\beta_1 \beta_2}$ connecting β_1 and β_2 in the G_2-subgraph. Since β_1 and β_2 are on opposite sides of the circuit L, $P_{\beta_1 \beta_2}$ must cross L, showing an edge of $P_{\beta_1 \beta_2}$ crosses an edge of L. But by construction process such an edge of $P_{\beta_1 \beta_2}$ was removed when the corresponding edge of L was inserted. Thus, when the nullity of the G_1-subgraph is increased by one after adding an edge, the number of components in the G_2-subgraph is also increased by one after the deletion of the corresponding edge in G_2. To verify the second part of our assertion, suppose that we construct the whole of the graph G_1 by this process, resulting in the increase in nullity by M_1, the nullity of G_1. This implies that the number of components of the G_2-subgraph is at least $M_1 + 1$, because G_2 initially contains at least one component and each increase in nullity of the G_1-subgraph is accompanied by an increase in the number of components of the associated G_2-subgraph. But once G_1 is constructed, what is left of G_2 is the null graph consisting only of N_2 nodes. Since by construction $N_2 = M_1 + 1$, the number of components in the G_2-subgraph is exactly $M_1 + 1$ instead of at least $M_1 + 1$. Thus, G_2 is connected and the number of components increases only when the nullity of the G_1-subgraph increases.

Return to g_1 and g_2 and observe that g_2 is a spanning subgraph of G_2. Then the increase in the number of components when g_2 is constructed from G_2 is m_1. Since G_2 is connected, its rank is $R_2 = N_2 - 1$. Hence the rank r_2 of g_2 is given by

$$r_2 = N_2 - 1 - m_1 = R_2 - m_1 \tag{1.45}$$

showing that G_2 is a combinatorial dual of G_1.

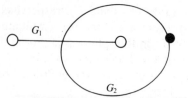

Fig. 1.47. The geometric duals of graphs containing one edge.

Sufficiency. To prove sufficiency, we show that if G_2 is a combinatorial dual of a graph G_1, then G_1 is planar. This also establishes the equivalency of the geometric dual and the combinatorial dual. The result is sufficiently important to be stated separately as a theorem.

THEOREM 1.19

A graph has a geometric dual if and only if it has a combinatorial dual.

Proof. We have already established that if a graph has a geometric dual, then it has a combinatorial dual. Thus, from Theorem 1.10 it is sufficient to consider a nonseparable graph G_1 possessing a combinatorial dual G_2. We show that G_2 is a geometric dual of G_1.

We prove this theorem by induction over the number of edges of G_1 and G_2. If the graphs G_1 and G_2 contain only one edge each, they can be mapped as shown in Fig. 1.47. Assume that the theorem is true for all G_1 and G_2 with $B-1$ edges or less, $B \geqq 2$. We show that the assertion is true for any G_1 and G_2 with B edges. To facilitate our discussion, two cases are distinguished.

Case 1

G_1 contains a node of degree 2. Let j be a node of G_1 of degree 2, and let (i, j) and (j, k) be the two edges incident at j. From Theorem 1.6, we see that since G_1 is nonseparable, every edge of G_1 is contained in a circuit. In particular, there is a circuit containing (i, j) and (j, k). Thus, removing either (i, j) or (j, k) alone will not alter the rank of G_1, but the removal of both of them reduces the rank of G_1 by one. Since G_2 is a combinatorial dual of G_1, by Theorem 1.15 G_1 is a combinatorial dual of G_2. Let (β_1, β_2) and (β_3, β_4) be the two edges in G_2 corresponding to (i, j) and (j, k) in G_1, respectively. From Definition 1.23, if $g_2 = (\beta_1, \beta_2)$ or (β_3, β_4), then $g_1 = G_1 - (i, j)$ or $G_1 - (j, k)$ and the ranks r_1 and R_1 of g_1 and G_1, respectively, and the nullity m_2 of g_2 are related by

$$r_1 = R_1 - m_2 = R_1 \qquad (1.46)$$

implying that the nullity m_2 of g_2 is zero. If, on the other hand, $g_2 = (\beta_1, \beta_2)(\beta_3, \beta_4)$, then $g_1 = G_1 - (i, j)(j, k)$ and

$$r_1 = R_1 - m_2 = R_1 - 1 \tag{1.47}$$

or $m_2 = 1$. The conclusion is that the subgraph composed of either (β_1, β_2) or (β_3, β_4) but not both is of nullity zero, and that the subgraph $(\beta_1, \beta_2)(\beta_3, \beta_4)$ is of nullity one. This is possible only if (β_1, β_2) and (β_3, β_4) are connected in parallel. Without loss of generality, let $\beta_1 = \beta_3$ and $\beta_2 = \beta_4$ and write $(\beta_1, \beta_2) = (\beta_1, \beta_2)_1$ and $(\beta_3, \beta_4) = (\beta_1, \beta_2)_2$, whose corresponding edges in G_1 are (i, j) and (j, k), respectively.

Let G_1' be the graph obtained from G_1 by shorting the edge (j, k), and let $G_2' = G_2 - (\beta_1, \beta_2)_2$. By Theorem 1.17, G_1' and G_2' are combinatorial duals and preserve the same corresponding edges as in G_1 and G_2. Since these graphs contain $B - 1$ edges, by induction hypothesis they are also geometric duals and can be mapped together onto the sphere as described in Definition 1.22. In particular, edge $(\beta_1, \beta_2)_1$ crosses (i, k), the edge connecting i and k in G_1' after shorting (j, k) in G_1. Mark a point on the edge (i, k) of G_1' between the node k and the point at which the edge $(\beta_1, \beta_2)_1$ of G_2' crosses it. Let this point be the node j, dividing the edge (i, k) into the two edges (i, j) and (j, k). Draw the edge $(\beta_1, \beta_2)_2$ crossing the edge (j, k). This reconstructs the graphs G_1 and G_2 such that they map together onto the sphere in accordance with Definition 1.22. Thus, G_2 is a geometric dual of G_1.

Case 2

Each node of G_1 is of at least degree 3. In this case, there is an edge (i, j) in G_1 whose removal results in a graph $G_1' = G_1 - (i, j)$ that is still nonseparable. Let (β_1, β_2) be the edge in G_2 corresponding to (i, j) in G_1. Since G_2 is nonseparable, $\beta_1 \neq \beta_2$ and the two endpoints of (β_1, β_2) are distinct. Let G_2' be the graph obtained from G_2 by shorting the edge (β_1, β_2). By Theorem 1.17, G_1' and G_2' are combinatorial duals and preserve the same corresponding edges as in G_1 and G_2. Notice that at this point, G_1' and G_2' are both nonseparable. Therefore, there are no cutpoints in G_1' and G_2'. We next show that edges incident with a node in either G_1' or G_2' correspond to a circuit in the other.

Let Q_i' be the subgraph of G_2' composed of all the edges incident at node i. Let $\bar{g}_1'$ be the complement of the subgraph g_1' in G_1' corresponding to the edges of Q_i' in G_2'. From Definition 1.23, the ranks $\bar{r}_2'$ and R_2' of $\bar{Q}_i' = G_2' - Q_i'$, the complement of Q_i' in G_2' and G_2', and the nullity m_1' of g_1' are related by

$$\bar{r}_2' = R_2' - m_1' = R_2' - 1 \tag{1.48}$$

where $\bar{r}_2' = R_2' - 1$, giving $m_1' = 1$. Thus, g_1' is a subgraph of nullity 1.

Furthermore, since G'_1 and G'_2 contain $B - 1$ edges, by induction hypothesis they can be mapped together onto the sphere in accordance with Definition 1.22 or G'_1 and G'_2 are also geometric duals. Let node i of G'_2 lie inside the circuit L' of g'_1 in G'_1. If $g'_1 \neq L'$, the subgraph $g'_1 - L'$ of G'_1 must lie inside L' because every edge of g'_1 must be crossed by an edge of Q'_i. This is possible only if G'_1 contains a cutpoint, contradicting the fact that G'_1 is nonseparable. This shows that the edges of G'_1 corresponding to those of Q'_i in G'_2 constitute a circuit or $g'_1 = L'$. By the same argument, we can show that edges incident with a node in either G_1 or G_2 correspond to a subgraph of nullity 1 in the other, because G_1 and G_2 are also nonseparable. Furthermore, this subgraph of nullity 1 must be a circuit. To see this, let Q_i be the subgraph composed of the edges incident at node i in G_2. Let $\bar{g}_1$ be the complement of the subgraph g_1 in G_1 corresponding to the edges of Q_i in G_2. Then g_1 is of nullity 1 and contains a circuit L such that $g_1 - L \neq \varnothing$, the null graph. This implies that the complement $\bar{g}_2$ of the subgraph g_2 in G_2 corresponding to the edges of L in G_1 is a spanning subgraph of G_2 because g_2 is a proper subgraph of Q_i, and is, therefore, connected. From Definition 1.23, the ranks $\bar{r}_2$ and R_2 of $\bar{g}_2$ and G_2 and the nullity m_1 of g_1 are related by

$$\bar{r}_2 = R_2 - m_1 = R_2 \qquad (1.49)$$

or $m_1 = 0$, a contradiction. Thus, the edges incident with a node in either G_1 or G_2 correspond to a circuit in the other.

Return to (i, j) in G_1 and (β_1, β_2) in G_2. Let Q_{β_1} and Q_{β_2} be the subgraphs of G_2 composed of the edges incident at nodes β_1 and β_2, respectively. Let L_1 and L_2 be the circuits in G_1 corresponding to the edges of Q_{β_1} and Q_{β_2} in G_2, respectively. One of these edges in L_1 and L_2 is (i, j). Write

$$L_1 = P_1 \cup (i, j) \qquad (1.50a)$$

$$L_2 = P_2 \cup (i, j) \qquad (1.50b)$$

where P_1 and P_2 are paths in G_1 with endpoints i and j. Recall that $G'_1 = G_1 - (i, j)$ and G'_2 is obtained from G_2 by shorting the edge (β_1, β_2) with the combined node being denoted by β'. If $Q_{\beta'}$ is the subgraph composed of the edges incident at node β' in G'_2, the circuit L'_β in G'_1 corresponding to the edges of $Q_{\beta'}$ in G'_2 is formed by the edges of the paths P_1 and P_2, because they correspond to edges incident at nodes β_1 and β_2 except the edge (β_1, β_2). Now, as before, G'_1 and G'_2 can be mapped onto the sphere in accordance with Definition 1.22. On the map, the node β' lies inside a region within the circuit L'_β of G'_1. Each edge of L'_β is crossed by an edge incident at β'. There are no other edges of G'_2 crossing L'_β. No other part of G'_2 other than the node β' can lie inside L'_β; for otherwise such a part can only have the node β' in common with its complement, indicating the existence of a cutpoint in

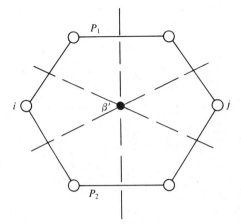

Fig. 1.48. The mapping of L'_β in G'_1 and $Q_{\beta'}$ in G'_2, where L'_β is the circuit composed of the paths P_1 and P_2.

G'_2. This is impossible for a nonseparable G'_2. Likewise, there is no part of G'_1 lying inside L'_β, because any such edge must be crossed by an edge of G'_2, resulting in a cutpoint in G'_1, whereas G'_1 is nonseparable. Thus, the mapping of L'_β in G'_1 and $Q_{\beta'}$ in G'_2 is of the form shown in Fig. 1.48, where the circuit L'_β is composed of the paths P_1 and P_2.

Observe that all the edges incident at node β_1 in G_2 except the edge (β_1, β_2) cross individually the edges of the path P_1, and that all the edges incident at node β_2 except (β_1, β_2) cross the edges of P_2. Thus, we can separate the node β' into two nodes β_1 and β_2 in such a way that no two edges of $G_2 - (\beta_1, \beta_2)$ cross each other. We now connect an edge between nodes i and j to form G_1, crossing none of the other edges. This edge (i, j) divides the circuit L'_β into two parts, with β_1 in one part and β_2 in the other, as depicted in Fig. 1.49. Now we join an edge (β_1, β_2) between β_1 and β_2, crossing only (i, j) in G_1, and obtain G_2. The graphs G_1 and G_2 are now mapped onto the sphere in accordance with Definition 1.22, as required. This shows that G_2 is a geometric dual of G_1, and our proof is complete.

In Definition 1.23 and the various theorems following it, we state that G_2 is *a dual* of G_1 or G_1 is *a dual* of G_2. One may ask whether or not a planar graph can have more than one dual. We can conceive of a simple way to construct two nonisomorphic graphs to be the duals of a planar graph, as follows: We begin by constructing a geometric dual G_2 of an unconnected planar graph G_1 by the procedure of Definition 1.22. Then G_2 is connected. We next use the same procedure to construct a geometric dual G_3 of G_2. Then G_3 is also connected. Thus, G_1 and G_3 are both duals of G_2 and they are not isomorphic, since one is connected and the other is not.

As a result of Theorem 1.19, it is not necessary to say that the graphs G_1

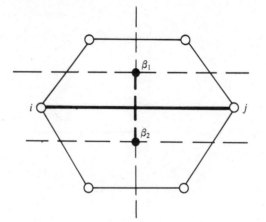

Fig. 1.49. The mapping of the graphs G_1 and G_2 onto the sphere.

and G_2 are geometric duals or combinatorial duals. It suffices to say that G_1 and G_2 are dual graphs.

As an illustration, consider the planar graph G_1 of Fig. 1.50(a) whose dual G_2 as constructed by the procedure of Definition 1.22 is shown in Fig. 1.50(b). We next use the same procedure to construct a dual G_3 of G_2 as given in Fig. 1.50(c). Then G_1 and G_3 are duals of G_2. The graphs G_1 and G_3 are not isomorphic because G_1 is unconnected whereas G_3 is connected. One natural question is that if the duals of a planar graph are not unique, how are they related? The answer to the question can be stated in terms of the notion of 2-isomorphism.

1.6   2-ISOMORPHISM

In Section 1.1, we introduced the notion of isomorphism to mean that two graphs are identical or the same. If a graph is separable, we can decompose it into blocks by splitting off the cutpoints. Now, if we like, we can reconnect the two blocks by coalescing any node i of one block with any node j of the other. The graph of Fig. 1.51(a) can be decomposed by splitting off the cutpoint k into k' and k''. Now, suppose that we reconnect the blocks at the nodes i and j. The resulting graph is shown in Fig. 1.51(b). In the present section, we consider the interchange of series-connected subgraphs. The resulting class of equivalent graphs is said to be 2-*isomorphic*, and was first studied by Whitney (1933*b*). The 2-isomorphic graphs are of great interest in electrical network theory.

DEFINITION 1.24

2-Isomorphism. Two graphs G_1 and G_2 are said to be 2-*isomorphic* if one can be made isomorphic to the other by a series of the following

(a)

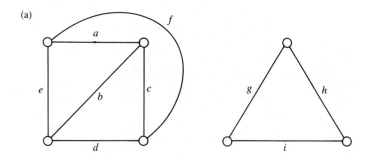

(b)

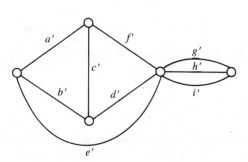

(c)

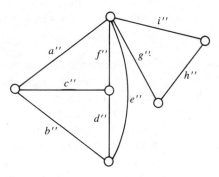

Fig. 1.50. The graph G_2 possessing two nonisomorphic duals G_1 and G_3: (a) G_1; (b) G_2; (c) G_3.

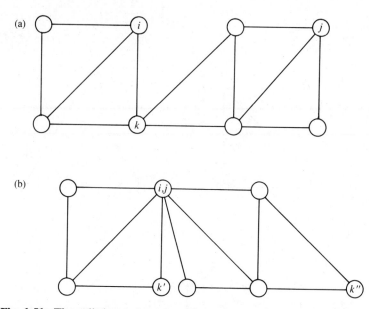

Fig. 1.51. The splitting and reconnecting of subgraphs at a cutpoint.

operations:

(a) Decompose a separable graph into blocks and then reconnect them at the single nodes to form a cutpoint.

(b) If g is a proper nonnull subgraph of G_1 or G_2 such that it has only two nodes i and j in common with its complement $\bar{g}$, decompose G_1 or G_2 into g and $\bar{g}$ by splitting off the nodes i and j and then reconnect at the same nodes after turning around at these nodes for either g or $\bar{g}$.

To illustrate the concept of 2-isomorphism, we consider the two graphs G_1 and G_2 of Fig. 1.52. To show that these two graphs are 2-isomorphic, we choose the subgraph $g = abcdefghij$ and its complement $\bar{g} = kmnpqrt$ in G_1. Next decompose G_1 into g and $\bar{g}$ by splitting off the nodes i and j and then reconnect at the same nodes after turning around at these nodes for g. The resulting graph G_3 is shown in Fig. 1.53(a). In G_3, let $g = abcdefghijkmn$. Then $\bar{g} = pqrt$. Turning around and reconnecting at the nodes u and j for $\bar{g}$ yields the graph G_4 as shown in Fig. 1.53(b). Finally, let $g = kmn$. Then $\bar{g} = abcdefghijpqrt$. Turning around and reconnecting at the nodes i and u for g gives the desired graph G_2 of Fig. 1.52(b). Thus, G_1 and G_2 are 2-isomorphic.

The most important result in characterizing 2-isomorphic graphs is given by Whitney (1933b), and is stated as a theorem.

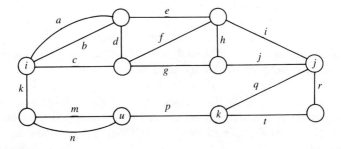

(a)

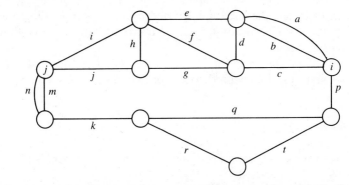

(b)

Fig. 1.52. Graphs used to illustrate the concept of 2-isomorphism: (a) G_1; (b) G_2.

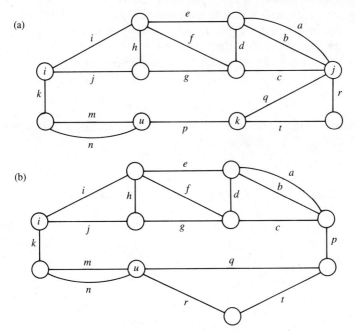

(a)

(b)

Fig. 1.53. Graphs used to illustrate the concept of 2-isomorphism: (a) G_3; (b) G_4.

THEOREM 1.20

Two graphs are 2-isomorphic if and only if there is a one-to-one correspondence between their edges such that circuits in one correspond to circuits
formed by the corresponding edges in the other.

The necessary part of the theorem is fairly evident. The proof of the
sufficient part is too long to be given here. For the interested reader, we
refer to the original paper of Whitney (1933b). As an example, consider the
2-isomorphic graphs G_1 and G_2 of Fig. 1.52, where the corresponding edges
are designated by the same labels. If we pick, for instance, the circuit
$L = ieakmptr$ in G_1, the subgraph formed by the corresponding edges in G_2
is also a circuit. This holds for all such circuits and we say that circuits
correspond to circuits.

To answer an earlier question on the relations of the duals of a planar
graph, we state the following theorem of Whitney (1933a, b).

THEOREM 1.21

The duals of a planar graph are unique within a 2-isomorphism.

Proof. Let G_α and G_β be two duals of a planar graph G. Take any circuit
L_α of G_α. Then following a proof similar to that for Theorem 1.19, we can
show that the subgraph C of G corresponding to the edges of L_α is a
minimal subgraph (cutset) whose removal from G reduces the rank by one.
Likewise, we can show that the subgraph L_β of G_β corresponding to the
edges of C is a circuit. Thus, circuits of G_α correspond to circuits of G_β, and
by Theorem 1.20, the graphs G_α and G_β are 2-isomorphic. This completes
the proof of the theorem.

The theorem states that if G_1 and G_2 are two duals of a planar graph G,
then G_1 and G_2 are 2-isomorphic.

1.7   MATRICES ASSOCIATED WITH A GRAPH

The most convenient algebra used in the study of graphs is the algebra of
the residue class modulo 2, which consists of two elements denoted by the
symbols 1 and 0. Two operations, *addition* "+" and *multiplication* "·", are
defined in this algebra by the rules

$$0 + 0 = 0, \qquad 0 + 1 = 1 + 0 = 1, \qquad 1 + 1 = 0 \qquad (1.51a)$$

$$0 \cdot 0 = 0, \qquad 0 \cdot 1 = 1 \cdot 0 = 0, \qquad 1 \cdot 1 = 1 \qquad (1.51b)$$

Except for the addition rule $1 + 1 = 0$, the others are the same for the real numbers zero and one in the real field.

1.7.1   Incidence Matrix

A graph is completely specified by its edge and node incidence relations. These relations are most conveniently expressed by means of a matrix.

DEFINITION 1.25

Node–Edge Incidence Matrix or Incidence Matrix. The *node–edge incidence matrix* or simply the *incidence matrix* A_a of an n-node, b-edge graph G without self-loops is a matrix of order $n \times b$ such that if $A_a = [a_{ij}]$, then

$$a_{ij} = 1 \quad \text{if edge } e_j \text{ is incident at node } i \qquad (1.52a)$$

$$a_{ij} = 0 \quad \text{otherwise} \qquad (1.52b)$$

Thus, the incidence matrix A_a of a graph G is a matrix, each of whose rows corresponds to a node and each of whose columns corresponds to an edge. For the graph G of Fig. 1.54, the incidence matrix is found to be

$$
A_a =
\begin{array}{c}
 \\ 1 \\ 2 \\ 3 \\ 4 \\ 5
\end{array}
\begin{array}{c}
\begin{array}{cccccccc}
e_1 & e_2 & e_3 & e_4 & e_5 & e_6 & e_7 & e_8
\end{array} \\
\begin{bmatrix}
1 & 1 & 0 & 0 & 1 & 0 & 0 & 0 \\
0 & 1 & 1 & 0 & 0 & 1 & 0 & 0 \\
1 & 0 & 0 & 1 & 0 & 0 & 0 & 1 \\
0 & 0 & 1 & 1 & 0 & 0 & 1 & 0 \\
0 & 0 & 0 & 0 & 1 & 1 & 1 & 1
\end{bmatrix}
\end{array}
\qquad (1.53)
$$

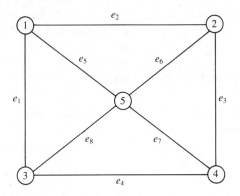

Fig. 1.54. A graph used to illustrate the incidence matrix.

Observe that each column of A_a contains exactly two ones. Hence, the sum of all the rows of A_a over the algebra of the residue class modulo 2 is a row of zeros, showing that not all the rows of A_a are linearly independent.

THEOREM 1.22

The rank of the incidence matrix of a graph is equal to the rank of the graph.

Proof. Let A_a be the incidence matrix of an n-node graph G. We shall only prove the case where G is connected, leaving the unconnected case as an obvious simple extension. Since the sum of all the rows of A_a is a row of zeros, the rank of A_a over the modulo 2 algebra is at most $n-1$. To complete the proof, we demonstrate that the rank of A_a is at least $r = n - 1$, the rank of G.

We claim that the sum of any k rows of A_a, $k < n$, contains at least one nonzero element. Suppose that the assertion is false, and let k rows of A_a add to a row of zeros. Then we can rearrange the rows of A_a so that these k rows appear at the top of the matrix. Since thse k rows add to a row of zeros, each column in these k rows must either contain two ones or all zeros. Now permute the columns of A_a so that the columns with all zeros in the first k rows appear in the last columns. There must be some columns like this; for, otherwise, the last $n - k$ rows of A_a contain only zeros, implying that G contains isolated nodes. This is impossible for a connected G. As a result, the matrix A_a can be partitioned as

$$A_a = \begin{bmatrix} A_{11} & 0 \\ 0 & A_{22} \end{bmatrix} \tag{1.54}$$

where the rows of A_{11} correspond to the first k rows of A_a, and the columns correspond to those where the first k rows contain both ones. Therefore, the nodes of G corresponding to the first k rows of A_a have no edges connecting to the nodes corresponding to the last $n - k$ rows. Hence, the graph G is not connected, contradicting the assumption. The assertion follows.

Let $A_1, A_2, \ldots, A_n$ be the rows of A_a. Since the sum of any k rows of A_a, $k < n$, contains at least one nonzero element, the equation

$$c_1 A_1 + c_2 A_2 + \ldots + c_n A_n = 0 \tag{1.55}$$

where c_j $(j = 1, 2, \ldots, n)$ are scalars from the field modulo 2, has only one nonzero solution for c_js with

$$c_1 = c_2 = \ldots = c_n = 1 \tag{1.56}$$

showing that any $n-1$ rows of A_a are linearly independent. The theorem follows. This completes the proof of the theorem.

This property was first established by Kirchhoff (1847). As a result, all the information contained in A_a is contained in the submatrix of order $r \times b$ and of rank r, the rank of the graph G.

DEFINITION 1.26

Basis Incidence Matrix. A *basis incidence matrix* A of a b-edge graph G of rank r is a submatrix of order $r \times b$ and of rank r of the incidence matrix A_a of G.

In the literature, the incidence matrix is frequently referred to as the *complete incidence matrix* because it contains rows corresponding to all the nodes of the graph G. In forming a basis incidence matrix A from A_a, the nodes in G corresponding to the deleted rows of A_a are called the *reference nodes* of the components of G because they correspond to the potential-reference points in the associated electrical network. For the graph G of Fig. 1.54, its complete incidence matrix A_a was obtained in (1.53). If we delete row 5, we obtain a basis incidence matrix

$$A = \begin{array}{c} \\ 1 \\ 2 \\ 3 \\ 4 \end{array} \begin{array}{cccccccc} e_1 & e_2 & e_3 & e_4 & e_5 & e_6 & e_7 & e_8 \\ \left[\begin{array}{cccccccc} 1 & 1 & 0 & 0 & 1 & 0 & 0 & 0 \\ 0 & 1 & 1 & 0 & 0 & 1 & 0 & 0 \\ 1 & 0 & 0 & 1 & 0 & 0 & 0 & 1 \\ 0 & 0 & 1 & 1 & 0 & 0 & 1 & 0 \end{array} \right] \end{array} \tag{1.57}$$

of G. This matrix is of rank $r = 4$, being equal to the rank of G.

DEFINITION 1.27

Tree. A spanning subgraph of a graph is said to be a *tree* if and only if it is connected and contains no circuits.

For the graph of Fig. 1.55, its trees are presented in Fig. 1.56. Observe that a tree contains $n-1$ edges, n being the number of nodes of the graph.

DEFINITION 1.28

Branch. An edge of a tree is called a *branch*.

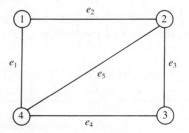

Fig. 1.55. A graph used to illustrate the concept of a tree.

DEFINITION 1.29

Major Submatrix. For a matrix F of order $p \times q$ and of rank p, a *major submatrix* of F is a nonsingular submatrix of order p.

The edges in each of the trees of Fig. 1.56 are the branches of the tree. For the basis incident matrix A of (1.57), a major submatrix is given by

$$M = \begin{array}{c} \\ 1 \\ 2 \\ 3 \\ 4 \end{array} \begin{array}{cccc} e_1 & e_2 & e_3 & e_5 \\ \begin{bmatrix} 1 & 1 & 0 & 1 \\ 0 & 1 & 1 & 0 \\ 1 & 0 & 0 & 0 \\ 0 & 0 & 1 & 0 \end{bmatrix} \end{array} \tag{1.58}$$

which is nonsingular over the field modulo 2.

THEOREM 1.23

A square submatrix of a basis incidence matrix of a connected graph is a major submatrix if and only if the columns of this submatrix correspond to the branches of a tree of the graph.

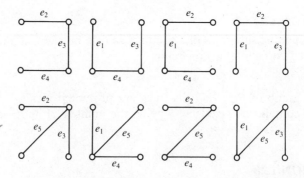

Fig. 1.56. Trees of the graph of Fig. 1.55.

Proof. Let M be the submatrix of a basis incidence matrix A of a connected graph G in question. If the columns of M correspond to the branches of a tree, then by Theorem 1.22 M is nonsingular because M is a basis incidence matrix of the tree. To prove necessity, we first demonstrate that if M is nonsingular, the subgraph g corresponding to its columns cannot contain any circuits. Suppose that the assertion is false. Let L be a circuit of length k in g and let M_1 be the submatrix of M formed by the columns corresponding to the edges of L. Relabel G if necessary so that the columns and the leading rows (corresponding to the nodes in L) of M_1 are arranged in the orders of the edges and nodes appearing in L, respectively. In M_1 it is not difficult to see that if the reference node of G is contained in L, the number of nonzero rows in M_1 is $k - 1$. Thus, the columns of M_1 are linearly dependent. On the other hand, if the reference node is not contained in L, the number of nonzero rows in M_1 is k. Since, in this case, each of these columns contains two ones, the rank of M_1 is at most $k - 1$. This shows that the columns of M_1 and hence M are linearly dependent, contradicting the hypothesis that M is nonsingular so that its columns are linearly independent.

Our conclusion is that if M is nonsingular, the subgraph g of G corresponding to its columns cannot contain any circuit. This together with the fact that g contains $n - 1$ edges implies that the subgraph g is a tree of G, completing the proof of the theorem.

COROLLARY 1.5

There exists a one-to-one correspondence between the trees of a graph and the major submatrices of its basis incidence matrix.

A basis incidence matrix A of the graph G of Fig. 1.55 is found to be

$$A = \begin{array}{c} \\ 1 \\ 2 \\ 3 \end{array} \begin{array}{c} e_1 \ \ e_2 \ \ e_3 \ \ e_4 \ \ e_5 \\ \begin{bmatrix} 1 & 1 & 0 & 0 & 0 \\ 0 & 1 & 1 & 0 & 1 \\ 0 & 0 & 1 & 1 & 0 \end{bmatrix} \end{array} \qquad (1.59)$$

It is straightforward to verify that the only major submatrices of A are those whose columns correspond to the branches of the trees of Fig. 1.56.

1.7.2   Circuit Matrix

In addition to the node–edge incidence matrix, we can define the circuit–edge incidence matrix.

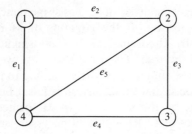

Fig. 1.57. A graph used to illustrate the orthogonal property of the incidence and circuit matrices.

DEFINITION 1.30

Circuit–Edge Incidence Matrix (Circuit Matrix). The *circuit–edge incidence matrix* or simply the *circuit matrix* B_a of a b-edge graph is a matrix of order $p \times b$, where p is the number of circuits of the graph, such that if $B_a = [b_{ij}]$, then

$$b_{ij} = 1 \quad \text{if edge } e_j \text{ is in circuit } i \tag{1.60a}$$

$$b_{ij} = 0 \quad \text{otherwise} \tag{1.60b}$$

For the graph G of Fig. 1.57, there are three circuits:

$$L_1 = e_1 e_2 e_5, \qquad L_2 = e_3 e_4 e_5, \qquad L_3 = e_1 e_2 e_3 e_4 \tag{1.61}$$

The circuit matrix B_a is found to be

$$
B_a = \begin{array}{c} \\ 1 \\ 2 \\ 3 \end{array}
\begin{array}{c}
\begin{array}{ccccc} e_1 & e_2 & e_3 & e_4 & e_5 \end{array} \\
\left[
\begin{array}{ccccc}
1 & 1 & 0 & 0 & 1 \\
0 & 0 & 1 & 1 & 1 \\
1 & 1 & 1 & 1 & 0
\end{array}
\right]
\end{array}
\tag{1.62}
$$

DEFINITION 1.31

Cotree. The complement of a tree in a connected graph is called a *cotree*.

DEFINITION 1.32

Chord (Link). An edge in a cotree is called a *chord* or a *link*.

Therefore, a cotree of a connected n-node, b-edge graph contains $m = b - n + 1$ chords. Because a tree is connected and contains no circuit, there is a unique path connecting any two of its nodes. The addition of any chord to the tree produces a unique circuit in the resulting graph. There are a total m such circuits, one corresponding to each chord. This leads to the following definition.

DEFINITION 1.33

Fundamental Circuits (f-Circuits). The *fundamental circuits* or simply the f-*circuits* of a connected graph of nullity m with respect to a tree are the m circuits, each being formed by a chord and the unique tree path connecting the two endpoints of the chord in the tree.

The submatrix B_f of the circuit matrix B_a corresponding to a set of f-circuits of a graph G has a very special form. For example, if the f-circuits are labeled in some manner from L_1 to L_m, and if the chord that appears in circuit i is numbered as edge e_i for $i = 1, 2, \ldots, m$, then B_f can be partitioned as

$$B_f = [U_m \quad B_{f12}] \tag{1.63}$$

where U_m is the identity matrix of order m. For the graph G of Fig. 1.54, if we choose the tree composed of the branches e_5, e_6, e_7 and e_8, the f-circuits, labeled as L_1, L_2, L_3 and L_4, of G corresponding to the chords e_1, e_2, e_3 and e_4 are found to be

$$L_1 = e_1 e_5 e_8, \quad L_2 = e_2 e_5 e_6, \quad L_3 = e_3 e_6 e_7, \quad L_4 = e_4 e_7 e_8 \tag{1.64}$$

respectively. The submatrix B_f of B_a formed by these f-circuits is given by

$$B_f = \begin{array}{c} \\ L_1 \\ L_2 \\ L_3 \\ L_4 \end{array} \begin{array}{cccccccc} e_1 & e_2 & e_3 & e_4 & e_5 & e_6 & e_7 & e_8 \\ \left[\begin{array}{cccc:cccc} 1 & 0 & 0 & 0 & 1 & 0 & 0 & 1 \\ 0 & 1 & 0 & 0 & 1 & 1 & 0 & 0 \\ 0 & 0 & 1 & 0 & 0 & 1 & 1 & 0 \\ 0 & 0 & 0 & 1 & 0 & 0 & 1 & 1 \end{array}\right] \end{array} \tag{1.65}$$

which is partitioned in accordance with (1.63).

DEFINITION 1.34

Fundamental Circuit Matrix (f-Circuit Matrix). For a connected graph G of nullity m, the submatrix of the circuit matrix of G corresponding to a set of m f-circuits in G is called a *fundamental circuit matrix* or simply an f-*circuit matrix* B_f of G.

The f-circuit matrix $\boldsymbol{B}_f$ obviously has rank m because it contains the identity matrix of order m, as shown in (1.63). Therefore, the rank of $\boldsymbol{B}_a$ is at least m. To show that m is also an upper bound for the rank of $\boldsymbol{B}_a$, we need the following theorem. Apart from establishing the rank of $\boldsymbol{B}_a$, the result is extremely important in its own right and was first established by Veblen (1931). It is also fundamental to electrical network theory.

THEOREM 1.24

If the columns of the matrices $\boldsymbol{A}_a$ and $\boldsymbol{B}_a$ of a graph are arranged in the same edge order, then

$$\boldsymbol{A}_a\boldsymbol{B}_a' = \boldsymbol{0} \quad \text{and} \quad \boldsymbol{B}_a\boldsymbol{A}_a' = \boldsymbol{0} \tag{1.66}$$

where the prime denotes the matrix transpose.

Proof. We only prove the first identity; the second one follows immediately after taking transpose on both sides of the first.

Consider the ith row of $\boldsymbol{A}_a$ and the jth column of $\boldsymbol{B}_a'$ or the jth row of $\boldsymbol{B}_a$. The entries in the corresponding positions in the ith row of $\boldsymbol{A}_a$ and the jth row of $\boldsymbol{B}_a$ are nonzero if and only if the corresponding edge is incident at node i and is also contained in circuit j. If node i is not contained in circuit j, then there is no such edge and the product is zero, giving the required result. If circuit j does include node i, there will be precisely two edges of the circuit j incident at node i, meaning that there are only two nonzero entries in the ith row of $\boldsymbol{A}_a$ with the property that the corresponding entries in the jth row of $\boldsymbol{B}_a$ are also nonzero. Therefore, the product of the ith row of $\boldsymbol{A}_a$ and the jth column of $\boldsymbol{B}_a'$ will be zero over the modulo 2 algebra. This completes the proof of the theorem.

As an example of the theorem, consider the graph G of Fig. 1.57. The product of the incidence matrix $\boldsymbol{A}_a$ and the transpose of the circuit matrix $\boldsymbol{B}_a$ is computed as

$$\boldsymbol{A}_a\boldsymbol{B}_a' = \begin{bmatrix} 1 & 1 & 0 & 0 & 0 \\ 0 & 1 & 1 & 0 & 1 \\ 0 & 0 & 1 & 1 & 0 \\ 1 & 0 & 0 & 1 & 1 \end{bmatrix} \begin{bmatrix} 1 & 0 & 1 \\ 1 & 0 & 1 \\ 0 & 1 & 1 \\ 0 & 1 & 1 \\ 1 & 1 & 0 \end{bmatrix} = \begin{bmatrix} 0 & 0 & 0 \\ 0 & 0 & 0 \\ 0 & 0 & 0 \\ 0 & 0 & 0 \end{bmatrix} \tag{1.67}$$

confirming (1.66).

THEOREM 1.25

The rank of the circuit matrix of a graph is equal to the nullity of the graph.

Proof. We have already established that the rank of the circuit matrix B_a of a connected graph G is at least m, the nullity of G. If G is not connected, by partitioning B_a in accordance with the nodes and edges in the components of G, it is easy to confirm that the assertion remains valid in general. To complete our proof, we show that m is also an upper bound for the rank of B_a.

From Theorem 1.24, we see that since $A_a B_a' = 0$, the columns of B_a' are in the null-space of A_a. By Theorem 1.22, the rank of A_a is r, the rank of G, showing that the dimension of the null-space of A_a is $b - r = m$, where b is the number of edges of G. Thus, the maximum number of linearly independent rows of B_a is m, and the theorem follows. This completes the proof of the theorem.

As a result of Theorem 1.25, there is really no need to write down all the rows of B_a. Only m linearly independent ones are sufficient.

DEFINITION 1.35

Basis Circuit Matrix. A *basis circuit matrix* B of a b-edge graph G of nullity m is a submatrix of order $m \times b$ and of rank m of the circuit matrix B_a of G.

Thus, a basis circuit matrix B contains all the information that is contained in B_a, which is also frequently referred to as the *complete circuit matrix* because all the circuits of the graph are represented by the rows of B_a. Evidently, the f-circuit matrix is a basis circuit matrix.

THEOREM 1.26

A square submatrix of a basis circuit matrix of a connected graph is a major submatrix if and only if the columns of this submatrix correspond to the chords of a cotree in the graph.

Proof. Necessity. Let B be a basis circuit matrix of a connected graph G of nullity m. By permuting the columns of B if necessary, we may assume that the leading columns of B form a major submatrix. Let B be partitioned as

$$B = [B_{11} \quad B_{12}] \tag{1.68}$$

where B_{11} is nonsingular and of order m. Since there are r columns in B_{12}, it is sufficient to show that the subgraph corresponding to these columns does not contain any circuits. Assume otherwise, and let B_i be the row of B_a corresponding to such a circuit. Consider the submatrix of B_a consisting of the rows of B and B_i. Then the submatrix can be partitioned as

$$\begin{bmatrix} B \\ B_i \end{bmatrix} = \begin{bmatrix} B_{11} & B_{12} \\ 0 & B_{22} \end{bmatrix} \tag{1.69}$$

Then there is at least one nonzero element in B_{22}. Since B_{11} is nonsingular, the rank of the matrix (1.69) is $m + 1$. But this matrix is also a submatrix of B_a, which by Theorem 1.25 is of rank m. This is impossible and the assertion follows.

Sufficiency. Assume that the columns of a submatrix of B correspond to the chords of a cotree in G. Let B_f be the f-circuit matrix formed by the chords of this cotree in G. By permuting the columns of B and B_f if necessary, the matrices B and B_f can be partitioned as

$$B = [B_{11} \quad B_{12}] \tag{1.70a}$$

$$B_f = [U_m \quad B_{f12}] \tag{1.70b}$$

Since the rows of B and B_f are the two bases for the vector space spanned by the rows of B_a, there exists a nonsingular matrix D of order m such that

$$B = DB_f \tag{1.71}$$

giving

$$B_{11} = DU_m = D \tag{1.72}$$

Hence B_{11} is nonsingular. This completes the proof of the theorem.

COROLLARY 1.6

There exists a one-to-one correspondence between the cotrees of a graph and the major submatrices of a basis circuit matrix of the graph.

As an illustration, consider the graph G of Fig. 1.57. The graph G is of nullity 2. A basis circuit matrix B of G is, therefore, of order 2×5. It is easy to verify that the submatrix of B_a of (1.62) formed by any two of its rows is a basis circuit matrix of G. The basis circuit matrix B formed by the first two rows of B_a corresponding to the meshes formed by the boundary edges of

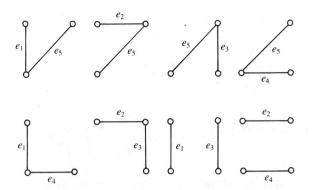

Fig. 1.58. Cotrees of the graph of Fig. 1.57.

the two interior regions of G is given by

$$B = \begin{matrix} & e_1 & e_2 & e_3 & e_4 & e_5 \\ & \begin{bmatrix} 1 & 1 & 0 & 0 & 1 \\ 0 & 0 & 1 & 1 & 1 \end{bmatrix} \end{matrix} \qquad (1.73)$$

The set of cotrees of G is shown in Fig. 1.58, and is given by

$$\bar{T} = \{e_1 e_5,\ e_2 e_5,\ e_3 e_5,\ e_4 e_5,\ e_1 e_4,\ e_2 e_3,\ e_1 e_3,\ e_2 e_4\} \qquad (1.74)$$

each of whose elements corresponds to the complement of a tree shown in Fig. 1.56. The submatrix formed by the columns corresponding to the chords of a cotree in $\bar{T}$ is a major submatrix of B, and these are the only major submatrices of B.

1.7.3 Cut Matrix

Another important class of subgraphs is called the *cutset*, which finds extensive use in electrical network theory because it generalizes the Kirchhoff's current law. The concept of cutsets was originally introduced by Whitney (1933a) and systematically developed by Seshu and Reed (1956). Our discussion here is to show that cutsets bear the same relationships to circuits that circuits bear to incidence relationships. Thus, we will find the duals of a number of theorems proved earlier for the circuits.

DEFINITION 1.36

Cutset. A *cutset* of a graph is a subgraph consisting of a minimal collection of edges whose removal reduces the rank of the graph by one.

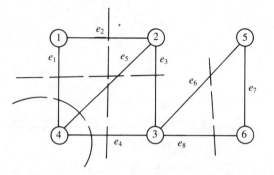

Fig. 1.59. The broken lines showing the cutsets.

The definition implies that if a graph G has more than one component, a cutset can only be formed from the edges of one of its components; for otherwise, the collection will not be minimal. Intuitively, if we "cut" the edges of a cutset, one of the components of G will be cut into two pieces. The name *cutset* has its origin in this interpretation. Note that a component of G may consist of an isolated node. For the graph G of Fig. 1.59, the subgraphs $e_1 e_3 e_5$, $e_2 e_4 e_5$, $e_1 e_4 e_5$, and $e_6 e_8$ are examples of cutsets. The broken lines shown in Fig. 1.59 indicate how these cutsets "cut" the graph. However, the subgraph $e_1 e_3 e_5 e_6 e_7$ is not a cutset because if we remove these edges from G, the rank of G is reduced from 5 to 3 ($=6-3$), a reduction of two instead of one as required. For the subgraph $e_3 e_4 e_6$, although its removal from G will reduce the rank of G by one, it is not a cutset because the removal of $e_3 e_4$ from G will also reduce the rank of G by one, showing that $e_3 e_4 e_6$ is not a minimal collection of edges.

DEFINITION 1.37

Incidence Cut. The subgraph formed by the edges incident at a node of a graph is called an *incidence cut* of the graph.

Thus, an incidence cut may either be a cutset or an edge-disjoint union of cutsets. For the graph G of Fig. 1.59, the subgraphs $e_1 e_4 e_5$ and $e_3 e_4 e_6 e_8$ are examples of incidence cuts. The former is also a cutset and the latter is an edge-disjoint union of two cutsets $e_3 e_4$ and $e_6 e_8$.

DEFINITION 1.38

Cut. A cutset or an edge-disjoint union of cutsets of a graph is called a *cut*.

A cut can also be interpreted in another useful fashion. Let V_1 be a nonempty proper subset of the node set V of a graph G, and let

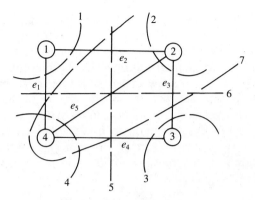

Fig. 1.60. A graph and its seven cuts denoted by the broken lines.

$V_2 = V - V_1$. Then the set of edges of G each of which is incident with one of its two endpoints in V_1 and the other in V_2 is a cut of G. In particular, if the removal of these edges from G increases the number of components of G by one, then the cut is also a cutset. For the graph G of Fig. 1.59, let $V_1 = \{1, 2, 5\}$. Then $V_2 = \{3, 4, 6\}$, and a cut is formed by the edges e_1, e_3, e_5, e_6 and e_7. Of course, the cutsets and incidence cuts are special types of cuts.

DEFINITION 1.39

Cut–Edge Incidence Matrix (Cut Matrix). The *cut–edge incidence matrix* or simply the *cut matrix* Q_a of a b-edge graph is a matrix of order $q \times b$, where q is the number of nonempty cuts in the graph, such that if $Q_a = [q_{ij}]$, then

$$q_{ij} = 1 \quad \text{if edge } e_j \text{ is in cut } i \tag{1.75a}$$

$$q_{ij} = 0 \quad \text{otherwise} \tag{1.75b}$$

The graph G of Fig. 1.60 contains seven cuts, as indicated by the broken lines drawn across the edges. The cut matrix is found to be

$$
Q_a =
\begin{array}{c}
\\ 1 \\ 2 \\ 3 \\ 4 \\ 5 \\ 6 \\ 7
\end{array}
\begin{array}{c}
\begin{array}{ccccc} e_1 & e_2 & e_3 & e_4 & e_5 \end{array} \\
\left[
\begin{array}{ccccc}
1 & 1 & 0 & 0 & 0 \\
0 & 1 & 1 & 0 & 1 \\
0 & 0 & 1 & 1 & 0 \\
1 & 0 & 0 & 1 & 1 \\
0 & 1 & 0 & 1 & 1 \\
1 & 0 & 1 & 0 & 1 \\
1 & 1 & 1 & 1 & 0
\end{array}
\right]
\end{array}
\tag{1.76}
$$

Clearly, not all the rows of Q_a are linearly independent. Then what is the rank of Q_a? Since Q_a contains the incidence matrix A_a as a submatrix, we know right away that the rank of Q_a is at least r, the rank of G. For example, in (1.76) the submatrix formed by the first four rows of Q_a is the incidence matrix of G. To show that r is also an upper bound, we need to establish a relationship between B_a and Q_a similar to that between B_a and A_a of (1.66). This relationship follows immediately from the observation that the number of edges common to a cut and a circuit is always even, giving a zero entry in the product of a row of Q_a, which corresponds to a cut, and a column of the transpose of B_a, which corresponds to a circuit, over the modulo 2 algebra.

THEOREM 1.27

If the columns of the matrices B_a and Q_a of a graph are arranged in the same edge order, then

$$Q_a B_a' = 0 \quad \text{and} \quad B_a Q_a' = 0 \tag{1.77}$$

where the prime denotes the matrix transpose.

Since the rank of B_a is m, the nullity of the graph G, and since $B_a Q_a' = 0$, it follows that the dimension of the null space of B_a is r ($=b - m$), where b is the number of edges of G. Thus, there are at most r linearly independent rows in Q_a, and we obtain the following theorem.

THEOREM 1.28

The rank of the cut matrix of a graph is equal to the rank of the graph.

Therefore, there is no need to write down all the rows of Q_a; only r linearly independent ones are sufficient.

DEFINITION 1.40

Basis Cut Matrix. A *basis cut matrix* Q of a b-edge graph G of rank r is a submatrix of order $r \times b$ and of rank r of the cut matrix Q_a of G.

Like the basis circuit matrix, a basis cut matrix contains all the information that is contained in Q_a. Earlier, we indicated how a cut of G can be used to partition its node set. In the following, we demonstrate how this partitioning of nodes of G can be done by means of a tree.

Let t be a tree of a connected graph G, and let e be a branch of t. Since t is connected and contains no circuits, the removal of e from t results in a subgraph consisting of two components. If V_1 and V_2 are the node sets of these two components, then V_1 and V_2 are mutually exclusive and together include all the nodes of G. Hence, the branch e of t defines a partition of the nodes of G in a unique way. The subgraph composed of all the edges each of which is incident with one of its two endpoints in V_1 and the other in V_2 is a cutset of G. This cutset contains only one branch of t, namely e, and some chords of the cotree $\bar{t}$ (with respect to t). Clearly, there are r such cutsets.

DEFINITION 1.41

Fundamental Cutsets (f-Cutsets). The *fundamental cutsets* or simply the *f-cutsets* of a connected graph of rank r with respect to a tree t are the r cutsets in which each cutset includes only one branch of t.

DEFINITION 1.42

Fundamental Cutset Matrix (f-Cutset Matrix). For a connected graph G of rank r, the submatrix of its cut matrix corresponding to a set of r f-cutsets in G is called a *fundamental cutset matrix* or simply an *f-cutset matrix* Q_f of G.

Like the f-circuit matrix, if the edges of G are numbered in such a way that the last r columns of Q_f correspond to the branches of t and if the f-cutsets are numbered correspondingly, the f-cutset matrix Q_f can be partitioned as

$$Q_f = [Q_{f11} \quad U_r] \tag{1.78}$$

where U_r is the identity matrix of order r. Thus, the f-cutset matrix is also a basis cut matrix.

We illustrate the above results by the following example.

Example 1.1

For the complete graph K_4 of Fig. 1.61, let us choose a tree $t = e_1 e_3 e_4$. The three f-cutsets C_1, C_2 and C_3 with respect to the branches e_1, e_3 and e_4 are found to be

$$C_1 = e_1 e_2 e_6, \qquad C_2 = e_2 e_4 e_5 e_6, \qquad C_3 = e_2 e_3 e_5 \tag{1.79}$$

and are shown in Fig. 1.62, respectively, where the thick edges represent

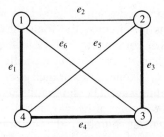

Fig. 1.61. A graph used to illustrate the concept of f-cutsets and f-circuits.

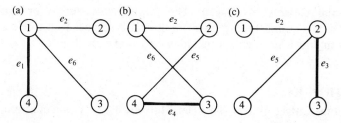

Fig. 1.62. The three f-cutsets defined for the tree $t = e_1 e_3 e_4$: (a) C_1; (b) C_2; (c) C_3.

the defining tree branches. The f-cutset matrix is given by

$$
Q_f = \begin{array}{c} \\ C_1 \\ C_2 \\ C_3 \end{array}
\begin{array}{cccccc} e_2 & e_5 & e_6 & e_1 & e_4 & e_3 \end{array}
\left[\begin{array}{ccc:ccc}
1 & 0 & 1 & 1 & 0 & 0 \\
1 & 1 & 1 & 0 & 1 & 0 \\
1 & 1 & 0 & 0 & 0 & 1
\end{array}\right]
\tag{1.80}
$$

For each chord in $\bar{t} = e_2 e_5 e_6$, the complement of t in G, there is an f-circuit. The three f-circuits

$$ L_1 = e_1 e_2 e_3 e_4, \qquad L_2 = e_3 e_4 e_5, \qquad L_3 = e_1 e_4 e_6 \tag{1.81} $$

are shown in Fig. 1.63 with the heavy lines denoting the defining chords. The f-circuit matrix is obtained as

$$
B_f = \begin{array}{c} \\ L_1 \\ L_2 \\ L_3 \end{array}
\begin{array}{cccccc} e_2 & e_5 & e_6 & e_1 & e_4 & e_3 \end{array}
\left[\begin{array}{ccc:ccc}
1 & 0 & 0 & 1 & 1 & 1 \\
0 & 1 & 0 & 0 & 1 & 1 \\
0 & 0 & 1 & 1 & 1 & 0
\end{array}\right]
\tag{1.82}
$$

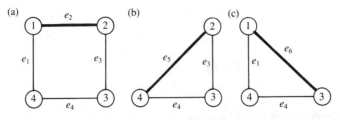

Fig. 1.63. The three f-circuits defined for the cotree $\bar{t} = e_2 e_5 e_6$: (a) L_1; (b) L_2; (c) L_3.

Using (1.80) and (1.82) in (1.77) yields

$$
\begin{bmatrix} 1 & 0 & 1 & 1 & 0 & 0 \\ 1 & 1 & 1 & 0 & 1 & 0 \\ 1 & 1 & 0 & 0 & 0 & 1 \end{bmatrix}
\begin{bmatrix} 1 & 0 & 0 \\ 0 & 1 & 0 \\ 0 & 0 & 1 \\ 1 & 0 & 1 \\ 1 & 1 & 1 \\ 1 & 1 & 0 \end{bmatrix}
= \begin{bmatrix} 0 & 0 & 0 \\ 0 & 0 & 0 \\ 0 & 0 & 0 \end{bmatrix}
\tag{1.83}
$$

confirming (1.77).

Finally, we mention that since the rows of Q and Q_f are the two bases of the vector space spanned by the rows of Q_a, it follows that one can be obtained from the other by a nonsingular transformation:

$$
Q = MQ_f \tag{1.84}
$$

where M is a nonsingular matrix of order r over the modulo 2 algebra. This leads directly to the following theorem.

THEOREM 1.29

A square submatrix of a basis cut matrix of a connected graph is a major submatrix if and only if the columns of this submatrix correspond to the branches of a tree of the graph.

COROLLARY 1.7

There exists a one-to-one correspondence between trees of a connected graph and the major submatrices of a basis cut matrix of the graph.

For the graph G of Fig. 1.61, the set of trees is given by

$$T = \{e_1e_2e_3,\ e_1e_2e_4,\ e_1e_3e_4,\ e_2e_3e_4,\ e_1e_2e_6,\ e_2e_3e_5,\ e_3e_4e_6,$$

$$e_1e_4e_5,\ e_2e_4e_5,\ e_2e_4e_6,\ e_2e_5e_6,\ e_3e_5e_6,\ e_4e_5e_6,\ e_1e_5e_6,$$

$$e_1e_3e_5,\ e_1e_3e_6\} \tag{1.85}$$

It is straightforward to verify that each of the major submatrices of Q_f of (1.80) is composed of the columns corresponding to a term in T.

1.7.4 Interrelationships Among the Matrices A, B_f and Q_f

Recall that a basis incidence matrix A of a graph G completely characterizes the graph in that if A is given the graph itself can be drawn in a straightforward manner. It is logical to expect that the matrices B_f and Q_f be expressible in terms of the submatrices of A.

THEOREM 1.30

If the columns of a basis incidence matrix A, an f-circuit matrix B_f and an f-cutset matrix Q_f of a graph of rank r and nullity m are arranged in the order of chords and branches for the tree defining B_f and Q_f such that, in partitioned forms

$$A = [A_{11}\quad A_{12}] \tag{1.86a}$$

$$B_f = [U_m\quad B_{f12}] \tag{1.86b}$$

$$Q_f = [Q_{f11}\quad U_r] \tag{1.86c}$$

then

$$B_f = [U_m\quad A'_{11}A'^{-1}_{12}] \tag{1.87a}$$

$$Q_f = A^{-1}_{12}A = [A^{-1}_{12}A_{11}\quad U_r] \tag{1.87b}$$

where the prime denotes the matrix transpose, and U_m and U_r are identity matrices of orders m and r, respectively.

Proof. The identities (1.87) follow immediately by substituting (1.86) in (1.66) and (1.77).

COROLLARY 1.8

Let t be a tree of a connected graph G, and let e be a branch of t. Then the f-cutset determined by e contains exactly those chords of G for which e is in each of the f-circuits determined by these chords.

In the graph G of Fig. 1.61, let $t = e_1 e_3 e_4$. Also let $e = e_4$. The f-circuits defined by the chords e_2, e_5 and e_6 and containing e_4 are $e_1 e_2 e_3 e_4$, $e_3 e_4 e_5$, and $e_1 e_4 e_6$. Thus, the f-cutset determined by the branch e_4 contains exactly those chords e_2, e_5 and e_6 in $e_1 e_2 e_3 e_4$, $e_3 e_4 e_5$, and $e_1 e_4 e_6$, respectively, so the f-cutset is composed of the branch e_4 and chords e_2, e_5 and e_6.

Example 1.2

We verify formulas (1.87) for the graph G of Fig. 1.61. A basis incidence matrix of G is found to be

$$
A = \begin{array}{c} \\ 1 \\ 2 \\ 3 \end{array}
\begin{array}{c} \begin{array}{cccccc} e_2 & e_5 & e_6 & e_1 & e_4 & e_3 \end{array} \\
\left[\begin{array}{ccc:ccc}
1 & 0 & 1 & 1 & 0 & 0 \\
1 & 1 & 0 & 0 & 0 & 1 \\
0 & 0 & 1 & 0 & 1 & 1
\end{array} \right] \end{array}
\tag{1.88}
$$

from which we calculate

$$
A_{12}^{-1} A_{11} = \begin{bmatrix} 1 & 0 & 0 \\ 0 & 0 & 1 \\ 0 & 1 & 1 \end{bmatrix}^{-1} \begin{bmatrix} 1 & 0 & 1 \\ 1 & 1 & 0 \\ 0 & 0 & 1 \end{bmatrix}
$$

$$
= \begin{bmatrix} 1 & 0 & 0 \\ 0 & 1 & 1 \\ 0 & 1 & 0 \end{bmatrix} \begin{bmatrix} 1 & 0 & 1 \\ 1 & 1 & 0 \\ 0 & 0 & 1 \end{bmatrix} = \begin{bmatrix} 1 & 0 & 1 \\ 1 & 1 & 1 \\ 1 & 1 & 0 \end{bmatrix}
\tag{1.89}
$$

From (1.87) we obtain

$$
B_{\mathrm{f}} = [U_3 \quad A_{11}' A_{12}'^{-1}] = \left[\begin{array}{ccc:ccc}
1 & 0 & 0 & 1 & 1 & 1 \\
0 & 1 & 0 & 0 & 1 & 1 \\
0 & 0 & 1 & 1 & 1 & 0
\end{array} \right]
\tag{1.90}
$$

$$
Q_{\mathrm{f}} = [A_{12}^{-1} A_{11} \quad U_3] = \left[\begin{array}{ccc:ccc}
1 & 0 & 1 & 1 & 0 & 0 \\
1 & 1 & 1 & 0 & 1 & 0 \\
1 & 1 & 0 & 0 & 0 & 1
\end{array} \right]
\tag{1.91}
$$

confirming (1.82) and (1.80).

1.7.5 Node-to-Datum Path Matrix

Formulas (1.87) require the inversion of a major submatrix A_{12} of A. For higher order matrices, it is a time-consuming process. To circumvent this difficulty, in the following we give a useful interpretation of the inverse of A_{12}.

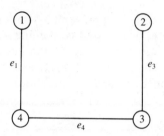

Fig. 1.64. The tree used to compute the node-to-datum path matrix (1.93).

DEFINITION 1.43

Node-to-Datum Path Matrix. For an n-node tree, the *node-to-datum path matrix* P of the tree with reference node n is a matrix of order $n-1$ such that if $P = [p_{ij}]$ then

$p_{ij} = 1$ if branch e_i is contained in the unique path connecting

the nodes j and n (1.92a)

$p_{ij} = 0$ otherwise   (1.92b)

As an illustration, consider the tree $t = e_1 e_3 e_4$ of the graph of Fig. 1.61 used in partitioning the incidence matrix A of (1.88). The tree is redrawn in Fig. 1.64. Then the node-to-datum path matrix P of t with reference node 4 is obtained as

$$P = \begin{array}{c} \\ e_1 \\ e_4 \\ e_3 \end{array} \begin{array}{c} 1 \quad 2 \quad 3 \\ \begin{bmatrix} 1 & 0 & 0 \\ 0 & 1 & 1 \\ 0 & 1 & 0 \end{bmatrix} \end{array} \qquad (1.93)$$

THEOREM 1.31

The inverse of a major submatrix of the basis incidence matrix of a connected graph with reference node n is equal to the node-to-datum path matrix of the tree corresponding to the columns of the major submatrix with n used as the reference node of the tree.

Proof. Let A be the basis incidence matrix of a connected graph G with reference node n. Let A_{12} be the major submatrix of A corresponding to a tree t in G. Also let P be the node-to-datum matrix of t with reference node

n. We show that

$$P = A_{12}^{-1} \tag{1.94}$$

or

$$\sum_{j=1}^{n-1} p_{ij} a_{jk} = \delta_{ik}, \qquad i, k = 1, 2, \ldots, n-1 \tag{1.95}$$

where δ_{ik} is the Kronecker delta, and

$$P = [p_{ij}] \quad \text{and} \quad A_{12} = [a_{ij}] \tag{1.96}$$

If nodes x and y are the two endpoints of a branch e_k of t, then (1.95) can be simplified to

$$p_{ix} a_{xk} + p_{iy} a_{yk} = \delta_{ik} \tag{1.97}$$

Observe that the branch e_k partitions the nodes of t into two mutually exclusive subsets V_1 and V_2. If $i \neq k$, then p_{ix} and p_{iy} are both one or both zero since the two endpoints of the branch e_i are both in V_1 or in V_2. Furthermore, if both p_{ix} and p_{iy} are 1, both a_{xk} and a_{yk} are also 1 and (1.97) becomes

$$p_{ix} a_{xk} + p_{iy} a_{yk} = 0, \qquad i \neq k \tag{1.98}$$

If $i = k$, two cases are distinguished: $p_{kx} = 0$ and $p_{kx} = 1$. For $p_{kx} = 0$, then $p_{ky} = 1$ and $a_{yk} = 1$. For $p_{kx} = 1$, then $p_{ky} = 0$ and $a_{xk} = 1$. In either situation, we have

$$p_{kx} a_{xk} + p_{ky} a_{yk} = 1 \tag{1.99}$$

This completes the proof of the theorem.

For the graph G of Fig. 1.61, the basis incidence matrix A with reference node 4 is shown in (1.88). Consider the submatrix A_{12} of A formed by the last three columns corresponding to the tree $t = e_1 e_4 e_3$ in G. This submatrix A_{12} is nonsingular and is given by

$$A_{12} = \begin{array}{c} \\ 1 \\ 2 \\ 3 \end{array} \begin{array}{ccc} e_1 & e_4 & e_3 \\ \begin{bmatrix} 1 & 0 & 0 \\ 0 & 0 & 1 \\ 0 & 1 & 1 \end{bmatrix} \end{array} \tag{1.100}$$

The node-to-datum path matrix P of the tree $t = e_1 e_4 e_3$ of Fig. 1.64 with reference node 4 was computed earlier in (1.93) as

$$
\boldsymbol{P} = \begin{array}{c} \\ e_1 \\ e_4 \\ e_3 \end{array} \begin{array}{c} 1 \quad 2 \quad 3 \\ \begin{bmatrix} 1 & 0 & 0 \\ 0 & 1 & 1 \\ 0 & 1 & 0 \end{bmatrix} \end{array} \tag{1.101}
$$

It is straightforward to verify that

$$
\boldsymbol{P} = \boldsymbol{A}_{12}^{-1} \tag{1.102}
$$

So far we have considered the problem of expressing $\boldsymbol{B}_f$ and $\boldsymbol{Q}_f$ in terms of the submatrices of $\boldsymbol{A}$. The reverse process of expressing $\boldsymbol{A}$ in terms of the submatrices of $\boldsymbol{B}_f$ and $\boldsymbol{Q}_f$ is much more difficult; it amounts to realizing a graph with a prescribed f-circuit or f-cutset matrix. A complete solution to this problem was first given by Tutte (1958, 1959).

1.8   DIRECTED GRAPHS

In many applications, it is necessary to associate with each edge of a graph an orientation or direction. For some the orientation of the edges is a "true" orientation in the sense that the system represented by the graph exhibits some unilateral property. For example, the directions of the one-way streets of a city and the orientations representing the unilateral property of a communication network are true orientations of the physical systems. In others, the orientation employed is a "pseudo"-orientation, used in lieu of an elaborate reference system such as in electrical network theory where the edges of a graph are assigned arbitrary orientations to represent the references of the branch currents and voltages. In this section, we introduce the basic concepts and terms associated with directed graphs. Since most of the concepts are directly analogous to those presented for undirected graphs, they will be mentioned only briefly. Terms that have no undirected counterpart will be discussed in detail.

DEFINITION 1.44

Abstract Directed Graph. An *abstract directed graph* $G_d(V, E)$, or simply a *directed graph* or *digraph* G_d consists of a set V of elements called *nodes* together with a set E of *ordered pairs* of the form (i, j), $i, j \in V$, called the *arcs* or *directed edges* of G_d. Node i is called the *initial node* and node j the *terminal node* of (i, j). Together they are the *endpoints* of (i, j).

Thus, the only difference between a graph and a directed graph is that the arcs of a directed graph are ordered pairs of nodes while the edges of a graph are not. For simplicity, we shall use the term arc instead of directed edge in the remainder of this book.

We say that the arc (i, j) is *directed* or *oriented* from node i to node j, and that (i, j) is *incident* with the nodes i and j or alternatively that (i, j) is *directed away* or *outgoing* from i and *directed toward* or *terminating* at j. A directed graph can also be represented equivalently by a geometric diagram in which the nodes are indicated by small circles or dots, while any two of them, i and j, are joined by an arrowheaded continuous curve, or even a straight line, from i to j if and only if (i, j) is in E.

We extend the directed graph concept by permitting several distinct edges with the same initial and terminal nodes; they are called the *parallel arcs* of G_d. As before, the parallel arcs directed from node i to node j are denoted by the symbols $(i, j)_1, (i, j)_2, \ldots, (i, j)_k, k \geqq 2$. If no particular arc is specified, (i, j) denotes any, but otherwise fixed, arc from i to j. Also, we admit arcs with the same endpoints; they are called the *self-loops* of G_d.

The terms *subgraph, sectional subgraph, rank, nullity,* the *complement* of a subgraph, and the other graph operations outlined in Section 1.2 can similarly be defined for G_d, and there is hardly any point going through the same ground all over again.

As an illustration, consider the directed graph $G_d(V, E)$ of Fig. 1.65, which is obtained from the graph of Fig. 1.1 by assigning orientations to the edges. Thus, we have

$$V = \{1, 2, 3, 4, 5, 6, 7, 8\}$$

$$E = \{(1, 2), (3, 3)_1, (3, 3)_2, (3, 6), (6, 6), (6, 4)_1, (6, 4)_2, (4, 5),$$

$$(4, 3), (5, 3), (7, 8)_1, (7, 8)_2, (8, 7)\} \tag{1.103}$$

The directed graph has two parallel arcs from node 6 to node 4 and two from 7 to 8. There are two self-loops at node 3 and one at node 6. The

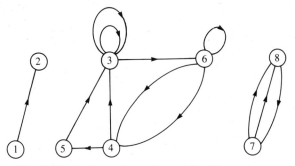

Fig. 1.65. A directed graph used for illustration.

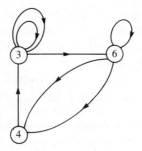

Fig. 1.66. The sectional subgraph $G_d[3, 4, 6]$ of the directed graph of Fig. 1.65.

sectional subgraph $G_d[3, 4, 6]$ induced by the nodes 3, 4 and 6 is shown in Fig. 1.66.

DEFINITION 1.45

Associated Undirected Graph. To every directed graph G_d there is an *associated undirected graph* G_u whose node and edge sets are the same as those in G_d except that the directions of the arcs or the orders in the pairs (i, j) of G_d are removed.

Intuitively, the associated undirected graph G_u of G_d is obtained by simply omitting the arrowheads in G_d. For example, the associated undirected graph of the directed graph shown in Fig. 1.65 is presented in Fig. 1.1. By the same token, sometimes it is desirable to change an undirected graph into a directed one by the process of duplication: We replace each edge of the graph by a pair of arcs with the same endpoints but with opposite directions. For example, in Fig. 1.67, G_d is the directed graph obtained from G by the procedure just outlined.

(a)

(b)

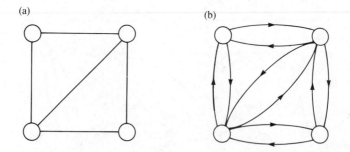

Fig. 1.67. The conversion of a graph into a directed graph: (a) G; (b) G_d.

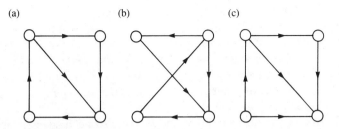

Fig. 1.68. Directed graphs used to illustrate the concept of isomorphism: (a) G_d; (b) G'_d; (c) G''_d.

DEFINITION 1.46

Isomorphism. Two directed graphs are said to be *isomorphic* if (1) their associated undirected graphs are isomorphic, and (2) the directions of their corresponding arcs are preserved for some correspondences of (1).

In other words, if G_d and G'_d are two isomorphic n-node directed graphs, then we can label their nodes $1, 2, \ldots, n$ and $1', 2', \ldots, n'$, respectively, so that for any i and j, the arc (i, j) is in G_d if and only if the corresponding arc (i', j') is in G'_d, containing the same number of parallel arcs if they exist. As an example, consider the directed graphs G_d, G'_d and G''_d of Fig. 1.68. It is easy to verify that G_d and G'_d are isomorphic, but G_d and G''_d are not even though their associated undirected graphs are isomorphic.

A directed graph G_d is said to be *connected* if its associated undirected graph G_u is connected. This is similarly valid for G_d to be *planar, separable,* or *nonseparable.* A subgraph G_s of G_d is an *arc sequence* if the associated undirected graph of G_s is an edge sequence of G_u. Similarly, in G_d we define *arc train, path, circuit, tree, branch, cotree, chord* and *component.* Also, in G_d we speak of *circuit arcs, noncircuit arcs, cutpoints, blocks, length* of an arc sequence. They are again defined in terms of G_u.

In the directed graph G_d of Fig. 1.69, the arc set $E_s =$

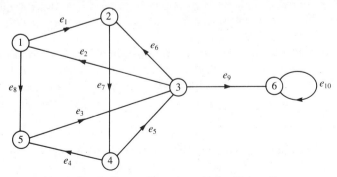

Fig. 1.69. A directed graph used for illustration.

$e_1 e_2 e_3 e_4 e_5 e_6 e_7 e_4 e_8 e_2$ is an arc sequence of length 10. If we delete the last three arcs from E_s, we obtain an arc train $E_t = e_1 e_2 e_3 e_4 e_5 e_6 e_7$. The arc train becomes a path P after the removal of the arcs e_5, e_6 and e_7 from E_t, or $P = e_1 e_2 e_3 e_4$. G_d has one component, and the nodes 3 and 6 are the cutpoints. The blocks are e_{10}, e_9, and $e_1 e_2 e_3 e_4 e_5 e_6 e_7 e_8$. Finally, the subgraph $e_1 e_8 e_4 e_5 e_6$ is a circuit of length 5, and all the arcs of G_d except e_9 are circuit arcs, while e_9 is the only noncircuit arc.

In addition to the terms defined above, we also need special subclasses of the class of arc sequences.

DEFINITION 1.47

Directed-Arc Sequence. A *directed-arc sequence of length* $k-1$ in a directed graph is an arc sequence in which the arcs along the arc sequence are of the form

$$(i_1, i_2), (i_2, i_3), \ldots, (i_{k-1}, i_k) \tag{1.104}$$

$k \geqq 2$. The directed-arc sequence is said to be *closed* if $i_1 = i_k$, and *open* otherwise. In an open directed-arc sequence, the node i_1 is called the *initial node*, and node i_k the *terminal node*.

Intuitively speaking, a directed-arc sequence is simply an arc sequence in which all the arcs are oriented in the same direction. For example, in Fig. 1.69, the arc sequence

$$(1, 2), (2, 4), (4, 3), (3, 1), (1, 5), (5, 3), (3, 2), (2, 4), (4, 3) \tag{1.105}$$

constitutes an open directed-arc sequence with initial node 1 and terminal node 3. The directed-arc sequence is directed from node 1 to node 3.

DEFINITION 1.48

Directed-Arc Train. If all the arcs appearing in a directed-arc sequence are distinct, the directed-arc sequence is called a *directed-arc train*.

Like the concepts of a path and a circuit, if in addition we require that all the nodes in a directed-arc train except the initial and terminal nodes be distinct, we have the concepts of a directed path and a directed circuit.

DEFINITION 1.49

Directed Path. An open directed-arc train as shown in (1.104) in which all the nodes $i_1, i_2, \ldots, i_k$ are distinct is called a *directed path of length* $k-1$.

DEFINITION 1.50

Directed Circuit. A closed directed-arc train as shown in (1.104), in which all the nodes $i_1, i_2, \ldots, i_{k-1}$ are distinct with $i_1 = i_k$, is called a *directed circuit of length* $k - 1$.

Thus, a self-loop is a directed circuit of length 1. For our purposes, it is convenient to define an isolated node as a directed path of zero length.

For the directed graph G_d of Fig. 1.69, the arc sequence

$$(1, 2), (2, 4), (4, 3), (3, 1), (1, 5), (5, 3), (3, 6), (6, 6) \qquad (1.106)$$

is an open directed-arc train of length 8, directing from node 1 to node 6. The open directed-arc train

$$(1, 2), (2, 4), (4, 3), (3, 6) \qquad (1.107)$$

is a directed path of length 4, and the closed directed-arc train

$$(1, 2), (2, 4), (4, 5), (5, 3), (3, 1) \qquad (1.108)$$

is a directed circuit of length 5.

The local structure of a directed graph is described by the degrees of its nodes.

Another term which is useful for describing certain structural features of a directed graph and which has no undirected counterpart is known as strong connectedness.

DEFINITION 1.51

Strong Connectedness. A directed graph is said to be *strongly connected* if, for every pair of distinct nodes i and j, there is a directed path from i to j as well as one from j to i.

A strongly connected directed graph implies the connectedness of the directed graph, but the converse is not generally true. The directed graph G_d of Fig. 1.70 is strongly connected, but the connected directed graph of

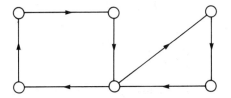

Fig. 1.70. A strongly connected directed graph.

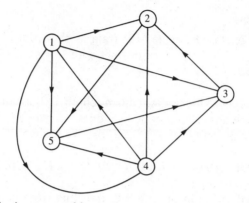

Fig. 1.71. A connected but not strongly connected directed graph.

Fig. 1.71 is not. Observe that strong connectedness does not depend on the number of arcs that a directed graph possesses, but rather their strategic locations.

DEFINITION 1.52

Strong Component. A *strong component* or a *strongly connected component* of a directed graph is a strongly connected subgraph containing the maximal number of arcs. An isolated node is a strong component.

In Fig. 1.71, the sectional subgraphs $G_d[1, 4]$ and $G_d[2, 3, 5]$ are strong components of G_d, and are shown in Fig. 1.72. The characterization of a strongly connected directed graph is given below.

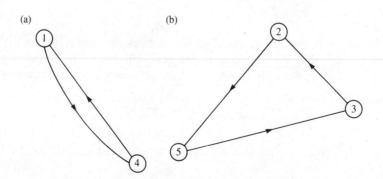

Fig. 1.72. Strongly connected sectional subgraphs of the directed graph of Fig. 1.71: (a) G_d [1, 4]; (b) G_d [2, 3, 5].

THEOREM 1.32

A necessary and sufficient condition for a directed graph to be strongly
connected is that there exists a closed directed-arc sequence containing
all of its nodes.

The proof of the theorem is straightforward, and is omitted. In the
theorem, if we replace the word *nodes* by *arcs*, we find that the theorem
remains valid.

1.8.1 Matrices Associated with a Directed Graph

As in the case for an undirected graph, a directed graph can be conveniently
described by a number of matrices. Since the results are very similar and
since their proofs can be carried out in exactly the same manner, we will
review only the highlights and concentrate our discussions on the
differences, leaving the details as obvious.

DEFINITION 1.53

Incidence Matrix. The *incidence matrix* A_a of an *n*-node *b*-arc directed
graph is a matrix of order $n \times b$ such that if $A_a = [a_{ij}]$, then

$$a_{ij} = 1 \text{ if arc } e_j \text{ is incident at node } i \text{ and is directed away}$$

$$\text{from node } i \qquad\qquad (1.109a)$$

$$a_{ij} = -1 \text{ if arc } e_j \text{ is incident at node } i \text{ and is directed toward}$$

$$\text{node } i \qquad\qquad (1.109b)$$

$$a_{ij} = 0 \text{ if arc } e_j \text{ is not incident at node } i \qquad\qquad (1.109c)$$

We remark that the entries in A_a are now treated as real integers. The
choice of symbolism here, as in the case of circuit and cut matrices to
follow, is guided by the fact that the essential structure of the matrix A_a is
the same for directed and undirected graphs. In fact, the properties of these
matrices, and to a large extent the methods of proving them, are identical to
those in the undirected case. Hence, the proofs in this section are given in
outlined form only and are often omitted.

THEOREM 1.33

The rank of the incidence matrix of a directed graph is equal to the rank of
the directed graph.

A *basis incidence matrix* A of a b-arc directed graph G_d of rank r is a submatrix of order $r \times b$ and of rank r of its incidence matrix A_a. The submatrix obtained from A_a by deleting any of its rows is a basis incidence matrix. The node corresponding to the deleted row of A_a is referred to as the *reference node* of G_d.

THEOREM 1.34

A square submatrix of a basis incidence matrix A of a connected directed graph is a major submatrix if and only if the columns of this submatrix correspond to the branches of a tree in the directed graph.

Likewise, we define the circuit matrix. Since we are dealing with a directed graph, it is natural to orient the circuits.

DEFINITION 1.54

Oriented Circuit. A circuit of a directed graph with an orientation assigned by a cyclic ordering of nodes along the circuit is called an *oriented circuit*.

As an illustration, consider the directed graph G_d of Fig. 1.73. The circuit $L_1 = e_1 e_2 e_5$ composed of the arcs e_1, e_2 and e_5 can be oriented either as $(1, 2, 4)$ or as $(1, 4, 2)$. These orientations can be represented pictorially by an arrowhead. For the orientation $(1, 2, 4)$, it can be represented by a clockwise arrowhead as shown in Fig. 1.73. Likewise, the circuits $L_2 = e_3 e_4 e_5$ and $L_3 = e_1 e_2 e_3 e_4$ with orientations $(2, 3, 4)$ and $(1, 2, 3, 4)$ are depicted pictorially in Fig. 1.73 by clockwise arrowheads. We shall say that the orientations of an arc of a circuit and the circuit *coincide* if the nodes of the arc appear in the same order both in the ordered-pair representation of the arc and in the ordered-node representation of the circuit. Otherwise, they are *opposite*. Pictorially, the meaning is obvious. For example, the arc $(1, 2)$ coincides with the circuit $(1, 2, 4)$, and $(4, 2)$ is opposite to the circuit. Note that a circuit of a directed graph need not be a directed circuit.

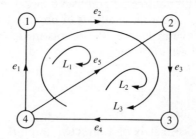

Fig. 1.73. Three oriented circuits in a directed graph.

DEFINITION 1.55

Circuit Matrix. The *circuit matrix* B_a of a b-arc directed graph is a matrix of order $p \times b$, where p is the number of circuits in the directed graph, such that if $B_a = [b_{ij}]$, then

$b_{ij} = 1$ if arc e_j is in circuit i and the orientations of the

circuit and the arc coincide   (1.110a)

$b_{ij} = -1$ if arc e_j is in circuit i and the orientations of the

circuit and the arc are opposite   (1.110b)

$b_{ij} = 0$ if the arc e_j is not in circuit i (1.110c)

As in the case for an undirected graph, a *basis circuit matrix* B of a b-arc directed graph G_d of nullity m is a submatrix of order $m \times b$ and of rank m of its circuit matrix B_a. This matrix contains all the essential information that is contained in B_a.

Similarly we define the *fundamental circuits* or simply the *f-circuits* with respect to a tree t of a directed graph G_d and the *fundamental circuit matrix* or the *f-circuit matrix* B_f. The orientation of an f-circuit is chosen to agree with that of the defining chord. As before, an f-circuit matrix can be partitioned as in (1.63), and the orthogonal relations (1.66) remain valid.

THEOREM 1.35

If the columns of the incidence matrix A_a and the circuit matrix B_a of a directed graph are arranged in the same arc order, then

$$A_a B_a' = 0 \quad \text{and} \quad B_a A_a' = 0 \tag{1.111}$$

THEOREM 1.36

The rank of the circuit matrix of a directed graph is equal to the nullity of the directed graph.

THEOREM 1.37

A square submatrix of a basis circuit matrix of a connected directed graph is a major submatrix if and only if the columns of this submatrix correspond to the chords of a cotree in the directed graph.

We illustrate the above results by the following example.

Example 1.3

Consider the directed graph G_d of Fig. 1.73. The incidence matrix A_a of G_d is found to be

$$
A_a = \begin{array}{c} \\ 1 \\ 2 \\ 3 \\ 4 \end{array}
\begin{array}{ccccc} e_1 & e_2 & e_3 & e_4 & e_5 \end{array}
\left[\begin{array}{ccccc}
-1 & 1 & 0 & 0 & 0 \\
0 & -1 & 1 & 0 & -1 \\
0 & 0 & -1 & 1 & 0 \\
1 & 0 & 0 & -1 & 1
\end{array}\right] \tag{1.112}
$$

By deleting row 4 from A_a, we obtain a basis incidence matrix

$$
A = \begin{array}{c} 1 \\ 2 \\ 3 \end{array}
\left[\begin{array}{ccccc}
-1 & 1 & 0 & 0 & 0 \\
0 & -1 & 1 & 0 & -1 \\
0 & 0 & -1 & 1 & 0
\end{array}\right] \tag{1.113}
$$

with node 4 serving as the reference node. Observe that each column of A_a contains two nonzero elements, a plus 1 and a minus 1. Thus, if A is given, A_a can be recovered completely.

Refer to the three oriented circuits L_1, L_2 and L_3, as shown in Fig. 1.73. The circuit matrix B_a is obtained as

$$
B_a = \begin{array}{c} \\ L_1 \\ L_2 \\ L_3 \end{array}
\begin{array}{ccccc} e_1 & e_2 & e_3 & e_4 & e_5 \end{array}
\left[\begin{array}{ccccc}
1 & 1 & 0 & 0 & -1 \\
0 & 0 & 1 & 1 & 1 \\
1 & 1 & 1 & 1 & 0
\end{array}\right] \tag{1.114}
$$

A basis circuit matrix B is found by deleting the third row from B_a:

$$
B = \begin{array}{c} L_1 \\ L_2 \end{array}
\left[\begin{array}{ccccc}
1 & 1 & 0 & 0 & -1 \\
0 & 0 & 1 & 1 & 1
\end{array}\right] \tag{1.115}
$$

Each major submatrix of A corresponds to a tree in G_d, and each major submatrix of B to a cotree of G_d. The sets T and $\bar{T}$ of trees and cotrees are found to be

$$
T = \{e_2e_3e_4,\ e_1e_3e_4,\ e_1e_2e_4,\ e_1e_2e_3,\ e_2e_3e_5,\ e_2e_4e_5,\ e_1e_4e_5,\ e_1e_3e_5\} \tag{1.116}
$$

$$
\bar{T} = \{e_1e_5,\ e_2e_5,\ e_3e_5,\ e_4e_5,\ e_1e_4,\ e_1e_3,\ e_2e_3,\ e_2e_4\} \tag{1.117}
$$

From (1.112) and (1.114), it is straightforward to verify (1.111), as follows:

$$A_aB_a' = \begin{bmatrix} -1 & 1 & 0 & 0 & 0 \\ 0 & -1 & 1 & 0 & -1 \\ 0 & 0 & -1 & 1 & 0 \\ 1 & 0 & 0 & -1 & 1 \end{bmatrix} \begin{bmatrix} 1 & 0 & 1 \\ 1 & 0 & 1 \\ 0 & 1 & 1 \\ 0 & 1 & 1 \\ -1 & 1 & 0 \end{bmatrix} = \begin{bmatrix} 0 & 0 & 0 \\ 0 & 0 & 0 \\ 0 & 0 & 0 \\ 0 & 0 & 0 \end{bmatrix}$$

$$(1.118)$$

Suppose that we pick a tree, say, $t = e_2e_4e_5$ in G_d. The f-circuit matrix B_f with respect to t is identical to that of (1.115). If the columns of B_f are arranged in the order of chords e_1 and e_3 and the branches e_2, e_4 and e_5, then B_f can be partitioned as

$$B_f = \begin{array}{c} e_1e_2e_5 \\ e_3e_4e_5 \end{array} \begin{array}{ccccc} e_1 & e_3 & e_2 & e_4 & e_5 \\ \begin{bmatrix} 1 & 0 & \vdots & 1 & 0 & -1 \\ 0 & 1 & \vdots & 0 & 1 & 1 \end{bmatrix} \end{array} \qquad (1.119)$$

which contains the identity matrix of order 2 formed by the first two columns corresponding to the chords e_1 and e_3.

Like the oriented circuit, we next define the orientation of a cut.

DEFINITION 1.56

Cut Orientation. For a directed graph G_d, let V_1 and V_2 be the sets of nodes partitioned by a cut of G_d. The cut is said to be *oriented* if the sets V_1 and V_2 are ordered either as (V_1, V_2) or as (V_2, V_1).

In most cases, the orientation of a cut may be represented by an arrow. For example, we can place an arrow near the broken line defining the cut. In Fig. 1.74, the orientations of the cuts of the directed graph G_d are as indicated by the arrows. However, the cutset $C_7 = e_1e_2e_3e_4$ cannot be represented in this way unless we redraw G_d such as by interchanging the positions of the nodes 3 and 4.

Let a cut C be ordered as (V_1, V_2). We say that the orientations of the arc (i, j) and the cut C *coincide* if i is in V_1 and j in V_2. Otherwise, they are *opposite*. Pictorially, the meaning is obvious. In Fig. 1.74 the orientations of the arc $e_2 = (1, 2)$ and the cutsets C_4 and C_6 coincide, and the orientations of e_2 and the cutset C_1 are opposite.

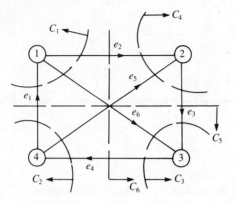

Fig. 1.74. A directed graph and its oriented cutsets denoted by the broken lines.

DEFINITION 1.57

Cut Matrix. The *cut matrix* Q_a of a b-arc directed graph is a matrix of order $q \times b$, where q is the number of nonempty cuts in the directed graph, such that if $Q_a = [q_{ij}]$, then

$$q_{ij} = 1 \text{ if arc } e_j \text{ is in cut } i \text{ and the orientations of the}$$
$$\text{cut and the arc coincide} \tag{1.120a}$$

$$q_{ij} = -1 \text{ if arc } e_j \text{ is in cut } i \text{ and the orientations of the}$$
$$\text{cut and the arc are opposite} \tag{1.120b}$$

$$q_{ij} = 0 \text{ if the arc } e_j \text{ is not in cut } i \tag{1.120c}$$

A result similar to that given in (1.77) follows from the observation that since the number of arcs common to a cut and a circuit is always even, say, $2k$, then k of these arcs have the same relative orientation in the cut and in the circuit and the other k arcs have one orientation in the cut and the opposite orientation in the circuit.

THEOREM 1.38

If the columns of the cut matrix Q_a and the circuit matrix B_a of a directed graph are arranged in the same arc order, then

$$Q_a B_a' = 0 \quad \text{and} \quad B_a Q_a' = 0 \tag{1.121}$$

THEOREM 1.39

The rank of the cut matrix of a directed graph is equal to the rank of the directed graph.

A *basis cut matrix* $\boldsymbol{Q}$ of a b-arc directed graph G_d of rank r is a submatrix of order $r \times b$ and of rank r of its cut matrix $\boldsymbol{Q}_a$. This matrix contains all the essential information that is contained in $\boldsymbol{Q}_a$. Likewise, we define the *fundamental cutsets* or simply the f-*cutsets* with respect to a tree t of G_d and the *fundamental cutset matrix* or the f-*cutset matrix* $\boldsymbol{Q}_f$. The orientation of an f-cutset is chosen to agree with that of the defining branch. As before, an f-cutset matrix $\boldsymbol{Q}_f$ can be partitioned as in (1.78).

THEOREM 1.40

A square submatrix of a basis cut matrix of a connected directed graph is a major submatrix if and only if the columns of this submatrix correspond to the branches of a tree of the directed graph.

We illustrate the above results by the following example.

Example 1.4

Consider the directed graph G_d of Fig. 1.74. Except the cutset $C_7 = e_1 e_2 e_3 e_4$, the other six oriented cutsets are as indicated in Fig. 1.74. The cut matrix is obtained as

$$
\boldsymbol{Q}_a = \begin{array}{c} \\ C_1 \\ C_2 \\ C_3 \\ C_4 \\ C_5 \\ C_6 \\ C_7 \end{array}
\begin{array}{c} \begin{array}{cccccc} e_1 & e_2 & e_3 & e_4 & e_5 & e_6 \end{array} \\
\left[\begin{array}{cccccc}
1 & -1 & 0 & 0 & 0 & -1 \\
-1 & 0 & 0 & 1 & -1 & 0 \\
0 & 0 & 1 & -1 & 0 & 1 \\
0 & 1 & -1 & 0 & 1 & 0 \\
-1 & 0 & 1 & 0 & -1 & 1 \\
0 & 1 & 0 & -1 & 1 & 1 \\
-1 & 1 & -1 & 1 & 0 & 0
\end{array}\right]
\end{array}
\tag{1.122}
$$

Suppose that we pick the tree $t = e_2 e_4 e_6$ in G_d. The f-cutset matrix $\boldsymbol{Q}_f$ corresponding to the three f-cutsets C_{f1}, C_{f2} and C_{f3} as depicted in Fig. 1.75 is given by

$$
\boldsymbol{Q}_f = \begin{array}{c} \\ C_{f1} \\ C_{f2} \\ C_{f3} \end{array}
\begin{array}{c} \begin{array}{cccccc} e_1 & e_3 & e_5 & e_2 & e_6 & e_4 \end{array} \\
\left[\begin{array}{ccc:ccc}
0 & -1 & 1 & 1 & 0 & 0 \\
-1 & 1 & -1 & 0 & 1 & 0 \\
-1 & 0 & -1 & 0 & 0 & 1
\end{array}\right]
\end{array}
\tag{1.123}
$$

the last three columns of which correspond to the branches of t. Thus, $\boldsymbol{Q}_f$

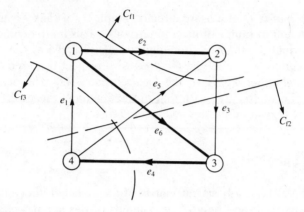

Fig. 1.75. Three f-cutsets with respect to the tree $t = e_2 e_4 e_6$.

is a basis cut matrix, each of whose major submatrices corresponds to a tree in G_d. These trees are found to be

$$T = \{e_1 e_2 e_3,\ e_2 e_3 e_4,\ e_1 e_3 e_4,\ e_1 e_2 e_4,\ e_1 e_2 e_6,\ e_2 e_3 e_5,\ e_3 e_4 e_6,$$

$$e_1 e_4 e_5,\ e_2 e_4 e_5,\ e_1 e_3 e_5,\ e_2 e_4 e_6,\ e_1 e_3 e_6,\ e_1 e_5 e_6,$$

$$e_2 e_5 e_6,\ e_3 e_5 e_6,\ e_4 e_5 e_6\} \tag{1.124}$$

Finally, with respect to the same tree $t = e_2 e_4 e_6$ the f-circuit matrix $\boldsymbol{B}_f$ for the three f-circuits $L_{f1} = e_1 e_4 e_6$, $L_{f2} = e_2 e_3 e_6$ and $L_{f3} = e_2 e_4 e_5 e_6$ is obtained as

$$
\boldsymbol{B}_f =
\begin{array}{c}
L_{f1} \\
L_{f2} \\
L_{f3}
\end{array}
\!\!\begin{array}{cccccc}
e_1 & e_3 & e_5 & e_2 & e_6 & e_4 \\
\left[\begin{array}{ccc|ccc}
1 & 0 & 0 & 0 & 1 & 1 \\
0 & 1 & 0 & 1 & -1 & 0 \\
0 & 0 & 1 & -1 & 1 & 1
\end{array}\right]
\end{array}
\tag{1.125}
$$

giving from (1.123) and (1.125)

$$
\boldsymbol{Q}_f \boldsymbol{B}_f' =
\begin{bmatrix}
0 & -1 & 1 & 1 & 0 & 0 \\
-1 & 1 & -1 & 0 & 1 & 0 \\
-1 & 0 & -1 & 0 & 0 & 1
\end{bmatrix}
\begin{bmatrix}
1 & 0 & 0 \\
0 & 1 & 0 \\
0 & 0 & 1 \\
0 & 1 & -1 \\
1 & -1 & 1 \\
1 & 0 & 1
\end{bmatrix}
= \boldsymbol{0} \quad (1.126)
$$

confirming (1.121).

1.8.2 Interrelationships among the Matrices

As in the case for an undirected graph, the basis incidence matrix, the f-circuit matrix and the f-cutset matrix are related in a similar fashion.

THEOREM 1.41

If the columns of a basis incidence matrix A, an f-circuit matrix B_f and an f-cutset matrix Q_f of a directed graph of rank r and nullity m are arranged in the order of chords and branches for the tree defining B_f and Q_f such that, in partitioned forms,

$$A = [A_{11} \quad A_{12}] \tag{1.127a}$$

$$B_f = [U_m \quad B_{f12}] \tag{1.127b}$$

$$Q_f = [Q_{f11} \quad U_r] \tag{1.127c}$$

then

$$B_f = [U_m \quad -A'_{11}A'^{-1}_{12}] \tag{1.128a}$$

$$Q_f = A_{12}^{-1}A = [-B'_{f12} \quad U_r] \tag{1.128b}$$

To avoid the calculation of the inverse of A_{12} in (1.128), we define the node-to-datum path matrix for a directed graph.

DEFINITION 1.58

Node-to-Datum Path Matrix. For an n-node tree in a directed graph, the *node-to-datum path matrix* P of the tree with reference node n is a matrix of order $n-1$ such that if $P = [p_{ij}]$ then

$p_{ij} = 1$ if branch e_i is contained in the unique path connecting

the nodes j and n, and is directed toward the node n

in the path $\qquad\qquad\qquad$ (1.129a)

$p_{ij} = -1$ if the branch e_i is contained in the unique path connecting

the nodes j and n, and is directed away from the node n

in the path $\qquad\qquad\qquad$ (1.129b)

$p_{ij} = 0$ if branch e_i is not contained in the unique path connecting

the nodes j and n $\qquad\qquad\qquad$ (1.129c)

In the directed graph G_d of Fig. 1.75, choose the tree $t = e_2e_4e_6$ as shown

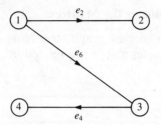

Fig. 1.76. A tree used to calculate the node-to-datum path matrix.

in Fig. 1.76. The node-to-datum path matrix P of this tree with reference node 4 is found to be

$$P = \begin{array}{c} \\ e_2 \\ e_6 \\ e_4 \end{array} \begin{array}{ccc} 1 & 2 & 3 \\ \left[\begin{array}{ccc} 0 & -1 & 0 \\ 1 & 1 & 0 \\ 1 & 1 & 1 \end{array}\right] \end{array} \qquad (1.130)$$

THEOREM 1.42

The inverse of a major submatrix of the basis incidence matrix of a connected directed graph with reference node n is equal to the node-to-datum path matrix of the tree corresponding to the columns of the major submatrix with n used as the reference node of the tree.

Example 1.5

Consider the directed graph G_d of Fig. 1.75, the basis incidence matrix A of which with reference node 4 is given by

$$A = \begin{array}{c} \\ 1 \\ 2 \\ 3 \end{array} \begin{array}{cccccc} e_1 & e_3 & e_5 & e_2 & e_6 & e_4 \\ \left[\begin{array}{cccccc} -1 & 0 & 0 & 1 & 1 & 0 \\ 0 & 1 & -1 & -1 & 0 & 0 \\ 0 & -1 & 0 & 0 & -1 & 1 \end{array}\right] \end{array} \qquad (1.131)$$

Choose the tree $t = e_2 e_4 e_6$. The submatrix A_{12} formed by the last three columns of A corresponding to the branches of t is a major submatrix, whose inverse is the node-to-datum path matrix P of t with reference node 4:

$$A_{12}^{-1} = P = \begin{array}{c} \\ e_2 \\ e_6 \\ e_4 \end{array} \begin{array}{ccc} 1 & 2 & 3 \\ \left[\begin{array}{ccc} 0 & -1 & 0 \\ 1 & 1 & 0 \\ 1 & 1 & 1 \end{array}\right] \end{array} \qquad (1.132)$$

obtaining from (1.128) the f-circuit matrix B_f and the f-cutset matrix Q_f as

$$Q_f = A_{12}^{-1} A = \begin{bmatrix} 0 & -1 & 0 \\ 1 & 1 & 0 \\ 1 & 1 & 1 \end{bmatrix} \begin{bmatrix} -1 & 0 & 0 & 1 & 1 & 0 \\ 0 & 1 & -1 & -1 & 0 & 0 \\ 0 & -1 & 0 & 0 & -1 & 1 \end{bmatrix}$$

$$= \begin{bmatrix} 0 & -1 & 1 & 1 & 0 & 0 \\ -1 & 1 & -1 & 0 & 1 & 0 \\ -1 & 0 & -1 & 0 & 0 & 1 \end{bmatrix} \qquad (1.133)$$

$$B_f = [U_3 \quad -Q'_{f11}] = \begin{bmatrix} 1 & 0 & 0 & 0 & 1 & 1 \\ 0 & 1 & 0 & 1 & -1 & 0 \\ 0 & 0 & 1 & -1 & 1 & 1 \end{bmatrix} \qquad (1.134)$$

confirming (1.123) and (1.125).

1.8.3   Some Important Classes of Directed Graphs

We have already seen graphs and directed graphs classified on the basis of whether they are planar or nonplanar, and separable or nonseparable. In the present section, we introduce three other useful classifications.

DEFINITION 1.59

Symmetric Directed Graph. A directed graph G_d is said to be *symmetric* if, for every arc (i, j) of G_d, it is matched by an arc (j, i) of G_d with the same number of parallel arcs in each direction if they exist.

The definition implies that if there are k arcs directed from i to j then there are k arcs directed from j to i. We remark that the number of self-loops at a node has no effect on its symmetry. Thus, if G_d is symmetric then the number of arcs outgoing from a node must be equal to the number of arcs terminating at the node. The converse, however, is not generally true. Fig. 1.77 is an example of a symmetric directed graph.

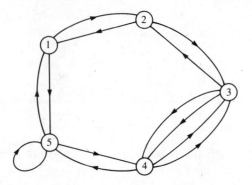

Fig. 1.77. A symmetric directed graph.

DEFINITION 1.60

Acyclic Directed Graph. A directed graph is said to be *acyclic* if it contains no directed circuits.

DEFINITION 1.61

Complete Directed Graph. A directed graph having no self-loops is said to be *complete* and *of order k* if, for each pair of nodes, there are k and only k parallel arcs in each direction. A complete directed graph of order 1 is simply called a *complete directed graph*.

DEFINITION 1.62

Directed Bipartite Graph. A directed graph $G(V, E)$ is said to be *bipartite* if its node set V can be partitioned into two disjoint subsets V_1 and V_2 such that each of the arcs has its initial node in V_1 and the terminal node in V_2.

The directed graph of Fig. 1.78 is acyclic, because it does not contain any

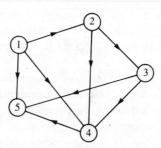

Fig. 1.78. An acyclic directed graph.

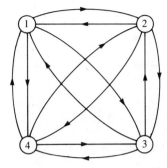

Fig. 1.79. The four-node complete directed graph.

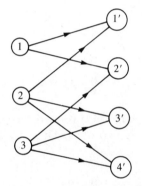

Fig. 1.80. A directed bipartite graph $K_{3,4}$.

directed circuits. Fig. 1.79 is the four-node complete directed graph. Fig. 1.80 is an example of a directed bipartite graph.

1.9 THE CIRCUIT MATRIX ASSOCIATED WITH A PLANAR GRAPH OR DIRECTED GRAPH

In Sections 1.4 and 1.5, a planar graph is characterized in terms of certain forbidden subgraphs or its dual graph. In the present section, we give another criterion for planarity due to MacLane (1937) in terms of the existence of a certain basis circuit matrix. As before, we use the modulo 2 algebra for undirected graphs and the real number system for directed graphs.

Recall that in a planar graph, a mesh is a circuit formed by the boundary edges of a region because of its appearance as mesh in a fishing net. For the planar graph G of Fig. 1.81, the circuit matrix $\boldsymbol{B}_\text{p}$ corresponding to the

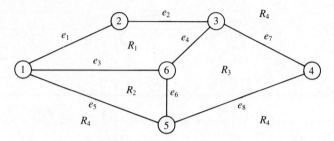

Fig. 1.81. A planar graph.

meshes of the regions R_1, R_2, R_3 and R_4 of G is found to be

$$\boldsymbol{B}_\text{p} = \begin{array}{c} \\ R_1 \\ R_2 \\ R_3 \\ R_4 \end{array} \begin{array}{cccccccc} e_1 & e_2 & e_3 & e_4 & e_5 & e_6 & e_7 & e_8 \\ \begin{bmatrix} 1 & 1 & 1 & 1 & 0 & 0 & 0 & 0 \\ 0 & 0 & 1 & 0 & 1 & 1 & 0 & 0 \\ 0 & 0 & 0 & 1 & 0 & 1 & 1 & 1 \\ 1 & 1 & 0 & 0 & 1 & 0 & 1 & 1 \end{bmatrix} \end{array} \qquad (1.135)$$

Observe that since each edge is traversed by exactly two meshes, each column of $\boldsymbol{B}_\text{p}$ contains exactly two ones. Thus, by the Euler formula (1.21) the rank of $\boldsymbol{B}_\text{p}$ is at most

$$q - 1 = b - n + 1 = m \qquad (1.136)$$

the nullity of G.

Likewise, for the directed graph G_d of Fig. 1.82, if all the interior meshes are oriented clockwise and the exterior mesh counterclockwise, as indicated, the circuit matrix $\boldsymbol{B}_\text{p}$ becomes

$$\boldsymbol{B}_\text{p} = \begin{array}{c} \\ R_1 \\ R_2 \\ R_3 \\ R_4 \end{array} \begin{array}{cccccccc} e_1 & e_2 & e_3 & e_4 & e_5 & e_6 & e_7 & e_8 \\ \begin{bmatrix} 1 & 1 & -1 & -1 & 0 & 0 & 0 & 0 \\ 0 & 0 & 1 & 0 & 1 & 1 & 0 & 0 \\ 0 & 0 & 0 & 1 & 0 & -1 & 1 & 1 \\ -1 & -1 & 0 & 0 & -1 & 0 & -1 & -1 \end{bmatrix} \end{array} \qquad (1.137)$$

Again, each arc of G_d is traversed by exactly two meshes oriented in opposite directions. Thus, each column of $\boldsymbol{B}_\text{p}$ contains exactly two nonzero elements, a +1 and a −1, again showing that the rank of this matrix is at most m. By induction over the number of edges over G or arcs over G_d, we can show that m is also the minimum rank of $\boldsymbol{B}_\text{p}$.

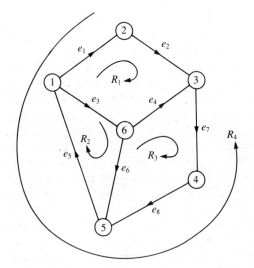

Fig. 1.82. A directed planar graph with oriented meshes.

THEOREM 1.43

The circuit matrix corresponding to the interior meshes of a planar graph or
a planar directed graph is a basis circuit matrix.

In fact, the above properties can also be used to characterize planarity of
a graph.

THEOREM 1.44

A graph is planar if and only if every block of the graph with at least three
nodes has a basis circuit matrix B and one additional row corresponding
to a circuit such that the augmented matrix formed by B and this
additional row contains exactly two ones in each column.

We only indicate the necessity. Since by Theorem 1.10 a graph is planar
if and only if each of its blocks is planar, it suffices to consider a planar
nonseparable graph G of nullity m with at least three nodes. Then there are
m interior meshes and one exterior mesh. By Theorem 1.43, the circuit
matrix of these m interior meshes is a basis circuit matrix B of G. This
together with the row corresponding to the exterior mesh constitutes the
desired augmented matrix, each of whose columns contains exactly two
ones.

To prove sufficiency, it is necessary to construct a plane embedding of G
with the stipulated properties. We refer to MacLane (1937) for its proof.

1.10 SUMMARY AND SUGGESTED READING

We began the chapter by introducing basic definitions of abstract graphs in order to establish the vocabulary for describing graphs and to provide a number of results that are needed in the subsequent analysis. We then defined a number of operations on graphs that are useful in expressing the structure of a given graph in terms of smaller or simpler graphs. Depending upon the structure, graphs are classified in many different ways such as nonseparable and separable graphs, bipartite graphs, and planar graphs.

Our discussions on the planar graphs were rather detailed. We showed that a graph is planar if and only if it does not contain certain forbidden subgraphs. These forbidden graphs are subgraphs homeomorphic to either K_5 or $K_{3,3}$. Alternatively, a planar graph can be characterized in terms of its dual graphs. Two types of dual graphs were defined: a geometric dual and a combinatorial dual. We showed that a graph is planar if and only if it has a combinatorial dual. Furthermore, a graph has a combinatorial dual if and only if it has a geometric dual, thereby establishing the equivalency of the geometric dual and the combinatorial dual. As a result, it is not necessary to say that two graphs are either geometric duals or combinatorial duals. It suffices to say that they are dual graphs. In addition, we demonstrated that every planar graph that does not contain any parallel edges and self-loops can be drawn on a plane without intersection using only straight lines as edges.

For the purposes of interchanging of series-connected subgraphs, we introduced the notion of 2-isomorphism of two graphs, that is of great interest in electrical network theory. Specifically, we showed that two graphs are 2-isomorphic if and only if there is a one-to-one correspondence between their edges such that circuits in one correspond to circuits formed by the corresponding edges in the other.

The most convenient way to study the properties of a graph is to express the incidence relations between the edges and nodes, circuits, cuts or paths by means of a matrix. For this we defined the incidence matrix, the circuit matrix, the cut matrix, and the node-to-datum path matrix. We showed that over the modulo 2 algebra the rank of the incidence matrix or the cut matrix of a graph is equal to the rank of the graph, whereas the rank of the circuit matrix of a graph is equal to the nullity of the graph. As a result, the basis incidence matrix, the basis circuit matrix and the basis cut matrix contain all the essential information that is contained in the original matrices. Furthermore, we established that there is a one-to-one correspondence between trees or cotrees of a graph and the major submatrices of these basis matrices. A simple and systematic way to construct a basis circuit or cut matrix is the use of the fundamental circuits or cutsets. For this we introduced the notion of f-circuits and f-cutsets with respect to a chosen tree of a graph. The basis matrices formed by these f-circuits and f-cutsets are the f-circuit matrix and the f-cutset matrix. If the columns of these matrices are arranged in the order of chords and branches for the defining tree, the matrices, in partitioned forms, contain the identity matrix, thereby making it possible for them to be expressible in terms of the submatrices of a basis incidence matrix. However, these expressions require the inversion of a major submatrix of the basis incidence matrix. To circumvent this difficulty, we introduced the node-to-datum path matrix of a tree, and showed that the inverse of a major submatrix of the basis incidence matrix of a connected graph with reference node n is equal to the node-to-datum path matrix of the tree corresponding to the columns of the major submatrix with n used as the reference node of the tree.

In many applications, it is necessary to associate with each edge of a graph an orientation or direction. For this we studied the basic concepts and terms associated with directed graphs. Since most of the concepts are directly analogous to those presented for undirected graphs, they were mentioned only briefly. Terms that have no undirected counterparts were discussed in detail. These are directed-arc sequence, directed-arc train, directed path, directed circuit, strong connectedness and strong component. As in the case for an undirected graph, a directed graph can be conveniently described by the incidence matrix, the circuit matrix, the cut matrix and the node-to-datum path matrix. Their properties are identical to those for the undirected graphs except that we now use the real numbers instead of the modulo 2 algebra and that we deal with the oriented circuits and cuts.

Finally, we introduced some important classes of directed graphs such as the symmetric directed graph, the acyclic directed graph, the complete directed graph, and the directed bipartite graph, and gave another criterion for planarity in terms of the existence of a certain basis circuit matrix. Specifically, we demonstrated that the circuit matrix corresponding to the interior meshes of a planar graph or a planar directed graph is a basis circuit matrix, and that a graph is planar if and only if every block of the graph with at least three nodes has a basis circuit matrix and one additional row corresponding to a circuit such that the augmented matrix formed by the basis circuit matrix and this additional row contains exactly two ones in each column.

For general information and other aspects of graph theory, we refer to the well written books of Berge (1962) and Harary (1969). For applications of graphs to electrical network theory, we refer to Chen (1976). For algorithms related to graph problems, see Nijenhuis and Wilf (1975) and Hu (1982).

REFERENCES

Berge, C. (1962), *Theory of Graphs and its Applications,* London, England: Methuen.

Branin, F. H. Jr (1962), "The relation between Kron's method and the classical methods of network analysis," *Matrix Tensor Quart.*, vol. 13, pp. 69–105.

Chen, W. K. (1976), *Applied Graph Theory: Graphs and Electrical Networks*, Amsterdam, The Netherlands: North-Holland, 2nd revised edition.

Dirac, G. A. and Schuster, S. (1954), "A theorem of Kuratowski," *Nederl. Akad. Wetensch. Proc.*, Ser. A., vol. 57, pp. 343–348.

Fáry, I. (1948), "On straight line representation of planar graphs," *Acta Sci. Math. Szeged.*, vol. 11, pp. 229–233.

Harary, F. (1969), *Graph Theory*, Reading, Mass.: Addison–Wesley.

Harary, F. and Tutte, W. T. (1965), "A dual form of Kuratowski's theorem," *Can. Math. Bull.*, vol. 8, pp. 17–20, and p. 373.

Hu, T. C. (1982), *Combinatorial Algorithms*, Reading, Mass.: Addison–Wesley.

Kirchhoff, G. (1847), "Über die Auflösung der Gleichungen, auf welche man bei der Untersuchungen der linearen Verteilung galvanischer Ströme geführt wird, *Ann. Phys. Chem.*, vol. 72, pp. 497–508.

König, D. (1950), *Theorie der endlichen und unendlichen Graphen*, New York: Chelsea.

Kuratowski, K. (1930), "Sur le probléme des courbes gauches en topologie," *Fund. Math.*, vol. 15, pp. 271–283.

MacLane, S. (1937), "A structural characterization of planar combinatorial graphs," *Duke Math. J.*, vol. 3, pp. 460–472.

Nijenhuis, A. and Wilf, H. S. (1975), *Combinatorial Algorithms*, New York: Academic Press.

Ore, O. (1962), *Theory of Graphs*, Providence, Rhode Island: Amer. Math. Soc. Colloq. Publ. 38.

Seshu, S. and Reed, M. B. (1956), "On the cut sets of electrical networks," *Proc. 2nd Midwest Symposium on Circuit Theory*, Michigan State University, East Lansing, Michigan, pp. 1.1–1.13.

Stein, S. K. (1951), "Convex maps," *Proc. Amer. Math. Soc.*, vol. 2, pp. 464–466.

Tutte, W. T. (1958), "A homotopy theorem for matroids," *Trans. Amer. Math. Soc.*, vol. 88, pp. 144–174.

Tutte, W. T. (1959), "Matroids and graphs," *Trans. Amer. Math. Soc.*, vol. 90, pp. 527–552.

Tutte, W. T. (1963), "How to draw a graph," *Proc. London Math. Soc.*, vol. 13, pp. 743–767.

Veblen, O. (1931), *Analysis Situs*, Providence, Rhode Island: Amer. Math. Soc. Colloq. Publ. 5.

Wagner, K. (1936), "Bemerkungen zum Vierfarbenproblem," *Jber. Deutsch. Math.-Verein.*, vol. 46, pp. 26–32.

Wagner, K. (1937), "Über eine Eigenschaft der ebenen Komplexe," *Math. Ann.*, vol. 114, pp. 570–590.

Whitney, H. (1932), "Non-separable and planar graphs," *Trans. Amer. Math. Soc.*, vol. 34, pp. 339–362.

Whitney, H. (1933a), "Planar graphs," *Fund. Math.*, vol. 21, pp. 73–84.

Whitney, H. (1933b), "2-isomorphic graphs," *Amer. J. Math.*, vol. 55, pp. 245–254.

2

THE SHORTEST DIRECTED PATH PROBLEM

A weighted directed graph is called a *directed network* or simply a *net*. The real numbers assigned to the arcs of the net may be positive, negative, or zero, and may be considered as the 'lengths' of the arcs. For example, if the streets of a city are represented by a net, where the nodes denote the intersections of the one-way and/or two-way streets and the arcs denote the streets, then the lengths associated with the arcs represent the true lengths of the streets from one intersection to the next. Likewise, an electrical system may be modeled by a net whose nodes denote the various states of the system and whose arcs represent all permissible transitions among the states. The length associated with an arc (i, j) is then the energy required in transforming the state i to the state j with positive length indicating energy absorption and negative length indicating energy release.

The *length* of a directed edge train is the sum of lengths of all the arcs in the directed edge train. In general, there are many directed edge trains from a specified node s to another t in a given net. A directed edge train with minimum length from s to t is called a *shortest directed edge train* from s to t in the net. The *length* of a directed circuit is the sum of lengths of all the arcs in the directed circuit. If the length of a directed circuit is negative, we say that the directed circuit is *negative* and the net contains a *negative directed circuit*. The problem of finding a shortest directed edge train in a net is not always well defined if the net contains a negative directed circuit. To see this, let C be such a negative directed circuit and let i be a node on C. If i is also on a directed edge train from node s to node t, then by proceeding from s to i, traversing the directed circuit C a sufficient number of times, and finally following the directed edge train from i to t, we obtain a directed edge train with arbitrarily small length, which may approach $-\infty$.

Thus, in such a situation the problem is not well defined. For our purposes, we shall restrict ourselves to the class of nets that do not contain any negative directed circuits. Then the problem of finding a shortest directed edge train from s to t is equivalent to that of finding a shortest directed path from s to t. This follows from the fact that a shortest directed path from s to t is as short as any shortest directed edge train from s to t provided that the net does not contain any negative directed circuits. Under this assumption, it is sufficient to consider the shortest directed path problem in a net that does not contain any negative directed circuits.

The shortest directed path problem is important in that it often occurs as a subproblem of other optimization problems. For instance, a minimal cost flow problem to be discussed in Chapter 5 can be formulated as a shortest directed path problem in a net in which the lengths of the arcs denote the costs in establishing the flows in the arcs. Or, in setting up a distribution system, it is frequently required to choose a minimal cost route among many alternate shipping routes. Cartaino and Dreyfus (1957) have shown that the problem of determining the least time for an airplane to climb to a given altitude can be formulated, in its discrete form, as a shortest directed path problem. Furthermore, the shortest directed path problem can usually be modified to solve other optimum path problems such as the longest directed path problem.

The purpose of this chapter is to describe a number of combinatorial algorithms for the shortest directed path problem in a net that does not contain any negative directed circuits.

2.1 SHORTEST DIRECTED PATHS

Given a net $G(V, E)$ with node set V and arc set E, suppose that each arc $(i, j) \in E$ is associated with a real number $l(i, j)$ called the *length* of the arc (i, j). The function l from the arc set E to the reals is the *length function*. Sometimes, it is convenient to consider arcs not in E to be arcs of infinite length in G. Therefore, a net is a triplet and can be compactly written as $G(V, E, l)$. To simplify the notation, we adopt the following convention for any nonempty subgraph $g(V_\alpha, E_\alpha)$ of G:

$$l(g) = \sum_{(i,j) \in E_\alpha} l(i, j) \qquad (2.1)$$

Thus, if P_{st} is a directed path from node s to node t in G, then $l(P_{st})$ is the *length* of the directed path P_{st}. This length is different from that defined in Definition 1.49. To distinguish, sometimes the length in Definition 1.49 is referred to as the *arc length*. This should not create any confusion as the context will reveal. This leads to the notion of distance.

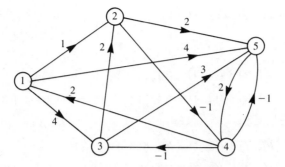

Fig. 2.1. A net $G(V, E, l)$ used to illustrate the length function.

DEFINITION 2.1

Distance. The length of a shortest directed path from a node s to a node t in a net is called the *distance* from s to t in the net.

Fig. 2.1 is a net $G(V, E, l)$ with node set V and arc set E given as

$$V = \{1, 2, 3, 4, 5\} \tag{2.2a}$$

$$E = \{(1, 2), (1, 3), (1, 5), (2, 4), (2, 5), (3, 2), (3, 5),$$
$$(4, 1), (4, 3), (4, 5), (5, 4)\} \tag{2.2b}$$

The length function l from E to the reals is defined as

$$l(1, 2) = 1, \qquad l(1, 3) = 4, \qquad l(1, 5) = 4,$$
$$l(2, 4) = -1, \qquad l(2, 5) = 2, \qquad l(3, 2) = 2,$$
$$l(3, 5) = 3, \qquad l(4, 1) = 2, \qquad l(4, 3) = -1,$$
$$l(4, 5) = -1, \qquad l(5, 4) = 2 \tag{2.3}$$

There are seven directed paths $P_{15}^{(k)}$ $(k = 1, 2, \ldots, 7)$ from node 1 to node 5, and they are found to be

$$P_{15}^{(1)} = (1, 2)(2, 5) \tag{2.4a}$$

$$P_{15}^{(2)} = (1, 2)(2, 4)(4, 5) \tag{2.4b}$$

$$P_{15}^{(3)} = (1, 2)(2, 4)(4, 3)(3, 5) \tag{2.4c}$$

$$P_{15}^{(4)} = (1, 5) \tag{2.4d}$$

$$P_{15}^{(5)} = (1, 3)(3, 2)(2, 5) \tag{2.4e}$$

$$P_{15}^{(6)} = (1, 3)(3, 2)(2, 4)(4, 5) \tag{2.4f}$$

$$P_{15}^{(7)} = (1, 3)(3, 5) \tag{2.4g}$$

the lengths of which are computed as

$$l(P_{15}^{(1)}) = l(1, 2) + l(2, 5) = 1 + 2 = 3 \tag{2.5a}$$

$$l(P_{15}^{(2)}) = l(1, 2) + l(2, 4) + l(4, 5) = 1 - 1 - 1 = -1 \tag{2.5b}$$

$$l(P_{15}^{(3)}) = l(1, 2) + l(2, 4) + l(4, 3) + l(3, 5) = 1 - 1 - 1 + 3 = 2 \tag{2.5c}$$

$$l(P_{15}^{(4)}) = l(1, 5) = 4 \tag{2.5d}$$

$$l(P_{15}^{(5)}) = l(1, 3) + l(3, 2) + l(2, 5) = 4 + 2 + 2 = 8 \tag{2.5e}$$

$$l(P_{15}^{(6)}) = l(1, 3) + l(3, 2) + l(2, 4) + l(4, 5)$$
$$= 4 + 2 - 1 - 1 = 4 \tag{2.5f}$$

$$l(P_{15}^{(7)}) = l(1, 3) + l(3, 5) = 4 + 3 = 7 \tag{2.5g}$$

Thus, the directed path $P_{15}^{(2)}$ of length -1 is the shortest path from node 1 to node 5 in G. There is one directed path $P_{15}^{(3)}$ of length 2, one $P_{15}^{(1)}$ of length 3, two $P_{15}^{(4)}$ and $P_{15}^{(6)}$ of length 4, one $P_{15}^{(7)}$ of length 7, and one $P_{15}^{(5)}$ of length 8.

Consider the directed subpath $P_{12}^{(6)} = (1, 3)(3, 2)$ of the directed path $P_{15}^{(6)}$. The length of the subpath $P_{12}^{(6)}$ is 6 whereas the length of $P_{15}^{(6)}$ is 4. Thus, the length of a directed path need not always be longer than that of its subpath. However, if all the arcs are of positive length, then the length of a directed path is always longer than that of any of its subpaths.

Let P_{st} be a shortest directed path from s to t in $G(V, E, l)$. Then any of its subpaths must itself be a shortest directed path in G. To see this, suppose that P_{ij} is a subpath of P_{st} from node i to node j. If there is a shorter directed path $\hat{P}_{ij}$ from i to j in G, then by proceeding from s to i on P_{st}, following the shorter directed path $\hat{P}_{ij}$, and finally proceeding from j to t on P_{st}, we produce a directed path from s to t which is shorter than P_{st}, contradicting the assumption that P_{st} is the shortest directed path from s to t. Thus, any subpath of a shortest directed path must itself be a shortest directed path. Since any path in a directed graph of n nodes contains at most $n - 1$ arcs, any shortest directed path in an n-node net contains at most $n - 1$ arcs. Note that in most applications, we can replace an undirected edge between nodes i and j by two arcs of the same length, one from i to j and the other from j to i, denoted by (i, j) and (j, i). Thus, any undirected graph or mixed graph can be converted into a directed graph. In this sense, an undirected edge with negative length in an undirected or mixed graph is equivalent to a negative directed circuit in its associated directed graph. As in other methods for solving the shortest directed path problem, the algorithms described in this chapter also yield, on one application, the shortest directed paths from a given node to all other nodes of the net that can be reached from the given node. Therefore, we shall discuss the problem of finding the shortest directed paths from one node, called the *source node*, to all other nodes in a net. A more general problem is that of finding the shortest directed paths between all pairs of nodes. These and other related problems will be treated in the following.

2.2 SHORTEST DIRECTED PATH ALGORITHMS

In this section, we describe several simple and efficient combinatorial algorithms for finding the shortest directed paths from a given node to all other nodes of a net that does not contain any negative directed circuits. The first algorithm is valid for the special situation where the arc lengths of a net are all nonnegative. The remainder of the algorithms are general and can be used in any nets with positive, zero or negative arc lengths as long as they do not contain any negative directed circuits. The special situation is considered first because it occurs most frequently in practice and the algorithm is most efficient in relation to the more complicated general algorithms. It is sufficiently important to be considered separately.

2.2.1 Dijkstra Algorithm

The most efficient algorithm for finding the shortest directed paths from a given node s to all other nodes in a net $G(V, E, l)$ with nonnegative arc lengths

$$l(i, j) \geqq 0 \quad \text{for all } (i, j) \in E \tag{2.6}$$

was first given by Dijkstra (1959). The algorithm is based on assigning labels to the nodes. The labels are continuously updated by an iterative procedure. At each stage, the number assigned to each node represents an upper bound on the directed path length from s to that node. At the end of the procedure, the node label becomes the exact length of a shortest directed path from s to that node in question.

To proceed, let each node i of G be assigned a nonnegative real number $l(i)$ called the *label* of i. Initially, all the labels are temporary. At each iteration, one of the temporary labels is made permanent, say $l(j)$. To distinguish a temporary label from a permanent one, we use $l^*(j)$ to indicate that node j has received the permanent label $l^*(j)$. The details of the algorithm are described as follows: Arcs not in E are considered as arcs of infinite length.

Step 1. Set $l^*(s) = 0$ and $l(i) = l(s, i)$ for $i \neq s$ and $i \in V$, where $l(s, i) = \infty$ for $i \neq s$ and $(s, i) \notin E$.

Step 2. Among all temporary labels $l(i)$, pick

$$l(k) = \min_{i} l(i) \tag{2.7}$$

Change $l(k)$ to $l^*(k)$. Stop if there is no temporary label left.

Step 3. Update all temporary labels of the nodes i with $(k, i) \in E$ for all i by

$$l(i) = \min [l(i), l^*(k) + l(k, i)] \qquad (2.8)$$

Return to Step 2.

To show that the algorithm indeed produces the shortest directed paths from the source node s to all other nodes, assume that all the shortest directed paths P_{si} from s to i $(i = 1, 2, \ldots, n - 1)$ in the n-node net $G(V, E, l)$ have been ordered in accordance with their lengths. Without loss of generality, we assume that all arc lengths are positive and write

$$l(P_{s1}) \leqq l(P_{s2}) \leqq \ldots \leqq l(P_{sk}) \leqq \ldots \leqq l(P_{s(n-1)}) \qquad (2.9)$$

since we can always rename the nodes, if necessary. If P_{s1} contains more than one arc, then it contains a subpath which is shorter than P_{s1}, contradicting our assumption that P_{s1} is the shortest among all the shortest directed paths P_{si} $(i = 1, 2, \ldots, n - 1)$. Thus, P_{s1} contains only one arc. We claim that P_{sk} contains at most k arcs. Assume to the contrary that P_{sk} contains more than k arcs. Then there are at least k nodes j on P_{sk} other than s and k. Since all the arc lengths are positive, each of the subpaths from s to j in P_{sk} must be shorter than P_{sk}, and we would have k shortest directed paths shorter than P_{sk}, a contradiction. Thus, P_{sk} contains at most k arcs. We next demonstrate that the above algorithm will calculate $l(P_{s1})$ first, $l(P_{s2})$ second, . . . , until $l(P_{s(n-1)})$ is found.

Clearly, at the end of the first iteration in Step 2 we generate $l(P_{s1}) = l^*(1)$. To find P_{s2} we need consider only one-arc or two-arc directed paths, the minimum length of which must be P_{s2}. If P_{s2} is a two-arc directed path with the last arc being $(j, 2)$, $j \neq 1$, the subpath (s, j) of P_{s2} is shorter than P_{s2}, a contradiction. Thus, P_{s2} can be either a one-arc directed path or a two-arc directed path with the last arc being $(1, 2)$. In other words, $l(P_{s2})$ is generated by means of the operation (2.8) from the permanent labels $l^*(s)$ and $l^*(1)$, yielding $l^*(2) = l(P_{s2})$ at the end of the second iteration in Step 2.

To complete the proof by induction, we assume that at the end of the kth iteration $l(P_{sk})$ can be generated by means of (2.8) from the permanent labels $l^*(s)$, $l^*(1)$, $l^*(2)$, . . . , $l^*(k - 1)$, $1 < k < n - 1$. We show that $l(P_{s(k+1)})$ can be generated by means of (2.8) from the permanent labels $l^*(s)$, $l^*(1)$, . . . , $l^*(k)$. If not all the internal nodes of $P_{s(k+1)}$ are permanently labeled, let j, $j \leqq k$, be the first such node with temporary label in $P_{s(k+1)}$ from s to $k + 1$. Since all the arcs are of positive length, the subpath from s to j in $P_{s(k+1)}$ is shorter than $P_{s(k+1)}$, implying that $P_{s(k+1)}$ is not the $(k + 1)$th shortest directed path in (2.9), a contradiction. Thus, all the internal nodes of $P_{s(k+1)}$ are permanently labeled. This means that to find $P_{s(k+1)}$ we need only search for those directed paths composed of a sequence of arcs whose endpoints are all permanently labeled followed by one arc reaching a temporary labeled node, the minimum length of which is $P_{s(k+1)}$. If $(q, k+1)$ is the last arc in $P_{s(k+1)}$, then

$$l(P_{s(k+1)}) = l^*(q) + l(q, k+1) \qquad (2.10)$$

where $q = s, 1, 2, \ldots, k-1$ or k, and the operation (2.8) will yield a temporary label equal to $l(P_{s(k+1)})$. A node with this temporary label is identified at the end of the $(k+1)$th iteration in Step 2, and its label is changed to $l^*(k+1)$.

In the case where a net contains arcs with zero length, we can first modify the net as follows: For each arc (i, j) of zero length, remove the arc (i, j) and then identify the nodes i and j with the combined node being designated as i. The shortest directed path from s to j in the original net can be obtained from that from s to i in the modified net by the insertion of the zero length arc (i, j). In fact, the algorithm remains valid even with the inclusion of zero length arcs.

Observe that in ordering the shortest directed paths P_{sk} ($k = 1, 2, \ldots, n-1$) in accordance with (2.9), we use one arc to reach node 1, one or two arcs to reach node 2, and at most k arcs to reach node k. By the very nature of our search process, the union of all these shortest directed paths P_{sk} ($k = 1, 2, \ldots, n-1$) is a tree of the net.

The algorithm consists of operations of comparisons and additions. We shall count these numbers. In Step 2, the first time there are $n-2$ comparisons; the second time, $n-3$ comparisons; so that there are a total

$$(n-2) + (n-3) + (n-4) + \ldots + 2 + 1 = \tfrac{1}{2}(n-1)(n-2) \qquad (2.11)$$

comparisons. Likewise, in Step 3 there are $n-2$ additions and the same number of comparisons the first time, and $n-3$ additions and the same number of comparisons the second time, and so forth. Thus, there are $\tfrac{1}{2}(n-1)(n-2)$ additions and comparisons in Step 3. As a result, the algorithm requires $(n-1)(n-2)$ comparisons and $\tfrac{1}{2}(n-1)(n-2)$ additions for an n-node net, and therefore its computational complexity is $O(n^2)$.

After we have determined the lengths of the shortest directed paths from node s to all other nodes j ($j = 1, 2, \ldots, n-1$) in the net, we have not yet identified the shortest directed paths themselves that will give the desired lengths. One way to track down these paths is as follows: Suppose that we wish to identify a shortest directed path from s to j. If node j is not permanently labeled, then there is no directed path from s to j. If j is permanently labeled, we look for all arcs $(i, j) \in E$ to determine a node i such that

$$l^*(i) + l(i, j) = l^*(j) \qquad (2.12)$$

We then repeat the process for node i. In this way, we can track back from node j to node s, and identify a shortest directed path from s to j.

Another approach is to modify the algorithm by assigning two numbers to each node j as a label of the form $[i, l(j)]$, as follows:

Step 1. Set $l^*(s) = 0$ and $l(i) = l(s, i)$ for $i \neq s$ and $i \in V$, where $l(s, i) = \infty$ for $i \neq s$ and $(s, i) \notin E$, and node i is labeled as $[s, l(i)]$

Step 2. Among all temporary labels $l(i)$, pick

$$l(k) = \min_i l(i) \tag{2.13}$$

Change $l(k)$ to $l^*(k)$. Stop if there is no temporary label left.

Step 3. Update all temporary labels of the nodes i with $(k, i) \in E$ for all i by

$$l(i) = \min [l(i), l^*(k) + l(k, i)] \tag{2.14}$$

Change the label on node i to $[k, l(i)]$ if $l(i)$ is decreased. Otherwise, keep the same label. Return to Step 2.

We illustrate the above results by the following examples.

Example 2.1

Consider the 7-node net $G(V, E)$ of Fig. 2.2, in which each undirected edge between nodes i and j denotes a pair of arcs of the same length, one from i to j and the other from j to i. We shall apply the algorithm to generate the shortest paths from node s to all other nodes 1, 2, 3, 4, 5, 6, as follows. For simplicity, only updated temporary labels are listed. The others remain the same.

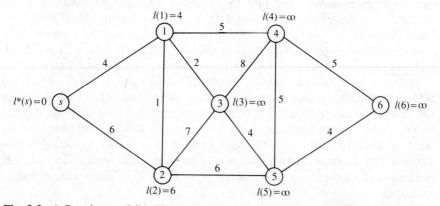

Fig. 2.2. A 7-node net $G(V, E)$ in which each undirected edge between nodes i and j denotes a pair of arcs of the same length, one from i to j and the other from j to i.

Step 1. Node s receives the permanent label $l^*(s) = 0$, and all other nodes receive the temporary labels indicated in Fig. 2.2.

First iteration

Step 2. Pick

$$l(1) = \min [l(1), l(2), l(3), l(4), l(5), l(6)]$$
$$= \min [4, 6, \infty, \infty, \infty, \infty] = 4 \tag{2.15}$$

Thus, $k = 1$. Change $l(1)$ to $l^*(1) = 4$ for node 1.

Step 3.

$$l(i) = \min [l(i), l^*(1) + l(1, i)], \quad i = 2, 3, 4, 5, 6 \tag{2.16}$$

This gives

$$l(2) = \min [l(2), l^*(1) + l(1, 2)] = \min [6, 4 + 1] = 5 \tag{2.17a}$$
$$l(3) = \min [l(3), l^*(1) + l(1, 3)] = \min [\infty, 4 + 2] = 6 \tag{2.17b}$$
$$l(4) = \min [l(4), l^*(1) + l(1, 4)] = \min [\infty, 4 + 5] = 9 \tag{2.17c}$$

The labels of the resulting net are shown in Fig. 2.3.

Second iteration

Step 2. Pick

$$l(2) = \min [l(2), l(3), l(4), l(5), l(6)]$$
$$= \min [5, 6, 9, \infty, \infty] = 5 \tag{2.18}$$

Thus, $k = 2$. Change $l(2)$ to $l^*(2) = 5$ for node 2.

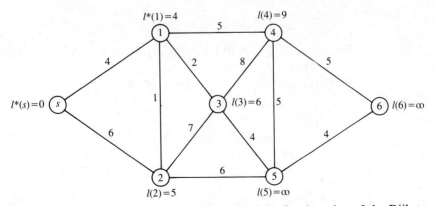

Fig. 2.3. The labeled net of Fig. 2.2 at the end of the first iteration of the Dijkstra algorithm.

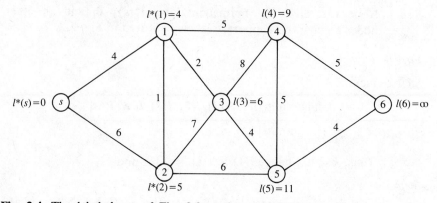

Fig. 2.4. The labeled net of Fig. 2.2 at the end of the second iteration of the Dijkstra algorithm.

Step 3.

$$l(i) = \min [l(i), l^*(2) + l(2, i)], \qquad i = 3, 4, 5, 6 \quad (2.19)$$

This gives

$$l(3) = \min [l(3), l^*(2) + l(2, 3)] = \min [6, 5 + 7] = 6 \quad (2.20a)$$
$$l(5) = \min [l(5), l^*(2) + l(2, 5)] = \min [\infty, 5 + 6] = 11 \quad (2.20b)$$

The labels of the resulting net are shown in Fig. 2.4.

Third iteration

Step 2. Pick

$$l(3) = \min [l(3), l(4), l(5), l(6)]$$
$$= \min [6, 9, 11, \infty] = 6 \quad (2.21)$$

Thus, $k = 3$. Change $l(3)$ to $l^*(3) = 6$ for node 3.

Step 3.

$$l(i) = \min [l(i), l^*(3) + l(3, i)], \qquad i = 4, 5, 6 \quad (2.22)$$

This gives

$$l(4) = \min [l(4), l^*(3) + l(3, 4)] = \min [9, 6 + 8] = 9 \quad (2.23a)$$
$$l(5) = \min [l(5), l^*(3) + l(3, 5)] = \min [11, 6 + 4] = 10 \quad (2.23b)$$

Fourth iteration

Step 2. Pick

$$l(4) = \min [l(4), l(5), l(6)]$$
$$= \min [9, 10, \infty] = 9 \tag{2.24}$$

Thus, $k = 4$. Change $l(4)$ to $l^*(4) = 9$ for node 4.

Step 3.

$$l(i) = \min [l(i), l^*(4) + l(4, i)], \qquad i = 5, 6 \tag{2.25}$$

This gives

$$l(5) = \min [l(5), l^*(4) + l(4, 5)] = \min [10, 9 + 5] = 10 \tag{2.26a}$$
$$l(6) = \min [l(6), l^*(4) + l(4, 6)] = \min [\infty, 9 + 5] = 14 \tag{2.26b}$$

Fifth iteration

Step 2. Pick

$$l(5) = \min [l(5), l(6)] = \min [10, 14] = 10 \tag{2.27}$$

Thus, $k = 5$. Change $l(5)$ to $l^*(5) = 10$ for node 5.

Step 3.

$$l(6) = \min [l(6), l^*(5) + l(5, 6)]$$
$$= \min [14, 10 + 4] = 14 \tag{2.28}$$

Sixth iteration

Step 2. Pick $l(6) = \min l(6) = 14$. Thus, $k = 6$. Change $l(6)$ to $l^*(6) = 14$. Stop.

The final labels of the nodes are shown in Fig. 2.5. Suppose that we wish to track down a shortest directed path P_{s6} from s to 6. We first look at all arcs $(i, 6) \in E$ to determine a node i such that

$$l^*(i) + l(i, 6) = l^*(6) = 14 \tag{2.29}$$

For $i = 4$ and 5 we have

$$l^*(4) + l(4, 6) = 9 + 5 = 14 = l^*(6) \tag{2.30a}$$
$$l^*(5) + l(5, 6) = 10 + 4 = 14 = l^*(6) \tag{2.30b}$$

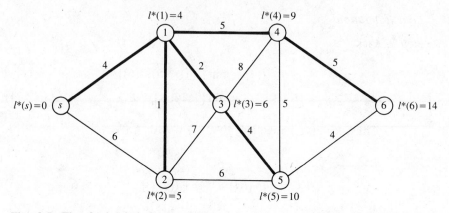

Fig. 2.5. The final labeled net of Fig. 2.2 after the application of the Dijkstra algorithm.

Thus, we can choose either $i = 4$ or $i = 5$. Let $i = 4$. We next consider all arcs $(i, 4) \in E$ to determine a node i such that

$$l^*(i) + l(i, 4) = l^*(4) = 9, \qquad i = 1, 3, 5 \tag{2.31}$$

identifying $i = 1$. We repeat this for node 1 with

$$l^*(i) + l(i, 1) = l^*(1) = 4, \qquad i = s, 2, 3 \tag{2.32}$$

giving $i = s$. Thus, a desired shortest directed path P_{s6} consists of the node sequence $s, 1, 4, 6$ or

$$P_{s6} = (s, 1)(1, 4)(4, 6) \tag{2.33}$$

Had we picked $i = 5$ in (2.30b), we would have generated the shortest directed path

$$P_{s6} = (s, 1)(1, 3)(3, 5)(5, 6) \tag{2.34}$$

Repeating this for all other nodes identifies all other shortest directed paths. The union of these paths forms a tree rooted at node s as shown in Fig. 2.6.

Alternatively, if we follow the modified procedure by assigning two numbers to a node, the final labeled net is shown in Fig. 2.7. To identify, for example, P_{s6} we first check the label of node 6, which is $[4, 14^*]$, showing that arc $(4, 6)$ is in P_{s6}. We next check the label of node 4 which is $[1, 9^*]$, indicating that arc $(1, 4)$ is in P_{s6}. Finally, the label of node 1 is $[s, 4^*]$, and we include $(s, 1)$ in P_{s6}. Likewise, we can identify other directed paths, the union of which is a rooted tree shown in Fig. 2.6.

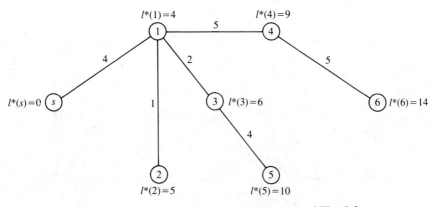

Fig. 2.6. A tree rooted at node s of the net of Fig. 2.2.

Example 2.2

Consider the net $G(V, E)$ of Fig. 2.8. We apply the modified algorithm to generate all the shortest directed paths P_{sk} ($k = 1, 2, \ldots, 13$) from s to k. Initially, node s is permanently labeled as $l^*(s) = 0$, node 1 is labeled by $[s, 1]$, node 4 by $[s, 2]$, and all other nodes are labeled by $[s, \infty]$, where $l(1) = 1$, $l(4) = 2$ and $l(j) = \infty$ for $j \neq s$, 1 and 4.

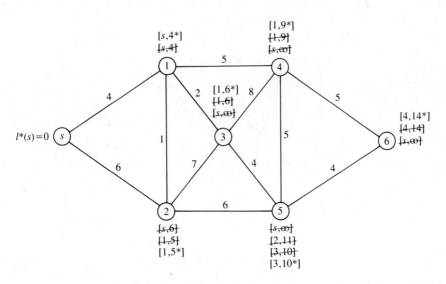

Fig. 2.7. The final labeled net of Fig. 2.2 after the application of the modified Dijkstra algorithm by assigning two numbers to a node.

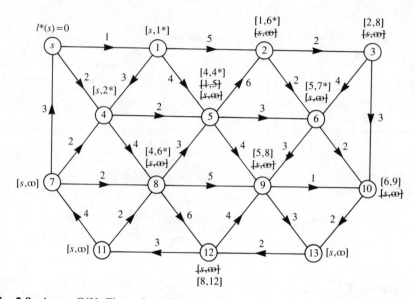

Fig. 2.8. A net $G(V, E)$ used to illustrate the modified Dijkstra algorithm with the labels showing the first six iterations.

First iteration

Step 2. Pick

$$l(1) = \min_i l(i) = 1 \tag{2.35}$$

Step 3. Change $l(1)$ in $[s, l(1)]$ to $[s, l^*(1)]$ or $[s, 1^*]$.

$$l(i) = \min [l(i), l^*(1) + l(1, i)], \qquad i = 2, 4, 5 \tag{2.36}$$

This gives $l(2) = 6$, $l(4) = 2$ and $l(5) = 5$. The labels of nodes 2, 4, and 5 are changed to $[1, 6]$, $[s, 2]$, and $[1, 5]$, respectively.

Second iteration

Step 2. Pick

$$l(4) = \min_i l(i) = 2 \tag{2.37}$$

Change $l(4)$ in $[s, l(4)]$ to $[s, l^*(4)]$ or $[s, 2^*]$.

Step 3.

$$l(i) = \min [l(i), l^*(4) + l(4, i)], \qquad i = 5, 8 \qquad (2.38)$$

This gives $l(5) = 4$ and $l(8) = 6$. The labels of nodes 5 and 8 are changed to $[4, 4]$ and $[4, 6]$, respectively.

These steps will now be repeated for the nodes in the following order: 5, 2, 8, 6, 3, 9, 10, 13, 12, 11, and 7. The details of the operations of the algorithm are described in Table 2.1, where the underlined entry in the ith row signifies that the label of the node corresponding to the entry is changed from a temporary label to a permanent one at the ith iteration. The first six iterations are indicated in Fig. 2.8, and the last seven are given in Fig. 2.9. The tree formed by the 13 shortest directed paths P_{sj} $(j = 1, 2, \ldots, 13)$ from s to j in the net is shown in Fig. 2.10.

2.2.2   Ford–Moore–Bellman Algorithm

The Dijkstra algorithm described in the preceding section is valid only for those nets whose arc lengths are nonnegative. In this section, we consider the general situation where the arc lengths may be positive, zero or negative. As mentioned before, in order for the shortest directed path problem to be meaningfully defined, we assume that the nets do not contain any negative directed circuits. The algorithm was originally proposed by Ford (1956), Moore (1957) and Bellman (1958), and is based on the notion that a shortest directed path from node s to node j containing at most $k + 1$ arcs can be obtained from those from s to j containing at most k arcs. Thus, at the end of the kth iteration the labels of the nodes represent the lengths of those shortest directed paths from s containing $k + 1$ or fewer arcs.

Let $l_j^{(k)}$ denote the length of a shortest directed path $P_{sj}^{(k)}$ from s to j in a given n-node net $G(V, E, l)$ using at most k arcs. To initialize the algorithm, set $l_s = l_s^{(k)} = 0$ and

$$l_j^{(1)} = l(s, j), \qquad j = 1, 2, \ldots, n - 1 \qquad (2.39)$$

It is convenient to define $l(i, j) = \infty$ for $(i, j) \notin E$, $i \neq j$. When $l_j^{(k)}$ $(j = 1, 2, \ldots, n - 1)$ are all known, $l_j^{(k+1)}$ can be calculated by the following recurrence relation: For all $(i, j) \in E$

$$l_j^{(k+1)} = \min \{l_j^{(k)}, \min_i [l_i^{(k)} + l(i, j)]\}, \qquad i \neq j, s; \quad j = 1, 2, \ldots, n - 1 \qquad (2.40)$$

Observe that a shortest directed path $P_{sj}^{(k+1)}$ from s to j using at most $k + 1$ arcs may consist of $k + 1$ arcs or less. If it uses exactly $k + 1$ arcs, let

TABLE 2.1

					Nodes							
1	2	3	4	5	6	7	8	9	10	11	12	13
s, 1*	s, 8	8	s, 2	s, 8	s, 8	8	s, 8	s, 8	8	s, 8	8	8
s, 1*	1, 6	s, 8	s, 2*	1, 5	s, 8	s, 8	s, 8	s, 8	s, 8	s, 8	s, 8	s, 8
s, 1*	1, 6	s, 8	s, 2*	4, 4*	s, 8	s, 8	4, 6	s, 8	s, 8	s, 8	s, 8	s, 8
s, 1*	1, 6*	s, 8	s, 2*	4, 4*	5, 7	s, 8	4, 6	5, 8	s, 8	s, 8	s, 8	s, 8
s, 1*	1, 6*	2, 8	s, 2*	4, 4*	5, 7	s, 8	4, 6*	5, 8	s, 8	s, 8	8, 12	s, 8
s, 1*	1, 6*	2, 8	s, 2*	4, 4*	5, 7*	s, 8	4, 6*	5, 8	s, 8	s, 8	8, 12	s, 8
s, 1*	1, 6*	2, 8*	s, 2*	4, 4*	5, 7*	s, 8	4, 6*	5, 8	s, 8	s, 8	8, 12	s, 8
s, 1*	1, 6*	2, 8*	s, 2*	4, 4*	5, 7*	s, 8	4, 6*	5, 8*	6, 9	s, 8	8, 12	9, 11
s, 1*	1, 6*	2, 8*	s, 2*	4, 4*	5, 7*	s, 8	4, 6*	5, 8*	6, 9	s, 8	8, 12	9, 11*
s, 1*	1, 6*	2, 8*	s, 2*	4, 4*	5, 7*	s, 8	4, 6*	5, 8*	6, 9*	s, 8	8, 12*	9, 11*
s, 1*	1, 6*	2, 8*	s, 2*	4, 4*	5, 7*	s, 8	4, 6*	5, 8*	6, 9*	s, 8	8, 12*	9, 11*
s, 1*	1, 6*	2, 8*	s, 2*	4, 4*	5, 7*	s, 8	4, 6*	5, 8*	6, 9*	12, 15*	8, 12*	9, 11*
s, 1*	1, 6*	2, 8*	s, 2*	4, 4*	5, 7*	11, 19*	4, 6*	5, 8*	6, 9*	12, 15*	8, 12*	9, 11*

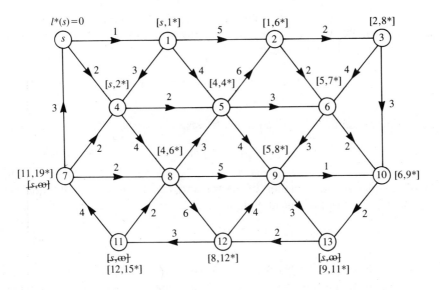

Fig. 2.9. The net used to indicate the labels of the last seven iterations after applying the modified Dijkstra algorithm to the net of Fig. 2.8.

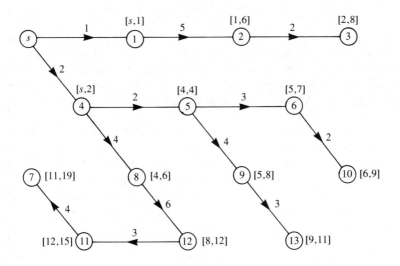

Fig. 2.10. The tree formed by the 13 shortest directed paths P_{sj} from s to j in the net of Fig. 2.8.

(i, j) be the last arc in $P_{sj}^{(k+1)}$. Then, $P_{sj}^{(k+1)}$ can be viewed as a k-arc shortest directed path $P_{si}^{(k)}$ from s to i followed by the arc (i, j). Thus, by considering all is we obtain the length of $P_{sj}^{(k+1)}$ as

$$l_j^{(k+1)} = l(P_{sj}^{(k+1)}) = \min_i \left[l_i^{(k)} + l(i, j) \right] \tag{2.41}$$

On the other hand, if $P_{sj}^{(k+1)}$ contains k arcs or less, then

$$l_j^{(k+1)} = l_j^{(k)} \tag{2.42}$$

Thus, by picking the smaller of (2.41) and (2.42) we arrive at equation (2.40). It is easy to see that the algorithm terminates when

$$l_j^{(k+1)} = l_j^{(k)}, \qquad j = 1, 2, \ldots, n-1 \tag{2.43}$$

for $k \leq n - 1$. If $l_j^{(k+1)} \neq l_j^{(k)}$ for some j when $k = n - 1$, then the net must contain a negative directed circuit. Thus, the existence of a negative directed circuit will be detected by the failure of the algorithm to terminate at the $(n - 1)$th iteration.

Observe that the algorithm consists of comparisons and additions. We shall count the numbers. After initialization, for each j with a fixed k, (2.40) requires at most $n - 2$ additions and the same number of comparisons. Since there are $n - 1$ nodes to be examined, for each iteration the algorithm needs to perform at most $(n - 1)(n - 2)$ additions and the same number of comparisons. Finally, there are at most $n - 1$ iterations, and therefore the computational complexity of the algorithm is $O(n^3)$. This is to be compared with the computational complexity required for the Dijkstra algorithm, which is $O(n^2)$. Thus, the Dijkstra algorithm is most efficient in relation to the Ford–Moore–Bellman algorithm. However, the Dijkstra algorithm is valid only for nets with nonnegative arc lengths, whereas the Ford–Moore–Bellman algorithm is more general and is applicable to any nets with positive, negative or zero arc lengths. In the latter case, no negative directed circuit is allowed.

The above counting of additions and comparisons required for the algorithm considers the worst case where the directed graph is nearly complete. In many practical situations, the nets are sparse with missing arcs. Also, as the above example demonstrated, the algorithm may terminate before $k = n - 1$ is reached. Thus, if b is the number of arcs of a net, and q is the number of iterations required for termination or the maximum number of arcs contained in any shortest directed path, then for each iteration the algorithm requires at most b additions and the same number of comparisons. Therefore, the computational complexity of the algorithm can also be written as $O(qb)$. For problems with $b \ll n^2$ and $q \ll n$, the required computation $O(qb)$ can be less than the $O(n^2)$ requirement of the Dijkstra algorithm.

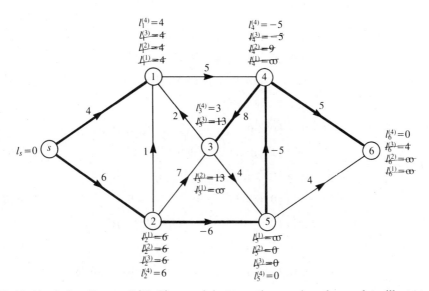

Fig. 2.11. A 7-node net $G(V, E)$ containing negative arc lengths used to illustrate the Ford–Moore–Bellman algorithm.

Example 2.3

Consider the 7-node net $G(V, E)$ of Fig. 2.11 where some of the arcs are of negative length. We apply the algorithm to generate the shortest directed paths P_{sj} $(j = 1, 2, \ldots, 6)$ from s to j, as follows: Initialization

$$l_1^{(1)} = 4, \qquad l_2^{(1)} = 6, \qquad l_i^{(1)} = \infty \quad \text{for } i = 3, 4, 5, 6 \qquad (2.44)$$

First iteration $(k = 1)$

$$l_1^{(2)} = \min \{l_1^{(1)}, \min [l_2^{(1)} + l(2, 1), l_3^{(1)} + l(3, 1)]\}$$
$$= \min \{4, \min [6 + 1, \infty + 2]\} = 4 \qquad (2.45a)$$

$$l_2^{(2)} = \min \{l_2^{(1)}\} = l_2^{(1)} = 6 \qquad (2.45b)$$

$$l_3^{(2)} = \min \{l_3^{(1)}, \min [l_2^{(1)} + l(2, 3), l_4^{(1)} + l(4, 3)]\}$$
$$= \min \{\infty, \min [6 + 7, \infty + 8]\} = 13 \qquad (2.45c)$$

$$l_4^{(2)} = \min \{l_4^{(1)}, \min [l_1^{(1)} + l(1, 4), l_5^{(1)} + l(5, 4)]\}$$
$$= \min \{\infty, \min [4 + 5, \infty - 5]\} = 9 \qquad (2.45d)$$

$$l_5^{(2)} = \min \{l_5^{(1)}, \min [l_2^{(1)} + l(2, 5), l_3^{(1)} + l(3, 5)]\}$$
$$= \min \{\infty, \min [6 - 6, \infty + 4]\} = 0 \qquad (2.45e)$$

$$l_6^{(2)} = \min \{l_6^{(1)}, \min [l_4^{(1)} + l(4, 6), l_5^{(1)} + l(5, 6)]\}$$
$$= \min \{\infty, \min [\infty + 5, \infty + 4]\} = \infty \qquad (2.45f)$$

Second iteration $(k = 2)$

$$l_1^{(3)} = \min \{l_1^{(2)}, \min [l_2^{(2)} + l(2, 1), l_3^{(2)} + l(3, 1)]\}$$

$$= \min \{4, \min [6 + 1, 13 + 2]\} = 4 \qquad (2.46a)$$

$$l_2^{(3)} = \min \{l_2^{(2)}\} = l_2^{(2)} = 6 \qquad (2.46b)$$

$$l_3^{(3)} = \min \{l_3^{(2)}, \min [l_2^{(2)} + l(2, 3), l_4^{(2)} + l(4, 3)]\}$$

$$= \min \{13, \min [6 + 7, 9 + 8]\} = 13 \qquad (2.46c)$$

$$l_4^{(3)} = \min \{l_4^{(2)}, \min [l_1^{(2)} + l(1, 4), l_5^{(2)} + l(5, 4)]\}$$

$$= \min \{9, \min [4 + 5, 0 - 5]\} = -5 \qquad (2.46d)$$

$$l_5^{(3)} = \min \{l_5^{(2)}, \min [l_2^{(2)} + l(2, 5), l_3^{(2)} + l(3, 5)]\}$$

$$= \min \{0, \min [6 - 6, 13 + 4]\} = 0 \qquad (2.46e)$$

$$l_6^{(3)} = \min \{l_6^{(2)}, \min [l_4^{(2)} + l(4, 6), l_5^{(2)} + l(5, 6)]\}$$

$$= \min \{\infty, \min [9 + 5, 0 + 4]\} = 4 \qquad (2.46f)$$

Third iteration $(k = 3)$

$$l_1^{(4)} = \min \{l_1^{(3)}, \min [l_2^{(3)} + l(2, 1), l_3^{(3)} + l(3, 1)]\} = 4 \qquad (2.47a)$$

$$l_2^{(4)} = \min \{l_2^{(3)}\} = l_2^{(3)} = 6 \qquad (2.47b)$$

$$l_3^{(4)} = \min \{l_3^{(3)}, \min [l_2^{(3)} + l(2, 3), l_4^{(3)} + l(4, 3)]\}$$

$$= \min \{13, \min [6 + 7, -5 + 8]\} = 3 \qquad (2.47c)$$

$$l_4^{(4)} = \min \{l_4^{(3)}, \min [l_1^{(3)} + l(1, 4), l_5^{(3)} + l(5, 4)]\}$$

$$= \min \{-5, \min [4 + 5, 0 - 5]\} = -5 \qquad (2.47d)$$

$$l_5^{(4)} = \min \{l_5^{(3)}, \min [l_2^{(3)} + l(2, 5), l_3^{(3)} + l(3, 5)]\}$$

$$= \min \{0, \min [6 - 6, 13 + 4]\} = 0 \qquad (2.47e)$$

$$l_6^{(4)} = \min \{l_6^{(3)}, \min [l_4^{(3)} + l(4, 6), l_5^{(3)} + l(5, 6)]\}$$

$$= \min \{4, \min [-5 + 5, 0 + 4]\} = 0 \qquad (2.47f)$$

Fourth iteration $(k = 4)$

$$l_j^{(5)} = \min \{l_j^{(4)}, \min_i [l_i^{(4)} + l(i, j)]\} = l_j^{(4)}, \qquad j = 1, 2, \ldots, 6 \quad (2.48)$$

The algorithm terminates at the end of the fourth iteration with $k = 4 \leqq n - 1 = 6$. The length of each shortest directed path is as indicated in Fig. 2.11 without the slashes. To identify a shortest directed path P_{sj} from s to j, we follow (2.12). For example, to find P_{s6} we first look for all arcs $(i, 6) \in E$ so that

$$l_6^{(4)} - l_i^{(4)} = l(i, 6), \qquad i = 4, 5 \tag{2.49}$$

or

$$l_6^{(4)} - l_4^{(4)} = 0 - (-5) = 5 = l(4, 6) \tag{2.50a}$$

$$l_6^{(4)} - l_5^{(4)} = 0 - 0 = 0 \neq l(5, 6) = 4 \tag{2.50b}$$

Thus, the arc $(4, 6)$ is in P_{s6}. We next consider the node 4 with

$$l_4^{(4)} - l_i^{(4)} = l(i, 4), \qquad i = 1, 5 \tag{2.51}$$

or

$$l_4^{(4)} - l_1^{(4)} = -5 - 4 = -9 \neq l(1, 4) = 5 \tag{2.52a}$$

$$l_4^{(4)} - l_5^{(4)} = -5 - 0 = -5 = l(5, 4) \tag{2.52b}$$

This shows that the arc $(5, 4)$ is in P_{s6}. We then consider node 5 with

$$l_5^{(4)} - l_i^{(4)} = l(i, 5), \qquad i = 2, 3 \tag{2.53}$$

or

$$l_5^{(4)} - l_2^{(4)} = 0 - 6 = -6 = l(2, 5) \tag{2.54a}$$

$$l_5^{(4)} - l_3^{(4)} = 0 - 3 = -3 \neq l(3, 5) = 4 \tag{2.54b}$$

Thus, arc $(2, 5)$ is in P_{s6}. Finally, we consider node 2 with

$$l_2^{(4)} - l_s = 6 - 0 = 6 = l(s, 2) \tag{2.55}$$

and identifies the arc $(s, 2)$. A desired shortest directed path P_{s6} from s to 6 is found to be

$$P_{s6} = (s, 2)(2, 5)(5, 4)(4, 6) \tag{2.56}$$

Note that if more than one node satisfies the equation (2.49), (2.51) or (2.53), then either node is permitted. The resulting solution is not unique, and more than one shortest directed path exists. For the net of Fig. 2.11, only one shortest directed path exists from s to any particular node. The tree formed by the shortest directed paths P_{sj} $(j = 1, 2, \ldots, 6)$ from s to j with root s is shown in Fig. 2.12.

Example 2.4

The net $G(V, E, l)$ of Fig. 2.13 is a weighted mixed graph. We use the algorithm to generate all the shortest directed paths P_{sj} $(j = 1, 2, \ldots, 13)$

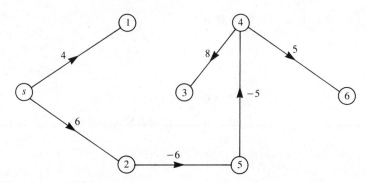

Fig. 2.12. The tree formed by the six shortest directed paths P_{sj} from s to j with root s in the net of Fig. 2.11.

from s to j, as follows:

Initialization $(k = 0)$

$$l_4^{(1)} = 2, \qquad l_i^{(1)} = \infty, \qquad i \neq 4 \tag{2.57}$$

First iteration $(k = 1)$

$$l_1^{(2)} = 5, \qquad l_4^{(2)} = 2, \qquad l_5^{(2)} = 0, \qquad l_7^{(2)} = 4$$
$$l_8^{(2)} = 6, \qquad l_i^{(2)} = \infty, \qquad i = 2, 3, 6, 9, 10, 11, 12, 13 \tag{2.58}$$

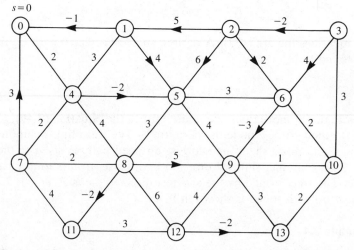

Fig. 2.13. A weighted mixed graph used to illustrate the Ford–Moore–Bellman algorithm.

TABLE 2.2

$k+1$ $\diagdown$ j	1	2	3	4	5	6	7	8	9	10	11	12	13
						Nodes							
$l_j^{(1)}$	∞	∞	∞	2	∞	∞	∞	∞	∞	∞	∞	∞	∞
$l_j^{(2)}$	5	∞	∞	2	0	∞	4	6	∞	∞	∞	∞	∞
$l_j^{(3)}$	5	∞	∞	2	0	3	4	3	4	∞	4	12	∞
$l_j^{(4)}$	5	∞	∞	2	0	3	4	3	0	5	1	7	7
$l_j^{(5)}$	5	∞	8	2	0	3	4	3	0	1	1	4	3
$l_j^{(6)}$	5	6	4	2	0	3	4	3	0	1	1	4	2
$l_j^{(7)}$	5	2	4	2	0	3	4	3	0	1	1	4	2
$l_j^{(8)}$	5	2	4	2	0	3	4	3	0	1	1	4	2

Second iteration $(k=2)$

$$l_1^{(3)} = 5, \qquad l_4^{(3)} = 2, \qquad l_5^{(3)} = 0, \qquad l_6^{(3)} = 3$$
$$l_7^{(3)} = 4, \qquad l_8^{(3)} = 3, \qquad l_9^{(3)} = 4, \qquad l_{11}^{(3)} = 4$$
$$l_{12}^{(3)} = 12, \qquad l_i^{(3)} = \infty, \qquad i = 2, 3, 10, 13 \qquad (2.59)$$

The results of other iterations together with the first two are shown in Table 2.2 where the columns represent nodes j and the rows represent $l_j^{(k+1)}$.

Observe from Table 2.2 that for $k=7$ we have

$$l_j^{(8)} = l_j^{(7)}, \qquad j = 1, 2, \ldots, 13 \qquad (2.60)$$

Thus, the algorithm terminates at the end of the seventh iteration, and the entries in the last row or next to the last row give the lengths of the shortest directed paths P_{sj} $(j = 1, 2, \ldots, 13)$ from s to j. To find the shortest directed paths P_{sj}, we need to identify the node i of the last arc (i, j) in P_{sj}. The results are presented in Table 2.3, from which a shortest

TABLE 2.3

	1	2	3	4	5	6	7	8	9	10	11	12	13
						Nodes							
Length from s to j	5	2	4	2	0	3	4	3	0	1	1	4	2
Last node i	4	3	10	s	4	5	4	5	6	9	8	9 or 11	12

directed path P_{sj} can be tracked back to s from j. For example, to find P_{s13} the table shows that its next to last node 13 is node 12. For node 12, its next to last node 12 is node 9 or 11. Continuing this process yields one of the following node sequences:

$$13, 12, 9, 6, 5, 4, s \quad \text{or} \quad 13, 12, 11, 8, 5, 4, s \qquad (2.61a)$$

which correspond to the shortest directed path

$$P_{s13} = (s, 4)(4, 5)(5, 6)(6, 9)(9, 12)(12, 13) \qquad (2.61b)$$

or

$$P_{s13} = (s, 4)(4, 5)(5, 8)(8, 11)(11, 12)(12, 13) \qquad (2.61c)$$

The final labels of the nodes and all the shortest directed paths P_{sj} are indicated in Fig. 2.14, where the tree formed by P_{sj} is denoted by the heavy lines. Each label consists of two real numbers except node s, the first of which represents the last node i to node j and the second the length of P_{sj}.

2.2.3   Yen Algorithm

The Yen algorithm is the same as the Ford–Moore–Bellman algorithm except that it has a different interpretation of the symbol $l_j^{(k)}$, and requires roughly half the computations.

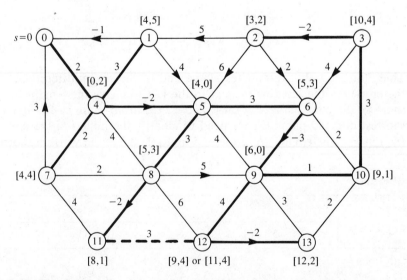

Fig. 2.14. The final labels of the nodes and all the shortest directed paths P_{sj} from s to j in the net of Fig. 2.13.

In a given net $G(V, E, l)$, let the source node s be designated as node 0, and the other $n - 1$ nodes be assigned the integers $1, 2, \ldots, n - 1$. Consider a k-arc directed path

$$P_{si_w} = (0, i_1)(i_1, i_2) \ldots (i_{p-1}, i_p)(i_p, i_{p+1}) \ldots (i_{q-1}, i_q) \ldots (i_{w-1}, i_w) \quad (2.62)$$

from node 0 to node i_w in G. This path can also be expressed as a sequence of nodes from 0 to i_w along the directed path as

$$\{0, i_1, i_2, \ldots, i_{p-1}, i_p, i_{p+1}, \ldots, i_{q-1}, i_q, \ldots, i_w\} \quad (2.63)$$

A subsequence of this sequence is called a *block* if it is maximal and is either monotonically increasing or decreasing. For example, the sub-sequence $\{0, i_1, i_2, \ldots, i_p\}$ is a block if $i_{x-1} < i_x$ ($x = 2, 3, \ldots, p$) and $i_p > i_{p+1}$. Likewise, the subsequence $\{i_p, i_{p+1}, \ldots, i_q\}$ is a block if $i_{x-1} > i_x$ ($x = p + 1, p + 2, \ldots, q$) and $i_q < i_{q+1}$. Thus, the sequence (2.62) can be decomposed into, say, m overlapping blocks. We say that the directed path P_{si_w} consists of m blocks. The sequence

$$\{0, 2, 3, 7, 4, 1, 5, 6, 9\} \quad (2.64)$$

for example, is uniquely decomposable into three blocks: $\{0, 2, 3, 7\}$, $\{7, 4, 1\}$, and $\{1, 5, 6, 9\}$. With the notion of block, we can now attach a new interpretation to the symbol $l_j^{(k)}$.

Recall that in the preceding section the symbol $l_j^{(k)}$ denotes the length of a shortest directed path from s to j in G using at most k arcs. We now use the same symbol $l_j^{(k)}$ to mean the length of a shortest directed path from node 0 to node j in G with at most k blocks. Since a block may contain any number of nodes, a directed path $P_{sj}^{(k)}$ from 0 to j with at most k blocks may contain as many as $n - 1$ arcs. In fact, $l_j^{(1)}$ may represent the length of a shortest directed path from 0 to j containing $n - 1$ arcs. In this case, the nodes of the directed path increase from 0 to j. On the other hand, a directed path in an n-node net can at most contain $n - 1$ blocks.

With these preliminaries, we now proceed to describe a modified Ford–Moore–Bellman algorithm, first proposed by Yen (1970). Define

$$l_j^{(0)} = l(0, j), \quad j = 1, 2, \ldots, n - 1 \quad (2.65)$$

and use $\{P_{sj}^{(k)}\}$ to denote the set of all directed paths $P_{sj}^{(k)}$ from 0 to j with at most k blocks. Then for $j = 1$ and $k = 1$ we have

$$l_1^{(1)} = l_1^{(0)} = l(0, 1) \quad (2.66)$$

and $\{P_{s1}^{(1)}\}$ consists only of one element $P_{s1}^{(1)} = (0, 1)$. For $j = 2$ and $k = 1$ two single blocks can be formed from the nonnegative integers 0, 1 and 2. They are 0, 2 and 0, 1, 2. For the block 0, 2, the corresponding directed path is the arc $(0, 2)$. For the block 0, 1, 2, the corresponding directed path consists of the arcs $(0, 1)$ and $(1, 2)$. The shorter of these two path lengths is $l_2^{(1)}$ or

$$l_2^{(1)} = \min \{l(0, 2), l_1^{(1)} + l(1, 2)\}$$
$$= \min \{l_2^{(0)}, \min_{i<2} [l_i^{(1)} + l(i, 2)]\} \tag{2.67}$$

where

$$\{P_{s2}^{(1)}\} = \{(0, 2), (0, 1)(1, 2)\} \tag{2.68}$$

For $j = 3$, $k = 1$, the single blocks that can be formed from 0, 1, 2, 3 are 0, 3; 0, 1, 3; 0, 2, 3; and 0, 1, 2, 3. We can write from (2.65) and (2.67)

$$l_3^{(1)} = \min \{l(0, 3), l_1^{(1)} + l(1, 3), l(0, 2) + l(2, 3), l_1^{(1)} + l(1, 2) + l(2, 3)\}$$
$$= \min \{l_3^{(0)}, l_1^{(1)} + l(1, 3), l_2^{(1)} + l(2, 3)\}$$
$$= \min \{l_3^{(0)}, \min_{i<3} [l_i^{(1)} + l(i, 3)]\} \tag{2.69}$$

where

$$\{P_{s3}^{(1)}\} = \{(0, 3), (0, 1)(1, 3), (0, 2)(2, 3), (0, 1)(1, 2)(2, 3)\} \tag{2.70}$$

Thus, knowing $l_1^{(1)}$ we can calculate $l_2^{(1)}$, and knowing $l_2^{(1)}$ we can calculate $l_3^{(1)}$. The above procedure can be generalized to yield the expression

$$l_j^{(1)} = \min \{l_j^{(0)}, \min_{i<j} [l_i^{(1)} + l(i, j)]\}, \qquad j = 2, 3, \ldots, n - 1 \tag{2.71}$$

Likewise, for $j = n - 1$ and $k = 2$ define

$$l_{n-1}^{(2)} = l_{n-1}^{(1)} \tag{2.72}$$

and for $j = n - 2$ and $k = 2$, a two-block sequence consists of an increasing sequence from 0 to $n - 1$ followed by the decreasing sequence $n - 1$, $n - 2$. Since $l_{n-1}^{(1)}$ denotes the length of a shortest directed path from 0 to $n - 1$ in G with at most one block, $l_{n-2}^{(2)}$ can be written as

$$l_{n-2}^{(2)} = \min \{l_{n-2}^{(1)}, l_{n-1}^{(1)} + l(n - 1, n - 2)\}$$
$$= \min \{l_{n-2}^{(1)}, \min_{i>n-2} [l_i^{(2)} + l(i, n - 2)]\} \tag{2.73}$$

For $j = n - 3$ and $k = 2$, a two-block sequence consists of an increasing sequence from 0 to $n - 1$ followed by a decreasing sequence $n - 1$, $n - 2$, $n - 3$ or $n - 1$, $n - 3$; or from 0 to $n - 2$ followed by $n - 2$, $n - 3$. In either case, we can write from (2.72) and (2.73)

$$l^{(2)}_{n-3} = \min \{l^{(1)}_{n-3}, l^{(1)}_{n-1} + l(n-1, n-3), l^{(1)}_{n-2} + l(n-2, n-3),$$
$$l^{(1)}_{n-1} + l(n-1, n-2) + l(n-2, n-3)\}$$
$$= \min \{l^{(1)}_{n-3}, l^{(2)}_{n-1} + l(n-1, n-3), l^{(2)}_{n-2} + l(n-2, n-3)\}$$
$$= \min \{l^{(1)}_{n-3}, \min_{i>n-3} [l^{(2)}_i + l(i, n-3)]\} \qquad (2.74)$$

This shows that knowing $l^{(2)}_{n-1} = l^{(1)}_{n-1}$, we can calculate $l^{(2)}_{n-2}$, and from $l^{(2)}_{n-2}$ we can calculate $l^{(2)}_{n-3}$. These equations can be generalized to yield

$$l^{(2)}_j = \min \{l^{(1)}_j, \min_{i>j} [l^{(2)}_i + l(i, j)]\}, \quad j = n-2, n-3, \ldots, 1 \qquad (2.75)$$

In general, for any k the expressions corresponding to (2.71) and (2.75) are given by

$$l^{(k)}_j = \min \{l^{(k-1)}_j, \min_{i<j} [l^{(k)}_i + l(i, j)]\} \qquad (2.76)$$

for odd k and $j = 2, 3, \ldots, n-1$, where $l^{(k)}_1 = l^{(k-1)}_1$; and

$$l^{(k)}_j = \min \{l^{(k-1)}_j, \min_{i>j} [l^{(k)}_i + l(i, j)]\} \qquad (2.77)$$

for even k and $j = n-2, n-3, \ldots, 1$, where $l^{(k)}_{n-1} = l^{(k-1)}_{n-1}$. Therefore, we can find all the distances from 0 to j using successive approximations with kth-order approximations giving the lengths of the shortest directed paths from 0 to j ($j = 1, 2, \ldots, n-1$) using at most k blocks. Since there are at most $n-1$ blocks, the algorithm should terminate if

$$l^{(k+1)}_j = l^{(k)}_j \quad \text{for all } j \qquad (2.78)$$

If $l^{(k+1)}_j \neq l^{(k)}_j$ for some j when $k = n-1$, this indicates that the net contains a negative directed circuit.

Observe that from (2.76) and (2.77) we either try those indices i which are less than j or those which are greater than j. Thus, we perform roughly half the work of the Ford–Moore–Bellman algorithm. The computational complexity in this case remains to be $O(n^3)$. However, an additional advantage of the Yen algorithm is that we can erase $l^{(k)}_j$ as soon as $l^{(k+1)}_j$ is generated, thereby reducing the storage requirement of the program.

Example 2.5

We use the Yen algorithm to generate the distances from node 0 to node j ($j = 1, 2, 3, 4, 5$) in the net $G(V, E, l)$ of Fig. 2.15.

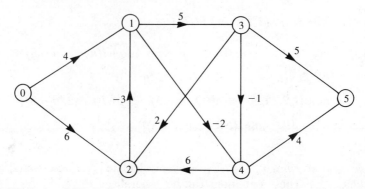

Fig. 2.15. A net $G(V, E, l)$ used to illustrate the Yen algorithm for the calculation of the distances from node 0 to nodes j ($j = 1, 2, 3, 4, 5$).

Initialization $(k = 0)$

$$l_1^{(0)} = 4, \qquad l_2^{(0)} = 6, \qquad l_i^{(0)} = \infty, \qquad i = 3, 4, 5 \qquad (2.79)$$

First iteration $(k = 1)$

$$l_j^{(1)} = \min \{l_j^{(0)}, \min_{i<j} [l_i^{(1)} + l(i, j)]\}, \qquad j = 2, 3, 4, 5 \qquad (2.80)$$

where $l_1^{(1)} = l_1^{(0)} = 4$. We need only consider those $i < j$ such that $(i, j) \in E$, obtaining

$$l_2^{(1)} = \min \{l_2^{(0)}\} = 6 \qquad (2.81a)$$

$$l_3^{(1)} = \min \{l_3^{(0)}, l_1^{(1)} + l(1, 3)\}$$
$$= \min \{\infty, 4 + 5\} = 9 \qquad (2.81b)$$

$$l_4^{(1)} = \min \{l_4^{(0)}, \min [l_1^{(1)} + l(1, 4), l_3^{(1)} + l(3, 4)]\}$$
$$= \min \{\infty, \min [4 - 2, 9 - 1]\} = 2 \qquad (2.81c)$$

$$l_5^{(1)} = \min \{l_5^{(0)}, \min [l_3^{(1)} + l(3, 5), l_4^{(1)} + l(4, 5)]\}$$
$$= \min \{\infty, \min [9 + 5, 2 + 4]\} = 6 \qquad (2.81d)$$

Second iteration $(k = 2)$

$$l_j^{(2)} = \min \{l_j^{(1)}, \min_{i>j} [l_i^{(2)} + l(i, j)]\}, \qquad j = 4, 3, 2, 1 \qquad (2.82)$$

where $l_5^{(2)} = l_5^{(1)} = 6$. We need only consider those $i > j$ such that $(i, j) \in E$, giving

$$l_4^{(2)} = \min \{l_4^{(1)}\} = 2 \tag{2.83a}$$

$$l_3^{(2)} = \min \{l_3^{(1)}\} = 9 \tag{2.83b}$$

$$l_2^{(2)} = \min \{l_2^{(1)}, \min [l_3^{(2)} + l(3, 2), l_4^{(2)} + l(4, 2)]\}$$
$$= \min \{6, \min [9 + 2, 2 + 6]\} = 6 \tag{2.83c}$$

$$l_1^{(2)} = \min \{l_1^{(1)}, l_2^{(2)} + l(2, 1)\} = \min \{4, 6 - 3\} = 3 \tag{2.83d}$$

Third iteration ($k = 3$)

$$l_j^{(3)} = \min \{l_j^{(2)}, \min_{i<j} [l_i^{(3)} + l(i, j)]\}, \qquad j = 2, 3, 4, 5 \tag{2.84}$$

where $l_1^{(3)} = l_1^{(2)} = 3$. It is sufficient to consider only those $i < j$ such that $(i, j) \in E$, yielding

$$l_2^{(3)} = \min \{l_2^{(2)}\} = 6 \tag{2.85a}$$

$$l_3^{(3)} = \min \{l_3^{(2)}, l_1^{(3)} + l(1, 3)\} = \min \{9, 3 + 5\} = 8 \tag{2.85b}$$

$$l_4^{(3)} = \min \{l_4^{(2)}, \min [l_1^{(3)} + l(1, 4), l_3^{(3)} + l(3, 4)]\}$$
$$= \min \{2, \min [3 - 2, 8 - 1]\} = 1 \tag{2.85c}$$

$$l_5^{(3)} = \min \{l_5^{(2)}, \min [l_3^{(3)} + l(3, 5), l_4^{(3)} + l(4, 5)]\}$$
$$= \min \{6, \min [8 + 5, 1 + 4]\} = 5 \tag{2.85d}$$

Fourth iteration ($k = 4$)

$$l_j^{(4)} = \min \{l_j^{(3)}, \min_{i>j} [l_i^{(4)} + l(i, j)]\}, \qquad j = 4, 3, 2, 1 \tag{2.86}$$

where $l_5^{(4)} = l_5^{(3)} = 5$. We need only consider those $i > j$ such that $(i, j) \in E$, obtaining

$$l_4^{(4)} = \min \{l_4^{(3)}\} = 1 \tag{2.87a}$$

$$l_3^{(4)} = \min \{l_3^{(3)}\} = 8 \tag{2.87b}$$

$$l_2^{(4)} = \min \{l_2^{(3)}, \min [l_3^{(4)} + l(3, 2), l_4^{(4)} + l(4, 2)]\}$$
$$= \min \{6, \min [8 + 2, 1 + 6]\} = 6 \tag{2.87c}$$

$$l_1^{(4)} = \min \{l_1^{(3)}, l_2^{(4)} + l(2, 1)\} = 3 \tag{2.87d}$$

The algorithm terminates at the end of the fourth iteration, since for

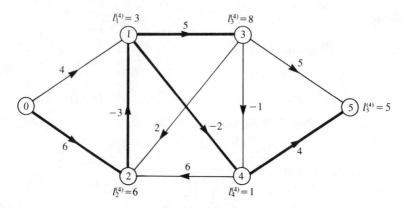

Fig. 2.16. A net used to show the distances from 0 to j ($j = 1, 2, 3, 4, 5$) in the net of Fig. 2.15 with the tree formed by the shortest directed paths being denoted by the heavy lines.

$k = 4$ we have

$$l_j^{(4)} = l_j^{(3)} \quad \text{for} \quad j = 1, 2, 3, 4, 5 \qquad (2.88)$$

The distances from 0 to j ($j = 1, 2, 3, 4, 5$) in the net are as indicated in Fig. 2.16 with the tree formed by the shortest directed paths being denoted by the heavy lines.

Example 2.6

Consider the net $G(V, E, l)$ of Fig. 2.17. We use the Yen algorithm to calculate the distances from node 0 to nodes j ($j = 1, 2, \ldots, 13$).

Initialization ($k = 0$)

$$l_1^{(0)} = -1, \quad l_4^{(0)} = 2, \quad l_i^{(0)} = \infty, \qquad i = 2, 3, 5, 6, \ldots, 13 \qquad (2.89)$$

The results of first three iterations are shown in Table 2.4. Observe from the table that for $k = 3$ we have

$$l_j^{(3)} = l_j^{(2)}, \qquad j = 1, 2, \ldots, 13 \qquad (2.90)$$

Thus, the algorithm terminates at the end of the third iteration or $k = 3$, which is considerably less than $n - 1 = 13$ as required for a general net. The distances together with the tree formed by the shortest directed paths are as indicated in Fig. 2.18 with the heavy lines denoting the tree branches.

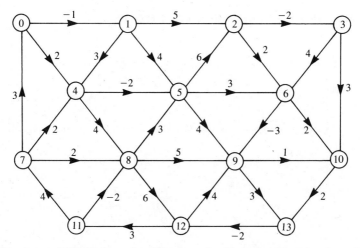

Fig. 2.17. A net $G(V, E, l)$ used to illustrate the Yen algorithm for the calculation of the distances from node 0 to nodes j $(j = 1, 2, \ldots, 13)$.

TABLE 2.4

k \\ j		1	2	3	4	5	6	7	8	9	10	11	12	13
	Nodes													
$l_j^{(1)}$		−1	4	2	2	0	3	∞	6	0	1	∞	12	3
$l_j^{(2)}$		−1	4	2	2	0	3	8	2	0	1	4	1	3
$l_j^{(3)}$		−1	4	2	2	0	3	8	2	0	1	4	1	3

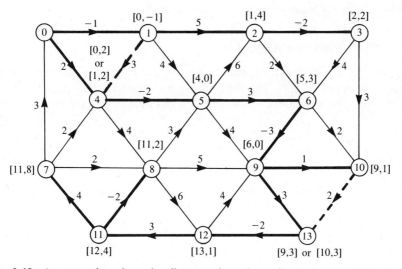

Fig. 2.18. A net used to show the distances from 0 to j $(j = 1, 2, \ldots, 13)$ in the net of Fig. 2.17 with the tree formed by the shortest directed paths being denoted by the heavy lines.

129

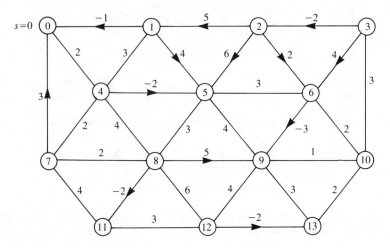

Fig. 2.19. A weighted mixed graph used to illustrate the Yen algorithm for the calculation of the distances from node 0 to nodes j ($j = 1, 2, \ldots, 13$).

Example 2.7

We use the Yen algorithm to calculate the distances from node 0 to nodes j ($j = 1, 2, \ldots, 13$) in the net $G(V, E, l)$ of Fig. 2.19. The details of the procedure are shown in Table 2.5.

The algorithm terminates at the end of the third iteration and the resulting distances and the tree rooted at node 0 are indicated in Fig. 2.20 with the heavy lines denoting the tree branches.

2.2.4 Ford–Fulkerson Algorithm

The present algorithm is applicable to any nets that do not contain any negative directed circuits, but the nets are allowed to have negative or zero arc lengths. The procedure is due to Ford and Fulkerson (1962), and is very

TABLE 2.5

k \ j	1	2	3	4	5	6	7	8	9	10	11	12	13
$l_j^{(0)}$	∞	∞	∞	2	∞	∞	∞	∞	∞	∞	∞	∞	∞
$l_j^{(1)}$	∞	∞	∞	2	0	3	4	3	0	1	1	4	2
$l_j^{(2)}$	5	2	4	2	0	3	4	3	0	1	1	4	2
$l_j^{(3)}$	5	2	4	2	0	3	4	3	0	1	1	4	2

Nodes

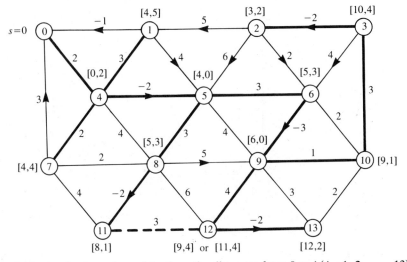

Fig. 2.20. A mixed graph used to show the distances from 0 to j ($j = 1, 2, \ldots, 13$) in the net of Fig. 2.19 with the tree rooted at node 0 being denoted by the heavy lines.

similar to the Ford–Moore–Bellman algorithm in that it sequentially reduces the labels on the nodes by examining arcs. The final labels on the nodes will also permit us to trace back from every node the shortest directed path from the origin to that node.

Let $G(V, E, l)$ be an n-node net, in which a node is designated as the origin or source $s = 0$ and the other nodes are denoted by the integers $1, 2, \ldots, n - 1$. Each node i of G will be assigned a label consisting of an ordered pair of real numbers of the form $[x, l(i)]$. The first number indicates a node designation of G, and the second the conditional distance from s to i. These labels will be updated sequentially until the conditional distances from s become the true distances. The details of the Ford–Fulkerson algorithm are described below:

Step 1. Set $l(s) = 0$ and $l(i) = \infty$ for $i \neq s$. Assign each node i a label $[\cdot, l(i)]$.
Step 2. Find an arc $(i, j) \in E$ such that

$$l(i) + l(i, j) < l(j) \qquad (2.91)$$

and change the label on node j to $[i, l(i) + l(i, j)]$, and repeat. If no such arc is found, terminate.

After termination of the algorithm, the second number of the label on a node j shows the distance from s to j in the net, and the first number is the initial node q of the last arc (q, j) to j in a shortest directed path from s to j.

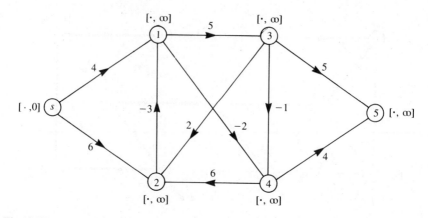

Fig. 2.21. A net $G(V, E, l)$ used to illustrate the Ford–Fulkerson algorithm for the generation of the shortest directed paths.

Thus, to identify the sequence of nodes of a shortest directed path from s to j, we follow the steps below:

Step 1. Set $i = j$.

Step 2. Identify k from the label $[k, l(i)]$ on node i. If i is not labeled, there is no such directed path.

Step 3. Set $i = k$. If $i = s$, terminate. Otherwise, return to Step 2.

Example 2.8

We use the Ford–Fulkerson algorithm to generate the shortest directed paths from node s to node j ($j = 1, 2, 3, 4, 5$) in the net $G(V, E, l)$ of Fig. 2.21, as follows:

Step 1. Assign the label $[\cdot, 0]$ to node s, and the label $[\cdot, \infty]$ to all other nodes j ($j = 1, 2, 3, 4, 5$) as indicated in Fig. 2.21.

Step 2. $l(1) = \infty > l(s) + l(s, 1) = 0 + 4 = 4$. Change the label $[\cdot, \infty]$ on node 1 to $[s, 4]$.

$l(2) = \infty > l(s) + l(s, 2) = 0 + 6 = 6$. Change the label $[\cdot, \infty]$ on node 2 to $[s, 6]$.

$l(3) = \infty > l(1) + l(1, 3) = 4 + 5 = 9$. Change the label $[\cdot, \infty]$ on node 3 to $[1, 9]$.

$l(4) = \infty > l(1) + l(1, 4) = 4 - 2 = 2$. Change the label $[\cdot, \infty]$ on node 4 to $[1, 2]$.

$l(5) = \infty > l(4) + l(4, 5) = 2 + 4 = 6$. Change the label $[\cdot, \infty]$ on node 5 to $[4, 6]$.

$l(1) = 4 > l(2) + l(2, 1) = 6 - 3 = 3$. Change the label $[s, 4]$ on node 1 to $[2, 3]$.

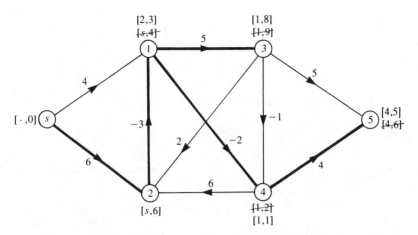

Fig. 2.22. The final labels of the nodes of the net of Fig. 2.21 after the application of the Ford–Fulkerson algorithm.

$l(3) = 9 > l(1) + l(1, 3) = 3 + 5 = 8$. Change the label $[1, 9]$ on node 3 to $[1, 8]$.

$l(4) = 2 > l(1) + l(1, 4) = 3 - 2 = 1$. Change the label $[1, 2]$ on node 4 to $[1, 1]$.

$l(5) = 6 > l(4) + l(4, 5) = 1 + 4 = 5$. Change the label $[4, 6]$ on node 5 to $[4, 5]$.

At the end of the above operations, no more arcs $(i, j) \in E$ can be found such that $l(i) + l(i, j) < l(j)$. The algorithm terminates and the final labels of the nodes are shown in Fig. 2.22. To identify the sequence of nodes of a shortest directed path from s to, say, $j = 5$, we follow the steps below:

Step 1. Set $i = 5$.
Step 2. Identify node 4 from the label $[4, 5]$ on node $i = 5$.
Step 3. Set $i = 4$. Return to Step 2.
Step 2. Identify node 1 from the label $[1, 1]$ on node $i = 4$.
Step 3. Set $i = 1$. Return to Step 2.
Step 2. Identify node 2 from the label $[2, 3]$ on node $i = 1$.
Step 3. Set $i = 2$. Return to Step 2.
Step 2. Identify node s from the label $[s, 6]$ on node $i = 2$.
Step 3. Set $i = s$. Terminate.

Thus, we can trace back the nodes from node 5 to node s as 4, 1, 2, and s. The node sequence from s to 5 is therefore $\{s, 2, 1, 4, 5\}$, and the

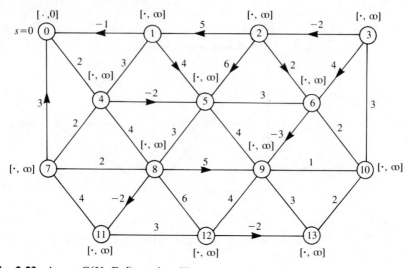

Fig. 2.23. A net $G(V, E, l)$ used to illustrate the Ford–Fulkerson algorithm for the generation of the shortest directed paths.

corresponding shortest directed path P_{s5} is found to be

$$P_{s5} = (s, 2)(2, 1)(1, 4)(4, 5) \qquad (2.92)$$

This directed path together with others are shown in Fig. 2.22 with the heavy lines.

Example 2.9

We use the Ford–Fulkerson algorithm to generate the shortest directed paths from node s to nodes j ($j = 1, 2, \ldots, 13$) in the net $G(V, E, l)$ of Fig. 2.23, as follows:

Step 1. Assign the label $[\cdot, 0]$ to node s, and the label $[\cdot, \infty]$ to all other nodes j ($j = 1, 2, \ldots, 13$).

Step 2. $l(4) = \infty > l(s) + l(s, 4) = 0 + 2 = 2$. Label node 4 as $[s, 2]$.
$l(5) = \infty > l(4) + l(4, 5) = 2 - 2 = 0$. Label node 5 as $[4, 0]$.
$l(6) = \infty > l(5) + l(5, 6) = 0 + 3 = 3$. Label node 6 as $[5, 3]$.
$l(7) = \infty > l(4) + l(4, 7) = 2 + 2 = 4$. Label node 7 as $[4, 4]$.
$l(8) = \infty > l(4) + l(4, 8) > l(5) + l(5, 8) = 3$. Label node 8 as $[5, 3]$.
$l(9) = \infty > l(8) + l(8, 9) > l(5) + l(5, 9) > l(6) + l(6, 9) = 0$.   Label node 9 as $[6, 0]$.
$l(10) = \infty > l(6) + l(6, 10) > l(9) + l(9, 10) = 1$. Label node 10 as $[9, 1]$.

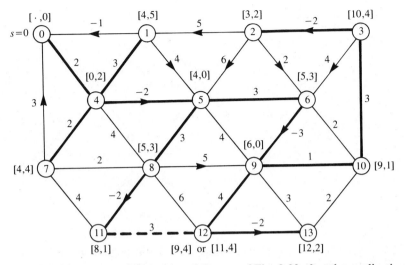

Fig. 2.24. The final labels of the nodes of the net of Fig. 2.23 after the application of the Ford–Fulkerson algorithm.

$l(11) = \infty > l(7) + l(7, 11) > l(8) + l(8, 11) = 1$. Label node 11 as $[8, 1]$.

$l(12) = \infty > l(8) + l(8, 12) > l(9) + l(9, 12) = l(11) + l(11, 12) = 4$. Label node 12 either as $[9, 4]$ or as $[11, 4]$.

$l(1) = \infty > l(4) + l(4, 1) = 5$. Label node 1 as $[4, 5]$.

$l(3) = \infty > l(10) + l(10, 3) = 4$. Label node 3 as $[10, 4]$.

$l(2) = \infty > l(3) + l(3, 2) = 2$. Label node 2 as $[3, 2]$.

$l(13) = \infty > l(9) + l(9, 13) = l(10) + l(10, 13) > l(12) + l(12, 13) = 2$. Label node 13 as $[12, 2]$.

The algorithm terminates and the final labels of the nodes are as shown in Fig. 2.24 with the heavy lines denoting the tree formed by all the shortest directed paths from s to j $(j = 1, 2, \ldots, 13)$.

Example 2.10

We use the Ford–Fulkerson algorithm to generate the shortest directed paths from node s to nodes j $(j = 1, 2, \ldots, 13)$ in the net $G(V, E, l)$ of Fig. 2.25, as follows:

Step 1. Assign the label $[\cdot, 0]$ to node s, and the label $[\cdot, \infty]$ to all other nodes j $(j = 1, 2, \ldots, 13)$.

Step 2. $l(1) = \infty > l(s) + l(s, 1) = -1$. Label node 1 as $[s, -1]$.

$l(2) = \infty > l(1) + l(1, 2) = 4$. Label node 2 as $[1, 4]$.

$l(3) = \infty > l(2) + l(2, 3) = 2$. Label node 3 as $[2, 2]$.

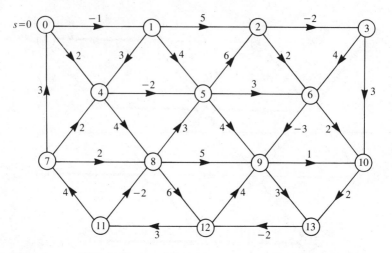

Fig. 2.25. A net $G(V, E, l)$ containing negative arc lengths used to illustrate the Ford–Fulkerson algorithm for the generation of the shortest directed paths.

$l(4) = \infty > l(s) + l(s, 4) = l(1) + l(1, 4) = 2$. Label node 4 as $[s, 2]$ or $[1, 2]$.

$l(5) = \infty > l(4) + l(4, 5) = 0$. Label node 5 as $[4, 0]$.

$l(6) = \infty > l(5) + l(5, 6) = 3$. Label node 6 as $[5, 3]$.

$l(8) = \infty > l(4) + l(4, 8) = 6$. Label node 8 as $[4, 6]$.

$l(9) = \infty > l(6) + l(6, 9) = 0$. Label node 9 as $[6, 0]$.

$l(10) = \infty > l(9) + l(9, 10) = 1$. Label node 10 as $[9, 1]$.

$l(12) = \infty > l(8) + l(8, 12) = 12$. Label node 12 as $[8, 12]$.

$l(13) = \infty > l(9) + l(9, 13) = l(10) + l(10, 13) = 3$. Label node 13 as $[9, 3]$ or $[10, 3]$.

$l(12) = \infty > l(13) + l(13, 12) = 1$. Label node 12 as $[13, 1]$.

$l(11) = \infty > l(12) + l(12, 11) = 4$. Label node 11 as $[12, 4]$.

$l(8) = 6 > l(11) + l(11, 8) = 2$. Label node 8 as $[11, 2]$.

$l(7) = \infty > l(11) + l(11, 7) = 8$. Label node 7 as $[11, 8]$.

The algorithm terminates and the final labels of the nodes are as shown in Fig. 2.26 with the heavy lines denoting the tree formed by all the shortest directed paths from s to j ($j = 1, 2, \ldots, 13$).

We now proceed to justify the algorithm by showing that under the assumption that the net does not contain any negative directed circuits, the algorithm will terminate. At termination, the node labels give the distances from s to the nodes, and the shortest directed paths can be identified from these labels.

After initialization in Step 1 and at any stage of the iteration in Step 2, if

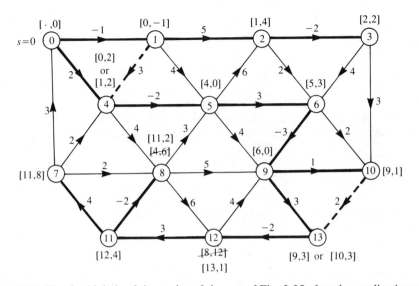

Fig. 2.26. The final labels of the nodes of the net of Fig. 2.25 after the application of the Ford–Fulkerson algorithm.

$l(j) < \infty$ for $j \neq s$, then node j has a label $[i_1, l(j)]$ such that

$$l(i_1) + l(i_1, j) \leq l(j) \tag{2.93}$$

showing that $l(i_1) < \infty$. Notice that the existence of the label $[i_1, l(j)]$ on j indicates that at some early stage we have $l(i_1) + l(i_1, j) = l(j)$. It is possible that the label $[i_2, l(i_1)]$ on i_1 may be changed again at a later stage to produce an inequality in (2.93). Now the existence of a label $[i_2, l(i_1)]$ on i_1 signifies that

$$l(i_2) + l(i_2, i_1) \leq l(i_1) \tag{2.94}$$

showing $l(i_2) < \infty$. It follows that if we start at any stage at a node j with $l(j) < \infty$ and follow the labels as outlined above, we generate a sequence of nodes $j, i_1, i_2, \ldots$, which either terminates at s or continues indefinitely. If it continues indefinitely, the nodes of the sequence will have to be repeated and a directed circuit can be identified.

Suppose that the sequence of nodes

$$j_1, j_2, \ldots, j_k = j_1 \tag{2.95}$$

represents a directed circuit yielded by the labels as outlined above. If j_m was the last node of the directed circuit to receive a label from its predecessor, then at the time immediately before j_m was labeled from j_{m-1}

we had

$$l(j_m) > l(j_{m-1}) + l(j_{m-1}, j_m) \tag{2.96}$$

$$l(j_{m+1}) \geqq l(j_m) + l(j_m, j_{m+1}) \tag{2.97}$$

Observe that immediately after j_m received a label from j_{m-1}, $l(j_m)$ is reduced to $l(j_{m-1}) + l(j_{m-1}, j_m)$ to produce an inequality in (2.97). Thus, if the primes are used to denote the node numbers after j_m received a label from j_{m-1}, we have

$$l'(j_{m+1}) > l'(j_m) + l(j_m, j_{m+1}) \tag{2.98}$$

For other arcs around the directed circuit, we have

$$l'(j_{p+1}) \geqq l'(j_p) + l(j_p, j_{p+1}), \qquad p \neq m, \quad p = 1, 2, \ldots, k-1 \tag{2.99}$$

Summing (2.98) and (2.99) around the directed circuit and noting the strict inequality of (2.98) results in the strict inequality

$$\sum_{i=1}^{k-1} l(j_i, j_{i+1}) < 0 \tag{2.100}$$

contradicting our assumption that the net does not contain any negative directed circuits. Thus, at every stage of the iterations in Step 2, the sequence of nodes generated from the labels of any node j with $l(j) < \infty$ eventually arrives at s and terminates with $l(s) = 0$; for otherwise s would be labeled from some node and a negative directed circuit is identified.

After termination in Step 2, let

$$s = j_1, j_2, \ldots, j_{q-1}, j_q = j \tag{2.101}$$

be a directed path from s to j yielded by the labels as outlined above. Then we have

$$l(j_{p+1}) = l(j_p) + l(j_p, j_{p+1}), \qquad p = 1, 2, \ldots, q-1 \tag{2.102}$$

for otherwise the algorithm would not have been terminated in Step 2. Summing (2.102) along the directed path gives

$$l(j) = l(s) + \sum_{i=1}^{q-1} l(j_i, j_{i+1}) \tag{2.103}$$

Since $l(s) = 0$, (2.103) becomes

$$l(j) = \sum_{i=1}^{q-1} l(j_i, j_{i+1}) \tag{2.104}$$

Suppose that there were a shorter directed path from s to j other than the one shown in (2.101) yielded by the labels, say

$$s = i_1, i_2, \ldots, i_w = j \tag{2.105}$$

Then along this directed path we have as in (2.102)

$$l(i_{x+1}) = l(i_x) + l(i_x, i_{x+1}), \qquad x = 1, 2, \ldots, w - 1 \tag{2.106}$$

the sum of which is

$$l(j) = \sum_{x=1}^{w-1} l(i_x, i_{x+1}) \tag{2.107}$$

Combining (2.104) and (2.107) gives

$$\sum_{i=1}^{q-1} l(j_i, j_{i+1}) = \sum_{x=1}^{w-1} l(i_x, i_{x+i}) \tag{2.108}$$

This shows that the two directed paths (2.101) and (2.105) are of the same length, contradicting the assumption that the latter is shorter than the former. Thus, if the net does not contain any negative directed circuits, the algorithm terminates and the resulting node labels give the distances and the shortest directed paths from s to all other nodes of the net that can be reached from s by directed paths.

2.3 MULTITERMINAL SHORTEST DIRECTED PATHS

In the foregoing, we discussed procedures for finding all shortest directed paths from a preassigned source node s to all other nodes. In the present section, we shall look for shortest directed paths between all pairs of nodes in a net. One obvious way for obtaining the solution is to apply the single source algorithms of Section 2.2 n times, each time with a different node chosen as the source node s. Since for each choice of s the computational complexity is $O(n^3)$ for a general n-node net, the resulting procedure would require $O(n^4)$. In the following, we describe several other more efficient algorithms for solving this problem. The methods are applicable to general nets without negative directed circuits.

2.3.1 Matrix Algorithm

Consider an n-node net $G(V, E, l)$ in which the nodes have been designated as $1, 2, \ldots, n$. For our purposes, we introduce two matrices based on G.

DEFINITION 2.2

Connection Matrix. The *connection matrix* $C = [c_{ij}]$ of an *n*-node net $G(V, E, l)$ is an $n \times n$ matrix whose *i*th row and *j*th column element c_{ij} is the length of the arc (i, j) or $c_{ij} = l(i, j)$, where $c_{ii} = 0$ for all i and $c_{ij} = \infty$ for all $(i, j) \notin E$.

DEFINITION 2.3

Distance Matrix. The *distance matrix* $D = [d_{ij}]$ of an *n*-node net $G(V, E, l)$ is an $n \times n$ matrix whose *i*th row and *j*th column element d_{ij} is the distance from node i to node j in G, where $d_{ii} = 0$ for all i.

We first define a special matrix binary operation, denoted by the symbol $\otimes$, called the *minaddition*. Given two square matrices of order n

$$A = [a_{ij}] \tag{2.109}$$

$$B = [b_{ij}] \tag{2.110}$$

the minaddition of A and B is a matrix

$$W = A \otimes B = [w_{ij}] \tag{2.111}$$

of the same order whose *i*th row and *j*th column element w_{ij} is determined by the equation

$$w_{ij} = \min_k (a_{ik} + b_{kj}) \tag{2.112}$$

Recall that in the ordinary matrix product, the element w_{ij} is defined by

$$w_{ij} = \sum_k a_{ik} b_{kj} \tag{2.113}$$

If in (2.113) the summation is replaced by the minimum operation, and the product $a_{ik}b_{kj}$ is changed to addition, we obtain the minaddition operation (2.112). It is straightforward to verify that minaddition is associative, but is not commutative. In what follows, we shall use power, product and similar terms in the sense of minaddition. Thus, we write

$$C^2 = C \otimes C \tag{2.114}$$

and C^3 is the third power of C in the sense of minaddition. Also, we shall use the symbol $c_{ij}^{(k)}$ to denote the *i*th row and *j*th column element of C^k:

$$C^k = [c_{ij}^{(k)}] \tag{2.115}$$

It is not difficult to see that the entry $c_{ij}^{(2)}$ gives the length of a shortest directed path from i to j in G using at most two arcs, because in this case

$$c_{ij}^{(2)} = \min_k (c_{ik} + c_{kj}) \qquad (2.116)$$

and we have tried every node k as a possible intermediate node of a two-arc or one-arc directed path from i to j, where the one-arc path corresponds to $k = i$ or $k = j$. The entries $c_{ij}^{(3)}$ of $C^3 = C \otimes C \otimes C$ represent the lengths of the shortest directed paths from i to j using at most three arcs. By induction, we can show that the entries $c_{ij}^{(k)}$ of C^k gives the lengths of the shortest directed paths from i to j using at most k arcs. Since we have already calculated C^2, there is no need to calculate C^3 first in order to calculate C^4. We can calculate C^4 directly from C^2 by virtue of the fact that the minaddition is associative:

$$C^4 = C \otimes C \otimes C \otimes C = (C \otimes C) \otimes (C \otimes C) = C^2 \otimes C^2 \qquad (2.117)$$

Once we obtain C^4, we can use it to calculate C^8. This squaring process can be continued until C^k, $k = 2^\alpha$, is obtained, where α is the least integer greater than or equal to $\log_2 (n - 1)$. This follows from the fact that the number of arcs in any path in an n-node net is at most $n - 1$. Therefore, we have

$$D = C^k = C^{n-1} \quad \text{for all } k \geq n - 1 \qquad (2.118)$$

Example 2.11

Consider the net $G(V, E, l)$ of Fig. 2.21, which is redrawn in Fig. 2.27.

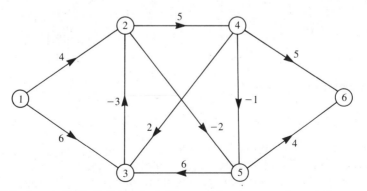

Fig. 2.27. A net $G(V, E, l)$ used to illustrate the construction of the connection matrix and the matrix binary operation called the minaddition.

The connection matrix of the net is found to be

$$
C = 3 \quad
\begin{array}{c@{}c}
 & \begin{array}{cccccc} 1 & 2 & 3 & 4 & 5 & 6 \end{array} \\
\begin{array}{c} 1 \\ 2 \\ 3 \\ 4 \\ 5 \\ 6 \end{array} &
\left[
\begin{array}{cccccc}
0 & 4 & 6 & \infty & \infty & \infty \\
\infty & 0 & \infty & 5 & -2 & \infty \\
\infty & -3 & 0 & \infty & \infty & \infty \\
\infty & \infty & 2 & 0 & -1 & 5 \\
\infty & \infty & 6 & \infty & 0 & 4 \\
\infty & \infty & \infty & \infty & \infty & 0
\end{array}
\right]
\end{array}
\tag{2.119}
$$

the square of which in the sense of minaddition is given by

$$
C^2 = C \otimes C = 3 \quad
\begin{array}{c@{}c}
 & \begin{array}{cccccc} 1 & 2 & 3 & 4 & 5 & 6 \end{array} \\
\begin{array}{c} 1 \\ 2 \\ 3 \\ 4 \\ 5 \\ 6 \end{array} &
\left[
\begin{array}{cccccc}
0 & 3 & 6 & 9 & 2 & \infty \\
\infty & 0 & 4 & 5 & -2 & 2 \\
\infty & -3 & 0 & 2 & -5 & \infty \\
\infty & -1 & 2 & 0 & -1 & 3 \\
\infty & 3 & 6 & \infty & 0 & 4 \\
\infty & \infty & \infty & \infty & \infty & 0
\end{array}
\right]
\end{array}
\tag{2.120}
$$

This matrix can again be squared to yield

$$
C^4 = C^2 \otimes C^2 = 3 \quad
\begin{array}{c@{}c}
 & \begin{array}{cccccc} 1 & 2 & 3 & 4 & 5 & 6 \end{array} \\
\begin{array}{c} 1 \\ 2 \\ 3 \\ 4 \\ 5 \\ 6 \end{array} &
\left[
\begin{array}{cccccc}
0 & 3 & 6 & 8 & 1 & 5 \\
\infty & 0 & 4 & 5 & -2 & 2 \\
\infty & -3 & 0 & 2 & -5 & -1 \\
\infty & -1 & 2 & 0 & -3 & 1 \\
\infty & 3 & 6 & 8 & 0 & 4 \\
\infty & \infty & \infty & \infty & \infty & 0
\end{array}
\right]
\end{array}
\tag{2.121}
$$

It is straightforward to verify that

$$
D = C^k = C^4 \quad \text{for all } k \geqq 4
\tag{2.122}
$$

We now count the number of additions and comparisons in (2.118). For each entry $c_{ij}^{(2)}$ of C^2, (2.116) requires n additions and $n-1$ comparisons. For C^2 we require a total of n^3 additions and $n^2(n-1)$ comparisons. Therefore, the computational complexity of the algorithm is $O(an^3)$.

In calculating C^k, if instead of using the minaddition operation we use the ordinary matrix multiplication and addition, the ith row and jth column element $c_{ij}^{(k)}$ of $\boldsymbol{C}^k$ can be written explicitly as

$$c_{ij}^{(k)} = \sum_{j_1=1}^{n} \sum_{j_2=1}^{n} \cdots \sum_{j_{k-1}=1}^{n} c_{ij_1} c_{j_1 j_2} \cdots c_{j_{k-1} j} \qquad (2.123)$$

where $c_{ij} = c_{ij}^{(1)}$ for all i and j. This shows that each product

$$c_{ij_1} c_{j_1 j_2} \cdots c_{j_{k-1} j} \qquad (2.124)$$

in the sum represents a directed edge sequence

$$(i, j_1)(j_1, j_2) \cdots (j_{k-1}, j) \qquad (2.125)$$

from i to j using exactly k arcs in the n-node complete directed graph with $c_{ij} = (i, j)$. Equation (2.123) gives all the directed edge sequences from i to j using exactly k arcs. It follows that if $\boldsymbol{C}$ is the connection matrix of $G(V, E, l)$ and if the summations in (2.123) are replaced by the minimum operations and the products are changed to additions, $c_{ij}^{(k)}$ is the length of a shortest directed path from i to j in G using at most k arcs. The reason for this is that using the minaddition operation and setting $c_{xx} = 0$ for all x, for any term in (2.123) corresponding to a directed edge sequence containing a directed circuit, there is a term corresponding to a directed path not longer than the directed edge sequence, because the net does not contain any negative directed circuits.

To reduce the number of operations in (2.118), Narahari Pandit (1961) proposed a revised matrix algorithm. The idea is that an entry of the 'product' matrix in the sense of minaddition, once calculated, immediately replaces the corresponding entries in the two matrices that form the product before the next entry of the product matrix is calculated. Clearly, in such a process, the order of the computation is important in that the entry calculated last uses the entries calculated earlier in the minaddition operations. We call the minaddition procedure the *forward process* if the calculations of the matrix product start from top row and from left to right in forming the minadditions. Let

$$\boldsymbol{C}^{(f)} = [c_{ij}^{(f)}] \qquad (2.126)$$

be the matrix calculated by this process, written as

$$\boldsymbol{C}^{(f)} = \boldsymbol{C} \otimes_{f} \boldsymbol{C} \qquad (2.127)$$

where f signifies the forward process, and

$$\boldsymbol{C} = \boldsymbol{C}^{(1)} = [c_{ij}^{(1)}] = [c_{ij}] \qquad (2.128)$$

The elements $c_{ij}^{(f)}$ of $C^{(f)}$ can be expressed explicitly as

$$c_{ij}^{(f)} = \min_{k} [c_{ik}^{(p)} + c_{kj}^{(q)}] \tag{2.129}$$

where

$$p = 1, \qquad j \leq k \tag{2.130a}$$

$$p = f, \qquad j > k \tag{2.130b}$$

$$q = 1, \qquad i \leq k \tag{2.130c}$$

$$q = f, \qquad i > k \tag{2.130d}$$

After obtaining $C^{(f)}$, the calculations of the matrix 'product' of $C^{(f)}$ by itself start from bottom row and from right to left, reversing the order of the first matrix multiplication of (2.127) using the operation $\otimes_f$. This reverse procedure is referred to as the *backward process*:

$$C^{(b)} = [c_{ij}^{(b)}] = C^{(f)} \otimes_b C^{(f)} \tag{2.131}$$

The elements $c_{ij}^{(b)}$ of $C^{(b)}$ can be written explicitly as

$$c_{ij}^{(b)} = \min_{k} [c_{ik}^{(p)} + c_{kj}^{(q)}] \tag{2.132}$$

where

$$p = f, \qquad k \leq j \tag{2.133a}$$

$$p = b, \qquad k > j \tag{2.133b}$$

$$q = f, \qquad k \leq i \tag{2.133c}$$

$$q = b, \qquad k > i \tag{2.133d}$$

In the case where all the arcs of a net $G(V, E, l)$ are nonnegative, Farbey, Land and Murchland (1967) showed that one forward process followed by one backward process is sufficient to generate all the distances between all pairs of nodes. On the other hand, Hu (1967) proved that while two forward processes are not enough, three are always sufficient. More recently, Yang and Chen (1989) demonstrated that one forward process followed by one backward process, three forward processes, one backward process followed by one forward process, or three backward processes are sufficient to generate all the distances between all pairs of nodes in a net with negative arcs but with no negative directed circuits.

We illustrate the above results by the following example.

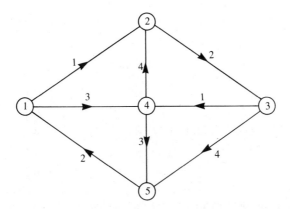

Fig. 2.28. A net $G(V, E, l)$ used to illustrate the forward and backward processes in the matrix calculation of the distances between all pairs of nodes.

Example 2.12

Consider the net $G(V, E, l)$ of Fig. 2.28, the connection matrix of which is found to be

$$
C = \begin{array}{c} \\ 1 \\ 2 \\ 3 \\ 4 \\ 5 \end{array} \begin{array}{ccccc} 1 & 2 & 3 & 4 & 5 \\ \begin{bmatrix} 0 & 1 & \infty & 3 & \infty \\ \infty & 0 & 2 & \infty & \infty \\ \infty & \infty & 0 & 1 & 4 \\ \infty & 4 & \infty & 0 & 3 \\ 2 & \infty & \infty & \infty & 0 \end{bmatrix} \end{array} \qquad (2.134)
$$

In the forward process, we calculate

$$c_{12}^{(f)} = \min \{0 + 1, 1 + 0, \infty + \infty, 3 + 4, \infty + \infty\} = 1 \qquad (2.135a)$$

$$c_{13}^{(f)} = \min \{0 + \infty, 1 + 2, \infty + 0, 3 + \infty, \infty + \infty\} = 3 \qquad (2.135b)$$

At this point, the original entry $c_{13} = \infty$ in C is replaced by $c_{13}^{(f)} = 3$ before continuing the calculation. Note that in machine computation, the replacement operation is automatic, and there is no need to check to see if $c_{ij}^{(f)} = c_{ij}$. To continue, we calculate

$$c_{14}^{(f)} = \min \{0 + 3, 1 + \infty, 3 + 1, 3 + 0, \infty + \infty\} = 3 \qquad (2.136a)$$

$$c_{15}^{(f)} = \min \{0 + \infty, 1 + \infty, 3 + 4, 3 + 3, \infty + 0\} = 6 \qquad (2.136b)$$

At this stage, we replace the entry $c_{15} = \infty$ by $c_{15}^{(f)} = 6$ before proceeding to the computation of the next element. The final result at the end of the forward process is given by

$$C^{(f)} = C \otimes_f C = \begin{matrix} & \begin{matrix} 1 & 2 & 3 & 4 & 5 \end{matrix} \\ \begin{matrix} 1 \\ 2 \\ 3 \\ 4 \\ 5 \end{matrix} & \begin{bmatrix} 0 & 1 & 3 & 3 & 6 \\ \infty & 0 & 2 & 3 & 6 \\ 6 & 5 & 0 & 1 & 4 \\ 5 & 4 & 6 & 0 & 3 \\ 2 & 3 & 5 & 5 & 0 \end{bmatrix} \end{matrix} \qquad (2.137)$$

This matrix is used to form $C^{(b)}$ by the backward process, as follows:

$$c_{54}^{(b)} = \min \{2+3, 3+3, 5+1, 5+0, 0+5\} = 5 \qquad (2.138a)$$

$$c_{53}^{(b)} = \min \{2+3, 3+2, 5+0, 5+6, 0+5\} = 5 \qquad (2.138b)$$

$$\vdots$$

$$c_{23}^{(b)} = \min \{\infty+3, 0+2, 2+0, 3+6, 6+5\} = 2 \qquad (2.138c)$$

$$c_{21}^{(b)} = \min \{\infty+0, 0+\infty, 2+6, 3+5, 6+2\} = 8 \qquad (2.138d)$$

At this point, we replace the entry $c_{21}^{(f)} = \infty$ by $c_{21}^{(b)} = 8$ before proceeding to calculate $c_{15}^{(b)}$. At the end of the backward process, the matrix becomes

$$C^{(b)} = C^{(f)} \otimes_b C^{(f)} = \begin{matrix} & \begin{matrix} 1 & 2 & 3 & 4 & 5 \end{matrix} \\ \begin{matrix} 1 \\ 2 \\ 3 \\ 4 \\ 5 \end{matrix} & \begin{bmatrix} 0 & 1 & 3 & 3 & 6 \\ 8 & 0 & 2 & 3 & 6 \\ 6 & 5 & 0 & 1 & 4 \\ 5 & 4 & 6 & 0 & 3 \\ 2 & 3 & 5 & 5 & 0 \end{bmatrix} \end{matrix} = D \qquad (2.139)$$

the distance matrix, the elements of which are the distances between all pairs of nodes in the net $G(V, E, l)$ of Fig. 2.28.

2.3.2   Floyd–Warshall Algorithm

Recall that a subpath of a shortest directed path in a net $G(V, E, l)$ is itself a shortest directed path. In particular, each arc of a shortest directed path is itself a shortest directed path. An arc (i, j) is termed a *basic arc* if it is the shortest directed path from i to j. Thus, arcs belonging to shortest directed paths are all basic arcs. If there is a pair of nodes i and j not connected directly by a basic arc (i, j), we can replace such a nonbasic arc by a basic

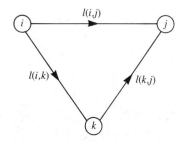

Fig. 2.29. Symbolic representation of the triple operation.

arc whose length is equal to the shortest distance from i to j in G, assuming that arcs not in G are arcs of infinite length in G. The present algorithm describes a simple procedure of creating basic arcs between each pair of nodes not connected by a basic arc, and was first proposed by Floyd (1962) and Warshall (1962).

In a given net $G(V, E, l)$, perform the following operation for a fixed k and all $i, j \neq k$:

$$l(i, j) \leftarrow \min\left[l(i, j), l(i, k) + l(k, j)\right] \tag{2.140}$$

As depicted in Fig. 2.29, the operation compares the length of an arc (i, j) with that of a two-arc directed path $(i, k)(k, j)$, the smaller of which is used to replace the length of arc (i, j), and is called the *triple operation*. We begin by setting $k = 1$ and apply the triple operation (2.140) for all $i, j = 2, 3, \ldots, n$. Then we set $k = 2$, and perform the triple operation for all $i, j = 1, 3, \ldots, n$. Notice that in performing the triple operation for $k = 2$, we use all the new arcs created when $k = 1$. We continue in this way until the triple operation is performed for $k = n$. We claim that at the end of the triple operation for $k = n$, the resulting net G' consists only of basic arcs. In other words, the arc length $l(i, j)$ in G' represents the shortest distance from i to j in $G(V, E, l)$. We now proceed to justify this assertion.

Consider an arbitrary shortest directed path, say, $(2, 5)(5, 3)(3, 4)(4, 6)$ as shown in Fig. 2.30(a). We show that the triple operation will create an arc $(2, 6)$, the length of which is equal to the sum of all the basic arcs in $(2, 5)(5, 3)(3, 4)(4, 6)$. Once we verify the assertion for this particular directed path, the procedure can be generalized to any arbitrary shortest directed path, from which a formal proof can be stated. However, we do not find it necessary; only the verification of this arbitrarily chosen path is provided here.

When $k = 2$, the triple operation does not create any new arcs for the directed path of Fig. 2.30(a). When $k = 3$, the triple operation creates a new arc $(5, 4)$ with

$$l(5, 4) = l(5, 3) + l(3, 4) \tag{2.141}$$

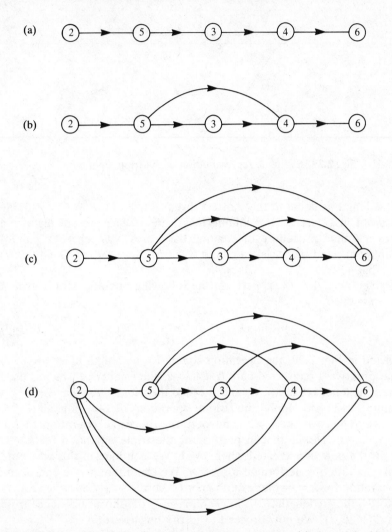

Fig. 2.30. A graph used to illustrate the triple operation: (a) the original graph and $k = 2$, (b) $k = 3$, (c) $k = 4$, (d) $k = 5$.

as shown in Fig. 2.30(b). When $k = 4$, two more arcs $(3, 6)$ and $(5, 6)$ as shown in Fig. 2.30(c) are created with

$$l(3, 6) = l(3, 4) + l(4, 6) \qquad (2.142a)$$

$$l(5, 6) = l(5, 4) + l(4, 6) = l(5, 3) + l(3, 4) + l(4, 6) \qquad (2.142b)$$

When $k = 5$, three more arcs $(2, 3)$, $(2, 4)$ and $(2, 6)$ are created as indicated in Fig. 2.30(d) with

$$l(2, 3) = l(2, 5) + l(5, 3) \tag{2.143a}$$

$$l(2, 4) = l(2, 5) + l(5, 4) = l(2, 5) + l(5, 3) + l(3, 4) \tag{2.143b}$$

$$l(2, 6) = l(2, 5) + l(5, 6) = l(2, 5) + l(5, 3) + l(3, 4) + l(4, 6) \tag{2.143c}$$

confirming that $(2, 6)$ is a basic arc.

The Floyd–Warshall algorithm is applicable to any net $G(V, E, l)$ that does not contain any negative directed circuits. For our purposes, we assume that $l(i, i) = 0$ $(i = 1, 2, \ldots, n)$ and $l(i, j) = \infty$ for $(i, j) \notin E$.

Step 1. Set $k = 0$.

Step 2. $k = k + 1$.

Step 3. For all $i \neq k$, $l(i, k) \neq \infty$ and all $j \neq k$, $l(k, j) \neq \infty$, perform the triple operation

$$l(i, j) \leftarrow \min \left[l(i, j), l(i, k) + l(k, j) \right] \tag{2.144}$$

Step 4. If $l(i, i) \geqq 0$ $(i = 1, 2, \ldots, n)$ and $k < n$, return to Step 2.
    If $l(i, i) < 0$ for some i, there is no solution. Stop.
    If $l(i, i) \geqq 0$ $(i = 1, 2, \ldots, n)$ and $k = n$, stop.

We remark that in Step 4 if $l(i, i) < 0$ for some i, then a negative directed circuit containing the node i exists in G, and no meaningful solution can be found. If $l(i, i) \geqq 0$ for all i and $k = n$, the solution is found and the arc length $l(i, j)$ in the resulting net G' gives the distance from i to j in G for all i and j. Once the distances between all pairs of nodes are calculated, the shortest directed paths themselves can be determined by using a recursive relation similar to that of (2.12). Alternatively, we can use a bookkeeping mechanism to record information about the directed paths themselves, as follows.

When we perform the triple operation, we keep track of the internal nodes of the directed paths. We use an $n \times n$ matrix

$$\boldsymbol{P} = [p_{ij}] \tag{2.145}$$

for storage and updating purposes. The ith row and jth column entry p_{ij} gives the first internal node on the directed path from i to j. If $p_{ij} = x$, then the first arc of the shortest directed path from i to j is (i, x). Likewise, if $p_{xj} = y$, then the first arc of the shortest directed path from x to j is (x, y). In this way, we can trace back to any of the other nodes. Initially, we assume that in going from i to j the first arc is (i, j). Thus, we set $p_{ij} = j$ for all i and j. When we perform the triple operation, we also update the information in

P with its entries being changed in accordance with the following rule:

$$p_{ij} = p_{ik}, \quad \text{if} \quad l(i, j) > l(i, k) + l(k, j) \tag{2.146a}$$

$$= p_{ij}, \quad \text{if} \quad l(i, j) \leq l(i, k) + l(k, j) \tag{2.146b}$$

We recognize that the triple operation performed on the net G can easily be performed on the connection matrix $C = [c_{ij}]$ of G. When $k = 1$, we compare every entry c_{ij} $(i \neq 1, j \neq 1)$ with $c_{i1} + c_{1j}$. If c_{ij} is greater than $c_{i1} + c_{1j}$, we replace the entry c_{ij} by $c_{i1} + c_{1j}$. Otherwise, the entry remains unaltered. For $k = 2$, we compare every entry c_{ij} $(i \neq 2, j \neq 2)$ with $c_{i2} + c_{2j}$. If c_{ij} is greater than $c_{i2} + c_{2j}$, we replace c_{ij} by $c_{i2} + c_{2j}$. Otherwise, the entry remains the same. Notice that in computing for $k = 2$, we have already used the results for $k = 1$. We continue in this way until $k = n$ is computed. Observe that each entry is compared with the sum of two other entries, one in the same row and one in the same column. For each entry, we have to check $(n - 1)^2$ entries. Since there are n nodes to consider, the computational complexity of the Floyd–Warshall algorithm is O(n^3).

Example 2.13

We use the Floyd–Warshall algorithm to find the distances between all pairs of nodes in the net $G(V, E, l)$ of Fig. 2.31. Initially, we set $l(i, i) = 0$ for all i and $l(i, j) = \infty$ for $(i, j) \notin E$.

Step 1. Set $k = 0$.
Step 2. Set $k = k + 1$ or $k = 1$.
Step 3.

$$l(4, 2) \leftarrow \min [\infty, 2 + 1] = 3 \tag{2.147a}$$

$$l(4, 3) \leftarrow \min [-1, 2 + 4] = -1 \tag{2.147b}$$

$$l(4, 5) \leftarrow \min [-1, 2 + 4] = -1 \tag{2.147c}$$

At the end of this step, an arc $(4, 2)$ is created with $l(4, 2) = 3$.

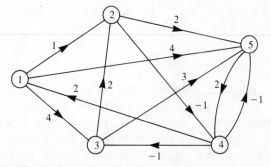

Fig. 2.31. A net $G(V, E, l)$ used to illustrate the Floyd–Warshall algorithm for the calculation of the distances between all pairs of nodes.

Step 4. Return to Step 2.

Step 2. $k = 2$.

Step 3. From here on we list only those arcs whose lengths will be changed after performing the triple operation.

$$l(1, 4) \leftarrow \min[\infty, 1 - 1] = 0 \qquad (2.148a)$$

$$l(3, 4) \leftarrow \min[\infty, 2 - 1] = 1 \qquad (2.148b)$$

$$l(1, 5) \leftarrow \min[4, 1 + 2] = 3 \qquad (2.148c)$$

At the end of this step, two new arcs $(1, 4)$ and $(3, 4)$ are created with $l(1, 4) = 0$ and $l(3, 4) = 1$, and the arc length of $(1, 5)$ is changed from 4 to 3.

Step 4. Return to Step 2.

Step 2. $k = 3$

Step 3.

$$l(4, 2) \leftarrow \min[3, -1 + 2] = 1 \qquad (2.149)$$

At the end of this step, the arc length $l(4, 2)$ is changed from 3 to 1.

Step 4. Return to Step 2.

Step 2. $k = 4$

Step 3.

$$l(2, 1) \leftarrow \min[\infty, -1 + 2] = 1 \qquad (2.150a)$$

$$l(3, 1) \leftarrow \min[\infty, 1 + 2] = 3 \qquad (2.150b)$$

$$l(1, 3) \leftarrow \min[4, 0 - 1] = -1 \qquad (2.150c)$$

$$l(5, 1) \leftarrow \min[\infty, 2 + 2] = 4 \qquad (2.150d)$$

$$l(2, 3) \leftarrow \min[\infty, -1 - 1] = -2 \qquad (2.150e)$$

$$l(5, 2) \leftarrow \min[\infty, 2 + 1] = 3 \qquad (2.150f)$$

$$l(2, 5) \leftarrow \min[2, -1 - 1] = -2 \qquad (2.150g)$$

$$l(3, 5) \leftarrow \min[3, 1 - 1] = 0 \qquad (2.150h)$$

$$l(5, 3) \leftarrow \min[\infty, 2 - 1] = 1 \qquad (2.150i)$$

$$l(1, 5) \leftarrow \min[3, 0 - 1] = -1 \qquad (2.150j)$$

At the end of this step, the resulting net is shown in Fig. 2.32.

Step 4. Return to Step 2.

Step 2. $k = 5$.

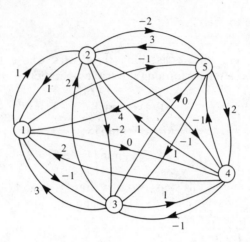

Fig. 2.32. The final net after the application of the Floyd–Warshall algorithm to the net of Fig. 2.31.

Step 3. Nothing is changed.

Step 4. Stop. The final net is shown in Fig. 2.32. Each of its arcs (i, j) is a basic arc, meaning that its length is the distance from i to j in the net of Fig. 2.31 or 2.32.

Having found the distances between all pairs of nodes, we need to ascertain the internal nodes along a shortest directed path. For this we define a 5×5 matrix P of (2.145). Initially, we let $p_{ij} = j$ for all i and j or

$$
P = \begin{matrix} & \begin{matrix} 1 & 2 & 3 & 4 & 5 \end{matrix} \\ \begin{matrix} 1 \\ 2 \\ 3 \\ 4 \\ 5 \end{matrix} & \begin{bmatrix} 1 & 2 & 3 & 4 & 5 \\ 1 & 2 & 3 & 4 & 5 \\ 1 & 2 & 3 & 4 & 5 \\ 1 & 2 & 3 & 4 & 5 \\ 1 & 2 & 3 & 4 & 5 \end{bmatrix} \end{matrix} = [p_{ij}] \tag{2.151}
$$

In (2.147a), when we set $l(4, 2)$ to $l(4, 1) + l(1, 2) = 2 + 1 = 3$, we also set

$$
p_{42} = p_{41} = 1.
$$

Likewise, in (2.148) when we set

$$
l(1, 4) = l(1, 2) + l(2, 4) = 1 - 1 = 0 \tag{2.152a}
$$

$$
l(3, 4) = l(3, 2) + l(2, 4) = 2 - 1 = 1 \tag{2.152b}
$$

$$
l(1, 5) = l(1, 2) + l(2, 5) = 1 + 2 = 3 \tag{2.152c}
$$

we also set

$$p_{14} = p_{12} = 2 \tag{2.153a}$$

$$p_{34} = p_{32} = 2 \tag{2.153b}$$

$$p_{15} = p_{12} = 2 \tag{2.153c}$$

respectively. At the end of computation, the resulting matrix becomes

$$\boldsymbol{P} = \begin{bmatrix} 1 & 2 & 2 & 2 & 2 \\ 4 & 2 & 4 & 4 & 4 \\ 2 & 2 & 3 & 2 & 2 \\ 1 & 3 & 3 & 4 & 5 \\ 4 & 4 & 4 & 4 & 5 \end{bmatrix} \tag{2.154}$$

To find a shortest directed path from 1 to 5, we first look at the entry p_{15} and find the first arc $(1, x)$. Since $p_{15} = 2$, $x = 2$. We next look at the entry $p_{25} = 4$. The second arc of the shortest directed path from 1 to 5 is $(2, 4)$. We then look at the entry $p_{45} = 5$, giving the third arc $(4, 5)$. Thus, a shortest directed path from 1 to 5 in the net of Fig. 2.31 is $(1, 2)(2, 4)(4, 5)$, whose length is -1 as indicated in Fig. 2.32.

2.4   ENUMERATION OF THE SHORTEST DIRECTED PATHS BY DECOMPOSITION

In many applications, a net $G(V, E, l)$ is sparse in that many of its node pairs are not connected directly by arcs. In such situations, we can regard the net as being composed of two overlapping nets $G_\alpha(V_\alpha, E_\alpha, l)$ and $G_\beta(V_\beta, E_\beta, l)$, as depicted symbolically in Fig. 2.33 with

$$V = V_\alpha \cup V_\beta \tag{2.155a}$$

$$Y = V_\alpha \cap V_\beta \tag{2.155b}$$

$$E = E_\alpha \cup E_\beta \tag{2.156a}$$

$$E_Y = E_\alpha \cap E_\beta \tag{2.156b}$$

where Y denotes the set of overlapping nodes and E_Y denotes the set of arcs (i, j) with $i, j \in Y$. The net $G(V, E, l)$ of Fig. 2.34, for example, may be decomposed into two overlapping nets $G_\alpha(V_\alpha, E_\alpha, l)$ and $G_\beta(V_\beta, E_\beta, l)$ as shown in Fig. 2.35 with $Y = \{2, 6\}$ and $E_Y = \{(6, 2)\}$. The nets G_α and G_β are the sectional directed graphs of G defined by the node sets V_α and V_β, and denoted by $G_\alpha = G[V_\alpha]$ and $G_\beta = G[V_\beta]$, respectively.

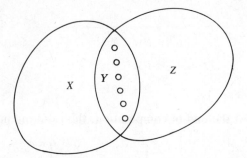

Fig. 2.33. Symbolic representation of a net as being composed of two overlapping nets.

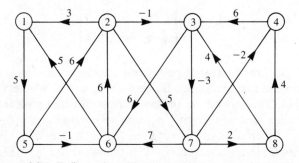

Fig. 2.34. A net $G(V, E, l)$ used to illustrate the decomposition of a net into two overlapping nets.

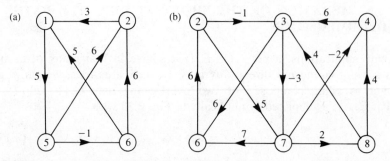

Fig. 2.35. A decomposition of the net of Fig. 2.34 into two overlapping nets: (a) $G_\alpha(V_\alpha, E_\alpha, l)$, (b) $G_\beta(V_\beta, E_\beta, l)$.

Let the node set V be partitioned into three subsets Y, X and Z:

$$V = X \cup Y \cup Z \tag{2.157}$$

where

$$X = V_\alpha - Y \tag{2.158a}$$

$$Z = V_\beta - Y \tag{2.158b}$$

If D is the distance matrix of $G(V, E, l)$, it can be partitioned in accordance with (2.157), as follows:

$$D = [d_{ij}] = \begin{array}{c} \\ X \\ Y \\ Z \end{array} \begin{bmatrix} D_{XX} & D_{XY} & D_{XZ} \\ D_{YX} & D_{YY} & D_{YZ} \\ D_{ZX} & D_{ZY} & D_{ZZ} \end{bmatrix} \qquad (2.159)$$

To simplify our notation, we shall use the symbol $d_{ij}(W)$ to denote the length of a shortest directed path from i to j in G subject to the restriction that all the nodes of the directed path belong to a subset W of the node set V. Thus, $d_{ij} = d_{ij}(V)$. Also, we use the symbol

$$D_{XY}(W) = [d_{ij}(W)] \qquad (2.160)$$

to denote the matrix of distances $d_{ij}(W)$ with $i \in X$ and $j \in Y$ with $D_{XY} = D_{XY}(V)$.

Recall that the original net $G(V, E, l)$ is composed of two nets $G_\alpha(V_\alpha, E_\alpha, l)$ and $G_\beta(V_\beta, E_\beta, l)$ overlapping at the nodes of Y. First, we apply the Floyd–Warshall algorithm to the net G_α, and obtain the matrix

$$\begin{bmatrix} D_{XX}(V_\alpha) & D_{XY}(V_\alpha) \\ D_{YX}(V_\alpha) & D_{YY}(V_\alpha) \end{bmatrix} \qquad (2.161)$$

of distances $d_{ij}(V_\alpha)$ between each pair of nodes in G_α. We then replace the lengths of the arcs between each pair of nodes of Y in G_β by those of $D_{YY}(V_\alpha)$. Note that arcs not in E_β are considered as arcs in E_β with infinite length. Let the resulting net be designated as $G'_\beta(V_\beta, E'_\beta, l')$. We shall now apply the Floyd–Warshall algorithm to G'_β again. At the end of the triple operations, we claim that we obtain the matrix

$$\begin{bmatrix} D_{YY}(V) & D_{YZ}(V) \\ D_{ZY}(V) & D_{ZZ}(V) \end{bmatrix} \qquad (2.162)$$

of distances $d_{ij}(V) = d_{ij}$ between each pair of nodes of V_β in G, the original net.

To verify our assertion, let P_{ij} be a shortest directed path from i to j in G with $i, j \in V_\beta$. If all the nodes of P_{ij} lie in Z, then $d_{ij}(V) = d_{ij}(Z)$ and the triple operations on G'_β will yield the correct distance. Thus, assume that P_{ij} contains nodes in X and/or Y. Such a path P_{ij} is symbolically shown in Fig. 2.36. Since i and j are in V_β and Y is the set of overlapping nodes, the subpaths of P_{ij} that contain the nodes of X must begin and end in the set Y. The subpath $P_{y_1 y_2}$ from y_1 to y_2 and the subpath $P_{y_3 y_4}$ from y_3 to y_4 in Fig. 2.36 are two typical such subpaths. They may be the shortest directed paths

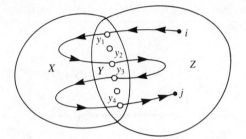

Fig. 2.36. A symbolic representation of a path P_{ij} containing nodes in X and/or Y.

from y_1 to y_2 and from y_3 to y_4 in G_α, respectively. Knowing $d_{y_1y_2}(V_\alpha)$ and $d_{y_3y_4}(V_\alpha)$ from (2.161), we effectively created two arcs (y_1, y_2) and (y_3, y_4) in G'_β with $l'(y_1, y_2) = d_{y_1y_2}(V_\alpha)$ and $l'(y_3, y_4) = d_{y_3y_4}(V_\alpha)$, as shown in Fig. 2.37. The shortest directed path P_{ij} from i to j can be replaced by another directed path of the same length in G'_β consisting of the subpath P_{iy_1}, (y_1, y_2), the subpath $P_{y_2y_3}$, (y_3, y_4), and the subpath P_{y_4j}. This means that the triple operations performed on G'_β will give the correct distance from i to j in G.

Having obtained the distances between each pair of nodes in V_β, we now replace the distances between each pair nodes of Y in G_α by those of $D_{YY}(V)$ of (2.162), and denote the resulting net by $G'_\alpha(V_\alpha, E'_\alpha, l')$. We apply the Floyd–Warshall algorithm again to G'_α. At the end of the triple operations, we obtain the matrix

$$\begin{bmatrix} D_{XX}(V) & D_{XY}(V) \\ D_{YX}(V) & D_{YY}(V) \end{bmatrix} \qquad (2.163)$$

of distances $d_{ij}(V) = d_{ij}$ between each pair of nodes of V_α in G, the original net.

Finally, to calculate the elements in $D_{XZ} = D_{XZ}(V)$ and $D_{ZX} = D_{ZX}(V)$,

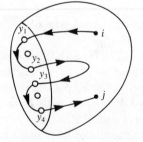

Fig. 2.37. A symbolic representation of the creation of two arcs (y_1, y_2) and (y_3, y_4) of equivalent lengths.

we use the formulas

$$d_{ij} = d_{ij}(V) = \min_{y \in Y} [d_{iy}(V) + d_{yj}(V)] \qquad (2.164a)$$

$$d_{ji} = d_{ji}(V) = \min_{y \in Y} [d_{jy}(V) + d_{yi}(V)] \qquad (2.164b)$$

for $i \in X$ and $j \in Z$. This follows directly from the observation that any directed path from $i \in X$ to $j \in Z$ or from j to i must pass at least one node y in Y, the minimum of which is certainly the minimum distance in G.

We now demonstrate the reduction in the number of operations required when distances are calculated by the decomposition procedure. Recall that the Floyd–Warshall algorithm requires approximately n^3 operations to find the distances between every pair of nodes in an n-node net. If the node set is decomposed as in (2.157) with $|X| = n_1$, $|Y| = n_2$ and $|Z| = n_3$, then we need approximately $(n_1 + n_2)^3$ operations in calculating (2.161), $(n_2 + n_3)^3$ operations in calculating (2.162), $(n_1 + n_2)^3$ in recalculating (2.163), and $2n_1 n_2 n_3$ operations in applying (2.164). Thus, the total number of operations required is

$$2(n_1 + n_2)^3 + (n_2 + n_3)^3 + 2n_1 n_2 n_3 \qquad (2.165)$$

As a specific example, let $n_1 = n_3 = 20$ and $n_2 = 5$. The decomposition algorithm requires approximately 50875 operations, whereas the direct application of the Floyd–Warshall algorithm will need 91125 operations, showing that decomposition can reduce the number of operations by a factor 1.8.

We illustrate the decomposition procedure by the following examples.

Example 2.14

Consider the sparse net $G(V, E, l)$ of Fig. 2.38 which can be decomposed into two nets $G_\alpha(V_\alpha, E_\alpha, l)$ and $G_\beta(V_\beta, E_\beta, l)$ as shown in Fig. 2.39.

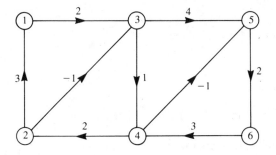

Fig. 2.38. A sparse net $G(V, E, l)$ used to illustrate the decomposition procedure.

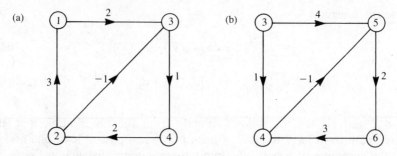

Fig. 2.39. The net of Fig. 2.38 decomposed into two overlapping nets: (a) $G_\alpha(V_\alpha, E_\alpha, l)$, (b) $G_\beta(V_\beta, E_\beta, l)$.

Following (2.157) and (2.158), we can make the following identifications:

$$X = \{1, 2\}, \qquad Y = \{3, 4\}, \qquad Z = \{5, 6\} \qquad (2.166a)$$

$$V_\alpha = \{1, 2, 3, 4\}, \qquad V_\beta = \{3, 4, 5, 6\} \qquad (2.166b)$$

Applying the Floyd–Warshall algorithm to G_α, we obtain the net of Fig. 2.40, whose distance matrix is given by

$$
\begin{array}{c}
\begin{array}{cccc} 1 & 2 & 3 & 4 \end{array} \\
\begin{array}{c} 1 \\ 2 \\ 3 \\ 4 \end{array}
\left[
\begin{array}{cc|cc}
0 & 5 & 2 & 3 \\
3 & 0 & -1 & 0 \\ \hline
6 & 3 & 0 & 1 \\
5 & 2 & 1 & 0
\end{array}
\right]
=
\begin{bmatrix}
\boldsymbol{D}_{XX}(V_\alpha) & \boldsymbol{D}_{XY}(V_\alpha) \\
\boldsymbol{D}_{YX}(V_\alpha) & \boldsymbol{D}_{YY}(V_\alpha)
\end{bmatrix}
\end{array}
\qquad (2.167)
$$

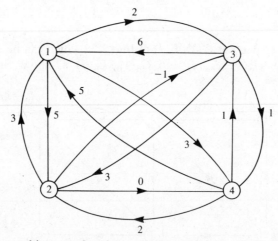

Fig. 2.40. The resulting net after the application of the Floyd–Warshall algorithm to G_α.

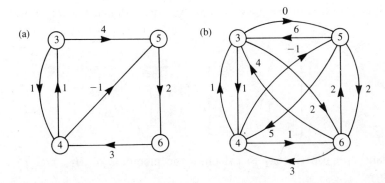

Fig. 2.41. (a) The net $G'_\beta(V_\beta, E'_\beta, l')$ obtained from G_β after the insertion of an arc $(4, 3)$ of length 1. (b) The resulting net after the application of the Floyd–Warshall algorithm to G'_β.

We next insert an arc $(4, 3)$ of length 1 in G_β to yield the net G'_β of Fig. 2.41(a), and then apply the Floyd–Warshall algorithm to G'_β. The resulting net is shown in Fig. 2.41(b), the distance matrix of which is found to be

$$
\begin{array}{c}
 \\
3 \\
4 \\
5 \\
6
\end{array}
\begin{array}{cc}
\begin{array}{cccc} 3 & 4 & 5 & 6 \end{array} & \\
\left[
\begin{array}{cc|cc}
0 & 1 & 0 & 2 \\
1 & 0 & -1 & 1 \\
\hline
6 & 5 & 0 & 2 \\
4 & 3 & 2 & 0
\end{array}
\right]
=
\begin{bmatrix}
\boldsymbol{D_{YY}(V)} & \boldsymbol{D_{YZ}(V)} \\
\boldsymbol{D_{ZY}(V)} & \boldsymbol{D_{ZZ}(V)}
\end{bmatrix}
\end{array}
\qquad (2.168)
$$

We now insert an arc $(4, 3)$ of length 1 in G_α to yield the net G'_α of Fig. 2.42(a), and then apply the Floyd–Warshall algorithm to G'_α. The

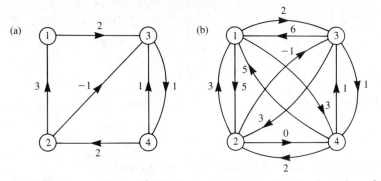

Fig. 2.42. (a) The net $G'_\alpha(V_\alpha, E'_\alpha, l')$ obtained from G_α after the insertion of an arc $(4, 3)$ of length 1. (b) The resulting net after the application of the Floyd–Warshall algorithm to G'_α.

resulting net is shown in Fig. 2.42(b), the distance matrix of which is obtained as

$$
\begin{array}{c}
 \quad 1 \;\; 2 \quad\; 3 \;\; 4 \\
\begin{array}{c} 1 \\ 2 \\ 3 \\ 4 \end{array}
\left[\begin{array}{cc:cc}
0 & 5 & 2 & 3 \\
3 & 0 & -1 & 0 \\
\hdashline
6 & 3 & 0 & 1 \\
5 & 2 & 1 & 0
\end{array}\right]
=\left[\begin{array}{cc}
\boldsymbol{D}_{XX}(V) & \boldsymbol{D}_{XY}(V) \\
\boldsymbol{D}_{YX}(V) & \boldsymbol{D}_{YY}(V)
\end{array}\right]
\end{array}
\tag{2.169}
$$

Finally, we use (2.164) to calculate the elements of $\boldsymbol{D}_{XZ}$ and $\boldsymbol{D}_{ZX}$, as follows:

$$d_{15} = \min\left[d_{13}+d_{35},\, d_{14}+d_{45}\right] = \min[2+0,\, 3-1] = 2 \tag{2.170a}$$

$$d_{16} = \min\left[d_{13}+d_{36},\, d_{14}+d_{46}\right] = \min\left[2+2,\, 3+1\right] = 4 \tag{2.170b}$$

$$d_{25} = \min\left[d_{23}+d_{35},\, d_{24}+d_{45}\right] = \min\left[-1+0,\, 0-1\right] = -1 \tag{2.170c}$$

$$d_{26} = \min\left[d_{23}+d_{36},\, d_{24}+d_{46}\right] = \min\left[-1+2,\, 0+1\right] = 1 \tag{2.170d}$$

$$d_{51} = \min\left[d_{53}+d_{31},\, d_{54}+d_{41}\right] = \min\left[6+6,\, 5+5\right] = 10 \tag{2.171a}$$

$$d_{61} = \min\left[d_{63}+d_{31},\, d_{64}+d_{41}\right] = \min\left[4+6,\, 3+5\right] = 8 \tag{2.171b}$$

$$d_{52} = \min\left[d_{53}+d_{32},\, d_{54}+d_{42}\right] = \min\left[6+3,\, 5+2\right] = 7 \tag{2.171c}$$

$$d_{62} = \min\left[d_{63}+d_{32},\, d_{64}+d_{42}\right] = \min\left[4+3,\, 3+2\right] = 5 \tag{2.171d}$$

Combining (2.168)–(2.170) gives the complete distance matrix of G:

$$
\boldsymbol{D} =
\begin{array}{c}
\quad 1 \;\; 2 \quad\; 3 \;\; 4 \quad\; 5 \;\; 6 \\
\begin{array}{c} 1 \\ 2 \\ 3 \\ 4 \\ 5 \\ 6 \end{array}
\left[\begin{array}{cc:cc:cc}
0 & 5 & 2 & 3 & 2 & 4 \\
3 & 0 & -1 & 0 & -1 & 1 \\
\hdashline
6 & 3 & 0 & 1 & 0 & 2 \\
5 & 2 & 1 & 0 & -1 & 1 \\
\hdashline
10 & 7 & 6 & 5 & 0 & 2 \\
8 & 5 & 4 & 3 & 2 & 0
\end{array}\right]
\end{array}
=\left[\begin{array}{ccc}
\boldsymbol{D}_{XX} & \boldsymbol{D}_{XY} & \boldsymbol{D}_{XZ} \\
\boldsymbol{D}_{YX} & \boldsymbol{D}_{YY} & \boldsymbol{D}_{YZ} \\
\boldsymbol{D}_{ZX} & \boldsymbol{D}_{ZY} & \boldsymbol{D}_{ZZ}
\end{array}\right]
\tag{2.172}
$$

each of whose elements d_{ij} is the distance from i to j in the original net $G(V, E, l)$ of Fig. 2.38.

2.5 SUMMARY AND SUGGESTED READING

In this chapter, we discussed the problem of finding the shortest directed paths from one node to all the other nodes and between all pairs of nodes in a weighted directed network called a net. The weights of the arcs of the net are real numbers that can be positive, zero or negative. However, for the problem to be meaningful, we assume that all the nets under consideration do not contain any negative directed circuits. The shortest directed path problem is fundamental in that it often occurs as a subproblem of other optimization problems.

For the problem of finding the shortest directed paths from one node to all other nodes, we presented four algorithms. The Dijkstra algorithm is most efficient because the required computation for an n-node net is $O(n^2)$. However, the algorithm is applicable only to those nets whose arc lengths are nonnegative. The basic idea of the Dijkstra algorithm is that it iterates on the length of the shortest directed paths. Initially, the shortest among the shortest directed paths is identified. At each iteration, the next shortest among the shortest directed paths is generated. The algorithm terminates at the end of the $(n-1)$th iteration. The Ford–Moore–Bellman algorithm is general and is applicable to nets with negative arc lengths. The algorithm iterates on the number of arcs in a directed path. At the end of the kth iteration, the labels on the nodes represent the lengths of those shortest directed paths from the source node containing $k+1$ or fewer arcs. The algorithm terminates with at most $n-1$ iterations, and requires $O(n^3)$ rather than $O(n^2)$ as in the Dijkstra algorithm. The Yen algorithm is basically the same as the Ford–Moore–Bellman algorithm except that it iterates on the number of blocks in a directed path. At the end of the kth iteration, it gives the lengths of all the shortest directed paths using at most k blocks. The algorithm terminates with at most $n-1$ iterations, and requires roughly half the work of the Ford–Moore–Bellman algorithm. An additional advantage of the Yen algorithm is that the storage requirement of the program is also reduced. Finally, the Ford–Fulkerson algorithm is very similar to the Ford–Moore–Bellman algorithm in that it sequentially reduces the labels on the nodes by examining the arcs until the conditional distances become the true distances.

For the problem of finding the shortest directed paths between all pairs of nodes, we presented two algorithms. The matrix algorithm uses the binary operation minaddition. The elements of the kth power of the connection matrix of a net in the sense of minaddition represent the lengths of the shortest directed paths in the net using at most k arcs. The algorithm terminates with at most α iterations, where α is the least integer greater than or equal to $\log_2(n-1)$, and requires $O(\alpha n^3)$ computations. To reduce the number of operations, we introduced two minaddition procedures known as the forward process and the reverse process. It can be shown that for a net with nonnegative arc lengths one forward process followed by one backward process is sufficient to generate all the distances between all pairs of nodes, and that while two forward processes are not enough, three are always sufficient. The Floyd–Warshall algorithm iterates on a set of nodes and uses the triple operation to create basic arcs between each pair of nodes not connected by a basic arc. At the end of the triple operation, the resulting net consists only of basic arcs. The computational complexity of the algorithm is $O(n^3)$, the same as if the Dijkstra algorithm was repeated for each node chosen as the source node.

In many applications, the nets are sparse in that many of the node pairs are not connected directly by arcs. In such cases, we can decompose a net into two overlapping nets. We showed that the distances between all pairs of nodes in the original net can be calculated from those of the component nets, and that the resulting reduction in the number of operations may be considerable.

Finally, we mention an intuitive way of solving the shortest path problem suggested by Minty (1957) for the case of undirected nets. One simply builds a physical model of the net using strings to connect the nodes, the lengths of which are proportional to the given arc lengths. By taking the source in one hand and the sink in the other, one solves the shortest path problem by stretching the source and the sink.

For general information and other aspects of the shortest directed path problem, see Dreyfus (1969) and Yen (1975). Yen's extensive survey article is 169 pages long and contains a bibliography of 300 papers on the subject. For the algorithms discussed in this chapter, we refer the reader to the original papers cited in the text. For the matrix algorithm, see Pollack and Wiebenson (1960), Narahari Pandit (1961), and Hu (1967). For decomposition of a sparse net, see Land and Stairs (1967), Hu (1968), Hu and Torres (1969), Yen (1971a), and Blewett and Hu (1977).

REFERENCES

Beardwood, J., Halton, J. H. and Hammersley, J. M. (1959), "The shortest path through many points," *Proc. Cambridge Phil. Soc.*, vol. 55, pp. 299–327.

Bellman, R. E. (1958), "On a routing problem," *Quart. Appl. Math.*, vol. 16, pp. 87–90.

Bilde, O. and Krarup, J. (1969), "A modified cascade algorithm for shortest paths," *Metra*, vol. 8, pp. 231–241.

Blewett, W. J. and Hu, T. C. (1977), "Tree decomposition algorithm for large networks," *Networks*, vol. 7, pp. 289–296.

Butas, L. F. (1968), "A directionally oriented shortest path algorithm," *Transportation Res.*, vol. 2, pp. 253–268.

Carson, J. S. and Law, A. M. (1977), "A note on Spira's algorithm for all-pairs shortest paths problem," *SIAM J. Computing*, vol. 6, pp. 696–699.

Cartaino, T. F. and Dreyfus, S. E. (1957), "Application of dynamic programming to the airplane minimum time-to-climb problem," *Aero Engr. Rev.*, vol. 16, pp. 74–77.

Chen, W. K. (1966a), "Boolean matrices and switching nets," *Math. Mag.*, vol. 39, pp. 1–8.

Chen, W. K. (1966b), "On directed trees and directed k-trees of a digraph and their generation," *SIAM J. Applied Math.*, vol. 14, pp. 550–559.

Cooke, K. L. and Halsey, E. (1966), "The shortest route through a network with times," *J. Math. Anal. and Appl.*, vol. 14, pp. 493–498.

Dantzig, G. B. (1967), "All shortest routes in a graph," in *Theory of Graphs*, International Symposium. New York: Gordon and Breach, pp. 91–92.

Dial, R. B. (1969), "Algorithm 360: Shortest path forest with topological ordering," *Comm. ACM*, vol. 12, pp. 632–633.

Dial, R. B., Glover, F., Karney, D. and Klingman, D. (1979), "A computational analysis of alternative algorithms for finding shortest path trees," *Networks*, vol. 9, pp. 215–248.

Dijkstra, E. W. (1959), "A note on two problems in connexion with graphs," *Numerische Math.*, vol. 1, pp. 269–271.

Dreyfus, S. E. (1969), "An appraisal of some shortest path algorithms," *Operations Res.*, vol. 17, pp. 395–412.

Farbey, B. A., Land, A. H. and Murchland, J. D. (1967), "The cascade algorithm for finding all shortest distances in a directed graph," *Mangement Sci.*, vol. 14, pp. 19–28.

Floyd, R. W. (1962), "Algorithm 97, shortest path," *Comm. ACM*, vol. 5, p. 345.

Ford, L. R. Jr (1956), "Network flow theory," The RAND Corp., P-923, Santa Monica, Calif.

Ford, L. R. Jr and Fulkerson, D. R. (1962), *Flows in Networks*, Chapter 3, Princeton, N.J.: Princeton University Press.

Frederickson, G. N. (1987), "Fast algorithms for shortest paths in planar graphs, with applications," *SIAM J. Computing*, vol. 16, pp. 1004–1022.

Fredman, M. L. (1976), "New bounds on the complexity of the shortest path problem," *SIAM J. Computing*, vol. 5, pp. 83–89.

Glover, F., Klingman, D. and Napier, A. (1974), "A note on finding all shortest paths," *Transportation Sci.*, vol. 8, pp. 3–12.

Hakimi, S. L. and Yau, S. S. (1965), "Distance matrix of a graph and its realizability," *Quart. Appl. Math.*, vol. 22, pp. 305–317.

Hesse, R. (1972), "Solution of the shortest route problem using the assignment technique," *Decision Sci.*, vol. 3, pp. 1–13.

Hoffman, W. and Pavley, R. (1959), "A method for the solution of the Nth best path problem," *J. ACM*, vol. 6, pp. 506–514.

Hoffman, A. J. and Winograd, S. (1972), "Finding all shortest distances in a directed network," *IBM J. Res. Develop.*, vol. 16, pp. 412–414.

Hu, T. C. (1967), "Revised matrix algorithms for shortest paths," *SIAM J. Applied Math.*, vol. 15, pp. 207–218.

Hu, T. C. (1968), "A decomposition algorithm for shortest paths in a network," *Operations Res.*, vol. 16, pp. 91–102.

Hu, T. C. (1982), *Combinatorial Algorithms*, Chapter 1, Reading, Mass.: Addison–Wesley.

Hu, T. C. and Torres, W. T. (1969), "Shortcut in the decomposition algorithm for shortest paths in a network," *IBM J. Res. Develop.*, vol. 13, pp. 387–390.

Ibaraki, T. (1970), "Shortest path problems visiting specified nodes," *Trans. Inst. Elec. Comm. Engr Japan,* vol. 53-A, pp. 639–646.

Johnson, D. B. (1973), "A note on Dijkstra's shortest path algorithm," *J. ACM,* vol. 20, pp. 385–388.

Johnson, D. B. (1977), "Effcient algorithms for shortest paths in sparse networks," *J. ACM,* vol. 24, pp. 1–13.

Kershenbaum, A. (1981), "A note on finding shortest path trees," *Networks,* vol. 11, pp. 399–400.

Knuth, D. E. (1977), "A generalization of Dijkstra's algorithm," *Inf. Process. Lett.,* vol. 6, pp. 1–5.

Land, A. H. and Stairs, S. W. (1967), "The extension of the cascade algorithm to large graphs," *Management Sci.,* vol. 14, pp. 29–33.

Lawler, E. L. (1972), "A procedure for computing the K best solutions to discrete optimization problems and its application to the shortest path problem," *Management Sci.,* vol. 18, pp. 401–405.

Mills, G. (1966), "A decomposition algorithm for the shortest-route problem," *Operations Res.,* vol. 14, pp. 279–291.

Mills, G. (1968), "A heuristic approach to some shortest route problems," *Can. Operational Res. Soc. J.,* vol. 6, pp. 20–25.

Minieka, E. (1974), "On computing sets of shortest paths in a graph," *Comm. ACM,* vol. 17, pp. 351–353.

Minty, G. J. (1957), "A comment on the shortest-route problem," *Operations Res.,* vol. 5, p. 724.

Minty, G. J. (1958), "A variant on the shortest-route problem," *Operations Res.,* vol. 6, pp. 882–883.

Moffat, A. and Takaoka, T. (1987), "An all pairs shortest path algorithm with expected time $O(n^2 \log n)$," *SIAM J. Computing,* vol. 16, pp. 1023–1031.

Moore, E. F. (1957), "The shortest path through a maze," *Proc. Int. Symp. on the Theory of Switching,* Part II, April 2–5, p. 285. The Annals of the Computation Laboratory of Harvard University, vol. 30, Cambridge, Mass.: Harvard University Press.

Mori, M. and Nishimura, T. (1968), "Solution of the routing problem through a network by matrix method with auxiliary nodes," *Transportation Res.,* vol. 1, pp. 165–180.

Murchland, J. D. (1969), "Bibliography of the shortest route problem," London School of Business Studies, Report LBS-TNT-6.2 (revised 1969).

Nakamori, M. (1972), "A note on the optimality of some all-shortest-path algorithms," *J. Operations Res. Soc. Japan,* vol. 15, pp. 201–204.

Narahari Pandit, S. N. (1961), "The shortest-route problem—an addendum," *Operations Res.,* vol. 9, pp. 129–132.

Nemhauser, G. L. (1972), "A generalized permanent label setting algorithm for the shortest path between specified nodes," *J. Math. Anal. and Appl.,* vol. 38, pp. 328–334.

Nicholson, T. A. J. (1966), "Finding the shortest route between two points in a network," *Computer J.,* vol. 9, pp. 275–280.

Pape, U. (1974), "Implementation and efficiency of Moore-algorithms for the shortest route problem," *Math. Programming,* vol. 7, pp. 212–222.

Peart, R. M., Randolph, P. H. and Bartlett, T. E. (1960), "The shortest-route problem," *Operations Res.,* vol. 8, pp. 866–867.

Perko, A. (1965), "Some computational notes on the shortest route problem," *Computer J.,* vol. 8, pp. 19–20.

Petitfrere, M. (1972), "Sur l'Algorithme de Dijkstra l'Obtention des plus Courts Chemins dans un Graphe," *Cahiers du Centre d'Etudes de Recherche Operationelle (Belgium),* vol. 13, pp. 111–123.

Pollack, M. and Wiebenson, W. (1960), "Solution of the shortest-route problem—a review," *Operations Res.,* vol. 8, pp. 224–230.

Shier, D. R. (1973), "A decomposition algorithm for optimality problems in tree-structured networks," *Discrete Math.,* vol. 6, pp. 175–189.

Shimbel, A. (1951), "Application of matrix algebra to communication nets," *Bull. Math. Biophysics,* vol. 13, pp. 165–178.

Spira, P. M. (1973), "A new algorithm for finding all shortest paths in a graph of positive arcs in average time $O(n^2 \log_2 b)$," *SIAM J. Computing,* vol. 2, pp. 28–32.

Tabourier, Y. (1973), "All shortest distances in a graph: An improvement to Dantzig's inductive algorithm," *Discrete Math.,* vol. 4, pp. 83–87.

Tarjan, R. E. (1981), "A unified approach to path problems," *J. ACM,* vol. 28, pp. 577–593.

Wagner, R. A. (1976), "A shortest path algorithm for edge-sparse graphs," *J. ACM,* vol. 23, pp. 50–57.

Warshall, S. (1962), "A theorem on Boolean matrices," *J. ACM,* vol. 9, pp. 11–12.

Weimer, D. L. (1963), "A serial technique to determine minimum paths," *Comm. ACM,* vol. 6, p. 664.

Whiting, P. D. and Hillier, J. A. (1960), "A method for finding the shortest route through a road network," *Operational Res. Quart.,* vol. 11, pp. 37–40.

Williams, T. A. and White, G. P. (1973), "A note on Yen's algorithm for finding the length of all shortest paths in *N*-node nonnegative-distance networks," *J. ACM,* vol. 20, pp. 389–390.

Yang, L. and Chen, W. K. (1989), "An extension of the revised matrix algorithm," *IEEE Proc. Int. Symp. on Circuits and Systems,* Portland, Oregon, May 8–11, pp. 1996–1999.

Yen, J. Y. (1970), "An algorithm for finding shortest routes from all source nodes to a given destination in general networks," *Quart. Appl. Math.,* vol. 27, pp. 526–530.

Yen, J. Y. (1971*a*), "On Hu's decomposition algorithm for shortest paths in a network," *Operations Res.,* vol. 19, pp. 983–985.

Yen, J. Y. (1971*b*), "On the efficiencies of algorithms for detecting negative loops in networks," *Santa Clara Business Rev.,* pp. 52–58.

Yen, J. Y. (1972*a*), "Finding the lengths of all shortest paths in *N*-node nonnegative-distance complete networks using $\frac{1}{2}N^3$ additions and N^3 comparisons," *J. ACM,* vol. 19, pp. 423–425.

Yen, J. Y. (1972*b*), "On the efficiency of a direct search method to locate negative cycles in a network," *Management Sci.,* vol. 19, pp. 333–335.

Yen, J. Y. (1975), "Shortest path network problems," *Math. Systems in Economics,* vol. 18, pp. 1–169.

3

MAXIMUM FLOWS IN NETWORKS

In Chapter 2, we discussed the shortest directed path problem. There, a network or simply a net is a weighted directed graph $G(V, E)$ in which each arc is associated with a real number called the length of the arc. The length may be positive, negative or zero. In the case of positive length, it may represent the physical length of a street or highway, or the energy absorption property of a system when it is changed from one state to another. On the other hand, a negative length may signify the release of energy when the system is transformed from one state to another. If we think of the network as an interconnection of pipelines or communication wires, the nodes represent the junctions of the pipelines or the communication centers and the arcs denote the pipelines or wires themselves. Then the nonnegative real number of an arc may represent the cross-sectional area of the corresponding pipeline or the message-carrying capacity of the corresponding wire. Such a problem comes up naturally in the study of transportation or communication networks. For this reason, we introduce a new concept of flows in a network and use nonnegative real numbers to indicate the maximum flow that can transfer through the arc. The nonnegative real number is called the arc capacity. In this chapter, we discuss various problems associated with the flows in a capacitated network.

3.1 FLOWS

A net is a directed graph $G(V, E)$ in which each arc (i, j) is assigned a nonnegative weight $c(i, j)$ called the *capacity* of the arc. The capacities of arcs of $G(V, E)$ can be considered as a function c from the arc set E to the nonnegative reals. Sometimes, it is convenient to allow infinite arc capacities. Also, to each arc $(i, j) \in E$ we assign a nonnegative weight $f(i, j)$ called the *flow* in arc (i, j). Thus, the flows in $G(V, E)$ are a function f from E to the nonnegative reals. More precisely, the net considered in this chapter is a *quadruplet* $G(V, E, c, f)$ with node set V, arc set E, capacity function c and flow function f. The set of flows associated with E denoted by $\{f(i, j)\}$ is called a *flow pattern*.

A flow pattern $\{f(i, j)\}$ is said to be *feasible* in $G(V, E, c, f)$ and of value f_{st} from node s to node t if it satisfies the following constraints: For each $i \in V$,

$$\sum_j f(i, j) - \sum_j f(j, i) = f_{st}, \qquad i = s \qquad (3.1a)$$

$$= 0, \qquad i \neq s, t \qquad (3.1b)$$

$$= -f_{st}, \qquad i = t \qquad (3.1c)$$

$$c(i, j) \geqq f(i, j) \geqq 0, \qquad (i, j) \in E \qquad (3.2)$$

Thus, to define a feasible flow pattern, two nodes s and t are distinguished. We call node s the *source* and node t the *sink*. All other nodes are referred to as the *intermediate nodes*. If the net flow out of node i is defined to be

$$\sum_j f(i, j) - \sum_j f(j, i) \qquad (3.3)$$

then equation (3.1) states that the net flow out of the source s is f_{st}, the net flow into the sink t is f_{st} or the net flow out of the sink t is $-f_{st}$, and the net flow out of an intermediate node is zero. Equation (3.1b) is called a *conservation equation*, similar to Kirchhoff's current law equation for electrical networks. Our objective here is to determine a maximum possible feasible flow pattern, the value f_{st} of which is called the *maximum flow*.

We remark that since $f = 0$ and $f_{st} = 0$ are permitted, there is no question about the existence of a feasible flow pattern. While the arc set E is a subset of all the ordered pairs (i, j), $i \neq j$ and $i, j \in V$, with capacity function c nonnegative on E, we could assume the net G to be a complete directed graph by taking $c = 0$ for arcs not originally in E, or we could assume strict positivity of the capacity function c by deleting from E arcs having zero capacity. Notice that not all the equations of (3.1) are linearly independent. To see this, let A_a be the complete incidence matrix of G, and let F be the column vector of the arc flows of E, arranged in the same arc order as the columns of A_a. Now row-partition the matrix A_a in accordance with the source s, intermediate nodes i and sink t:

$$A_a = \begin{bmatrix} A_s \\ A_i \\ A_t \end{bmatrix} \qquad (3.4)$$

Equation (3.1) can be rewritten as

$$A_a F = \begin{bmatrix} A_s \\ A_i \\ A_t \end{bmatrix} \quad F = \begin{bmatrix} f_{st} \\ 0 \\ -f_{st} \end{bmatrix} \tag{3.5}$$

Observe that by adding all the equations of (3.5) we produce a row of zeros, implying that not all the equations are linearly independent. Therefore, we could omit any one of them without loss of generality. We prefer, however, to retain the one-to-one correspondence between the equations and nodes. Finally, we mention that by adding an arc (t, s) in G with capacity $c(t, s) \geq f_{st}$, all equations in the resulting net can be taken as conservative equations.

We illustrate the above result by the following example.

Example 3.1

Consider the net $G(V, E, c, f)$ of Fig. 3.1, where node s is the source, t is the sink, and a, b, c and d are the intermediate nodes. The capacities of the arcs are given by

$$\begin{array}{lll}
c(s, a) = 2, & c(a, s) = 1, & c(s, b) = 3 \\
c(a, b) = 3, & c(a, c) = 1, & c(b, c) = 1 \\
c(b, d) = 4, & c(d, a) = 2, & c(d, c) = 1 \\
c(c, t) = 2, & c(d, t) = 4, & c(t, d) = 1
\end{array} \tag{3.6}$$

These are given as the first members of the pairs of numbers written adjacent to the arcs of the net of Fig. 3.1. A feasible flow pattern given as the second members of the pairs of numbers written adjacent to the arcs

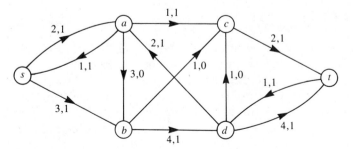

Fig. 3.1. A net $G(V, E, c, f)$ used to illustrate the flow problem.

of Fig. 3.1 is found to be

$$f(s, a) = 1, \qquad f(a, s) = 1, \qquad f(s, b) = 1$$
$$f(a, b) = 0, \qquad f(a, c) = 1, \qquad f(b, c) = 0$$
$$f(b, d) = 1, \qquad f(d, a) = 1, \qquad f(d, c) = 0$$
$$f(c, t) = 1, \qquad f(d, t) = 1, \qquad f(t, d) = 1 \qquad (3.7)$$

The constraints corresponding to (3.5) are obtained from Fig. 3.1 as

	(s, a)	(a, s)	(s, b)	(a, b)	(a, c)	(b, c)	(b, d)	(d, a)	(d, c)	(c, t)	(d, t)	(t, d)
s	1	−1	1	0	0	0	0	0	0	0	0	0
a	−1	1	0	1	1	0	0	−1	0	0	0	0
b	0	0	−1	−1	0	1	1	0	0	0	0	0
c	0	0	0	0	−1	−1	0	0	−1	1	0	0
d	0	0	0	0	0	0	−1	1	1	0	1	−1
t	0	0	0	0	0	0	0	0	0	−1	−1	1

$$
\times \begin{bmatrix} 1 \\ 1 \\ 1 \\ 0 \\ 1 \\ 0 \\ 1 \\ 1 \\ 0 \\ 1 \\ 1 \\ 1 \end{bmatrix}
=
\begin{array}{c} s \\ a \\ b \\ c \\ d \\ t \end{array}
\begin{bmatrix} 1 \\ 0 \\ 0 \\ 0 \\ 0 \\ -1 \end{bmatrix}
\qquad (3.8)
$$

showing that the value f_{st} of this feasible flow pattern is 1.

3.2 *s–t* CUTS

A *cutset* of a directed graph or a net $G(V, E, c, f)$ is a subgraph consisting of a minimal collection of arcs whose removal reduces the rank of G by one. Intuitively, if we "cut" the arcs of a cutset, one of the components of G will be cut into two pieces. The name *cutset* has its origin in this interpretation. As examples of cutsets, consider the net $G(V, E, c, f)$ of Fig. 3.1. The subgraphs $(a, c)(d, a)(a, b)(s, b)$, $(a, c)(d, a)(b, c)(b, d)$, and $(c, t)(t, d)(d, t)$ are examples of cutsets. The broken lines of Fig. 3.2 show how these cutsets "cut" G. The subgraph

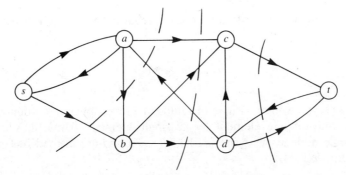

Fig. 3.2. A graph used to illustrate the concepts of a cut and a cutset.

$(a, c)(d, a)(a, b)(s, b)(c, t)(t, d)(d, t)$ is not a cutset because the removal of these arcs from G reduces the rank of G from 5 to 3, a reduction of two instead of one as required. This brings out the concept of a cut. A *cut* of G is either a cutset or an arc-disjoint union of cutsets of G. The subgraph $(a, c)(d, a)(a, b)(s, b)(c, t)(t, d)(d, t)$ is a cut but not a cutset. A cut can also be interpreted in another useful fashion. Let X be a nonempty proper subset of the node set V of G, and write $\bar{X} = V - X$. Then the set of arcs of G each of which is incident with one of its two endpoints in X and the other in $\bar{X}$ is a cut of G. In particular, if the removal of these arcs from G increases the number of components of G by one, then the cut is also a cutset. In Fig. 3.2, let $X = \{s, a\}$ and $\bar{X} = \{b, c, d, t\}$. Then the set of arcs (a, c), (a, b), (s, b) and (d, a) forms a cut of G. It is also a cutset of G. On the other hand, if we let $X = \{s, a, t\}$ and $\bar{X} = \{b, c, d\}$, the set of arcs (a, c), (d, a), (a, b), (s, b), (c, t), (t, d) and (d, t) forms a cut but not a cutset.

DEFINITION 3.1

s–t **Cutset.** For two distinguished nodes s and t of a directed graph, an *s–t cutset* is a minimal set of arcs, the removal of which breaks all the directed paths from s to t in the directed graph.

The term minimal in the definition needs some clarification. A set S or a subgraph W is said to be *minimal* with respect to property P if no proper subset of S or no proper subgraph of W has property P.

To simplify the notation, we adopt the following conventions. Let X and Y be two subsets of the node set V of a net $G(V, E, c, f)$. We use the symbol (X, Y) to denote the set of all arcs (x, y) directed from $x \in X$ to $y \in Y$. For any function g from the arc set E to the reals, write

$$g(X, Y) = \sum_{(x,y)\in(X,Y)} g(x, y) \qquad (3.9)$$

Likewise, when we deal with a function h from the node set V to the reals, we write

$$h(X) = \sum_{x \in X} h(x) \qquad (3.10)$$

where $h(x)$ is the weight assigned to node x. For simplicity, we denote a set consisting only of one element by its single element. Thus, if X contains only a single node x, we write (x, Y), $g(x, Y)$ or $h(x)$ instead of $(\{x\}, Y)$, $g(\{x\}, Y)$ or $h(\{x\})$.

DEFINITION 3.2

$s\text{-}t$ **Cut.** For two distinguished nodes s and t of a directed graph $G(V, E)$, an $s\text{-}t$ *cut* is the set of arcs $(X, \bar{X})$ of G with $s \in X$ and $t \in \bar{X}$, where X is a subset of V and $\bar{X} = V - X$.

We remark that an $s\text{-}t$ cut may not be an $s\text{-}t$ cutset. Consider, for example, the directed graph $G(V, E)$ of Fig. 3.3. Let $X = \{s, b\}$. Then

$$(X, \bar{X}) = \{(s, a), (b, a), (b, t)\} \qquad (3.11)$$

where $\bar{X} = \{a, t\}$, is an $s\text{-}t$ cut, but it is not an $s\text{-}t$ cutset, because $\{(b, t)\}$ is a proper subset of $(X, \bar{X})$ and the removal of (b, t) from G will also break all directed paths from s to t. However, we can show that every $s\text{-}t$ cutset is an $s\text{-}t$ cut. To see this, let Q be an $s\text{-}t$ cutset of a directed graph $G(V, E)$. Define the subset X of V recursively as follows:

(1) $s \in X$.
(2) If $x \in X$ and $(x, y) \in E - Q$, then $y \in X$.

Then $t \in \bar{X} = V - X$. We first show that every arc $(x, y) \in (X, \bar{X})$, $x \in X$ and $y \in \bar{X}$, is in Q. Suppose that (x, y) is not in Q. Then in $E - Q$ there is a directed path from s to y formed by a directed path from s to x followed by

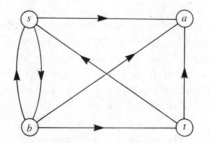

Fig. 3.3. An example of an $s\text{-}t$ cut that is not an $s\text{-}t$ cutset.

(x, y). This would imply that $y \in X$, a contradiction. Conversely, if there is an arc $(x, y) \in Q$ which is not in $(X, \bar{X})$, then Q is not an s−t cutset because the removal of $(X, \bar{X})$, a proper subset of Q, will also break all directed paths from s to t. Thus, every s−t cutset is an s−t cut.

In Fig. 3.3, (b, t) is an s−t cutset. Using the procedure outlined above yields the subset $X = \{s, a, b\}$. The corresponding s−t cut is found to be

$$(X, \bar{X}) = (\{s, a, b\}, t) = \{(b, t)\} \tag{3.12}$$

The *capacity* of an s−t cut $(X, \bar{X})$ in a net $G(V, E, c, f)$ is defined to be

$$c(X, \bar{X}) = \sum_{(x,y)\in(X,\bar{X})} c(x, y) \tag{3.13}$$

A minimum s−t cut C_{min} is an s−t cut with minimum capacity among all the s−t cuts:

$$c(C_{min}) = \min_i \{c(X_i, \bar{X}_i)\} \tag{3.14}$$

where $(X_i, \bar{X}_i)$ is an s−t cut of G. Likewise, the *capacity* of an s−t cutset Q in G is defined by

$$c(Q) = \sum_{(x,y)\in Q} c(x, y) \tag{3.15}$$

A minimum s−t cutset Q_{min} is an s−t cutset with minimum capacity among all the s−t cutsets:

$$c(Q_{min}) = \min_k \{c(Q_k)\} \tag{3.16}$$

where Q_k is an s−t cutset of G. We show that if all arc capacities are positive, then

$$c(C_{min}) = \min_i \{c(X_i, \bar{X}_i)\} = \min_k \{c(Q_k)\} = c(Q_{min}) \tag{3.17}$$

To justify (3.17), we use the fact that since every s−t cutset is an s−t cut, it is clear that

$$c(C_{min}) \leqq c(Q_{min}) \tag{3.18}$$

To complete the proof, we show that the reverse inequality is also true and hence the equality must hold. Since C_{min} is a minimum s−t cut and since all the arc capacities are positive by assumption, no proper subset of C_{min} can be an s−t cut; for, otherwise, the s−t cut formed by the proper subset would

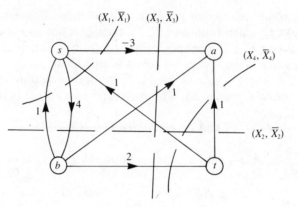

Fig. 3.4. An example showing that nonnegative arc capacities are necessary for identity (3.17) to hold.

have a smaller capacity than C_{min}. This means that no proper subset of C_{min} can break all directed paths from s to t in G. Consequently, C_{min} is a minimal set of arcs, the removal of which breaks all the directed paths from s to t in G; and, by definition, it is also an s–t cutset. This implies

$$c(C_{min}) \geqq c(Q_{min}) \tag{3.19}$$

Combining this with (3.18) gives (3.17). The proof is completed.

To see that the hypothesis that all arc capacities be nonnegative is necessary for (3.17) to hold, consider the net $G(V, E, c, f)$ of Fig. 3.4. There are four s–t cuts, as follows:

$$(X_1, \bar{X}_1) = (s, \{a, b, t\}) = \{(s, a), (s, b)\} \tag{3.20a}$$

$$(X_2, \bar{X}_2) = (\{s, a\}, \{b, t\}) = \{(s, b)\} \tag{3.20b}$$

$$(X_3, \bar{X}_3) = (\{s, b\}, \{a, t\}) = \{(b, t), (b, a), (s, a)\} \tag{3.20c}$$

$$(X_4, \bar{X}_4) = (\{s, a, b\}, t) = \{(b, t)\} \tag{3.20d}$$

whose capacities are

$$c(X_1, \bar{X}_1) = c(s, a) + c(s, b) = -3 + 4 = 1 \tag{3.21a}$$

$$c(X_2, \bar{X}_2) = c(s, b) = 4 \tag{3.21b}$$

$$c(X_3, \bar{X}_3) = c(b, t) + c(b, a) + c(s, a) = 2 + 1 - 3 = 0 \tag{3.21c}$$

$$c(X_4, \bar{X}_4) = c(b, t) = 2 \tag{3.21d}$$

On the other hand, there are two s–t cutsets $Q_1 = \{(s, b)\}$ and $Q_2 = \{(b, t)\}$

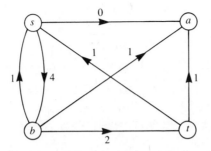

Fig. 3.5. An example showing that the zero arc capacity is permitted for identity (3.17) to hold.

whose capacities are $c(Q_1) = 4$ and $c(Q_2) = 2$. This gives $C_{\min} = 0$ and $Q_{\min} = 2$ and (3.17) fails to hold. The reason is that the net contains an arc (s, a) with negative arc capacity $c(s, a) = -3$. In passing, we mention that $Q_1 = (X_2, \bar{X}_2)$ and $Q_2 = (X_4, \bar{X}_4)$, confirming an earlier assertion that every $s–t$ cutset is also an $s–t$ cut.

With the exclusion of nets with negative arc capacity, (3.17) remains valid for nets with nonnegative arc capacities, zero included. Fig. 3.5 is a net containing a zero capacity arc (s, a). Since the nets of Figs. 3.4 and 3.5 are isomorphic, they possess the same $s–t$ cuts and $s–t$ cutsets. However, their capacities are different and are given below:

$$c(X_1, \bar{X}_1) = c(s, a) + c(s, b) = 4, \qquad c(X_2, \bar{X}_2) = c(s, b) = 4$$

$$c(X_3, \bar{X}_3) = c(b, t) + c(b, a) + c(s, a) = 3, \qquad c(X_4, \bar{X}_4) = c(b, t) = 2 \quad (3.22a)$$

$$c(Q_1) = c(s, b) = 4, \qquad c(Q_2) = c(b, t) = 2 \qquad (3.22b)$$

showing that $C_{\min} = Q_{\min} = 2$ and (3.17) holds. To justify this extension, we observe that if an $s–t$ cut is not an $s–t$ cutset, then a proper subset of the $s–t$ cut is an $s–t$ cutset. Since all arc capacities are nonnegative, the capacity of this $s–t$ cut is at least as large as that of the proper subset. Hence, the $s–t$ cutsets determine the minimum $s–t$ cut.

Finally, we mention that a directed circuit L of G contains an equal number of arcs in common with the $s–t$ cut $(X, \bar{X})$ and $t–s$ cut $(\bar{X}, X)$. This follows from the observation that a directed circuit L and a cut $(X, \bar{X}) \cup (\bar{X}, X)$ have an even number of arcs in common, zero included, that in traversing along L the common arcs will alternately appear in $(X, \bar{X})$ and $(\bar{X}, X)$ because starting from a node x on L, eventually it has to return to x to complete the circuit.

Since an $s–t$ cut $(X, \bar{X})$ breaks all directed paths from s to t, it is intuitively clear that the value f_{st} of a flow f in a net $G(V, E, c, f)$ cannot exceed the capacity of any $s–t$ cut. Before we prove this, we rewrite the constraints (3.1) in terms of the simplified notation of (3.9): For each $i \in V$,

$$f(s, V) - f(V, s) = f_{st} \tag{3.23a}$$

$$f(i, V) - f(V, i) = 0, \qquad i \neq s, t \tag{3.23b}$$

$$f(t, V) - f(V, t) = -f_{st} \tag{3.23c}$$

These together with the capacity constraints

$$c(i, j) \geqq f(i, j) \geqq 0, \qquad (i, j) \in E \tag{3.24}$$

define a feasible flow pattern $\{f(i, j)\}$.

THEOREM 3.1

Let $(X, \bar{X})$ be an s–t cut of a net $G(V, E, c, f)$. Then the flow value f_{st} from s to t in G is given by

$$f_{st} = f(X, \bar{X}) - f(\bar{X}, X) \leqq c(X, \bar{X}) \tag{3.25}$$

Proof. Since f is a flow of G, it satisfies the equations (3.23). Summing these equations over $x \in X$ gives

$$f_{st} = \sum_{x \in X} [f(x, V) - f(V, x)] = f(X, V) - f(V, X) \tag{3.26}$$

Writing $V = X \cup \bar{X}$ in (3.26) and expanding the resulting terms yields

$$\begin{aligned} f_{st} &= f(X, X \cup \bar{X}) - f(X \cup \bar{X}, X) \\ &= f(X, X) + f(X, \bar{X}) - f(X, X) - f(\bar{X}, X) \\ &= f(X, \bar{X}) - f(\bar{X}, X) \end{aligned} \tag{3.27}$$

Since $f(\bar{X}, X) \geqq 0$ and $f(X, \bar{X}) \leqq c(X, \bar{X})$ by virtue of (3.24), (3.25) follows immediately. This completes the proof of the theorem.

The theorem states that the value of a flow from s to t is equal to the net flow across any s–t cut. In the net $G(V, E, c, f)$ of Fig. 3.1, which is redrawn in Fig. 3.6, the first member of a pair of numbers written adjacent to an arc denotes the arc capacity, and the second member denotes the flow in the arc. Three cuts are indicated in Fig. 3.6, the net flows of which are found to be

$$f(X_1, \bar{X}_1) - f(\bar{X}_1, X_1) = f(a, c) + f(a, b) + f(s, b) - f(d, a)$$

$$= 1 + 0 + 1 - 1 = 1 \leqq c(X_1, \bar{X}_1) = 1 + 3 + 3 = 7 \tag{3.28a}$$

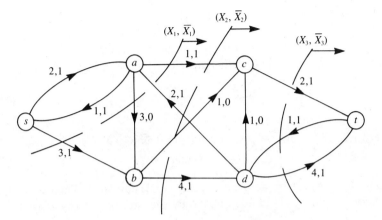

Fig. 3.6. A labeled net with a pair of numbers written adjacent to an arc, the first number denoting the arc capacity and the second number denoting the flow in the arc.

$$f(X_2, \bar{X}_2) - f(\bar{X}_2, X_2) = f(a, c) + f(b, c) + f(b, d) - f(d, a)$$
$$= 1 + 0 + 1 - 1 = 1 \leqq c(X_2, \bar{X}_2) = 1 + 1 + 4 = 6 \quad (3.28b)$$
$$f(X_3, \bar{X}_3) - f(\bar{X}_3, X_3) = f(c, t) + f(d, t) - f(t, d)$$
$$= 1 + 1 - 1 = 1 \leqq c(X_3, \bar{X}_3) = 2 + 4 = 6 \quad (3.28c)$$

The value of this flow from s to t is 1, being equal to the net flow across any one of the three s–t cuts.

3.3 MAXIMUM FLOW

A basic problem in flows is to find a feasible flow pattern that maximizes the value f_{st} of a flow in a given net $G(V, E, c, f)$. In this section, we state and prove the fundamental result concerning the maximum flow known as the max-flow min-cut theorem. The theorem was independently discovered by Ford and Fulkerson (1956) and Elias, Feinstein and Shannon (1956). Ford and Fulkerson (1956) gave a combinatorial proof which constructs a maximum flow and locates a minimum s–t cut. Their proof shows that there always exists a flow with value equal to the capacity of a minimum s–t cut. The proof will also serve as a basis for a number of other algorithms in this chapter. Elias, Feinstein and Shannon (1956) used an ingenious graph–theoretic approach by breaking a net into simpler nets until a solution for the simpler nets become evident. A third proof was given by Dantzig and Fulkerson (1956) using the Duality Theorem of linear programming.

THEOREM 3.2

(Max-flow min-cut theorem). The maximum flow value f_{max} from s to t in a net $G(V, E, c, f)$ is equal to the capacity of a minimum s–t cut, i.e.

$$f_{max} = \max \{f_{st}\} = \min_i \{c(X_i, \bar{X}_i)\} \tag{3.29}$$

where $(X_i, \bar{X}_i)$ is an s–t cut, and $\max \{f_{st}\}$ is taken over all feasible flow patterns in G.

Proof. Let $(X, \bar{X})$ be an arbitrary s–t cut. Then from Theorem 3.1 the value f_{st} of any flow f is bounded above by the capacity of any s–t cut:

$$f_{st} \leq f(X, \bar{X}) \leq c(X, \bar{X}) \tag{3.30}$$

In particular, the maximum flow value f_{max} is bounded above by the capacity of a minimum s–t cut, or

$$f_{max} = \max \{f_{st}\} \leq \min_i \{c(X_i, \bar{X}_i)\} \tag{3.31}$$

Thus, to prove the theorem, it suffices to establish the existence of a flow f and an s–t cut $(X, \bar{X})$ such that the flow value equals the capacity of this s–t cut $(X, \bar{X})$ or

$$f(X, \bar{X}) = c(X, \bar{X}) \tag{3.32a}$$
$$f(\bar{X}, X) = 0 \tag{3.32b}$$

which is equivalent to stating that

$$f_{max} = \max \{f_{st}\} = f(X, \bar{X}) - f(\bar{X}, X) = f(X, \bar{X})$$
$$= c(X, \bar{X}) = \min_i \{c(X_i, \bar{X}_i)\} \tag{3.33}$$

and the equality holds throughout (3.25). We now proceed to establish such a flow and to locate the desired s–t cut $(X, \bar{X})$.

Let f be a maximum flow in $G(V, E, c, f)$. Using f, define a subset X of the node set V recursively as follows:

(1) $s \in X$.
(2) If $x \in X$ and $f(x, y) < c(x, y)$, then $y \in X$.
(3) If $x \in X$ and $f(y, x) > 0$, then $y \in X$.

We assert that $t \in \bar{X} = V - X$; for, if not, there exists a path, not necessarily a directed path, between nodes s and t,

$$P_{st} = (s, i_2)(i_2, i_3) \ldots (i_{k-1}, t) \tag{3.34}$$

such that all forward arcs $(i_\alpha, i_{\alpha+1})$ of P_{st} are not saturated,

$$f(i_\alpha, i_{\alpha+1}) < c(i_\alpha, i_{\alpha+1}) \tag{3.35}$$

and all reverse arcs $(i_{\alpha+1}, i_\alpha)$ of P_{st} are not flowless,

$$f(i_{\alpha+1}, i_\alpha) > 0 \tag{3.36}$$

Here, an arc $(i_\alpha, i_{\alpha+1})$ of P_{st} is said to be a *forward arc* of P_{st} if in traversing from s to t on P_{st} the arc $(i_\alpha, i_{\alpha+1})$ is directed from i_α to $i_{\alpha+1}$. Otherwise, it is a *reverse arc* of P_{st}. Thus, an arc is a forward arc from s to t on P_{st} and becomes a reverse arc from t to s on P_{st}. We say that an arc (i, j) is *saturated* with respect to a flow f if $f(i, j) = c(i, j)$ and is *flowless* with respect to f if $f(i, j) = 0$. Thus, an arc that is both saturated and flowless can only have zero capacity. Let

$$w_1 = \min \{c(i_\alpha, i_{\alpha+1}) - f(i_\alpha, i_{\alpha+1})\} \tag{3.37}$$

taken over all forward arcs $(i_\alpha, i_{\alpha+1})$ of P_{st},

$$w_2 = \min \{f(i_{\alpha+1}, i_\alpha)\} \tag{3.38}$$

taken over all reverse arcs $(i_{\alpha+1}, i_\alpha)$ of P_{st}, and

$$w = \min (w_1, w_2) \tag{3.39}$$

We now define a new flow f^* based on the original flow f, as follows:

$$f^*(i_\alpha, i_{\alpha+1}) = f(i_\alpha, i_{\alpha+1}) + w \tag{3.40a}$$

for all forward arcs $(i_\alpha, i_{\alpha+1})$ of P_{st},

$$f^*(i_{\alpha+1}, i_\alpha) = f(i_{\alpha+1}, i_\alpha) - w \tag{3.40b}$$

for all reverse arcs $(i_{\alpha+1}, i_\alpha)$ of P_{st}, and

$$f^*(i, j) = f(i, j) \tag{3.40c}$$

for all other arcs (i, j) of G. It is straightforward to verify that the new flow function f^* thus defined is a feasible flow pattern having value $f_{st} + w$ from s to t, where f_{st} is the value of the original flow f. This shows that f is not a maximum flow, contrary to our assumption. Thus, t must be in $\bar{X}$, and $(X, \bar{X})$ is an s–t cut.

By construction, we see that

$$f(i, j) = c(i, j) \tag{3.41a}$$

for $(i, j) \in (X, \bar{X})$, $i \in X$ and $j \in \bar{X}$, and

$$f(j, i) = 0 \tag{3.41b}$$

for $(j, i) \in (\bar{X}, X)$, $j \in \bar{X}$ and $i \in X$; for otherwise j would be in X. Hence

$$f(X, \bar{X}) = c(X, \bar{X}) \tag{3.42a}$$

$$f(\bar{X}, X) = 0 \tag{3.42b}$$

This completes the proof of the theorem.

DEFINITION 3.3

Flow Augmenting Path. A path P_{st}, not necessarily a directed path, between nodes s and t in a given net $G(V, E, c, f)$ is said to be a *flow augmenting path* with respect to f if all forward arcs (i, j) of P_{st} are not saturated, $f(i, j) < c(i, j)$, and all reverse arcs (j, i) are not flowless, $f(j, i) > 0$, in traversing from s to t on P_{st}.

The path P_{st} defined in (3.34) is a flow augmenting path. Thus, a flow f is maximum if and only if there is no flow augmenting path with respect to f. The result is useful in that in order to increase the value of a flow, it suffices to look for flow augmenting paths. In a similar way, we see that an s–t cut $(X, \bar{X})$ is minimum if and only if for every maximum flow f, all arcs of $(X, \bar{X})$ are saturated and all arcs $(\bar{X}, X)$ are flowless.

Example 3.2

In the net $G(V, E, c, f)$ of Fig. 3.7, a feasible flow pattern is shown in the figure. The s–t cut

$$(X, \bar{X}) = (s, \{a, b, c, d, t\}) = \{(s, a), (s, b)\} \tag{3.43}$$

has minimum capacity

$$c(X, \bar{X}) = c(s, a) + c(s, b) = 2 + 3 = 5 \tag{3.44}$$

among all the s–t cuts. Thus, by Theorem 3.2 the maximum flow from s

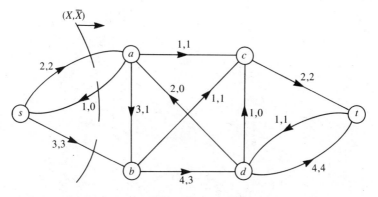

Fig. 3.7. A net showing a feasible flow pattern.

to t in G is equal to $c(X, \bar{X})$ or

$$f_{\max} = c(X, \bar{X}) = 5 \tag{3.45}$$

Observe that all arcs in $(X, \bar{X})$ are saturated and the arc in $(\bar{X}, X) = \{(a, s)\}$ is flowless. The $s-t$ cut

$$(Y, \bar{Y}) = (\{s, a, b\}, \{c, d, t\}) = \{(a, c), (b, c), (b, d)\} \tag{3.46}$$

is not minimum because not all arcs in $(Y, \bar{Y})$ are saturated. Also, it is easy to check that there is no flow augmenting path in G.

We now state and prove other properties of the minimum $s-t$ cuts.

THEOREM 3.3

Let $(X, \bar{X})$ and $(Y, \bar{Y})$ be two minimum $s-t$ cuts in a net $G(V, E, c, f)$. Then $(X \cup Y, \overline{X \cup Y})$ and $(X \cap Y, \overline{X \cap Y})$ are also minimum $s-t$ cuts of G, where $\overline{X \cup Y} = V - X \cup Y$ and $\overline{X \cap Y} = V - X \cap Y$.

Proof. If X is contained in Y, then $X \cup Y = Y$ and $X \cap Y = X$, giving

$$(X \cup Y, \overline{X \cup Y}) = (Y, \bar{Y}) \tag{3.47a}$$

$$(X \cap Y, \overline{X \cap Y}) = (X, \bar{X}) \tag{3.47b}$$

Likewise, if Y is contained in X, similar results are obtained, and the theorem is trivial. Thus, we assume that the intersections

$$A = X \cap Y, \qquad B = \bar{X} \cap Y$$
$$C = X \cap \bar{Y}, \qquad D = \bar{X} \cap \bar{Y} \tag{3.48}$$

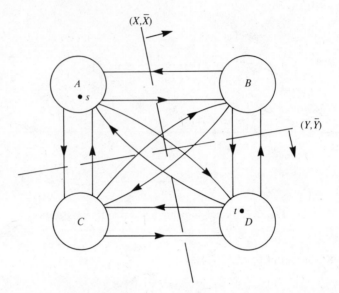

Fig. 3.8. A symbolic representation of the partition of the nodes of a net by the two minimum s–t cuts $(X, \bar{X})$ and $(Y, \bar{Y})$.

are not empty, as depicted in Fig. 3.8, where $s \in A$ and $t \in D$. Since $(X, \bar{X})$ and $(Y, \bar{Y})$ are minimum s–t cuts and $(A \cup B \cup C, D)$ and $(A, B \cup C \cup D)$ are s–t cuts, we must have the following inequalities:

$$c(A \cup B \cup C, D) + c(A, B \cup C \cup D) \geqq c(X, \bar{X}) + c(Y, \bar{Y}) \quad (3.49)$$

each of which can be expanded as

$$c(A \cup B \cup C, D) = c(A, D) + c(B, D) + c(C, D) \quad (3.50a)$$

$$c(A, B \cup C \cup D) = c(A, B) + c(A, C) + c(A, D) \quad (3.50b)$$

$$c(X, \bar{X}) = c(A \cup C, B \cup D) = c(A, B) + c(A, D) + c(C, B) + c(C, D)$$
$$(3.51a)$$

$$c(Y, \bar{Y}) = c(A \cup B, C \cup D) = c(A, C) + c(A, D) + c(B, C) + c(B, D)$$
$$(3.51b)$$

Substituting these in (3.49) yields

$$c(C, B) + c(B, C) \leqq 0 \quad (3.52)$$

Since $c(C, B)$ and $c(B, C)$ are both nonnegative, (3.52) can only be satisfied with the equality. Using this in (3.49) obtains

$$c(A \cup B \cup C, D) + c(A, B \cup C \cup D) = c(X, \bar{X}) + c(Y, \bar{Y}) \quad (3.53)$$

which can be rewritten as

$$c(X \cup Y, \overline{X \cup Y}) + c(X \cap Y, \overline{X \cap Y}) = c(X, \bar{X}) + c(Y, \bar{Y}) \quad (3.54)$$

Since $c(X, \bar{X})$ and $(Y, \bar{Y})$ are minimum s–t cuts, it is necessary that

$$c(X \cup Y, \overline{X \cup Y}) \geqq c(X, \bar{X}) = c(Y, \bar{Y}) \quad (3.55a)$$
$$c(X \cap Y, \overline{X \cap Y}) \geqq c(X, \bar{X}) = c(Y, \bar{Y}) \quad (3.55b)$$

These in conjunction with (3.54) shows that the equality must hold in (3.55), and $(X \cup Y, \overline{X \cup Y})$ and $(X \cap Y, \overline{X \cap Y})$ are minimum s–t cuts. This completes the proof of the theorem.

In words, Theorem 3.3 states that if there are two minimum s–t cuts that cross each other as in (3.48), then there are two more minimum s–t cuts that do not cross each other.

Example 3.3

A maximum feasible flow pattern is shown in Fig. 3.9 for the net $G(V, E, c, f)$. Two minimum s–t cuts are found to be

$$(X, \bar{X}) = (\{s, b, c\}, \{a, t\}) = \{(s, a), (s, t), (b, t)\} \quad (3.56a)$$
$$(Y, \bar{Y}) = (\{s, a\}, \{b, c, t\}) = \{(a, t), (s, t), (s, c)\} \quad (3.56b)$$

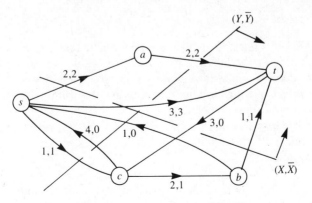

Fig. 3.9. A net with a maximum feasible flow pattern.

whose capacity is given by

$$c(X, \bar{X}) = c(Y, \bar{Y}) = 6 \qquad (3.57)$$

Then according to Theorem 3.3 the $s-t$ cuts

$$(X \cup Y, \overline{X \cup Y}) = (\{s, a, b, c\}, t) = \{(a, t), (s, t), (b, t)\} \quad (3.58a)$$
$$(X \cap Y, \overline{X \cap Y}) = (s, \{a, b, c, t\}) = \{(s, a), (s, t), (s, c)\} \quad (3.58b)$$

are also minimum. It is easy to confirm that the capacity of the $s-t$ cuts in (3.58) is 6, being equal to the minimum $s-t$ cut capacity.

3.4   FORD–FULKERSON ALGORITHM

The proof of the max-flow min-cut theorem given as Theorem 3.2 provides a simple and efficient algorithm for constructing a maximum flow and locating a minimum $s-t$ cut in a given net $G(V, E, c, f)$. The Ford–Fulkerson algorithm is a procedure which systematically searches for a flow augmenting path, and then increases the flow along this path. It can be carried out by two routines: The Labeling Routine and the Augmentation Routine. The labeling routine searches for a flow augmenting path and the augmentation routine increases the flow along the flow augmenting path. The algorithm may start with zero flow, and terminates when the maximum flow is generated. With rare exception where the arc capacities are irrational, the algorithm terminates after a finite iteration.

The algorithm assigns labels to the nodes of a given net $G(V, E, c, f)$. The label assigned to a node is represented by an ordered triplet $(x, +, w)$ or $(x, -, w)$, where $x \in V$ and w is a positive number or ∞. During the labeling process, a node is always considered to be in one of the following three states:

(i) *Unlabeled node.* A node is *unlabeled* if it receives no label. At the beginning of the labeling process, every node is unlabeled.

(ii) *Labeled and unscanned node.* A node x is said to be *labeled and unscanned* if it has a label and if its neighboring nodes y, $(x, y) \in E$, have not all been labeled.

(iii) *Labeled and scanned node.* A node x is *labeled and scanned* if it has a label and if all of its neighboring nodes y, $(x, y) \in E$, have also been labeled.

We now describe Ford–Fulkerson's labeling routine and augmentation routine.

Labeling Routine

Step 1. Label s by $(s, +, \infty)$. Now s is labeled and unscanned and all other nodes are unlabeled and unscanned.

Step 2. Select any labeled and unscanned node x, and perform the following operations:

(a) For all nodes y, $(x, y) \in E$, that are unlabeled such that $f(x, y) < c(x, y)$, label y by $(x, +, w(y))$ where

$$w(y) = \min [w(x), c(x, y) - f(x, y)] \qquad (3.59)$$

Then y is labeled and unscanned.

(b) For all nodes y, $(y, x) \in E$, that are unlabeled such that $f(y, x) > 0$, label y by $(x, -, w(y))$ where

$$w(y) = \min [w(x), f(y, x)] \qquad (3.60)$$

Now change the label on x by circling the $+$ or $-$ entry. Then x is now labeled and scanned.

Step 3. Repeat Step 2 until either t is labeled or until no more labels can be assigned and t is unlabeled. In the former case, go to the Augmentation Routine; in the latter case, terminate.

Augmentation Routine

Step 1. Let $z = t$ and go to Step 2 below.

Step 2. If the label on z is $(q, +, w(z))$, increase the flow $f(q, z)$ by $w(t)$. If the label on z is $(q, -, w(z))$, decrease the flow $f(z, q)$ by $w(t)$.

Step 3. If $q = s$, discard all labels and return to Step 1 of the Labeling Routine. Otherwise, let $z = q$ and return to Step 2 of the Augmentation Routine.

We illustrate the Ford–Fulkerson algorithm by the following examples.

Example 3.4

Consider the net $G(V, E, c, f)$ of Fig. 3.1 which is redrawn in Fig. 3.10. The flow shown in the net G is not maximum and we shall apply the Ford–Fulkerson algorithm to generate a maximum flow, as follows:

First iteration

Labeling routine

Step 1. Label s by $(s, +, \infty)$.

Step 2. Node a is labeled by $(s, +, 1)$, and node b by $(s, +, 2)$. Circle the $+$ in $(s, +, \infty)$, giving $(s, \oplus, \infty)$.

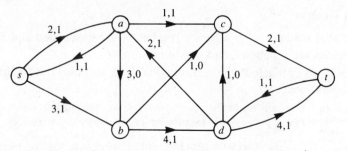

Fig. 3.10. A net used to illustrate the Ford–Fulkerson algorithm for the calculation of a maximum flow.

Step 3. Return to Step 2.

Step 2. Node c is labeled by $(b, +, 1)$ and change $(s, +, 2)$ to $(s, \oplus, 2)$. Node d is labeled by $(a, -, 1)$ and change $(s, +, 1)$ to $(s, \oplus, 1)$.

Step 3. Return to Step 2.

Step 2. Node t is labeled by $(c, +, 1)$, and change $(b, +, 1)$ to $(b, \oplus, 1)$.

Step 3. Go to Augmentation Routine.

Augmentation routine

Step 1. Let $z = t$.

Step 2. Increase the flow $f(c, t)$ by $w(t) = 1$.

Step 3. Set $z = c$.

Step 2. Increase the flow $f(b, c)$ by 1.

Step 3. Set $z = b$.

Step 2. Increase the flow $f(s, b)$ by 1.

Step 3. Discard all labels and return to Step 1 of the Labeling Routine.

The details of the first iteration are indicated in Fig. 3.11.

Second iteration

Labeling routine

Step 1. Label s by $(s, +, \infty)$.

Step 2. Node a is labeled by $(s, -, 1)$, and node b by $(s, +, 1)$. Change $(s, +, \infty)$ to $(s, \oplus, \infty)$.

Step 3. Return to Step 2.

Step 2. Node d is labeled by $(a, -, 1)$. Change $(s, -, 1)$ to $(s, \ominus, 1)$.

Step 3. Return to Step 2.

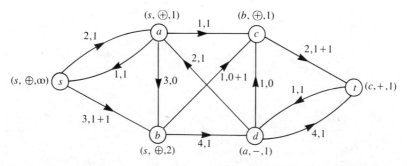

Fig. 3.11. The resulting net after the completion of the first iteration of the Ford–Fulkerson algorithm.

Step 2. Nodes c and t are labeled by $(d, +, 1)$. Change $(a, -, 1)$ to $(a, \ominus, 1)$.

Step 3. Go to Augmentation Routine.

Augmentation routine

Step 1. Let $z = t$.

Step 2. Increase the flow $f(d, t)$ by $w(t) = 1$.

Step 3. Set $z = d$.

Step 2. Decrease the flow $f(d, a)$ by 1.

Step 3. Set $z = a$.

Step 2. Decrease the flow $f(a, s)$ by 1.

Step 3. Discard all labels and return to Step 1 of the Labeling Routine.

The details of the second iteration are illustrated in Fig. 3.12.

The third, fourth and fifth iterations are shown in Figs. 3.13, 3.14 and 3.15, respectively. At the end of the fifth iteration, the algorithm terminates and the flow pattern shown in Fig. 3.15 is maximum. The

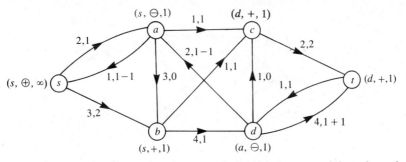

Fig. 3.12. The resulting net after the completion of the second iteration of the Ford–Fulkerson algorithm.

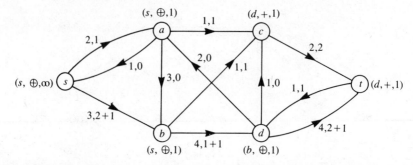

Fig. 3.13. The resulting net after the completion of the third iteration of the Ford–Fulkerson algorithm.

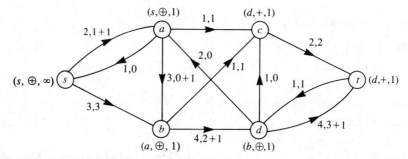

Fig. 3.14. The resulting net after the completion of the fourth iteration of the Ford–Fulkerson algorithm.

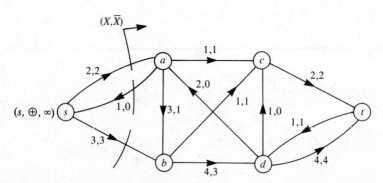

Fig. 3.15. The resulting maximum flow pattern after the application of the Ford–Fulkerson algorithm to the net of Fig. 3.10.

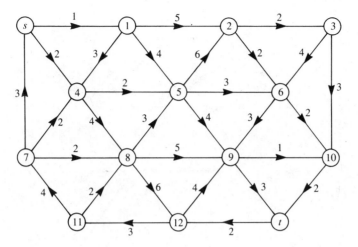

Fig. 3.16. A net used to illustrate the Ford–Fulkerson algorithm for the generation of a maximum flow pattern.

desired minimum s–t cut $(X, \bar{X})$ is found to be

$$(X, \bar{X}) = (s, \{a, b, c, d, t\}) = \{(s, a), (s, b)\} \tag{3.61}$$

the capacity of which is $c(X, \bar{X}) = c(s, a) + c(s, b) = 5$. The s–t cut $(X, \bar{X})$ is indicated in Fig. 3.15.

Example 3.5

We use the Ford–Fulkerson algorithm to generate a maximum flow in the net $G(V, E, c, f)$ of Fig. 3.16 from node s to node t. Initially, the flow f is set to zero. The algorithm proceeds as follows:

First iteration

Labeling routine. The routine finds an augmentation path

$$P_{st} = (s, 4)(4, 8)(8, 9)(9, t) \tag{3.62}$$

Augmentation routine. Since there is no reverse arc in P_{st}, the flow in each forward arc is increased by $w(t) = 2$.

The details of the first iteration are shown in Fig. 3.17.

Second iteration

Labeling routine. The routine finds an augmentation path

$$P_{st} = (s, 1)(1, 5)(5, 9)(9, t) \tag{3.63}$$

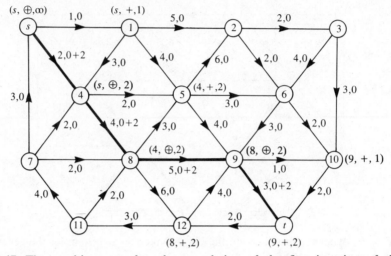

Fig. 3.17. The resulting net after the completion of the first iteration of the Ford–Fulkerson algorithm.

Augmentation routine. Since there is no reverse arc in P_{st}, the flow in each forward arc is increased by $w(t) = 1$.

The details of the second iteration are shown in Fig. 3.18.

Third iteration

Labeling routine. Node s is labeled by $(s, +, \infty)$, but no more labels can be assigned to other nodes. The program terminates.

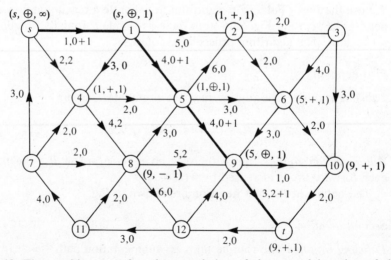

Fig. 3.18. The resulting net after the completion of the second iteration of the Ford–Fulkerson algorithm.

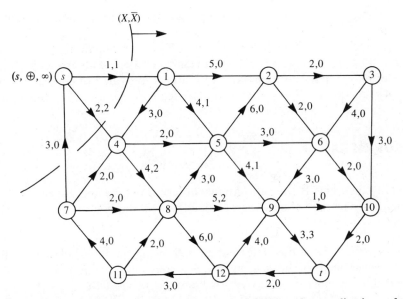

Fig. 3.19. The resulting maximum flow pattern after the application of the Ford–Fulkerson algorithm to the net of Fig. 3.16.

A maximum flow pattern is shown in Fig. 3.19. The desired minimum $s-t$ cut $(X, \bar{X})$ shown in the figure is found to be

$$(X, \bar{X}) = (s, \bar{s}) = \{(s, 1), (s, 4)\} \tag{3.64}$$

whose capacity is $c(X, \bar{X}) = 3$.

3.4.1 Integrity Theorem

The Ford–Fulkerson algorithm is used not only to prove the max-flow min-cut theorem, but also to solve the maximum flow problem. The speed of the algorithm depends on the arc capacities in the net as well as on the numbers of nodes and arcs of the net. Indeed, in certain cases where the arc capacities are irrational, the algorithm might not converge at all. This will be elaborated in Section 3.4.2.

To ensure the termination of the algorithm, it will be necessary to assume that the capacity function c is integral valued. In the case of rational capacities for the arcs, they can always be converted to a problem with integral capacities by clearing fractions. Therefore, confining our attention to rational numbers is really no restriction for computational purposes. If the flow is integral and if the labeling routine identifies a flow augmenting path, then the maximum allowable flow change $w(t)$ of the augmentation routine, being the minimum of positive integers or the difference of two positive integers, is a positive integer, provided that the computation is initiated with an integral flow. For each flow augmenting path, the flow value is increased by at least one unit. Upon termination, a maximum integral flow has been generated. As a result, the Ford–Fulkerson algorithm must terminate in a finite number of iterations, provided of course that the capacity function c is integral valued. This leads to the following theorem.

THEOREM 3.4

(Integrity theorem) If the capacity function of a net is integral valued, then there exists a maximum integral valued flow in the net.

In the search for a flow augmenting path using the labeling routine, the first time we need to check at most $n-1$ nodes in an n-node net and the second time at most $n-2$ nodes, so there are at most $(n-1)+(n-2)+ \dots + 1 = n(n-1)/2$ nodes to be checked before a flow augmenting path is identified. If all arc capacities are integers, the maximum flow value f_{st} from s to t, being equal to the minimum s–t cut capacity, is also an integer. Since the flow value is increased by at least 1 unit per flow augmenting path, the Ford–Fulkerson algorithm requires at most $O(f_{st}n^2)$ steps. Since the flow value f_{st} is really an unknown quantity at the beginning, we do not have a bound in terms of the numbers of nodes and arcs of a net. In fact, it is possible to assign arc capacities to a very small net, so the algorithm will take a very long time to run. This will be shown by an example in the following section.

3.4.2 Irrational Arc Capacities

The Ford–Fulkerson algorithm is very popular because it is simple to understand and easy to implement. For many problems in practice, the algorithm terminates fairly quickly. However, in the case where the arc capacities are allowed to be irrational, it is possible to construct a net so that the algorithm not only will not terminate but also will converge to a wrong limit. In the following, we describe the steps of the algorithm for such a net due to Ford and Fulkerson (1962).

Before proceeding, we introduce a few terms that will be needed in the discussion. In a given net $G(V, E, c, f)$ with capacity function c and flow function f from s to t, the term $[c(x, y) - f(x, y)]$ is called the *residual capacity* of arc $(x, y) \in E$ with respect to f. Now consider the recursion

$$a_{k+2} = a_k - a_{k+1} \qquad (3.65)$$

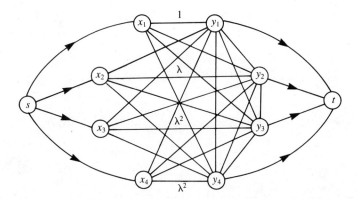

Fig. 3.20. The construction of a 10-node net, in which an undirected edge represents a pair of oppositely directed arcs, each having capacity equal to that of the undirected edge.

for all $k \geq 0$, which has the solution

$$a_k = \lambda^k \tag{3.66}$$

where

$$\lambda = \frac{-1 + \sqrt{5}}{2} < 1 \tag{3.67}$$

Thus, we have the following convergent series:

$$\sum_{k=0}^{\infty} \lambda^k = \frac{3 + \sqrt{5}}{2} = S \tag{3.68}$$

We construct a 10-node net $G(V, E, c, f)$ as shown in Fig. 3.20, where an undirected edge represents a pair of oppositely directed arcs, each having capacity equal to that of the undirected edge. Four arcs (x_1, y_1), (x_2, y_2), (x_3, y_3) and (x_4, y_4) are distinguished, and are referred to as the *special arcs*. To every arc of E except the four special arcs we assign the capacity S. The special arcs are given the capacities

$$c(x_1, y_1) = 1 \tag{3.69a}$$

$$c(x_2, y_2) = \lambda \tag{3.69b}$$

$$c(x_3, y_3) = \lambda^2 \tag{3.69c}$$

$$c(x_4, y_4) = \lambda^2 \tag{3.69d}$$

For the first iteration using the labeling routine, we find the flow

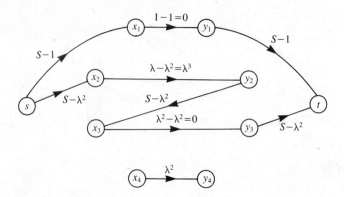

Fig. 3.21. A net showing the residual capacities of the arcs after augmenting the flow on the flow-augmenting path (3.70) by λ^2 units.

augmenting path $(s, x_1)(x_1, y_1)(y_1, t)$. We then increase the flow by 1 unit, the maximum permissible amount, along this path. The four special arcs will then have residual capacities 0, λ, λ^2, λ^2, respectively.

For the second iteration, we choose the flow augmenting path

$$P_{st1} = (s, x_2)(x_2, y_2)(y_2, x_3)(x_3, y_3)(y_3, t) \qquad (3.70)$$

The only special arcs that are on this path are (x_2, y_2) and (x_3, y_3). Augmenting the flow on this path by λ^2, the maximum permissible amount, yields a flow pattern, the residual capacities of which are shown in Fig. 3.21. All other undisplayed arcs have residual capacity S. The residual capacities of the four special arcs now become 0, $\lambda - \lambda^2 = \lambda^3$, 0, λ^2, respectively, where we have used the fact that

$$\lambda^{k+2} = \lambda^k - \lambda^{k+1} \qquad (3.71)$$

for all nonnegative integer k. Next, we choose the flow augmenting path

$$P_{st2} = (s, x_2)(x_2, y_2)(y_2, y_1)(x_1, y_1)(x_1, y_3)(x_3, y_3)(x_3, y_4)(y_4, t) \quad (3.72)$$

Observe that only the special arcs (x_1, y_1) and (x_3, y_3) are reverse arcs in this path, and all other arcs are forward arcs. Now augment the flow along this path by λ^3 units, again the maximum permissible amount. The residual capacities of the resulting arcs are shown in Fig. 3.22, where all the undisplayed arcs have residual capacity S except the arcs (y_2, x_3) and (y_3, t), which have residual capacity $S - \lambda^2$. The two augmentation steps together have increased the flow value by $\lambda^2 + \lambda^3 = \lambda$ units.

Observe that the residual capacities of the four special arcs are now changed to λ^3, 0, λ^3, λ^2. By relabeling the nodes of the special arcs, the special arcs have the residual capacities 0, λ^2, λ^3, λ^3, respectively.

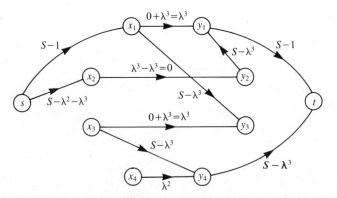

Fig. 3.22. A net showing the residual capacities of the arcs after augmenting the flow on the flow-augmenting path (3.72) by λ^3 units.

To complete our construction, we use the inductive process. Suppose that at the end of the kth iteration, the four special arcs (x'_1, y'_1), (x'_2, y'_2), (x'_3, y'_3), (x'_4, y'_4), after relabeling if necessary, have residual capacities

$$0, \lambda^k, \lambda^{k+1}, \lambda^{k+1} \qquad (3.73)$$

and the augmentation steps have increased the flow value by $\lambda^k + \lambda^{k+1} = \lambda^{k-1}$ units. We show that if the above procedure of using two flow augmentation steps is repeated, the special arcs of the resulting net will have residual capacities $0, \lambda^{k+1}, \lambda^{k+2}, \lambda^{k+2}$, respectively. This is considered to be the $(k + 1)$th iteration.

First, we choose the flow augmenting path

$$P'_{st1} = (s, x'_2)(x'_2, y'_2)(y'_2, x'_3)(x'_3, y'_3)(y'_3, t) \qquad (3.74)$$

as shown in Fig. 3.23. Augment the flow along this path by the maximum amount of λ^{k+1} units. The resulting residual capacities of the four special arcs are as indicated in Fig. 3.23. Next, select the flow augmenting path

$$P'_{st2} = (s, x'_2)(x'_2, y'_2)(y'_2, y'_1)(x'_1, y'_1)(x'_1, y'_3)(x'_3, y'_3)(x'_3, y'_4)(y'_4, t) \quad (3.75)$$

As before, the special arcs (x'_1, y'_1) and (x'_3, y'_3) are reverse arcs in P'_{st2}, and all others are forward arcs. Augment the flow along this path by λ^{k+2} units. The residual capacities of the four special arcs in the resulting net are shown in Fig. 3.24, and are given by $\lambda^{k+2}, 0, \lambda^{k+2}, \lambda^{k+1}$, respectively. By relabeling the nodes of the special arcs, the residual capacities of the four special arcs at the end of the $(k + 1)$th iteration are given by

$$0, \lambda^{k+1}, \lambda^{k+2}, \lambda^{k+2} \qquad (3.76)$$

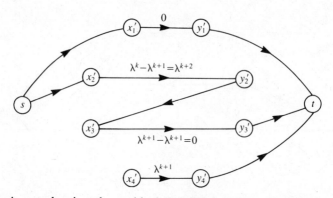

Fig. 3.23. A net showing the residual capacities of the four special arcs after augmenting the flow on the flow-augmenting path (3.74) by λ^{k+1} units.

The two augmentation steps together have increased the flow value by

$$\lambda^{k+1} + \lambda^{k+2} = \lambda^k \tag{3.77}$$

We now determine the flow value at the end of the $(k + 1)$th iteration. Recall that at the end of the first iteration, the flow value is increased by 1 unit. At the end of the second iteration, the flow value is increased by λ units; at the end of the kth iteration, by λ^{k-1} units, and at the end of the $(k + 1)$th iteration, by λ^k units. Therefore, the total flow value at the end of the $(k + 1)$th iteration is given by

$$1 + \lambda + \ldots + \lambda^{k-1} + \lambda^k = \sum_{j=0}^{k} \lambda^j \tag{3.78}$$

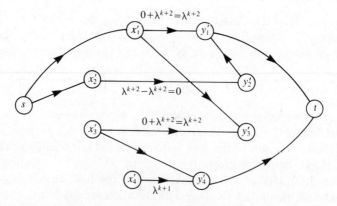

Fig. 3.24. A net showing the residual capacities of the four special arcs after augmenting the flow on the flow-augmenting path (3.75) by λ^{k+2} units.

showing from (3.68) that no non-special arc is ever required to carry more than

$$S = \sum_{u=0}^{\infty} \lambda^u \tag{3.79}$$

units of flow in repeating the inductive step. The process converges to a flow having value S, whereas the maximum flow value from s to t in the net of Fig. 3.20 is $4S$, being equal to the minimum s–t cut.

The conclusion is that if we allow irrational arc capacities, it is possible to construct a net with finite arc capacities, so that the Ford–Fulkerson algorithm will never terminate and the sequence of flow values will converge to a number that is not the maximum flow in the net. Because of this difficulty, many new algorithms have been proposed. They are guaranteed to terminate within a time bound that is independent of the arc capacities, and depends only on the numbers of nodes and arcs of the net.

We now turn our attention to the discussion of other algorithms. Many of these algorithms are based on the concept of the layered net, and are much more efficient than the Ford–Fulkerson algorithm.

3.5 LAYERED NETS

Given a net $G(V, E, c, f)$, we discuss how to induce a *layered net* $N(G)$ or simply N from G. An arc (i, j) of G is said to be *useful* from i to j if either (i, j) is not saturated, $f(i, j) < c(i, j)$, or $(j, i) \in E$ is not flowless, $f(j, i) > 0$. The layered net N will be constructed one layer at a time from the nodes of G, using the flow f as a guide. By definition, the source s is at the 0th layer. Then a node j is at layer 1 if there is a useful arc $(s, j) \in E$. We include arc (s, j) in N for each j and assign a capacity

$$c'(s, j) = c(s, j) - f(s, j) + f(j, s) \tag{3.80}$$

to (s, j). The set of all such j forms layer 1 nodes of N. To construct layer 2, we pick a node i in layer 1 and look for a useful arc $(i, u) \in E$, where u is not a node in layer 1 or $u \neq s$. We then include arc (i, u) in N for each i and u and assign a capacity

$$c'(i, u) = c(i, u) - f(i, u) + f(u, i) \tag{3.81}$$

to (i, u). The set of all such u forms layer 2 nodes of N. In general, a node y is in layer k if there is a useful arc $(x, y) \in E$, where x is a layer $k - 1$ node and y does not belong to any of the previous layers $1, 2, \ldots, k - 1$ or $y \neq s$. We then include arc (x, y) in N for each x and y and assign a capacity

$$c'(x, y) = c(x, y) - f(x, y) + f(y, x) \tag{3.82}$$

Note that the new capacity function c' represents the total residual or unused flow-carrying capacity of the arcs in both directions between their endpoints.

The layering process continues until we reach a layer where there is a useful arc (v, t) from some node v of this layer to the sink t, or else until no additional layers can be created by the above procedure. In the former case, we include arc (v, t) in N for each v and assign a capacity

$$c'(v, t) = c(v, t) - f(v, t) + f(t, v) \qquad (3.83)$$

to (v, t), and the layering process is complete. In the latter case where no additional layers can be created but the sink has not been reached, the present flow function f in G is maximum and the maximum flow problem has been solved. Observe that not all the nodes of G need appear in N, and that in N all the arcs are directed from layer $k - 1$ to layer k regardless of the direction of the useful arcs in G. In addition, even after an arc (x, y) is included in N, additional arcs (w, y) are included in N for all such layer $k - 1$ nodes w. Finally, we remove all arcs that do not belong to any directed path from s to t in the resulting net. Fig. 3.25 shows the typical appearance of a layered net. In contrast to a general net, in a layered net N every directed path from the source s to some fixed node y in layer k contains exactly k arcs. These properties of layered nets are extremely useful in devising ways of finding their flows.

We summarize the above by presenting an algorithm for generating a layered net $N(V', E', c', f')$ from a given net $G(V, E, c, f)$, as follows: Let $U_i \subset V$ and $V_i \subset U_i$ for $i = 0, 1, 2, \ldots, k \leqq n - 1$.

Step 1. $U_0 = \{s\}$. Set $i = 0$.
Step 2. $U_{i+1} = \{y \mid (x, y) \in E, x \in U_i, y \notin U_0 \cup U_1 \cup \cdots \cup U_i$, and $c(x, y) - f(x, y) + f(y, x) > 0\}$.

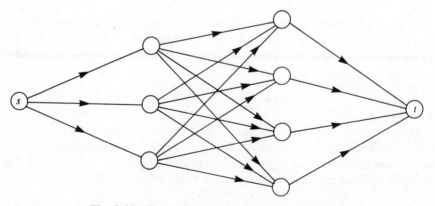

Fig. 3.25. The typical appearance of a layered net.

Step 3. If $t \in U_{i+1}$, set $k = i + 1$ and stop. Go to Step 5.
Step 4. Set $i = i + 1$. Return to Step 2.
Step 5. $V_k = \{t\}$. Set $j = k$.
Step 6. $V_{j-1} = \{x \mid (x, y) \in E, \quad y \in V_j, \quad x \in U_{j-1}, \quad \text{and} \quad c(x, y) - f(x, y) + f(y, x) > 0\}$.
Step 7. If $j = 1$, stop.
Step 8. Set $j = j - 1$. Return to Step 6.

The layered net $N(V', E', c', f')$ is a net defined by the sets

$$V' = V_0 \cup V_1 \cup \cdots \cup V_k \tag{3.84a}$$

$$E' = \{(x, y) \mid x \in V_j, y \in V_{j+1} \quad \text{for} \quad j = 0, 1, \ldots, k-1, \quad (x, y) \in E$$
$$\text{and} \quad c(x, y) - f(x, y) + f(y, x) > 0\} \tag{3.84b}$$

$$c'(x, y) = c(x, y) - f(x, y) + f(y, x), \quad (x, y) \in E' \tag{3.84c}$$

and f' is initially set to zero.

The algorithm consists of two parts. The first part from Step 1 to Step 4 generates the subsets U_i, in which U_k may contain nodes other than the sink t. The second part from Step 5 to Step 8 identifies the layers V_i from U_i, so that V_k contains only the sink t. Fig. 3.26 shows the typical appearance of

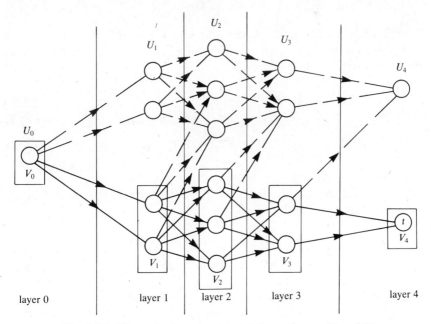

Fig. 3.26. The typical appearance of the node sets U_i and V_i.

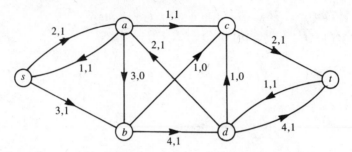

Fig. 3.27. A net used to illustrate the construction of a layered net.

the node sets U_i and V_i. The net consists of both the solid and broken lines. The layered net N is the subnet and consists only of the solid lines.

Example 3.6

Consider the net $G(V, E, c, f)$ shown in Fig. 3.1, which is redrawn in Fig. 3.27. To construct a layered net N of G, we proceed as follows:

The source s is at the layer 0. Nodes a and b are at layer 1 because arcs (s, a) and (s, b) are useful arcs. Thus, they belong to N with capacities

$$c'(s, a) = c(s, a) - f(s, a) + f(a, s) = 2 - 1 + 1 = 2 \qquad (3.85a)$$

$$c'(s, b) = c(s, b) - f(s, b) = 3 - 1 = 2 \qquad (3.85b)$$

Thus, layer 1 consists of the nodes a and b. For layer 2, we consider arcs (a, c), (a, d), (b, c) and (b, d). Only the last three (a, d), (b, c) and (b, d) are useful arcs with capacities

$$c'(a, d) = f(d, a) = 1 \qquad (3.86a)$$

$$c'(b, c) = c(b, c) - f(b, c) = 1 - 0 = 1 \qquad (3.86b)$$

$$c'(b, d) = c(b, d) - f(b, d) = 4 - 1 = 3 \qquad (3.86c)$$

Thus, nodes c and d belong to layer 2 and arcs (a, d), (b, c) and (b, d) are included in N. Finally, for layer 3, we consider arcs (c, t) and (d, t). They are useful arcs with capacities

$$c'(c, t) = c(c, t) - f(c, t) = 2 - 1 = 1 \qquad (3.87a)$$

$$c'(d, t) = c(d, t) - f(d, t) + f(t, d) = 4 - 1 + 1 = 4 \qquad (3.87b)$$

Therefore, node t is at layer 3 and arcs (c, t) and (d, t) are in N. The layered net N that results from the net G of Fig. 3.27 for the flow pattern shown therein is presented in Fig. 3.28.

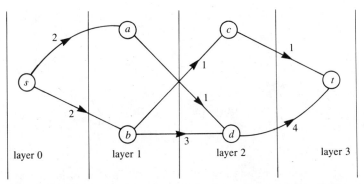

Fig. 3.28. The layered net that results from the net of Fig. 3.27.

Once the layered net N of G is found with respect to a flow f, we then look for a maximum flow in the layered net N. A flow function f' is said to be a *blocking flow* in N if every directed path from s to t contains at least one saturated arc. In the next section, we shall discuss an elegant procedure for finding a blocking flow in a layered net.

We now describe a general procedure for finding a maximum flow in a given net $G(V, E, c, f)$. We start with the zero flow in G, construct a layered net N from G using f as a guide, find a blocking flow in N, and then augment the flow in G. With a new flow f^* in G, we construct a new layered net N' from $G(V, E, c, f^*)$ using f^* as a guide, find a new blocking flow in N', and then augment the flow in $G(V, E, c, f^*)$, etc. We call the part of the procedure that

   (i) constructs a layered net
  (ii) finds a blocking flow
 (iii) augments the flow in G

a *phase*. The procedure consists of a sequence of these phases with increasing height so that there are at most $n - 1$ phases for an n-node net G. By the *height* of a layered net N, we mean the number of arcs in any directed path from s to t in N. The layered net N of Fig. 3.28, for example, is of height 3. In the following, we show that the heights of the layered nets increase with the phases.

THEOREM 3.5

The heights of the layered nets constructed during the phase-to-phase computation in the solution of a net flow problem form a strictly increasing sequence of positive integers.

Proof. Let N_k be the layered net constructed during the kth phase of the computation and let h_k denote the height of N_k. We first prove that if

$$P_1 = (v_0, v_1)(v_1, v_2) \ldots (v_{w-1}, v_w) \qquad (3.88)$$

is a directed path from $s = v_0$ to v_w in N_{k+1}, and if each node v_i ($i = 1, 2, \ldots, w$) of P_1 is also contained in N_k, then

$$j \geqq \alpha_j, \qquad j = 0, 1, 2, \ldots, w \qquad (3.89)$$

where node v_j was contained in layer α_j of N_k, and is in layer j of N_{k+1}.

We shall prove the above assertion by induction. The result (3.89) is obviously true for $j = 0$, since $v_0 = s$ was in layer $\alpha_0 = 0$ of N_k and remains in layer $j = 0$ of N_{k+1}, giving $j = \alpha_0 = 0$. Assume that (3.89) holds for any $j \leqq u < w$. We show that for $j = u + 1$ it is true that if node v_{u+1} was in layer β of N_k, then

$$u + 1 \geqq \beta \qquad (3.90)$$

Suppose otherwise that $u + 1 < \beta$. Consider node v_u which, by induction hypothesis, was contained in a layer p of N_k such that $p \leqq u$. It follows that the arc (v_u, v_{u+1}) cannot be in N_k because, for v_u in layer $p \leqq u$ and v_{u+1} in layer $\beta > u + 1$, nodes v_u and v_{u+1} were not in two consecutive layers. As a result, the flow in the original net G from v_u to v_{u+1} could not have been affected by the augmentation procedure of phase k. On the other hand, arc (v_u, v_{u+1}) is in N_{k+1}, meaning that it was a useful arc from v_u to v_{u+1} in G at the beginning of phase $k + 1$, and its flow in G was unaffected by phase k. Therefore, (v_u, v_{u+1}) must be a useful arc from v_u to v_{u+1} at the beginning of phase k. Since v_u was in N_k, (v_u, v_{u+1}) must be in N_k. This contradicts an earlier assertion that (v_u, v_{u+1}) is not in N_k. Hence, (3.89) holds for all j.

We now proceed to complete the proof of the theorem. Let

$$P_2 = (s, v_1)(v_1, v_2) \ldots (v_{p-2}, v_{p-1})(v_{p-1}, t) \qquad (3.91)$$

where $p = h_{k+1}$, be a directed path from s to t in N_{k+1}. To facilitate our proof, two cases are distinguished.

Case 1

All the nodes of P_2 are in N_k. Then appealing to (3.89) by letting $v_w = t$ with $w = p = h_{k+1}$ in (3.88) shows that

$$j \geqq \alpha_j, \qquad j = 0, 1, \ldots, p = h_{k+1} \qquad (3.92)$$

where $s = v_0$ and v_j was in layer α_j of N_k. In particular, for $j = p = h_{k+1}$

we have $p \geqq \alpha_p$. This is equivalent to saying that

$$h_{k+1} \geqq h_k \tag{3.93}$$

If $h_{k+1} = h_k$ or $p = \alpha_p$, then

$$j = \alpha_j, \qquad j = 0, 1, \ldots, p \tag{3.94}$$

This is possible if the directed path P_2 is in both N_k and N_{k+1}. As a result, all the arcs of P_2 in the original net G were useful arcs both before and after the augmentation procedure of phase k. This contradicts the fact that the blocking flow used in the augmentation stage of phase k saturated some arcs of P_2. Therefore, in this case we have

$$h_{k+1} > h_k \tag{3.95}$$

Case 2

Not all the nodes of P_2 are in N_k. Let (v_u, v_{u+1}) be the first arc of P_2 such that v_{u+1} was not in N_k. Then the flow in (v_u, v_{u+1}) in G was unaffected by flow augmentation in phase k. Because (v_u, v_{u+1}) is in N_{k+1}, it was a useful arc at the beginning of phase $k + 1$, but it was unaffected by phase k, yet it was not in N_k. This is possible only if v_u is in layer h_{k-1} of N_k and $v_{u+1} \neq t$. In other words, v_{u+1} would have entered into N_k in layer h_k, had all such nodes been included in N_k. But layer h_k is special in that it contains only sink t. Thus, if v_u was in layer α_u of N_k, then $\alpha_u + 1 = h_k$. Since all the nodes of the subpath from s to u in P_2 are also in N_k, we obtain from (3.89) that

$$u \geqq \alpha_u \tag{3.96a}$$

or

$$u + 1 \geqq \alpha_u + 1 = h_k \tag{3.96b}$$

Now $v_{u+1} \neq t$ and t is in the layer $h_{k+1} > u + 1$ of N_{k+1}. We conclude that

$$h_{k+1} > h_k \tag{3.97}$$

This completes the proof of the theorem.

The novel idea of layering nets is due to Dinic (1970). Because the height of the layered net is increased from one phase to the next, there are at most $n - 1$ phases for an n-node net G. The labor involved in constructing a layered net is obviously $O(m)$, so is the labor in augmenting the flow in G with a blocking flow, where m is the number of arcs of G. In the following

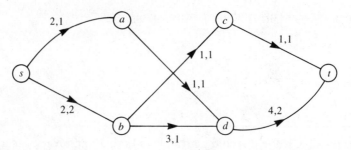

Fig. 3.29. A blocking flow for the layered net of Fig. 3.28 with respect to the flow f.

section, we show that a blocking flow can be found in $O(n^2)$ time in a layered net. Then the whole maximum flow problem can be solved in $O(mn^2)$ or $O(n^4)$, since $m < n^2$.

Example 3.7

Consider the net $G(V, E, c, f)$ of Fig. 3.27. The layered net $N(G)$ of G with respect to the flow f was shown in Fig. 3.28. A blocking flow of $N(G)$ is presented in Fig. 3.29. Observe that each directed path from s to t in $N(G)$ contains at least one saturated arc. No additional flow can be added from s to t in $N(G)$. Since each directed path from s to t in $N(G)$ is composed of three arcs, the height of $N(G)$ is 3 or

$$h_1 = 3 \tag{3.98}$$

Using the flow pattern of Fig. 3.29, additional flows can be added to the arcs of G. The resulting net $G^*(V, E, c, f^*)$ is shown in Fig. 3.30. Using the new flow f^* as a guide, the layered net $N(G^*)$ of G^* is given in Fig. 3.31. This layered net is clearly of height 4 or

$$h_2 = 4 \tag{3.99}$$

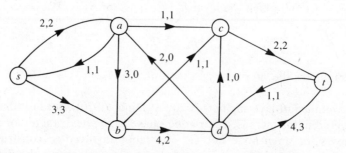

Fig. 3.30. The resulting net after additional flows are added to the arcs of the net of Fig. 3.27.

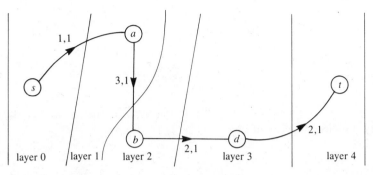

Fig. 3.31. The layered net that results from the net of Fig. 3.30, using the flow f^* as a guide.

Thus, in solving the network flow problem by the layered net approach, two phases of the computations are required. In going from phase 1 to phase 2, the heights of the layered nets are increased from 3 to 4. The five partitioned layers and a blocking flow for the layered net $N(G^*)$ are also indicated in Fig. 3.31. Using this flow in $N(G^*)$ to augment the flow f^* in G^* yields the final maximum flow as shown in Fig. 3.32.

3.6 A BLOCKING FLOW ALGORITHM

In the preceding section, we showed how to construct a layered net $N(V', E', c', f')$ from a given net $G(V, E, c, f)$, using flow f as a guide. In the present section, we give a procedure for finding a blocking flow in N. The procedure known as the *MPM algorithm* is due to Malhotra, Pramodh-Kumar and Maheshwari (1978), and is a very clever modification of the algorithm proposed by Karzanov (1974).

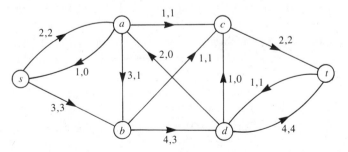

Fig. 3.32. The final maximum flow that results from the net of Fig. 3.27 by means of the layered net approach.

For each node y in the layered net $N(V', E', c', f')$, the *in-flow potential* $P_{in}(y)$ of y is the sum of the capacities of all arcs (x, y) directed towards y:

$$P_{in}(y) = \sum_{(x,y) \in E'} c'(x, y) \tag{3.100}$$

The *out-flow potential* $P_{out}(y)$ of y is the sum of the capacities of all arcs (y, x) directed away from y:

$$P_{out}(y) = \sum_{(y,x) \in E'} c'(y, x) \tag{3.101}$$

The *flow potential* $P(y)$ of y is the smaller of either the in-potential or the out-potential:

$$P(y) = \min [P_{in}(y), P_{out}(y)] \tag{3.102}$$

In other words, the flow potential of a node is the minimum of either the total incoming arc capacities or the total outgoing arc capacities of the node. Clearly, the flow potential of a node is the maximum amount of flow that can be forced through the node, and the maximum amount of flow that can pass through all the nodes cannot exceed the smallest flow potential among all the nodes with nonzero flow potential.

MPM algorithm

Step 1. Find a node $x \neq s, t$ of smallest flow potential

$$P_{min} = \min_{j} \{P(j)\} \tag{3.103}$$

in $N(V', E', c', f')$.

Step 2. Send P_{min} units of flow along the outgoing arcs (x, y), $(x, y) \in E'$, of N by saturating as many of them as possible in some order.

Step 3. Follow the flow $f'(x, y) \neq 0$, $(x, y) \in E'$, to the next higher layer for each y, and repeat Step 2 by sending $f'(x, y)$ units of flow along the outgoing arcs of y. Repeat for the next higher layer until the sink t is reached.

Step 4. Assign P_{min} units of flow to the incoming arcs (y, x), $(y, x) \in E'$, of N by saturating as many of them as possible in some order.

Step 5. Follow the flow $f'(y, x) \neq 0$, $(y, x) \in E'$, to the next lower layer for each y, and repeat Step 4 by assigning $f'(y, x)$ units of flow along the incoming arcs of y. Repeat for the next lower layer until the source s is reached.

Step 6. Augment the flow $f(x, y)$, $(x, y) \in E$, of G by the flow $f'(x, y)$, $(x, y) \in E'$, of N by replacing each $f(x, y)$ by $f(x, y) + f'(x, y)$. At the same time, update each arc capacity of N from $c'(x, y)$ to $c'(x, y) - f'(x, y)$.

Step 7. Remove all arcs of zero residual capacity and all nodes other than s and t of zero flow potential together with all their incident arcs from the resulting net obtained in Step 6. If the source s and sink t are still connected by a directed path, return to Step 1 and repeat all the steps. Otherwise, stop.

Notice that the node of minimum flow potential in Step 1 will become a node of zero flow potential at the end of Step 6, and, therefore, this node together with all its incident arcs will be removed in Step 7. We now estimate the number of operations required in establishing a blocking flow. First of all, to find a node of minimum flow potential in Step 1, we need $n - 3$ comparisons the first time for an n-node layered net, and at most $n - 4$ comparisons the second time, so that there are at most $(n - 3) + (n - 4) + \ldots + 1 = (n - 2)(n - 3)/2$ comparisons, and we need at most $O(n^2)$ comparisons in Step 1. In Steps 2–6, since each arc can be saturated only once, the time of saturating all arcs of G is at most $O(m)$, where m is the number of arcs in G. For each minimum flow potential node, we visit at most $n - 1$ other nodes and there are at most n minimum flow potential nodes altogether. So the amount of work required to update the arc capacities is at most $O(n^2)$. As a result, the work required for the MPM algorithm to find a blocking flow in a layered net is

$$O(n^2) + O(m) + O(n^2) = O(n^2) \tag{3.104}$$

where $m < n^2$. Recall that there are at most $n - 1$ layered nets that we have to look at in order to find a maximum flow in the original net. Each layered net corresponds to a phase. Hence, a maximum flow in a net can be found in $O(n^3)$ time. In contrast to the Ford–Fulkerson algorithm, the number of operations of which depends on the arc capacities, the layered-net approach using the MPM algorithm is dependent only on the number of nodes of a net.

We illustrate the MPM algorithm by the following examples.

Example 3.8

Consider the net $G(V, E, c, f)$ of Fig. 3.33, which was considered in Examples 3.6 and 3.7. Assume initially that the flow in G is zero or $f = 0$. The layered net N_1 of G with respect to this $f = 0$ is shown in Fig. 3.34 with flow potentials of the nodes indicated by numbers adjacent to the

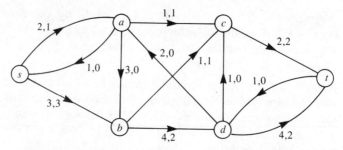

Fig. 3.33. A net used to illustrate the MPM algorithm.

nodes. The flow potentials of the nodes of N_1 are found to be

$$P(a) = \min [P_{\text{in}}(a), P_{\text{out}}(a)] = \min [2, 1] = 1 \qquad (3.105a)$$

$$P(b) = \min [P_{\text{in}}(b), P_{\text{out}}(b)] = \min [3, 5] = 3 \qquad (3.105b)$$

$$P(c) = \min [P_{\text{in}}(c), P_{\text{out}}(c)] = \min [2, 2] = 2 \qquad (3.105c)$$

$$P(d) = \min [P_{\text{in}}(d), P_{\text{out}}(d)] = \min [4, 4] = 4 \qquad (3.105d)$$

the minimum of which is

$$P_{\min} = \min \{P(a), P(b), P(c), P(d)\} = \min \{1, 3, 2, 4\} = 1 \quad (3.106)$$

We now follow the seven steps of the MPM algorithm to find a blocking flow in N_1, as follows:

Step 1. $P_{\min} = P(a) = 1$.
Step 2. Send 1 unit of flow along (a, c) or $f'(a, c) = 1$.
Step 3. Follow $f'(a, c)$ and send $f'(a, c) = 1$ unit of flow along (c, t), obtaining $f'(c, t) = 1$.

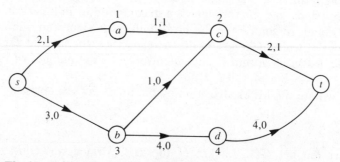

Fig. 3.34. The layered net that results from the net of Fig. 3.33 with respect to the flow $f = 0$, where flow potentials of the nodes are indicated by numbers adjacent to the nodes.

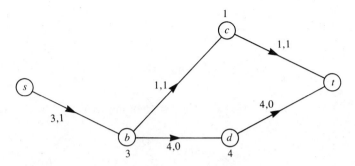

Fig. 3.35. The resulting net after the completion of the first iteration of the MPM algorithm.

Step 4. Assign 1 unit of flow to the incoming arc (s, a), giving $f'(s, a) = 1$.

Step 5. It is not needed.

Step 6. Change the flow f of G to

$$f(s, a) = 1, \qquad f(a, c) = 1, \qquad f(c, t) = 1 \qquad (3.107)$$

All others remain to be zero. Update the capacities of the arcs (s, a), (a, c) and (c, t) from 2, 1 and 2 to

$$c'(s, a) - f'(s, a) = 2 - 1 = 1 \qquad (3.108a)$$

$$c'(a, c) - f'(a, c) = 1 - 1 = 0 \qquad (3.108b)$$

$$c'(c, t) - f'(c, t) = 2 - 1 = 1 \qquad (3.108c)$$

respectively.

Step 7. Remove node a and all arcs (s, a) and (a, c) incident at a. The resulting net N_1' is shown in Fig. 3.35 with flow function f'. Return to Step 1.

Step 1. $P_{\min} = P(c) = 1$ in N_1'.

Step 2. Send 1 unit of flow along (c, t) or $f'(c, t) = 1$ in N_1'.

Step 3. It is not needed.

Step 4. Assign 1 unit of flow to (b, c) or $f'(b, c) = 1$ in N_1'.

Step 5. Assign 1 unit of flow to (s, b) or $f'(s, b) = 1$ in N_1'.

Step 6. Augment the flow f of G as follows:

$$f(s, b) = 0 + 1 = 1 \qquad (3.109a)$$

$$f(b, c) = 0 + 1 = 1 \qquad (3.109b)$$

$$f(c, t) = 1 + 1 = 2 \qquad (3.109c)$$

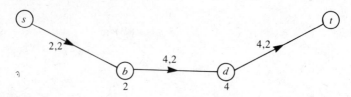

Fig. 3.36. The resulting net after the completion of the second iteration of the MPM algorithm.

$f(s, a) = 1$, $f(a, c) = 1$, and all others are zero. Update the arc capacities of arcs (s, b), (b, c) and (c, t) from 3, 1 and 1 to $3 - 1 = 2$, $1 - 1 = 0$ and $1 - 1 = 0$, respectively.

Step 7. Remove node c and all arcs (b, c) and (c, t) incident at c. The resulting net N_1'' is shown in Fig. 3.36 with flow function f''. Return to Step 1.

Step 1. $P_{\min} = P(b) = 2$ in N_1''.

Step 2. Send 2 units of flow along (b, d) or $f''(b, d) = 2$ in N_1''.

Step 3. Send 2 units of flow along (d, t) or $f''(d, t) = 2$ in N_1''.

Step 4. Assign 2 units of flow to (s, b) or $f''(s, b) = 2$ in N_1''.

Step 5. It is not needed.

Step 6. Augment the flow of G and the result is shown in Fig. 3.33.

Step 7. Stop.

A blocking flow of N_1 is obtained by superimposing the flow patterns of Figs. 3.34–3.36, and is shown in Fig. 3.37. Observe that every directed path from s to t in N_1 of Fig. 3.37 contains at least one saturated arc. This completes the first phase of operations for finding a maximum flow in G using the layered-net approach. A feasible flow pattern is presented in Fig. 3.33.

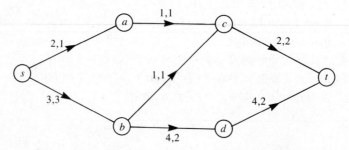

Fig. 3.37. A blocking flow of N_1 obtained by superimposing the flow patterns of Figs 3.34–3.36.

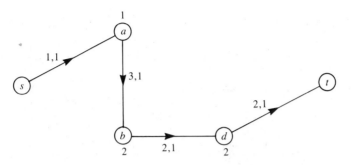

Fig. 3.38. The layered net that results from the net of Fig. 3.33 with respect to the flow pattern of Fig. 3.33.

To continue with phase 2, we construct a layered net N_2 of G using the flow pattern of Fig. 3.33. The layered net N_2 is shown in ·Fig. 3.38. We again follow the seven steps of the MPM algorithm to find a blocking flow, as follows:

Step 1. $P_{min} = P(a) = 1$.
Step 2. Send 1 unit of flow along (a, b) or $f'(a, b) = 1$.
Step 3. Send 1 unit of flow along (b, d) and (d, t) or $f'(b, d) = f'(d, t) = 1$.
Step 4. Assign 1 unit of flow to (s, a) or $f'(s, a) = 1$.
Step 5. It is not needed.
Step 6. Augment the flow of G of Fig. 3.33 and the result is shown in Fig. 3.39.
Step 7. Stop.

The algorithm terminates with two iterations, and a desired maximum

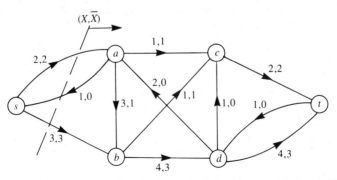

Fig. 3.39. The final maximum flow that results from the net of Fig. 3.33 after the completion of the MPM algorithm.

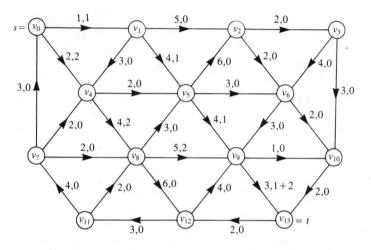

Fig. 3.40. A net used to illustrate the MPM algorithm.

flow is shown in Fig. 3.39 with maximum flow value 5. The corresponding minimum s–t cut is found to be $(X, \bar{X}) = (s, \{a, b, c, d, t\})$, as indicated in Fig. 3.39.

Example 3.9

We use the layered-net approach in conjunction with the MPM algorithm to find a maximum flow in the net $G(V, E, c, f)$ of Fig. 3.40. Initially, set $f = 0$.

First, we follow the layering process of Section 3.5 to construct a net N_1 of G using $f = 0$ as a guide. The result is shown in Fig. 3.41 with flow potentials of the nodes indicated by numbers adjacent to the nodes. To introduce the layered net N_1' of G, we remove all arcs that do not belong to any directed path from s to t in N_1. The resulting layered net N_1' of G with respect to $f = 0$ is shown in Fig. 3.42 with nodal flow potential written adjacent to the node. The layered net N_1' is of height 4.

Step 1. $P_{\min} = P(v_1) = 1$ in N_1'.

Step 2. Send 1 unit of flow along the arc (v_1, v_5).

Step 3. Send 1 unit of flow along the arcs (v_5, v_9) and (v_9, t).

Step 4. Assign 1 unit of flow to arc (s, v_1).

Step 5. It is not needed.

Step 6. Augment the flow of G and record the result in Fig. 3.40. Update the arc capacities of arcs (s, v_1), (v_1, v_5), (v_5, v_9) and (v_9, t) from 1, 4, 4, 3 to 0, 3, 3 and 2, respectively.

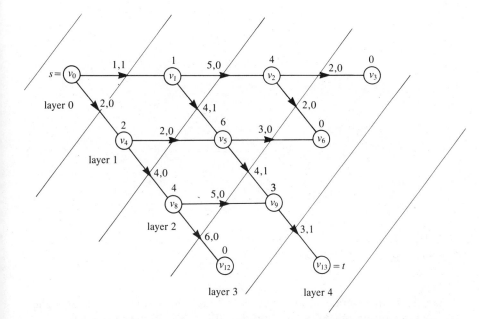

Fig. 3.41. The layered net that results from the net of Fig. 3.40 with respect to the flow $f = 0$, where flow potentials of the nodes are indicated by numbers adjacent to the nodes.

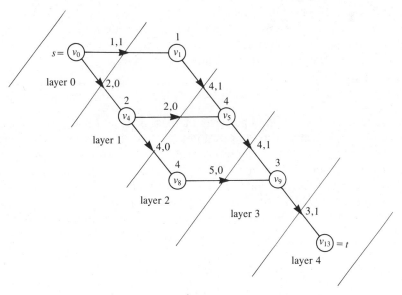

Fig. 3.42. The resulting layered net N_1' obtained from N_1 by removing all arcs that do not belong to any directed paths from s to t in N_1.

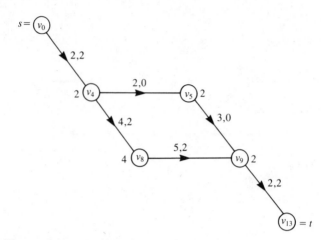

Fig. 3.43. The resulting net after the completion of the first iteration of the MPM algorithm.

Step 7. Remove node v_1 and arcs (s, v_1) and (v_1, v_5) incident at v_1. The resulting net N_1'' is presented in Fig. 3.43. Return to Step 1.

Step 1. $P_{\min} = P(v_4) = P(v_5) = P(v_9) = 2$ in N_1''. Choose, say, node v_4.

Step 2. Send 2 units of flow along the arc (v_4, v_8).

Step 3. Send 2 units of flow along the arcs (v_8, v_9) and (v_9, t).

Step 4. Assign 2 units of flow to arc (s, v_4).

Step 5. It is not needed.

Step 6. Augment the flow of G and record the result in Fig. 3.40. Update the arc capacities of arcs (s, v_4), (v_4, v_8), (v_8, v_9) and (v_9, t) from 2, 4, 5, 2 to 0, 2, 3 and 0, respectively.

Step 7. Stop.

By superimposing the flow patterns of Figs. 3.42 and 3.43, we obtain a desired blocking flow of the layered net N_1', and the result is presented in Fig. 3.44. Observe that every directed path from s to t in N_1' contains at least one saturated arc, and that, although the maximum number of phases required for the net G is $n - 1 = 13$, the algorithm terminates in only one phase. The final flow pattern is shown in Fig. 3.45 with maximum flow value 3. The corresponding minimum s–t cut is found to be

$$(X, \bar{X}) = (s, \{v_1, v_2, \ldots, v_{12}, v_{13} = t\}) \qquad (3.110)$$

as indicated in Fig. 3.45.

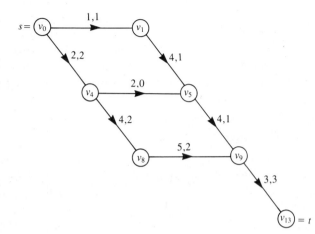

Fig. 3.44. A blocking flow of the layered net N_1' obtained by superimposing the flow patterns of Figs 3.42 and 3.43.

3.7 VARIANTS OF THE FORD–FULKERSON ALGORITHM

Recall that the Ford–Fulkerson algorithm is carried out in two steps using two routines—the labeling routine and the augmentation routine. The labeling routine searches for a flow augmenting path and, after the flow augmenting path is found, the augmentation routine increases the flow along the flow augmenting path. However, in searching for a flow

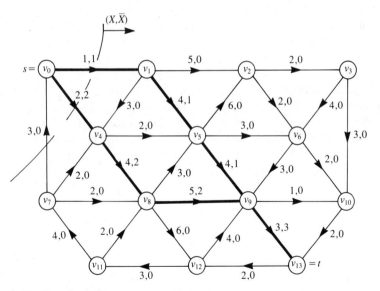

Fig. 3.45. The final flow pattern obtained from the net of Fig. 3.40 after the application of the MPM algorithm.

augmenting path, the labeling routine does not specify the order with which the nodes are labeled or with which the labeled nodes are scanned. If the nodes are labeled and scanned in a certain order, a significant improvement in computational efficiency of the Ford–Fulkerson algorithm results. In the following, we present several refinements and modifications of the Ford–Fulkerson approach.

3.7.1 Edmonds–Karp Algorithm

Edmonds and Karp (1972) suggested that the labeling routine of the Ford–Fulkerson algorithm be implemented on a first-labeled-first-scanned basis. The approach is commonly known as the *breadth-first search* in computer science.

Let $G(V, E, c, f)$ be an n-node net. In labeling the nodes of V using the labeling routine, let x be a node that has been labeled but not yet scanned. To scan x, we assign labels to all the unlabeled nodes $y \in V$ such that $(x, y) \in E$ is a useful arc. The nodes y are then scanned in the order that they are labeled. The flow augmenting path obtained in this way always contains the minimum number of arcs from the source s to the sink t. For our purposes, we say that a flow augmenting path is of *arc length k* if it contains k arcs. This should not be confused with the length of a path or directed path discussed in the preceding chapter, where the length of a path or directed path is defined as the sum of lengths of the arcs in the path or directed path. The two concepts coincide when each arc in the path or directed path is of length 1.

The Edmonds–Karp algorithm proceeds as follows: We first use a flow augmenting path of arc length 1 and augment flow along this path. When there are no flow augmenting paths of arc length 1, we use a flow augmenting path of arc length 2 and augment flow along this path. This is repeated until the shortest flow augmenting path is of arc length $n - 1$. Thus, there are a total $n - 1$ phases, and each phase consists of finding a flow augmenting path of arc length k $(k = 1, 2, \ldots, n - 1)$ using the breadth-first search and augmenting flow along this path. At the end of each phase, we construct a residue net induced by the existing flow and composed of the useful arcs of G. The crux of the procedure is that the shortest augmenting path increases in arc length from phase to phase.

Given a flow f in $G(V, E, c, f)$, the *residue net* $M(V, E', c', f')$ of G induced by the existing flow f is the net with the same node set V such that $(x, y) \in E'$ if and only if $(x, y) \in E$ is a useful arc in G with

$$c'(x, y) = c(x, y) - f(x, y) + f(y, x) \qquad (3.111)$$

It is straightforward to verify that for each directed path from s to t in M, there corresponds a flow augmenting path from s to t in G. We now divide all the nodes of the residue net M into different layers. By definition, the source s is in layer 0. Then a node x is in layer k if the shortest directed path from s to x in M is of arc length k. In other words, the shortest directed path consists of k useful arcs in M. The subnet N_r of M consisting only of the arcs $(x, y) \in E'$ connecting nodes in layer i to nodes in layer $i + 1$ for $i = 0, 1, 2, \ldots, n - 1$ is called the *layered residue net* of G induced by the flow f, and has the typical appearance as that shown in Fig. 3.26.

We call the part of the algorithm that (1) finds the residue net M, (2) partitions the nodes of M into layers and constructs the layered residue net N_r, and (3) finds a blocking flow from s to t in N_r, a *phase*. The algorithm consists of a sequence of these phases with increasing arc lengths of the shortest flow augmenting paths, as required by Theorem 3.5. Thus, the algorithm terminates with at most $n - 1$ phases.

In constructing the residue net, we look at each arc at most twice, once in each direction, so the total amount of work is $O(m)$, where m is the number of arcs in G. In searching for a flow augmenting path by breadth-first search, it takes at most $O(m)$ steps. This is also the labor involved in constructing the layered residue net. To find a blocking flow, we increase the flow along each flow augmenting path. There are at most m flow augmenting paths in each phase, and each flow augmenting path requires at most $O(m)$ steps. Thus, the work in each phase is bounded by $O(m^2)$. Since there are at most $n - 1$ phases, the total work is bounded by $O(nm^2)$. With $m < n^2$, the Edmonds–Karp algorithm has a worst-case bound $O(nm^2) = O(n^5)$. This is in contrast to the layered-net approach using the MPM algorithm that requires at most $O(n^3)$.

Example 3.10

Consider the net $G(V, E, c, f)$ of Fig. 3.33, which is redrawn in Fig. 3.46. We use the Edmonds–Karp algorithm to calculate a maximum flow.

Using the flow f of Fig. 3.46, we construct the residue net $M(V, E', c', f')$ of G such that $(x, y) \in E'$ if and only if $(x, y) \in E$ is a useful arc in G with $c'(x, y)$ being determined by (3.111). For example,

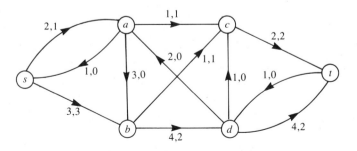

Fig. 3.46. A net used to illustrate the Edmonds–Karp algorithm.

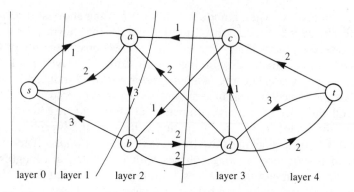

layer 0 | layer 1 | layer 2 | layer 3 | layer 4

Fig. 3.47. The residue net M of the net of Fig. 3.46 with respect to the flow f.

arc (b, d) is in M because it is a useful arc in G with capacity

$$c'(b, d) = c(b, d) - f(b, d) + f(d, b) = 4 - 2 + 0 = 2 \quad (3.112a)$$

Likewise, arc (d, b) is in M because

$$c'(d, b) = c(d, b) - f(d, b) + f(b, d) = 0 - 0 + 2 = 2 \quad (3.112b)$$

We remark that arcs not in G may be regarded as arcs with zero capacity. The residue net M of G with respect to f is presented in Fig. 3.47.

We next partition the nodes of M into different layers. A node x is in layer k if the shortest directed path from s to x in M is of arc length k. Thus, nodes s, a, b and d are in layers 0, 1, 2 and 3, respectively. Nodes c and t are in layer 4. The shortest directed paths used to partition the nodes of M are shown in Fig. 3.48. Finally, the layered residue net N_r of

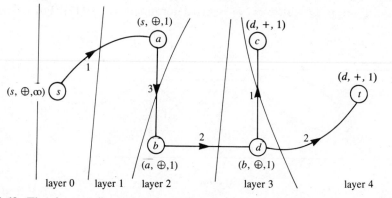

layer 0 | layer 1 | layer 2 | layer 3 | layer 4

Fig. 3.48. The shortest directed paths used to partition the nodes of the residue net M of Fig. 3.47.

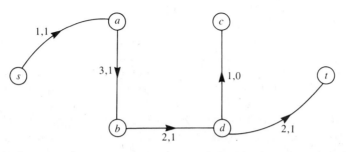

Fig. 3.49. The net showing the assignment of a unit of flow to the directed path (3.113).

G with respect to the flow f is the subnet of M consisting only of the arcs $(x, y) \in E'$ connecting nodes in layer i to nodes in layer $i+1$ for $i = 0, 1, 2, 3$: (s, a), (a, b), (b, d), (d, c) and (d, t). This layered residue net N_r of G is presented in Fig. 3.48. Applying Ford–Fulkerson's labeling routine on a first-labeled-first-scanned basis, the labels are also given in Fig. 3.48, yielding a directed path

$$P_{st} = (s, a)(a, b)(b, d)(d, t) \tag{3.113}$$

A unit of flow can be assigned to this path as indicated in Fig. 3.49. Augmenting the flow of G in Fig. 3.46 with this flow results in the final feasible flow pattern of Fig. 3.50. Since the algorithm terminates at the end of this phase, the flow shown in Fig. 3.50 is maximum with the minimum s–t cut $(X, \bar{X})$ as indicated.

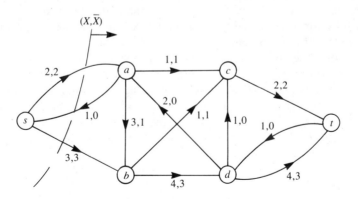

Fig. 3.50. The final maximum flow pattern obtained from the net of Fig. 3.46 after the application of the Edmonds–Karp algorithm.

3.7.2 Dinic Algorithm

The Edmonds–Karp algorithm has a worst-case bound $O(nm^2) = O(n^5)$ by assuming that we search each flow augmenting path independently in the residue net M of a given net $G(V, E, c, f)$ induced by the flow f. This bound can be improved to $O(n^2m) = O(n^4)$ if we coordinate the search for flow augmenting paths of a given arc length in a phase. This improvement was suggested by Dinic (1970) and is known as the *Dinic algorithm*.

The Dinic algorithm is very similar to the Edmonds–Karp algorithm in that it consists of a sequence of phases with increasing arc lengths of the shortest flow augmenting paths so that the algorithm terminates in at most $n - 1$ phases. Each phase includes (1) the construction of the residue net of G, (2) the construction of a layered net, and (3) finding a blocking flow in the layered net. The residue net M and the layered residue net N_r of G induced by the current flow f are constructed in the same way as before. The layered net N of G induced by the flow f is the subnet of N_r consisting of all the directed paths from s to t. The layered net N constructed in this way is identical to that obtained in Section 3.5. Once the layered net N is constructed, we apply the labeling and scanning processes of the labeling routine to N, using the *depth-first search* to reach t. In the depth-first search, nodes of N are visited on a last-labeled-first-scanned basis. In general, suppose x is the most recently labeled node. We immediately scan x by searching for an unlabeled node y such that (x, y) is a useful arc of N. Node y is then labeled and the search starts anew at y. If no such y can be found, the search returns to w, the node from which x was reached. When we have to "back-up" from a node x during the search, we can delete all the arcs incident at x in N. If we reach sink t, a flow augmenting path is found. Then we increase flow along this path, update the residue capacities, remove arcs with zero residue capacity from N, and repeat the search for a new flow augmenting path. After all flow augmentations have been made in N corresponding to a blocking flow, the layered net N is destroyed and we proceed to the next phase. On the other hand, if a layered net cannot be successfully constructed using the current flow, the current flow is maximum and the algorithm terminates.

As before, the construction of a layered net N requires $O(m)$ steps. The depth-first search for an augmenting path in N takes at most $O(n)$ time, because we look at a node at most once during the search. In general, there are at most m augmenting paths in a phase, so the total amount of work in a phase is $O(nm)$. Since there are at most $n - 1$ phases, the total work required for the Dinic algorithm in the worst case is $O(n^2m) = O(n^4)$ with $m < n^2$.

Example 3.11

In the net $G(V, E, c, f)$ of Fig. 3.51, assume initially that the flow is zero, $f = 0$. The layered net N of G with respect to this zero flow is shown in

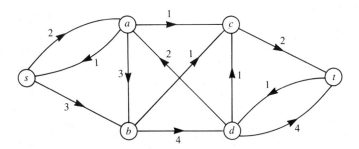

Fig. 3.51. A net used to illustrate the Dinic algorithm.

Fig. 3.52. After applying the labeling routine to N using the depth-first search, the resulting labels are indicated in Fig. 3.52. Thus, a unit flow can be assigned to the directed path $(s, b)(b, c)(c, t)$. We now update the residue capacities and remove arcs with zero capacity in N. This yields the flow augmenting paths $(s, a)(a, c)(c, t)$ and $(s, b)(b, d)(d, t)$ as shown in Fig. 3.53(a) and (b), respectively. Superimposing the flow patterns of Figs. 3.52 and 3.53 gives the flow pattern of Fig. 3.46. Repeating the above procedure for the net of Fig. 3.46 yields the corresponding nets of Figs. 3.48 and 3.49. The final maximum flow is shown in the net of Fig. 3.50.

3.7.3 Other Variations

In addition to the above two variants of the Ford–Fulkerson algorithm, other refinements and modifications of the Ford–Fulkerson algorithm are possible. They will be briefly described below.

Recall that the order in which the nodes are labeled and scanned is crucial to the efficiency of the Ford–Fulkerson algorithm. However, no such order is explicitly known for optimum efficiency. Two particular ordering

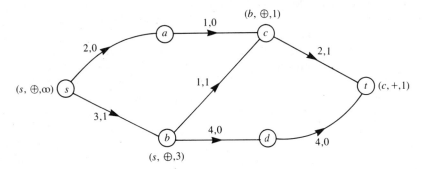

Fig. 3.52. The layered net of the net of Fig. 3.51 with respect to the flow $f = 0$.

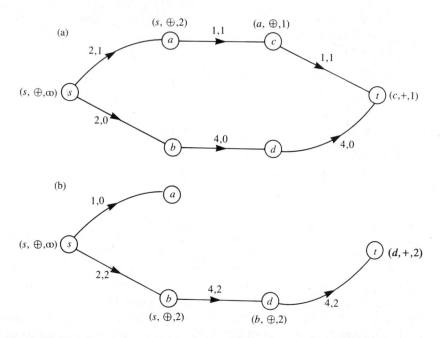

Fig. 3.53. The flow-augmenting paths P_{st} obtained from the net of Fig. 3.52 after updating the residue capacities and removing arcs with zero capacity: (a) $P_{st} =$ $(s, a)(a, c)(c, t)$, (b) $P_{st} = (s, b)(b, d)(d, t)$.

methods, known as the breadth-first search used in the Edmonds–Karp algorithm and the depth-first search used in the Dinic algorithm, have been widely used for solving the maximum flow problem. In fact, a computer program based on the breadth-first search technique is given by Bayer (1968).

In applying the Ford–Fulkerson algorithm, in general only a small portion of the large number of labeled nodes is included in a flow augmenting path. Lin and Leon (1974) proposed a "two-end" labeling algorithm in which labeling and scanning start from both the source s and the sink t and advance from both directions. Thus, instead of a large-sized tree rooted at the source, their technique generates two relatively smaller ones rooted at the source and the sink. They used two small-sized nets with one containing 49 nodes and 196 arcs and the other 48 nodes and 72 arcs with certain special structures to demonstrate their approach, and showed that the technique is better performed than the "one-end" approach.

Edmonds and Karp (1972) also suggested another improvement. Their idea is to determine, at each phase of the labeling process, a flow augmenting path that allows the largest possible flow augmentation. If U denotes the set of nodes already labeled but not including the sink t, and if W is the set of unlabeled nodes w adjacent to a node $u \in U$ such that (u, w)

is a useful arc in $G(V, E, c, f)$, if W is empty the current flow is maximum. Otherwise, we look for an arc (u, w), $u \in U$ and $w \in W$, with largest possible residue arc capacity

$$c'(u, w) = \max \{c(u, w) - f(u, w) + f(w, u) \mid u \in U, w \in W\} \quad (3.114)$$

and label the node w. If $w = t$, the program terminates and we find a flow augmenting path from s to t that allows the largest possible flow augmentation. If $w \neq t$, then

$$U = U \cup \{w\}, \qquad W = W - \{w\} \quad (3.115)$$

and the process is repeated. Edmonds and Karp (1972) showed that if the net has integral capacities, then a maximum flow will be obtained within at most

$$1 + \log_{M/(M-1)} f_{st} \quad (3.116)$$

augmentations, where f_{st} is the value of the maximum flow and M is the maximum number of arcs across an s–t cut.

In addition, Johnson (1966) proposed the use of triple labels, and Srinivasan and Thompson (1972) introduced the notion of the predecessor and distance labels. Finally, Cheung (1980) combined many of the above approaches, and suggested the layer-updating method. The main idea is to maintain by updating without destruction a two-way layered subnet throughout the whole process. In constructing the layered net, instead of starting from the source and advancing in one direction, his method starts the construction from both the source and the sink and advances, alternately, in both directions. When two front layers meet, a flow augmenting path is found through which the flow is immediately augmented. After each flow augmentation, instead of destroying the whole two-way layered subnet and starting all over again, only a small portion of it is reconstructed by relinking some of the nodes.

3.8 KARZANOV ALGORITHM

There are two distinct characteristics associated with the Ford–Fulkerson algorithm. First, flow is augmented through a flow augmenting path from the source to the sink. Secondly, throughout the solution process, the flow pattern is always conservative for all the nodes except the source and the sink. The present algorithm, first suggested by Karzanov (1974), has two contrasting features. Instead of using the flow augmenting paths, flow is augmented, level by level, through layers. During the solution process, the flow conservation property may not hold at some of the nodes. However, flow conservation is achieved by flow elimination. The Karzanov algorithm is important in that it provides a new approach substantially different from the classical approach of Ford and Fulkerson, and has an upper bound $O(n^3)$.

Given a net $G(V, E, c, f)$, a function g from the arc set E to the nonnegative reals is said to be a *preflow* of G if for each arc $(x, y) \in E$,

$$g(x, y) \leq c(x, y) \tag{3.117}$$

and for each node $y \in V$

$$\sum_x g(x, y) \geq \sum_z g(y, z) \tag{3.118}$$

A node y satisfying (3.118) with a strict inequality is called an *unbalanced node*. Otherwise, it is *balanced*. If every node is balanced, then the preflow g becomes a flow f of G. The Karzanov algorithm consists of many phases and each phase involves two stages: Advance of preflow and balance of preflow. The general setup is very similar to that of the Dinic algorithm in that both use layered nets to find a maximum flow in G. However, the major difference is that in the Dinic algorithm we find the maximum flow in a layered net of G by saturating one arc at a time, while in the Karzanov algorithm we find the maximum flow in a layered net by saturating one node at a time. We start each phase by pushing the preflow from the source s and then from layer to layer until the sink t is reached. Then we balance the preflow at each node until every node is balanced. The former is called the *advance of preflow* and the latter the *balance of preflow*. These two operations are iterated until the flow becomes maximum in the layered net.

Let N be a layered net of G and V_i ($i = 0, 1, 2, \ldots, k$) be the layers of N. A layer j is said to be *unbalanced* if

$$\sum_{x \in V_{j-1}} \sum_{y \in V_j} g(x, y) \neq \sum_{y \in V_j} \sum_{z \in V_{j+1}} g(y, z) \tag{3.119}$$

for $j = 1, 2, \ldots, k - 1$. In finding a maximum flow in N, we say that an arc (x, y) is *closed* if the current flow $g(x, y)$ cannot be changed. Otherwise, it is *open*. Initially, all the arcs in N are open until some of them are declared closed. The flows in the closed arcs remain the same for the remainder of the phase.

For our purposes, we assume that all the outgoing arcs (x, y) of node x are ordered in a certain way, say, in increasing order of the index y. This ordering of arcs is fixed during the phase. The incoming arcs (w, x) of node x are not ordered at first, but we keep track of the order in which the preflow $g(w, x)$ are added to the node x.

Stage 1. Advance of Preflow

We begin at the source s at the layer 0 by pushing as much preflow as possible into nodes x at the layer 1 by setting $g(s, x) = c(s, x)$ for all $x \in V_1$. We have moved the preflow from layer 0 to layer 1.

In general, during an advance of preflow operation at layer i, we consider an unbalanced node $x \in V_i$ and increase the preflow in each of the outgoing arcs (x, y) from x to all $y \in V_{i+1}$ until either the arc is saturated or the node x is balanced. The increases follow the preassigned arc order by first pushing as much flow as possible in the first open arc which is not saturated, and then as much as possible in the second open arc, etc. Thus, the outgoing arcs (x, y) of x are much like a *queue*. The advance operation stops when it is not possible to push any preflow forward from any node $x \in V_i$. This occurs when the outgoing arcs (x, y) of x are either closed or saturated.

Stage 2. Balance of Preflow

We start from an unbalanced node y in the highest layer j, and reduce the incoming flows to y in the last-in-first-out fashion until the node y is balanced. Recall that we keep track of the order of the incoming arcs (x, y), $x \in V_{j-1}$, to y when $g(x, y)$ is added to node y. When we reduce the incoming flow to y, we reduce the latest addition first in a last-in-first-out fashion, so it is like a *stack*.

In general, during a balance operation at layer i, we consider an unbalanced node $y \in V_i$, and reduce the preflow in the arcs (x, y) incoming from all $x \in V_{i-1}$ to y in a last-in-first-out fashion until node y is balanced. Then all the arcs (x, y) to the newly balanced node y are declared closed. Thus, all the arcs incident at node y can be deleted from the layered net N. If all unbalanced nodes are balanced in this layer, return to Stage 1 even though there may be unbalanced nodes in lower layers. Observe that in balancing the nodes in layer i we may create unbalanced nodes in layer $i - 1$. Since all nodes in layers $i - 2, i - 3, \ldots, 0$ have not been disturbed, when we return to Stage 1 we can start from layer $i - 1$ and push as much preflow as possible to the higher layers until sink t is reached.

We summarize the above by stating the following steps for the Karzanov algorithm. Let $N(V', E', c', f')$ be the layered net of $G(V, E, c, f)$.

Karzanov Algorithm

Step 1. Set $f = 0$.

Step 2. Based on current flow f, construct a layered net N of G with the layered node sets V_i $(i = 0, 1, 2, \ldots, k)$. If $t \notin V_k$, stop.

Step 3. Set $i = 1$ and $f'(s, y) = c'(s, y)$, $(s, y) \in E'$.

Step 4. Perform the preflow advance operations at the layers $i, i + 1, \ldots, k - 1$ consecutively.

Step 5. Search for an unbalanced node y in the highest layer j, $1 \le j \le k-1$, and perform a preflow balance operation for each $y \in V_j$. If $j = 1$ or if all the nodes are balanced except s and t, return to Step 2. If $j > 1$, set $i = j - 1$ and return to Step 4.

We now show that the Karzanov algorithm indeed will generate a maximum flow in a layered net N of G induced by the current flow f, and requires at most $O(n^2)$ operations.

A node x of N is said to be *blocked* if every directed path from x to t contains at least one saturated arc. Thus, once a node is blocked, no more flow can be pushed through that node. We first show that an unbalanced node x becomes blocked after the application of the preflow advance operations, and this node remains blocked during the whole phase of operations. We prove this assertion by induction over the number of preflow balance operations.

Initially, during the first stage of preflow advancement, the source and all the unbalanced nodes are blocked because every outgoing arc from these nodes is saturated. A blocked node y at the highest layer j cannot become unblocked because no arc flow $g(y, z)$, $z \in V_{j+1}$, is reduced after the preflow balance operation, and, therefore, each directed path from y to t contains at least a saturated arc. Assume that the assertion is true after the application of q or less preflow balance operations. We show that it is true for $q + 1$ preflow balance operations.

Let y be a blocked node at the highest layer j after the qth preflow balance operation. By induction hypothesis, every directed path from y to t contains at least a saturated arc. During the preflow balance operation, the incoming flow of every such node y is reduced and this reduction in turn reduces the outgoing arc flows of some of the nodes at the layer $j - 1$. Let x be a node at layer $j - 1$ that was originally blocked before the reduction of its outgoing arc flow. Since every directed path from x to t must pass through a blocked node y, node x remains blocked after the preflow balance operation. If node x becomes unbalanced after the flow reduction of its outgoing arcs, and if it is processed in the next preflow balance operation, node x will become balanced and each of its outgoing arcs is either saturated or closed. Therefore, each directed path from x to t contains either a saturated arc or a closed arc that must pass through the blocked node y. As a result, node x remains blocked and the assertion follows.

Recall that once a node is balanced, it can be removed from the layered net. Thus, every node is balanced at most once. This in conjunction with the facts that each unbalanced node can be processed at most once to become a blocked node and that it will remain blocked during the whole phase shows that the source s, which is blocked after the first iteration, remains blocked at the end of the phase. Hence, the induced flow is maximum.

We now determine the maximum number of operations needed to find a maximum flow in a layered net. During the stage of a preflow balance operation, if the flow in an arc is decreased, the arc is then declared closed. The number of flow reductions is, therefore, bounded by the number of arcs or $O(m)$ time. During the stage of a preflow advance operation, if the flow in an arc is increased, the arc is either saturated or unsaturated. Since any decrease in flow in an arc will close that arc, saturation can occur at most once for any arc. Thus, the number of saturations during a phase is also bounded by $O(m)$. On the other hand, if an arc flow is increased but not to saturation, this can occur at most $n - 1$ times in the initial preflow advance operation, and at most $n - 2$ times during the second preflow advance operation, etc., so that there are at most

$$(n - 1) + (n - 2) + \ldots + 2 + 1 = \tfrac{1}{2}n(n - 1) \tag{3.120}$$

occurrences at each phase. Thus, to find a maximum flow in a layered net we require an upper bound of

$$O(m) + O(m) + O(n^2) = O(n^2), \qquad m \leqq n^2 \tag{3.121}$$

Since there are at most $n - 1$ phases, the Karzanov algorithm is bounded by $O(n^3)$.

Finally, we mention that using a similar approach, Kinariwala and Rao (1977) proposed a flow switching algorithm and reported computational improvements over the breadth-first search approach. Like the Karzanov algorithm, their method can start with an arbitrary flow pattern. The flow pattern is then augmented through layers and the flow conservation property at the nodes is achieved by eliminating the surplus flow.

Example 3.12

Consider the net $G(V, E, c, f)$, of Fig. 3.51, which is redrawn in Fig. 3.54. Initially, assume that $f = 0$. Based on this zero flow, the layered net $N(V', E', c', f')$ of G is obtained in Fig. 3.55 containing four layers. We

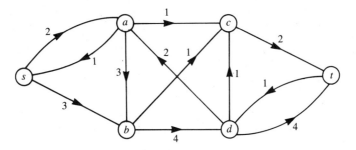

Fig. 3.54. A net used to illustrate the Karzanov algorithm.

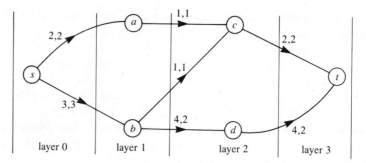

Fig. 3.55. The layered net of the net of Fig. 3.54 with respect to zero flow.

follow the five steps of the Karzanov algorithm:

Step 1. Set $f = 0$.

Step 2. Construct N of G as shown in Fig. 3.55 with $V_0 = \{s\}$, $V_1 = \{a, b\}$, $V_2 = \{c, d\}$, and $V_3 = \{t\}$. Then $k = 3$

Step 3. Set $i = 1$, $f'(s, a) = c'(s, a) = 2$, and $f'(s, b) = c'(s, b) = 3$.

Step 4. Perform preflow advance operations at layers 1 and 2. The results are shown in Fig. 3.55.

Step 5. Node a is the unbalanced node in the highest layer 1. Perform a preflow balance operation for node a. This is equivalent to reducing the arc flow $f'(s, a)$ from 2 to 1. The final flow pattern is shown in Fig. 3.56. Return to Step 2.

Step 2. Based on the flow pattern of Fig. 3.56, construct a layered net N of G as shown in Fig. 3.57 with nodes s, a, b, d and t belonging to layers 0, 1, 2, 3, and 4, respectively. Then $k = 4$.

Step 3. Set $i = 1$ and $f'(s, a) = 1$.

Step 4. Perform preflow advance operations at layers 1, 2 and 3. The results are shown in Fig. 3.57.

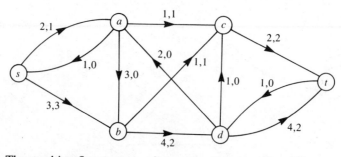

Fig. 3.56. The resulting flow pattern after performing a preflow balance operation for node a in the net of Fig. 3.55.

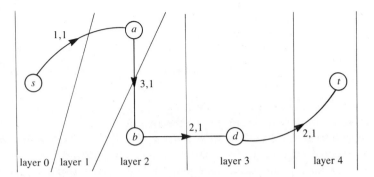

Fig. 3.57. A layered net constructed from the net of Fig. 3.56.

Step 5. Since nodes a, b and d are all balanced, return to Step 2.
Step 2. Stop.

Combining the feasible flow patterns of Figs. 3.56 and 3.57 yields a desired maximum flow of Fig. 3.58.

3.9 FLOWS IN UNDIRECTED AND MIXED NETS

So far we have considered a net $G(V, E, c, f)$ as a weighted directed graph with two real functions c and f defined from the arc set E to the nonnegative reals. In the case where the weighted graph is undirected or mixed, the maximum flow problem can be solved in a similar manner. If an edge $(x, y) = (y, x)$ is undirected with capacity $c(x, y) = c(y, x)$, we interpret this to mean that

$$f(x, y) \leqq c(x, y) \qquad (3.122a)$$

$$f(y, x) \leqq c(x, y) \qquad (3.122b)$$

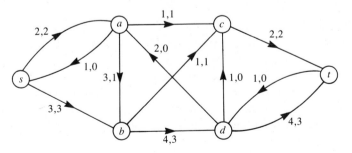

Fig. 3.58. A maximum flow obtained by combining the feasible flow patterns of Figs 3.56 and 3.57.

where $f(x, y)$ is the flow from x to y in (x, y), and that the flow is permitted in only one of the two directions or

$$f(x, y)f(y, x) = 0 \qquad (3.122c)$$

In other words, the arc (x, y) has a flow capacity $c(x, y)$ in either direction but the flow can only move in one of the two directions.

To find a maximum flow in such a net $G'(V, E', c', f')$, we first replace each undirected edge (x, y) by a pair of oppositely directed edges (x, y) and (y, x), each having the capacity equal to that of the original undirected edge. We now apply any of the existing techniques to find a maximum flow in the resulting directed net $G(V, E, c, f)$. Once a solution f is found with flow value f_{st}, we can construct a feasible flow pattern f' in the original net $G'(V, E', c', f')$ with the same flow value f_{st} by taking

$$f'(x, y) = \max[0, f(x, y) - f(y, x)] \qquad (3.123)$$

yielding

$$f'(x, y)f'(y, x) = 0 \qquad (3.124)$$

The operation (3.123) is equivalent to canceling flows in opposite directions. Since the maximum flow value for any specific orientation of the given net is no greater than the maximum flow value obtained by the above procedure of replacing each undirected edge by a pair of oppositely directed edges, the maximum flow problem in an undirected or mixed net can always be solved in this way.

One of the applications of this consideration is that one might think of a network of city streets, each street having a traffic flow capacity. If one is asked to put up one-way signs on streets not already oriented in order to permit the largest traffic flow from some points to the others, the procedure outlined above provides a convenient solution.

Example 3.13

Consider the mixed net $G'(V, E', c', f')$ of Fig. 3.59. By replacing each of the three undirected edges (a, c), (a, d) and (b, d) by a pair of oppositely directed edges, we obtain the directed net $G(V, E, c, f)$ of Fig. 3.60. Using any of the techniques described in the foregoing results in a maximum feasible flow pattern as shown in Fig. 3.60, the first number adjacent to an arc being the arc capacity and the second number the arc flow.

To construct a feasible flow pattern in the original mixed net G', we

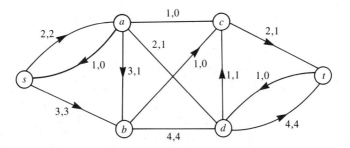

Fig. 3.59. A mixed net $G'(V, E', c', f')$ used to illustrate the maximum flow problem.

apply (3.123) and obtain

$$f'(a, c) = \max [0, f(a, c) - f(c, a)] = \max [0, 1 - 1] = 0 \quad (3.125a)$$
$$f'(a, d) = \max [0, f(a, d) - f(d, a)] = \max [0, 1 - 0] = 1 \quad (3.125b)$$
$$f'(b, d) = \max [0, f(b, d) - f(d, b)] = \max [0, 4 - 0] = 4 \quad (3.125c)$$

and the flow in all other arcs (x, y) remains unaltered, i.e. $f'(x, y) = f(x, y)$. The result is shown in Fig. 3.59. Note that $f'(c, a) = f'(d, a) = f'(d, b) = 0$.

3.10   FLOWS IN NODE-AND-ARC CAPACITATED NETS

Given a net $G(V, E, c, f)$, suppose that in addition to the arc capacity c, each node $i \in V$ is associated with a nonnegative real number $h(i)$ called the *node capacity* of i. The node capacity h is, therefore, a function from the node set V to the nonnegative reals. Our objective is to find a maximum

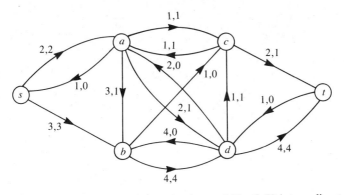

Fig. 3.60. The conversion of the mixed net of Fig. 3.59 into a directed net.

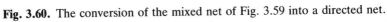

flow from the source s to the sink t in G subject to both arc and node capacities: For each $i \in V$

$$f(s, V) - f(V, s) = f_{st} \tag{3.126a}$$

$$f(i, V) - f(V, i) = 0, \qquad i \neq s, t \tag{3.126b}$$

$$f(t, V) - f(V, t) = -f_{st} \tag{3.126c}$$

$$c(i, j) \geqq f(i, j) \geqq 0, \qquad (i, j) \in E \tag{3.126d}$$

$$f(i, V) \leqq h(i), \qquad i \neq t \tag{3.126e}$$

$$f(V, t) \leqq h(t) \tag{3.126f}$$

This problem can be converted to the arc capacity case by the following procedure. Let $G^*(V^*, E^*, c^*, f^*)$ be the net derived from $G(V, E, c, f, h)$ in accordance with the following rules: To each node $i \in V$, there correspond two nodes $i', i'' \in V^*$ such that if $(i, j) \in E$, then $(i', j'') \in E^*$. In addition, for each $i \in V$, there is an $(i'', i') \in E^*$. The arc capacity c^* defined on E^* is given by

$$c^*(i', j'') = c(i, j), \qquad (i, j) \in E \tag{3.127a}$$

$$c^*(i'', i') = h(i), \qquad i \in V \tag{3.127b}$$

In the net $G(V, E, c, f, h)$ of Fig. 3.61, the numbers adjacent to the arcs are the arc capacities, and those adjacent to the nodes are the node capacities. The net $G^*(V^*, E^*, c^*, f^*)$ derived from G is shown in Fig. 3.62. Observe that there are twice as many nodes in G^* than in G. The operation is equivalent to splitting each node i into two nodes, a left node i'' and a right node i', so that all arcs terminating at i now terminate at i'', whereas all arcs outgoing from i now outgo from i'. The node capacity $h(i)$ is then imposed as an arc capacity for the arc (i'', i') directed from i'' to i'.

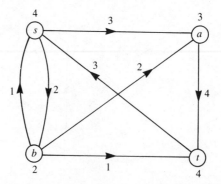

Fig. 3.61. A node-and-arc-capacitated net, in which the numbers adjacent to the arcs are the arc capacities and those adjacent to the nodes are the node capacities.

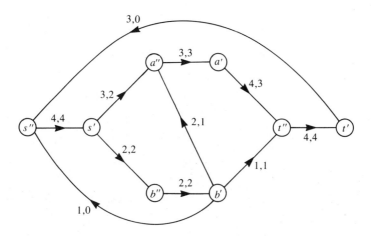

Fig. 3.62. The conversion of a node-and-arc-capacitated net into an arc-capacitated net.

With this representation, it is clear that for any flow from s to t in G that does not exceed the node capacities, there corresponds an equivalent flow f^* from s'' to t' in G^* by taking

$$f^*(i', j'') = f(i, j), \qquad (i, j) \in E \tag{3.128a}$$

$$f^*(i'', i') = f(i, V), \qquad i \neq t \tag{3.128b}$$

$$f^*(t'', t') = f(V, t) \tag{3.128c}$$

and vice versa.

Example 3.14

Consider the net $G(V, E, c, f, h)$ of Fig. 3.61, which has both arc and node capacities. The net can be converted into an equivalent arc capacity net $G^*(V^*, E^*, c^*, f^*)$ of Fig. 3.62. Using any of the techniques discussed in this chapter, a maximum flow from s'' to t' is as indicated in Fig. 3.62. Applying (3.128) yields a feasible flow pattern for the original net G as shown in Fig. 3.63.

It is interesting to observe that without nodal capacity constraints, the maximum flow value from s to t in G is 5, whereas with nodal capacity the maximum flow value is reduced to 4.

3.11 SUMMARY AND SUGGESTED READING

We began this chapter by defining a flow pattern for a net. A flow pattern is feasible if it satisfies the arc capacity constraints and the conservation

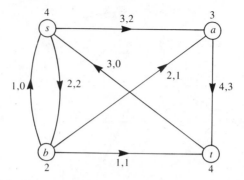

Fig. 3.63. A feasible flow pattern for the node-and-arc-capacitated net of Fig. 3.61.

equation for all the intermediate nodes. Our objective is to find a maximum feasible flow pattern for a general net. For this we introduced the notion of an s–t cut, which is different from the usual concepts of a cutset or a cut. We then showed that the maximum flow value from the source to the sink in a net is equal to the capacity of a minimum s–t cut separating the source and the sink. This is known as the max-flow min-cut theorem in the literature. The remainder of the chapter is primarily concerned with the various algorithms for finding a maximum flow in a net.

We first introduced the classical Ford–Fulkerson algorithm, which is a systematical procedure searching for a flow augmenting path and then increasing the flow along this path. The algorithm can be carried out by two routines known as the labeling routine and the augmentation routine. It is popular because it is simple to understand and easy to implement. For many practical problems, the algorithm terminates fairly quickly. However, we demonstrated by an example that in the case where the arc capacities are irrational, it is possible to construct a net so that the algorithm not only will not terminate but also will converge to a wrong limit. Because of this, many new algorithms have been proposed. Some are simple modifications of the Ford–Fulkerson algorithm, and others are completely different.

There are many variants of the Ford–Fulkerson algorithm. Recall that in searching for a flow augmenting path, the labeling routine does not specify the order with which the nodes are labeled or the order with which the labeled nodes are scanned. If the nodes are labeled and scanned on a breadth-first search basis, we essentially have the Edmonds–Karp algorithm. On the other hand, if the nodes are labeled and scanned on a depth-first search basis, we obtain the Dinic algorithm which also uses the layered net. The concept of the layered net was due to Dinic, and is extremely useful in devising ways to find its flows. A layered net is a directed net in which every arc is directed from one layer to the next adjacent one, and is derived from a given net using the current flow as a guide. The significance of the layered nets is that their heights form a strictly increasing sequence of positive integers when they are constructed during the phase-to-phase computation in the solution of a net flow problem. To find a blocking flow in a layered net, we presented a procedure known as the MPM algorithm, which is a clever modification of the Karzanov algorithm, and uses the notion of flow potential.

In contrast to the Ford–Fulkerson algorithm, the Karzanov algorithm provides a substantially different approach. We start each phase by pushing the preflow from the source to the sink, layer by layer. Then we balance the preflow at each node until every node is balanced. The former is called the advance of preflow and the latter the balance of preflow. These two operations constitute a phase and are iterated until the flow becomes maximum in the layered net.

Finally, we discussed the situations where a given net contains either undirected edges or nodes with flow capacities. In the former, the mixed net can be converted into an equivalent directed net that provides a solution. In the latter, the problem can be changed to the arc capacity case and a solution follows.

The speed of the Ford–Fulkerson algorithm depends not only on the number n of nodes and the number m of arcs but also on the arc capacities in the net. Indeed, for certain irrational arc capacities, the algorithm might not converge at all. For integral arc capacities, the Ford–Fulkerson algorithm runs in time $O(f_{st}n^2)$ where f_{st} is the maximum flow value or the minimum s–t cut capacity. Since then many algorithms have been proposed, the speeds of which are bounded by a polynomial function of m and n only; they provide a steady procession of improvements in computational efficiency. The chronology is presented in Table 3.1.

We remark that for an n-node net, the maximum number of arcs in the net is bounded by $O(n^2)$. Thus, for a complete or nearly complete directed graph, all of the computational complexities in Table 3.1 starting from the Karzanov algorithm are in the neighborhood of $O(n^3)$. On the other hand, for a sparse net with relatively few arcs, the later algorithms result in a significant improvement in performance.

There is no clear winner among the algorithms in the table that are based on Dinic's approach. The Karzanov, MPM, Shiloach and Vishkin, and Tarjan algorithms are suitable for the dense nets, whereas the Cherkasky, Galil, Galil and Naamad, Shiloach, Sleator and Tarjan, and Gabow algorithms are designed for the sparse nets. For a small range of densities, Galil's bound of $O(n^{5/3}m^{2/3})$ seems to be the best. For sparse nets with integer arc capacities of moderate size, Gabow's scaling algorithm is the best. Finally, among the algorithms based on Dinic's approach, the only parallel algorithm is that of Shiloach and Vishkin, which has a parallel running time of $O(n^2 \log n)$ with n processors but requires $O(mn)$ space.

The standard book for the network flow problem and its variants is Ford and Fulkerson (1962). For a lucid exposition, we refer to Wilf (1986). For a concise presentation on the subject matter, we recommend Hu (1982). For

TABLE 3.1

Author(s)	Year	Computational Complexity†
Ford and Fulkerson	1956	$O(f_{st}n^2)$, integral capacities
Edmonds and Karp	1969	$O(m^2n)$
Dinic	1970	$O(mn^2)$
Karzanov	1974	$O(n^3)$
Cherkasky	1977	$O(m^{1/2}n^2)$
Malhotra, Pramodh-Kumar and Maheshwari	1978	$O(n^3)$
Galil	1978	$O(m^{2/3}n^{5/3})$
Galil and Naamad; Shiloach	1978	$O(mn \log^2 n)$
Sleator and Tarjan	1980	$O(mn \log n)$
Shiloach and Vishkin	1982	$O(n^3)$
Gabow	1983	$O(nm \log U)$
Tarjan	1984	$O(n^3)$
Goldberg	1985	$O(n^3)$
Goldberg and Tarjan	1986	$O(nm \log (n^2/m))$
Ahuja and Orlin	1986	$O(nm + n^2 \log U)$

† Where U denotes an upper bound on the arc capacities.

further study on the various algorithms, the reader is referred to the original papers listed in the references. A computational comparison of eight methods for the maximum network flow problem with networks up to 1500 nodes and 7960 arcs tested can be found in Cheung (1980).

REFERENCES

Ahuja, R. K. and Orlin, J. B. (1987), "A fast and simple algorithm for the maximum flow problem," Tech. Rept 1905–87, Sloan School of Management, Massachusetts Institute of Technology, Cambridge, Mass.

Bayer, G. (1968), "Algorithm 324. Maxflow," *Comm. ACM,* vol. 11, pp. 117–118.

Chen, W. K. (1976), *Applied Graph Theory: Graphs and Electrical Networks,* Amsterdam, The Netherlands: North-Holland, 2nd revised edition.

Chen, W. K. (1983), "Recent advances in the application of graph theory to networks," *Circuits and Systems Mag.,* vol. 5, pp. 12–21.

Cherkasky, R. V. (1977), "An algorithm for constructing maximal flows in networks with complexity of $O(V^2\sqrt{E})$ operations," Akad. Nauk USSR, *Mathematical Methods for the Solution of Economical Problems,* vol. 7, pp. 112–125.

Cheung, T. Y. (1980), "Computational comparison of eight methods for the maximum network flow problem," *ACM Trans. Math. Software,* vol. 6, pp. 1–16.

Dantzig, G. B. and Fulkerson, D. R. (1956), "On the max-flow min-cut theorem of networks," in *Linear Inequalities and Related Systems, Ann. Math. Studies,* vol. 38, pp. 215–221.

Dinic, E. A. (1970), "Algorithm for solution of a problem of maximal flow in networks with power estimation," *Soviet Math. Dokl.,* vol. 11, pp. 1277–1280.

Edmonds, J. and Karp, R. M. (1972), "Theoretical improvements in algorithmic efficiency for network flow problems," *J. ACM,* vol. 19, pp. 248–264.

Elias, P., Feinstein, A. and Shannon, C. E. (1956), "A note on the maximum flow through a network," *IRE Trans. Inform. Theory,* vol. IT-2, pp. 117–119.

Even, S. and Tarjan, R. (1975), "Network flow and testing graph connectivity," *SIAM J. Computing,* vol. 4, pp. 507–518.

Ford, L. R. Jr and Fulkerson, D. R. (1956), "Maximal flow through a network," *Can. J. Math.,* vol. 8, pp. 399–404.

Ford, L. R. Jr and Fulkerson, D. R. (1957), "A simple algorithm for finding maximal network flows and an application to the Hitchcock problem," *Can. J. Math.,* vol. 9, pp. 210–218.

Ford, L. R. Jr and Fulkerson, D. R. (1962), *Flows in Networks,* Princeton, N.J.: Princeton University Press.

Gabow, H. N. (1985), "Scaling algorithms for network problems," *J. Comput. Sci.,* vol. 31, pp. 148–168.

Galil, Z. (1978), "A new algorithm for the maximal flow problem," *Proc. 19th IEEE Symp. on the Foundations of Computer Sci.,* October. Michigan: Ann Arbor, pp. 231–245.

Galil, Z. (1980), "An $O(V^{5/3}E^{2/3})$ algorithm for the maximal flow problem," *Acta Inf.,* vol, 14, pp. 221–242.

Galil, Z. and Naamad, A. (1979), "Network flow and generalized path compression," *Proc. 11th ACM Symp. on Theory of Computing,* Atlanta, Georgia, pp. 13–26.

Galil, Z. and Naamad, A. (1980), "An $O(EV \log^2 V)$ algorithm for the maximal flow problem," *J. Comput. System Sci.,* vol. 21, pp. 203–217.

Goldberg, A. V. (1985), "A new max-flow algorithm," Tech. Rept MIT/LCS/TM-291, Laboratory for Computer Science, Massachusetts Institute of Technology, Cambridge, Mass.

Goldberg, A. V. and Tarjan, R. E. (1986), "A new approach to the maximum flow problem," *Proc. 18th ACM Symp. on Theory of Computing,* New York, pp. 136–146.

Goldberg, A. V. and Tarjan, R. E. (1988), "A new approach to the maximum-flow problem," *J. ACM,* vol. 35, pp. 921–940.

Gusfield, D., Martel, C. and Fernandez-Baca, D. (1987), "Fast algorithms for bipartite network flow," *SIAM J. Computing,* vol. 16, pp. 237–251.

Hassin, R. (1981), "Maximum flow in (s, t)-planar networks," *Inf. Process. Lett.,* vol. 13, p. 107.

Hassin, R. and Johnson, D. B. (1985), "An $O(n \log^2 n)$ algorithm for maximum flow in undirected planar networks," *SIAM J. Computing,* vol. 14, pp. 612–624.

Hu, T. C. (1982), *Combinatorial Algorithms,* Reading, Mass.: Addison–Wesley.

Itai, A. and Shiloach, Y. (1979), "Maximum flow in planar networks," *SIAM J. Computing,* vol. 8, pp. 135–150.

Janiga, L. and Koubek, V. (1985), "A note on finding minimum cuts in directed planar networks by parallel computation," *Inf. Process. Lett.*, vol. 21, pp. 75–78.

Johnson, D. B. (1987), "Parallel algorithms for minimum cuts and maximum flows in planar networks," *J. ACM*, vol. 34, pp. 950–967.

Johnson, D. B. and Venkatesan, S. (1982), "Using divide and conquer to find flows in directed planar networks on $O(n^{3/2} \log n)$ time," *Proc. 20th Annual Allerton Conf. on Communication, Control, and Computing*, Urbana-Champaign, Ill., October, pp. 899–905.

Johnson, E. L. (1966), "Networks and basic solutions," *Operations Res.*, vol. 14, pp. 619–623.

Karzanov, A. V. (1974), "Determining the maximal flow in a network by the method of preflows," *Soviet Math. Dokl.*, vol. 15, pp. 434–437.

Kinariwala, B. and Rao, A. G. (1977), "Flow switching approach to the maximum flow problem: I," *J. ACM*, vol. 24, pp. 630–645.

Lin, P. M. and Leon, B. J. (1974), "Improving the efficiency of labeling algorithms for maximum flow in networks," *Proc. IEEE Int. Symp. on Circuits and Systems*, San Francisco, Calif., April, pp. 162–166.

Malhotra, V. M., Pramodh-Kumar, M. and Maheshwari, S. N. (1978), "An $O(V^3)$ algorithm for finding maximum flows in networks," *Inf. Process. Lett.*, vol. 7, pp. 277–278.

Picard, J. C. and Ratliff, H. D. (1975), "Minimum cuts and related problems," *Networks*, vol. 5, pp. 357–370.

Queyranne, M. (1980), "Theoretical efficiency of the algorithm 'capacity' for the maximum flow problem," *Math. Oper. Res.*, vol. 5, pp. 258–266.

Reif, J. H. (1983), "Minimum s–t cut of a planar undirected network in $O(n \log^2 (n))$ time,"*SIAM J. Computing*, vol. 12, pp. 71–81.

Shiloach, Y. (1978), "An $O(nI \log^2 I)$ maximum flow algorithm," Tech. Rept STAN-CS-78-802, Computer Science Dept, Stanford Univ., Stanford, Calif.

Shiloach, Y. and Vishkin, U. (1982), "An $O(n^2 \log n)$ parallel max-flow algorithm," *J. Algorithms*, vol. 3, pp. 128–146.

Sleator, D. D. (1980), "An $O(nm \log n)$ algorithm for maximum network flow," Tech. Rept STAN-CS-80-831, Computer Science Dept, Stanford Univ., Stanford, Calif.

Sleator, D. D. and Tarjan, R. E. (1983), "A data structure for dynamic trees," *J. Comput. System Sci.*, vol. 26, pp. 362–391.

Srinivasan, V. and Thompson, G. L. (1972), "Accelerated algorithms for labeling and relabeling trees, with applications to distribution problems," *J. ACM*, vol. 19, pp. 712–726.

Tarjan, R. E. (1983), *Data Structures and Network Algorithms*, Philadelphia, Penn.: Society for Industrial and Applied Mathematics.

Tarjan, R. E. (1984), "A simple version of Karzanov's blocking flow algorithm," *Operations Res. Lett.*, vol. 2, pp. 265–268.

Wilf, H. S. (1986), *Algorithms and Complexity*, Englewood Cliffs, N.J.: Prentice-Hall.

Zadeh, N. (1972), "Theoretical efficiency of the Edmonds–Karp algorithm for computational maximal flows," *J. ACM*, vol. 19, pp. 184–192.

Zadeh, N. (1973*a*), "More pathological examples for network flow problems," *Math. Programming*, vol. 5, pp. 217–224.

Zadeh, N. (1973*b*), "A bad network problem for the simplex method and other minimum cost flow algorithms," *Math. Programming*, vol. 5, pp. 255–266.

4

MINIMUM TREES AND COMMUNICATION NETS

In the preceding chapter, we considered the problem of determining the maximum flow from the source to the sink in a net $G(V, E, c, f)$ with node set V, arc set E, and capacity function c and flow function f both from E to the nonnegative reals. In the present chapter, instead of focusing on the value of a maximum flow from one specified node to another, we are primarily concerned with the problem of finding the maximum flows between all pairs of nodes when each of these flows is to be sent through the net $G(V, E, c, f)$ separately and the corresponding synthesis problem of constructing a net to satisfy all the flow requirements individually. Such a system, known as a *communication net*, occurs naturally in practice. For example, the nodes of a net may represent communication centers that can communicate to each other through the communication channels of limited capacity denoted by weighted arcs. The arc capacity then represents the maximum amount of information that can be transferred through the arc. In reality, all the centers are communicating simultaneously, and the resulting maximum flow problem is known as the *simultaneous maximum flow problem*. To simplify our study here, we shall concentrate on one pair of nodes at a time. In other words, at any given time, only one pair of nodes serves as the source and the sink while all other nodes serve as intermediate nodes.

Even with this simplification, many questions arise. Does one have to solve the maximum flow problem for each of the $\binom{n}{2}$ pairs of nodes in an n-node communication net or will something simpler suffice? What are the necessary and sufficient conditions for a given set of real nonnegative numbers to represent maximum flow values between pairs of nodes in some communication net? If the flow requirement between each pair of nodes is specified, we certainly can construct a communication net, whose maximum flow value between each pair of nodes exceeds the flow requirement. This can easily be achieved by assigning sufficiently large arc capacities between each pair of nodes. The problem is then to synthesize a communication net that meets specified lower bounds on all maximum flow values at a minimum total arc capacity. In this chapter, we shall answer these and other related questions. However, before we do this, we need to introduce the notions of forest, subtree and tree of a graph that will be used in the remainder of this chapter.

4.1 FORESTS, SUBTREES AND TREES

The tree is perhaps one of the most important subgraphs in graph theory insofar as engineering applications are concerned. Many of the fundamental relations such as the number of independent Kirchhoff's equations in electrical network theory, the formulation of the state equation, the scheduling and distributing problems, and a variety of other applications can all be stated in terms of the single concept of a tree. Since this concept is equally valid for both directed graphs and undirected graphs, in this section we shall only deal with the undirected graph.

DEFINITION 4.1
Tree. A spanning subgraph of a graph is said to be a *tree* if and only if it is connected and contains no circuits. An edge of a tree is called a *branch*.

The definition differs slightly from the conventional mathematical usage in that the term "spanning" is usually omitted. The alternative is to use the term *spanning tree* for the concept we need. However, in most practical applications, the terminology is in accordance with Definition 4.1. As an illustration, consider the graph G of Fig. 4.1, all the trees of which are shown in Fig. 4.2.

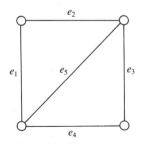

Fig. 4.1. A graph used to illustrate various subgraphs.

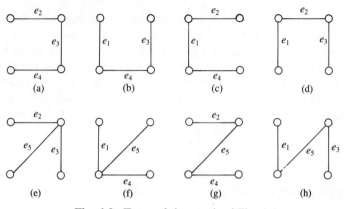

Fig. 4.2. Trees of the graph of Fig. 4.1.

DEFINITION 4.2

Cotree. The complement of a tree in a graph is called a *cotree*. An edge in a cotree is called a *chord* or *link*.

For an n-node, b-edge connected graph G, a tree contains $n-1$ branches and a cotree contains $b-n+1$ chords. Since there is a unique path connected between any two nodes in a tree, the addition of a chord to the tree produces a unique circuit in the resulting graph. Thus, each chord in a cotree defines a circuit with respect to the chosen tree in the graph in a unique way. These circuits are referred to as the *fundamental circuits* or *f-circuits* for short. For the graph of Fig. 4.1, the cotrees associated with the trees of Fig. 4.2 are shown in Fig. 4.3. The f-circuits formed by the chords e_1 and e_5 with respect to the tree $t = e_2 e_3 e_4$ of Fig. 4.2(a) are given by $e_1 e_2 e_3 e_4$ and $e_3 e_4 e_5$, respectively, and are depicted in Fig. 4.4.

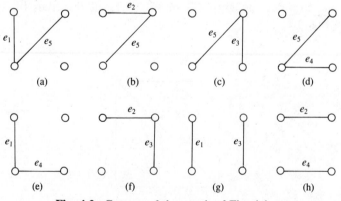

Fig. 4.3. Cotrees of the graph of Fig. 4.1.

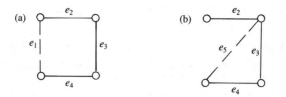

Fig. 4.4. The fundamental circuits in the graph of Fig. 4.1 with respect to the tree $t = e_2 e_3 e_4$.

DEFINITION 4.3

Forest. A spanning subgraph of a graph is said to be a *forest* if it does not contain any circuits. One or many of its components may each consist of an isolated node.

DEFINITION 4.4

Subtree. A component of a forest of a graph is called a *subtree*.

The subgraphs of Fig. 4.5 are some examples of forests of the graph of Fig. 4.1. The forests in Fig. 4.5(a) and (b) each contain two components, whereas the forest in (c) contains three components. Each component of the forests of Fig. 4.5 is a subtree. Thus, an isolated node may be considered as a subtree.

As simple consequences of the definition, trees can be characterized in many other ways, and we shall in the future make use of these equivalences given in the following theorem.

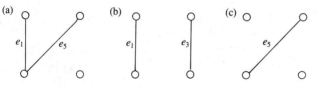

Fig. 4.5. Forests of the graph of Fig. 4.1.

THEOREM 4.1

An n-node graph G is a tree if and only if any one of the following properties is true:

(1) G is connected and does not contain any circuits,

(2) G has $n - 1$ edges and does not contain any circuits,

(3) G is connected and has $n - 1$ edges,

(4) G is connected and is of zero nullity,

(5) G is connected but loses this property if any edge is removed,

(6) there exists a unique path between any two of its nodes.

As a consequence, a subgraph can be made part of a tree if and only if it contains no circuits. Likewise, a subgraph can be made part of a cotree if and only if it contains no cuts of the graph. Then what are the necessary and sufficient conditions for a subgraph to be part of a tree and another subgraph to be part of the corresponding cotree? The characterization of this problem is given below.

THEOREM 4.2

Let g_1 and g_2 be two edge-disjoint subgraphs of a connected graph G. Let t_1 be a tree of G containing g_1, and let $\bar{t}_2$ be a cotree of G with respect to the tree t_2 and containing g_2. Then there exists a tree t for which g_1 is a subgraph of t and g_2 is a subgraph of the cotree $\bar{t}$ with respect to t.

Proof. Let G^* be the graph obtained from G by removing all the edges of g_2. Because the tree t_2 is contained in G^*, G^* is connected and contains all the nodes of G. Since g_1 and g_2 are edge-disjoint, g_1 is also contained in G^*. Hence, the subgraph g_1, being part of t_1, is circuitless, and can be made part of a tree of G^*. Let this tree be t. Then t is the desired tree of G.   Q.E.D.

A different version of the theorem is the following.

COROLLARY 4.1

Let g_1 and g_2 be two edge-disjoint subgraphs of a connected graph G. Then there exists a tree t of G for which g_1 is a subgraph of t and g_2 is a subgraph of the cotree $\bar{t}$ with respect to t if, and only if, g_1 contains no circuits and g_2 contains no cuts of G.

DEFINITION 4.5

Distance between Two Trees. The *distance* between two trees of a graph is the number of edges contained in one but not in the other.

For example, consider the trees $t_1 = e_2e_3e_4$, $t_2 = e_1e_3e_4$ and $t_3 = e_2e_3e_5$ of Fig. 4.2. The trees t_1 and t_2 are of distance 1 because t_1 contains only one edge e_2 that is not contained in t_2, or t_2 contains only one edge e_1 that is not contained in t_1. Likewise, t_1 and t_3 are of distance 1 but t_2 and t_3 are of distance 2. We next introduce a useful operation called the elementary tree transformation.

DEFINITION 4.6
Elementary Tree Transformation. Let t be a tree of a graph G and let e_1 be an edge of G but not in t. Then the operation

$$e_1 \cup t - e_2 = t^* \tag{4.1}$$

is called an *elementary tree transformation* if t^* is a tree of G, where e_2 is an edge of t.

The following result, originally due to Whitney (1935), is stated as a theorem.

THEOREM 4.3

Every tree of a connected graph can be obtained from any other one by a finite sequence of elementary tree transformations.

Proof. Let t_1 and t_2 be any two trees of a connected graph G. If $t_1 \neq t_2$, there exists a branch e_2 in t_2 but not in t_1. Since not all the edges of the f-circuit L in $t_1 \cup e_2$ defined by the chord e_2 of t_1 can be in t_2, there is a branch e_1 of t_1 in L but not in t_2. Consider the tree $t^* = e_2 \cup t_1 - e_1$, which is closer to t_2 than t_1. Thus, if $t^* \neq t_2$, the process may be repeated. Since t_2 contains a finite number of edges, we will eventually arrive at t_2 by a finite sequence of elementary tree transformations.   Q.E.D.

We illustrate the above results by the following example.

Example 4.1
Two of the trees of the graph of Fig. 4.1 are shown in Fig. 4.6 as

$$t_1 = e_1 e_3 e_4, \qquad t_2 = e_2 e_3 e_5 \tag{4.2}$$

Fig. 4.6. Two trees of the graph of Fig. 4.1: (a) t_1; (b) t_2.

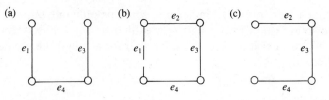

Fig. 4.7. An elementary tree transformation converting t_1 to t^*: (a) t_1; (b) $t_1 \cup e_2$; (c) t^*.

We show that t_2 can be obtained from t_1 by two elementary tree transformations.

Edge e_2 is in t_2 but not in t_1. The elementary tree transformation

$$e_2 \cup t_1 - e_1 = e_2 e_3 e_4 \tag{4.3}$$

results in a tree $t^* = e_2 e_3 e_4$ of G, which is of distance 1 to t_2, whereas t_1 is of distance 2 to t_2. Thus, t^* is closer to t_2 than t_1. Now observe that e_5 is an edge of t_2 not contained in t^*. The second elementary tree transformation

$$e_5 \cup t^* - e_4 = e_2 e_3 e_5 \tag{4.4}$$

yields the desired tree t_2. These operations are depicted in Figs. 4.7 and 4.8.

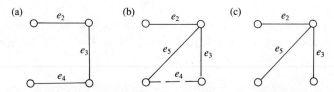

Fig. 4.8. An elementary tree transformation converting t^* to t_2: (a) t^*; (b) $t^* \cup e_5$; (c) t_2.

4.2 MINIMUM AND MAXIMUM TREES

An *undirected net* is a weighted undirected graph with node set V and edge set E. Each edge $(i, j) \in E$ has associated with it a real number $l(i, j)$ called the *length* of the edge (i, j), as previously defined in Section 2.1. The function l from the edge set E to the reals is the *length function*. Edges not in E are considered to be edges of infinite length in the undirected net. Therefore, an undirected net is a triplet and can be compactly written as $G(V, E, l)$. We remark that edge length can be positive, negative or zero, and that since $G(V, E, l)$ is undirected, $(i, j) = (j, i)$ and the length function is symmetric with $l(i, j) = l(j, i)$ for all $(i, j) \in E$.

The *length* of a tree t of $G(V, E, l)$ is the sum of the lengths of its branches:

$$l(t) = \sum_{(i,j) \in t} l(i, j) \tag{4.5}$$

Among all the trees t of $G(V, E, l)$, there is a "longest" one called a *maximum tree* of G:

$$l(t_{\max}) = \max_t l(t) \tag{4.6}$$

Likewise, among all the trees t of G, a "shortest" one is referred to as a *minimum tree*:

$$l(t_{\min}) = \min_t l(t) \tag{4.7}$$

In studying communication nets, maximum trees of G are of considerable use. We shall therefore state and prove a maximality criterion for a maximum tree, and then describe several simple algorithms that have been devised for constructing maximum or minimum trees.

THEOREM 4.4

A tree of an undirected net $G(V, E, l)$ is maximum if and only if the inequality

$$l(x_1, x_k) \leqq \min [l(x_1, x_2), l(x_2, x_3), \ldots, l(x_{k-1}, x_k)] \tag{4.8}$$

holds for each chord (x_1, x_k) with respect to the tree, where $(x_1, x_2)(x_2, x_3) \ldots (x_{k-1}, x_k)$ is the unique path between the nodes x_1 and x_k in the tree.

Proof. Necessity. Let t be a maximum tree of G. If (4.8) is not satisfied, then there is a branch (x_i, x_{i+1}), $1 \leqq i \leqq k-1$, in the unique tree path such that

$$l(x_1, x_k) > l(x_i, x_{i+1}) \tag{4.9}$$

Then the elementary tree transformation

$$(x_1, x_k) \cup t - (x_i, x_{i+1}) = t^* \tag{4.10}$$

would result in a tree t^* which is longer than t, contradicting the assumption that t is a maximum tree. Thus, the inequality (4.8) holds for every chord (x_1, x_k) with respect to the tree t.

Sufficiency. We first show that if t_1 and t_2 are two trees of G, each satisfying the inequality (4.8), then t_1 and t_2 are of the same length. To this end, we divide the edges of t_1 and t_2 into three classes: Edges belonging to t_1 only are called the t_1-*edges*, edges belonging to t_2 only are called the t_2-*edges*, and those belonging to both t_1 and t_2 are called the *common edges*.

Suppose that t_1 and t_2 are distinct. Let (x_1, x_k) be a t_2-edge and consider the f-circuit

$$(x_1, x_k)(x_1, x_2)(x_2, x_3) \ldots (x_{k-1}, x_k) \tag{4.11}$$

formed by the chord (x_1, x_k) and the unique tree path $P_{1k}(t_1) = (x_1, x_2)(x_2, x_3) \ldots (x_{k-1}, x_k)$ between nodes x_1 and x_k in t_1, not all of which can be the common edges; for, otherwise, (4.11) will be a circuit of t_2, not possible for a tree. Thus, there are t_1-edges in $P_{1k}(t_1)$. Appealing to (4.8) shows that each $(x_\alpha, x_{\alpha+1})$ of these t_1-edges has length of at least $l(x_1, x_k)$. We next demonstrate that at least one of them is of length $l(x_1, x_k)$. Suppose that each $(x_\alpha, x_{\alpha+1})$ of these t_1-edges had length longer than $l(x_1, x_k)$. Then the f-circuit formed by the chord $(x_\alpha, x_{\alpha+1})$ and the unique tree path $P_{\alpha(\alpha+1)}(t_2)$ between the nodes x_α and $x_{\alpha+1}$ in t_2 cannot contain the edge (x_1, x_k), since t_2 satisfies the inequality (4.8). It follows that if we replace each $(x_\alpha, x_{\alpha+1})$ of these t_1-edges in (4.11) by its unique tree path $P_{\alpha(\alpha+1)}(t_2)$ in t_2, we obtain a subgraph of t_2 containing a circuit, a contradiction. Therefore, at least one of these t_1-edges in (4.11) has length equal to $l(x_1, x_k)$, as asserted. Let $(x_\alpha, x_{\alpha+1})$ be such a t_1-edge with $l(x_\alpha, x_{\alpha+1}) = l(x_1, x_k)$. Then the elementary tree transformation

$$(x_1, x_k) \cup t_1 - (x_\alpha, x_{\alpha+1}) = t^* \tag{4.12}$$

would yield a tree t^* that has the same length as t_1. Furthermore, the distance between t^* and t_2 is one shorter than that between t_1 and t_2, and the hypothesis (4.8) is again satisfied for t^*, as is readily verified. Hence, we can repeat the argument and show that t_1 can be transformed to t_2 by a finite sequence of elementary tree transformations, having a succession of equal length trees, the last of which is t_2. This shows that if t_1 and t_2 satisfy (4.8), then t_1 and t_2 have the same length. In particular, we can let t_2 be a maximum tree, because every maximum tree satisfies the condition (4.8). This implies that every tree t_1 satisfying the inequality (4.8) must be a maximum tree, and the theorem follows.   Q.E.D.

We illustrate this result by the following example.

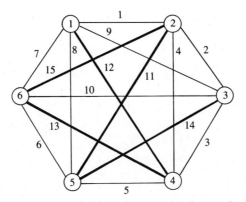

Fig. 4.9. An undirected net with edge lengths given by the numbers adjacent to the edges.

Example 4.2

Consider the undirected net $G(V, E, l)$ of Fig. 4.9, where the nodes are labeled by the integers 1, 2, 3, 4, 5, 6 and the edge lengths are given by the numbers adjacent to the edges. It is claimed that the tree shown in Fig. 4.10 is a maximum tree t_{max}. To verify this assertion by Theorem 4.4, we apply condition (4.8) to each chord of the cotree:

$$\bar{t}_{max} = (1, 2)(1, 3)(1, 5)(1, 6)(2, 3)(2, 4)(3, 4)(3, 6)(4, 5)(5, 6) \quad (4.13)$$

For the chord $(1, 2)$, the inequality (4.8) becomes

$$l(1, 2) = 1 \leqq \min [l(1, 4), l(4, 6), l(6, 2)]$$
$$= \min [12, 13, 15] = 12 \quad (4.14)$$

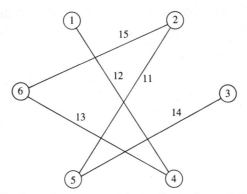

Fig. 4.10. A maximum tree of the undirected net of Fig. 4.9.

For the chord $(1, 3)$, we have the inequality

$$l(1, 3) = 9 \leqq \min [l(3, 5), l(5, 2), l(2, 6), l(6, 4), l(4, 1)]$$
$$= \min [14, 11, 15, 13, 12] = 11 \qquad (4.15)$$

Likewise, the inequalities for the remainder of the chords are as follows:

$$l(1, 5) = 8 \leqq \min [12, 13, 15, 11] = 11 \qquad (4.16a)$$

$$l(1, 6) = 7 \leqq \min [12, 13] = 12 \qquad (4.16b)$$

$$l(2, 3) = 2 \leqq \min [14, 11] = 11 \qquad (4.16c)$$

$$l(2, 4) = 4 \leqq \min [13, 15] = 13 \qquad (4.16d)$$

$$l(3, 4) = 3 \leqq \min [13, 15, 11, 14] = 11 \qquad (4.16e)$$

$$l(3, 6) = 10 \leqq \min [15, 11, 14] = 11 \qquad (4.16f)$$

$$l(4, 5) = 5 \leqq \min [11, 15, 13] = 11 \qquad (4.16g)$$

$$l(5, 6) = 6 \leqq \min [15, 11] = 11 \qquad (4.16h)$$

Thus, condition (4.8) is satisfied for each chord, and the tree $t_{\max}$ of Fig. 4.10 is a maximum tree.

It is important to note that since the edge lengths are allowed to be negative, when we can solve the maximum tree problem, we can also solve the minimum tree problem. All we have to do is to multiply each edge length by -1 and solve the corresponding maximum tree problem. Thus, we will only state the algorithms for solving the minimum tree problem, leaving the maximum tree problem as obvious, or vice versa. We remark that the shortest tree found in Section 2.2 by the shortest path algorithms is different from the minimum tree that we shall construct in this chapter. Consider, for example, the undirected net $G(V, E, l)$ of Fig. 4.11(a). The tree formed by the shortest paths from node 1 to nodes 2, 3, and 4 is presented in Fig. 4.11(b), whereas the minimum tree of G is shown in Fig. 4.11(c). The former has total length 10, and the latter has length 7. In addition, if all edge lengths are positive then a minimum tree will be a minimum spanning subgraph of G. In this case, the problem of finding a minimum tree is the

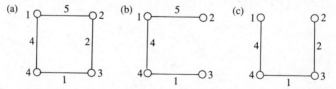

Fig. 4.11. A net (a) containing a tree formed by the shortest paths (b) and a minimum tree (c).

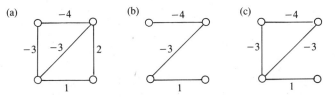

Fig. 4.12. A net (a) containing a minimum tree (b) and a minimum spanning subgraph (c).

same as that of finding a minimum connecting subgraph. These are not generally valid if G contains negative edge lengths. In the net $G(V, E, l)$ of Fig. 4.12(a), a minimum tree t_{min} is shown in (b). This minimum tree is not a minimum spanning subgraph of G because the subgraph of Fig. 4.12(c) is shorter than the minimum tree. The minimum tree t_{min} is of length -6, whereas the minimum spanning subgraph is of length -9.

Example 4.3

The undirected net $G(V, E, l)$ of Fig. 4.13 contains edges of negative lengths, a minimum tree of which is shown in Fig. 4.14. To verify that the tree t_{min} of Fig. 4.14 is indeed minimum, we multiply each edge length of Figs 4.13 and 4.14 by -1 and apply Theorem 4.4 for a maximum tree. This is equivalent to reversing the inequality sign in (4.8), changing min operation to max operation and then applying the resulting condition to the original net G and the minimum tree t_{min} of Figs. 4.13 and 4.14. The cotree with respect to t_{min} is given by

$$\bar{t}_{min} = (1, 3)(2, 5)(3, 4)(4, 5)(4, 6)(5, 7) \tag{4.17}$$

For the chord $(4, 5)$, we have the inequality

$$l(4, 5) = 8 \geqq \max \left[l(5, 6), l(6, 3), l(3, 2), l(2, 4) \right]$$
$$= \max \left[-5, -6, 1, -2 \right] = 1 \tag{4.18}$$

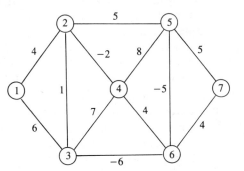

Fig. 4.13. An undirected net containing edges of negative lengths.

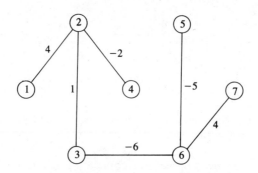

Fig. 4.14. A minimum tree of the undirected net of Fig. 4.13.

Likewise, the inequalities corresponding to other chords are obtained as follows:

$$l(1, 3) = 6 \geqq \max [4, 1] = 4 \qquad (4.19a)$$

$$l(2, 5) = 5 \geqq \max [-5, -6, 1] = 1 \qquad (4.19b)$$

$$l(3, 4) = 7 \geqq \max [1, -2] = 1 \qquad (4.19c)$$

$$l(4, 6) = 4 \geqq \max [-6, 1, -2] = 1 \qquad (4.19d)$$

$$l(5, 7) = 5 \geqq \max [4, -5] = 4 \qquad (4.19e)$$

Since all the conditions are satisfied, t_{min} of Fig. 4.14 is indeed a minimum tree of G. In fact, it is the only minimum tree of G.

4.3 MINIMUM AND MAXIMUM TREE ALGORITHMS

In this section, we study the minimum tree and maximum tree enumeration algorithms. Since the algorithms for finding a minimum tree in an undirected net $G(V, E, l)$ are equally valid for finding a maximum tree, *mutatis mutandis*, in the following we shall only focus our attention on the development of algorithms for the minimum tree problem.

We use a simple incremental technique known as the *greedy method*, which builds up a minimum tree edge by edge by including appropriate short edges and excluding appropriate long edges until a minimum tree is constructed. The method, due to Tarjan (1981), is sufficiently general to include all known efficient algorithms for the minimum tree problem.

Given an undirected net $G(V, E, l)$, an edge coloring process is described as follows: Initially all edges of G are uncolored. We color one edge at a time either blue or red in accordance with the following rules:

Blue rule. Select a cut that is devoid of any blue edges. Among the uncolored edges in the cut, select one of minimum length and color it blue.

Red rule. Select a circuit that is devoid of any red edges. Among the uncolored edges on the circuit, select one of maximum length and color it red.

The method is nondeterministic in that we are free to apply either rule at any time and in arbitrary order until all edges of G are colored. As will be shown, the greedy method will color all the edges of G, and when all the edges are colored, the blue ones form a minimum tree. Thus, the blue color signifies the acceptance of an edge, and the red color means rejection.

DEFINITION 4.7

Color Invariant. In applying the blue rule and the red rule in coloring the edges of an undirected net, if at every stage of the process there is a minimum tree containing all of the blue edges and none of the red ones, then the process is said to maintain *color invariant*.

The significance of the edge-coloring process is contained in the following theorem.

THEOREM 4.5

The greedy method colors all the edges of a connected undirected net, and maintains the color invariant.

Proof. Let $G(V, E, l)$ be a connected undirected net. Initially, none of the edges of G is colored, and since G is connected there exists at least one minimum tree satisfying the color invariant property. Suppose that the color invariant is true before the application of the blue rule. We show that it remains to be true after the application of the blue rule. Let $(X, \bar{X}) = (\bar{X}, X)$, $\bar{X} = V - X$, be the cut to which the blue rule is applied to color the edge $(x, y) \in (X, \bar{X})$, and let t be a minimum tree satisfying the color invariant before the edge (x, y) is colored. If (x, y) is in t, then t satisfies the color invariant after (x, y) is colored. Assume that (x, y) is not in t and consider the f-circuit formed by the chord (x, y) and the unique path connected between the nodes x and y in t. Since a cut and a circuit have an even number of edges in common, let (x, y) and (u, v) be two of these edges that belong to both the f-circuit and the cut $(X, \bar{X})$. By construction, none of the edges of t is red, and by the blue rule the edge (u, v) is uncolored with $l(u, v) \geq l(x, y)$. Applying the elementary tree transformation

$$(x, y) \cup t - (u, v) = t^* \tag{4.20}$$

yields a minimum tree t^* of G that maintains the color invariant after the edge (x, y) is colored.

We next show that the red rule also maintains the color invariant. To this end, let L be the circuit to which the red rule is applied to color the edge $(x, y) \in L$, and let t be a minimum tree satisfying the color invariant before the edge (x, y) is colored. If (x, y) is not in t, then t satisfies the color invariant after (x, y) is colored red. Thus, we assume that (x, y) is in t. Then the removal of (x, y) from t partitions the node set V of G into subsets X and $\bar{X} = V - X$. Since the cut $(X, \bar{X}) = (\bar{X}, X)$ must contain an even number of edges in common with the circuit L, let (x, y) and (u, v) be two of these edges that belong to both the circuit L and the cut $(X, \bar{X})$. By construction, none of the edges of t is red, and by the red rule the edge (u, v) is uncolored with $l(u, v) \leqq l(x, y)$. Applying the elementary tree transformation

$$(u, v) \cup t - (x, y) = t^* \tag{4.21}$$

produces a minimum tree t^* of G that maintains the color invariant after the edge (x, y) is colored.

Finally, we must show that the process will not terminate prematurely, and all the edges of G will be colored. Suppose otherwise that some of the edges are not colored and neither the blue rule nor the red rule applies. By color invariant, there is a minimum tree t in G containing all the blue edges and none of the red ones. If we remove all the uncolored edges from this tree t, we obtain a forest, each of whose subtrees consists of either all blue edges or an isolated node. Let (x, y) be an uncolored edge of G. If both nodes x and y are in a nontrivial subtree, the red rule applies to the circuit formed by (x, y) and the unique path of blue edges connected between the nodes x and y of the subtree. If the nodes x and y are in two different subtrees t_α and t_β, the blue rule applies to either of the two cuts $(X_\alpha, \bar{X}_\alpha) = (\bar{X}_\alpha, X_\alpha)$ and $(X_\beta, \bar{X}_\beta) = (\bar{X}_\beta, X_\beta)$, where X_α and X_β are the node sets of t_α and t_β, respectively, and $\bar{X}_\alpha = V - X_\alpha$ and $\bar{X}_\beta = V - X_\beta$. Consequently, all the edges of G are guaranteed to be colored, and the process maintains the color invariant.   Q.E.D.

The greedy method is applicable to a wide variety of problems besides the minimum tree problem. In the following, we shall examine three well-known minimum tree algorithms that are variants of the greedy method.

4.3.1 Borůvka Algorithm

Borůvka (1926) was the first to develop a fully realized minimum tree algorithm. The same algorithm was rediscovered by Choquet (1938), Lukasziewicz, Florek, Perkal, Steinhaus and Zubrzycki (1951), and Sollin [see Berge and Ghouila-Houri (1965)].

In applying the coloring process to the edges of $G(V, E, l)$, the blue edges always form subtrees of a forest. We shall consider the forest consisting of the blue subtrees and a number of trivial subtrees of isolated nodes. These trivial subtrees of isolated nodes are considered trivial blue subtrees of the forest. Thus, at each stage during the coloring process, there is a forest composed only of the blue subtrees, trivial blue subtrees included. The Borůvka algorithm combines these blue subtrees two at a time until finally only one blue tree, a minimum tree, remains.

Borůvka Algorithm

Step 1. Let f_0 be the initial blue forest composed of n blue subtrees, each of which is an isolated node, where n is the number of nodes in G. Set $i = 0$.

Step 2. For each blue subtree t_α of f_i, find a minimum-length edge (x_α, y_α) incident to t_α, where x_α is in t_α but y_α is not. Color all these selected edges (x_α, y_α) blue.

Step 3. Let

$$f_{i+1} = f_i \cup \left[\bigcup_\alpha (x_\alpha, y_\alpha) \right] \tag{4.22}$$

Step 4. Set $i = i + 1$.

Step 5. If f_i is a tree, stop. Otherwise, return to Step 2.

The Borůvka algorithm starts initially with n blue subtrees, each of which is an isolated node and contains no edges, and then applies the blue rule to build up a minimum tree. Since every edge has two endpoints, an edge may be selected twice in Step 2, once for each endpoint. Such an edge, however, is colored only once. The algorithm is guaranteed to work correctly only if all the edge lengths are distinct, because in this case the edges can be ordered so that the blue rule will color them one at a time. In the case where the edge lengths are nondistinct, we can distinguish them by assigning numbers to the edges and ordering edges lexicographically by length and number. The Borůvka algorithm can be implemented in several ways and is well suited for parallel computation. We illustrate the algorithm by the following examples.

Example 4.4

We apply the Borůvka algorithm to find a minimum tree for the undirected net $G(V, E, l)$ of Fig. 4.15. We follow the above five steps of the algorithm.

Step 1. f_0 is a forest of G consisting of the isolated nodes 1, 2, 3, 4, 5, 6, 7 and set $i = 0$.

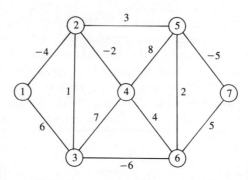

Fig. 4.15. An undirected net used to illustrate the Borùvka algorithm.

Step 2. For node 1, the minimum-length edge incident at this node is
(1, 2) with $l(1, 2) = -4$. For node 2, the minimum-length edge
incident at this node is also $(1, 2) = (2, 1)$ with $l(1, 2) = l(2, 1) =$
-4. The minimum-length edges incident at nodes 3, 4, 5, 6 and 7
are (3, 6), (2, 4), (5, 7), (3, 6) and (5, 7), respectively, with
$l(3, 6) = -6$, $l(2, 4) = -2$ and $l(5, 7) = -5$. Color the edges
(1, 2), (2, 4), (3, 6) and (5, 7) blue.

Step 3. Let the resulting forest be

$$f_1 = f_0 \cup (1, 2)(2, 4)(3, 6)(5, 7) = (1, 2)(2, 4)(3, 6)(5, 7) \quad (4.23)$$

as shown in Fig. 4.16.

Step 4. Set $i = 1$.

Step 5. Return to Step 2.

Step 2. For the blue subtree $(1, 2)(2, 4)$, the minimum-length edge
incident to this subtree is (2, 3) with $l(2, 3) = 1$. For the blue
subtree (3, 6), the minimum-length edge incident to this subtree
is also (2, 3). Finally, the minimum-length edge incident to the
blue subtree (5, 7) is (5, 6) with $l(5, 6) = 2$. Color the edges (2, 3)
and (5, 6) blue.

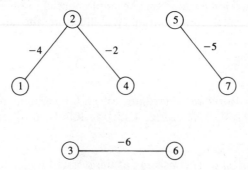

Fig. 4.16. A forest generated by the Borùvka algorithm.

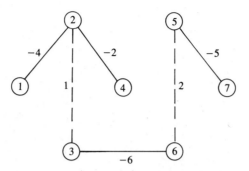

Fig. 4.17. A minimum tree of the undirected net of Fig. 4.15 generated by the Borůvka algorithm.

Step 3. Let the resulting forest be

$$f_2 = f_1 \cup (2, 3)(5, 6)$$
$$= (1, 2)(2, 3)(2, 4)(3, 6)(5, 6)(5, 7) \qquad (4.24)$$

as shown in Fig. 4.17.

Step 4. Set $i = 2$.

Step 5. Since f_2 is a tree of G, stop. The desired minimum tree is shown in Fig. 4.17 with total length -14.

Example 4.5

Consider the net $G(V, E, l)$ of Fig. 4.18, where the edge lengths are not all distinct. We demonstrate that if the edges of the same length are not properly distinguished, the Borůvka algorithm may result in an incorrect solution. Therefore, if not all the edge lengths are distinct, care should be taken by first ordering the edges of the same length before the algorithm is applied.

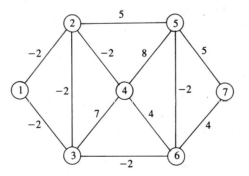

Fig. 4.18. An undirected net in which the edge lengths are not all distinct.

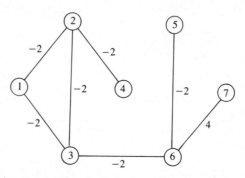

Fig. 4.19. A subgraph generated by the Borùvka algorithm without prior ordering of the edges of the same length.

Suppose that we apply the algorithm directly to the net G of Fig. 4.18 without prior ordering of the edges of the same length. Initially, the forest f_0 consists of seven isolated nodes. In Step 2 the minimum-length edges incident to nodes 1, 2, 3, 4, 5, 6, and 7 may be selected as $(1, 2)$, $(2, 3)$, $(3, 1)$, $(4, 2)$, $(5, 6)$, $(6, 3)$ and $(6, 7)$, respectively. The corresponding subgraph f_1 of these edges is shown in Fig. 4.19. Clearly, it is not a tree. Alternatively, the minimum-length edges incident to nodes 1, 2, 3, 4, 5, 6 and 7 may be chosen to be $(1, 2)$, $(1, 2)$, $(3, 6)$, $(2, 4)$, $(5, 6)$, $(3, 6)$ and $(6, 7)$, respectively. The corresponding forest f_1 of these edges is presented in Fig. 4.20. Observe now that the minimum-length edge incident to the blue subtree $(1, 2)(2, 4)$ of Fig. 4.20 may be either $(2, 3)$ or $(1, 3)$. Likewise, the minimum-length edge incident to the blue subtree $(3, 6)(5, 6)(6, 7)$ may also be $(2, 3)$ or $(1, 3)$. If we pick $(2, 3)$ for one and $(1, 3)$ for the other, the resulting subgraph f_2 is shown in Fig. 4.19 and is not a tree.

To avoid this difficulty, we shall order the edges of G lexicographically

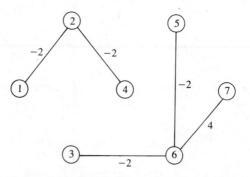

Fig. 4.20. A forest generated by the Borùvka algorithm without prior ordering of the edges of the same length.

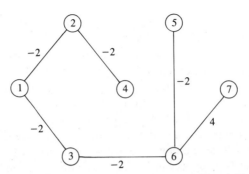

Fig. 4.21. A minimum tree of the undirected net of Fig. 4.18 generated by the Borůvka algorithm.

by length and by assigning numbers to the edges, as follows:

$$(3, 6), (5, 6), (1, 2), (1, 3), (2, 3), (2, 4), (4, 6), (6, 7),$$

$$(2, 5), (5, 7), (3, 4), (4, 5) \tag{4.25}$$

Using this in Step 2, the minimum-length edges incident to nodes 1, 2, 3, 4, 5, 6 and 7 can now be uniquely selected to be $(1, 2)$, $(1, 2)$, $(1, 3)$, $(2, 4)$, $(5, 6)$, $(3, 6)$ and $(6, 7)$, respectively. The corresponding subgraph f_1 formed by these edges is a desired minimum tree as shown in Fig. 4.21.

4.3.2 Kruskal Algorithm

The algorithm was first suggested by Kruskal (1956), and is a variant of the greedy method. To implement the algorithm, we must first order the edges of $G(V, E, l)$ in nondecreasing order by length, and represent the blue subtrees of the forest so that we can test whether two nodes are in the same blue subtree. The Kruskal algorithm consists of applying the following steps to the edges already arranged in nondecreasing order by length.

Kruskal Algorithm

Step 1. Select a shortest edge of $G(V, E, l)$ and color it blue. Set $i = 0$.

Step 2. Among the edges not yet chosen, select a shortest edge (x, y). If nodes x and y belong to the same blue subtree, color (x, y) red; otherwise, color it blue.

Step 3. Set $i = i + 1$.

Step 4. If $i = m - 1$, stop, where m is the number of edges of G. Otherwise, return to Step 2.

In words, it states that we begin the algorithm by selecting a shortest edge of G. At each successive stage, we select a shortest edge among the edges that have not yet been selected and that does not form a circuit with those edges already selected. By changing the word shortest to longest, the algorithm also finds a maximum tree of G. Alternatively, we can start with a complete graph and remove the edges one at a time. Among the edges not yet removed, we remove a longest edge that will not disconnect the graph.

The total running time for the Kruskal algorithm is $O(m \log n)$, where m is the number of edges and n is the number of nodes of G. The algorithm is best in situations where the edges are given in sorted order or can be sorted fast. We illustrate this algorithm by the following example.

Example 4.6

We apply the Kruskal algorithm to find a minimum tree in the net $G(V, E, l)$ of Fig. 4.18. First, we arrange the edges of G in nondecreasing order by edge length, as shown in (4.25). We then follow the four steps to build up a minimum tree.

Step 1. Select edge $(3, 6)$ and color it blue. Set $i = 0$.
Step 2. Select edge $(5, 6)$ and color it blue.
Step 3. Set $i = 1$.
Step 4. Return to Step 2.
Step 2. Select edge $(1, 2)$ and color it blue.
Step 3. Set $i = 2$.
Step 4. Return to Step 2.
Step 2. Select edge $(1, 3)$ and color it blue.
Step 3. Set $i = 3$.
Step 4. Return to Step 2.
Step 2. Select edge $(2, 3)$ and color it red.
Step 3. Set $i = 4$.
Step 4. Return to Step 2.
Step 2. Select edge $(2, 4)$ and color it blue.
Step 3. Set $i = 5$.
Step 4. Return to Step 2.
Step 2. Select edge $(4, 6)$ and color it red.
Step 3. Set $i = 6$.
Step 4. Return to Step 2.
Step 2. Select edge $(6, 7)$ and color it blue.
Step 3. Set $i = 7$.
Step 4. Return to Step 2.
Step 2. Select edge $(2, 5)$ and color it red.

Step 3. Set $i = 8$.

Step 4. Return to Step 2.

Step 2. Select edge $(5, 7)$ and color it red.

Step 3. Set $i = 9$.

Step 4. Return to Step 2.

Step 2. Select edge $(3, 4)$ and color it red.

Step 3. Set $i = 10$.

Step 4. Return to Step 2.

Step 2. Select edge $(4, 5)$ and color it red.

Step 3. Set $i = 11$.

Step 4. Stop.

After the termination of the coloring process, the final colored net is presented in Fig. 4.22, where the solid lines denote the blue edges and the broken lines the red edges.

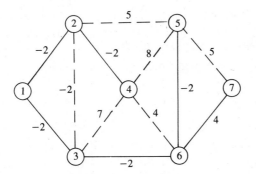

Fig. 4.22. The final colored net of the undirected net of Fig. 4.18 generated by the Kruskal algorithm.

4.3.3 Prim Algorithm

The Prim algorithm was originally proposed by Jarník (1930), and rediscovered by Prim (1957) and Dijkstra (1959). The procedure is commonly known as the Prim algorithm, and is a variant of the greedy method. It uses an arbitrary starting node and builds only one nontrivial blue subtree.

Let s be an arbitrary starting node of an undirected connected net $G(V, F, l)$. Let t_α be the blue subtree containing s. A node y is said to *border* t_α if y is not in t_α and if there is a node x in t_α such that the edge $(x, y) \in E$. For each node y bordering t_α, let (i, y) be a minimum-length edge incident to y and t_α:

$$l(i, y) = \min_{x \in t_\alpha} l(x, y) \qquad (4.26)$$

For our purposes, we color the edge (i, y) light blue. Thus, we associate every node bordering t_α a light blue edge. These light blue edges are candidates to become blue, and they together with the blue edges form a subtree spanning t_α and its bordering nodes. To proceed with the coloring process, we select a light blue edge (i, y) that is of minimum length among all the light blue edges and color it blue. This adds the edge (i, y) to the blue subtree t_α and yields a new blue subtree

$$t_\alpha^* = t_\alpha \cup (i, y) \tag{4.27}$$

We next examine each edge (y, u) incident at y. If node u is not in t_α^* and has no incident light blue edge, we color (y, u) light blue. If node u is not in t_α^* but has an incident light blue edge (x, u), x in t_α^*, of greater length than $l(y, u)$, we color (x, u) red and color (y, u) light blue. The process is repeated until a minimum tree is constructed.

Prim Algorithm

Step 1. Pick an arbitrary node of $G(V, E, l)$ as the initial blue subtree t_0 and set $i = 0$. For each node y bordering t_0, color a minimum-length edge incident to y and t_0 with light blue.

Step 2. Select a minimum-length light blue edge (x, y), x in t_i, and color it blue. Let

$$t_{i+1} = t_i \cup (x, y) \tag{4.28}$$

Step 3. For each edge (y, z), z not in t_{i+1}, if there is no light blue edge incident at z, color (y, z) light blue; and if there is an incident light blue edge (w, z) at z with $l(w, z) > l(y, z)$, color (w, z) red and (y, z) light blue. Otherwise, no operation is required.

Step 4. Set $i + 1$.

Step 5. If $i = n - 1$, stop. If $i < n - 1$, return to Step 2.

The Prim algorithm described above has a running time of $O(n^2)$, $O(n)$ time per coloring phase, where n is the number of nodes of G. We illustrate this algorithm by the following example.

Example 4.7

Consider the net $G(V, E, l)$ of Fig. 4.18, which is redrawn in Fig. 4.23. We use the Prim algorithm to generate a minimum tree, as follows:

Step 1. Pick node 1 as the initial blue subtree t_0 and set $i = 0$. Edges $(1, 2)$ and $(1, 3)$ are colored light blue.

Step 2. Select edge $(1, 2)$ and color it blue and let $t_1 = (1, 2)$.

Step 3. Color edges $(2, 5)$ and $(2, 4)$ light blue.

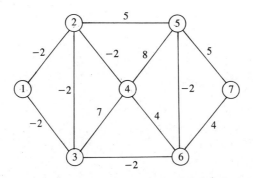

Fig. 4.23. An undirected net used to illustrate the Prim algorithm.

Step 4. Set $i = 1$.
Step 5. Return to Step 2.

The resulting net at the end of Step 5 is presented in Fig. 4.24, where the solid line denotes the blue edge, and the dashed lines the light blue edges.

Step 2. Color edge $(2, 4)$ blue and let $t_2 = (1, 2)(2, 4)$.
Step 3. Color edge $(4, 6)$ light blue.
Step 4. Set $i = 2$.
Step 5. Return to Step 2.

At the end of Step 5, the resulting net is shown in Fig. 4.25.

Step 2. Color edge $(1, 3)$ blue and let $t_3 = (1, 2)(1, 3)(2, 4)$.
Step 3. Color $(4, 6)$ red and $(3, 6)$ light blue.
Step 4. Set $i = 3$.
Step 5. Return to Step 2.

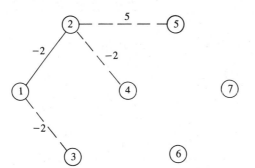

Fig. 4.24. A colored subnet generated by the Prim algorithm at the end of the first cycle.

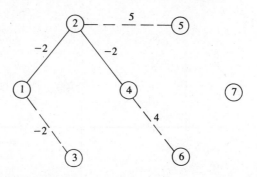

Fig. 4.25. A colored subnet generated by the Prim algorithm at the end of the second cycle.

At the end of this phase, the resulting net is shown in Fig. 4.26 with the heavy line denoting the red edge.

Step 2. Color edge $(3, 6)$ blue and let $t_4 = (1, 2)(1, 3)(2, 4)(3, 6)$.
Step 3. Color edges $(6, 5)$ and $(6, 7)$ light blue, and edge $(2, 5)$ red.
Step 4. Set $i = 4$.
Step 5. Return to Step 2.

At the end of this phase, the resulting net is shown in Fig. 4.27.

Step 2. Color edge $(6, 5)$ blue and let $t_5 = (1, 2)(1, 3)(2, 4)(3, 6)(6, 5)$.
Step 3. No operation is required.
Step 4. Set $i = 5$.
Step 5. Return to Step 2.

At the end of this phase, the resulting net is presented in Fig. 4.28.

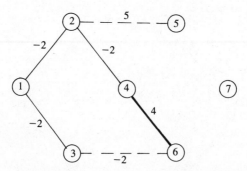

Fig. 4.26. A colored subnet generated by the Prim algorithm at the end of the third cycle.

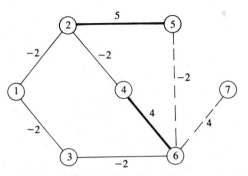

Fig. 4.27. A colored subnet generated by the Prim algorithm at the end of the fourth cycle.

Step 2. Color edge $(6, 7)$ blue and let

$$t_6 = (1, 2)(1, 3)(2, 4)(3, 6)(6, 5)(6, 7) \qquad (4.29)$$

Step 3. No operation is required.
Step 4. Set $i = 6$.
Step 5. Stop.

The tree t_6 of (4.29) is a desired minimum tree with total length -6 and is indicated in Fig. 4.29 by the thin solid lines.

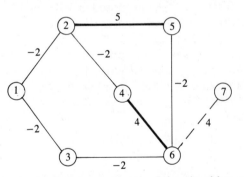

Fig. 4.28. A colored subnet generated by the Prim algorithm at the end of the fifth cycle.

4.3.4 General Remarks

All three algorithms presented in the foregoing use maninly the blue rule. It should be possible to find the dual algorithms using mainly the red rule, but such procedures seem to be less efficient.

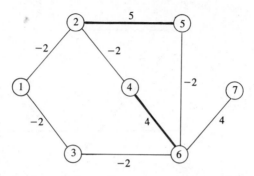

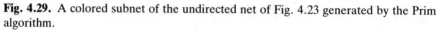

Fig. 4.29. A colored subnet of the undirected net of Fig. 4.23 generated by the Prim algorithm.

The Kruskal algorithm generates blue subtrees in an irregular fashion dictated solely by the edge lengths, and the Prim algorithm grows the blue subtree from a single root. The Borůvka algorithm, on the other hand, builds up blue subtrees uniformly throughout the net, and is therefore well suited for parallel computation. In fact, Yao (1975) proposed a Borůvka-like algorithm using the appropriate data structures, which runs in $O(m \log \log n)$ time but needs a linear-time selection algorithm [see, for example, Blum, Floyd, Pratt, Rivest and Tarjan (1973) and Schönhage, Paterson and Pippenger (1976)], and is therefore not very practical. However, a similar but more practical algorithm with $O(m \log \log n)$ time was proposed by Cheriton and Tarjan (1976).

More recently, Tarjan (1981) proposed a general blue rule algorithm using two data structures for each blue subtree. The algorithm is called the *round robin algorithm*. For sparse nets, the round robin algorithm is asymptotically faster than any of the other three algorithms. However, for dense nets, it is slower by a factor of $O(\log \log n)$ than the Prim algorithm. Other results on the minimum tree problem may be found in the survey paper by Maffioli (1981).

4.4   TERMINAL CAPACITY MATRIX

In this section and the remainder of the chapter, we study the maximum flows for all pairs of nodes in a communication net $G(V, E, c, f)$. To simplify the problem, we assume that at any given time, only one pair of nodes serves as the source and the sink while all other nodes serve as intermediate nodes.

DEFINITION 4.8

Terminal Capacity. Given a pair of nodes i and j of a communication net $G(V, E, c, f)$, the *terminal capacity* τ_{ij} from i to j is the value of the minimum $i–j$ cut.

The concept of terminal capacity has a number of physical significances. For example, if all arc capacities are unity, the terminal capacity τ_{ij} represents the minimum number of arcs that must be removed to break all directed paths from i to j in G. In a communication system, the terminal capacity τ_{ij} may actually represent the capacity available for communication from i to j at any given time when all other nodes serve as intermediate or relaying nodes. The communication capability between all pairs of nodes in G is best described by a matrix called the terminal capacity matrix.

DEFINITION 4.9

Terminal Capacity Matrix. The *terminal capacity matrix* $T = [\tau_{ij}]$ of an n-node communication net $G(V, E, c, f)$ is a square matrix of order n, whose ith row and jth column element τ_{ij}, $i \neq j$, is the terminal capacity from i to j and whose diagonal elements τ_{ii} are defined to be infinite.

We illustrate the above result by the following example.

Example 4.8

We compute the terminal capacity matrix for the communication net $G(V, E, c, f)$ of Fig. 4.30. Since G is a 5-node net, the terminal capacity matrix T is of order 5 with one row and one column corresponding to each node of the net.

Consider, for example, the element τ_{13} which is the value of a minimum 1–3 cut $(X, \bar{X}) = (\{1, 5\}, \{2, 3, 4\})$ or

$$(X, \bar{X}) = (\{1, 5\}, \{2, 3, 4\}) = (1, 2)(4, 5)(3, 5) \qquad (4.30)$$

giving

$$\tau_{13} = c(X, \bar{X}) = c(\{1, 5\}, \{2, 3, 4\})$$
$$= c(1, 2) + c(4, 5) + c(3, 5) = 2 + 2 + 1 = 5 \qquad (4.31)$$

Likewise, for the element τ_{23} the corresponding minimum 2–3 cut is

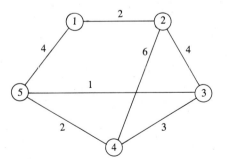

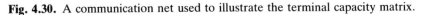

Fig. 4.30. A communication net used to illustrate the terminal capacity matrix.

found to be

$$(Y, \bar{Y}) = (\{1, 2, 4, 5\}, 3) = (2, 3)(3, 5)(3, 4) \qquad (4.32)$$

yielding

$$\tau_{23} = c(Y, \bar{Y}) = c(\{1, 2, 4, 5\}, 3)$$
$$= c(2, 3) + c(3, 5) + c(3, 4) = 4 + 1 + 3 = 8 \qquad (4.33)$$

The other elements can be computed in a similar manner. The terminal capacity matrix of the net of Fig. 4.30 is obtained as

$$
T =
\begin{array}{c}
 \\
1 \\
2 \\
3 \\
4 \\
5
\end{array}
\begin{array}{ccccc}
1 & 2 & 3 & 4 & 5 \\
\begin{bmatrix}
\infty & 5 & 5 & 5 & 6 \\
5 & \infty & 8 & 11 & 5 \\
5 & 8 & \infty & 8 & 5 \\
5 & 11 & 8 & \infty & 5 \\
6 & 5 & 5 & 5 & \infty
\end{bmatrix}
\end{array}
\qquad (4.34)
$$

So far the communication nets that we are concerned with can either be directed or undirected. A basic question arises naturally at this point: 'What are the necessary and sufficient conditions for a given matrix of real nonnegative elements with infinity along the main diagonal to be the terminal capacity matrix of a communication net?' The general characterization for such a matrix is not known. However, necessary and sufficient conditions for such a matrix to be the terminal capacity matrix of an undirected communication net are available. They provide concise and elegant answers to the question posted above. Therefore, we will focus on the undirected communication nets first, leaving the discussion on oriented or directed communication nets until later.

THEOREM 4.6

A symmetric real matrix $T = [\tau_{ij}]$ of nonnegative elements with infinity along its main diagonal is the terminal capacity matrix of an undirected communication net if and only if for all i, j and k,

$$\tau_{ij} \geq \min [\tau_{ik}, \tau_{kj}] \qquad (4.35)$$

Proof. Necessity. Let $G(V, E, c, f)$ be the undirected communicaton net. Let $(X, \bar{X})$ be a minimum i–j cut of G. Then $\tau_{ij} = c(X, \bar{X})$. If node $k \in X$, then $(X, \bar{X})$ is also a k–j cut and

$$\tau_{ij} = c(X, \bar{X}) \geqq \tau_{kj} \qquad (4.36)$$

and the inequality (4.35) holds. If node $k \in \bar{X}$, then $(X, \bar{X})$ is also an i–k cut and

$$\tau_{ij} = c(X, \bar{X}) \geqq \tau_{ik} \qquad (4.37)$$

and condition (4.35) holds.

Sufficiency. Construct the n-node complete undirected graph $G(V, E)$ and associate with each of its edges (i, j) the number τ_{ij}, which is considered as the length of the edge. Let $t_{\max}$ be a maximum tree in the resulting net $G(V, E, l)$ with $l(i, j) = \tau_{ij}$. It follows from Theorem 4.4 that if $(i, x_1)(x_1, x_2) \ldots (x_{u-1}, x_u)(x_u, j)$ is the unique path between the nodes i and j in $t_{\max}$, then

$$l(i, j) \leqq \min [l(i, x_1), l(x_1, x_2), \ldots, l(x_{u-1}, x_u), l(x_u, j)] \qquad (4.38)$$

or

$$\tau_{ij} \leqq \min [\tau_{ix_1}, \tau_{x_1 x_2}, \ldots, \tau_{x_{u-1} x_u}, \tau_{x_u j}] \qquad (4.39)$$

Since by assumption (4.35) holds for all i, j and $k \in V$, it follows that

$$\tau_{ij} \geqq \min [\tau_{ix_1}, \tau_{x_1 j}]$$
$$\geqq \min [\tau_{ix_1}, \tau_{x_1 x_2}, \tau_{x_2 j}]$$
$$\geqq \min [\tau_{ix_1}, \tau_{x_1 x_2}, \tau_{x_2 x_3}, \tau_{x_3 j}]$$
$$\vdots$$
$$\geqq \min [\tau_{ix_1}, \tau_{x_1 x_2}, \ldots, \tau_{x_{u-1} x_u}, \tau_{x_u j}] \qquad (4.40)$$

Combining (4.39) and (4.40) shows that

$$\tau_{ij} = \min [\tau_{ix_1}, \tau_{x_1 x_2}, \ldots, \tau_{x_{u-1} x_u}, \tau_{x_u j}] \qquad (4.41)$$

Hence, if each branch (x, y) of $t_{\max}$ is now assigned the capacity

$$c(x, y) = l(x, y) \qquad (4.42)$$

and if each chord of the cotree $\bar{t}_{\max}$ is removed from $\bar{G}(V, E, l)$, we obtain an undirected communication net $t_{\max}(V, E_t, c)$, the terminal capacity of which is T. This completes the proof of the theorem.   Q.E.D.

An important consequence of the proof is that if T is realizable, it is realizable by a tree. Since an n-node tree contains $n - 1$ branches, the matrix T can have at most $n - 1$ numerically different elements. We summarize these results as a corollary. However, before we do this, we introduce the notion of flow equivalency.

DEFINITION 4.10

Flow Equivalency. Two n-node communication nets are said to be *flow equivalent*, or briefly, *equivalent*, if they have the same terminal capacity matrix.

With this term, we can now state the corollary.

COROLLARY 4.2

Every n-node undirected communication net is equivalent to a tree and there are at most $n - 1$ numerically distinct terminal capacities.

In Section 4.5 we will demonstrate that it is possible to construct an equivalent tree by solving precisely $n - 1$ maximum flow problems instead of first determining the terminal capacity matrix by solving a large number of maximum flow problems and then constructing a τ-maximum tree, as discussed in the proof of Theorem 4.6.

We remark that condition (4.35) is a kind of triangle inequality, and imposes severe limitations on the elements of the terminal capacity matrix. For example, by applying (4.35) to each side of the triangle, it is straightforward to verify that, among the three terminal capacities appearing in (4.35), two of them must be equal and the third must be no smaller than their common value. As a consequence, there are at most $n - 1$ numerically distinct values.

We illustrate the above by the following example.

Example 4.9

The terminal capacity matrix T of the communication net $G(V, E, c, f)$ of Fig. 4.30 was obtained earlier in (4.34), and is given by

$$T = \begin{bmatrix} \infty & 5 & 5 & 5 & 6 \\ 5 & \infty & 8 & 11 & 5 \\ 5 & 8 & \infty & 8 & 5 \\ 5 & 11 & 8 & \infty & 5 \\ 6 & 5 & 5 & 5 & \infty \end{bmatrix} \qquad (4.43)$$

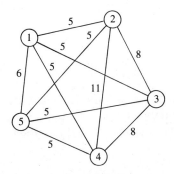

Fig. 4.31. A weighted five-node complete graph.

For $i = 1$, $j = 2$ and $k = 3$, we have the inequality

$$\tau_{12} = 5 \geqq \min [\tau_{13}, \tau_{32}] = \min [5, 8] = 5 \qquad (4.44)$$

Likewise, we can verify inequality (4.35) for all other values of i, j and k.

To construct a flow-equivalent tree of the net of Fig. 4.30, we associate with each edge (x, y) of the 5-node complete graph the length $l(x, y) = \tau_{xy}$, the xth row and yth column element of T, to obtain a weighted graph of Fig. 4.31. Applying any of the algorithms outlined in Section 4.3 yields a maximum tree t_{max} as shown in Fig. 4.32. This tree is flow-equivalent to the communication net of Fig. 4.30, as can easily be verified by computing its terminal capacity matrix. Observe that since t_{max} contains four numerically distinct branch capacities, its terminal capacity matrix has four numerically different entries, excluding the infinity.

DEFINITION 4.11

Principal Partition. A real symmetric matrix T is said to be *principally partitionable* if after possibly permuting rows and the corresponding

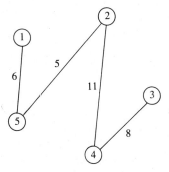

Fig. 4.32. A flow-equivalent tree of the net of Fig. 4.30.

columns, it can be partitioned into the form

$$T = \begin{bmatrix} T_a & T_c \\ T_c' & T_b \end{bmatrix} \tag{4.45}$$

where (i) every element in T_c is identical and is the smallest number in T, (ii) T_a and T_b are symmetric submatrices, and (iii) every diagonal element in T is ∞. T_a and T_b are referred to as the *resultant main submatrices* by a principal partition.

The significance of the principal partition is contained in the following theorem.

THEOREM 4.7

A real symmetric matrix of nonnegative elements with ∞ along its main diagonal is the terminal capacity matrix of an undirected communication net if, and only if, the matrix and all of its resultant main submatrices can be principally partitioned until all the final resultant main submatrices are of order 1.

Proof. Necessity. Let T be the terminal capacity matrix of an n-node undirected communication net $G(V, E, c, f)$. By Corollary 4.2, there is an n-node tree t that is flow-equivalent to G. Let the branches (x_i, x_{i+1}) $(i = 1, 2, \ldots, n-1)$ of t be arranged in nondecreasing order by capacity:

$$c(x_1, x_2) \leqq c(x_2, x_3) \leqq \ldots \leqq c(x_{n-1}, x_n) \tag{4.46}$$

Since T is also the terminal capacity matrix of tree t, the removal of the branch (x_1, x_2) from t partitions the node set V into the subset X and $\bar{X} = V - X$. By permuting the rows and the corresponding columns if necessary, the matrix T can be partitioned as

$$T = \begin{matrix} & X & \bar{X} \\ X & \begin{bmatrix} T_a & T_c \\ \bar{X} & T_c' & T_b \end{bmatrix} \end{matrix} \tag{4.47}$$

Since $(X, \bar{X}) = (x_1, x_2)$ is the minimum i–j cut for all $i \in X$ and $j \in \bar{X}$, every element in T_c is identical and is the smallest number in T. In addition, T_a and T_b are symmetric, the diagonal elements of which are all ∞. We complete the proof of necessity by induction over the number of tree branches removed from t. Assume that the above partitioning process is valid for all the resultant main submatrices T_k after the removal of the kth branch (x_k, x_{k+1}), $1 \leq k < n - 1$. We show that it remains to be true after the removal of the $(k + 1)$th branch (x_{k+1}, x_{k+2}).

Observe that after the removal of the kth branch (x_k, x_{k+1}) from t, the resulting subgraph is a forest containing $k + 1$ subtrees, some of which may consist only of an isolated node. Let t_k be the subtree corresponding to the submatrix T_k and let (x_{k+1}, x_{k+2}) be a branch of t_k. If V_k is the node set of t_k, then the removal of (x_{k+1}, x_{k+2}) from t_k partitions the node set V_k into two disjoint subsets X_k and $\bar{X}_k = V_k - X_k$ such that $c(X_k, \bar{X}_k) = c(x_{k+1}, x_{k+2})$ among all the remaining cut capacities $c(X_u, \bar{X}_u) = c(x_{u+1}, x_{u+2})$, $u = k, k + 1, \ldots, n - 2$. After possibly permuting rows and the corresponding columns, the submatrix T_k can further be partitioned in accordance with the node sets X_k and $\bar{X}_k$, as follows:

$$T_k = \begin{array}{c} \\ X_k \\ \bar{X}_k \end{array} \overset{\displaystyle \begin{array}{cc} X_k & \bar{X}_k \end{array}}{\left[\begin{array}{cc} T_{ka} & T_{kc} \\ T'_{kc} & T_{kb} \end{array} \right]} \tag{4.48}$$

where every element in T_{kc} is identical and is the smallest number in T_k. In addition, T_{ka} and T_{kb} are symmetric, the diagonal elements of which are all ∞. Thus, the principal partition is applicable to T and all of its resultant main submatrices.

Sufficiency. Suppose that the matrix T is principally partitioned as in (4.47), where every element T_c is identical and is the smallest number in T. Let G_a and G_b be two nets composed of the nodes corresponding to the node sets X and $\bar{X}$, respectively. The structures of the nets G_a and G_b have not been ascertained at this point. Let an edge (x_1, x_2) be connected between the nets G_a and G_b with x_1 in G_a and x_2 in G_b and assign the edge capacity $c(x_1, x_2)$ equal to the common element value in T_c, as depicted in Fig. 4.33.

Since by hypothesis the resultant main submatrices T_a and T_b can further

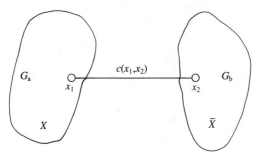

Fig. 4.33. The structures of the nets G_a and G_b connected by the an edge (x_1, x_2) having capacity equal to the common element value in T_c.

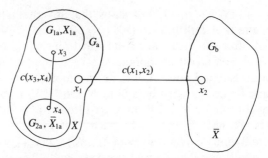

Fig. 4.34. The construction of the subnets G_{1a} and G_{2a}.

be principally partitioned, for our purposes we consider only T_a and write

$$T_a = \begin{matrix} & X_{1a} & \bar{X}_{1a} \\ X_{1a} & \begin{bmatrix} T_{1a} & T_{1c} \\ \bar{X}_{1a} & T'_{1c} & T_{1b} \end{bmatrix} \end{matrix} \tag{4.49}$$

where every element in T_{1c} is identical and is the smallest number in T_a. Let the node set X of G_a be partitioned in accordance with the node sets X_{1a} and $\bar{X}_{1a}$, respectively, and let the resulting subnets be denoted by G_{1a} and G_{2a}. We next connect an edge (x_3, x_4) between G_{1a} and G_{2a} with x_3 in G_{1a} and x_4 in G_{2a} and assign the edge capacity $c(x_3, x_4)$ equal to the common element value in T_{1c}, as depicted in Fig. 4.34. The process can be continued until every resultant main submatrix is composed only of one element ∞. The resulting net is a tree, the branch capacities of which are the terminal capacities of T. This completes the proof of the theorem.   Q.E.D.

The result was first given by Mayeda (1960). The proof of sufficiency also serves as a basis for realizing an undirected communication net having a preassigned realizable terminal capacity matrix.

Example 4.10

Consider the real symmetric matrix

$$T = \begin{matrix} & & 1 & 2 & 3 & 4 & 5 \\ & 1 & \begin{bmatrix} \infty & 5 & 5 & 5 & 6 \\ 2 & 5 & \infty & 8 & 11 & 5 \\ 3 & 5 & 8 & \infty & 8 & 5 \\ 4 & 5 & 11 & 8 & \infty & 5 \\ 5 & 6 & 5 & 5 & 5 & \infty \end{bmatrix} \end{matrix} \tag{4.50}$$

discussed in Example 4.9. After permuting the rows and the corresponding columns, the matrix T can be principally partitioned as

$$
T = \begin{array}{c} \\ 1 \\ 5 \\ 3 \\ 2 \\ 4 \end{array}
\begin{array}{ccccc}
1 & 5 & 3 & 2 & 4 \\
\end{array}
\left[
\begin{array}{cc:c:cc}
\infty & 6 & 5 & 5 & 5 \\
\hdashline
6 & \infty & 5 & 5 & 5 \\
\hdashline
5 & 5 & \infty & 8 & 8 \\
\hdashline
5 & 5 & 8 & \infty & 11 \\
5 & 5 & 8 & 11 & \infty
\end{array}
\right] \tag{4.51}
$$

Thus, according to Theorem 4.7, the matrix T is realizable because the principal partition is applicable to T and all of its resultant main submatrices

To construct an undirected communication net $G(V, E, c, f)$ having terminal capacity matrix T, we first partition the node set of G into the subsets $X = \{1, 5\}$ and $\bar{X} = \{2, 3, 4\}$ in accordance with the partition of (4.51), and then connect an edge (x_1, x_2) between the net G_a of node set X and the net G_b of node set $\bar{X}$ with capacity $c(x_1, x_2) = 5$, as depeicted in Fig. 4.35(a) in which we arbitrarily set $x_1 = 5$ and $x_2 = 4$. We next partition the node set $\bar{X}$ of G_b into the subsets $X_{1b} = \{3\}$ and $\bar{X}_{1b} = \{2, 4\}$ in accordance with the partition of (4.51) and then insert an edge (x_3, x_4) between the net G_{1b} of node set X_{1b} and the net G_{2b} of node set $\bar{X}_{1b}$ with capacity $c(x_3, x_4) = 8$, as shown in Fig. 4.35(b) where $x_3 = 3$ and x_4 is arbitrarily chosen to be node 4. Finally, we insert edges $(1, 5)$ and $(2, 4)$ of capacities $c(1, 5) = 6$ and $c(2, 4) = 11$ in the net of Fig. 4.35(b), and obtain the tree structure of Fig. 4.35(c). Had node 2 been chosen as x_4, we would have obtained the linear tree of Fig. 4.35(d).

4.5 SYNTHESIS OF A FLOW-EQUIVALENT TREE

In the foregoing, we demonstrated that every undirected communication net is flow-equivalent to a tree, and there are at most $n - 1$ numerically distinct terminal capacity values in an n-node net. Is there a better way of constructing an equivalent tree other than by first obtaining the terminal capacity matrix, and then principally partitioning it?

Gomory and Hu (1961) have answered the question decidedly in the affirmative. They devised a procedure that involves the successive solution of precisely $n - 1$ maximum flow problems. Moreover, many of these problems are solved in smaller and more simplified nets than the original one. In this section, we describe their procedure in detail.

To begin our discussion, let $G(V, E, c, f)$ be an n-node undirected communication net. Let us pick two arbitrary nodes x_1 and x_2 as the source and the sink, respectively, and apply any one of the algorithms discussed in

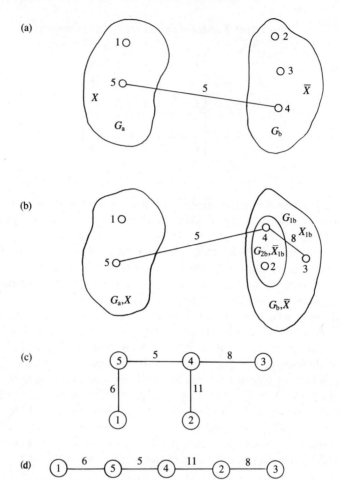

Fig. 4.35. The construction of an undirected communication net having terminal capacity matrix (4.51): (a) G_a and G_b; (b) G_a, G_{1b}, and G_{2b}; (c) tree structure; and (d) linear tree.

Chapter 3 to locate a minimum cut $(X, \bar{X})$ with $x_1 \in X$ and $x_2 \in \bar{X}$, as depicted in Fig. 4.36. Suppose that we wish to determine the maximum flow from x_3 to x_4 in G, where x_3 and x_4 both belong to the subnet G_1 or the subnet G_2 of Fig. 4.36. Without loss of generality, assume that both x_3 and x_4 are in X. We now show that in computing the maximum flow from x_3 to x_4, nodes in $\bar{X}$ can be "condensed" into a single node to which all the edges of the minimum cut $(X, \bar{X})$ are attached, as depicted in Fig. 4.37, where the parallel edges are combined and represented by a single edge, whose capacity is equal to the sum of the capacities of the individual edges. The resulting net is referred to as the *condensed net*.

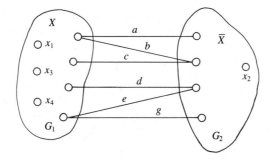

Fig. 4.36. A symbolic representation of a minimum cut.

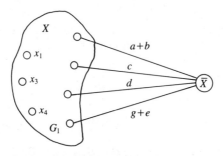

Fig. 4.37. The condensation of the subnet G_2 into a single node to which all the edges of the minimum cut in Fig. 4.36 are attached.

THEOREM 4.8

The maximum flow value between any two nodes of a condensed net is equal to the maximum flow value between the corresponding pair of nodes in the original net.

Proof. Let x_1 and x_2 be any two nodes of an undirected communication net $G(V, E, c, f)$, and let $(X, \bar{X})$ be a minimum x_1–x_2 cut in G. Let $G^*(V^*, E^*, c^*, f^*)$ be the condensed net obtained from G by condensing the nodes of $\bar{X}$ into a single node. Choose any two nodes x_3 and x_4 in G^* and let $(Y, \bar{Y})$ be a minimum x_3–x_4 cut in the original net G. Define

$$A = X \cap Y, \qquad \bar{A} = X \cap \bar{Y} \qquad (4.52a)$$

$$B = \bar{X} \cap Y, \qquad \bar{B} = \bar{X} \cap \bar{Y} \qquad (4.52b)$$

where $\bar{A}$ denotes the complement of A in X, and $\bar{B}$ denotes the complement of B in $\bar{X}$, as depicted symbolically in Fig. 4.38. Without loss of generality, we may assume that $x_1 \in A$, $x_3 \in A$ and $x_4 \in \bar{A}$. Two cases are distinguished.

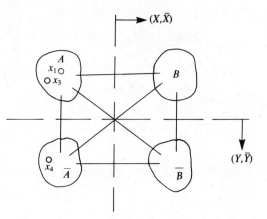

Fig. 4.38. A symbolic representation of an undirected communication net partitioned by a minimum x_1–x_2 cut and a minimum x_3–x_4 cut.

Case 1

$x_2 \in B$. Then we have the following expansions:

$$c(X, \bar{X}) = c(A \cup \bar{A}, B \cup \bar{B}) = c(A, B)$$
$$+ c(A, \bar{B}) + c(\bar{A}, B) + c(\bar{A}, \bar{B}) \qquad (4.53a)$$

$$c(Y, \bar{Y}) = c(A \cup B, \bar{A} \cup \bar{B}) = c(A, \bar{A})$$
$$+ c(A, \bar{B}) + c(B, \bar{A}) + c(B, \bar{B}) \qquad (4.53b)$$

Since from Fig. 4.38, $(A \cup B \cup \bar{B}, \bar{A})$ is an x_3–x_4 cut and since $(Y, \bar{Y})$ is a minimum x_3–x_4 cut, it follows that

$$c(Y, \bar{Y}) - c(A \cup B \cup \bar{B}, \bar{A}) = c(A, \bar{B}) + c(B, \bar{B}) - c(\bar{B}, \bar{A}) \leqq 0 \quad (4.54)$$

Likewise, since $(A \cup \bar{A} \cup \bar{B}, B)$ is an x_1–x_2 cut and since $(X, \bar{X})$ is a minimum x_1–x_2 cut, we have

$$c(X, \bar{X}) - c(A \cup \bar{A} \cup \bar{B}, B) = c(A, \bar{B}) + c(\bar{A}, \bar{B}) - c(\bar{B}, B) \leqq 0 \quad (4.55)$$

Adding (4.54) and (4.55) and invoking the fact that since G is undirected, $c(B, \bar{B}) = c(\bar{B}, B)$ and $c(\bar{A}, \bar{B}) = c(\bar{B}, \bar{A})$, we obtain

$$c(\bar{B}, A) = c(A, \bar{B}) \leqq 0 \qquad (4.56)$$

Because all the edge capacities of G are nonnegative, it follows that

$$c(\bar{B}, A) = c(A, \bar{B}) = 0 \qquad (4.57)$$

and the sum of (4.54) and (4.55) becomes

$$[c(Y, \bar{Y}) - c(A \cup B \cup \bar{B}, \bar{A})] + [c(X, \bar{X}) - c(A \cup \bar{A} \cup \bar{B}, B)] = 0 \quad (4.58)$$

This shows that if either term inside the brackets is negative, the other term will be positive, violating either (4.54) or (4.55). Therefore, they must be identically zero or

$$c(Y, \bar{Y}) = c(A \cup B \cup \bar{B}, \bar{A}) \qquad (4.59a)$$

$$c(X, \bar{X}) = c(A \cup \bar{A} \cup \bar{B}, B) \qquad (4.59b)$$

In other words, if $(Y, \bar{Y})$ is a minimum x_3–x_4 cut of G, then $(A \cup B \cup \bar{B}, \bar{A})$ is also a minimum x_3–x_4 cut of G. Consequently, condensing $\bar{X}$ to a single node does not affect the value of a maximum flow from x_3 to x_4, and we can use the condensed net G^* to calculate this maximum flow.

Case 2

$x_2 \in \bar{B}$. Following a similar argument as in Case 1, we can show that $(A, \bar{A} \cup B \cup \bar{B})$ is also a minimum x_3–x_4 cut of G, and condensing $\bar{X}$ to a single node does not affect the value of a maximum flow from x_3 to x_4. Thus, we again can use the condensed net G^* to calculate this maximum flow. This completes the proof of the theorem.   Q.E.D.

This theorem is fundamental to the Gomory–Hu procedure for constructing a flow-equivalent tree by solving precisely $n - 1$ maximum flow problems. Before we proceed to describe their algorithm, we mention that not only every undirected communication net is flow-equivalent to a tree, but is also equivalent to a path called a *linear tree*.

COROLLARY 4.3

Every undirected communication net is flow-equivalent to a linear tree.

Proof. Let

$$T = [\tau_{ij}] \qquad (4.60)$$

be the terminal capacity matrix of an n-node undirected communication net $G(V, E, c, f)$. Then according to Theorem 4.7, T can be principally partitioned until all the resultant main submatrices are of order 1. The principally partitioned matrix T is realizable as the linear tree shown in Fig. 4.39.   Q.E.D.

Fig. 4.39. A linear tree realization of a principally partitioned matrix.

This procedure in realizing a flow-equivalent tree from a given net G is ineffective in that in general it requires to solve $n(n-1)/2$ maximum flow problems in order to ascertain the terminal capacities τ_{ij} of T. In the following, we present the Gomory–Hu algorithm which reduces the number of maximum flow problems to be solved from $n(n-1)/2$ to $n-1$, a substantial saving in computation.

4.5.1 Gomory–Hu Algorithm

The algorithm was first proposed by Gomory and Hu (1961) for constructing a flow-equivalent tree by solving precisely $n-1$ maximum flow problems.

Gomory–Hu Algorithm

Step 1. Set $i = 1$. Select two nodes x_1 and y_1 arbitrarily in $G(V, E, c, f)$ and locate a minimum x_1–y_1 cut (X_1, X_2) where $X_2 = V - X_1$. Represent the node sets X_1 and X_2 by two nodes and connect them by an edge of capacity $c(X_1, X_2)$, as depicted in Fig. 4.40. The resulting tree is denoted by t_1.

Step 2. Select a node set X_k ($1 \leq k \leq i + 1$) of at least two elements from the sets $X_1, X_2, \ldots, X_{i+1}$, and pick two nodes y and z arbitrarily in X_k. Removing the node X_k and all of its incident edges from t_i results in a forest containing many subtrees. Construct a condensed net $G^*(V^*, E^*, c^*, f^*)$ from G by condensing the nodes contained in each subtree. A typical t_i is shown in Fig. 4.41.

Step 3. Locate a minimum y–z cut (Y, Z) of G^*, which partitions the node set X_k into X_{k1} and X_{k2} with $y \in X_{k1}$ and $z \in X_{k2}$. Connect X_{k1} and X_{k2} by an edge having capacity $c^*(Y, Z)$. The other nodes of the tree t_i are attached to X_{k1} if they are in the X_{k1} part of the cut (Y, Z), and to X_{k2} otherwise. The new tree is denoted by t_{i+1}, as indicated in Fig. 4.42.

Step 4. Set $X_k = X_{k1}$ and $X_{i+2} = X_{k2}$. Set $i = i + 1$.

Step 5. If $i = n - 1$, stop. Otherwise, return to Step 2.

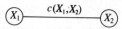

Fig. 4.40. A symbolic representation of the node sets X_1 and X_2 connected by an edge of capacity $c(X_1, X_2)$.

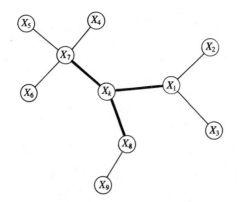

Fig. 4.41. The construction of a cut-tree by the Gomory–Hu algorithm.

The beauty of the algorithm is that not only is a flow-equivalent tree constructed with a minimum effort by solving precisely $n - 1$ maximum flow problems, but also it is the kind of tree whose branches represent the relevant $n - 1$ minimum cuts in the original net. It is not just any equivalent tree; it is the tree structure corresponding precisely to the multi-terminal cut structure of the net. Such a tree is referred to as a *cut-tree* of the communication net. Notice that there are usually many flow-equivalent trees to a net. For example, as indicated in Corollary 4.3, every undirected communication net is equivalent to a linear tree. The maximum tree of the weighted complete graph constructed from the terminal capacity matrix of the net is another flow-equivalent tree. However, before we show that the tree constructed by the above algorithm is indeed an equivalent tree of the original net, we illustrate the procedure by the following examples, postponing the proof to the following section.

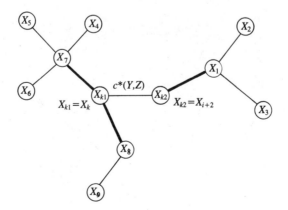

Fig. 4.42. A new tree t_{i+1} obtained from the tree t_i of Fig. 4.41.

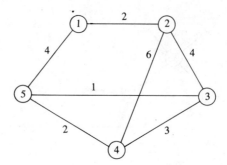

Fig. 4.43. An undirected communication net used to illustrate the construction of a cut-tree.

Example 4.11

Consider the undirected communication net $G(V, E, c, f)$ of Fig. 4.30 which is redrawn in Fig. 4.43. We follow the five steps of the algorithm to construct a cut-tree of G, as follows:

Step 1. Set $i = 1$. Arbitrarily select nodes 1 and 3 in G, and locate a minimum 1–3 cut $(X_1, X_2) = (\{1, 5\}, \{2, 3, 4\})$. Construct t_1 as shown in Fig. 4.44(a).

Step 2. Pick nodes 1 and 5 in $X_1 = \{1, 5\}$. Removing the node X_1 and its incident edge from t_1 results in a forest containing a subtree of an isolated node $X_2 = \{2, 3, 4\}$. Construct a condensed net $G^*(V^*, E^*, c^*, f^*)$ from G by condensing the nodes 2, 3 and 4 in G, as shown in Fig. 4.44(b).

Step 3. Locate a minimum 1–5 cut $(Y, Z) = (1, \{5, X_2\})$ in G^* with $c^*(Y, Z) = 6$, and construct t_2 as in Fig. 4.44(c).

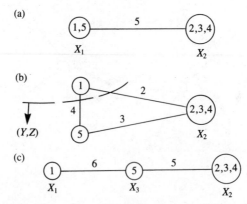

Fig. 4.44. The construction of a cut-tree for the net of Fig. 4.43: (a) t_1; (b) G^*; (c) t_2.

Step 4. Set $i = 2$, $X_1 = \{1\}$, and $X_3 = \{5\}$.

Step 5. Return to Step 2.

Step 2. Pick nodes 2 and 3 in $X_2 = \{2, 3, 4\}$. Removing node X_2 and its incident edge from t_2 results in a forest containing the subtree consisting only of the edge $(1, 5)$ in t_2. Construct a condensed net G^* from G by condensing the nodes 1 and 5 in G, as in Fig. 4.45(a).

Step 3. Locate a minimum 2–3 cut $(Y, Z) = (\{W_1, 2, 4\}, 3)$ in G^* with $c^*(Y, Z) = 8$, where W_1 is the combined node of 1 and 5, and construct t_3 as in Fig. 4.45(b).

Step 4. Set $i = 3$, $X_2 = \{2, 4\}$, and $X_4 = \{3\}$.

Step 5. Return to Step 2.

Step 2. Pick nodes 2 and 4 in $X_2 = \{2, 4\}$. Removing node X_2 and its incident edges from t_3 results in a forest containing the subtrees $(1, 5)$ and an isolated node 3. Construct a condensed net G^* from G by condensing nodes 1 and 5 in G, as shown in Fig. 4.46(a).

Step 3. Locate a minimum 2–4 cut $(Y, Z) = (\{W_1, 2, 3\}, 4)$ in G^* with $c^*(Y, Z) = 11$, where W_1 is the combined node of 1 and 5, and construct t_4 as in Fig. 4.46(b).

Step 4. Set $i = 4$, $X_2 = \{2\}$, and $X_5 = \{4\}$.

Step 5. Stop.

The desired cut-tree is shown in Fig. 4.46(b). This cut-tree is more than just another equivalent tree; its structure corresponds precisely to the multi-terminal cut structure of G. In fact, the capacity of a branch is equal to the capacity of a minimum cut separating the two endpoints of the branch in the original net. In Fig. 4.46(b), the removal of the branch $(2, 5)$ from t_4 partitions the node set V of G into the subsets $X = \{1, 5\}$ and $\bar{X} = \{2, 3, 4\}$. Then the cut $(X, \bar{X}) = (\{1, 5\}, \{2, 3, 4\})$ is precisely a minimum 2–5 cut in G. Likewise, the removal of the branch $(2, 4)$ from t_4 partitions the node set V into the subsets $Y = \{1, 2, 3, 5\}$ and $\bar{Y} = \{4\}$. Then $(Y, \bar{Y}) = (\{1, 2, 3, 5\}, 4)$ is precisely a minimum 2–4 cut in G.

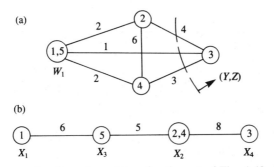

Fig. 4.45. The construction of a cut-tree for the net of Fig. 4.43: (a) G^*; (b) t_3.

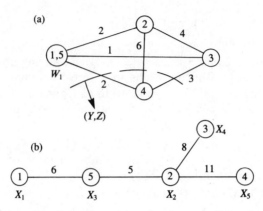

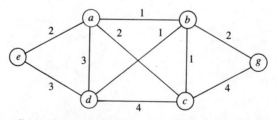

Fig. 4.46. The construction of a cut-tree for the net of Fig. 4.43: (a) G^*; (b) t_4.

Example 4.12

We use the Gomory–Hu algorithm to construct a cut-tree for the undirected communication net $G(V, E, c, f)$ of Fig. 4.47, as follows:

Step 1. Set $i = 1$. Select nodes e and g, and locate a minimum e–g cut $(X_1, X_2) = (e, \{a, b, c, d, g\})$ having capacity 5. Construct tree t_1 as shown in Fig. 4.48(a).

Step 2. Select nodes a and b in X_2 and construct $G^* = G$.

Step 3. Locate a minimum a–b cut $(Y, Z) = (b, \{a, c, d, e, g\})$ with $c^*(Y, Z) = 5$, and construct t_2 as in Fig. 4.48(b).

Step 4. Set $i = 2$, $X_2 = \{a, c, d, g\}$, and $X_3 = \{b\}$.

Step 5. Return to Step 2.

Step 2. Select nodes a and c in X_2 and construct $G^* = G$.

Step 3. Locate a minimum a–c cut $(Y, Z) = (\{a, d, e\}, \{b, c, g\})$ with $c^*(Y, Z) = 8$, and construct t_3 as in Fig. 4.48(c).

Step 4. Set $i = 3$, $X_2 = \{a, d\}$, and $X_4 = \{c, g\}$.

Step 5. Return to Step 2.

Fig. 4.47. An undirected communication net used to illustrate the construction of a cut-tree by the Gomory–Hu algorithm.

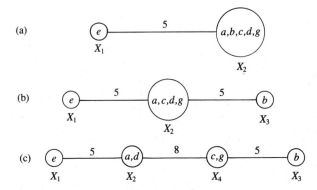

Fig. 4.48. The construction of a cut-tree for the net of Fig. 4.47: (a) t_1; (b) t_2; (c) t_3.

Step 2. Select nodes a and d in X_2 and construct G^* as shown in Fig. 4.49(a).

Step 3. Locate a minimum a–d cut $(Y, Z) = (a, \{d, e, W_1\})$ in G^* with $c^*(Y, Z) = 8$, and construct t_4 as in Fig. 4.49(b), where W_1 is the combined node of b, c and g.

Step 4. Set $i = 4$, $X_2 = \{d\}$, and $X_5 = \{a\}$.

Step 5. Return to Step 2.

Step 2. Select nodes c and g in X_4 and construct G^* as in Fig. 4.50(a).

Step 3. Locate a minimum c–g cut $(Y, Z) = (g, \{b, c, W_2\})$ in G^* with $c^*(Y, Z) = 6$, and construct t_5 as in Fig. 4.50(b), where W_2 is the combined node of a, d and e.

Step 4. Set $i = 5$, $X_4 = \{g\}$, and $X_6 = \{c\}$.

Step 5. Stop.

The desired flow-equivalent cut-tree t_5 is shown in Fig. 4.50(b). If we remove branch (c, d) from t_5, the node set V of G is partitioned into the subsets $X = \{b, c, g\}$ and $\bar{X} = \{a, d, e\}$. Then the cut $(X, \bar{X}) =$

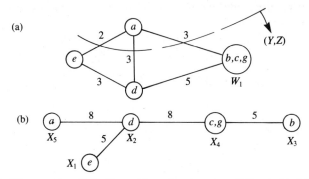

Fig. 4.49. The construction of a cut-tree for the net of Fig. 4.47: (a) G^*; (b) t_4.

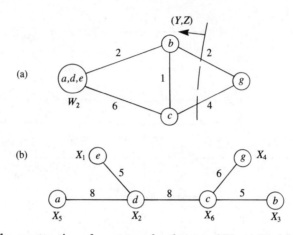

Fig. 4.50. The construction of a cut-tree for the net of Fig. 4.47: (a) G^*; (b) t_5.

$(\{b, c, g\}, \{a, d, e\})$ is precisely a minimum c–d cut in G. This is similarly valid for other branches of t_5. Hence, the structure corresponds precisely to the multi-terminal cut structure of G. The terminal capacity matrix T of the cut-tree t_5 of Fig. 4.50(b) is found to be

$$
T = \begin{array}{c@{\,}c}
 & \begin{array}{cccccc} a & b & c & d & e & g \end{array} \\
\begin{array}{c} a \\ b \\ c \\ d \\ e \\ g \end{array} &
\left[\begin{array}{cccccc}
\infty & 5 & 8 & 8 & 5 & 6 \\
5 & \infty & 5 & 5 & 5 & 5 \\
8 & 5 & \infty & 8 & 5 & 6 \\
8 & 5 & 8 & \infty & 5 & 6 \\
5 & 5 & 5 & 5 & \infty & 5 \\
6 & 5 & 6 & 6 & 5 & \infty
\end{array}\right]
\end{array}
\tag{4.61}
$$

Rearranging the rows and columns yields the principally partitioned terminal capacity matrix:

$$
T = [\tau_{ij}] = \begin{array}{c@{\,}c}
 & \begin{array}{cccccc} b & e & g & a & c & d \end{array} \\
\begin{array}{c} b \\ e \\ g \\ a \\ c \\ d \end{array} &
\left[\begin{array}{cc:c:cc:c}
\infty & 5 & 5 & 5 & 5 & 5 \\ \hdashline
5 & \infty & 5 & 5 & 5 & 5 \\ \hline
5 & 5 & \infty & 6 & 6 & 6 \\ \hdashline
5 & 5 & 6 & \infty & 8 & 8 \\
5 & 5 & 6 & 8 & \infty & 8 \\ \hdashline
5 & 5 & 6 & 8 & 8 & \infty
\end{array}\right]
\end{array}
\tag{4.62}
$$

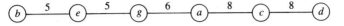

Fig. 4.51. A linear tree realization of the terminal capacity matrix (4.62).

This matrix can be realized by the linear tree of Fig. 4.51, where the branch capacities of the path from node b to node d correspond to the up-diagonal elements $\tau_{12} = 5$, $\tau_{23} = 5$, $\tau_{34} = 6$, $\tau_{45} = 8$, and $\tau_{56} = 8$ of T. This linear tree is not a cut-tree. For example, if we remove branch (g, a) from this linear tree, the node set V of G is partitioned into the subsets $X = \{b, e, g\}$ and $\bar{X} = \{a, c, d\}$. However, the cut $(X, \bar{X}) = (\{b, e, g\}, \{a, c, d\})$ is not a minimum a–g cut in G of Fig. 4.47, because its capacity is 12 whereas the capacity of a minimum a–g cut is 6.

Example 4.13

We use the Gomory–Hu algorithm to construct a cut-tree for the 14-node undirected communication net $G(V, E, c, f)$ of Fig. 4.52, as follows:

Step 1. Set $i = 1$. Select arbitrarily nodes 6 and 10 and locate a minimum 6–10 cut (X_1, X_2) with

$$X_1 = \{1, 5, 8, 9, 10, 12, 13, 14\} \qquad (4.63a)$$

$$X_2 = \{2, 3, 4, 6, 7, 11\} \qquad (4.63b)$$

as indicated in Fig. 4.52, where $c(X_1, X_2) = 19$. Construct the tree t_1 as in Fig. 4.53(a).

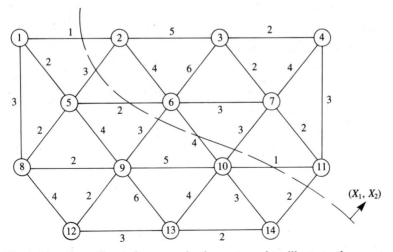

Fig. 4.52. A 14-node undirected communication net used to illustrate the construction of a cut-tree by the Gomory–Hu algorithm.

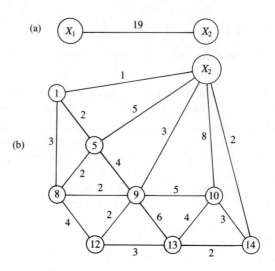

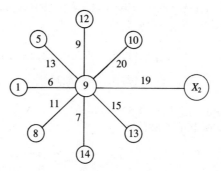

Fig. 4.53. The construction of a cut-tree for the net of Fig. 4.52: (a) t_1; (b) G_1^*.

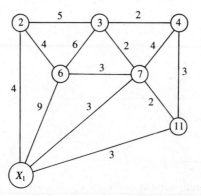

Fig. 4.54. The resulting tree t_8 after the first seven iterations of the Gomory–Hu algorithm applied to the net of Fig. 4.52.

Fig. 4.55. The condensed net G_2^* used in the construction of a cut-tree for the net of Fig. 4.52 by the Gomory–Hu algorithm.

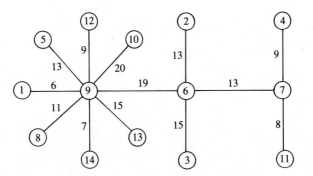

Fig. 4.56. A cut-tree t_{13} for the net of Fig. 4.52 constructed by the Gomory–Hu algorithm.

By repeatedly selecting node pairs in X_1, we can use the condensed net G_1^* of Fig. 4.53(b) for the first seven iterations of Steps 2–5. This results in the tree t_8 shown in Fig. 4.54. Likewise, for the next five iterations, we can use the condensed net G_2^* of Fig. 4.55 for all the node pairs in X_2, resulting in the desired cut-tree t_{13} of Fig. 4.56.

Finally, from the cut-tree t_{13} we compute the terminal capacity matrix T of G, and obtain

$$
T =
\begin{array}{c|cccccccccccccc}
 & 1 & 2 & 3 & 4 & 5 & 6 & 7 & 8 & 9 & 10 & 11 & 12 & 13 & 14 \\
\hline
1 & \infty & 6 & 6 & 6 & 6 & 6 & 6 & 6 & 6 & 6 & 6 & 6 & 6 & 6 \\
2 & 6 & \infty & 13 & 9 & 13 & 13 & 13 & 11 & 13 & 13 & 8 & 9 & 13 & 7 \\
3 & 6 & 13 & \infty & 9 & 13 & 15 & 13 & 11 & 15 & 15 & 8 & 9 & 15 & 7 \\
4 & 6 & 9 & 9 & \infty & 9 & 9 & 9 & 9 & 9 & 9 & 8 & 9 & 9 & 7 \\
5 & 6 & 13 & 13 & 9 & \infty & 13 & 13 & 11 & 13 & 13 & 8 & 9 & 13 & 7 \\
6 & 6 & 13 & 15 & 9 & 13 & \infty & 13 & 11 & 19 & 19 & 8 & 9 & 15 & 7 \\
7 & 6 & 13 & 13 & 9 & 13 & 13 & \infty & 11 & 13 & 13 & 8 & 9 & 13 & 7 \\
8 & 6 & 11 & 11 & 9 & 11 & 11 & 11 & \infty & 11 & 11 & 8 & 9 & 11 & 7 \\
9 & 6 & 13 & 15 & 9 & 13 & 19 & 13 & 11 & \infty & 20 & 8 & 9 & 15 & 7 \\
10 & 6 & 13 & 15 & 9 & 13 & 19 & 13 & 11 & 20 & \infty & 8 & 9 & 15 & 7 \\
11 & 6 & 8 & 8 & 8 & 8 & 8 & 8 & 8 & 8 & 8 & \infty & 8 & 8 & 7 \\
12 & 6 & 9 & 9 & 9 & 9 & 9 & 9 & 9 & 9 & 9 & 8 & \infty & 9 & 7 \\
13 & 6 & 13 & 15 & 9 & 13 & 15 & 13 & 11 & 15 & 15 & 8 & 9 & \infty & 7 \\
14 & 6 & 7 & 7 & 7 & 7 & 7 & 7 & 7 & 7 & 7 & 7 & 7 & 7 & \infty \\
\end{array}
$$

$$(4.64)$$

After permuting the rows and the corresponding columns, the terminal capacity matrix T of (4.64) can be principally partitioned as

$$
T =
\begin{array}{c|cccccccccccccc}
 & 1 & 14 & 11 & 4 & 12 & 8 & 2 & 5 & 7 & 3 & 13 & 6 & 9 & 10 \\
\hline
1 & \infty & 6 & 6 & 6 & 6 & 6 & 6 & 6 & 6 & 6 & 6 & 6 & 6 & 6 \\
14 & 6 & \infty & 7 & 7 & 7 & 7 & 7 & 7 & 7 & 7 & 7 & 7 & 7 & 7 \\
11 & 6 & 7 & \infty & 8 & 8 & 8 & 8 & 8 & 8 & 8 & 8 & 8 & 8 & 8 \\
4 & 6 & 7 & 8 & \infty & 9 & 9 & 9 & 9 & 9 & 9 & 9 & 9 & 9 & 9 \\
12 & 6 & 7 & 8 & 9 & \infty & 9 & 9 & 9 & 9 & 9 & 9 & 9 & 9 & 9 \\
8 & 6 & 7 & 8 & 9 & 9 & \infty & 11 & 11 & 11 & 11 & 11 & 11 & 11 & 11 \\
2 & 6 & 7 & 8 & 9 & 9 & 11 & \infty & 13 & 13 & 13 & 13 & 13 & 13 & 13 \\
5 & 6 & 7 & 8 & 9 & 9 & 11 & 13 & \infty & 13 & 13 & 13 & 13 & 13 & 13 \\
7 & 6 & 7 & 8 & 9 & 9 & 11 & 13 & 13 & \infty & 13 & 13 & 13 & 13 & 13 \\
3 & 6 & 7 & 8 & 9 & 9 & 11 & 13 & 13 & 13 & \infty & 15 & 15 & 15 & 15 \\
13 & 6 & 7 & 8 & 9 & 9 & 11 & 13 & 13 & 13 & 15 & \infty & 15 & 15 & 15 \\
6 & 6 & 7 & 8 & 9 & 9 & 11 & 13 & 13 & 13 & 15 & 15 & \infty & 19 & 19 \\
9 & 6 & 7 & 8 & 9 & 9 & 11 & 13 & 13 & 13 & 15 & 15 & 19 & \infty & 20 \\
10 & 6 & 7 & 8 & 9 & 9 & 11 & 13 & 13 & 13 & 15 & 15 & 19 & 20 & \infty
\end{array}
$$

$$(4.65)$$

This matrix can be realized by the linear tree of Fig. 4.57, the branch capacities of which from node 1 to node 10 along the tree path correspond to its up-diagonal elements $\tau_{12} = 6$, $\tau_{23} = 7$, $\tau_{34} = 8$, $\tau_{45} = 9$, $\tau_{56} = 9$, $\tau_{67} = 11$, $\tau_{78} = 13$, $\tau_{89} = 13$, $\tau_{9,10} = 13$, $\tau_{10,11} = 15$, $\tau_{11,12} = 15$, $\tau_{12,13} = 19$, and $\tau_{13,14} = 20$, respectively. This tree, however, is not a cut-tree.

4.5.2 Proof of the Gomory–Hu Algorithm

In this section, we show that the Gomory–Hu algorithm indeed generates a cut-tree that is flow-equivalent to the undirected communication net

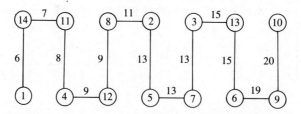

Fig. 4.57. A linear tree realization of the net of Fig. 4.52.

$G(V, E, c, f)$. Consider any two nodes x and y. Let

$$P_{xy} = (x, x_1)(x_1, x_2) \ldots (x_r, y) \tag{4.66}$$

be the unique path connecting the nodes x and y in the final tree t. We show that the terminal capacity τ_{xy} between x and y in G is equal to

$$\tau_{xy} = \min [c_t(x, x_1), c_t(x_1, x_2), \ldots, c_t(x_r, y)] \tag{4.67}$$

where c_t is the capacity function of the tree t. To this end, we first demonstrate that the inequality

$$\tau_{xy} \leqq \min [c_t(x, x_1), c_t(x_1, x_2), \ldots, c_t(x_r, y)] \tag{4.68}$$

holds. Recall that the removal of any branch (u, v) of t from t results in a forest of two subtrees that partitions the node set V of G into two subsets X and $\bar{X} = V - X$. The corresponding cut $(X, \bar{X})$ in G separates the nodes u and v with $c(X, \bar{X}) = c_t(u, v)$, and therefore is a u–v cut. That this is the case follows immediately from the construction, where each new tree produced in the construction represents cuts in this way provided that the old tree does. This implies that the terminal capacity τ_{xy} of G cannot exceed any of those x–y cuts corresponding to the tree branches $(x, x_1), (x_1, x_2), \ldots, (x_r, y)$, and (4.68) follows.

We next show that the reverse inequality

$$\tau_{xy} \geqq \min [c_t(x, x_1), c_t(x_1, x_2), \ldots, c_t(x_r, y)] \tag{4.69}$$

also holds. This is accomplished by showing that, at any stage of the construction, if an edge of capacity c_1 connects nodes X and Y in the tree, then there is an x in X and a y in Y such that $\tau_{xy} = c_1$. We prove this by induction over the number of stages. This is certainly true at the first stage of Step 1. We show that this property is maintained. Suppose that a node Y is about to be split with node X attached to it by an edge of capacity c_1. By induction hypothesis there is an x in X and a y in Y in the tree with $c_1 = \tau_{xy}$. Select nodes u and v arbitrarily in Y in Step 2 for locating a minimum u–v cut in G^* of cut capacity c_2 in Step 3. This u–v cut partitions the node set Y into the subsets Y_1 and Y_2 with u in Y_1 and v in Y_2. Without loss of generality, we may assume that X is connected to node Y_1 in the new tree as depicted symbolically in Fig. 4.58, where u and v provide the two nodes such that $\tau_{uv} = c_2$. As to the old edge of capacity c_1, two cases are possible. If y is in Y_1, then x and y provide the two nodes. If y is in Y_2, we show that nodes u and x provide the required nodes. Thus, we assume that y is in Y_2.

Observe that the removal of the cut of capacity c_2 from G separates the net into two parts with nodes u and x in one part and nodes v and y in the other. By Theorem 4.8, we can condense the nodes in Y_2 in G without

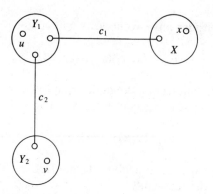

Fig. 4.58. A symbolic representation showing that X is connected to node Y_1 in the new tree.

affecting τ_{xu}. This is equivalent to saying that τ_{xu} remains unaffected if all pairs of nodes of Y_2 are connected by edges of infinite capacity. Let the resulting net be denoted by $G'(V, E', c', f')$ with τ'_{ij} representing the terminal capacity between nodes i and j. Then we have

$$\tau'_{xu} = \tau_{xu} \tag{4.70a}$$

$$\tau'_{xy} \geqq \tau_{xy} = c_1 \tag{4.70b}$$

$$\tau'_{uv} \geqq \tau_{uv} = c_2 \tag{4.70c}$$

$$\tau'_{yv} = \infty \tag{4.70d}$$

Appealing to (4.35) yields

$$\tau'_{xu} \geqq \min\,[\tau'_{xy},\, \tau'_{yv},\, \tau'_{vu}] = \min\,[\tau'_{xy},\, \tau'_{uv}] \tag{4.71}$$

showing that

$$\tau_{xu} = \tau'_{xu} \geqq \min\,[\tau'_{xy},\, \tau'_{uv}] \geqq \min\,[c_1, c_2] \tag{4.72}$$

Since the cut of capacity c_2 also separates nodes x and y, it follows that

$$c_2 \geqq c_1 \tag{4.73}$$

Hence, we have

$$\tau_{xu} \geqq c_1 \tag{4.74}$$

Because the cut of capacity c_1 is also a u–x cut, it is necessary that

$$\tau_{xu} = c_1 \tag{4.75}$$

and u and x provide the required nodes.

In other words, the branch capacities in the final tree t actually represent the terminal capacities between adjacent nodes of t. Applying (4.35) to the unique tree path P_{xy} of (4.66) establishes the inequality (4.69). Using this in conjunction with (4.68), we obtain the equality of (4.67). This completes the proof that the Gomory–Hu algorithm indeed produces a cut-tree that is flow-equivalent to the original net.

4.6 SYNTHESIS OF OPTIMUM UNDIRECTED COMMUNICATION NETS

In the foregoing, we have discussed ways to compute the maximum flows or the terminal capacities between all pairs of nodes in an undirected communication net. In the present section, we study the inverse problem of synthesizing a net having a preassigned lower bound on the maximum flow value between every pair of nodes. We certainly can construct a net, the flow values of which will exceed the lower bounds, simply by assigning arbitrarily large edge capacities between all pairs of nodes. Our objective here is to construct a net with maximum flow values exceeding all the lower bounds and with a minimum total edge capacity.

Let

$$R = [r_{ij}] \qquad (4.76)$$

where $r_{ii} = \infty$, be a symmetric matrix of nonnegative real elements of order n called the *requirement matrix*, and let

$$T = [\tau_{ij}] \qquad (4.77)$$

be the terminal capacity matrix of an n-node undirected communication net $G(V, E, c, f)$. We shall call the net G *feasible* if for $i \neq j$

$$\tau_{ij} \geq r_{ij}, \qquad i, j = 1, 2, \dots, n \qquad (4.78)$$

The problem is to construct a feasible net $G(V, E, c, f)$ that minimizes the total edge capacity of the net:

$$c(G) = \min_i c_i(G_i) \qquad (4.79)$$

where $G_i(V, E_i, c_i, f_i)$ is a feasible net.

DEFINITION 4.12

Requirement Graph. Given a symmetric $n \times n$ requirement matrix $R = [r_{ij}]$, the *requirement graph* of R is the n-node weighted complete graph $G_R(V, E, r)$ with $r(i, j) = r_{ij}$ for each edge $(i, j) \in E$, where the *requirement function* r is from E to the elements of R.

DEFINITION 4.13

Dominant Requirement Tree. If the weights of the edges of a requirement graph are considered as the lengths of the edges, then a *dominant requirement tree* is a maximum tree in the requirement graph.

Given the requirement matrix

$$
R = \begin{array}{c} \\ 1 \\ 2 \\ 3 \\ 4 \\ 5 \\ 6 \end{array}
\begin{array}{c} \begin{array}{cccccc} 1 & 2 & 3 & 4 & 5 & 6 \end{array} \\
\begin{bmatrix}
\infty & 1 & 9 & 12 & 8 & 7 \\
1 & \infty & 2 & 4 & 11 & 15 \\
9 & 2 & \infty & 3 & 14 & 10 \\
12 & 4 & 3 & \infty & 5 & 13 \\
8 & 11 & 14 & 5 & \infty & 6 \\
7 & 15 & 10 & 13 & 6 & \infty
\end{bmatrix} \end{array}
\tag{4.80}
$$

of order 6, its requirement graph G_R is the 6-node complete graph G_R of Fig. 4.59. Using any of the algorithms developed in Section 4.3, a maximum tree t_m of G_R is produced in Fig. 4.60. This maximum tree t_m is a dominant requirement tree of G_R.

The importance of the dominant requirement tree is enhanced considerably by the following theorem.

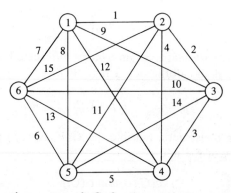

Fig. 4.59. The requirement graph G_R for the requirement matrix (4.80).

THEOREM 4.9

The necessary and sufficient condition that an undirected communication net be feasible is that (4.78) hold for all the branches of a dominant requirement tree.

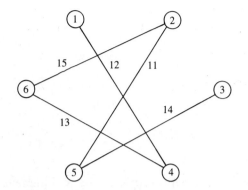

Fig. 4.60. A maximum tree for the requirement graph of Fig. 4.59.

Proof. The necessity is obvious because the conditions (4.78) for all the branches of a dominant requirement tree are a subset of all the inequalities given in (4.78).

To establish sufficiency, we show that if

$$\tau_{ij} \geq r_{ij} = r(i, j) \tag{4.81}$$

holds for each branch (i, j) of a dominant requirement tree t_m, where r is the requirement function of the communication net $G(V, E, r)$, then (4.81) holds for all i and j. Let (x, y) be a chord of the cotree with respect to the tree t_m, and let

$$P_{xy} = (x, x_1)(x_1, x_2) \ldots (x_k, y) \tag{4.82}$$

be the unique path in t_m connecting between nodes x and y. Then from (4.40) and (4.81) we have

$$\tau_{xy} \geq \min \left[\tau_{xx_1}, \tau_{x_1x_2}, \ldots, \tau_{x_ky} \right]$$
$$\geq \min \left[r_{xx_1}, r_{x_1x_2}, \ldots, r_{x_ky} \right] \tag{4.83}$$

Since the requirements r_{ij} are considered as the lengths of the edges in the requirement graph G_R and since t_m is a maximum tree, from Theorem 4.4 we have

$$r_{xy} \leq \min \left[r_{xx_1}, r_{x_1x_2}, \ldots, r_{x_ky} \right] \tag{4.84}$$

which when combined with (4.83) gives

$$\tau_{xy} \geq r_{xy} \tag{4.85}$$

This completes the proof of the theorem.   Q.E.D.

Therefore, there is no need to consider all the requirements. The requirements associated with the branches of a dominant requirement tree are sufficient. These tree branch requirements are called the *dominant requirements*.

Given an undirected communication net $G(V, E, c, f)$, the total edge capacity is the sum of all edge capacities, or

$$c(G) = \tfrac{1}{2} \sum_{\substack{i \\ i \neq j}} \sum_{\substack{j \\ i \neq j}} c(i, j) \tag{4.86}$$

Assume that G is feasible with respect to the requirement matrix $\boldsymbol{R} = [r_{ij}]$. For any node i of G, define

$$u_i = \max_{\substack{j \\ j \neq i}} r_{ij} \tag{4.87}$$

In other words, u_i is the largest flow requirement among those involving the node i. Thus, in any feasible net the sum of capacities of edges incident at a node i must be at least as large as u_i to allow flow out of node i, or

$$\sum_j c(i, j) \geqq u_i \tag{4.88}$$

Because an edge in G is counted once in each of its two endpoints, a lower bound to the total edge capacity $c(G)$ is then

$$C_\alpha = \tfrac{1}{2} \sum_i u_i \leqq c(G) \tag{4.89}$$

We now proceed to describe a procedure that produces a feasible net G such that (4.89) is satisfied with the equality sign. The resulting net is therefore optimum in the sense that its total capacity is minimum among all the feasible realizations. The technique was first proposed by Gomory and Hu (1961).

Recall that from Theorem 4.9 it is sufficient to consider only the dominant requirements. Therefore, in selecting u_i in (4.87) we need consider only those branches r_{ij} of the dominant requirement tree t_m that are incident at node i. Now suppose that the requirements for the branches of t_m are replaced by a new set of requirements r'_{ij}. For this new set, there corresponds to a new lower bound

$$C'_\alpha = \tfrac{1}{2} \sum_i u'_i \tag{4.90}$$

where

$$u'_i = \max_{\substack{j \\ j \neq i}} r'_{ij} \tag{4.91}$$

Finally, if the branches of t_m are assigned the requirements

$$r''_{ij} = r_{ij} + r'_{ij}, \qquad (i, j) \in t_m \tag{4.92}$$

the corresponding lower bound becomes

$$C''_\alpha = \tfrac{1}{2} \sum_i u''_i \tag{4.93}$$

where

$$u''_i = \max_{\substack{j \\ j \neq i}} r''_{ij} \tag{4.94}$$

Since u_i and u'_i may not be associated with the same branch, we have in general

$$u''_i \leq u_i + u'_i \tag{4.95}$$

or

$$C''_\alpha \leq C_\alpha + C'_\alpha \tag{4.96}$$

However, if r_{ij} or r'_{ij} are *uniform requirement* with $r_{ij} = r_0$ or $r'_{ij} = r'_0$ for all r_{ij} or r'_{ij} in t_m, then

$$C''_\alpha = C_\alpha + C'_\alpha \tag{4.97}$$

Let $G(V, E, c, f)$ and $G'(V', E', c', f')$ be two n-node undirected communication nets, and let $G''(V'', E'', c'', f'')$ be the net obtained by superimposing the nets G and G'. Then $V = V' = V''$, $E'' = E \cup E'$ and

$$c''(i, j) = c(i, j) + c'(i, j), \qquad (i, j) \in E'' \tag{4.98}$$

The terminal capacity τ''_{ij} between nodes i and j in G'' and those τ_{ij} and τ'_{ij} in G and G' are related by the inequality

$$\tau''_{ij} \geq \tau_{ij} + \tau'_{ij} \tag{4.99}$$

The Gomory–Hu procedure of synthesis uses the dominant requirement tree and then decomposes it into a sum of "uniform" requirement forests. Each such uniform requirement forest is synthesized at its total lower bound capacity. The resulting net satisfies the original flow requirements in view of (4.99) and is of minimum total edge capacity because of (4.97).

4.6.1 Gomory–Hu Procedure

The procedure for constructing a feasible net with minimum total edge capacity was first proposed by Gomory and Hu (1961). In the following, we describe their procedure in detail.

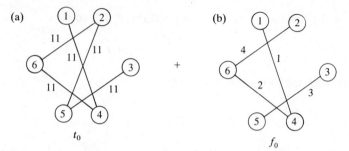

Fig. 4.61. The decomposition of the dominant requirement tree of Fig. 4.60 into the sum of a uniform dominant requirement tree t_0 (a) and a requirement forest f_0 (b).

Let t_m be the dominant requirement tree that we wish to satisfy. Let r_{min} be the smallest requirement associated with the branches of t_m. For each branch (i, j) in t_m with requirement r_{ij}, write

$$r_{ij} = r_{min} + (r_{ij} - r_{min}) \qquad (4.100)$$

The original requirement tree t_m can then be considered as the superposition of a uniform dominant requirement tree t_0 with uniform requirements r_{min} and a requirement forest f_0 with requirements $r_{ij} - r_{min}$. For example, the dominant requirement tree t_m of Fig. 4.60 can be decomposed into the sum of a uniform dominant requirement tree t_0 with uniform requirements $r_{min} = 11$ and a requirement forest f_0, as shown in Fig. 4.61. Clearly, the procedure can then further be applied to each subtree of the remaining

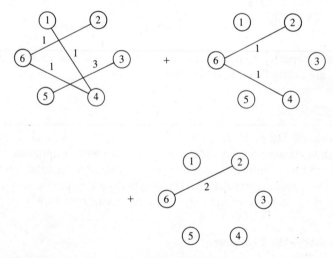

Fig. 4.62. The decomposition of the forest f_0 into the sum of uniform requirement subtrees.

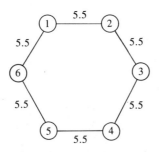

Fig. 4.63. The synthesis of the uniform dominant requirement tree t_0 of Fig. 4.61(a).

requirement forest f_0 until t_m has been expressed as a sum of uniform requirement subtrees t_α. In Fig. 4.61, the forest can further be decomposed into those shown in Fig. 4.62.

The uniform dominant requirement tree t_0 in the decomposition is then synthesized by a circuit through its nodes in any order, each of whose edges has capacity equal to $\frac{1}{2}r_{min}$, half the uniform requirement. Clearly, such a circuit will satisfy all requirements of the uniform dominant requirement tree t_0. Likewise, each uniform requirement subtree t_α can be synthesized by a circuit passing through its nodes in any order, each edge of which has a uniform edge capacity equal to half the uniform requirement of the subtree t_α. Therefore, by *synthesizing a uniform requirement tree or subtree*, we mean the construction of a net of one or more circuits as described above. We remark that in the case where a subtree is composed only of a single edge, it is convenient to use a single edge instead of two parallel edges, each having half the original edge capacity. For example, in Fig. 4.61 the uniform dominant requirement tree t_0 is synthesized as shown in Fig. 4.63, and those of Fig. 4.62 are shown in Fig. 4.64. Finally, to obtain the desired feasible

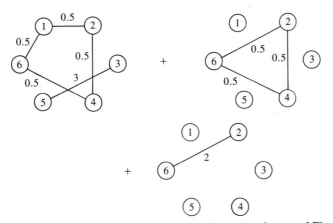

Fig. 4.64. The synthesis of the uniform requirement subtrees of Fig. 4.62.

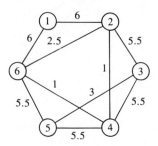

Fig. 4.65. A feasible net for the requirement matrix (4.80).

net, we superimpose the resulting circuit realizations to form a net G^* with each edge capacity equal to the sum of the corresponding edge capacities of the individual realizations. Thus, by superimposing the realizations of Figs. 4.63 and 4.64, we obtain the feasible net G^* of Fig. 4.65.

Before we justify our assertion that the final net G^* is indeed a feasible minimum capacity realization, we illustrate the Gomory–Hu procedure by the following example.

Example 4.14

Given the symmetric requirement matrix

$$
\boldsymbol{R} = \begin{array}{c} \\ 1 \\ 2 \\ 3 \\ 4 \\ 5 \end{array}
\begin{array}{c} \begin{array}{ccccc} 1 & 2 & 3 & 4 & 5 \end{array} \\
\begin{bmatrix}
\infty & 2 & 1 & 4 & 6 \\
2 & \infty & 5 & 1 & 4 \\
1 & 5 & \infty & 7 & 1 \\
4 & 1 & 7 & \infty & 6 \\
6 & 4 & 1 & 6 & \infty
\end{bmatrix}
\end{array}
\qquad (4.101)
$$

we synthesize a feasible net with a minimum total edge capacity.

From the requirement matrix $\boldsymbol{R}$, we first construct the requirement graph G_R of Fig. 4.66, from which we obtain a maximum tree called a dominant requirement tree t_m as shown in Fig. 4.67. This tree t_m can be decomposed into a sum of a uniform dominant requirement tree t_0 and a number of uniform requirement subtrees as indicated in Fig. 4.68. Each of such uniform tree or subtrees is then synthesized by a circuit or a number of circuits. The results are presented in Fig. 4.69. Finally, we superimpose the realizations of the nets of Fig. 4.69 to yield the desired realization G^* of Fig. 4.70. The net G^* is a feasible minimum-total-edge-capacity realization. The total edge capacity of G^* is 15.5 or $c^*(G^*) = 15.5$.

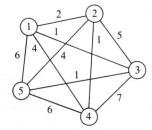

Fig. 4.66. The requirement graph G_R for the requirement matrix (4.101).

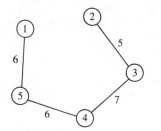

Fig. 4.67. A dominant requirement tree t_m for the requirement graph G_R of Fig. 4.66.

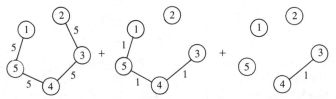

Fig. 4.68. The decomposition of the dominant requirement tree t_m of Fig. 4.67 into the sum of a uniform dominant requirement tree t_0 and a number of uniform requirement subtrees.

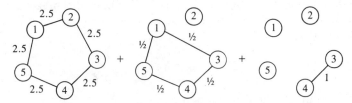

Fig. 4.69. The synthesis of the uniform dominant requirement tree t_0 and the uniform requirement subtrees of Fig. 4.68.

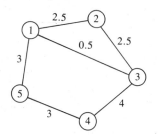

Fig. 4.70. A feasible minimum-total-edge-capacity realization for the requirement matrix (4.101).

THEOREM 4.10

The net G^* constructed above is a feasible minimum capacity net.

Proof. To show that G^* is feasible, it suffices to demonstrate that the requirements of the dominant requirement tree t_m are satisfied. Since each uniform requirement tree or subtree having uniform requirement r_0 is realized by a circuit through its nodes, every edge of which has capacity $\frac{1}{2}r_0$, each realization meets the flow requirements. From (4.99) we see that the terminal capacity τ_{ij}^* between nodes i and j in G^* is no less than the sum of the corresponding terminal capacities of individual circuit realizations. Thus, the net G^* is feasible.

As indicated in (4.88), for any feasible net $G(V, E, c, f)$ we must have

$$c(i, V) = \sum_j c(i, j) \geqq u_i, \qquad (i, j) \in E \qquad (4.102)$$

or

$$c(V, V) = 2c(G) \geqq 2C_\alpha = \sum_i u_i \qquad (4.103)$$

where $c(V, V)$ denotes twice the sum of the edge capacity $c(G)$ of G. We show that the net $G^*(V^*, E^*, c^*, f^*)$ constructed above achieves the lower bound C_α in (4.103), or

$$c^*(G^*) = C_\alpha \qquad (4.104)$$

To proceed, we first define $\hat{u}_i$ as in (4.87) where the max operation is taken over all branches incident at node i in the dominant requirement tree t_m. It follows that

$$u_i \geqq \hat{u}_i \qquad (4.105)$$

But by the nature of the construction of G^*, we have

$$c^*(i, V^*) = \hat{u}_i \qquad (4.106)$$

yielding from (4.105) and (4.106)

$$c^*(V^*, V^*) = \sum_i \hat{u}_i \leqq \sum_i u_i = 2C_\alpha \qquad (4.107)$$

Since (4.103) holds for any feasible net, in particular it holds for G^* or

$$c^*(V^*, V^*) \geqq 2C_\alpha \qquad (4.108)$$

Combining (4.107) and (4.108) gives

$$c^*(V^*, V^*) = 2C_\alpha \qquad (4.109)$$

Thus, G^* is a feasible minimum capacity realization. This completes the proof of the theorem.   Q.E.D.

A consequence of the proof of the above theorem is the following. From (4.109) we obtain

$$\sum_i u_i = \sum_i \hat{u}_i \qquad (4.110)$$

from which it follows that

$$u_i = \hat{u}_i \qquad (4.111)$$

meaning that in determining u_i in (4.87) we need only to check the requirements associated with the branches incident at node i of the dominant requirement tree t_m.

4.6.2 Dominant Flow Realization

Recall that in synthesizing a uniform tree or subtree, we have the freedom of passing the circuit through the nodes in any order, each resulting in a feasible minimum capacity realization. However, among all these realizations, there is one whose flow function dominates all others. In other words, there exists a feasible minimum capacity net $\hat{G}(\hat{V}, \hat{E}, \hat{c}, \hat{f})$ such that for any other feasible minimum capacity realization $G(V, E, c, f)$ we have

$$\hat{f}(i, j) \geqq f(i, j) \qquad (4.112)$$

for all edges (i, j) in $\hat{G}$ and G. In the following, we describe a procedure for constructing such a net $\hat{G}$ known as the *dominant flow net*.

Let $\boldsymbol{R} = [r_{ij}]$ be the symmetric requirement matrix, and let the elements r_{ij} of $\boldsymbol{R}$ be revised upward to yield a new requirement matrix

$$\hat{\boldsymbol{R}} = [\hat{r}_{ij}] \qquad (4.113)$$

where

$$\hat{r}_{ij} = \min [u_i, u_j] \qquad (4.114)$$

and u_i and u_j are defined in (4.87). As in (4.87), define

$$\hat{u}_i = \max_{\substack{j \\ j \neq i}} \hat{r}_{ij} \qquad (4.115)$$

Then we have $u_i = \hat{u}_i$ for all i or

$$\sum_i u_i = \sum_i \hat{u}_i = 2C_\alpha \qquad (4.116)$$

Let $\hat{G}(\hat{V}, \hat{E}, \hat{c}, \hat{f})$ be the net obtained by the Gomory–Hu procedure for the requirement matrix $\hat{R}$. We shall show that if $\hat{T}$ is the terminal capacity matrix of $\hat{G}$, then

$$\hat{T} = \hat{R} \qquad (4.117)$$

To establish (4.117), assume that $\hat{\tau}_{xy} > \hat{r}_{xy}$ where $\hat{T} = [\hat{\tau}_{xy}]$. Then

$$\hat{c}(x, \hat{V}) \geqq \hat{\tau}_{xy} > \hat{r}_{xy} = \min[u_x, u_y] \qquad (4.118)$$

Without loss of generality, suppose that $u_x \leqq u_y$. Then from (4.118)

$$\hat{c}(x, \hat{V}) > u_x \qquad (4.119)$$

or, summing over all $x \in \hat{V}$,

$$\hat{c}(\hat{V}, \hat{V}) > \sum_i u_i = 2C_\alpha \qquad (4.120)$$

This contradicts the fact that $\hat{G}$ is a minimum capacity realization with total edge capacity equal to C_α. Thus, $\hat{\tau}_{xy} = \hat{r}_{xy}$ for all x and y.

Now we show that if $T = [\tau_{ij}]$ is the terminal capacity matrix of any feasible minimum capacity net $G(V, E, c, f)$, then for all i and j

$$\hat{\tau}_{ij} \geqq \tau_{ij} \qquad (4.121)$$

To show this, we assume otherwise by letting $\hat{\tau}_{ij} < \tau_{ij}$ for some i and j with

$$\tau_{ij} > \hat{\tau}_{ij} = \hat{r}_{ij} \qquad (4.122)$$

and assume, say, that $\hat{u}_i < \hat{u}_j$. Then

$$c(i, V) \geqq \tau_{ij} > \hat{\tau}_{ij} = \hat{r}_{ij} = \hat{u}_i = u_i \qquad (4.123)$$

or

$$c(V, V) > \sum_i u_i = 2C_\alpha \qquad (4.124)$$

and the same contradiction results. Thus, $\hat{\tau}_{ij} \geqq \tau_{ij}$.

In other words, there exists a feasible minimum capacity realization $\hat{G}$ such that any other such realizations G would result in no greater flow value, and more flow between any pair of nodes in $\hat{G}$ can be obtained only by increasing the total edge capacity.

We illustrate the above results by the following example.

Example 4.15

Given the requirement matrix

$$R = \begin{array}{c} \\ 1 \\ 2 \\ 3 \\ 4 \\ 5 \end{array} \begin{array}{ccccc} 1 & 2 & 3 & 4 & 5 \\ \left[\begin{array}{ccccc} \infty & 5 & 9 & 2 & 4 \\ 5 & \infty & 6 & 5 & 3 \\ 9 & 6 & \infty & 3 & 4 \\ 2 & 5 & 3 & \infty & 7 \\ 4 & 3 & 4 & 7 & \infty \end{array}\right] \end{array} \tag{4.125}$$

we construct a dominant flow net $\hat{G}$.

Using (4.87), the elements u_i $(i = 1, 2, 3, 4, 5)$ are found from (4.125) to be

$$u_1 = 9, \qquad u_2 = 6, \qquad u_3 = 9, \qquad u_4 = 7, \qquad u_5 = 7 \tag{4.126}$$

obtaining from (4.114) the revised requirement matrix

$$\hat{R} = \begin{array}{c} \\ 1 \\ 2 \\ 3 \\ 4 \\ 5 \end{array} \begin{array}{ccccc} 1 & 2 & 3 & 4 & 5 \\ \left[\begin{array}{ccccc} \infty & 6 & 9 & 7 & 7 \\ 6 & \infty & 6 & 6 & 6 \\ 9 & 6 & \infty & 7 & 7 \\ 7 & 6 & 7 & \infty & 7 \\ 7 & 6 & 7 & 7 & \infty \end{array}\right] \end{array} \tag{4.127}$$

The requirement graph $\hat{G}_R$ of $\hat{R}$ is shown in Fig. 4.71, from which we obtain a dominant requirement tree $\hat{t}_m$ of Fig. 4.72. This tree $\hat{t}_m$ can be decomposed as a sum of a uniform tree and uniform subtrees as indicated in Fig. 4.73. These uniform tree and subtrees can be synthesized as those shown in Fig. 4.74. The superposition of these circuit realizations yields a dominant flow net $\hat{G}$ of Fig. 4.75, the terminal capacity matrix of which is

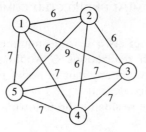

Fig. 4.71. The requirement graph $\hat{G}_R$ for the requirement matrix (4.127).

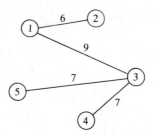

Fig. 4.72. A dominant requirement tree for the requirement graph of Fig. 4.71.

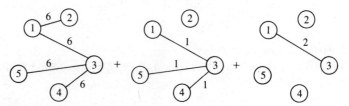

Fig. 4.73. The decomposition of the dominant requirement tree of Fig. 4.72 into the sum of a uniform tree and uniform subtrees.

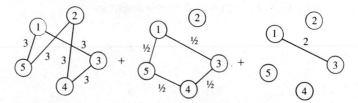

Fig. 4.74. The synthesis of the uniform tree and subtrees of Fig. 4.73.

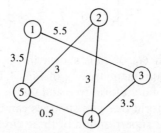

Fig. 4.75. A dominant flow net for the requirement matrix (4.127).

found to be

$$\hat{T} = \begin{array}{c} \\ 1 \\ 2 \\ 3 \\ 4 \\ 5 \end{array} \begin{array}{ccccc} 1 & 2 & 3 & 4 & 5 \\ \begin{bmatrix} \infty & 6 & 9 & 7 & 7 \\ 6 & \infty & 6 & 6 & 6 \\ 9 & 6 & \infty & 7 & 7 \\ 7 & 6 & 7 & \infty & 7 \\ 7 & 6 & 7 & 7 & \infty \end{bmatrix} \end{array} \tag{4.128}$$

showing that $\hat{R}$ is realized exactly.

Applying the Gomory–Hu procedure, we can construct other feasible minimum capacity nets. Two such nets G_1 and G_2 are presented in Fig. 4.76, whose terminal capacity matrices T_1 and T_2 are obtained as

$$T_1 = \begin{array}{c} \\ 1 \\ 2 \\ 3 \\ 4 \\ 5 \end{array} \begin{array}{ccccc} 1 & 2 & 3 & 4 & 5 \\ \begin{bmatrix} \infty & 6 & 9 & 6 & 6 \\ 6 & \infty & 6 & 6 & 6 \\ 9 & 6 & \infty & 6 & 6 \\ 6 & 6 & 6 & \infty & 7 \\ 6 & 6 & 6 & 7 & \infty \end{bmatrix} \end{array} \tag{4.129}$$

$$T_2 = \begin{array}{c} \\ 1 \\ 2 \\ 3 \\ 4 \\ 5 \end{array} \begin{array}{ccccc} 1 & 2 & 3 & 4 & 5 \\ \begin{bmatrix} \infty & 6 & 9 & 5 & 5 \\ 6 & \infty & 6 & 5 & 5 \\ 9 & 6 & \infty & 5 & 5 \\ 5 & 5 & 5 & \infty & 7 \\ 5 & 5 & 5 & 7 & \infty \end{bmatrix} \end{array} \tag{4.130}$$

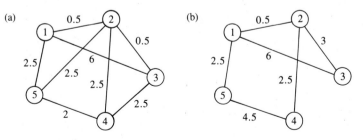

Fig. 4.76. Two feasible minimum capacity nets obtained by the Gomory–Hu procedure: (a) G_1; (b) G_2.

It is straightforward to verify that $\hat{G}$ is indeed a dominant flow net, because each element of its terminal capacity matrix is no smaller than the corresponding element in either T_1 or T_2, and the three nets G, G_1 and G_2 have the same total edge capacity of 19.

4.7   ORIENTED COMMUNICATION NETS

So far we have been concerned only with undirected communication nets. These nets can be concisely and elegantly characterized in terms of the triangle inequality (4.35) or the principal partitions of (4.45). However, in the case of an oriented or directed communication net, where the flow can only be sent in the direction of an arc, no simple necessary and sufficient conditions are known. Only algorithms have been proposed to construct an oriented communication net having a preassigned real square asymmetric matrix to be its terminal capacity matrix. Examples of such algorithms can be found in Frisch and Sen (1967) and Matsui (1970). In the present section, we discuss a number of known properties of the terminal capacity matrix of an oriented communication net.

Let T be the terminal capacity matrix of an oriented communication net $G(V, E, c, f)$, which in general is real but asymmetric. The elements of T, however, still satisfy the triangle inequality (4.35).

THEOREM 4.11

If $T = [\tau_{ij}]$ is the terminal capacity matrix of an oriented communication net, then for all i, j and k,

$$\tau_{ij} \geqq \min [\tau_{ik}, \tau_{kj}] \tag{4.131}$$

The proof of the theorem is identical to the proof of necessity of Theorem 4.6 except that the net is now oriented instead of undirected. This triangle inequality (4.131) can easily be extended to the polygon inequality, as follows: For any i, $x_1, x_2, \ldots, x_r$, and j, we have

$$\tau_{ij} \geqq \min [\tau_{ix_1}, \tau_{x_1j}]$$
$$\geqq \min [\tau_{ix_1}, \tau_{x_1x_2}, \tau_{x_2j}]$$
$$\vdots$$
$$\geqq \min [\tau_{ix_1}, \tau_{x_1x_2}, \ldots, \tau_{x_rj}] \tag{4.132}$$

or for any i, $x_1, x_2, \ldots, x_r$ and j

$$\tau_{ij} \geqq \min [\tau_{ix_1}, \tau_{x_1x_2}, \ldots, \tau_{x_rj}] \tag{4.133}$$

However, this condition is not sufficient for the realizability of T.

DEFINITION 4.14

Semi-principal Partition. A real matrix T is said to be *semi-principally partitionable* if after possibly permuting rows and the corresponding columns, it can be partitioned into the form

$$T = \begin{bmatrix} T_a & T_c \\ T_d & T_b \end{bmatrix} \tag{4.134}$$

where (i) every element in T_c is identical and is the smallest number in T, (ii) T_a and T_b are square submatrices, and (iii) every diagonal element in T is ∞. T_a and T_b are called the *resultant main submatrices* by a semi-principal partition.

The definition is very similar to principal partition except tht T is not necessarily symmetric. Like the triangle inequality, the semi-principal partition is only a necessary condition for the realizability of a terminal capacity matrix but not sufficient.

THEOREM 4.12

If T is the terminal capacity matrix of an oriented communication net, then the semi-principal partition can be applied to T and all of its resultant main submatrices until all the final resultant main submatrices are of order 1.

Proof. Let T be the terminal capacity matrix of an oriented communication net $G(V, E, c, f)$. Then among all the cuts from one node to another in G, there is a minimum capacity cut $(X, \bar{X})$. This cut partitions the node set V into subsets X and $\bar{X} = V - X$. Then the terminal capacity τ_{xy} from any node $x \in X$ and $y \in \bar{X}$ must be $c(X, \bar{X})$. Every other element in T corresponds to some cut capacity not smaller than $c(X, \bar{X})$. Thus, T can be semi-principally partitioned as

$$T = \begin{array}{c} \\ X \\ \bar{X} \end{array} \!\! \begin{array}{c} X \quad \bar{X} \\ \begin{bmatrix} T_a & T_c \\ T_d & T_b \end{bmatrix} \end{array} \tag{4.135}$$

Next, among all the cuts from one node in X to another in X, there exists a minimum capacity cut $(Y, \bar{Y})$ that partitions the node set X into the subsets W and Z such that every other such cut assumes a capacity not smaller than $c(Y, \bar{Y})$. Thus, T_a can be principally partitioned as

$$T_a = \begin{array}{c} \\ W \\ Z \end{array} \!\! \begin{array}{c} W \quad Z \\ \begin{bmatrix} T_{aa} & T_{ac} \\ T_{ad} & T_{ab} \end{bmatrix} \end{array} \tag{4.136}$$

Clearly, this process can be applied to any resultant main submatrices until they are of order 1. The theorem follows.   Q.E.D.

COROLLARY 4.4

The maximum number of numerically distinct entries in the terminal capacity matrix of an n-node oriented communication net is $(n+2)(n-1)/2$, excluding the entries on the main diagonal. Furthermore, there exists an n-node oriented communication net with $(n+2)(n-1)/2$ numerically distinct entries.

The corollary follows directly from the observation that in a semi-principally partitioned T, the maximum number of numerically distinct entries above the main diagonal is $n-1$, and the maximum number of such entries below the main diagonal is $n(n-1)/2$. The total number is therefore

$$(n-1) + \tfrac{1}{2}n(n-1) = \tfrac{1}{2}(n+2)(n-1) \tag{4.137}$$

Mayeda (1962) showed that an n-node oriented communication net with $(n+2)(n-1)/2$ numerically distinct entries can be constructed. The net has the general configuration of Fig. 4.77, the terminal capacity matrix of which is found to be

$$
T =
\begin{bmatrix}
\infty & n-1 & \cdots & 2 & 1 \\
n^n + (n-2) & \infty & \cdots & 2 & 1 \\
2n^{n-1} + (n-3) & n^{n-1} + (n-3) + (n-1) & \cdots & 2 & 1 \\
\vdots & \vdots & \vdots & \vdots & \vdots \\
(n-2)n^3 + 1 & (n-3)n^3 + 1 + (n-1) & \cdots & \infty & 1 \\
(n-1)n^2 & (n-2)n^2 + (n-1) & \cdots & n^2 + 2 & \infty
\end{bmatrix}
\tag{4.138}
$$

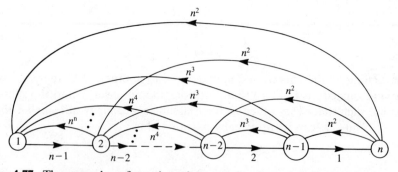

Fig. 4.77. The general configuration of an n-node oriented communication net with $(n+2)(n-1)/2$ numerically distinct entries in its terminal capacity matrix.

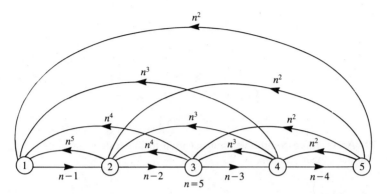

Fig. 4.78. The general configuration of a five-node oriented communication net with 14 numerically distinct entries in its terminal capacity matrix.

For $n = 5$ the net takes the form of Fig. 4.78, and its terminal capacity matrix becomes

$$
T =
\begin{bmatrix}
\infty & 5-1 & 5-2 & 2 & 1 \\
5^5+3 & \infty & 5-2 & 2 & 1 \\
2 \times 5^4+2 & 5^4+6 & \infty & 2 & 1 \\
3 \times 5^3+1 & 2 \times 5^3+5 & 5^3+4 & \infty & 1 \\
4 \times 5^2 & 3 \times 5^2+4 & 2 \times 5^2+3 & 5^2+2 & \infty
\end{bmatrix}
$$

$$
=
\begin{bmatrix}
\infty & 4 & 3 & 2 & 1 \\
3128 & \infty & 3 & 2 & 1 \\
1252 & 631 & \infty & 2 & 1 \\
376 & 255 & 129 & \infty & 1 \\
100 & 79 & 53 & 27 & \infty
\end{bmatrix}
\qquad (4.139)
$$

Example 4.16

Consider the oriented communication net $G(V, E, c, f)$ of Fig. 4.79, the terminal capacity matrix of which is found to be

$$
T =
\begin{array}{c c}
& \begin{array}{c c c c c} 1 & 2 & 3 & 4 & 5 \end{array} \\
\begin{array}{c} 1 \\ 2 \\ 3 \\ 4 \\ 5 \end{array} &
\begin{bmatrix}
\infty & 1 & 1 & 1 & 1 \\
3 & \infty & 2 & 1 & 3 \\
1 & 1 & \infty & 1 & 1 \\
3 & 3 & 4 & \infty & 3 \\
3 & 2 & 2 & 1 & \infty
\end{bmatrix}
\end{array}
\qquad (4.140)
$$

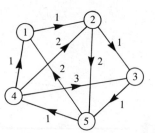

Fig. 4.79. An oriented communication net used to illustrate semi-principal partition of its terminal capacity matrix.

After permuting the rows and the corresponding columns, this matrix can be semi-principally partitioned to yield

$$
\begin{array}{c}
 \quad 1 \quad\ \ 3 \quad\ \ 5 \quad\ 2 \quad\ 4 \\[2pt]
\boldsymbol{T} =
\begin{array}{c}
1 \\ 3 \\ 5 \\ 2 \\ 4
\end{array}
\left[
\begin{array}{cc:c|cc}
\infty & 1 & 1 & 1 & 1 \\ \hdashline
1 & \infty & 1 & 1 & 1 \\ \hline
3 & 2 & \infty & 2 & 1 \\ \cdashline{3-4}
3 & 2 & 3 & \infty & 1 \\ \hline
3 & 4 & 3 & 3 & \infty
\end{array}
\right]
\end{array}
\qquad (4.141)
$$

The matrix has four numerically distinct entries out of a possible total $\frac{1}{2}(n+2)(n-1) = 14$.

Example 4.17

Consider the oriented communication net $G(V, E, c, f)$ of Fig. 4.80, the

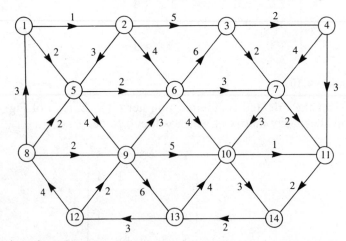

Fig. 4.80. An oriented communication net used to illustrate semi-principal partition of its terminal capacity matrix.

terminal capacity matrix of which is found to be

$$
T =
\begin{array}{c|cccccccccccccc}
 & 1 & 2 & 3 & 4 & 5 & 6 & 7 & 8 & 9 & 10 & 11 & 12 & 13 & 14 \\
\hline
1 & \infty & 1 & 3 & 2 & 3 & 3 & 3 & 3 & 3 & 3 & 3 & 3 & 3 & 3 \\
2 & 3 & \infty & 11 & 2 & 5 & 9 & 7 & 3 & 5 & 11 & 5 & 3 & 5 & 5 \\
3 & 2 & 1 & \infty & 2 & 2 & 2 & 4 & 2 & 2 & 4 & 4 & 2 & 2 & 4 \\
4 & 2 & 1 & 2 & \infty & 2 & 2 & 6 & 2 & 2 & 5 & 6 & 2 & 2 & 5 \\
5 & 3 & 1 & 6 & 2 & \infty & 6 & 6 & 3 & 6 & 6 & 5 & 3 & 6 & 5 \\
6 & 2 & 1 & 7 & 2 & 2 & \infty & 7 & 2 & 2 & 9 & 5 & 2 & 2 & 5 \\
7 & 2 & 1 & 2 & 2 & 2 & 2 & \infty & 2 & 2 & 5 & 5 & 2 & 2 & 5 \\
8 & 3 & 1 & 6 & 2 & 5 & 6 & 6 & \infty & 7 & 7 & 5 & 3 & 7 & 5 \\
9 & 3 & 1 & 6 & 2 & 3 & 6 & 6 & 3 & \infty & 14 & 5 & 3 & 8 & 5 \\
10 & 2 & 1 & 2 & 2 & 2 & 2 & 2 & 2 & 2 & \infty & 3 & 2 & 2 & 4 \\
11 & 2 & 1 & 2 & 2 & 2 & 2 & 2 & 2 & 2 & 2 & \infty & 2 & 2 & 2 \\
12 & 3 & 1 & 6 & 2 & 4 & 6 & 6 & 4 & 6 & 6 & 5 & \infty & 6 & 5 \\
13 & 3 & 1 & 3 & 2 & 3 & 3 & 3 & 3 & 3 & 7 & 4 & 3 & \infty & 5 \\
14 & 2 & 1 & 2 & 2 & 2 & 2 & 2 & 2 & 2 & 2 & 2 & 2 & 2 & \infty \\
\end{array}
$$

$$(4.142)$$

After permuting the rows and the corresponding columns, this matrix T can be semi-principally partitioned as follows:

$$
T =
\begin{array}{c|ccc|ccc|ccc|ccc|c|c}
 & 11 & 14 & 10 & 7 & 3 & 6 & 1 & 13 & 9 & 5 & 8 & 12 & 4 & 2 \\
\hline
11 & \infty & 2 & 2 & 2 & 2 & 2 & 2 & 2 & 2 & 2 & 2 & 2 & 2 & 1 \\
14 & 2 & \infty & 2 & 2 & 2 & 2 & 2 & 2 & 2 & 2 & 2 & 2 & 2 & 1 \\
10 & 3 & 4 & \infty & 2 & 2 & 2 & 2 & 2 & 2 & 2 & 2 & 2 & 2 & 1 \\
7 & 5 & 5 & 5 & \infty & 2 & 2 & 2 & 2 & 2 & 2 & 2 & 2 & 2 & 1 \\
3 & 4 & 4 & 4 & 4 & \infty & 2 & 2 & 2 & 2 & 2 & 2 & 2 & 2 & 1 \\
6 & 5 & 5 & 9 & 7 & 7 & \infty & 2 & 2 & 2 & 2 & 2 & 2 & 2 & 1 \\
1 & 3 & 3 & 3 & 3 & 3 & 3 & \infty & 3 & 3 & 3 & 3 & 3 & 2 & 1 \\
13 & 4 & 5 & 7 & 3 & 3 & 3 & 3 & \infty & 3 & 3 & 3 & 3 & 2 & 1 \\
9 & 5 & 5 & 14 & 6 & 6 & 6 & 3 & 8 & \infty & 3 & 3 & 3 & 2 & 1 \\
5 & 5 & 5 & 6 & 6 & 6 & 6 & 3 & 6 & 6 & \infty & 3 & 3 & 2 & 1 \\
8 & 5 & 5 & 7 & 6 & 6 & 6 & 3 & 7 & 7 & 5 & \infty & 3 & 2 & 1 \\
12 & 5 & 5 & 6 & 6 & 6 & 6 & 3 & 6 & 6 & 4 & 4 & \infty & 2 & 1 \\
4 & 6 & 5 & 5 & 6 & 2 & 2 & 2 & 2 & 2 & 2 & 2 & 2 & \infty & 1 \\
2 & 5 & 5 & 11 & 7 & 11 & 9 & 3 & 5 & 5 & 5 & 3 & 3 & 2 & \infty \\
\end{array}
$$

$$(4.143)$$

4.8   SUMMARY AND SUGGESTED READING

We began this chapter by introducing the notions of forests, subtrees and trees and showed that every tree of a connected graph can be obtained from any other one by a finite sequence of elementary tree transformations. We then considered the minimum and maximum tree problems by presenting the greedy method, which builds up a minimum tree edge by edge by including appropriate short edges and excluding appropriate long edges until a minimum tree is constructed. Since edge lengths are allowed to be negative, when we can solve the minimum tree problem, we can also solve the maximum tree problem. All we have to do is to multiply each edge length by -1 and solve the corresponding minimum tree problem. For this reason, we only state the algorithms for solving the minimum tree problem, leaving the maximum tree problem as obvious. Three well-known minimum tree algorithms that are variants of the greedy method were examined. The Kruskal algorithm generates blue subtrees in an irregular fashion dictated solely by the edge lengths, and the Prim algorithm grows a blue subtree from a single root. The Borùvka algorithm, on the other hand, builds up blue subtrees uniformly throughout the net, and is therefore well suited for parallel computation.

In the remainder of the chapter, we studied the terminal capacity matrix of a communication net and its realizability. We showed that a real symmetric matrix is the terminal capacity matrix of an undirected communication net if and only if its elements satisfy the triangle inequality or the matrix is principally partitionable, so do its resultant main submatrices. We demonstrated that every undirected communication net is flow-equivalent to a tree and there are at most $n - 1$ numerically distinct terminal capacity values in an n-node net. We gave an algorithm for determining the elements of the terminal capacity matrix of an n-node undirected communication net by solving precisely $n - 1$ maximum flow problems. Moreover, many of these problems are solved in smaller and more simplified nets than the original one. We also studied the inverse problem of synthesizing a net having a preassigned lower bound on the maximum flow value between every pair of nodes with a minimum total edge capacity. The procedure uses the dominant requirement tree and then decomposes it into a sum of uniform requirement forests. Each such uniform requirement forest is synthesized at its total lower bound capacity. The resulting net obtained by superposition of these individual realizations would satisfy the original flow requirements with a minimum total edge capacity. However, among many of these minimum-capacity realizations, there is one which dominates all others.

Finally, we discussed a number of known properties of the terminal capacity matrix of an oriented communication net. We showed that the elements of this matrix satisfy the triangle inequality, and that the matrix itself is semi-principally partitionable, so do its resultant main submatrices.

However, these conditions are not sufficient for its realizability. In the oriented case, the maximum number of numerically distinct entries in the terminal capacity matrix is $(n + 2)(n - 1)/2$, excluding the entries on the main diagonal.

The standard book for communication nets is Frank and Frisch (1971). For a concise exposition on minimum tree problems, we refer to Tarjan (1983), and for undirected communication net problems, see Hu (1982). For further study on the various algorithms, the reader is referred to the original papers listed in the references.

REFERENCES

Agarwal, A. K. and Arora, S. R. (1976), "Synthesis of multiterminal communication nets: Finding one or all solutions," *IEEE Trans. Circuits and Systems,* vol. CAS-23, pp. 141–146.

Akers, S. B. Jr (1960), "Use of the wye–delta transformation in network simplification," *Operations Res.,* vol. 8, pp. 311–323.

Ali, A. (1965), "Realizability conditions of special types of oriented communication nets," *IEEE Trans. Circuit Theory,* vol. CT-12, p. 417.

Barnard, H. M. (1965), "Note on completely partitionable terminal capacity matrices," *IEEE Trans. Circuit Theory,* vol. CT-12, p. 122.

Bentely, J. L. (1980), "A parallel algorithm for constructing minimum spanning trees," *J. Algorithms,* vol. 1, pp. 51–59.

Berge, C. and Ghouila-Houri, A. (1965), *Programming, Games, and Transportation Networks,* New York: John Wiley.

Blum, M., Floyd, R. W., Pratt, V. R., Rivest, R. L. and Tarjan, R.E. (1973), "Time bounds for selection," *J. Comput. System Sci.,* vol. 7, pp. 448–461.

Bock, F. (1971), "An algorithm to construct a minimum directed spanning tree in a directed network," in *Developments in Operations Research,* New York: Gordon and Breach, pp. 29–44.

Borůvka, O. (1926), "O jistém problému minimálnim," *Práca Moravské Přírodovědecké Společnosti,* vol. 3, pp. 37–58.

Chen, C. (1974), "Realizability of communication nets: An application of the Zadeh criterion," *IEEE Trans. Circuits and Systems,* vol. CAS-21, pp. 150–151.

Cheriton, D. and Tarjan, R. E. (1976), "Finding minimum spanning trees," *SIAM J. Computing,* vol. 5, pp. 724–742.

Chien, R. T. (1960), "Synthesis of a communication net," *IBM J. Res. Develop.,* vol. 4, pp. 311–320.

Choquet, G. (1938), "Etude de certains réseaux de routes," *C. R. Acad. Sci. Paris,* vol. 206, pp. 310–313.

Dalal, Y. K. (1987), "A distributed algorithm for constructing minimal spanning trees," *IEEE Trans. Software Engineering,* vol. SE-13, pp. 398–405.

Dijkstra, E. W. (1959), "A note on two problems in connexion with graphs," *Numerische Math.,* vol. 1, pp. 269–271.

Ford, L. R. Jr and Fulkerson, D. R. (1962), *Flows in Networks*, Princeton, N.J.: Princeton University Press.

Frank, H. and Frisch, I. T. (1971), *Communication, Transmission, and Transportation Networks*, Reading, Mass.: Addison–Wesley.

Frisch, I. T. and Sen, D. K. (1967), "Algorithms for synthesis of oriented communication nets," *IEEE Trans. Circuit Theory*, vol. CT-14, pp. 370–379.

Frisch, I. T. and Shein, N. P. (1969), "Necessary and sufficient conditions for realizability of vertex weighted nets," *IEEE Trans. Circuit Theory*, vol. CT-16, pp. 496–502.

Gallager, R. G., Humblet, P. A. and Spira, P. M. (1983), "A distributed algorithm for minimum-weight spanning trees," *ACM Trans. Program. Lang. Syst.*, vol. 5, pp. 66–77.

Gomory, R. E. and Hu, T. C. (1961), "Multiterminal network flows," *SIAM J. Applied Math.*, vol. 9, pp. 551–570.

Gomory, R. E. and Hu, T. C. (1964), "Synthesis of a communication network," *SIAM J. Applied Math.*, vol. 12, pp. 348–369.

Gupta, R. P. (1966), "On flows in pseudosymmetric networks," *SIAM J. Applied Math.*, vol. 14, pp. 215–225.

Gusfield, D. (1983), "Simple constructions for multi-terminal network flow synthesis," *SIAM J. Computing*, vol. 12, pp. 157–165.

Hu, T. C. (1974), "Optimum communication spanning tree," *SIAM J. Computing*, vol. 3, pp. 188–195.

Hu, T. C. (1982), *Combinatorial Algorithms*, Reading, Mass.: Addison–Wesley.

Jarník, V. (1930), "O jistém problému minimálním," *Práca Moravské Přírodovědecké Společnosti*, vol. 6, pp. 57–63.

Jelinek, F. (1963), "On the maximum number of different entries in the terminal capacity matrix of an oriented communication net," *IEEE Trans. Circuit Theory*, vol. CT-10, pp. 308–309.

Johnson, D. B. (1975), "Priority queues with update and finding minimum spanning trees," *Inf. Process. Lett.*, vol. 4, pp. 53–57.

Kruskal, J. B. (1956), "On the shortest spanning subtree of a graph and the traveling salesman problem," *Proc. Amer. Math. Soc.*, vol. 7, pp. 48–50.

Lukasziewicz, L., Florek, K., Perkal, J., Steinhaus, H. and Zubrzycki, S. (1951), "Sur la liaison et la division des points d'un ensemble fini," *Colloq. Math.*, vol. 2, pp. 282–285.

Maffioli, F. (1981), "Complexity of optimum undirected tree problems: A survey of recent results," in *Analysis and Design of Algorithms in Combinatorial Optimization*, International Center for Mechanical Sciences, Courses and Lectures 266. New York: Springer–Verlag.

Matsui, K. (1970), "Synthesis of oriented communication nets," *Electronics and Communications in Japan*, vol. 53-A, pp. 15–20.

Mayeda, W. (1960), "Terminal and branch capacity matrices of a communication net," *IRE Trans. Circuit Theory*, vol. CT-7, pp. 260–269.

Mayeda, W. (1962), "On oriented communication nets," *IRE Trans. Circuit Theory*, vol. CT-9, pp. 261–267.

Ozawa, T. (1980), "Realization of a symmetric terminal capacity matrix by a tree with the minimum diameter," *Networks,* vol. 10, pp. 129–141.

Pierce, A. R. (1975), "Bibliography on algorithms for shortest path, shortest spanning tree and related circuit routing problems (1956–1974)," *Networks,* vol. 5, pp. 129–149.

Prim, R. C. (1957), "Shortest connection networks and some generalizations," *Bell System Tech. J.,* vol. 36, pp. 1389–1401.

Resh, J. A. (1965), "On the synthesis of oriented communication nets," *IEEE Trans. Circuit Theory,* vol. CT-12, pp. 540–546.

Schönhage, A., Paterson, M. and Pippenger, N. (1976), "Finding the median," *J. Comput. System Sci.,* vol. 13, pp. 184–199.

Spira, P. M. and Pan, A. (1975), "On finding and updating spanning trees and shortest paths," *SIAM J. Computing,* vol. 4, pp. 375–380.

Tang, D. T. and Chien, R. T. (1961), "Analysis and synthesis techniques of oriented communication nets," *IRE Trans. Circuit Theory,* vol. CT-8, pp. 39–44.

Tapia, M. A. and Myers, B. R. (1967), "Generation of concave node weighted trees," *IEEE Trans. Circuit Theory,* vol. CT-14, pp. 229–230.

Tarjan, R. E. (1981), "Minimum spanning trees," Technical Memo., Bell Labs., Murray Hill, N.J.

Tarjan, R. E. (1982), "Sensitivity analysis of minimum spanning trees and shortest path trees," *Inf. Process. Lett.,* vol. 14, pp. 30–33.

Tarjan, R. E. (1983), *Data Structures and Network Algorithms,* Philadelphia, Penn.: Society for Industrial and Applied Mathematics.

Whitney, H. (1935), "On the abstract properties of linear dependence," *Amer. J. Math.,* vol. 57, pp. 509–533.

Wing, O. and Chien, R. T. (1961), "Optimal synthesis of a communication net," *IRE Trans. Circuit Theory,* vol. CT-8, pp. 44–49.

Yao, A. (1975), "An $O(|E| \log \log |V|)$ algorithm for finding minimum spanning trees," *Inf. Process. Lett.,* vol. 4, pp. 21–23.

Yau, S. S. (1961), "On the structure of a communication net," *IRE Trans. Circuit Theory,* vol. CT-8, p. 365.

Yau, S. S. (1962), "Synthesis of radio-communication nets," *IRE Trans. Circuit Theory,* vol. CT-9, pp. 62–68.

5

FEASIBILITY THEOREMS AND THEIR APPLICATIONS

In Chapter 3, we discussed the flow problems in a network. A flow pattern is said to be feasible if it satisfies the arc capacity constraints and the conservation equation for all the intermediate nodes. Our objective there was to find a maximum feasible flow pattern for a general net. We showed that the maximum flow value from the source s to the sink t in a net is equal to the capacity of a minimum s–t cut separating the source and the sink. This is known as the max-flow min-cut theorem. The remainder of Chapter 3 is primarily concerned with the various algorithms for finding a maximum flow in a net.

In the present chapter, we develop several theorems characterizing the existence of network flows that satisfy additional linear inequalities of various kinds. Specifically, we give necessary and sufficient conditions for the existence of a flow pattern that satisfies the "demands" at certain nodes from the "supplies" at some of the others, or that satisfies both the lower and upper bounds of the arc flows. Since the proofs of these theorems rely on the max-flow min-cut theorem, it follows from the integrity theorem (Theorem 3.4) that if the additional constraints are integral, then integral feasible flows exist provided that there are any feasible flows. These results are then used to pose and solve a number of combinatorial problems in operations research.

5.1 A SUPPLY–DEMAND THEOREM

Given a net $G(V, E, c, f)$ with node set V, arc set E, capacity function c and flow function f, partition the node set V into the disjoint source set S,

318

intermediate node set R, and the sink set T. Associate with each $x \in S$ a nonnegative real number $a(x)$ called the *supply* of some commodity at node x, and with each $x \in T$ a nonnegative real number $b(x)$, the *demand* for the commodity at node x. Thus, the supplies in G can be considered as a function a from the source set S to the nonnegative reals, and the demands as a function b from the sink set T to the nonnegative reals. The objective is to determine the existence of a flow pattern in G, so that the demands at the sink set T can be fulfilled from the supplies at the source set S satisfying the constraints

$$f(x, V) - f(V, x) \leq a(x), \qquad x \in S \qquad (5.1)$$

$$f(x, V) - f(V, x) = 0, \qquad x \in R \qquad (5.2)$$

$$f(V, x) - f(x, V) \geq b(x), \qquad x \in T \qquad (5.3)$$

$$c(x, y) \geq f(x, y) \geq 0, \qquad (x, y) \in E \qquad (5.4)$$

If such a solution exists, we say that the constraints (5.1)–(5.4) are *feasible*. Otherwise, they are *infeasible*.

Consider, for example, the net $G(V, E, c, f)$ of Fig. 5.1, having the arc capacities as indicated. The node set V is partitioned into the source set S, intermediate node set R, and the sink set T, as follows:

$$S = \{1, 2\}, \qquad R = \{3, 4, 5\}, \qquad T = \{6, 7\} \qquad (5.5)$$

Suppose that the supplies of some commodity at nodes in S and the demands for the commodity at nodes in T are specified as

$$a(1) = 7, \qquad a(2) = 10 \qquad (5.6)$$

$$b(6) = 7, \qquad b(7) = 8 \qquad (5.7)$$

respectively. A flow pattern in meeting the demands from the supplies is

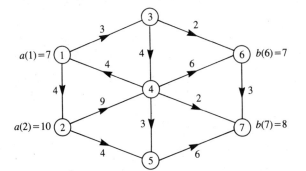

Fig. 5.1. A net with source nodes 1 and 2 and sink nodes 6 and 7.

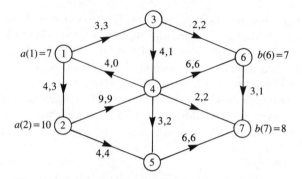

Fig. 5.2. A feasible flow pattern for the net of Fig. 5.1.

shown in Fig. 5.2, in which the second numbers adjacent to the arcs represent the amounts of flow in the arcs. The constraints (5.1)–(5.4) become

$$f(1, V) - f(V, 1) = 3 + 3 - 0 = 6 \leqq a(1) = 7 \tag{5.8a}$$

$$f(2, V) - f(V, 2) = 9 + 4 - 3 = 10 \leqq a(2) = 10 \tag{5.8b}$$

$$f(3, V) - f(V, 3) = 2 + 1 - 3 = 0 \tag{5.9a}$$

$$f(4, V) - f(V, 4) = 6 + 2 + 2 + 0 - 9 - 1 = 0 \tag{5.9b}$$

$$f(5, V) - f(V, 5) = 6 - 4 - 2 = 0 \tag{5.9c}$$

$$f(V, 6) - f(6, V) = 2 + 6 - 1 = 7 \geqq b(6) = 7 \tag{5.10a}$$

$$f(V, 7) - f(7, V) = 1 + 2 + 6 = 9 \geqq b(7) = 8 \tag{5.10b}$$

confirming that the flow pattern of Fig. 5.2 or the above supply–demand constraints are feasible.

The general necessary and sufficient conditions for the existence of a flow pattern in a net that satisfies the supply–demand constraints were first given by Gale (1957) and are stated below as a supply–demand theorem.

THEOREM 5.1

Partition the node set V of a given net $G(V, E, c, f)$ into three disjoint subsets S, R and T. Associate with each $x \in S$ a supply $a(x) \geqq 0$ at x and with each $y \in T$ a demand $b(y) \geqq 0$ at y. Then the constraints

$$f(x, V) - f(V, x) \leqq a(x), \qquad x \in S \tag{5.11}$$

$$f(x, V) - f(V, x) = 0, \qquad x \in R \tag{5.12}$$

$$f(V, x) - f(x, V) \geqq b(x), \qquad x \in T \tag{5.13}$$

$$c(x, y) \geqq f(x, y) \geqq 0, \qquad (x, y) \in E \tag{5.14}$$

are feasible if and only if

$$b(T \cap \bar{X}) - a(S \cap \bar{X}) \leqq c(X, \bar{X}) \qquad (5.15)$$

holds for every subset $X \subseteq V$, where $\bar{X} = V - X$.

Proof. Necessity. Assume that there is a flow f in G satisfying the constraints (5.11)–(5.14). Then by summing equations (5.12) and inequalities (5.11) and (5.13) over $x \in \bar{X}$ yields

$$f(S \cap \bar{X}, V) - f(V, S \cap \bar{X}) \leqq a(S \cap \bar{X}) \qquad (5.16)$$

$$f(R \cap \bar{X}, V) - f(V, R \cap \bar{X}) = 0 \qquad (5.17)$$

$$f(V, T \cap \bar{X}) - f(T \cap \bar{X}, V) \geqq b(T \cap \bar{X}) \qquad (5.18)$$

Rewriting (5.16) and (5.17) as

$$f(V, S \cap \bar{X}) - f(S \cap \bar{X}, V) \geqq -a(S \cap \bar{X}) \qquad (5.19)$$

$$f(V, R \cap \bar{X}) - f(R \cap \bar{X}, V) = 0 \qquad (5.20)$$

and combining these with (5.18), we obtain

$$f(V, T \cap \bar{X}) + f(V, S \cap \bar{X}) + f(V, R \cap \bar{X}) - f(T \cap \bar{X}, V) - f(S \cap \bar{X}, V)$$
$$- f(R \cap \bar{X}, V) \geqq b(T \cap \bar{X}) - a(S \cap \bar{X}) \qquad (5.21)$$

or equivalently

$$f(V, \bar{X}) - f(\bar{X}, V) \geqq b(T \cap \bar{X}) - a(S \cap \bar{X}) \qquad (5.22)$$

Using $V = X \cup \bar{X}$ in (5.22) gives

$$f(X, \bar{X}) - f(\bar{X}, X) \geqq b(T \cap \bar{X}) - a(S \cap \bar{X}) \qquad (5.23)$$

Since f satisfies (5.14), summing over $x \in X$ and $y \in \bar{X}$ results in

$$f(X, \bar{X}) - f(\bar{X}, X) \leqq c(X, \bar{X}) \qquad (5.24)$$

Combining this with (5.23) shows that the constraint

$$b(T \cap \bar{X}) - a(S \cap \bar{X}) \leqq c(X, \bar{X}) \qquad (5.25)$$

must hold for every subset $X \subseteq V$.

Sufficiency. To prove sufficiency, we construct a new net $G_1(V_1, E_1, c_1, f_1)$ from $G(V, E, c, f)$ by adjoining a fictitious source s, sink

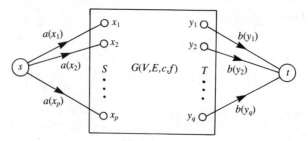

Fig. 5.3. The extended net $G_1(V_1, E_1, c_1, f_1)$ of the net $G(V, E, c, f)$.

t, and the arcs (s, S) and (T, t), as depicted in Fig. 5.3. Thus, we have

$$V_1 = V \cup \{s, t\}, \qquad E_1 = E \cup (s, S) \cup (T, t) \tag{5.26}$$

The capacity function c_1 on E_1 is defined by

$$c_1(s, x) = a(x), \qquad\qquad x \in S \tag{5.27a}$$

$$c_1(x, t) = b(x), \qquad\qquad x \in T \tag{5.27b}$$

$$c_1(x, y) = c(x, y), \qquad (x, y) \in E \tag{5.27c}$$

We now show that the inequality (5.15) holds for every subset $X \subseteq V$ if and only if it holds for the cut (T, t) in G_1. The implication is that (T, t) is a minimum s–t cut in G_1. To see this, let $(X_1, \bar{X}_1)$ be any s–t cut in G_1, and define

$$X = X_1 - \{s\}, \qquad \bar{X} = \bar{X}_1 - \{t\} \tag{5.28}$$

Consider the expansion

$$
\begin{aligned}
c_1(X_1, \bar{X}_1) - c_1(T, t) &= c_1(X, t) + c_1(X, \bar{X}) + c_1(s, \bar{X}) - c_1(T, t) \\
&= b(T \cap X) + c(X, \bar{X}) + a(S \cap \bar{X}) - b(T) \\
&= c(X, \bar{X}) + a(S \cap \bar{X}) - b(T \cap \bar{X}) \tag{5.29}
\end{aligned}
$$

By assumption, (5.15) holds for every subset $X \subseteq V$. Thus, the inequality

$$c_1(X_1, \bar{X}_1) - c_1(T, t) \geqq 0 \tag{5.30}$$

holds for all s–t cuts $(X_1, \bar{X}_1)$ of G_1, showing that (T, t) is a minimum s–t cut in G_1. Our conclusion is that (5.15) holds for all $X \subseteq V$ if and only if (5.30) holds for all s–t cuts in G_1.

Since (T, t) is a minimum s–t cut in G_1, by the max-flow min-cut theorem (Theorem 3.2) there exists a flow f_1 from s to t in G_1 that saturates all the arcs of (T, t). Define

$$f(x, y) = f_1(x, y), \qquad (x, y) \in E \tag{5.31}$$

Clearly, f satisfies (5.12) and (5.14). To see that f also satisfies (5.11) and (5.13), we consider for all $x \in S$ and $y \in T$ the equations

$$f_1(s, x) = f_1(x, V) - f_1(V, x) = f(x, V) - f(V, x) \tag{5.32}$$

$$f_1(y, t) = f_1(V, y) - f_1(y, V) = f(V, y) - f(y, V) \tag{5.33}$$

Since by construction

$$a(x) \geq f_1(s, x) \tag{5.34}$$

$$b(y) = f_1(y, t) \tag{5.35}$$

the inequalities (5.11) and (5.13) follow. This completes the proof of the theorem.

The necessary and sufficient conditions for the supply–demand feasibility constraints (5.15) are stated in terms of a set of inequalities. If a supply is considered as a negative demand, condition (5.15) states that the net demand over any subset of the node set of a net cannot exceed the capacity of the arcs leading into the subset. In other words, if the problem is feasible, then it must be possible to send into any subset of the node set a total amount that is at least equal to the excess of demand over supply for the subset. If this condition is satisfied for all subsets of the node set, then the problem is feasible. Otherwise, it is infeasible.

For example, consider the net $G(V, E, c, f)$ of Fig. 5.4 with source nodes 1 and 2 and sink nodes 6 and 7. The supplies and demands of these nodes are given by

$$a(1) = 10, \qquad a(2) = 3, \qquad b(6) = 5, \qquad b(7) = 8 \tag{5.36}$$

as indicated in Fig. 5.4. A flow pattern that almost succeeds in meeting the demands from the sources is presented in Fig. 5.5, in which the second numbers adjacent to the arcs denote their flow values.

To ascertain the feasibility of this problem, we apply Theorem 5.1 with

$$S = \{1, 2\}, \qquad R = \{3, 4, 5\}, \qquad T = \{6, 7\} \tag{5.37}$$

Using the cut

$$(X, \bar{X}) = (\{1, 3, 4, 6\}, \{2, 5, 7\}) \tag{5.38}$$

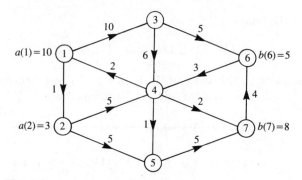

Fig. 5.4. A net used to illustrate the feasibility theorem.

in (5.15) yields

$$b(T \cap \bar{X}) - a(S \cap \bar{X}) = b(7) - a(2) = 8 - 3 = 5$$

$$\ngeqslant c(X, \bar{X}) = c(1, 2) + c(4, 5) + c(4, 7) = 4 \quad (5.39)$$

Thus, condition (5.15) is not satisfied for some $X \subseteq V$, and the problem is therefore infeasible. Alternatively, the cut

$$(X, \bar{X}) = (\{1, 2, 3, 4, 5, 6\}, \{7\}) \quad (5.40)$$

also violates condition (5.15):

$$b(T \cap \bar{X}) - a(S \cap \bar{X}) = b(7) - a(\{\ \}) = 8 \ngeqslant c(X, \bar{X}) = 7 \quad (5.41)$$

To see that the flow pattern of Fig. 5.5 represents the best one can do, we consider the extended net $G_1(V_1, E_1, c_1, f_1)$ of Fig. 5.6, which is obtained

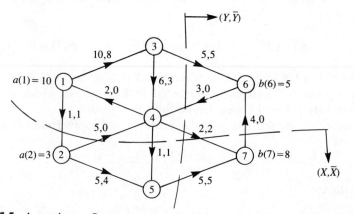

Fig. 5.5. A maximum flow pattern used to illustrate the feasibility theorem.

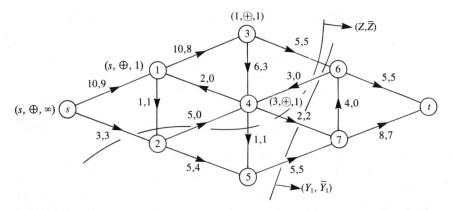

Fig. 5.6. An extended net of the net of Fig. 5.5 used to demonstrate that the flow pattern in Fig. 5.5 is maximum.

from G by adjoining a fictitious source s, sink t, and the arcs (s, S) and (T, t) with arc capacities as indicated in the figure. The flow in the net G_1 of Fig. 5.6 is maximum because by the max-flow min-cut theorem the s–t cut

$$(Y_1, \bar{Y}_1) = (\{s, 1, 2, 3, 4, 5\}, \{6, 7, t\}) \tag{5.42}$$

is minimum. The restriction of $(Y_1, \bar{Y}_1)$ in G gives the corresponding partition $(Y, \bar{Y})$ as depicted in Fig. 5.5.

In practice, if we are interested in ascertaining the feasibility of a given supply–demand net $G(V, E, c, f)$, the most efficient way to do this is to use the Ford–Fulkerson algorithm of Section 3.2 to solve the equivalent maximum flow problem in the extended net $G_1(V_1, E_1, c_1, f_1)$ of Fig. 5.3, rather than to check condition (5.15) for all subsets of the node set of G. If the problem is infeasible, a violation of condition (5.15) will be detected at the conclusion of the computation of the algorithm by taking X and $\bar{X}$ to be the labeled and unlabeled nodes of V, respectively.

For example, if we wish to ascertain the feasibility of the supply–demand net $G(V, E, c, f)$ of Fig. 5.5, we consider the extended net $G_1(V_1, E_1, c_1, f_1)$ of Fig. 5.6. Assume that the initial flow is as indicated in Fig. 5.6. Applying the Ford–Fulkerson algorithm yields the node labels as shown in Fig. 5.6. Then by taking

$$Z = \{s, 1, 3, 4\} \tag{5.43a}$$

$$\bar{Z} = \{2, 5, 6, 7, t\} \tag{5.43b}$$

to be the labeled and unlabeled nodes of V, respectively, a subset

$$X = Z - \{s\} = \{1, 3, 4\} \tag{5.44}$$

of V violating condition (5.15) is detected. To verify, we use (5.44) in (5.15) and obtain

$$b(T \cap \bar{X}) - a(S \cap \bar{X}) = b(\{6, 7\}) - a(2) = 5 + 8 - 3 = 10$$
$$\nleqq c(X, \bar{X}) = 1 + 1 + 2 + 5 = 9 \tag{5.45}$$

where

$$\bar{X} = \bar{Z} - \{t\} = \{2, 5, 6, 7\} \tag{5.46}$$

Recall that in the proof of Theorem 5.1 we appealed to the max-flow min-cut theorem (Theorem 3.2). In the following, we demonstrate that Theorem 5.1 implies the max-flow min-cut theorem. To see this, let $G(V, E, c, f)$ be a net with source s and sink t and let $(X, \bar{X})$ be a minimum s–t cut of G. Suppose that we place a demand equal to $c(X, \bar{X})$ at the sink t and an infinite supply at the source s. All other nodes of V are intermediate nodes. In terms of the symbols used in the supply–demand theorem (Theorem 5.1), we can make the following identifications:

$$a(s) = \infty, \qquad b(t) = c(X, \bar{X}) \tag{5.47a}$$
$$S = \{s\}, \qquad R = V - \{s, t\}, \qquad T = \{t\} \tag{5.47b}$$

Then according to Theorem 5.1 the constraints

$$f(s, V) - f(V, s) = f_{st} \tag{5.48a}$$
$$f(x, V) - f(V, x) = 0, \qquad x \neq s, t \tag{5.48b}$$
$$f(V, t) - f(t, V) \geq c(X, \bar{X}) \tag{5.48c}$$
$$c(x, y) \geq f(x, y) \geq 0, \qquad (x, y) \in E \tag{5.49}$$

are feasible if and only if

$$b(T \cap \bar{Y}) - a(S \cap \bar{Y}) \leq c(Y, \bar{Y}) \tag{5.50}$$

holds for all subsets $Y \subseteq V$, where $\bar{Y} = V - Y$. For $s \in \bar{Y}$

$$a(S \cap \bar{Y}) = a(s) = \infty \tag{5.51}$$

and for $t \in Y$

$$b(T \cap \bar{Y}) = b(\{ \}) = 0 \tag{5.52}$$

In either case, condition (5.50) is satisfied. Therefore, we assume that $s \in Y$ and $t \in \bar{Y}$ and (5.50) reduces to

$$b(t) = c(X, \bar{X}) \leq c(Y, \bar{Y}) \tag{5.53}$$

since $a(S \cap \bar{Y}) = 0$. But by assumption $(X, \bar{X})$ is a minimum s–t cut and $(Y, \bar{Y})$ is an arbitrary s–t cut. The inequality (5.53) is always satisfied. The constraints (5.48) and (5.49) are, therefore, feasible. In other words, there exists a flow from s to t in G with a value of at least $c(X, \bar{X})$. Invoking Theorem 3.1 which states that the flow value from s to t in G cannot exceed the capacity of any s–t cut, $c(X, \bar{X})$ is also the maximum flow value from s to t in G. The max-flow min-cut theorem follows.

Theorem 5.1 can also be stated in terms of the aggregate demand at the sinks. Specifically, we show that if, corresponding to each subset of the sinks, there is a flow satisfying the aggregate demand of the subset without exceeding the supply limitations at each of the sources, then there exists a flow in the net meeting all the individual demands. This result, due to Gale (1957), is stated as follows.

THEOREM 5.2

Partition the node set V of a given net $G(V, E, c, f)$ into three disjoint subsets S, R and T. Associate with each $x \in S$ a supply $a(x) \geq 0$ at x and with each $y \in T$ a demand $b(y)$ at y. Then the constraints

$$f(x, V) - f(V, x) \leq a(x), \qquad x \in S \qquad (5.54)$$

$$f(x, V) - f(V, x) = 0, \qquad x \in R \qquad (5.55)$$

$$f(V, x) - f(x, V) \geq b(x), \qquad x \in T \qquad (5.56)$$

$$c(x, y) \geq f(x, y) \geq 0, \qquad (x, y) \in E \qquad (5.57)$$

are feasible if and only if, for every subset $T_\alpha \subseteq T$, there exists a flow f_α in G satisfying

$$f_\alpha(x, V) - f_\alpha(V, x) \leq a(x), \qquad x \in S \qquad (5.58)$$

$$f_\alpha(x, V) - f_\alpha(V, x) = 0, \qquad x \in R \qquad (5.59)$$

$$c(x, y) \geq f_\alpha(x, y) \geq 0, \qquad (x, y) \in E \qquad (5.60)$$

and

$$f_\alpha(V, T_\alpha) - f_\alpha(T_\alpha, V) \geq b(T_\alpha) \qquad (5.61)$$

Proof. The necessity is obvious. To prove sufficiency, let X and $\bar{X} = V - X$ be a partition of the node set V such that $(T - T_\alpha) \subseteq X$ and $T_\alpha \subseteq \bar{X}$. Since by hypothesis the flow f_α satisfies (5.58), (5.59) and (5.61), it follows immediately by summing these equations and inequalities over the subsets $S \cap \bar{X}$, $R \cap \bar{X}$ and $T \cap \bar{X} = T_\alpha$, respectively, that

$$f_\alpha(S \cap \bar{X}, V) - f_\alpha(V, S \cap \bar{X}) \leqq a(S \cap \bar{X}) \qquad (5.62)$$

$$f_\alpha(R \cap \bar{X}, V) - f_\alpha(V, R \cap \bar{X}) = 0 \qquad (5.63)$$

$$f_\alpha(V, T \cap \bar{X}) - f_\alpha(T \cap \bar{X}, V) \geqq b(T \cap \bar{X}) \qquad (5.64)$$

Multiplying (5.62) and (5.63) by -1, reversing the inequality sign in (5.62), and adding the resulting inequality and equation to (5.64), we obtain

$$f_\alpha(V, S \cap \bar{X}) + f_\alpha(V, R \cap \bar{X}) + f_\alpha(V, T \cap \bar{X}) - f_\alpha(S \cap \bar{X}, V)$$
$$- f_\alpha(R \cap \bar{X}, V) - f_\alpha(T \cap \bar{X}, V) \geqq b(T \cap \bar{X}) - a(S \cap \bar{X}) \qquad (5.65)$$

or equivalently

$$b(T \cap \bar{X}) - a(S \cap \bar{X}) \leqq f_\alpha(V, \bar{X}) - f_\alpha(\bar{X}, V) = f_\alpha(X, \bar{X}) - f_\alpha(\bar{X}, X) \qquad (5.66)$$

Appealing to (5.60) by summing those equations over all $(x, y) \in (X, \bar{X})$ yields

$$c(X, \bar{X}) \geqq f_\alpha(X, \bar{X}) \geqq 0 \qquad (5.67)$$

Using this in (5.66) and noting that $f_\alpha(\bar{X}, X) \geqq 0$ gives

$$b(T \cap \bar{X}) - a(S \cap \bar{X}) \leqq c(X, \bar{X}) \qquad (5.68)$$

showing that condition (5.15) is fulfilled for all subsets $X \subseteq V$. Thus, by Theorem 5.1 the constraints (5.54)–(5.57) are feasible. This completes the proof of the theorem.

Dually, we can show that if, corresponding to each subset of the sources, there is a flow satisfying all individual demands without exceeding the aggregate supply of the subset with the supply at the sources outside the subset being infinite, then there exists a flow in the net meeting all the individual supplies and demands. We summarize this result as follows.

THEOREM 5.3

Partition the node set V of a given net $G(V, E, c, f)$ into three disjoint subsets S, R, and T. Associate with each $x \in S$ a supply $a(x) \geqq 0$ at x and with each $y \in T$ a demand $b(y)$ at y. Then the constraints

$$f(x, V) - f(V, x) \leqq a(x), \qquad x \in S \qquad (5.69)$$

$$f(x, V) - f(V, x) = 0, \qquad x \in R \qquad (5.70)$$

$$f(V, x) - f(x, V) \geqq b(x), \qquad x \in T \qquad (5.71)$$

$$c(x, y) \geqq f(x, y) \geqq 0, \qquad (x, y) \in E \qquad (5.72)$$

are feasible if and only if, for every subset $S_\alpha \subseteq S$, there exists a flow f_α in G satisfying

$$f_\alpha(x, V) - f_\alpha(V, x) = 0, \qquad x \in R \qquad (5.73)$$

$$f_\alpha(V, x) - f_\alpha(x, V) \geqq b(x), \qquad x \in T \qquad (5.74)$$

$$c(x, y) \geqq f_\alpha(x, y) \geqq 0, \qquad (x, y) \in E \qquad (5.75)$$

and

$$f_\alpha(S_\alpha, V) - f_\alpha(V, S_\alpha) \leqq a(S_\alpha) \qquad (5.76)$$

Observe that in proving Theorem 5.1 we used only the max-flow min-cut theorem (Theorem 3.2), and that Theorems 5.2 and 5.3 were derived directly from Theorem 5.1. As a result, if the functions a, b and c are integral valued and if there exists a feasible flow, then by the integrity theorem (Theorem 3.4) there is an integral feasible flow.

THEOREM 5.4

If there is a feasible flow for the constraints (5.11)–(5.14), (5.54)–(5.57), or (5.69)–(5.72), and if the supply function a, the demand function b, and the capacity function c are integral valued, then there is an integral feasible flow for these constraints.

We illustrate the above results by the following examples.

Example 5.1

We use the supply–demand net $G(V, E, c, f)$ of Fig. 5.1, which for convenience is redrawn in Fig. 5.7, to determine its feasibility.

Instead of applying Theorem 5.1 to determine the feasibility of the constraints for the net G of Fig. 5.7, which requires the checking of $2^7 = 128$ inequalities of the type (5.15), we use the Ford–Fulkerson algorithm of Section 3.2 to calculate the maximum flow from the source s to the sink t in the extended net $G_1(V_1, E_1, c_1, f_1)$ of Fig. 5.8. The extended net G_1 is obtained from G by adjoining a fictitious source s, sink t, and the arcs $(s, 1)$, $(s, 2)$, $(6, t)$ and $(7, t)$ with capacities

$$c_1(s, 1) = a(1) = 7, \qquad c_1(s, 2) = a(2) = 10$$

$$c_1(6, t) = b(6) = 7, \qquad c_1(7, t) = b(7) = 8 \qquad (5.77)$$

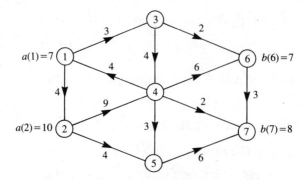

Fig. 5.7. A supply–demand net used to illustrate the feasibility theorem.

Applying the Ford–Fulkerson algorithm to G_1, a final feasible flow pattern together with the associated node labels is as indicated in Fig. 5.8. Since the s–t cut

$$(T, t) = (\{s, 1, 2, 3, 4, 5, 6, 7\}, t) = \{(6, t), (7, t)\} \qquad (5.78)$$

is minimum, being saturated, the problem is feasible. A feasible flow f for the net G is obtained by restricting f_1 to E. The result is shown in Fig. 5.9.   Q.E.D.

We remark that the feasible flow of Fig. 5.9 meets the demands at the sinks 6 and 7 without exceeding the supplies at 1 and 2. This does not imply that we cannot find other feasible flows that can do "better". For example, the feasible flow shown in Fig. 5.2 supplies 16 units to the sinks 6 and 7 from the sources 1 and 2 instead of the 15 for the flow of Fig. 5.9.

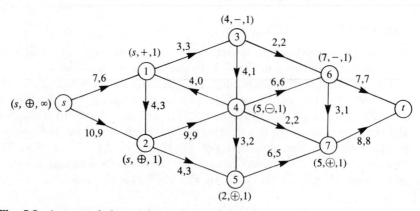

Fig. 5.8. An extended net of the supply–demand net of Fig. 5.7 used to calculate the maximum flow from s to t.

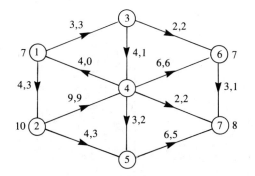

Fig. 5.9. A feasible flow pattern for the supply–demand net of Fig. 5.7.

Example 5.2

We use the net $G(V, E, c, f)$ of Fig. 5.7 to illustrate Theorems 5.2 and 5.3. From Fig. 5.7 we can make the following identifications:

$$S = \{1, 2\}, \qquad R = \{3, 4, 5\}, \qquad T = \{6, 7\} \qquad (5.79)$$

First, we apply Theorem 5.2 to verify that there is a feasible flow in G. To this end, we consider the subsets $T_\alpha = \{6\}$, $\{7\}$, and $\{6, 7\}$ of T. The empty subset is not included because the constraints (5.58)–(5.61) can always be fulfilled with zero flow. For $T_\alpha = \{6\}$, a flow $f_{\alpha 1}$ meeting the demand at sink 6 without exceeding the individual supplies at the sources 1 and 2 is shown in Fig. 5.10. This flow $f_{\alpha 1}$, however, does not meet the demand at sink 7. For $T_\alpha = \{7\}$, a flow $f_{\alpha 2}$ meeting the demand at sink 7 without exceeding the individual supplies at sources 1 and 2 is presented in Fig. 5.11. Observe that this flow $f_{\alpha 2}$ does not meet the demand at sink 6. Finally, for $T_\alpha = \{6, 7\}$ a flow $f_{\alpha 3}$ meeting the aggregate demand,

$$b(6) + b(7) = 7 + 8 = 15 \qquad (5.80)$$

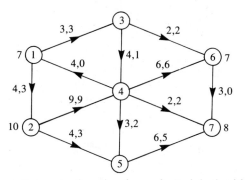

Fig. 5.10. A flow pattern meeting the demand at sink 6 without exceeding the individual supplies at sources 1 and 2.

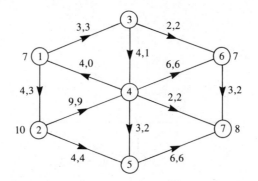

Fig. 5.11. A flow pattern meeting the demand at sink 7 without exceeding the individual supplies at sources 1 and 2.

without exceeding the individual supplies at sources 1 and 2 is given in Fig. 5.12. Notice that this flow $f_{\alpha 3}$ does not meet the individual demand at sink 7. Since, corresponding to each subset $T_\alpha \subseteq T$, there is a flow satisfying the aggregate demand of the subset without exceeding the supply limitations at each of the sources, according to Theorem 5.2 there exists a flow in the net G meeting all the individual demands without exceeding the supply limitations at each of the sources. Such a flow is shown in Fig. 5.9.

Next, we apply Theorem 5.3 to verify the existence of a feasible flow in G. For this we consider the subsets $S_\alpha = \{1\}$, $\{2\}$, and $\{1, 2\}$ of S. Again, the trivial empty subset is not included. For $S_\alpha = \{1\}$, a flow $f_{\alpha 4}$ meeting the individual demands at sinks 6 and 7 without exceeding the supply at source 1 is given in Fig. 5.13, where the supply at source 2 was set to infinity. Observe that in this case the supply at source 2 exceeds the original supply limitation by 3 ($= 13 - 10$). Likewise, for $S_\alpha = \{2\}$ a flow $f_{\alpha 5}$ meeting the individual demands at sinks 6 and 7 without exceeding the

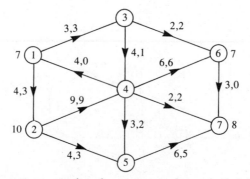

Fig. 5.12. A flow pattern meeting the aggregate demand of sinks 6 and 7 without exceeding the individual supplies at sources 1 and 2.

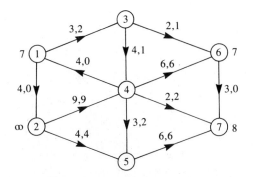

Fig. 5.13. A flow pattern meeting the individual demands at sinks 6 and 7 without exceeding the supply at source 1. The supply at source 2 was set to infinity.

supply at source 2 is presented in Fig. 5.14. Finally, for $S_\alpha = \{1, 2\}$ there is a flow $f_{\alpha 6}$ satisfying all individual demands at sinks 6 and 7 without exceeding the aggregate supply,

$$a(1) + a(2) = 7 + 10 = 17 \qquad (5.81)$$

at sources 1 and 2. This flow $f_{\alpha 6}$, being equal to $f_{\alpha 5}$, is again shown in Fig. 5.14. Thus, according to Theorem 5.3 there exists a flow in G meeting all the individual demands without exceeding the supply limitations at each of the sources. Such a flow is shown in Fig. 5.9 or 5.14.   Q.E.D.

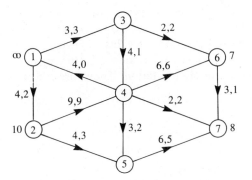

Fig. 5.14. A flow pattern meeting the individual demands at sinks 6 and 7 without exceeding the supply at source 2. The supply at source 1 was set to infinity.

Example 5.3

Consider the supply–demand net $G(V, E, c, f)$ of Fig. 5.15 with

$$a(1) = 10, \qquad a(2) = 3, \qquad b(6) = 5, \qquad b(7) = 8 \qquad (5.82)$$

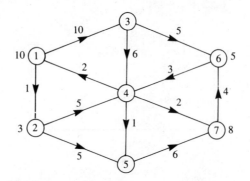

Fig. 5.15. An infeasible supply–demand net.

We wish to ascertain the feasibility of this net. From Fig. 5.15 we have

$$S = \{1, 2\}, \qquad R = \{3, 4, 5\}, \qquad T = \{6, 7\} \tag{5.83}$$

To apply Theorem 5.3, we consider the subsets $S_\alpha = \{1\}$, $\{2\}$, and $\{1, 2\}$. For $S_\alpha = \{1\}$ a flow $f_{\alpha 1}$ meeting the individual demands at sinks 6 and 7 without exceeding the supply at source 1 is shown in Fig. 5.16, where the supply at source 2 was set to infinity. This flow $f_{\alpha 1}$ does not exceed the aggregate supply

$$a(1) + a(2) = 10 + 3 = 13 \tag{5.84}$$

of the subset $S_\alpha = \{1, 2\}$ of sources 1 and 2. Finally, for the subset $S_\alpha = \{2\}$ we set $a(1) = \infty$ in Fig. 5.15. To meet the demand at sink 7, arcs $(4, 7)$ and $(5, 7)$ must be saturated. This in turn requires that the flow value in arc $(2, 5)$ be at least 5, or source 2 must provide a supply of at least 4, exceeding its supply limitation. Therefore, there does not exist a

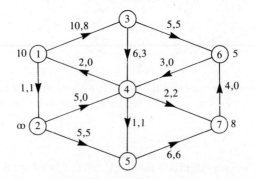

Fig. 5.16. A flow pattern meeting the individual demands at sinks 6 and 7 without exceeding the supply at source 1. The supply at source 2 was set to infinity.

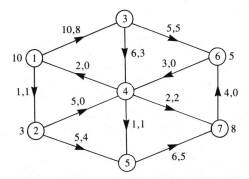

Fig. 5.17. A flow pattern meeting the demand at sink 6 without exceeding the individual supplies at sources 1 and 2.

flow that will meet the individual demands at sinks 6 and 7 that will not exceed the supply at source 2, even after setting the supply at the other source 1 to infinity. By Theorem 5.3, the problem is infeasible.

To verify this from the demand side, we consider the subsets $T_\alpha = \{6\}$, $\{7\}$, and $\{6, 7\}$. For $T_\alpha = \{6\}$ a flow $f_{\alpha 2}$ meeting the demand at sink 6 without exceeding the individual supplies at sources 1 and 2 is presented in Fig. 5.17. However, for $T_\alpha = \{7\}$ it is straightforward to show that there is no flow that will meet the demand at sink 7 without exceeding the supplies at sources 1 and 2. Thus, the problem is infeasible.   Q.E.D.

5.2   AN EXTENDED SUPPLY–DEMAND THEOREM

In the preceding section, we presented the necessary and sufficient conditions for the existence of a flow that meets all the individual demands at the sinks without exceeding the supply limitations at each of the sources. Neither the lower bounds for the supplies at each of the sources nor the upper bounds for the demands at each of the sinks are assumed. In the present section, we extend the problem by imposing these bounds on the net flow leaving each source and entering each sink. Our objective is to find the necessary and sufficient conditions for the resulting set of inequalities to be feasible. Specifically, we show that if there is a flow that meets the lower bound requirements at each of the sources and the upper bound requirements at each of the sinks, and if there is a flow that meets the upper bound requirements at each of the sources and the lower bound requirements at each of the sinks, then there is a flow that satisfies all the lower and upper bound requirements at each of the sources and sinks simultaneously. This results, due to Fulkerson (1959), is a kind of symmetry with respect to the demands and supplies, and is known as a *symmetric supply–demand theorem*.

THEOREM 5.5

Partition the node set V of a given net $G(V, E, c, f)$ into three disjoint subsets S, R and T. Associate with each $x \in S$ two nonnegative real functions $a(x)$ and $a'(x)$, $a(x) \leq a'(x)$, and with each $x \in T$ two nonnegative real functions $b(x)$ and $b'(x)$, $b(x) \leq b'(x)$. Then the constraints

$$a(x) \leq f(x, V) - f(V, x) \leq a'(x), \qquad x \in S \qquad (5.85)$$

$$f(x, V) - f(V, x) = 0, \qquad x \in R \qquad (5.86)$$

$$b(x) \leq f(V, x) - f(x, V) \leq b'(x), \qquad x \in T \qquad (5.87)$$

$$c(x, y) \geq f(x, y) \geq 0, \qquad (x, y) \in E \qquad (5.88)$$

are feasible if and only if

$$c(X, \bar{X}) \geq b(T \cap \bar{X}) - a'(S \cap \bar{X}) \qquad (5.89)$$

$$c(X, \bar{X}) \geq a(S \cap X) - b'(T \cap X) \qquad (5.90)$$

hold for every subset $X \subseteq V$, where $\bar{X} = V - X$.

Proof. We first construct an extended net $G'(V', E', c', f')$ of Fig. 5.18 by adjoining new nodes s, t, u and v and arcs (s, S), (u, S), (T, t), (T, v),

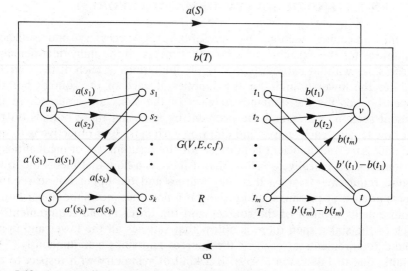

Fig. 5.18. An extended net $G'(V', E', c', f')$ obtained from the net $G(V, E, c, f)$ by adjoining nodes s, t, u and v and arcs as indicated.

(u, t), (s, v) and (t, s) with capacities defined as

$$c'(s, x) = a'(x) - a(x), \qquad x \in S \qquad (5.91a)$$

$$c'(u, x) = a(x), \qquad x \in S \qquad (5.91b)$$

$$c'(x, t) = b'(x) - b(x), \qquad x \in T \qquad (5.91c)$$

$$c'(x, v) = b(x), \qquad x \in T \qquad (5.91d)$$

$$c'(u, t) = b(T) \qquad (5.91e)$$

$$c'(s, v) = a(S) \qquad (5.91f)$$

$$c'(t, s) = \infty \qquad (5.91g)$$

$$c'(x, y) = c(x, y), \qquad (x, y) \in E \qquad (5.91h)$$

We assert that the constraints (5.85)–(5.88) are feasible if and only if the value of a maximum flow from u to v in G' is $a(S) + b(T)$. To see this, let f be a feasible flow in G. Extend f in G to f' in G' by defining

$$f'(s, x) = f(x, V) - f(V, x) - a(x), \qquad x \in S \qquad (5.92a)$$

$$f'(u, x) = a(x), \qquad x \in S \qquad (5.92b)$$

$$f'(x, t) = f(V, x) - f(x, V) - b(x), \qquad x \in T \qquad (5.92c)$$

$$f'(x, v) = b(x), \qquad x \in T \qquad (5.92d)$$

$$f'(u, t) = b(T) \qquad (5.92e)$$

$$f'(s, v) = a(S) \qquad (5.92f)$$

$$f'(t, s) = f(S, V) - f(V, S) \qquad (5.92g)$$

$$f'(x, y) = f(x, y), \qquad (x, y) \in E \qquad (5.92h)$$

It is straightforward to verify that f', as defined above, is a flow from u to v in G' having value $a(S) + b(T)$.

Conversely, if f' is a flow from u to v in G' of value $a(S) + b(T)$, then

$$f'(u, x) = a(x), \qquad x \in S \qquad (5.93a)$$

$$f'(x, v) = b(x), \qquad x \in T \qquad (5.93b)$$

Let f be f' restricted to E. Then for $x \in S$ we have

$$f'(u, x) + f'(s, x) = f(x, V) - f(V, x) \qquad (5.94)$$

Since from (5.91a)

$$a'(x) - a(x) \geq f'(s, x) \geq 0 \qquad (5.95)$$

equation (5.94) can be rewritten as

$$a'(x) \geq f(x, V) - f(V, x) \geq a(x), \qquad x \in S \tag{5.96}$$

after invoking (5.93a). Likewise, we can show that

$$b'(x) \geq f(V, x) - f(x, V) \geq b(x), \qquad x \in T \tag{5.97}$$

This completes the proof of our assertion that the constraints (5.85)–(5.88) are feasible if and only if the value of a maximum flow from u to v in G' is $a(S) + b(T)$. Thus, to prove the theorem, we need only show that the conditions (5.89) and (5.90) are necessary and sufficient for the existence of a flow f' from u to v in G' having value $a(S) + b(T)$, or equivalently a flow that saturates all source and sink arcs.

By appealing to the max-flow min-cut theorem (Theorem 3.2), we recognize that if we can show that every u–v cut in $G'(V', E', c', f')$ has capacity value of at least $a(S) + b(T)$, then G' has a flow from u to v of value $a(S) + b(T)$ and the problem is feasible. To this end, let $(X', \bar{X}')$ be a u–v cut in G'. Four cases are distinguished.

Case 1

$s \in X'$ and $t \in \bar{X}'$. Partition the subsets X' and $\bar{X}'$ of V' into

$$X' = \{u, s\} \cup X, \qquad \bar{X}' = \{v, t\} \cup \bar{X} \tag{5.98}$$

so that $\bar{X} = V - X$. Then

$$\begin{aligned}
c'(X', \bar{X}') &= c'(u, t) + c'(u, \bar{X}) + c'(s, v) + c'(s, \bar{X}) \\
&\quad + c'(X, v) + c'(X, t) + c'(X, \bar{X}) \\
&= b(T) + a(S \cap \bar{X}) + a(S) + a'(S \cap \bar{X}) - a(S \cap \bar{X}) \\
&\quad + b(T \cap X) + b'(T \cap X) - b(T \cap X) + c(X, \bar{X}) \tag{5.99}
\end{aligned}$$

Since $a'(S \cap \bar{X}) \geq a(S \cap \bar{X})$ and $b'(T \cap X) \geq b(T \cap X)$, it follows that

$$c'(X', \bar{X}') \geq a(S) + b(T) \tag{5.100}$$

Case 2

$s \in \bar{X}'$ and $t \in X'$. In this case, $c'(X', \bar{X}')$ is infinite and no condition is obtained.

Case 3

$s, t \in X'$. Partition X' and $\bar{X}'$ into

$$X' = \{s, t, u\} \cup X, \qquad \bar{X}' = \{v\} \cup \bar{X} \tag{5.101}$$

Then we have

$$c'(X', \bar{X}') = c'(s, v) + c'(s, \bar{X}) + c'(u, \bar{X}) + c'(X, v) + c'(X, \bar{X})$$
$$= a(S) + a'(S \cap \bar{X}) - a(S \cap \bar{X}) + a(S \cap \bar{X})$$
$$+ b(T \cap X) + c(X, \bar{X})$$
$$= a(S) + a'(S \cap \bar{X}) + b(T) - b(T \cap \bar{X}) + c(X, \bar{X}) \quad (5.102)$$

This shows that

$$c'(X', \bar{X}') \geqq a(S) + b(T) \tag{5.103}$$

if and only if

$$c(X, \bar{X}) \geqq b(T \cap \bar{X}) - a'(S \cap \bar{X}) \tag{5.104}$$

Case 4

$s, t \in \bar{X}'$. Partition X' and $\bar{X}'$ into

$$X' = \{u\} \cup X, \qquad \bar{X}' = \{s, t, v\} \cup \bar{X} \tag{5.105}$$

Then we have

$$c'(X', \bar{X}') = c'(u, t) + c'(u, \bar{X}) + c'(X, t) + c'(X, v) + c'(X, \bar{X})$$
$$= b(T) + a(S \cap \bar{X}) + b'(T \cap X) - b(T \cap X)$$
$$+ b(T \cap X) + c(X, \bar{X})$$
$$= b(T) + a(S) - a(S \cap X) + b'(T \cap X) + c(X, \bar{X}) \tag{5.106}$$

This shows that

$$c'(X', \bar{X}') \geqq a(S) + b(T) \tag{5.107}$$

if and only if

$$c(X, \bar{X}) \geqq a(S \cap X) - b'(T \cap X) \tag{5.108}$$

Thus, we have shown that the constraints (5.85)–(5.88) are feasible if and only if the value of a maximum flow from u to v in G' is $a(S) + b(T)$, and that such a flow exists in G' if and only if conditions (5.89) and (5.90) are satisfied for every subset of the node set of G. This completes the proof of the theorem.

Observe that if we set $a(x) = 0$ for $x \in S$ and $b'(y) = \infty$ for $y \in T$, then Theorem 5.5 reduces to Theorem 5.1, a supply–demand theorem. Theorem 5.5 is therefore an *extended supply–demand theorem*. Suppose that we interchange the roles of the sources and sinks in G by thinking of a as the demand function at the set S of sinks, b' as the supply function at the set T of sources, and reverse all arc directions of G. Then by Theorem 5.1 condition (5.90) is necessary and sufficient for the existence of a flow meeting all the supply and demand requirements in the reversed net. In this sense, the conditions (5.89) and (5.90) are symmetric, and Theorem 5.5 is also known as a *symmetric supply–demand theorem*. This leads directly to the following corollary.

COROLLARY 5.1

The constraints (5.85)–(5.88) are feasible if and only if each of the following constraint sets

$$a(x) \leqq f(x, V) - f(V, x), \qquad x \in S \qquad (5.109a)$$

$$f(x, V) - f(V, x) = 0, \qquad x \in R \qquad (5.109b)$$

$$f(V, x) - f(x, V) \leqq b'(x), \qquad x \in T \qquad (5.109c)$$

$$c(x, y) \geqq f(x, y) \geqq 0, \qquad (x, y) \in E \qquad (5.109d)$$

and

$$f(x, V) - f(V, x) \leqq a'(x), \qquad x \in S \qquad (5.110a)$$

$$f(x, V) - f(V, x) = 0, \qquad x \in R \qquad (5.110b)$$

$$b(x) \leqq f(V, x) - f(x, V), \qquad x \in T \qquad (5.110c)$$

$$c(x, y) \geqq f(x, y) \geqq 0, \qquad (x, y) \in E \qquad (5.110d)$$

is feasible.

In words, the corollary states that if there is a flow meeting the lower bound requirements at each of the sources and the upper bound requirements at each of the sinks, and if there is a flow satisfying the upper bound requirements at each of the sources and the lower bound requirements at each of the sinks, then there is a feasible flow in the supply–demand net.

We illustrate the above results by the following examples.

Example 5.4

In the supply–demand net $G(V, E, c, f)$ of Fig. 5.19, the sources are nodes 1 and 2 and the sinks are nodes 6 and 7. Thus, the node set V can be partitioned into the subsets

$$S = \{1, 2\}, \qquad R = \{3, 4, 5\}, \qquad T = \{6, 7\} \qquad (5.111)$$

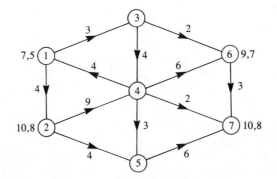

Fig. 5.19. A supply–demand net with lower and upper bounds specified for the supplies and demands of the sources and sinks.

The lower and upper bounds of the supplies and demands at the sources and the sinks are preassigned, respectively, as

$$a(1) = 5, \quad a'(1) = 7, \quad a(2) = 8, \quad a'(2) = 10 \quad (5.112)$$

$$b(6) = 7, \quad b'(6) = 9, \quad b(7) = 8, \quad b'(7) = 10 \quad (5.113)$$

They are given as pairs of numbers adjacent to the nodes in the net of Fig. 5.19, the first number being the upper bound and the second the lower bound.

Instead of directly applying Theorem 5.5 to ascertain the existence of a flow that meets the lower and upper bound requirements of the supplies and demands at the sources and the sinks simultaneously, which requires the checking of $2 \times 2^{|V|} = 2 \times 2^7 = 256$ inequalities (5.89) and (5.90), we use Corollary 5.1 to determine its feasibility. To this end, we consider the net G_α of Fig. 5.20, in which the supplies at sources 1 and 2 are required to be at least 5 and 8, and the demands at sinks 6 and 7 are not to exceed

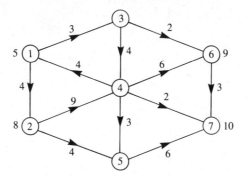

Fig. 5.20. A supply–demand net with lower bounds specified for the supplies at sources 1 and 2 and upper bounds specified for the demands at sinks 6 and 7.

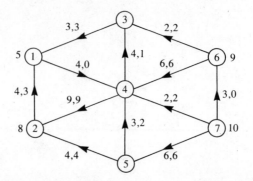

Fig. 5.21. A supply–demand net with lower bounds specified for the demands at sinks 1 and 2 and upper bounds specified for the supplies at sources 6 and 7.

9 and 10, respectively. A feasible flow in G_α exists if and only if there is a flow in the reversed net G_β of Fig. 5.21, which is obtained from G_α by reversing all arc directions, such that the supplies at sources 6 and 7 do not exceed 9 and 10, and the demands at sinks 1 and 2 are at least 5 and 8, respectively. The existence of a flow meeting all the requirements in G_β is shown in Fig. 5.21 with the arc flows given as the second numbers in the pairs of numbers adjacent to the arcs. Thus, the constraints (5.109) are feasible.

To check the feasibility of the constraints (5.110), we use the net of Fig. 5.1, in which the supplies at sources 1 and 2 cannot exceed 7 and 10, respectively, and the demands at sinks 6 and 7 are at least 7 and 8, respectively. A feasible flow is shown in Fig. 5.2. Thus, the constraints (5.110) are feasible. By Corollary 5.1, there is a feasible flow in the original net G meeting all the lower and upper bound requirements simultaneously. Such a flow is presented in Fig. 5.22.   Q.E.D.

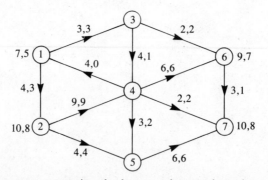

Fig. 5.22. A flow pattern meeting the lower and upper bound requirements of the supplies and demands at sources 1 and 2 and sinks 6 and 7.

Example 5.5

In the supply–demand net $G(V, E, c, f)$ of Fig. 5.23, the lower and upper bounds of the supplies and demands at sources 1 and 2 and at sinks 6 and 7 are specified as

$$a(1) = a'(1) = 5, \qquad a(2) = a'(2) = 10 \qquad (5.114)$$
$$b(6) = b'(6) = 7, \qquad b(7) = b'(7) = 8 \qquad (5.115)$$

respectively. They are shown in Fig. 5.23 as pairs of numbers adjacent to the nodes. We wish to determine if there is a feasible flow in G that satisfies the requirements (5.114) and (5.115).

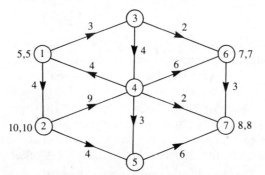

Fig. 5.23. A supply–demand net with the same lower and upper bounds specified for the supplies and demands of the sources and the sinks.

To apply Corollary 5.1, we need only consider the feasibility problems for the nets G_α of Fig. 5.24 and G_β of Fig. 5.25. The net G_α was obtained from G by reversing all arc directions with the stipulations that the demands at sinks 1 and 2 be at least 5 and 10, respectively, and that the

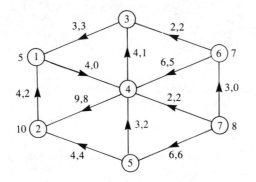

Fig. 5.24. A supply–demand net with lower bounds specified for the demands at sinks 1 and 2 and upper bounds specified for the supplies at sources 6 and 7.

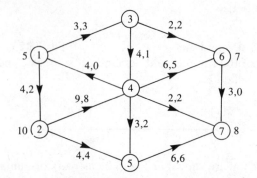

Fig. 5.25. A supply–demand net with lower bounds specified for the demands at sinks 6 and 7 and upper bounds specified for the supplies at sources 1 and 2.

supplies at sources 6 and 7 not exceed 7 and 8, respectively. A flow pattern meeting these requirements is shown in Fig. 5.24. Thus, the constraints (5.109) are feasible. For the net G_β, the requirements are that the demands at sinks 6 and 7 be at least 7 and 8, respectively, and that the supplies at sources 1 and 2 not exceed 5 and 10, respectively. A flow pattern satisfying these constraints is presented in Fig. 5.25, showing that the constraints (5.110) are feasible. The existence of the feasible flows in G_α and G_β implies the existence of a flow in G that meets all the requirements (5.114) and (5.115). Such a flow is shown in Fig. 5.26.   Q.E.D.

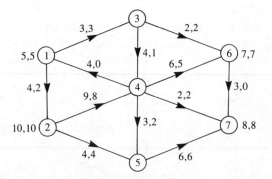

Fig. 5.26. A flow pattern meeting the same lower and upper bound requirements of the supplies and demands at sources 1 and 2 and sinks 6 and 7.

We remark that in the case where $a(x) = a'(x)$ for $x \in S$ and $b(y) = b'(y)$ for $y \in T$, (5.109) and (5.110) reduce to

$$f(x, V) - f(V, x) = a(x), \qquad x \in S \qquad (5.116a)$$

$$f(x, V) - f(V, x) = 0, \qquad x \in R \qquad (5.116b)$$

$$f(V, x) - f(x, V) = b(x), \qquad x \in T \qquad (5.116c)$$

$$c(x, y) \geqq f(x, y) \geqq 0, \qquad (x, y) \in E \qquad (5.116d)$$

Thus, in determining the feasibility for the net of Fig. 5.23, we need only consider the net G_β of Fig. 5.25 with the stipulations that the demands at the sinks 6 and 7 be exactly 7 and 8, and that the supplies at the sources 1 and 2 be exactly 5 and 10, respectively. A flow pattern meeting these requirements is shown in Fig. 5.25.   Q.E.D.

5.3 CIRCULATION THEOREM

In the foregoing, we studied the feasibility problem of a supply–demand net, in which the lower and upper bounds are set for the supplies and demands at the sources and sinks. No minimum flow values are required in individual arcs. In the present section, we are concerned with the existence of a flow in a source-free and sink-free net, that satisfies the prescribed lower and upper bounds on the flow values in arcs.

Let $G(V, E, c, f)$ be a source-free and sink-free net, and let l and c be the lower and upper bound functions from E to the nonnegative reals with

$$c(x, y) \geqq l(x, y) \geqq 0, \qquad (x, y) \in E \qquad (5.117)$$

Thus, for our purposes we write G as a quintuplet $G(V, E, l, c, f)$. A *feasible circulation* in G is a function f from E to the nonnegative reals satisfying

$$f(x, V) - f(V, x) = 0, \qquad x \in V \qquad (5.118)$$

$$c(x, y) \geqq f(x, y) \geqq l(x, y) \geqq 0, \qquad (x, y) \in E \qquad (5.119)$$

We now proceed to establish the *circulation theorem* due to Hoffman (1960) below.

THEOREM 5.6

A necessary and sufficient condition for the existence of a feasible circulation in a given net $G(V, E, l, c, f)$ is that the inequality

$$c(X, \bar{X}) \geqq l(\bar{X}, X) \qquad (5.120)$$

holds for all subsets $X \subseteq V$, where $\bar{X} = V - X$.

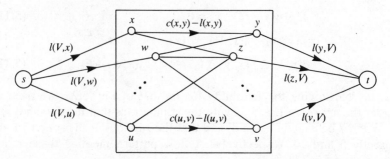

Fig. 5.27. An extended net obtained from G by adjoining nodes s and t and sets of arcs (s, V) and (V, t).

Proof. We first construct an extended net $G'(V', E', l', c', f')$ from G by adjoining two nodes s and t and the sets of arcs (s, V) and (V, t), as depicted in Fig. 5.27. The lower and upper functions l' and c' of G' are defined by

$$l'(x, y) = 0, \qquad (x, y) \in E' \qquad (5.121a)$$

$$c'(x, y) = c(x, y) - l(x, y), \qquad (x, y) \in E \qquad (5.121b)$$

$$c'(s, x) = l(V, x), \qquad x \in V \qquad (5.121c)$$

$$c'(x, t) = l(x, V), \qquad x \in V \qquad (5.121d)$$

It is straightforward to verify that if f is a feasible circulation in G, then the flow function f' defined by

$$f'(x, y) = f(x, y) - l(x, y), \qquad (x, y) \in E \qquad (5.122)$$

$$f'(s, x) = l(V, x), \qquad x \in V \qquad (5.123a)$$

$$f'(x, t) = l(x, V), \qquad x \in V \qquad (5.123b)$$

is a flow from s to t in G'. Conversely, if there is a flow f' in G' satisfying (5.123), then the flow function f defined by

$$f(x, y) = f'(x, y) + l(x, y), \qquad (x, y) \in E \qquad (5.124)$$

is a feasible circulation in G. Conditions (5.123) imply the existence of a flow f' from s to t in G' of value $l(V, V)$. Our conclusion is that a feasible circulation exists in G if and only if there is a flow from s to t in G' that has a value $l(V, V)$.

To complete the proof, it is sufficient to show that there is a flow from s to t in G' of value $l(V, V)$. By appealing to the max-flow min-cut theorem

(Theorem 3.2), we need only prove that all the $s-t$ cuts in G' have values of at least $l(V, V)$. To this end, let $(X', \bar{X}')$ be an arbitrary $s-t$ cut in G', and partition X' and $\bar{X}'$ into

$$X' = \{s\} \cup X, \qquad \bar{X}' = \{t\} \cup \bar{X} \tag{5.125}$$

Consider the expansion of the cut capacity

$$
\begin{aligned}
c'(X', \bar{X}') &= c'(s, \bar{X}) + c'(X, \bar{X}) + c'(X, t) \\
&= l(V, \bar{X}) + c(X, \bar{X}) - l(X, \bar{X}) + l(X, V) \\
&= l(\bar{X}, \bar{X}) + c(X, \bar{X}) + l(X, V) \\
&= l(V, V) - l(\bar{X}, X) + c(X, \bar{X}) \tag{5.126}
\end{aligned}
$$

It follows that

$$c'(X', \bar{X}') \geqq l(V, V) \tag{5.127}$$

if and only if

$$c(X, \bar{X}) \geqq l(\bar{X}, X) \tag{5.128}$$

This completes the proof of the theorem.

In words, the theorem states that the flow $l(\bar{X}, X)$ forced into any subset X of the node set must be able to escape through the cut $(X, \bar{X})$ having capacity of at least $l(\bar{X}, X)$. If this condition is satisfied for all subsets of the node set of G, then there is assured a feasible circulation.

In Section 3.9, we considered the flow problem in an undirected or mixed net $G(V, E, c, f)$. If an edge $(x, y) = (y, x)$ is undirected with capacity $c(x, y) = c(y, x)$, we interpret this to mean that

$$f(x, y) \leqq c(x, y) \tag{5.129a}$$
$$f(y, x) \leqq c(x, y) \tag{5.129b}$$

and that flow is permitted in only one of the two directions or

$$f(x, y)f(y, x) = 0 \tag{5.130}$$

In other words, the arc (x, y) has a flow capacity $c(x, y)$ in either direction but the flow can only move in one of the two directions. To find a maximum flow in such a net, we first replace each undirected edge (x, y) by a pair of oppositely directed edges (x, y) and (y, x), each having capacity equal to that of the original undirected edge, and obtain a directed net $G'(V, E', c', f')$.

We then apply any of the existing techniques to find a maximum flow. Once a solution f' is found with a certain maximum flow value, we can construct a feasible flow pattern f in the original net G with the same flow value by taking

$$f(x, y) = \max [0, f'(x, y) - f'(y, x)] \qquad (5.131)$$

yielding

$$f(x, y)f(y, x) = 0 \qquad (5.132)$$

The operation (5.131) is equivalent to canceling flows in opposite directions. This procedure can be extended to Theorems 5.1–5.5 to solve the feasibility problem in a supply–demand net. However, if nonzero lower bounds are imposed on undirected edge flows, then the above procedure cannot be used in determining a feasible circulation in a source-free and sink-free net, because the operation is no longer valid. Thus, there is a basic difference between the supply–demand theorem and the circulation theorem.

Theorem 5.6 gives a necessary and sufficient condition for the existence of a flow f in a net $G(V, E, c, f)$ that is flow conservative at each node $x \in V$ and that meets the lower and upper bound requirements in each arc $(x, y) \in E$. Like Theorem 5.5, this result can be extended to the situation where the net flow into a node $x \in V$ lies between prescribed bounds. The extension is due to Hoffman (1960) and is stated as follows.

THEOREM 5.7

In a given net $G(V, E, l, c, f)$, associate with each $x \in V$ two real functions $a(x)$ and $a'(x)$, $a(x) \leqq a'(x)$. Then the constraints

$$a(x) \leqq f(V, x) - f(x, V) \leqq a'(x), \qquad x \in V \qquad (5.133)$$

$$l(x, y) \leqq f(x, y) \leqq c(x, y), \qquad (x, y) \in E \qquad (5.134)$$

are feasible if and only if

$$c(X, \bar{X}) \geqq l(\bar{X}, X) + \max [a(\bar{X}), -a'(X)] \qquad (5.135)$$

holds for all subsets $X \subseteq V$.

Proof. We first construct an extended net $G'(V', E', l', c', f')$ from G by adjoining two nodes s and t and the sets of arcs (s, V) and (V, t) as depicted in Fig. 5.28. The lower and upper bound functions l' and c' for the

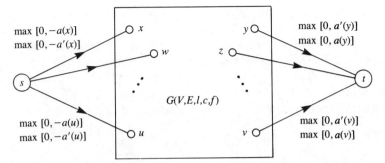

Fig. 5.28. An extended net obtained from G by adjoining nodes s and t and sets of arcs (s, V) and (V, t).

arcs in G' are defined by

$$l'(s, x) = \max [0, -a'(x)], \qquad x \in V \qquad (5.136a)$$

$$c'(s, x) = \max [0, -a(x)], \qquad x \in V \qquad (5.136b)$$

$$l'(x, t) = \max [0, a(x)], \qquad x \in V \qquad (5.137a)$$

$$c'(x, t) = \max [0, a'(x)], \qquad x \in V \qquad (5.137b)$$

$$l'(x, y) = l(x, y), \qquad (x, y) \in E \qquad (5.138a)$$

$$c'(x, y) = c(x, y), \qquad (x, y) \in E \qquad (5.138b)$$

Since $a'(x) \geq a(x)$, we have

$$c'(s, x) \geq l'(s, x), \qquad x \in V \qquad (5.139)$$

It is straightforward to verify that if there is a feasible flow f in G, then there is a flow f' from the source s to the sink t in G' meeting the lower and upper bound requirements (5.136)–(5.138) by defining

$$f'(s, x) = \max [0, f(x, V) - f(V, x)], \qquad x \in V \qquad (5.140a)$$

$$f'(x, t) = \max [0, f(V, x) - f(x, V)], \qquad x \in V \qquad (5.140b)$$

$$f'(x, y) = f(x, y), \qquad (x, y) \in E \qquad (5.140c)$$

Conversely, if there is a flow f' from s to t in G' satisfying the lower and upper bound requirements, then by restricting f' over E we obtain a feasible flow f in G. Our conclusion is that the constraints (5.133) and (5.134) are feasible if and only if there is a feasible flow in G' from s to t.

Suppose that we add arcs (s, t) and (t, s) to the net $G'(V', E', l', c', f')$

with infinite capacity and zero lower bound. Let the resulting net be denoted by $G''(V'', E'', l'', c'', f'')$. Then there is a feasible flow in G' from s to t if and only if there is a feasible circulation in G''. Thus, to complete our proof, it is sufficient to show that feasibility conditions (5.120) of Theorem 5.6, when applied to G'', yield the inequalities (5.135).

To this end, let X'' be a subset of V'' and define $\bar{X}'' = V'' - X''$. Then by Theorem 5.6 there is a feasible circulation in G'' if and only if

$$c''(X'', \bar{X}'') - l''(\bar{X}'', X'') \geqq 0 \tag{5.141}$$

for all $X'' \subseteq V''$. We show that (5.141) is satisfied if and only if (5.135) holds. To facilitate our discussion, four cases are distinguished.

Case 1

$s \in X''$ and $t \in \bar{X}''$. Partition the subsets X'' and $\bar{X}''$ into

$$X'' = \{s\} \cup X, \qquad \bar{X}'' = \{t\} \cup \bar{X} \tag{5.142}$$

Then the left-hand side of (5.141) can be expanded as

$$c''(X'', \bar{X}'') - l''(\bar{X}'', X'') = c''(\{s\} \cup X, \{t\} \cup \bar{X}) - l''(\{t\} \cup \bar{X}, \{s\} \cup X)$$
$$= c''(s, t) + c''(s, \bar{X}) + c''(X, t) + c''(X, \bar{X}) - l''(t, s) - l''(\bar{X}, X) = \infty \tag{5.143}$$

Thus, (5.141) is always satisfied. No condition is obtained in this case.

Case 2

$s \in \bar{X}''$ and $t \in X''$. Partition the subsets X'' and $\bar{X}''$ into

$$X'' = \{t\} \cup X, \qquad \bar{X}'' = \{s\} \cup \bar{X} \tag{5.144}$$

The left-hand side of (5.141) becomes

$$c''(X'', \bar{X}'') - l''(\bar{X}'', X'') = c''(\{t\} \cup X, \{s\} \cup \bar{X}) - l''(\{s\} \cup \bar{X}, \{t\} \cup X)$$
$$= c''(t, s) + c''(X, \bar{X}) - l''(s, X) - l''(\bar{X}, t) - l''(\bar{X}, X) = \infty \tag{5.145}$$

Equation (5.141) is always satisfied. No condition is obtained.

Case 3

$s, t \in X''$. Partition X'' into

$$X'' = \{s, t\} \cup X \tag{5.146}$$

and rewrite $\bar{X}'' = \bar{X}$. Then we have

$$
\begin{aligned}
c''(X'', \bar{X}'') - l''(\bar{X}'', X'') &= c''(\{s, t\} \cup X, \bar{X}) - l''(\bar{X}, \{s, t\} \cup X) \\
&= c''(s, \bar{X}) + c''(X, \bar{X}) - l''(\bar{X}, t) - l''(\bar{X}, X) \\
&= c(X, \bar{X}) - l(\bar{X}, X) + \sum_{y \in \bar{X}} \max [0, -a(y)] - \sum_{y \in \bar{X}} \max [0, a(y)] \\
&= c(X, \bar{X}) - l(\bar{X}, X) - \sum_{\substack{y \in \bar{X} \\ a(y) < 0}} a(y) - \sum_{\substack{y \in \bar{X} \\ a(y) \geq 0}} a(y) \\
&= c(X, \bar{X}) - l(\bar{X}, X) - a(\bar{X}) \qquad\qquad (5.147)
\end{aligned}
$$

Case 4

$s, t \in \bar{X}''$. Write $X'' = X$ and

$$\bar{X}'' = \{s, t\} \cup \bar{X} \qquad\qquad (5.148)$$

Then we have

$$
\begin{aligned}
c''(X'', \bar{X}'') - l''(\bar{X}'', X'') &= c''(X, \{s, t\} \cup \bar{X}) - l''(\{s, t\} \cup \bar{X}, X) \\
&= c''(X, t) + c''(X, \bar{X}) - l''(s, X) - l''(\bar{X}, X) \\
&= c(X, \bar{X}) - l(\bar{X}, X) + \sum_{x \in X} \max [0, a'(x)] - \sum_{x \in X} \max [0, -a'(x)] \\
&= c(X, \bar{X}) - l(\bar{X}, X) + \sum_{\substack{x \in X \\ a'(x) > 0}} a'(x) + \sum_{\substack{x \in X \\ a'(x) \leq 0}} a'(x) \\
&= c(X, \bar{X}) - l(\bar{X}, X) + a'(X) \qquad\qquad (5.149)
\end{aligned}
$$

Thus, condition (5.141) holds for all $X'' \subseteq V''$ if and only if (5.135) is satisfied for all $X \subseteq V$. This completes the proof of the theorem.

We illustrate the above results by the following examples.

Example 5.6

In the given net $G(V, E, l, c, f)$ of Fig. 5.29, the lower and upper bounds for the flow values in the arcs are shown in Fig. 5.29 as pairs of numbers adjacent to the arcs. Thus, we have

$$
\begin{array}{lll}
c(1, 3) = 4, & c(1, 4) = 4, & c(2, 1) = 7 \\
c(3, 2) = 3, & c(3, 4) = 3, & c(4, 2) = 5 \qquad (5.150) \\
l(1, 3) = 4, & l(1, 4) = 3, & l(2, 1) = 2 \\
l(3, 2) = 2, & l(3, 4) = 2, & l(4, 2) = 3 \qquad (5.151)
\end{array}
$$

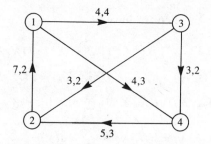

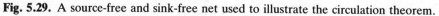

Fig. 5.29. A source-free and sink-free net used to illustrate the circulation theorem.

We use Theorem 5.6 to determine the existence of a feasible circulation in G. To this end, we apply (5.120) and obtain the following 14 inequalities:

$$c(1, \{2, 3, 4\}) = c(1, 3) + c(1, 4) = 4 + 4 = 8$$

$$\geq l(\{2, 3, 4\}, 1) = l(2, 1) = 2 \tag{5.152a}$$

$$c(2, \{1, 3, 4\}) = c(2, 1) = 7 \geq l(\{1, 3, 4\}, 2) = 5 \tag{5.152b}$$

$$c(3, \{1, 2, 4\}) = 6 \geq l(\{1, 2, 4\}, 3) = 4 \tag{5.152c}$$

$$c(4, \{1, 2, 3\}) = 5 \geq l(\{1, 2, 3\}, 4) = 5 \tag{5,152d}$$

$$c(\{1, 2\}, \{3, 4\}) = 8 \geq l(\{3, 4\}, \{1, 2\}) = 5 \tag{5.152e}$$

$$c(\{1, 3\}, \{2, 4\}) = 10 \geq l(\{2, 4\}, \{1, 3\}) = 2 \tag{5.152f}$$

$$c(\{1, 4\}, \{2, 3\}) = 9 \geq l(\{2, 3\}, \{1, 4\}) = 4 \tag{5.152g}$$

$$c(\{2, 3\}, \{1, 4\}) = 10 \geq l(\{1, 4\}, \{2, 3\}) = 7 \tag{5.152h}$$

$$c(\{2, 4\}, \{1, 3\}) = 7 \geq l(\{1, 3\}, \{2, 4\}) = 7 \tag{5.152i}$$

$$c(\{3, 4\}, \{1, 2\}) = 8 \geq l(\{1, 2\}, \{3, 4\}) = 7 \tag{5.152j}$$

$$c(\{1, 2, 3\}, 4) = 7 \geq l(4, \{1, 2, 3\}) = 3 \tag{5.152k}$$

$$c(\{1, 2, 4\}, 3) = 4 \geq l(3, \{1, 2, 4\}) = 4 \tag{5.152l}$$

$$c(\{2, 3, 4\}, 1) = 7 \geq l(1, \{2, 3, 4\}) = 7 \tag{5.152m}$$

$$c(\{1, 3, 4\}, 2) = 8 \geq l(2, \{1, 3, 4\}) = 2 \tag{5.152n}$$

The empty subset and the node itself are not included because the condition (5.120) is trivially satisfied for them. Since (5.120) holds for all subsets $X \subseteq V$, by Theorem 5.6 there is a feasible circulation in G, one of which is shown in Fig. 5.30. In Fig. 5.30, the upper bounds, the flow values and the lower bounds for the arcs are given in this order as triplets of nonnegative real numbers adjacent to the arcs. For the arc $(1, 4)$, for example, the upper bound is 4, the flow value is 3 and the lower bound is 3. They are written as a triplet 4, 3, 3 adjacent to the arc $(1, 4)$ in G.

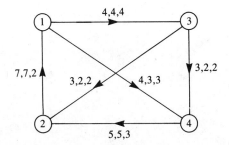

Fig. 5.30. A feasible circulation for the net of Fig. 5.29.

Suppose that we reduce the capacity of the arc $(2, 1)$ in G from 7 to 6, everything else being the same. Choose $X = \{2, 4\}$. Then

$$c(\{2, 4\}, \{1, 3\}) = c(2, 1) = 6$$
$$\not\geq l(\{1, 3\}, \{2, 4\}) = 2 + 3 + 2 = 7 \tag{5.153}$$

showing that condition (5.120) is violated and, therefore, the net of Fig. 5.29 with $c(2, 1) = 7$ being replaced by $c(2, 1) = 6$ does not possess a feasible circulation.

Intuitively, this can be interpreted as follows: The amount of flow forced into the subset $X = \{2, 4\}$ is required to be at least $l(\{1, 3\}, \{2, 4\}) = 7$, whereas the maximum available escape capacity is $c(\{2, 4\}, \{1, 3\}) = 6$. This is impossible to achieve for a feasible flow. The conclusion follows. Q.E.D.

Example 5.7

For the net $G(V, E, l, c, f)$ of Fig. 5.29, suppose that we stipulate that the net flow into each node must lie between the preassigned bounds, as follows:

$$a(1) = -4, \quad a'(1) = 0, \quad a(2) = -3, \quad a'(2) = 1$$
$$a(3) = -2, \quad a'(3) = 2, \quad a(4) = 2, \quad a'(4) = 4 \tag{5.154}$$

These are indicated in Fig. 5.31 as pairs of numbers adjacent to the nodes, the first being the upper bound and the second the lower bound.

To check to see if there is a feasible flow, we apply (5.135) and obtain

$$c(1, \{2, 3, 4\}) = 8 \geq l(\{2, 3, 4\}, 1) + \max\left[a(\{2, 3, 4\}), -a'(1)\right]$$
$$= 2 + \max\left[-3, 0\right] = 2 + 0 = 2 \tag{5.155a}$$
$$c(2, \{1, 3, 4\}) = 7 \geq l(\{1, 3, 4\}, 2) + \max\left[a(\{1, 3, 4\}), -a'(2)\right]$$
$$= 5 + \max\left[-4, -1\right] = 4 \tag{5.155b}$$

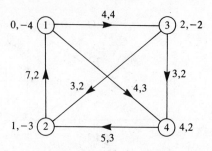

Fig. 5.31. A source-free and sink-free net used to illustrate the extended circulation theorem.

$$c(3, \{1, 2, 4\}) = 6 \geqq l(\{1, 2, 4\}, 3) + \max [a(\{1, 2, 4\}), -a'(3)]$$
$$= 4 + \max [-5, -2] = 2 \qquad (5.155c)$$

$$c(4, \{1, 2, 3\}) = 5 \geqq l(\{1, 2, 3\}, 4) + \max [a(\{1, 2, 3\}), -a'(4)]$$
$$= 5 + \max [-9, -4] = 1 \qquad (5.155d)$$

$$c(\{1, 2\}, \{3, 4\}) = 8 \geqq l(\{3, 4\}, \{1, 2\}) + \max [a(\{3, 4\}), -a'(\{1, 2\})]$$
$$= 5 + \max [0, -1] = 5 \qquad (5.155e)$$

$$c(\{1, 3\}, \{2, 4\}) = 10 \geqq l(\{2, 4\}, \{1, 3\}) + \max [a(\{2, 4\}), -a'(\{1, 3\})]$$
$$= 2 + \max [-1, -2] = 1 \qquad (5.155f)$$

$$c(\{1, 4\}, \{2, 3\}) = 9 \geqq l(\{2, 3\}, \{1, 4\}) + \max [a(\{2, 3\}), -a'(\{1, 4\})]$$
$$= 4 + \max [-5, -4] = 0 \qquad (5.155g)$$

$$c(\{2, 3\}, \{1, 4\}) = 10 \geqq l(\{1, 4\}, \{2, 3\}) + \max [a(\{1, 4\}), -a'(\{2, 3\})]$$
$$= 7 + \max [-2, -3] = 5 \qquad (5.155h)$$

$$c(\{2, 4\}, \{1, 3\}) = 7 \geqq l(\{1, 3\}, \{2, 4\}) + \max [a(\{1, 3\}), -a'(\{2, 4\})]$$
$$= 7 + \max [-6, -5] = 2 \qquad (5.155i)$$

$$c(\{3, 4\}, \{1, 2\}) = 8 \geqq l(\{1, 2\}, \{3, 4\}) + \max [a(\{1, 2\}), -a'(\{3, 4\})]$$
$$= 7 + \max [-7, -6] = 1 \qquad (5.155j)$$

$$c(\{1, 2, 3\}, 4) = 7 \geqq l(4, \{1, 2, 3\}) + \max [a(4), -a'(\{1, 2, 3\})]$$
$$= 3 + \max [2, -3] = 5 \qquad (5.155k)$$

$$c(\{1, 2, 4\}, 3) = 4 \geqq l(3, \{1, 2, 4\}) + \max [a(3), -a'(\{1, 2, 4\})]$$
$$= 4 + \max [-2, -5] = 2 \qquad (5.155l)$$

$$c(\{2, 3, 4\}, 1) = 7 \geqq l(1, \{2, 3, 4\}) + \max [a(1), -a'(\{2, 3, 4\})]$$
$$= 7 + \max [-4, -7] = 3 \qquad (5.155m)$$

$$c(\{1, 3, 4\}, 2) = 8 \geqq l(2, \{1, 3, 4\}) + \max\,[a(2), -a'(\{1, 3, 4\})]$$
$$= 2 + \max\,[-3, -6] = -1 \qquad (5.155n)$$

Since all the conditions are satisfied, by Theorem 5.6 there is a feasible flow in G. One such flow is shown in Fig. 5.32, in which the upper bounds, the flow values, and the lower bounds for the arc flows are given as triplets of real numbers adjacent to the arcs. Furthermore, the stipulated upper bounds, the net in-flow values, and the lower bounds associated with the nodes are also represented in this order by the triplets of real numbers adjacent to the nodes in Fig. 5.32.   Q.E.D.

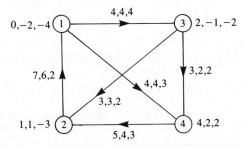

Fig. 5.32. A feasible circulation for the net of Fig. 5.31.

Example 5.8

For the net $G(V, E, l, c, f)$ of Fig. 5.33, the net flow into each node is required to lie between the prescribed bounds, as follows:

$$a(1) = -4, \quad a'(1) = 0, \quad a(2) = -3, \quad a'(2) = 1$$
$$a(3) = 0, \quad a'(3) = 2, \quad a(4) = 2, \quad a'(4) = 4 \qquad (5.156)$$

These are shown in Fig. 5.33 as pairs of numbers adjacent to the nodes.

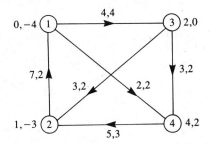

Fig. 5.33. A source-free and sink-free net used to illustrate the non-existence of a feasible circulation.

To check the feasibility of a circulation in G, we apply (5.135) for the subset $X = \{1, 2\}$ of V, and obtain

$$
\begin{aligned}
c(X, \bar{X}) = c(\{1, 2\}, \{3, 4\}) &= c(1, 3) + c(1, 4) = 4 + 2 = 6 \\
&\ngeqq l(\{3, 4\}, \{1, 2\}) + \max\,[a(\{3, 4\}), -a'(\{1, 2\})] \\
&= l(3, 2) + l(4, 2) + \max\,[0 + 2, 0 - 1] \\
&= 2 + 3 + 2 = 7
\end{aligned}
\tag{5.157}
$$

showing that (5.135) is violated. Therefore, there is no feasible flow in G meeting all the requirements.   Q.E.D.

Example 5.9

For the net $G(V, E, l, c, f)$ of Fig. 5.34, the net flow into each node is required to lie between the prescribed bounds, as follows:

$$
\begin{aligned}
&a(1) = -4, \quad &&a'(1) = -2, \quad &&a(2) = -3, \quad &&a'(2) = -2 \\
&a(3) = -2, \quad &&a'(3) = 2, \quad &&a(4) = 2, \quad &&a'(4) = 4 \quad (5.158)
\end{aligned}
$$

They are as indicated in Fig. 5.34.

To check the feasibility of a circulation in G, we apply (5.135) for the subset $X = \{1, 2\}$ of V, and obtain

$$
\begin{aligned}
c(X, \bar{X}) = c(\{1, 2\}, \{3, 4\}) &= c(1, 3) + c(1, 4) = 4 + 4 = 8 \\
&\ngeqq l(\{3, 4\}, \{1, 2\}) + \max\,[a(\{3, 4\}), -a'(\{1, 2\})] \\
&= l(3, 2) + l(4, 2) + \max\,[-2 + 2, 2 + 2] \\
&= 2 + 3 + 4 = 9
\end{aligned}
\tag{5.159}
$$

showing that condition (5.135) is violated, and there is no feasible circulation in G.   Q.E.D.

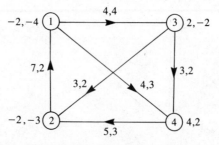

Fig. 5.34. A source-free and sink-free net used to illustrate the non-existence of a feasible circulation.

Before we move on to the construction of a feasible circulation, we give an intuitive interpretation of the condition (5.135). It states that either there must be sufficient cut capacity $c(X, \bar{X})$ from X to $\bar{X}$ to accommodate the required minimum net out-flow $l(\bar{X}, X)$ from $\bar{X}$ to X plus the net flow $a(\bar{X})$ into the nodes of $\bar{X}$, or the net flow $l(\bar{X}, X)$ forced into X from $\bar{X}$ cannot exceed the sum of maximum net flows $a'(X)$ into the nodes of X plus the escape cut capacity $c(X, \bar{X})$ from X to $\bar{X}$. If these conditions are satisfied for all subsets of the node set, the existence of a feasible circulation is assured.

In the net of Fig. 5.33, for example, the required minimum net out-flow from $\bar{X} = \{3, 4\}$ to $X = \{1, 2\}$ is $l(\bar{X}, X) = 5$, whereas the net flow into nodes 3 and 4 is $a(\{3, 4\}) = 2$. There is not sufficient cut capacity $c(X, \bar{X}) = c(\{1, 2\}, \{3, 4\}) = 6$ to meet the minimum need, which is $l(\bar{X}, X) + a(\bar{X}) = 5 + 2 = 7$. Thus, there is no feasible circulation in the net. Likewise, for the net of Fig. 5.34, the net flow forced into $X = \{1, 2\}$ from $\bar{X} = \{3, 4\}$ is $l(\{3, 4\}, \{1, 2\}) = 5$. The maximum net flow that can be retained in X is $a'(X) = a'(\{1, 2\}) = -4$. There is not sufficient escape cut capacity $c(X, \bar{X}) = c(\{1, 2\}, \{3, 4\}) = 8$ to accommodate the minimum need, which is $l(\bar{X}, X) - a'(X) = 5 + 4 = 9$. Therefore, no feasible circulation exists.

We now proceed to a discussion on the construction of a feasible circulation. However, before we do this we remark that in general if one is interested in checking the feasibility of a circulation in a given net, the most efficient method is to use the feasible circulation algorithm to be discussed in the following section rather than to check the conditions (5.120) for all subsets of the node set. If the problem is infeasible, a violation of (5.120) will be located at the conclusion of the computation.

5.4   FEASIBLE CIRCULATION ALGORITHM

In the preceding section, we discussed the conditions under which a feasible circulation exists. No procedure is given to the construction of a feasible circulation. In the present section, we describe a labeling process for constructing a feasible circulation provided that the capacity function and the lower bound function are rational valued. This restriction is necessary because the labeling routine is a variant of the Ford–Fulkerson algorithm described in Section 3.4.

Let $G(V, E, l, c, f)$ be a given net. The algorithm assigns labels to the nodes in V. The label assigned to a node is represented by an ordered triplet $(x, +, w)$ or $(x, -, w)$, where $x \in V$ and w is a positive number. During the labeling process, a node is always considered to be in one of the following three states: (1) unlabeled node, (2) labeled and unscanned node, and (3) labeled and scanned node, as described in Section 3.4.

Feasible Circulation Algorithm

Step 1.   Start with any integral valued conservative flow f or with $f = 0$.

Step 2.   Select an arc (s, t) for which either $f(s, t) > c(s, t)$ or $f(s, t) < l(s, t)$. If $f(s, t) > c(s, t)$, go to Step 3. If $f(s, t) < l(s, t)$, go to Step 9. Otherwise, go to Step 15.

Step 3.   Label s by $(t, -, w(s))$, where $w(s) = f(s, t) - c(s, t)$.

Step 4.   Select any labeled, unscanned node x, and perform the following operations:

(a) For all nodes y, $(x, y) \in E$, that are unlabeled such that $f(x, y) < c(x, y)$, assign y the label $(x, +, w(y))$ where

$$w(y) = \min \left[w(x), c(x, y) - f(x, y) \right] \qquad (5.160)$$

(b) For all nodes y, $(y, x) \in E$, that are unlabeled such that $f(y, x) > l(y, x)$, assign y the label $(x, -, w(y))$ where

$$w(y) = \min \left[w(x), f(y, x) - l(y, x) \right] \qquad (5.161)$$

Now change the label on x by circling the $+$ or $-$ entry. Then x is now labeled and scanned.

Step 5.   Repeat Step 4 until either t is labeled or no more labels can be assigned and t is unlabeled. In the former case, go to Step 6; and in the later case, terminate and there is no feasible circulation.

Step 6.   Let $z = t$.

Step 7.   If the label on z is $(q, +, w(z))$, increase the flow $f(q, z)$ by $w(t)$. If the label on z is $(q, -, w(z))$, decrease the flow $f(z, q)$ by $w(t)$.

Step 8.   If $q = s$, decrease $f(s, t)$ by $w(t)$ and discard all labels and return to Step 2. Otherwise, let $z = q$ and return to Step 7.

Step 9.   If $f(s, t) < l(s, t)$, label t by $(s, +, w(t))$ where $w(t) = l(s, t) - f(s, t)$.

Step 10. Select any labeled, unscanned node x, and perform the same labeling operations as in Step 4.

Step 11. Repeat Step 10 until either s is labeled or no more labels can be assigned and s is unlabeled. In the former case, go to Step 12; and in the later case, terminate and there is no feasible circulation.

Step 12. Let $z = s$.

Step 13. If the label on z is $(q, +, w(z))$, increase the flow $f(q, z)$ by $w(s)$. If the label on z is $(q, -, w(z))$, decrease the flow $f(z, q)$ by $w(s)$.

Step 14. If $q = t$, increase $f(s, t)$ by $w(s)$ and discard all labels and return to Step 2. Otherwise, let $z = q$ and return to Step 13.

Step 15. Stop. A feasible circulation has been constructed.

The above algorithm either constructs a feasible circulation in a finite number of steps or shows that there is no feasible circulation. To demonstrate that this is indeed the case, we observe that if t is labeled in Step 5, then a flow augmenting path P_{st} from s to t has been found, in which all forward arcs (x, y) of P_{st} are not saturated, $f(x, y) < c(x, y)$, and all reverse arcs (y, x) have flow values in excess of $l(y, x)$ in traversing from s to t on P_{st}. Likewise, if s is labeled in Step 11, a similar flow augmenting path P_{ts} from t to s has been found. Note that in the former case, t cannot be labeled from s via the arc (s, t); and that in the latter case, s cannot be labeled from t via (s, t). When the flow changes are made in Steps 6–8 or 12–14, a new flow f' satisfying the conservation equations is obtained. Furthermore, the new flow is at least one unit closer to feasibility than the old one. It follows that, after a finite number of steps, either a feasible circulation is constructed, or t in Step 5 or s in Step 11 is not labeled.

Suppose that t in Step 5 is not labeled, and let X and $\bar{X}$ be the labeled and unlabeled sets of nodes of G. Then $s \in X$ and $t \in \bar{X}$. From the rules of labeling outlined in Step 4, it follows that

$$f(x, y) \geqq c(x, y), \qquad (x, y) \in (X, \bar{X}) \tag{5.162a}$$

$$f(y, x) \leqq l(y, x), \qquad (y, x) \in (\bar{X}, X) \tag{5.162b}$$

In addition, there is at least one arc $(s, t) \in (X, \bar{X})$ which satisfies the strict inequality

$$f(s, t) > c(s, t) \tag{5.163}$$

Summing over all $x \in X$ and $y \in \bar{X}$ in conjunction with (5.163), (5.162) becomes

$$f(X, \bar{X}) > c(X, \bar{X}) \tag{5.164a}$$

$$f(\bar{X}, X) \leqq l(\bar{X}, X) \tag{5.164b}$$

which can be combined to yield

$$f(X, \bar{X}) - f(\bar{X}, X) > c(X, \bar{X}) - l(\bar{X}, X) \tag{5.165}$$

Since f satisfies the conservation equations at all nodes, the left-hand side of (5.165) is identically zero, and we obtain

$$c(X, \bar{X}) < l(\bar{X}, X) \tag{5.166}$$

violating the condition (5.120). Thus, there is no feasible circulation.

In an exactly similar manner, we can show that if s in Step 11 is not labeled, there is no feasible circulation. We illustrate this algorithm by the following examples.

Example 5.10

Consider the source-free and sink-free net $G(V, E, l, c, f)$ of Fig. 5.35, in which the upper and lower bounds for the arcs are shown as pairs of nonnegative real numbers adjacent to the arcs. For simplicity, the capacities $c(x, y)$, flow values $f(x, y)$ and lower bounds $l(x, y)$ for the arcs (x, y) will also be represented as triplets of nonnegative real numbers written adjacent to the arcs (x, y) in the order described. We follow the steps of the algorithm to construct a feasible circulation in the net.

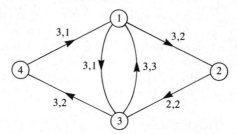

Fig. 5.35. A source-free and sink-free net used to illustrate the feasible circulation algorithm.

Step 1. Set $f = 0$. $c(x, y)$, $f(x, y)$ and $l(x, y)$ are shown as triplets adjacent to the arcs (x, y) in Fig. 5.36.

First iteration

Step 2. Select arc $(s, t) = (4, 1)$ with $f(4, 1) = 0 < l(4, 1) = 1$. Go to Step 9.

Step 9. Label $t = 1$ by $(4, +, 1)$, where $w(1) = l(4, 1) - f(4, 1) = 1 - 0 = 1$.

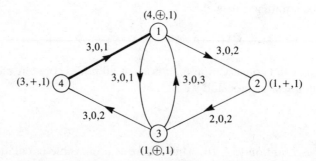

Fig. 5.36. A labeled net of Fig. 5.35 after selecting arc $(4, 1)$ for the first iteration in the use of the feasible circulation algorithm, where the initial flow is assumed to be zero.

Step 10. Select $x = 1$, and label nodes 2 and 3 as $(1, +, 1)$ and $(1, +, 1)$, respectively.

Step 11. Select $x = 3$ and label node $s = 4$ by $(3, +, 1)$. The labeled nodes are shown in Fig. 5.36.

Step 12. Let $z = s = 4$.

Step 13. Increase the flow $f(q, z) = f(3, 4)$ by $w(s) = w(4) = 1$.

Step 14. Let $z = q = 3$ and return to Step 13.

Step 13. Increase $f(q, z) = f(1, 3)$ by $w(s) = w(4) = 1$.

Step 14. Increase $f(s, t) = f(4, 1)$ by $w(s) = w(4) = 1$. Discard all labels and return to Step 2.

At the end of Step 14, the flow pattern is shown in Fig. 5.37.

Second iteration

Step 2. Select $(s, t) = (3, 1)$. Go to Step 9.

Step 9. Label $t = 1$ by $(3, +, 3)$.

Step 10. Select $x = 1$ and label nodes 2 and 3 by $(1, +, 3)$ and $(1, +, 2)$, respectively, as shown in Fig. 5.37.

Step 11. Go to Step 12.

Step 12. Let $z = s = 3$.

Step 13. Increase $f(q, z) = f(1, 3)$ by $w(s) = w(3) = 2$.

Step 14. Increase $f(s, t) = f(3, 1)$ by $w(s) = w(3) = 2$. Discard all labels and return to Step 2.

At the end of Step 14, the flow pattern is shown in Fig. 5.38.

Third iteration

Step 2. Select $(s, t) = (3, 4)$. Go to Step 9.

Step 9. Label $t = 4$ by $(3, +, 1)$.

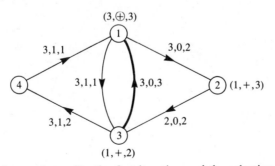

Fig. 5.37. The flow pattern after the first iteration and the selection of arc $(3, 1)$ for the second iteration.

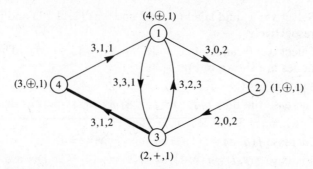

Fig. 5.38. The flow pattern after the second iteration and the selection of arc (3, 4) for the third iteration.

Step 10. Select $x = 4$ and label node 1 by $(4, +, 1)$.

Step 11. Go to Step 10.

Step 10. Select $x = 1$ and label node 2 by $(1, +, 1)$.

Step 11. Go to Step 10.

Step 10. Select $x = 2$ and label $s = 3$ by $(2, +, 1)$.

Step 11. Go to Step 12.

Step 12. Let $z = s = 3$.

Step 13. Increase $f(q, z) = f(2, 3)$ by $w(s) = w(3) = 1$.

Step 14. Let $z = q = 2$ and return to Step 13.

Step 13. Increase $f(q, z) = f(1, 2)$ by $w(s) = w(3) = 1$.

Step 14. Let $z = q = 1$ and return to Step 13.

Step 13. Increase $f(q, z) = f(4, 1)$ by $w(3) = 1$.

Step 14. Increase $f(s, t) = f(3, 4)$ by $w(3) = 1$. Discard all labels and return to Step 2.

At the end of Step 14, the flow pattern is shown in Fig. 5.39.

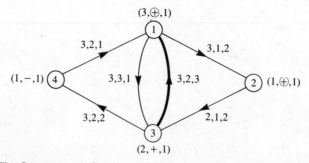

Fig. 5.39. The flow pattern after the third iteration and the selection of arc (3, 1) for the fourth iteration.

Fourth iteration

Step 2. Select $(s, t) = (3, 1)$. Go to Step 9.

Step 9. Label $t = 1$ by $(3, +, 1)$.

Step 10. Select $x = 1$ and label nodes 2 and 4 by $(1, +, 1)$ and $(1, -, 1)$, respectively.

Step 11. Go to Step 10.

Step 10. Select $x = 2$ and label node 3 by $(2, +, 1)$.

Step 11. Go to Step 12.

Step 12. Let $z = s = 3$.

Step 13. Increase $f(q, z) = f(2, 3)$ by $w(s) = w(3) = 1$.

Step 14. Let $z = q = 2$ and return to Step 13.

Step 13. Increase $f(q, z) = f(1, 2)$ by $w(3) = 1$.

Step 14. Increase $f(s, t) = f(3, 1)$ by $w(3) = 1$. Discard all labels and return to Step 2.

At the end of Step 14, the flow pattern is shown in Fig. 5.40.

Step 15. Stop. A feasible circulation has been constructed, and is given in Fig. 5.40.

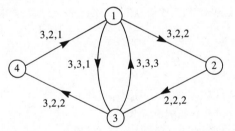

Fig. 5.40. A feasible circulation for the net of Fig. 5.35.

Example 5.11

In the net $G(V, E, l, c, f)$ of Fig. 5.41, the capacities, the conservative flow values, and the lower bounds of the arcs are as indicated in the figure by the triplets adjacent to the arcs. We use the algorithm to construct a feasible circulation.

Step 1. Start with the flow f as shown in Fig. 5.41.

Step 2. Select arc $(s, t) = (2, 1)$, as shown in Fig. 5.42.

Step 3. Label $s = 2$ by $(1, -, 1)$.

Step 4. Select $x = 2$ and label node 4 by $(2, -, 1)$

Step 5. Select $x = 4$ and label $t = 1$ by $(4, -, 1)$

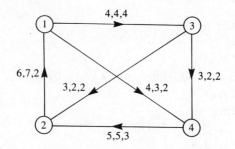

Fig. 5.41. A source-free and sink-free net used to illustrate the feasible circulation algorithm.

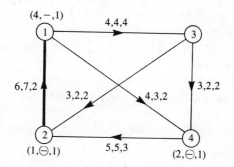

Fig. 5.42. A labeled net of Fig. 5.41 after selecting $(2, 1)$ as the initial arc for iteration.

Step 6. Let $z = t = 1$.

Step 7. Decrease $f(z, q) = f(1, 4)$ by $w(1) = 1$.

Step 8. Let $z = 4$ and return to Step 7.

Step 7. Decrease $f(z, q) = f(4, 2)$ by $w(1) = 1$.

Step 8. Decrease $f(s, t) = f(2, 1)$ by $w(1) = 1$, and return to Step 2.

Step 2. Go to Step 15.

Step 15. Stop. A feasible circulation has been constructed as shown in Fig. 5.43.

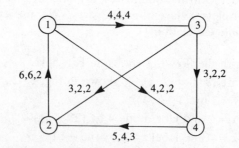

Fig. 5.43. A feasible circulation for the net of Fig. 5.41.

Example 5.12

The net $G(V, E, l, c, f)$ of Fig. 5.44 is the same as that of Fig. 5.41 except that the lower bound for the arc $(1, 4)$ has been increased from 2 to 3, everything else being the same. We use the algorithm to ascertain the feasibility of G.

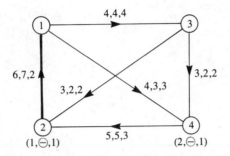

Fig. 5.44. A source-free and sink-free net used to illustrate the non-existence of a feasible circulation by means of the feasible circulation algorithm.

Step 1. Start with the flow f as shown in Fig. 5.44.

Step 2. Select arc $(s, t) = (2, 1)$.

Step 3. Label $s = 2$ by $(1, -, 1)$.

Step 4. Select $x = 2$ and label node 4 by $(2, -, 1)$.

Step 5. Select $x = 4$. No more labels can be assigned. Terminate and there is no feasible circulation in G.

Let X and $\bar{X}$ be the labeled and unlabeled sets of nodes of G. Then we have from Fig. 5.44

$$X = \{2, 4\}, \qquad \bar{X} = \{1, 3\} \tag{5.167}$$

giving

$$c(X, \bar{X}) = c(\{2, 4\}, \{1, 3\}) = c(2, 1) = 6$$

$$\ngeqslant l(\bar{X}, X) = l(\{1, 3\}, \{2, 4\}) = 2 + 3 + 2 = 7 \tag{5.168}$$

Thus, a violation of condition (5.120) is detected, and there is no feasible flow in G confirming (5.153).

Example 5.13

A source-free and sink-free net $G(V, E, l, c, f)$ is shown in Fig. 5.45. Applying the feasible circulation algorithm yields a feasible circulation shown in Fig. 5.45, in which the capacities, the flow values, and the lower bounds for the arcs are represented by the triplets of nonnegative real numbers adjacent to the arcs.

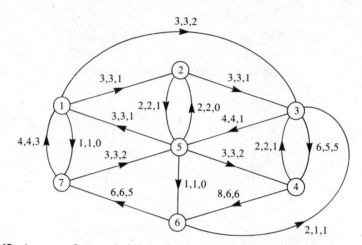

Fig. 5.45. A source-free and sink-free net with capacities, flow values and lower bounds for the arcs given as triplets of nonnegative real numbers adjacent to the arcs.

Thus, the most efficient way to check the feasibility of a circulation in a net is to use the feasible circulation algorithm outlined in this section rather than to check the conditions (5.120) for all subsets of the node set of the net. If the problem is infeasible, a violation of (5.120) will be located at the conclusion of the computation by taking X and $\bar{X}$ to be the labeled and unlabeled nodes of the node set, respectively. In the situation in which the net flow into a node is required to lie between prescribed bounds, we apply the algorithm to the extended net $G''(V'', E'', l'', c'', f'')$ of a given net $G(V, E, l, c, f)$ as defined in the proof of Theorem 5.7. Once a feasible circulation f'' is found in G'', the restriction f of f'' over E gives the desired flow in G. If a violation of the conditions (5.120) is located, the corresponding violation of (5.135) can be identified.

5.5 FLOWS IN NETS WITH LOWER BOUNDS ON ARCS

In Chapter 3, we considered the problem of determining the maximum flow value from a source to a sink in an arc capacitated net, where lower bounds of zero were assumed on all arc flows. In the present section, we extend the problem by requiring nonnegative real lower bounds on arc flows.

Let $G(V, E, l, c, f)$ be a net with source s and sink t, where l is a lower bound function from E to the nonnegative reals satisfying

$$c(x, y) \geqq l(x, y) \geqq 0, \qquad (x, y) \in E \tag{5.169}$$

A flow f is said to be *feasible* in G of value f_{st} from s to t if it satisfies the following constraints: For each $x \in V$

$$f(x, V) - f(V, x) = f_{st}, \qquad\qquad x = s \qquad\qquad (5.170a)$$

$$f(x, V) - f(V, x) = 0, \qquad\qquad x \neq s, t \qquad\qquad (5.170b)$$

$$f(x, V) - f(V, x) = -f_{st}, \qquad\qquad x = t \qquad\qquad (5.170c)$$

$$c(x, y) \geq f(x, y) \geq l(x, y) \geq 0, \qquad (x, y) \in E \qquad\qquad (5.171)$$

The maximum value of such flows from s to t in G is given by the following theorem, which is an extension of Theorem 3.2.

THEOREM 5.8

If there is a feasible flow from s to t in a given net $G(V, E, l, c, f)$, then the maximum flow value f_{max} from s to t is equal to the minimum of $[c(X, \bar{X}) - l(\bar{X}, X)]$ taken over all s–t cuts $(X, \bar{X})$ in G, i.e.

$$f_{max} = \max \{f_{st}\} = \min_{X} \{c(X, \bar{X}) - l(\bar{X}, X)\} \qquad\qquad (5.172)$$

Proof. If there is a feasible flow f from s to t in G, then by summing over all $x \in X$ and $y \in \bar{X}$, (5.170) and (5.171) become

$$f(X, V) - f(V, X) = f_{st} \qquad\qquad (5.173)$$

$$c(X, \bar{X}) \geq f(X, \bar{X}) \geq l(X, \bar{X}) \geq 0 \qquad\qquad (5.174)$$

giving

$$c(X, \bar{X}) - l(\bar{X}, X) \geq f(X, \bar{X}) - f(\bar{X}, X) = f_{st} \qquad\qquad (5.175)$$

This shows that the flow value f_{st} from s to t in G cannot exceed the minimum of $c(X, \bar{X}) - l(\bar{X}, X)$ taken over all s–t cuts $(X, \bar{X})$ in G. In particular, the maximum flow value f_{max} is bounded above by this minimum, i.e.

$$f_{max} \leq \min_{X} \{c(X, \bar{X}) - l(\bar{X}, X)\} \qquad\qquad (5.176)$$

It remains to be shown that a flow value equal to this minimum can be attained.

To this end, we apply the Ford–Fulkerson algorithm to G for constructing a maximum flow from s to t. The only change is in the labeling rules (3.60), as follows: For all nodes y, $(y, x) \in E$, that are unlabeled such that

$$f(y, x) > l(y, x) \qquad\qquad (5.177)$$

label y by $(x, -, w(y))$ where

$$w(y) = \min [w(x), f(y, x) - l(y, x)] \qquad (5.178)$$

and node x has been labeled $(z, \pm, w(x))$. As in the proof of the max-flow min-cut theorem, the modified algorithm will yield an $s-t$ cut $(Y, \bar{Y})$, all of whose arcs are saturated, and all the flow values in the arcs of $(\bar{Y}, Y)$ are equal to their lower bounds. Thus, we have

$$f_{\max} = c(Y, \bar{Y}) - l(\bar{Y}, Y) = \min_{X} \{c(X, \bar{X}) - l(\bar{X}, X)\} \qquad (5.179)$$

This completes the proof of the theorem.

The theorem states that if there is a feasible flow from s to t in G, then the maximum flow value from s to t is equal to $\min_{X} \{c(X, \bar{X}) - l(\bar{X}, X)\}$. To ascertain the existence of a feasible flow from s to t in G, we consider the extended net $G'(V', E', l', c', f')$ obtained from $G(V, E, l, c, f)$ by adding the arcs (s, t) and (t, s) with infinite capacity and zero lower bound, as depicted in Fig. 5.46. It follows that there is a feasible flow from s to t in G if and only if there is a feasible circulation in G'. According to Theorem 5.6, there is a feasible circulation in G' if and only if

$$c'(X', \bar{X}') \geqq l'(\bar{X}', X') \qquad (5.180)$$

holds for all subsets $X' \subseteq V'$, where $\bar{X}' = V' - X'$. If $s \in X'$ and $t \in \bar{X}'$ or if $s \in \bar{X}'$ and $t \in X'$, then $c'(X', \bar{X}')$ is infinite and condition (5.180) is always fulfilled. Therefore, we need only consider the situation where both s and t belong to X' or neither does. This implies that (5.180) is satisfied for all

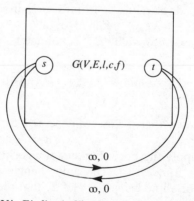

Fig. 5.46. The net $G'(V', E', l', c', f')$ obtained from $G(V, E, l, c, f)$ by adding arcs (s, t) and (t, s) with infinite capacity and zero lower bound.

subsets $X' \subseteq V'$ if and only if

$$c(X, \bar{X}) \geq l(\bar{X}, X) \tag{5.181}$$

holds for all subsets $X \subseteq V$ such that either both s and t are in X or neither is, where $\bar{X} = V - X$. To construct such a flow, we can solve the equivalent maximum flow problem, using the modified Ford–Fulkerson algorithm as outlined in the proof of Theorem 5.8.

Instead of finding a maximum flow from s to t in G, we can use a modified Ford–Fulkerson algorithm to generate a minimum flow from s to t, assuming of course the existence of a feasible flow from s to t in G. The modification of (3.59) and (3.60) in Step 2 of the labeling routine is as follows: Select any labeled and unscanned node x with label $(z, \pm, w(x))$, and perform the following operations:

(a) For all nodes y, $(x, y) \in E$, that are unlabeled such that $f(x, y) > l(x, y)$, label y by $(x, -, w(y))$ where

$$w(y) = \min [w(x), f(x, y) - l(x, y)] \tag{5.182}$$

(b) For all nodes y, $(y, x) \in E$, that are unlabeled such that $f(y, x) < c(y, x)$, label y by $(x, +, w(y))$ where

$$w(y) = \min [w(x), c(y, x) - f(y, x)] \tag{5.183}$$

The procedure will result in a minimum flow from s to t in G. A dual to Theorem 5.8 is stated as follows.

THEOREM 5.9

If there is a feasible flow from s to t in a given net $G(V, E, l, c, f)$, then the minimum flow value $f_{\min}$ from s to t is equal to the maximum of $[l(X, \bar{X}) - c(\bar{X}, X)]$ taken over all s–t cuts $(X, \bar{X})$ in G, i.e.

$$f_{\min} = \min \{f_{st}\} = \max_X \{l(X, \bar{X}) - c(\bar{X}, X)\} \tag{5.184}$$

The theorem can be proved in a manner similar to that of Theorem 5.8, the details of which are omitted. We illustrate the above by the following examples.

Example 5.14

A capacitated net $G(V, E, l, c, f)$ is shown in Fig. 5.47. A feasible flow from s to t is presented in Fig. 5.48, where, as before, the triplets of

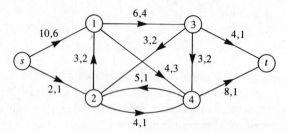

Fig. 5.47. A capacitated net with lower bounds on flows in arcs.

nonnegative real numbers adjacent to the arcs denote the capacities, the flow values, and the lower bounds for the arcs given in the order described.

Applying the modified Ford–Fulkerson algorithm outlined in the proof of Theorem 5.8, an augmenting path P_{st} from s to t is located by the labeling process:

$$P_{st} = (s, 2)(2, 4)(4, t) \tag{5.185}$$

A unit flow can now be increased along this path, and the resulting flow pattern is shown in Fig. 5.49. Applying the modified Ford–Fulkerson algorithm to the net of Fig. 5.49 yields the node labels as indicated. Since no more labels can be assigned and t is not reached, the flow is therefore maximum.

Let Y and $\bar{Y}$ be the sets of labeled and unlabeled nodes of the net of Fig. 5.49, respectively. Then we have $Y = \{s, 1\}$, $\bar{Y} = \{2, 3, 4, t\}$, and

$$
\begin{aligned}
f_{\max} &= c(Y, \bar{Y}) - l(\bar{Y}, Y) \\
&= c(\{s, 1\}, \{2, 3, 4, t\}) - l(\{2, 3, 4, t\}, \{s, 1\}) \\
&= c(1, 3) + c(1, 4) + c(s, 2) - l(2, 1) \\
&= 6 + 4 + 2 - 2 = 10
\end{aligned}
\tag{5.186}
$$

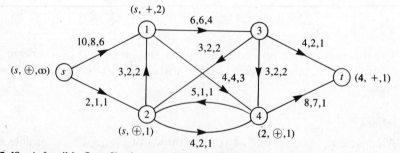

Fig. 5.48. A feasible flow for the net of Fig. 5.47 together with the labeled nodes for flow augmentation.

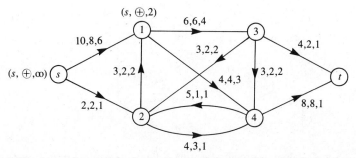

Fig. 5.49. A maximum flow from s to t and the resulting labels for the nodes.

giving the maximum flow value from s to t in G to be 10. Observe that all the arcs in $(Y, \bar{Y})$ are saturated and the arc in $(\bar{Y}, Y)$ equals to its lower bound.

Example 5.15

We wish to determine the minimum flow value from s to t in the capacitated net $G(V, E, l, c, f)$ of Fig. 5.47. An initial feasible flow f is shown in Fig. 5.48, and is redrawn in Fig. 5.50. Applying the modified Ford–Fulkerson algorithm of (5.182) and (5.183) to the net G of Fig. 5.50 locates a flow augmenting path $P_{st} = (s, 1)(1, 3)(3, t)$ from s to t. A unit flow reduction along this path is possible, and the resulting flow pattern is shown in Fig. 5.51. Repeating the labeling process once more for the net of Fig. 5.51 yields another flow augmenting path $P'_{st} = (s, 1)(2, 1)(2, 4)(4, t)$. In P'_{st} a unit flow reduction can be made for the arcs $(s, 1)$, $(2, 4)$ and $(4, t)$ and a unit flow increase is assigned to arc $(2, 1)$. The resulting flow pattern is presented in Fig. 5.52, in which if we repeat the labeling process, we find that except node s, no more labels can be assigned to other nodes and t is not reached. Thus, the flow from s to t of value 7 is the minimum among all the feasible flows.

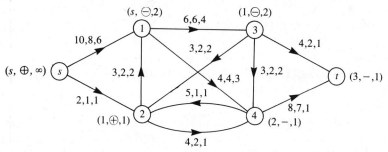

Fig. 5.50. A feasible flow from s to t together with the node labels locating a flow augmenting path for flow reduction.

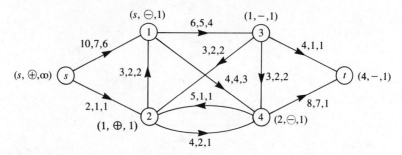

Fig. 5.51. A node labeling process locating a flow augmenting path from s to t for flow reduction.

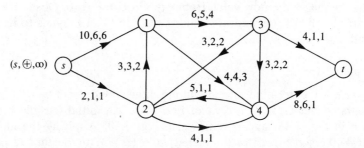

Fig. 5.52. A minimum flow from s to t with node labels identifying the associated $s–t$ cut.

To identify an $s–t$ cut having this minimum value, let X and $\bar{X}$ be the labeled and unlabeled nodes of G. Then from Fig. 5.52

$$X = \{s\}, \qquad \bar{X} = \{1, 2, 3, 4, t\} \tag{5.187}$$

giving the minimum flow value

$$
\begin{aligned}
f_{\min} &= l(X, \bar{X}) - c(\bar{X}, X) \\
&= l(\{s\}, \{1, 2, 3, 4, t\}) - c(\{1, 2, 3, 4, t\}, \{s\}) \\
&= l(s, 1) + l(s, 2) = 6 + 1 = 7
\end{aligned} \tag{5.188}
$$

5.6 FEASIBLE FLOWS IN NODE-AND-ARC CAPACITATED NETS

In Section 3.10, we studied the maximum flow problem in a node-and-arc capacitated net. In the present section, we extend the feasibility theorems to node-and-arc capacitated nets.

Let $G(V, E, c, f)$ be a given net. Suppose that in addition to the arc capacity function, each node $i \in V$ is associated with a nonnegative real number $h(i)$ called the *node capacity* of i. The node capacity h is, therefore, a function from the node set V to the nonnegative reals. For simplicity, we write G as a quintuplet $G(V, E, c, f, h)$. As before, we partition the node set V into the disjoint source set S, the intermediate node set R, and the sink set T. Associate with each $x \in S$ a nonnegative real number $a(x)$ called the *supply* function, and with each $x \in T$ a nonnegative real number $b(x)$ the *demand* function. The objective is to determine the existence of a flow pattern in G satisfying the constraints

$$f(x, V) - f(V, x) \leq a(x), \qquad x \in S \qquad (5.189)$$

$$f(x, V) - f(V, x) = 0, \qquad x \in R \qquad (5.190)$$

$$f(V, x) - f(x, V) \geq b(x), \qquad x \in T \qquad (5.191)$$

$$c(x, y) \geq f(x, y) \geq 0, \qquad (x, y) \in E \qquad (5.192)$$

$$f(x, V) \leq h(x), \qquad x \in V \qquad (5.193)$$

$$f(V, x) \leq h(x), \qquad x \in V \qquad (5.194)$$

If V_1 and V_2 are disjoint subsets of V, then a directed path from a node in V_1 to a node in V_2 is called a *directed path from V_1 to V_2*. Using this we introduce the notion of a generalized disconnecting set with respect to V_1 and V_2.

DEFINITION 5.1

Generalized Disconnecting Set. A *generalized disconnecting set from V_1 to V_2* in a directed graph $G(V, E)$ is a collection of nodes and arcs of G such that every directed path from V_1 to V_2 has at least a node or an arc belonging to the collection, where V_1 and V_2 are disjoint subsets of V.

Let X be a subset of V and write $\bar{X} = V - X$. Denote by $D_{X, \bar{X}}$ a generalized disconnecting set from X to $\bar{X}$ in $G(V, E, c, f, h)$. Then the *capacity* $k(D_{X, \bar{X}})$ of $D_{X, \bar{X}}$ is defined to be the sum of the capacities of its constituent elements:

$$k(D_{X, \bar{X}}) = \sum_{(x, y) \in D_{X, \bar{X}}} c(x, y) + \sum_{x \in D_{X, \bar{X}}} h(x) \qquad (5.195)$$

As in Section 3.10, the present problem can be converted to the arc capacity case by the following procedure. Let $G^*(V^*, E^*, c^*, f^*)$ be the net derived from $G(V, E, c, f, h)$ in accordance with the following rules: To each node $i \in V$, there correspond two nodes i', $i'' \in V^*$ such that if $(i, j) \in E$, then $(i', j'') \in E^*$. In addition, for each $i \in V$, there is an

$(i'', i') \in E^*$. The arc capacity defined on E^* is given by

$$c^*(i', j'') = c(i, j), \qquad (i, j) \in E \tag{5.196}$$

$$c^*(i'', i') = h(i), \qquad i \in V \tag{5.197}$$

An example for this conversion is shown in Figs. 3.61 and 3.62.

With this representation, it is clear that for any feasible flow in a supply–demand net $G(V, E, c, f, h)$ that does not exceed the node capacities, there corresponds an equivalent feasible flow in $G^*(V^*, E^*, c^*, f^*)$ by taking

$$f^*(i', j'') = f(i, j), \qquad (i, j) \in E \tag{5.198}$$

$$f^*(i'', i') = f(i, V), \qquad i \notin T \tag{5.199a}$$

$$f^*(i'', i') = f(V, i), \qquad i \in T \tag{5.199b}$$

and vice versa. Thus, we can apply Theorem 5.1 to ascertain the feasibility conditions for G. To this end, let the node set V^* be partitioned into the disjoint subsets

$$S^* = \{x' \mid x' \in V^* \quad \text{and} \quad x \in S\} \tag{5.200a}$$

$$T^* = \{x'' \mid x'' \in V^* \quad \text{and} \quad x \in T\} \tag{5.200b}$$

$$R^* = V^* - S^* - T^* \tag{5.200c}$$

corresponding to the source, sink and intermediate sets of G^*, respectively. The supply and demand functions a and b for the nodes of S^* and T^* are defined the same as in G:

$$a(x') = a(x), \qquad x' \in S^* \quad \text{and} \quad x \in S \tag{5.201a}$$

$$b(x'') = b(x), \qquad x'' \in T^* \quad \text{and} \quad x \in T \tag{5.201b}$$

According to Theorem 5.1, there is a feasible flow in G^* if and only if

$$b(T^* \cap \bar{X}^*) - a(S^* \cap \bar{X}^*) \leq c^*(X^*, \bar{X}^*) \tag{5.202}$$

holds for every subset $X^* \subseteq V^*$, where $\bar{X}^* = V^* - X^*$. Observe that for each cut $(X^*, \bar{X}^*)$, there corresponds a generalized disconnecting set $D_{X,\bar{X}}$ in G for some $X \subseteq V$ such that $(x, y) \in E$ or $x \in V$ is in $D_{X,\bar{X}}$ if and only if either (x', y'') or (x'', x') is in $(X^*, \bar{X}^*)$, respectively, and vice versa. Furthermore, we have

$$k(D_{X,\bar{X}}) = c^*(X^*, \bar{X}^*) \tag{5.203}$$

$$b(T \cap \bar{X}) = b(T^* \cap \bar{X}^*) \tag{5.204}$$

$$a(S \cap \bar{X}) = a(S^* \cap \bar{X}^*) \tag{5.205}$$

Thus, the constraints (5.189)–(5.194) are feasible if and only if

$$b(T \cap \bar{X}) - a(S \cap \bar{X}) \leq \min k(D_{X,\bar{X}}) \tag{5.206}$$

holds for every subset $X \subseteq V$. Thus, we have established a result of Duguid (1961).

THEOREM 5.10

Partition the node set V of a given net $G(V, E, c, f, h)$ into three disjoint subsets S, R and T with a supply function $a(x) \geq 0$, $x \in S$, and a demand function $b(y) \geq 0$, $y \in T$. Then the constraints

$$f(x, V) - f(V, x) \leq a(x), \qquad x \in S \qquad (5.207a)$$

$$f(x, V) - f(V, x) = 0, \qquad x \in R \qquad (5.207b)$$

$$f(V, x) - f(x, V) \geq b(x), \qquad x \in T \qquad (5.207c)$$

$$c(x, y) \geq f(x, y) \geq 0, \qquad (x, y) \in E \qquad (5.207d)$$

$$f(x, V) \leq h(x), \qquad x \in V \qquad (5.207e)$$

$$f(V, x) \leq h(x), \qquad x \in V \qquad (5.207f)$$

are feasible if and only if

$$b(T \cap \bar{X}) - a(S \cap \bar{X}) \leq \min_i k(D^i_{X,\bar{X}}) \qquad (5.208)$$

holds for every subset $X \subseteq V$, where $\bar{X} = V - X$ and $k(D^i_{X,\bar{X}})$ is the capacity of the ith generalized disconnecting set from X to $\bar{X}$ in G.

If a supply is considered to be a negative demand, then the theorem states that there is a feasible flow in G if and only if the net demand for every subset $\bar{X}$ of the node set does not exceed the minimum capacity of a generalized disconnecting set from its complement to $\bar{X}$. We remark that if there are no node capacity constraints, Theorem 5.10 reduces to Theorem 5.1 after setting $h(x) = \infty$ for $x \in V$.

In Section 3.10, we demonstrated that the solution of the maximum flow problem from s to t in a node-and-arc capacitated net $G(V, E, c, f, h)$ is equivalent to solving the maximum flow problem from s'' to t' in the corresponding arc capacitated net $G^*(V^*, E^*, c^*, f^*)$. This result can now be stated in terms of the generalized disconnecting set.

THEOREM 5.11

The maximum flow value f_{max} from s to t in a node-and-arc capacitated net $G(V, E, c, f, h)$ is equal to the minimum capacity of a generalized disconnecting set from s to t, i.e.

$$f_{max} = \max \{f_{st}\} = \min_i \{k(D^i_{s,t})\} \qquad (5.209)$$

where $D_{s,t}^i$ is the ith generalized disconnecting set from s to t, and f_{st} is taken over all feasible flow patterns in G.

Proof. Let $G^*(V^*, E^*, c^*, f^*)$ be the net derived from G by the rules outlined in Section 3.10 or above. Then it is clear that for any flow from s to t in G that does not exceed the node capacities, there corresponds an equivalent flow f^* from s'' to t' in G^* by taking

$$f^*(i', j'') = f(i, j), \qquad (i, j) \in E \qquad (5.210a)$$

$$f^*(i'', i') = f(i, V), \qquad i \neq t \qquad (5.210b)$$

$$f^*(t'', t') = f(V, t) \qquad (5.210c)$$

and vice versa. Then by the max-flow min-cut theorem (Theorem 3.2), the maximum flow value $f_{\max}^*$ from s'' to t' in G^* is equal to the capacity of a minimum s''–t' cut $(X^*, \bar{X}^*)$. By taking $(x, y) \in E$ or $x \in V$ in $D_{s,t}$ if and only if either (x', y'') or (x'', x') is in $(X^*, \bar{X}^*)$, we see that for each s''–t' cut $(X^*, \bar{X}^*)$ in G^*, there corresponds a generalized disconnecting set $D_{s,t}$ in G having the same capacity:

$$c^*(X^*, \bar{X}^*) = k(D_{s,t}) \qquad (5.211)$$

The theorem follows. This completes the proof of the theorem.

We illustrate the above results by the following examples.

Example 5.16

A node-and-arc capacitated net $G(V, E, c, f, h)$ is presented in Fig. 5.53 with the node capacities given as

$$h(s) = 14, \qquad h(1) = 9, \qquad h(2) = 5$$

$$h(3) = 5, \qquad h(4) = 10, \qquad h(t) = 15 \qquad (5.212)$$

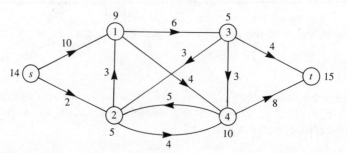

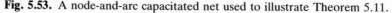

Fig. 5.53. A node-and-arc capacitated net used to illustrate Theorem 5.11.

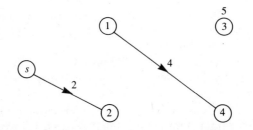

Fig. 5.54. A minimum capacity generalized disconnecting set from s to t for the net of Fig. 5.53.

They are shown in Fig. 5.53 as numbers $h(x)$ adjacent to the nodes $x \in V$ together with the arc capacities $c(x, y)$ given as numbers adjacent to the arcs (x, y).

The subgraph $D_{s,t}^1$ of Fig. 5.54 is a generalized disconnecting set from s to t in G because the removal of the subgraph corresponding to this set from G breaks all the the directed paths from s to t in G or, equivalently, every directed path from s to t has at least a node or an arc belonging to this subgraph. The set $D_{s,t}^2 = \{2, 3, (1, 4)\}$ is another generalized disconnecting set from s to t. The capacities of these generalized disconnecting sets $D_{s,t}^1$ and $D_{s,t}^2$ are found to be

$$k(D_{s,t}^1) = c(s, 2) + c(1, 4) + h(3) = 2 + 4 + 5 = 11 \qquad (5.213a)$$
$$k(D_{s,t}^2) = h(2) + h(3) + c(1, 4) = 5 + 5 + 4 = 14 \qquad (5.213b)$$

Since $D_{s,t}^1$ has the minimum capacity among all the generalized disconnecting sets from s to t, by Theorem 5.11 the maximum flow value f_{max} from s to t in G is equal to 11, or

$$f_{max} = \max \{f_{st}\} = \min_i \{k(D_{s,t}^i)\} = 11 \qquad (5.214)$$

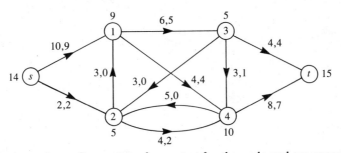

Fig. 5.55. A maximum flow pattern from s to t for the node-and-arc capacitated net of Fig. 5.53.

A flow pattern meeting the node and arc capacities is shown in Fig. 5.55 as pairs of numbers adjacent to the arcs, the first being the arc capacities and the second the arc flow values.

To illustrate the actual construction of a maximum feasible flow from s to t in G, we apply the rules of Section 3.10 by first converting the node-and-arc capacitated net G of Fig. 5.53 to the equivalent arc capacitated net $G^*(V^*, E^*, c^*, f^*)$ of Fig. 5.56, and then by using any of the existing maximum flow algorithms discussed in Chapter 3 we construct a maximum flow from s'' to t' in G^*. The resulting flow pattern is shown in Fig. 5.56, where as before the arc capacities $c^*(x, y)$ and arc flow values $f^*(x, y)$ are given as pairs of numbers adjacent to the arcs. Finally, applying the Ford–Fulkerson algorithm yields the node labels as indicated in Fig. 5.56. Let X^* and $\bar{X}^*$ be the sets of labeled and unlabeled nodes of V^*, respectively. Then we have

$$X^* = \{s'', s', 1''\}, \qquad \bar{X}^* = \{1', 2'', 2', 3'', 3', 4'', 4', t'', t'\} \quad (5.215)$$

giving

$$c^*(X^*, \bar{X}^*) = c^*(\{s'', s', 1''\}, \{1', 2'', 2', 3'', 3', 4'', 4', t'', t'\})$$
$$= c^*(s', 2'') + c^*(1'', 1') = 2 + 9 = 11 \quad (5.216)$$

Thus, $(X^*, \bar{X}^*)$ is a minimum s''–t' cut. The corresponding minimum generalized disconnecting set $D_{s,t}^3$ from s to t in G is identified as

$$D_{s,t}^3 = \{(s, 2), 1\} \quad (5.217)$$

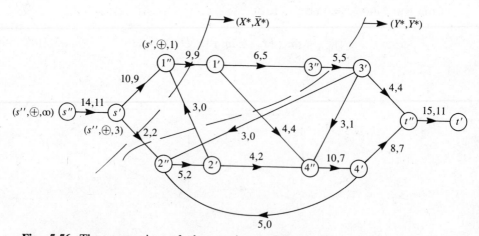

Fig. 5.56. The conversion of the maximum flow problem of a node-and-arc capacitated net to that of an equivalent arc capacitated net.

having capacity $k(D_{s,t}^3) = c(s, 2) + h(1) = 2 + 9 = 11$. As mentioned earlier, $D_{s,t}^1 = \{(s, 2), (1, 4), 3\}$ is another such minimum set, the corresponding minimum s''–t' cut $(Y^*, \bar{Y}^*)$ of which in G^* is found to be

$$(Y^*, \bar{Y}^*) = (\{s'', s', 1'', 1', 3''\}, \{2'', 2', 3', 4'', 4', t'', t\}) \quad (5.218)$$

Example 5.17

A node-and-arc capacitated net $G(V, E, c, f, h)$ is shown in Fig. 5.57, where the supplies $a(x)$, the demands $b(x)$, the node capacities $h(x)$ for the nodes $x \in V$ and the arc capacities $c(x, y)$, $(x, y) \in E$, are as indicated in the figure. We wish to ascertain the feasibility of this supply–demand problem.

To proceed, we first construct a preliminary flow pattern as shown in Fig. 5.58, which nearly succeeds in meeting the supply and demand

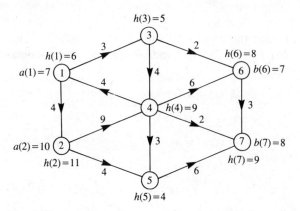

Fig. 5.57. A node-and-arc capacitated supply–demand net.

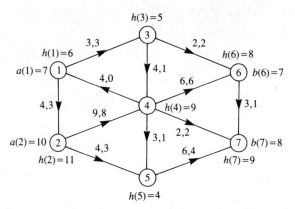

Fig. 5.58. A flow pattern that almost succeeds in meeting the supply and demand requirements.

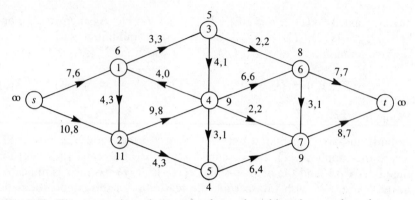

Fig. 5.59. The conversion of a supply–demand problem in a node-and-arc capacitated net to a maximum flow problem in an equivalent net.

requirements and satisfies the node and arc capacity constraints. We next construct an extended net $G'(V', E', c', f', h')$ from G by adjoining two nodes s and t and the arcs (s, S) and (T, t), as shown in Fig. 5.59, where $S = \{1, 2\}$ and $T = \{6, 7\}$. The node and arc capacity functions h' and c' of G' are defined by

$$h'(s) = h'(t) = \infty \qquad\qquad (5.219a)$$

$$c'(s, x) = a(x), \qquad\qquad x \in S \qquad (5.219b)$$

$$c'(x, t) = b(x), \qquad\qquad x \in T \qquad (5.219c)$$

$$h'(x) = h(x), \qquad\qquad x \in V \qquad (5.219d)$$

$$c'(x, y) = c(x, y), \qquad (x, y) \in E \qquad (5.219e)$$

Also, the flow values f' are taken to be

$$f'(s, 1) = f(1, V) - f(V, 1) = f(1, 3) + f(1, 2) - f(4, 1) = 3 + 3 - 0 = 6$$
$$(5.220a)$$

$$f'(s, 2) = f(2, V) - f(V, 2) = f(2, 4) + f(2, 5) - f(1, 2) = 8 + 3 - 3 = 8$$
$$(5.220b)$$

$$f'(6, t) = f(V, 6) - f(6, V) = f(3, 6) + f(4, 6) - f(6, 7) = 2 + 6 - 1 = 7$$
$$(5.220c)$$

$$f'(7, t) = f(V, 7) - f(7, V) = f(6, 7) + f(4, 7) + f(5, 7) = 1 + 2 + 4 = 7$$
$$(5.220d)$$

$$f'(x, y) = f(x, y), \qquad (x, y) \in E \qquad (5.220e)$$

These are as indicated in Fig. 5.59.

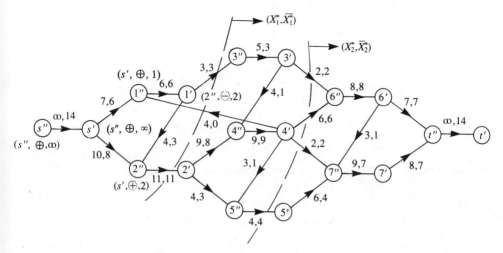

Fig. 5.60. The conversion of the feasibility problem of a node-and-arc capacitated net to the maximum flow problem in an equivalent arc capacitated net.

To convert the maximum flow problem in a node-and-arc capacitated net G', we apply the rules of Section 3.10 which were repeated briefly in this section and obtain the equivalent arc capacitated net $G^*(V^*, E^*, c^*, f^*)$ of Fig. 5.60. In Fig. 5.60, the arc capacities and flow values are again given as pairs of numbers adjacent to the arcs. Finally, using the Ford–Fulkerson algorithm yields the node labels shown in Fig. 5.60. Let X_1^* and $\bar{X}_1^*$ be the labeled and unlabeled nodes of G^*, respectively. Then

$$X_1^* = \{s'', s', 1'', 1', 2''\} \tag{5.221a}$$

$$\bar{X}_1^* = \{2', 3'', 3', 4'', 4', 5'', 5', 6'', 6', 7'', 7', t'', t'\} \tag{5.221b}$$

The s''–t' cut $(X_1^*, \bar{X}_1^*)$ is minimum in G^* with cut capacity

$$c^*(X_1^*, \bar{X}_1^*) = c^*(1', 3'') + c^*(2'', 2') = 3 + 11 = 14 \tag{5.222}$$

By the max-flow min-cut theorem, the flow f^* shown in Fig. 5.60 is maximum, so is the flow f' in Fig. 5.59. Since the arc $(7, t)$ in G' is not saturated, the supply–demand problem for the net G of Fig. 5.58 is infeasible.

To verify that condition (5.208) is indeed violated for some $X \subseteq V$, let $X = \{1, 2\}$. The subgraph of $D^1_{X,\bar{X}}$ in G corresponding to the cut $(X_1^*, \bar{X}_1^*)$ of G^* is a minimum generalized disconnecting set, as shown in Fig. 5.61, and is given by

$$D^1_{X,\bar{X}} = \{(1, 3), 2\} \tag{5.223}$$

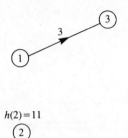

Fig. 5.61. A minimum generalized disconnecting set from $\{1, 2\}$ to $\{3, 4, 5, 6, 7\}$ for the net of Fig. 5.57.

yielding from (5.208)

$$
\begin{aligned}
b(T \cap \bar{X}) &- a(S \cap \bar{X}) \\
&= b(\{6, 7\} \cap \{3, 4, 5, 6, 7\}) - a(\{1, 2\} \cap \{3, 4, 5, 6, 7\}) \\
&= b(\{6, 7\}) - a(\{ \ \}) = b(6) + b(7) - 0 = 7 + 8 = 15 \\
\not\leqq k(D_{X, \bar{X}}^1) &= k(\{(1, 3), 2\}) = c(1, 3) + h(2) = 3 + 11 = 14
\end{aligned}
$$

$$(5.224)$$

confirming that the supply–demand problem for the net of Fig. 5.57 is infeasible.

In addition to the cut $(X_1^*, \bar{X}_1^*)$, there is another minimum $s''-t'$ cut $(X_2^*, \bar{X}_2^*)$ in G^*, as depicted in Fig. 5.60, where

$$X_2^* = \{s'', s', 1'', 1', 2'', 2', 3'', 3', 4'', 4', 5''\} \qquad (5.225a)$$

$$\bar{X}_2^* = \{6'', 6', 5', 7'', 7', t'', t'\} \qquad (5.225b)$$

whose capacity is found to be

$$
\begin{aligned}
c^*(X_2^*, \bar{X}_2^*) &= c^*(3', 6'') + c^*(4', 6'') + c^*(4', 7'') + c^*(5'', 5') \\
&= 2 + 6 + 2 + 4 = 14
\end{aligned}
$$

$$(5.226)$$

The subgraph of $D_{X, \bar{X}}^2$ in G corresponding to this cut $(X_2^*, \bar{X}_2^*)$ is another minimum generalized disconnecting set, as shown in Fig. 5.62, and is given by

$$D_{X, \bar{X}}^2 = \{(3, 6), (4, 6), (4, 7), 5\} \qquad (5.227)$$

where

$$X = \{1, 2, 3, 4, 5\}, \qquad \bar{X} = \{6, 7\} \qquad (5.228)$$

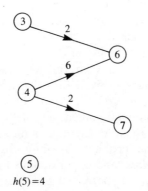

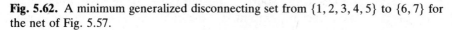

Fig. 5.62. A minimum generalized disconnecting set from $\{1,2,3,4,5\}$ to $\{6,7\}$ for the net of Fig. 5.57.

yielding from (5.208)

$$b(T \cap \bar{X}) - a(S \cap \bar{X}) = b(\{6, 7\}) - a(\{ \;\}) = 15$$
$$\nleq k(D^2_{X,\bar{x}}) = c(3, 6) + c(4, 6) + c(4, 7) + h(5)$$
$$= 2 + 6 + 2 + 4 = 14 \qquad (5.229)$$

a violation of (5.208).

We remark that if one is interested in checking the feasibility of a node-and-arc capacitated supply–demand net or in computing the maximum flow of a node-and-arc capacitated net, the most efficient method is to use the Ford–Fulkerson algorithm to solve the equivalent maximum flow problem in the enlarged arc capacitated net, rather than to check the conditions (5.208) for all subsets of the node set of the original net in determining the feasibility of the supply–demand problem.

5.7 SUMMARY AND SUGGESTED READING

In this chapter, we developed several theorems characterizing the existence of network flows that satisfy additional linear inequalities of various kinds. Specifically, we gave necessary and sufficient conditions for the existence of a flow pattern that satisfies the demands at certain nodes from the supplies at some of the others. If such a solution exists, we say that the constraints are feasible. Otherwise, they are infeasible. We showed that if, corresponding to each subset of sinks, there is a flow satisfying the aggregate demand of the subset, without exceeding the supply limitations at each of the sources, then there exists a flow in the net meeting all the individual demands. Likewise, if, corresponding to each subset of sources, there is a flow satisfying all individual demands without exceeding the aggregate supply of the subset with the supply at the sources outside the subset being infinite, then there exists a flow in the net meeting all the individual supplies. These results were derived directly from the max-flow min-cut theorem. As a result, if the supply function, the demand function, and the capacity function are all integral valued, and if there exists a feasible flow, then by the flow integrity theorem there is an integral feasible flow.

We then extended the problem by imposing lower bounds for the supplies at each of the sources and upper bounds for the demands at each of the sinks. We showed that if there is a flow that meets the lower bound requirements at each of the sources and the upper bound requirements at each of the sinks, and if there is a flow that meets the upper bound requirements at each of the sources and the lower bound requirements at each of the sinks, then there is a flow that satisfies all the lower and upper bound requirements at each of the sources and sinks simultaneously. This result, being symmetric with respect to the demands and supplies, is known as a symmetric supply–demand theorem.

In addition to the supply–demand problem, we also studied the existence of a flow in a source-free and sink-free net that satisfies the prescribed lower and upper bounds on the flow values in the arcs. If such a flow exists, we say that there is a feasible circulation in the net. Necessary and sufficient conditions for the existence of a feasible circulation were derived, and is known as the circulation theorem. The extension of this problem to the situation where the net flow into an individual node lies between prescribed bounds was also considered. Necessary and sufficient conditions were obtained. To construct a feasible circulation, we described a labeling process that is a variant of the Ford–Fulkerson algorithm. This process is valid for all nets having rational-valued capacity function as well as the lower-bound function. The procedure is efficient in that it either constructs a feasible circulation or detects a violation of the feasibility condition.

In Chapter 3, we considered the problem of finding a maximum flow from a source to a sink in a capacitated net with zero lower bound for all the arcs. We generalized this problem by requiring nonnegative real lower bounds on arc flows. We showed that if there is a feasible flow from the source s to the sink t in a net, then its maximum flow value is equal to the minimum of the difference of the capacity of an s–t cut $(X, \bar{X})$ and the sum of the lower bounds of the arcs in the cut $(\bar{X}, X)$. A similar result was obtained for the minimum flow value from s to t.

Finally, we studied the maximum flow problem in a node-and-arc capacitated net, in which each node is associated with a nonnegative real number. For this, we introduced the notion of a generalized disconnecting set. We showed that there is a feasible flow if and only if the net demand for every subset of the node set does not exceed the minimum capacity of a generalized disconnecting set from its complement to the subset. As a by-product, we demonstrated that the solution of the maximum flow problem in a node-and-arc capacitated net is equivalent to solving the maximum flow problem in an equivalent arc capacitated net. This result can also be stated in terms of a minimum capacity generalized disconnecting set. In words, it states that the maximum flow value from the source s to the sink t in a node-and-arc capacitated feasible net is equal to the minimum capacity of a generalized disconnecting set from s to t.

The classical book for feasibility problems and their variants is Ford and Fulkerson (1962). For further study on the various aspects of the problems, the reader is referred to the original papers listed in the references, particularly the papers by Gale (1957) and Hoffman (1960).

REFERENCES

Chen, W. K. (1976), *Applied Graph Theory: Graphs and Electrical Networks,* Amsterdam, The Netherlands: North-Holland, 2nd revised edition.

Dantzig, G. B. and Fulkerson, D. R. (1954), "Minimizing the number of tankers to meet a fixed schedule," *Naval Res. Logist. Quart.,* vol. 1, pp. 217–222.

Duguid, A. M. (1961), "Feasible flows and possible connection," *Pacific J. Math.,* vol. 11, pp. 483–488.

Ford, L. R. Jr and Fulkerson, D. R. (1962), *Flows in Networks,* Princeton, N.J.: Princeton University Press.

Fulkerson, D. R. (1959), "A network-flow feasibility theorem and combinatorial applications," *Can. J. Math.,* vol. 11, pp. 440–451.

Gale, D. (1957), "A theorem on flows in networks," *Pacific J. Math.,* vol. 7, pp. 1073–1082.

Hoffman, A. J. (1960), "Some recent applications of the theory of linear inequalities to extremal combinatorial analysis," *Proc. Symposia on Applied Math.,* vol. 10, pp. 113–127.

Lan, J. L. and Chen, W. K. (1985), "On f-factors of a graph," *J. Franklin Inst.,* vol. 320, pp. 55–62.

6

APPLICATIONS OF FLOW
THEOREMS TO SUBGRAPH
PROBLEMS

In the preceding chapter, we developed several theorems characterizing the existence of network flows that satisfy additional linear inequalities of various kinds. Specifically, we gave necessary and sufficient conditions for the existence of a flow pattern that satisfies the demands at certain nodes from the supplies at some of the others, or that satisfies both the lower and upper bounds of the arc flows. In the present chapter, we apply these theorems to the solutions of the subgraph problem for directed graphs, the matrix problem with prescribed row sums and column sums, and a number of other combinatorial problems in operations research.

6.1 THE SUBGRAPH PROBLEM OF A DIRECTED GRAPH

A problem that occurs in varying contexts is to establish a general criterion for the existence of subgraphs with prescribed degrees of a given directed graph. This problem has been studied extensively by many and a complete solution was given by Ore (1956a, 1956b, 1958b). A special case of the problem is to determine the necessary and sufficient conditions for the existence of a directed graph having the prescribed outgoing and incoming degrees. Various situations to this special case have been investigated by Chen (1966), Hakimi and Schmeichel (1978), and Eggleton and Holton (1979). In the following, we apply the flow theorems to generalize Ore's results by presenting criteria for the existence of (p, s) subgraphs with prescribed degrees and to show how this result allows the unification of many of the existing conditions. In general, we follow the recent work of Chen (1980).

A directed graph $G(V, E)$ consists of the node set V and edge set E of ordered pairs of the form $(i, j)_t$ called the *arcs*, where $i, j \in V$ and t is a positive integer. The arcs $(i, j)_t$ for $t = 1, 2, \ldots, k$, $k \geq 2$, are the *parallel arcs* of G if $(i, j)_t \in E$ for all t. This is in direct contrast to most of the nets considered so far where the existence of at most one arc directed from one node to another has been postulated. For $t = 1$, we write $(i, j)_t = (i, j)$, for simplicity. Also, (i, j) is used to represent any one of the parallel arcs $(i, j)_t \in E$. As before, the node i is called the *initial node* and j the *terminal node* of $(i, j)_t$. The local structure of a directed graph is described by the degrees of its nodes.

DEFINITION 6.1

Outgoing and Incoming Degrees. For a directed graph G, the number $d^+(i)$ of arcs of G having node i as their initial node is called the *outgoing degree* of node i in G, and the number $d^-(i)$ of arcs of G having node i as their terminal node is called the *incoming degree* of node i in G. Together $[d^+(i), d^-(i)]$ they are referred to as the *degree pair* of the node i in G.

Thus, there are two numbers defined for each node of G. These numbers sometimes are also referred to as *positive* and *negative degrees* of a node. If $d(i)$ denotes the number of arcs of G incident with node i, then

$$d(i) = d^+(i) + d^-(i) \tag{6.1}$$

Since every arc is outgoing from a node and terminating at another, it is evident that the number b of arcs of G is related to the degrees of its nodes by the equation

$$b = \sum_i d^+(i) = \sum_i d^-(i) \tag{6.2}$$

where the summations are over all i of G.

As an illustration, consider the directed graph G of Fig. 6.1, in which we have

$$d^+(1) = 2, \quad d^-(1) = 1, \quad d^+(2) = 1, \quad d^-(2) = 2$$
$$d^+(3) = 3, \quad d^-(3) = 2, \quad d^+(4) = 2, \quad d^-(4) = 1$$
$$d^+(5) = 1, \quad d^-(5) = 2, \quad d^+(6) = 1, \quad d^-(6) = 2 \tag{6.3}$$

It is straightforward to confirm that

$$b = \sum_{i=1}^{6} d^+(i) = 2 + 1 + 3 + 2 + 1 + 1$$

$$= \sum_{i=1}^{6} d^-(i) = 1 + 2 + 2 + 1 + 2 + 2 = 10 \tag{6.4}$$

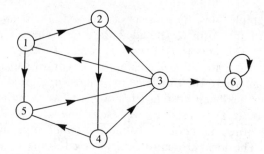

Fig. 6.1. A directed graph used for illustration.

The sequence of degree pairs $[d^+(i), d^-(i)]$ of the nodes i $(i = 1, 2, \ldots, 6)$ is given by

$$\{[d^+(i), d^-(i)]\} = \{[2, 1], [1, 2], [3, 2], [2, 1], [1, 2], [1, 2]\} \qquad (6.5)$$

In a given directed graph $G(V, E)$, suppose that each node $x \in V$ has associated with it a nonnegative integer $h(i)$ and that each arc $(x, y) \in E$ has associated with it a nonnegative integer $g(x, y)$. The function h is defined from V to the nonnegative integers, and the function g from E to the nonnegative integers. As in Section 3.2, if X and Y are subsets of V, then (X, Y) denotes the set of all arcs (x, y) directed from $x \in X$ to $y \in Y$; and, for any function h or g defined on V or E, write

$$h(X) = \sum_{x \in X} h(x) \qquad (6.6)$$

$$g(X, Y) = \sum_{(x,y) \in (X,Y)} g(x, y) \qquad (6.7)$$

We denote a set consisting of one element by its single element. Thus, if X contains only one element x, we write (x, Y), $h(x)$, $g(x, Y)$, and so on. In this connection, (x, y) has two different meanings. On the one hand, it represents any one of the parallel arcs $(x, y)_t$, $t = 1, 2, \ldots, k$, $k \geq 2$, in E. On the other hand, it denotes the set of parallel arcs from x to y in E. This should not create any difficulty as the context will tell. For a finite set S, the number of its elements is denoted by $|S|$. Thus, $|X|$ denotes the number of nodes in X and $|(X, Y)|$ denotes the number of arcs in (X, Y). In particular, $|(x, y)| = k$ denotes the number of parallel arcs from x to y in E.

DEFINITION 6.2

(p, s)-Digraph. A (p, s)-*digraph* is a directed graph $G(V, E)$, in which $|(x, y)| \leq p$ for all $(x, y) \in E$, $x \neq y$, and $|(x, x)| \leq s$ for all $x \in V$, where p

and s are two given nonnegative integers. When $p = s$, a (p, s)-digraph is simply called a *p-digraph*.

The letters p and s stand for the words *parallel* and *self-loop*, respectively. In Fig. 6.2, the directed graph $G(V, E)$ is a $(3, 2)$-digraph, because the maximum number of parallel arcs from one node to another is 3 or $|(1, 2)| = 3$, and the maximum number of self-loops at any node is 2 or $|(3, 3)| = 2$. Clearly, it is also a $(3, 3)$-digraph or a $(4, 3)$-digraph. As a matter of fact, it is a (p, s)-digraph for any $p \geq 3$ and $s \geq 2$. Its degree-pair sequence is found to be

$$\{[d^+(x), d^-(x)]\} = \{[4, 1], [3, 4], [4, 4], [3, 3], [3, 5]\} \qquad (6.8)$$

Given a directed graph $G(V, E)$, associate with each $x \in V$ four nonnegative integers $a(x)$, $a'(x)$, $b(x)$ and $b'(x)$ satisfying

$$0 \leq a(x) \leq a'(x), \qquad x \in V \qquad (6.9a)$$

$$0 \leq b(x) \leq b'(x), \qquad x \in V \qquad (6.9b)$$

The problem is to find necessary and sufficient conditions under which G possesses a (p, s)-digraph as a spanning subgraph H whose outgoing and incoming degrees $d_H^+(x)$ and $d_H^-(x)$ satisfy

$$a(x) \leq d_H^+(x) \leq a'(x), \qquad x \in V \qquad (6.10a)$$

$$b(x) \leq d_H^-(x) \leq b'(x), \qquad x \in V \qquad (6.10b)$$

To determine such conditions, we convert this to a flow problem, as follows: First construct from $G(V, E)$ a directed bipartite graph $B(V', V''; E')$: To each $x \in V$, there correspond two nodes $x' \in V'$ and $x'' \in V''$. The arc (x', y'') is in the arc set E' if and only if (x, y) is an arc of G. We remark that parallel arcs need not be considered in the present situation. If there are parallel arcs from x to y in G, there corresponds a

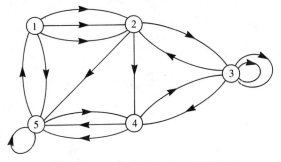

Fig. 6.2. A $(3, 2)$-digraph $G(V, E)$.

single arc $(x', y'') \in E'$. Thus, $B(V', V''; E')$ is a $(1, 0)$-digraph associated with $G(V, E)$. Associate with each arc $(x', y'') \in E'$ a nonnegative integer $c(x', y'')$ called the *capacity* of (x', y''). The *capacity function* c from E' to the nonnegative integers is defined by

$$c(x', y'') = \min \left[|(x, y)|, p \right], \quad x \neq y \qquad (6.11a)$$

$$= \min \left[|(x, y)|, s \right], \quad x = y \qquad (6.11b)$$

To complete the conversion to a supply–demand problem, associate with each $x' \in V'$ two nonnegative integers $a(x')$ and $a'(x')$, and with each $x'' \in V''$ two nonnegative integers $b(x'')$ and $b'(x'')$ satisfying

$$a(x') = a(x), \quad a'(x') = a'(x), \quad x \in V, \quad x' \in V' \qquad (6.12a)$$

$$b(x'') = b(x), \quad b'(x'') = b'(x), \quad x \in V, \quad x'' \in V'' \qquad (6.12b)$$

The directed bipartite graph $B(V', V''; E')$ can now be considered as a supply–demand net $B(V' \cup V'', E', c, f)$ with source set V' and sink set V''. Then according to Theorem 5.5, the constraints

$$a(x') \leqq f(x', V' \cup V'') - f(V' \cup V'', x') \leqq a'(x'), \quad x' \in V' \qquad (6.13)$$

$$b(x'') \leqq f(V' \cup V'', x'') - f(x'', V' \cup V'') \leqq b'(x''), \quad x'' \in V'' \qquad (6.14)$$

$$c(x', y'') \geqq f(x', y'') \geqq 0, \quad (x', y'') \in E' \qquad (6.15)$$

are feasible if and only if

$$c(X, \bar{X}) \geqq b(V'' \cap \bar{X}) - a'(V' \cap \bar{X}) \qquad (6.16a)$$

$$c(X, \bar{X}) \geqq a(V' \cap X) - b'(V'' \cap X) \qquad (6.16b)$$

hold for every subset $X \subseteq V' \cup V''$, where $\bar{X} = V' \cup V'' - X$. Since the net B is bipartite with arcs directing from a node in V' to a node in V'', we have

$$f(V' \cup V'', x') = 0 \qquad (6.17a)$$

$$f(x'', V' \cup V'') = 0 \qquad (6.17b)$$

Partition the subsets X and $\bar{X}$ into

$$X = X' \cup X'' \qquad (6.18a)$$

$$\bar{X} = \bar{X}' \cup \bar{X}'' \qquad (6.18b)$$

where $X' \subseteq V'$, $X'' \subseteq V''$, and

$$\bar{X}' = V' - X', \quad \bar{X}'' = V'' - X'' \qquad (6.19)$$

Invoking the bipartite property of the net B, constraints (6.16) can be simplified to

$$c(X', \bar{X}'') \geq b(\bar{X}'') - a'(\bar{X}') \tag{6.20a}$$

$$c(X', \bar{X}'') \geq a(X') - b'(X'') \tag{6.20b}$$

Our conclusion is that in the supply–demand net $B(V' \cup V'', E', c, f)$ with source set V' and sink set V'', the constraints

$$a(x') \leq f(x', V' \cup V'') \leq a'(x'), \qquad x' \in V' \tag{6.21}$$

$$b(x'') \leq f(V' \cup V'', x'') \leq b'(x''), \qquad x'' \in V'' \tag{6.22}$$

$$c(x', y'') \geq f(x', y'') \geq 0, \qquad (x', y'') \in E' \tag{6.23}$$

are feasible if and only if

$$c(X', \bar{X}'') \geq b(\bar{X}'') - a'(\bar{X}') \tag{6.24a}$$

$$c(X', \bar{X}'') \geq a(X') - b'(X'') \tag{6.24b}$$

hold for every subset $X' \subseteq V'$ and $X'' \subseteq V''$. It is clear that if the directed graph $G(V, E)$ possesses a (p, s) spanning subgraph H whose outgoing and incoming degrees satisfy the inequalities (6.10), then there is a feasible integral flow f in B satisfying (6.21)–(6.23) by defining the capacity function as in (6.11). Conversely, if there is a feasible integral flow f from V' to V'' in B satisfying the constraints (6.21)–(6.23), we can construct a (p, s) subgraph H satisfying (6.10) in G by putting arc (x, y) in H with multiplicity $f(x', y'')$ if and only if $f(x', y'') \neq 0$. Hence, by translating conditions (6.24) in terms of those in G, we obtain the desired conditions on the subgraphs.

THEOREM 6.1

In a directed graph $G(V, E)$, associate with each $x \in V$ four nonnegative integers $a(x)$, $a'(x)$, $b(x)$ and $b'(x)$ satisfying

$$0 \leq a(x) \leq a'(x) \tag{6.25a}$$

$$0 \leq b(x) \leq b'(x) \tag{6.25b}$$

and specify two nonnegative integers p and s. Then G has a (p, s) subgraph H whose outgoing and incoming degrees $d_H^+(x)$ and $d_H^-(x)$ satisfy

$$a(x) \leq d_H^+(x) \leq a'(x) \tag{6.26a}$$

$$b(x) \leq d_H^-(x) \leq b'(x) \tag{6.26b}$$

for each $x \in V$ if and only if

$$\sum_{y \in \gamma(X)} \min \left\{ b'(y), \sum_{x \in X} \min \left[|(x, y)|, \delta_{xy}(s - p) + p \right] \right\} \geq a(X) \quad (6.27a)$$

$$\sum_{y \in \gamma^*(X)} \min \left\{ a'(y), \sum_{x \in X} \min \left[|(y, x)|, \delta_{xy}(s - p) + p \right] \right\} \geq b(X) \quad (6.27b)$$

hold for all subsets $X \subseteq V$, where δ_{xy} is the Kronecker delta, $\gamma(X)$ denotes the set of terminal nodes of the arcs of G having their initial nodes in X, and $\gamma^*(X)$ denotes the set of initial nodes of the arcs of G having their terminal nodes in X.

Proof. It is sufficient to show that conditions (6.24) and (6.27) are equivalent. Observe that each of the conditions (6.24) is stated in terms of the selections of a pair of subsets $X' \subseteq V'$ and $X'' \subseteq V''$. We first demonstrate that each of these conditions (6.24) can be simplified to one involving the choice of but one subset. Consider (6.24b), for example. For a given subset $X' \subseteq V'$, define

$$U'' = \{ y'' \mid y'' \in V'', b'(y'') < c(X', y'') \} \quad (6.28)$$

For this pair of subsets $X' \subseteq V'$ and $U'' \subseteq V''$, the inequality (6.24b) can be written as

$$c(X', \bar{U}'') + b'(U'') = \sum_{y'' \in \gamma(X')} \min \left[b'(y''), c(X', y'') \right] \geq a(X') \quad (6.29)$$

For any fixed $X' \subseteq V'$, the left-hand side of (6.29) minimizes this sum over all $X'' \subseteq V''$, as can be demonstrated below:

$$\begin{aligned}
c(X', \bar{U}'') + b'(U'') &= c(X', \bar{U}'' \cap X'') + c(X', \bar{X}'') - c(X', U'' \cap \bar{X}'') \\
&\quad + b'(U'' \cap \bar{X}'') + b'(X'') - b'(\bar{U}'' \cap X'') \\
&\leq c(X', \bar{X}'') + b'(X'')
\end{aligned} \quad (6.30)$$

since

$$c(X', \bar{U}'' \cap X'') - b'(\bar{U}'' \cap X'') \leq 0 \quad (6.31a)$$

$$b'(U'' \cap \bar{X}'') - c(X', U'' \cap \bar{X}'') \leq 0 \quad (6.31b)$$

Thus, condition (6.24b) is satisfied for all $X' \subseteq V'$ and $X'' \subseteq V''$ if and only if (6.29) holds for all $X' \subseteq V'$. Similarly, condition (6.24a) reduces to

$$\sum_{x' \in \gamma^*(X'')} \min \left[a'(x'), c(x', X'') \right] \geq b(X'') \quad (6.32)$$

for all $X'' \subseteq V''$.

To compute $c(X', y'')$ and $c(x', X'')$, $y'' \in V''$ and $x' \in V'$, let

$$X = \{x \in V \mid x' \in X'\} \tag{6.33a}$$

$$Y = \{y \in V \mid y'' \in X''\} \tag{6.33b}$$

Then from (6.11) we obtain

$$c(X', y'') = \sum_{x \in X} \min \left[|(x, y)|, \, \delta_{xy}(s - p) + p \right] \tag{6.34a}$$

$$c(x', X'') = \sum_{y \in Y} \min \left[|(x, y)|, \, \delta_{xy}(s - p) + p \right] \tag{6.34b}$$

Translating (6.29) and (6.32) in terms of the specifications for the given directed graph G in conjunction with (6.34) gives conditions (6.27). This completes the proof of the theorem.

COROLLARY 6.1

A directed graph $G(V, E)$ has a subgraph H whose outgoing and incoming degrees $d_H^+(x)$ and $d_H^-(x)$ satisfy

$$a(x) \leq d_H^+(x) \leq a'(x), \qquad x \in V \tag{6.35a}$$

$$b(x) \leq d_H^-(x) \leq b'(x), \qquad x \in V \tag{6.35b}$$

if and only if the inequalities

$$\sum_{y \in \gamma(X)} \min \left[b'(y), |(X, y)| \right] \geq a(X) \tag{6.36a}$$

$$\sum_{y \in \gamma^*(X)} \min \left[a'(y), |(y, X)| \right] \geq b(X) \tag{6.36b}$$

hold for all $X \subseteq V$.

Proof. In (6.27), let

$$s = p = \sum_{(x,y) \in E} |(x, y)| \tag{6.37}$$

The corollary follows directly from the observation that

$$|(X, y)| = \sum_{x \in X} |(x, y)| = \sum_{x \in X} \min \left[|(x, y)|, p \right] \tag{6.38a}$$

$$|(y, X)| = \sum_{x \in X} |(y, x)| = \sum_{x \in X} \min \left[|(y, x)|, p \right] \tag{6.38b}$$

This completes the proof of the corollary.

In the case for which the outgoing and incoming degrees are specified exactly, we set $a(x) = a'(x)$ and $b(x) = b'(x)$ and obtain the following theorem.

THEOREM 6.2

A directed graph $G(V, E)$ has a (p, s) subgraph H with outgoing and incoming degrees satisfying

$$d_H^+(x) = a(x) \geq 0, \qquad x \in V \tag{6.39a}$$

$$d_H^-(x) = b(x) \geq 0, \qquad x \in V \tag{6.39b}$$

if and only if

$$a(V) = b(V) \tag{6.40}$$

and either

$$\sum_{y \in \gamma(X)} \min \left\{ b(y), \sum_{x \in X} \min \left[|(x, y)|, \delta_{xy}(s - p) + p \right] \right\} \geq a(X) \tag{6.41}$$

or

$$\sum_{y \in \gamma^*(X)} \min \left\{ a(y), \sum_{x \in X} \min \left[|(y, x)|, \delta_{xy}(s - p) + p \right] \right\} \geq b(X) \tag{6.42}$$

holds for all $X \subseteq V$.

Proof. For the subgraph H to exist, it is necessary that $a(V) = b(V)$. To complete the proof, it is sufficient to show that (6.40) and (6.41) imply (6.42), and (6.40) and (6.42) imply (6.41).

As indicated in the proof of Theorem 6.1, with $a(x) = a'(x)$ and $b(x) = b'(x)$, (6.41) and (6.42) are completely equivalent to (6.24). Using the symbols defined in (6.24) for the bipartite supply–demand net $B(V' \cup V'', E', c, f)$, we first demonstrate that (6.40) and (6.24b) imply (6.24a), as follows:

$$a(\bar{X}') + c(X', \bar{X}'') \geq a(\bar{X}') + a(X') - b'(X'')$$

$$= a(V') - b(X'') = b(V'') - b(X'')$$

$$= b(\bar{X}'') \tag{6.43}$$

Likewise, we can show that (6.40) and (6.24a) imply (6.24b):

$$b(X'') + c(X', \bar{X}'') \geq b(X'') + b(\bar{X}'') - a'(\bar{X}')$$
$$= b(V'') - a(\bar{X}') = a(V') - a(\bar{X}')$$
$$= a(X') \tag{6.44}$$

This completes the proof of the theorem.

Using (6.38) in (6.41) and (6.42) yields a result due to Ore (1956a) on the existence of a subgraph of a directed graph having prescribed outgoing and incoming degrees.

COROLLARY 6.2

A directed graph $G(V, E)$ has a subgraph H with outgoing and incoming degrees $d_H^+(x)$ and $d_H^-(x)$ satisfying

$$d_H^+(x) = a(x) \geq 0, \qquad x \in V \tag{6.45a}$$

$$d_H^-(x) = b(x) \geq 0, \qquad x \in V \tag{6.45b}$$

if and only if

$$a(V) = b(V) \tag{6.46}$$

and either

$$\sum_{y \in \gamma(X)} \min [b(y), |(X, y)|] \geq a(X) \tag{6.47}$$

or

$$\sum_{y \in \gamma^*(X)} \min [a(y), |(y, X)|] \geq b(X) \tag{6.48}$$

holds for all $X \subseteq V$.

We illustrate the above results by the following examples.

Example 6.1

The directed graph shown in Fig. 6.3 is a $(2, 2)$-digraph $G(V, E)$. We wish to determine if there is a $(1, 1)$ subgraph H whose outgoing and

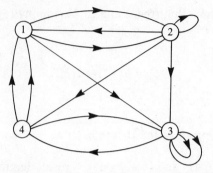

Fig. 6.3. A $(2, 2)$-digraph $G(V, E)$ used to study the subgraph problem.

incoming degrees $d_H^+(x)$ and $d_H^-(x)$ satisfy

$$a(1) = 1 \leqq d_H^+(1) \leqq 2 = a'(1) \qquad (6.49a)$$

$$a(2) = 1 \leqq d_H^+(2) \leqq 3 = a'(2) \qquad (6.49b)$$

$$a(3) = 2 \leqq d_H^+(3) \leqq 3 = a'(3) \qquad (6.49c)$$

$$a(4) = 0 \leqq d_H^+(4) \leqq 1 = a'(4) \qquad (6.49d)$$

$$b(1) = 0 \leqq d_H^-(1) \leqq 2 = b'(1) \qquad (6.50a)$$

$$b(2) = 1 \leqq d_H^-(2) \leqq 3 = b'(2) \qquad (6.50b)$$

$$b(3) = 2 \leqq d_H^-(3) \leqq 4 = b'(3) \qquad (6.50c)$$

$$b(4) = 1 \leqq d_H^-(4) \leqq 3 = b'(4) \qquad (6.50d)$$

To apply Theorem 6.1, we consider all the nonempty subsets X of $V = \{1, 2, 3, 4\}$ and use $p = s = 1$ in (6.27). The empty subset need not be considered because the inequalities (6.27) are trivially satisfied in this case. For the other 15 ($= 2^4 - 1$) subsets, conditions (6.27a) become

$$\min \{b'(2), \min [|(1, 2)|, 1]\} + \min \{b'(3), \min [|(1, 3)|, 1]\}$$

$$= \min \{3, \min [2, 1]\} + \min \{4, \min [1, 1]\}$$

$$= \min \{3, 1\} + \min \{4, 1\} = 1 + 1 = 2 \geqq a(1) = 1 \qquad (6.51a)$$

$$\min \{2, \min [1, 1]\} + \min \{3, \min [1, 1]\} + \min \{4, \min [1, 1]\}$$

$$+ \min \{3, \min [1, 1]\} = 1 + 1 + 1 + 1 = 4$$

$$\geqq a(2) = 1 \qquad (6.51b)$$

$$\min \{4, \min [2, 1]\} + \min \{3, \min [1, 1]\} = 2 \geqq a(3) = 2 \qquad (6.51c)$$

$$\min \{2, \min [2, 1]\} + \min \{4, \min [1, 1]\} = 2 \geqq a(4) = 0 \qquad (6.51d)$$

for the single element subsets;

$$\min\{2, \min[0,1] + \min[1, 1]\} + \min\{3, \min[2, 1] + \min[1, 1]\}$$
$$+ \min\{4, \min[1, 1] + \min[1, 1]\} + \min\{3, \min[0, 1] + \min[1, 1]\}$$
$$= 1 + 2 + 2 + 1 = 6 \geqq a(\{1, 2\}) = 1 + 1 = 2 \qquad (6.52a)$$
$$\min\{3, \min[2, 1] + \min[0, 1]\} + \min\{4, \min[1, 1] + \min[2, 1]\}$$
$$+ \min\{3, \min[0, 1] + \min[1, 1]\} = 4$$
$$\geqq a(\{1, 3\}) = 3 \qquad (6.52b)$$

$$\min\{2, \min[0, 1] + \min[2, 1]\} + \min\{3, \min[2, 1] + \min[0, 1]\}$$
$$+ \min\{4, \min[1, 1] + \min[1, 1]\} = 4$$
$$\geqq a(\{1, 4\}) = 1 \qquad (6.52c)$$
$$\min\{2, \min[1, 1] + \min[0, 1]\} + \min\{3, \min[1, 1] + \min[0, 1]\}$$
$$+ \min\{4, \min[1, 1] + \min[2, 1]\} + \min\{3, \min[1, 1] + \min[1, 1]\}$$
$$= 6 \geqq a(\{2, 3\}) = 3 \qquad (6.52d)$$

$$\min\{2, \min[1, 1] + \min[2, 1]\} + \min\{3, \min[1, 1] + \min[0, 1]\}$$
$$+ \min\{4, \min[1, 1] + \min[1, 1]\} + \min\{3, \min[1, 1] + \min[0, 1]\}$$
$$= 6 \geqq a(\{2, 4\}) = 1 \qquad (6.52e)$$

$$\min\{2, \min[0, 1] + \min[2, 1]\} + \min\{4, \min[2, 1] + \min[1, 1]\}$$
$$+ \min\{3, \min[1, 1] + \min[0, 1]\} = 4$$
$$\geqq a(\{3, 4\}) = 2 \qquad (6.52f)$$

for the two-element subsets;

$$\min\{2, \min[0, 1] + \min[1, 1] + \min[0, 1]\} + \min\{3, \min[2, 1]$$
$$+ \min[1, 1] + \min[0, 1]\} + \min\{4, \min[1, 1] + \min[1, 1]$$
$$+ \min[2, 1]\} + \min\{3, \min[0, 1] + \min[1, 1] + \min[1, 1]\}$$
$$= 8 \geqq a(\{1, 2, 3\}) = 4 \qquad (6.53a)$$
$$\min\{2, \min[0, 1] + \min[1, 1] + \min[2, 1]\} + \min\{3, \min[2, 1]$$
$$+ \min[1, 1] + \min[0, 1]\} + \min\{4, \min[1, 1] + \min[1, 1]$$
$$+ \min[1, 1]\} + \min\{3, \min[0, 1] + \min[1, 1] + \min[0, 1]\}$$
$$= 8 \geqq a(\{1, 2, 4\}) = 2 \qquad (6.53b)$$

$$\min \{2, \min [0, 1] + \min [0, 1] + \min [2, 1]\} + \min \{3, \min [2, 1]$$
$$+ \min [0, 1] + \min [0, 1]\} + \min \{4, \min [1, 1] + \min [2, 1]$$
$$+ \min [1, 1]\} + \min \{3, \min [0, 1] + \min [1, 1] + \min [0, 1]\}$$
$$= 6 \geqq a(\{1, 3, 4\}) = 3 \tag{6.53c}$$

$$\min \{2, \min [1, 1] + \min [0, 1] + \min [2, 1]\} + \min \{3, \min [1, 1]$$
$$+ \min [0, 1] + \min [0, 1]\} + \min \{4, \min [1, 1] + \min [2, 1]$$
$$+ \min [1, 1]\} + \min \{3, \min [1, 1] + \min [1, 1] + \min [0, 1]\}$$
$$= 8 \geqq a(\{2, 3, 4\}) = 3 \tag{6.53d}$$

for the three-element subsets; and

$$\min \{2, \min [0, 1] + \min [1, 1] + \min [0, 1] + \min [2, 1]\}$$
$$+ \min \{3, \min [2, 1] + \min [1, 1] + \min [0, 1] + \min [0, 1]\}$$
$$+ \min \{4, \min [1, 1] + \min [1, 1] + \min [2, 1] + \min [1, 1]\}$$
$$+ \min \{3, \min [0, 1] + \min [1, 1] + \min [1, 1] + \min [0, 1]\}$$
$$= 10 \geqq a(\{1, 2, 3, 4\}) = 4 \tag{6.54}$$

for the set itself. For conditions (6.27b), we have

$$\min \{3, \min [1, 1]\} + \min \{1, \min [2, 1]\} = 2$$
$$\geqq b(1) = 0 \tag{6.55a}$$

$$\min \{2, \min [2, 1]\} + \min \{3, \min [1, 1]\} = 2$$
$$\geqq b(2) = 1 \tag{6.55b}$$

$$\min \{2, \min [1, 1]\} + \min \{3, \min [1, 1]\} + \min \{3, \min [2, 1]\}$$
$$+ \min \{1, \min [1, 1]\} = 4 \geqq b(3) = 2 \tag{6.55c}$$

$$\min \{3, \min [1, 1]\} + \min \{3, \min [1, 1]\} = 2$$
$$\geqq b(4) = 1 \tag{6.55d}$$

for the single element subsets;

$$\min \{2, \min [0, 1] + \min [2, 1]\} + \min \{3, \min [1, 1] + \min [1, 1]\}$$
$$+ \min \{1, \min [2, 1] + \min [0, 1]\} = 4$$
$$\geqq b(\{1, 2\}) = 1 \tag{6.56a}$$

$\min \{2, \min [0, 1] + \min [1, 1]\} + \min \{3, \min [1, 1] + \min [1, 1]\}$

$\quad + \min \{3, \min [0, 1] + \min [2, 1]\} + \min \{1, \min [2, 1]$

$\quad + \min [1, 1]\} = 6 \geqq b(\{1, 3\}) = 2 \hspace{3cm} (6.56b)$

$\min \{3, \min [1, 1] + \min [1, 1]\} + \min \{3, \min [0, 1] + \min [1, 1]\}$

$\quad + \min \{1, \min [2, 1] + \min [0, 1]\} = 4$

$\quad \geqq b(\{1, 4\}) = 1 \hspace{4cm} (6.56c)$

$\min \{2, \min [2, 1] + \min [1, 1]\} + \min \{3, \min [1, 1] + \min [1, 1]\}$

$\quad + \min \{3, \min [0, 1] + \min [2, 1]\} + \min \{1, \min [0, 1] + \min [1, 1]\}$

$\quad = 6 \geqq b(\{2, 3\}) = 3 \hspace{3.5cm} (6.56d)$

$\min \{2, \min [2, 1] + \min [0, 1]\} + \min \{3, \min [1, 1] + \min [1, 1]\}$

$\quad + \min \{3, \min [0, 1] + \min [1, 1]\} + \min \{1, \min [0, 1] + \min [0, 1]\}$

$\quad = 4 \geqq b(\{2, 4\}) = 2 \hspace{3.5cm} (6.56e)$

$\min \{2, \min [1, 1] + \min [0, 1]\} + \min \{3, \min [1, 1] + \min [1, 1]\}$

$\quad + \min \{3, \min [2, 1] + \min [1, 1]\} + \min \{1, \min [1, 1] + \min [0, 1]\}$

$\quad = 6 \geqq b(\{3, 4\}) = 3 \hspace{3.5cm} (6.56f)$

for the two-element subsets;

$\min \{2, \min [0, 1] + \min [2, 1] + \min [1, 1]\} + \min \{3, \min [1, 1]$

$\quad + \min [1, 1] + \min [1, 1]\} + \min \{3, \min [0, 1] + \min [0, 1]$

$\quad + \min [2, 1]\} + \min \{1, \min [2, 1] + \min [0, 1] + \min [1, 1]\}$

$\quad = 7 \geqq b(\{1, 2, 3\}) = 3 \hspace{3cm} (6.57a)$

$\min \{2, \min [0, 1] + \min [2, 1] + \min [0, 1]\} + \min \{3, \min [1, 1]$

$\quad + \min [1, 1] + \min [1, 1]\} + \min \{3, \min [0, 1] + \min [0, 1]$

$\quad + \min [1, 1]\} + \min \{1, \min [2, 1] + \min [0, 1] + \min [0, 1]\}$

$\quad = 6 \geqq b(\{1, 2, 4\}) = 2 \hspace{3cm} (6.57b)$

$\min \{2, \min [0, 1] + \min [1, 1] + \min [0, 1]\} + \min \{3, \min [1, 1]$

$\quad + \min [1, 1] + \min [1, 1]\} + \min \{3, \min [0, 1] + \min [2, 1]$

$\quad + \min [1, 1]\} + \min \{1, \min [2, 1] + \min [1, 1] + \min [0, 1]\}$

$\quad = 7 \geqq b(\{1, 3, 4\}) = 3 \hspace{3cm} (6.57c)$

$$\min \{2, \min [2, 1] + \min [1, 1] + \min [0, 1]\} + \min \{3, \min [1, 1]$$
$$+ \min [1, 1] + \min [1, 1]\} + \min \{3, \min [0, 1]$$
$$+ \min [2, 1] + \min [1, 1]\} + \min \{1, \min [0, 1] + \min [1, 1]$$
$$+ \min [0, 1]\} = 8 \geqq b(\{2, 3, 4\}) = 4 \tag{6.57d}$$

for the three-element subsets; and

$$\min \{2, \min [0, 1] + \min [2, 1] + \min [1, 1] + \min [0, 1]\} + \min \{3,$$
$$\min [1, 1] + \min [1, 1] + \min [1, 1] + \min [1, 1]\} + \min \{3,$$
$$\min [0, 1] + \min [0, 1] + \min [2, 1] + \min [1, 1]\} + \min \{1,$$
$$\min [2, 1] + \min [0, 1] + \min [1, 1] + \min [0, 1]\}$$
$$= 8 \geqq b(\{1, 2, 3, 4\}) = 4 \tag{6.58}$$

for the set itself. Since conditions (6.27) are satisfied for all subsets X of V, by Theorem 6.1 we conclude that there is a $(1, 1)$ subgraph H whose outgoing and incoming degrees $d_H^+(x)$ and $d_H^-(x)$ satisfy the inequalities (6.49) and (6.50). One such $(1, 1)$ subgraph H is presented in Fig. 6.4.

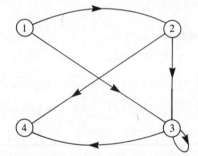

Fig. 6.4. A $(1, 1)$ subgraph H satisfying the degree constraints (6.49) and (6.50).

Example 6.2

For the directed graph $G(V, E)$ of Fig. 6.3, we wish to ascertain the existence of a subgraph H whose outgoing and incoming degrees $d_H^+(x)$ and $d_H^-(x)$ satisfy the inequalities

$$a(1) = 2 \leqq d_H^+(1) \leqq 3 = a'(1) \tag{6.59a}$$

$$a(2) = 2 \leqq d_H^+(2) \leqq 3 = a'(2) \tag{6.59b}$$

$$a(3) = 2 \leqq d_H^+(3) \leqq 3 = a'(3) \tag{6.59c}$$

$$a(4) = 1 \leqq d_H^+(4) \leqq 2 = a'(4) \tag{6.59d}$$

$$b(1) = 1 \leqq d_H^-(1) \leqq 2 = b'(1) \tag{6.60a}$$

$$b(2) = 2 \leqq d_H^-(2) \leqq 3 = b'(2) \qquad (6.60b)$$

$$b(3) = 3 \leqq d_H^-(3) \leqq 4 = b'(3) \qquad (6.60c)$$

$$b(4) = 2 \leqq d_H^-(4) \leqq 3 = b'(4) \qquad (6.60d)$$

From Corollary 6.1, such a subgraph H exists if and only if conditions (6.36) hold for all subsets $X \subseteq V$. As before, we consider only the nonempty subsets of V. For (6.36a) we have

$$\min [b'(2), |(1, 2)|] + \min [b'(3), |(1, 3)|] = \min [3, 2] + \min [4, 1]$$

$$= 2 + 1 = 3 \geqq a(1) = 2 \qquad (6.61a)$$

$$\min [2, |(2, 1)|] + \min [3, |(2, 2)|] + \min [4, |(2, 3)|] + \min [3, |(2, 4)|]$$

$$= \min [2, 1] + \min [3, 1] + \min [4, 1] + \min [3, 1]$$

$$= 1 + 1 + 1 + 1 = 4 \geqq a(2) = 2 \qquad (6.61b)$$

$$\min [4, |(3, 3)|] + \min [3, |(3, 4)|] = \min [4, 2] + \min [3, 1]$$

$$= 2 + 1 = 3 \geqq a(3) = 2 \qquad (6.61c)$$

$$\min [2, |(4, 1)|] + \min [4, |(4, 3)|] = \min [2, 2] + \min [4, 1]$$

$$= 2 + 1 = 3 \geqq a(4) = 1 \qquad (6.61d)$$

for the single element subsets;

$$\min [2, |(\{1, 2\}, 1)|] + \min [3, |(\{1, 2\}, 2)|] + \min [4, |(\{1, 2\}, 3)|]$$

$$+ \min [3, |(\{1, 2\}, 4)|]$$

$$= \min [2, 1] + \min [3, 3] + \min [4, 2] + \min [3, 1]$$

$$= 1 + 3 + 2 + 1 = 7 \geqq a(\{1, 2\}) = 2 + 2 = 4 \qquad (6.62a)$$

$$\min [3, |(\{1, 3\}, 2)|] + \min [4, |(\{1, 3\}, 3)|] + \min \{3, |(\{1, 3\}, 4)|\}$$

$$= \min [3, 2] + \min [4, 3] + \min [3, 1]$$

$$= 2 + 3 + 1 = 6 \geqq a(\{1, 3\}) = 2 + 2 = 4 \qquad (6.62b)$$

$$\min [2, |(\{1, 4\}, 1)|] + \min [3, |(\{1, 4\}, 2)|] + \min [4, |(\{1, 4\}, 3)|]$$

$$= \min [2, 2] + \min [3, 2] + \min [4, 2]$$

$$= 2 + 2 + 2 = 6 \geqq a(\{1, 4\}) = 2 + 1 = 3 \qquad (6.62c)$$

$$\min [2, |(\{2, 3\}, 1)|] + \min [3, |(\{2, 3\}, 2)|] + \min [4, |(\{2, 3\}, 3)|]$$

$$+ \min [3, |(\{2, 3\}, 4)|] = \min [2, 1] + \min [3, 1]$$

$$+ \min [4, 3] + \min [3, 2]$$

$$= 1 + 1 + 3 + 2 = 7 \geqq a(\{2, 3\}) = 2 + 2 = 4 \qquad (6.62d)$$

$$\min [2, |(\{2, 4\}, 1)|] + \min [3, |(\{2, 4\}, 2)|] + \min [4, |(\{2, 4\}, 3)|]$$
$$+ \min [3, |(\{2, 4\}, 4)|]$$
$$= \min [2, 3] + \min [3, 1] + \min [4, 2] + \min [3, 1]$$
$$= 2 + 1 + 2 + 1 = 6 \geqq a(\{2, 4\}) = 2 + 1 = 3 \qquad (6.62e)$$
$$\min [2, |(\{3, 4\}, 1)|] + \min [4, |(\{3, 4\}, 3)|] + \min [3, |(\{3, 4\}, 4)|]$$
$$= \min [2, 2] + \min [4, 3] + \min [3, 1]$$
$$= 2 + 3 + 1 = 6 \geqq a(\{3, 4\}) = 2 + 1 = 3 \qquad (6.62f)$$

for the two-element subsets;

$$\min [2, |(\{1, 2, 3\}, 1)|] + \min [3, |(\{1, 2, 3\}, 2)|]$$
$$+ \min [4, |(\{1, 2, 3\}, 3)|] + \min [3, |(\{1, 2, 3\}, 4)|]$$
$$= \min [2, 1] + \min [3, 3] + \min [4, 4] + \min [3, 2]$$
$$= 1 + 3 + 4 + 2 = 10$$
$$\geqq a(\{1, 2, 3\}) = 2 + 2 + 2 = 6 \qquad (6.63a)$$
$$\min [2, |(\{1, 2, 4\}, 1)|] + \min [3, |(\{1, 2, 4\}, 2)|]$$
$$+ \min [4, |(\{1, 2, 4\}, 3)|] + \min [3, |(\{1, 2, 4\}, 4)|]$$
$$= \min [2, 3] + \min [3, 3] + \min [4, 3] + \min [3, 1]$$
$$= 2 + 3 + 3 + 1 = 9 \geqq a(\{1, 2, 4\}) = 2 + 2 + 1 = 5 \qquad (6.63b)$$
$$\min [2, |(\{1, 3, 4\}, 1)|] + \min [3, |(\{1, 3, 4\}, 2)|]$$
$$+ \min \{4, |(\{1, 3, 4\}, 3)|] + \min [3, |(\{1, 3, 4\}, 4)|]$$
$$= \min [2, 2] + \min [3, 2] + \min [4, 4] + \min [3, 1]$$
$$= 2 + 2 + 4 + 1 = 9 \geqq a(\{1, 3, 4\}) = 2 + 2 + 1 = 5 \qquad (6.63c)$$
$$\min [2, |(\{2, 3, 4\}, 1)|] + \min [3, |(\{2, 3, 4\}, 2)|]$$
$$+ \min [4, |(\{2, 3, 4\}, 3|] + \min [3, |(\{2, 3, 4\}, 4)|]$$
$$= \min [2, 3] + \min [3, 1] + \min [4, 4] + \min [3, 2]$$
$$= 2 + 1 + 4 + 2 = 9 \geqq a(\{2, 3, 4\}) = 2 + 2 + 1 = 5 \qquad (6.63d)$$

for the three-element subsets; and

$$\min [2, |(\{1, 2, 3, 4\}, 1)|] + \min [3, |(\{1, 2, 3, 4\}, 2)|]$$
$$+ \min [4, |(\{1, 2, 3, 4\}, 3)|] + \min [3, |(\{1, 2, 3, 4\}, 4)|]$$
$$= \min [2, 3] + \min [3, 3] + \min [4, 5] + \min [3, 2]$$

$$= 2 + 3 + 4 + 2 = 11$$
$$\geqq a(\{1, 2, 3, 4\}) = 2 + 2 + 2 + 1 = 7 \tag{6.64}$$

for the set itself. For conditions (6.36*b*), we have

$$\min [a'(2), |(2, 1)|] + \min [a'(4), |(4, 1)|] = \min [3, 1]$$
$$+ \min [2, 2] = 1 + 2 = 3 \geqq b(1) = 1 \tag{6.65a}$$
$$\min [3, |(1, 2)|] + \min [3, |(2, 2)|] = \min [3, 2] + \min [3, 1]$$
$$= 2 + 1 = 3 \geqq b(2) = 2 \tag{6.65b}$$
$$\min [3, |(1, 3)|] + \min [3, |(2, 3)|] + \min [3, |(3, 3)|]$$
$$+ \min [2, |(4, 3)|] = \min [3, 1] + \min [3, 1] + \min [3, 2]$$
$$+ \min [2, 1] = 1 + 1 + 2 + 1 = 5 \geqq b(3) = 3 \tag{6.65c}$$
$$\min [3, |(2, 4)|] + \min [3, |(3, 4)|] = \min [3, 1] + \min [3, 1]$$
$$= 1 + 1 = 2 \geqq b(4) = 2 \tag{6.65d}$$

for the single element subsets;

$$\min [3, |(1, \{1, 2\})|] + \min [3, |(2, \{1, 2\})|] + \min [2, |(4, \{1, 2\})|]$$
$$= \min [3, 2] + \min [3, 2] + \min [2, 2]$$
$$= 2 + 2 + 2 = 6 \geqq b(\{1, 2\}) = 1 + 2 = 3 \tag{6.66a}$$
$$\min [3, |(1, \{1, 3\})|] + \min [3, |(2, \{1, 3\})|] + \min [3, |(3, \{1, 3\})|]$$
$$+ \min [2, |(4, \{1, 3\})|]$$
$$= \min [3, 1] + \min [3, 2] + \min [3, 2] + \min [2, 3]$$
$$= 1 + 2 + 2 + 2 = 7 \geqq b(\{1, 3\}) = 1 + 3 = 4 \tag{6.66b}$$
$$\min [3, |(2, \{1, 4\})|] + \min [3, |(3, \{1, 4\})|] + \min [2, |(4, \{1, 4\})|]$$
$$= \min [3, 2] + \min [3, 1] + \min [2, 2]$$
$$= 2 + 1 + 2 = 5 \geqq b(\{1, 4\}) = 1 + 2 = 3 \tag{6.66c}$$
$$\min [3, |(1, \{2, 3\})|] + \min [3, |(2, \{2, 3\})|] + \min [3, |(3, \{2, 3\})|]$$
$$+ \min [2, |(4, \{2, 3\})|]$$
$$= \min [3, 3] + \min [3, 2] + \min [3, 2] + \min [2, 1]$$
$$= 3 + 2 + 2 + 1 = 8 \geqq b(\{2, 3\}) = 2 + 3 = 5 \tag{6.66d}$$

$$\min [3, |(1, \{2, 4\})|] + \min [3, |(2, \{2, 4\})|] + \min [3, |(3, \{2, 4\})|]$$
$$= \min [3, 2] + \min [3, 2] + \min [3, 1]$$
$$= 2 + 2 + 1 = 5 \geqq b(\{2, 4\}) = 2 + 2 = 4 \tag{6.66e}$$

$$\min [3, |(1, \{3, 4\})|] + \min [3, |(2, \{3, 4\})|] + \min [3, |(3, \{3, 4\})|]$$
$$+ \min [2, |(4, \{3, 4\})|]$$
$$= \min [3, 1] + \min [3, 2] + \min [3, 3] + \min [2, 1]$$
$$= 1 + 2 + 3 + 1 = 7 \geqq b(\{3, 4\}) = 3 + 2 = 5 \tag{6.66f}$$

for the two-element subsets;

$$\min [3, |(1, \{1, 2, 3\})|] + \min [3, |(2, \{1, 2, 3\})|]$$
$$+ \min [3, |(3, \{1, 2, 3\})|] + \min [2, |(4, \{1, 2, 3\})|]$$
$$= \min [3, 3] + \min [3, 3] + \min [3, 2] + \min [2, 3]$$
$$= 3 + 3 + 2 + 2 = 10$$
$$\geqq b(\{1, 2, 3\}) = 1 + 2 + 3 = 6 \tag{6.67a}$$

$$\min [3, |(1, \{1, 2, 4\})|] + \min [3, |(2, \{1, 2, 4\})|]$$
$$+ \min [3, |(3, \{1, 2, 4\})|] + \min [2, |(4, \{1, 2, 4\})|]$$
$$= \min [3, 2] + \min [3, 3] + \min [3, 1] + \min [2, 2]$$
$$= 2 + 3 + 1 + 2 = 8$$
$$\geqq b(\{1, 2, 4\}) = 1 + 2 + 2 = 5 \tag{6.67b}$$

$$\min [3, |(1, \{1, 3, 4\})|] + \min [3, |(2, \{1, 3, 4\})|]$$
$$+ \min [3, |(3, \{1, 3, 4\})|] + \min [2, |(4, \{1, 3, 4\})|]$$
$$= \min [3, 1] + \min [3, 3] + \min [3, 3] + \min [2, 3]$$
$$= 1 + 3 + 3 + 2 = 9$$
$$\geqq b(\{1, 3, 4\}) = 1 + 3 + 2 = 6 \tag{6.67c}$$

$$\min [3, |(1, \{2, 3, 4\})|] + \min [3, |(2, \{2, 3, 4\})|]$$
$$+ \min [3, |(3, \{2, 3, 4\})|] + \min [2, |(4, \{2, 3, 4\})|]$$
$$= \min [3, 3] + \min [3, 3] + \min [3, 3] + \min [2, 1]$$
$$= 3 + 3 + 3 + 1 = 10$$
$$\geqq b(\{2, 3, 4\}) = 2 + 3 + 2 = 7 \tag{6.67d}$$

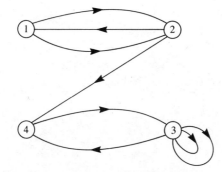

Fig. 6.5. A subgraph H of the directed graph of Fig. 6.3, whose outgoing and incoming degrees satisfy the constraints (6.59) and (6.60).

for the three-element subsets; and

$$\min\,[3, |(1, \{1, 2, 3, 4\})|] + \min\,[3, |(2, \{1, 2, 3, 4\})|]$$
$$+ \min\,[3, |(3, \{1, 2, 3, 4\})|] + \min\,[2, |(4, \{1, 2, 3, 4\})|]$$
$$= \min\,[3, 3] + \min\,[3, 4] + \min\,[3, 3] + \min\,[2, 3]$$
$$= 3 + 3 + 3 + 2 = 11$$
$$\geqq b(\{1, 2, 3, 4\}) = 1 + 2 + 3 + 2 = 8 \qquad\qquad (6.68)$$

for the set itself. Thus, conditions (6.36) of Corollary 6.1 are all satisfied, and the directed graph $G(V, E)$ of Fig. 6.3 possesses a subgraph H whose outgoing and incoming degrees $d_H^+(x)$ and $d_H^-(x)$ satisfy the inequalities (6.59) and (6.60). One such subgraph is shown in Fig. 6.5.

Example 6.3

Consider again the directed graph $G(V, E)$ of Fig. 6.3, which is redrawn in Fig. 6.6. The problem is to determine the existence of a $(1, 0)$ subgraph H whose outgoing and incoming degrees $d_H^+(x)$ and $d_H^-(x)$ are required to be

$$d_H^+(1) = 2, \qquad d_H^+(2) = 2, \qquad d_H^+(3) = 2, \qquad d_H^+(4) = 0 \quad (6.69a)$$
$$d_H^-(1) = 0, \qquad d_H^-(2) = 1, \qquad d_H^-(3) = 3, \qquad d_H^-(4) = 2 \quad (6.69b)$$

From Theorem 6.2, such a $(1, 0)$ subgraph exists if and only if (6.40) and either (6.41) or (6.42) holds for all subsets $X \subseteq V$. It is straightforward to verify that (6.40) holds:

$$a(V) = a(\{1, 2, 3, 4\}) = 2 + 2 + 2 + 0 = 6$$
$$= b(\{1, 2, 3, 4\}) = 0 + 1 + 3 + 2 = b(V) \qquad\qquad (6.70)$$

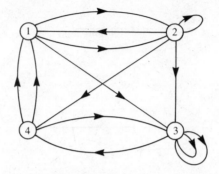

Fig. 6.6. A $(2, 2)$-digraph $G(V, E)$ used to study the subgraph problem.

where $a(x) = d_H^+(x)$ and $b(x) = d_H^-(x)$ for $x = 1, 2, 3, 4$. For our purposes, we use the subset $X = \{3\}$ in (6.41) with $p = 1$ and $s = 0$, and obtain

$$\min \{b(3), \min [|(3, 3)|, 0]\} + \min \{b(4), \min [|(3, 4)|, 1]\}$$

$$= \min \{3, \min [2, 0]\} + \min \{2, \min [1, 1]\}$$

$$= \min [3, 0] + \min [2, 1] = 0 + 1 = 1$$

$$\not\geqq a(3) = 2 \tag{6.71}$$

where $\gamma(X) = \gamma(3) = \{3, 4\}$. Thus, condition (6.41) is violated for the subset $X = \{3\}$, and according to Theorem 6.2 there is no $(1, 0)$ subgraph with outgoing and incoming degrees as prescribed in (6.69).

Instead of looking for a $(1, 0)$ subgraph, suppose that the problem is to determine the existence of any subgraph having outgoing and incoming degrees as prescribed in (6.69). Then according to Corollary 6.2, the problem is solvable if and only if (6.46) and either (6.47) or (6.48) holds for all subsets $X \subseteq V$. For illustrative purposes, we use (6.48) and obtain

$$\min [a(2), |(2, 1)|] + \min [a(4), |(4, 1)|] = \min [2, 1]$$

$$+ \min [0, 2] = 1 + 0 = 1 \geqq b(1) = 0 \tag{6.72a}$$

$$\min [2, |(1, 2)|] + \min [2, |(2, 2)|] = \min [2, 2]$$

$$+ \min [2, 1] = 2 + 1 = 3 \geqq b(2) = 1 \tag{6.72b}$$

$$\min [2, |(1, 3)|] + \min [2, |(2, 3)|] + \min [2, |(3, 3)|]$$

$$+ \min [0, |(4, 3)|] = 1 + 1 + 2 + 0 = 4 \geqq b(3) = 3 \tag{6.72c}$$

$$\min [2, |(2, 4)|] + \min [2, |(3, 4)|] = \min [2, 1]$$

$$+ \min [2, 1] = 1 + 1 = 2 \geqq b(4) = 2 \tag{6.72d}$$

for the single element subsets;

$$\min [a(1), |(1, \{1, 2\})|] + \min [a(2), |(2, \{1, 2\})|]$$
$$+ \min [a(4), |(4, \{1, 2\})|]$$
$$= \min [2, 2] + \min [2, 2] + \min [0, 2]$$
$$= 2 + 2 + 0 = 4 \geqq b(\{1, 2\}) = 0 + 1 = 1 \tag{6.73a}$$

$$\min [2, 1] + \min [2, 2] + \min [2, 2] + \min [0, 3]$$
$$= 1 + 2 + 2 + 0 = 5 \geqq b(\{1, 3\}) = 0 + 3 = 3 \tag{6.73b}$$

$$\min [2, 2] + \min [2, 1] + \min [0, 2] = 3 \geqq b(\{1, 4\}) = 2 \tag{6.73c}$$

$$\min [2, 3] + \min [2, 2] + \min [2, 2] + \min [0, 1]$$
$$= 6 \geqq b(\{2, 3\}) = 4 \tag{6.73d}$$

$$\min [2, 2] + \min [2, 2] + \min [2, 1]$$
$$= 5 \geqq b(\{2, 4\}) = 3 \tag{6.73e}$$

$$\min [2, 1] + \min [2, 2] + \min [2, 3] + \min [0, 1]$$
$$= 5 \geqq b(\{3, 4\}) = 5 \tag{6.73f}$$

for the two-element subsets;

$$\min [2, 3] + \min [2, 3] + \min [2, 2] + \min [0, 3]$$
$$= 6 \geqq b(\{1, 2, 3\}) = 4 \tag{6.74a}$$

$$\min [2, 2] + \min [2, 3] + \min [2, 1] + \min [0, 2]$$
$$= 5 \geqq b(\{1, 2, 4\}) = 3 \tag{6.74b}$$

$$\min [2, 1] + \min [2, 3] + \min [2, 3] + \min [0, 3]$$
$$= 5 \geqq b(\{1, 3, 4\}) = 5 \tag{6.74c}$$

$$\min [2, 3] + \min [2, 3] + \min [2, 3] + \min [0, 1]$$
$$= 6 \geqq b(\{2, 3, 4\}) = 6 \tag{6.74d}$$

for the three-element subsets; and

$$\min [2, 3] + \min [2, 4] + \min [2, 3] + \min [0, 3]$$
$$= 6 \geqq b(\{1, 2, 3, 4\}) = 6 \tag{6.75}$$

for the set itself. Thus, conditions (6.48) are satisfied. These together with (6.70) imply the existence of a subgraph H in $G(V, E)$ having its

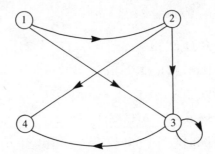

Fig. 6.7. A subgraph H of the directed graph of Fig. 6.6, whose outgoing and incoming degrees are given by (6.69).

outgoing and incoming degrees as prescribed in (6.69). An example of such a subgraph is presented in Fig. 6.7.

DEFINITION 6.3

Regular Directed Graph of Degree n. A directed graph is said to be *regular of degree n* if the outgoing and incoming degrees have the same value n for each of its nodes.

DEFINITION 6.4

n-Factor. An *n-factor* of a directed graph is a spanning regular subgraph of degree n.

The directed graph shown in Fig. 6.8, for example, is a regular directed graph of degree 2. A directed circuit is a regular directed graph of degree 1. However, not every regular directed graph of degree 1 is a directed circuit, an example of which is shown in Fig. 6.9. A connected regular directed graph of degree 1 is a directed circuit. Two subgraphs of the directed graph

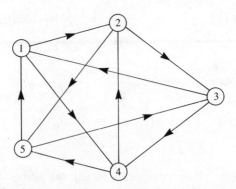

Fig. 6.8. A regular directed graph of degree 2.

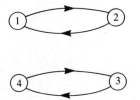

Fig. 6.9. A regular directed graph of degree 1.

$G(V, E)$ of Fig. 6.6 are presented in Fig. 6.10. The subgraph of Fig. 6.10(a) is a 1-factor of G, being regular of degree 1, whereas the spanning subgraph of Fig. 6.10(b) is a 2-factor of G. We shall apply Corollary 6.2 to derive a criterion when a directed graph possesses a 1-factor.

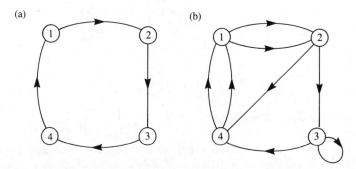

Fig. 6.10. Two subgraphs of the directed graph of Fig. 6.6: (a) a 1-factor and (b) a 2-factor of the directed graph.

THEOREM 6.3

The necessary and sufficient condition that a directed graph $G(V, E)$ possess a 1-factor is that either

$$|\gamma(X)| \geq |X| \tag{6.76}$$

or

$$|\gamma^*(X)| \geq |X| \tag{6.77}$$

holds for every subset $X \subseteq V$, where

$$\gamma(X) = \{y \mid x \in X, (x, y) \in E\} \tag{6.78}$$
$$\gamma^*(X) = \{y \mid x \in X, (y, x) \in E\} \tag{6.79}$$

Proof. We appeal to Corollary 6.2 by setting $a(x) = b(x) = 1$ for each

$x \in V$. Then we have

$$a(X) = b(X) = |X| \tag{6.80}$$

and (6.47) and (6.48) reduce to

$$\sum_{y \in \gamma(X)} \min [b(y), |(X, y)|] = \sum_{y \in \gamma(X)} \min [1, |(X, y)|]$$

$$= \sum_{y \in \gamma(X)} 1 = |\gamma(X)| \geqq a(X) = |X| \tag{6.81}$$

$$\sum_{y \in \gamma^*(X)} \min [a(y), |(y, X)|] = \sum_{y \in \gamma^*(X)} \min [1, |(y, X)|]$$

$$= \sum_{y \in \gamma^*(X)} 1 = |\gamma^*(X)| \geqq b(X) = |X| \tag{6.82}$$

since

$$|(X, y)| \geqq 1, \qquad |(y, X)| \geqq 1 \tag{6.83}$$

This completes the proof of the theorem.

Thus, every regular directed graph has a 1-factor, and can be decomposed as the direct sum of n 1-factors if it is regular of degree n. Theorem 6.3 also establishes the existence of a matching in a directed bipartite graph due to Hall (1935) and König (1950).

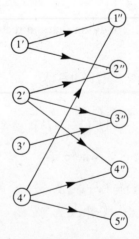

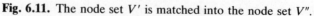
Fig. 6.11. The node set V' is matched into the node set V''.

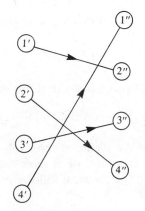

Fig. 6.12. The node set V' is matched onto the subset Y.

DEFINITION 6.5

Matching. A *matching* of a directed bipartite graph $B(V', V''; E')$ is a set of arcs E_x of E' such that no two arcs of E_x have a node in common. If a matching defines a one-to-one correspondence between a set $X \subseteq V'$ and a set $Y \subseteq V''$, then X is matched *onto* Y or X is matched *into* V''.

A directed bipartite graph $B(V', V''; E')$ is shown in Fig. 6.11 with $V' = \{1', 2', 3', 4'\}$ and $V'' = \{1'', 2'', 3'', 4'', 5''\}$. A matching from $X = V'$ onto $Y = \{1'', 2'', 3'', 4''\}$ is shown in Fig. 6.12, or putting it differently X is matched into V'' in Fig. 6.11.

THEOREM 6.4

In a directed bipartite graph $B(V', V''; E')$, V' can be matched into V'' if and only if

$$|\gamma(X)| \geqq |X| \tag{6.84}$$

for each subset $X \subseteq V'$, where $\gamma(X) \in V''$ is defined in (6.78) with E' replacing E.

Proof. The necessity follows immediately from the observation that if there is a matching from V' into V'', there are at least as many nodes in $\gamma(X)$ as in X. To prove sufficiency, we assume that (6.84) holds for each $X \subseteq V'$. In particular, we have $|\gamma(V')| \geqq |V'| = k$. Let Y be a subset of $\gamma(V')$ containing k elements. Let $G(V, E)$ be the k-node directed graph obtained from $B(V', V''; E')$ such that $(x, y) \in E$ if and only if $(x', y'') \in E'$; $x' \in V'$ and $y'' \in Y$. It is evident that there is a matching from V' onto Y in B

if and only if there is a 1-factor in G. But according to Theorem 6.3, there is a 1-factor in G if and only if

$$|\gamma(Z)| \geq |Z| \qquad (6.85)$$

holds for each subset $Z \subseteq V$. Condition (6.85) is equivalent to

$$|\gamma(W)| \geq |W| \qquad (6.86)$$

for each subset $W \subseteq V'$ in the sectional subgraph $B[V' \cup Y]$ of B, which is defined as the maximum subgraph of B over the node set $V' \cup Y$. Since (6.86) is implied by (6.84), the theorem follows.

We illustrate the above results by the following example.

Example 6.4

A directed bipartite graph $B(V', V''; E')$ is shown in Fig. 6.13. The problem is to determine whether or not there is a matching from V' into V''. To this end, we apply (6.84) as follows:

$$|\gamma(1')| = |\{1'', 2'', 4''\}| = 3 \geq |\{1'\}| = 1 \qquad (6.87a)$$

$$|\gamma(2')| = |\{2''\}| = 1 \geq |\{2'\}| = 1 \qquad (6.87b)$$

$$|\gamma(3')| = |\{1'', 3'', 4''\}| = 3 \geq |\{3'\}| = 1 \qquad (6.87c)$$

$$|\gamma(\{1', 2'\})| = |\{1'', 2'', 4''\}| = 3 \geq |\{1', 2'\}| = 2 \qquad (6.87d)$$

$$|\gamma(\{1', 3'\})| = |\{1'', 2'', 3'', 4''\}| = 4$$
$$\geq |\{1', 3'\}| = 2 \qquad (6.87e)$$

$$|\gamma(\{2', 3'\})| = |\{1'', 2'', 3'', 4''\}| = 4$$
$$\geq |\{2', 3'\}| = 2 \qquad (6.87f)$$

$$|\gamma(V')| = |\{1'', 2'', 3'', 4''\}| = 4 \geq |V'| = 3 \qquad (6.87g)$$

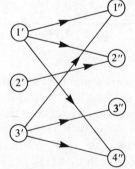

Fig. 6.13. A directed bipartite graph $B(V', V''; E')$.

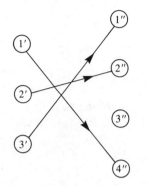

Fig. 6.14. A matching from the node set V' into the node set V'' for the directed bipartite graph $B(V', V''; E')$ of Fig. 6.13.

Since all the conditions are satisfied, there is a matching from V' into V'' in B, one of which is shown in Fig. 6.14.

6.2 DIGRAPHIC SEQUENCES

In this section, we present necessary and sufficient conditions for the existence of a directed graph with prescribed outgoing and incoming degrees. One motivation for considering this problem is the potential applications of the result in science and engineering in general and in electrical engineering and computer science in particular. Now, we demonstrate that the problem can be solved using the previous theory.

DEFINITION 6.6

Digraphic Sequence. A sequence of n nonnegative integer pairs

$$\pi = \{[a_i, b_i] \mid i = 1, 2, \ldots, n\} \tag{6.88}$$

is said to be (p, s) *digraphic* if there exists a (p, s)-digraph having π as the sequence of the degree pairs of its nodes, and such a directed graph is called a *realization* of π.

We consider the following generalization of this problem. Given a sequence of n nonnegative integer four-tuples

$$\pi' = \{(a_i, a_i', b_i, b_i') \mid a_i \leqq a_i', b_i \leqq b_i', i = 1, 2, \ldots, n\} \tag{6.89}$$

the problem is to find necessary and sufficient conditions under which there exists an n-node (p, s)-digraph $G(V, E)$, whose degree pairs $[d^+(i), d^-(i)]$

satisfy the inequalities

$$a_i \leqq d^+(i) \leqq a_i' \qquad (6.90a)$$

$$b_i \leqq d^-(i) \leqq b_i' \qquad (6.90b)$$

for each $i \in V$. Such a directed graph is called a *realization* of π', and π' is said to be (p, s) *digraphic*. To facilitate our discussion, let

$$S_a = \{a_i \mid i = 1, 2, \ldots, n\} \qquad (6.91a)$$

$$S_{a'} = \{a_i' \mid i = 1, 2, \ldots, n\} \qquad (6.91b)$$

$$S_b = \{b_i \mid i = 1, 2, \ldots, n\} \qquad (6.92a)$$

$$S_{b'} = \{b_i' \mid i = 1, 2, \ldots, n\} \qquad (6.92b)$$

To apply Theorem 6.1 to the present problem, we set $|(x, y)| = \infty$ for all x and y. The left-hand side of (6.27a) reduces to

$$\sum_{y \in \gamma(X)} \min\left\{b'(y), \sum_{x \in X} \min\left[|(x, y)|, \delta_{xy}(s - p) + p\right]\right\}$$

$$= \sum_{y \in V} \min\left[b'(y), \sum_{x \in X} \delta_{xy}(s - p) + p\right]$$

$$= \sum_{y \in X} \min\left[b'(y), \sum_{x \in X} \delta_{xy}(s - p) + p\right]$$

$$+ \sum_{y \in \bar{X}} \min\left[b'(y), \sum_{x \in X} \delta_{xy}(s - p) + p\right]$$

$$= \sum_{y \in X} \min\left[b'(y), (|X| - 1)p + s\right] + \sum_{y \in \bar{X}} \min\left[b'(y), |X|p\right]$$

$$= \sum_{b_j' \in X_{b'}} \min\left[b_j', (|X_{b'}| - 1)p + s\right] + \sum_{b_i' \in \bar{X}_{b'}} \min\left[b_i', |X_{b'}|p\right]$$

$$(6.93)$$

where $X_{b'}$ is a subset of $S_{b'}$ corresponding to X, and $\bar{X}_{b'}$ denotes the complement of $X_{b'}$ in $S_{b'}$. For each $X_{b'} \subseteq S_{b'}$, there is a corresponding $X_a \subseteq S_a$ with the property that $a_j \in X_a$ if and only if $b_j' \in X_{b'}$. We say that $X_{b'}$ and X_a are the *corresponding subsets* of $S_{b'}$ and S_a. This is similarly valid for other sets of (6.91) and (6.92). With this the right-hand side of (6.27a) can be written as

$$a(X) = \sum_{a_k \in X_a} a_k \qquad (6.94)$$

A similar result can be obtained for $(6.27b)$. The above results are summarized as a theorem.

THEOREM 6.5

A sequence $\pi' = \{(a_i, a_i', b_i, b_i') \mid a_i \leqq a_i', \, b_i \leqq b_i'\}$ is (p, s) digraphic if and only if, for each nonempty subset $X_a \subseteq S_a$,

$$\sum_{b_j' \in X_{b'}} \min [b_j', (|X_a| - 1)p + s] + \sum_{b_i' \in \bar{X}_{b'}} \min [b_i', |X_a|p] \geq \sum_{a_k \in X_a} a_k \quad (6.95a)$$

and, for each nonempty subset $X_b \subseteq S_b$,

$$\sum_{a_j' \in X_{a'}} \min [a_j', (|X_b| - 1)p + s] + \sum_{a_i' \in \bar{X}_{a'}} \min [a_i', |X_b|p] \geq \sum_{b_k \in X_b} b_k \quad (6.95b)$$

where X_a and $X_{b'}$ are the corresponding subsets of S_a and $S_{b'}$, and $X_{a'}$ and X_b are the corresponding subsets of $S_{a'}$ and S_b; and $\bar{X}_{b'}$ and $\bar{X}_{a'}$ denote the complements of $X_{b'}$ and $X_{a'}$ in $S_{b'}$ and $S_{a'}$, respectively. The sets S_a, $S_{a'}$, S_b and $S_{b'}$ are defined in (6.91) and (6.92).

In the special situation where $a_i = a_i'$ and $b_i = b_i'$, we obtain a result of Chen (1966).

COROLLARY 6.3

A sequence $\pi = \{[a_i, b_i]\}$ of nonnegative integer pairs is (p, s) digraphic if and only if

$$\sum_{a_i \in S_a} a_i = \sum_{b_j \in S_b} b_j \quad (6.96)$$

and either

$$\sum_{b_j \in X_b} \min [b_j, (|X_a| - 1)p + s] + \sum_{b_i \in \bar{X}_b} \min [b_i, |X_a|p] \geq \sum_{a_k \in X_a} a_k \quad (6.97)$$

or

$$\sum_{a_j \in X_a} \min [a_j, (|X_b| - 1)p + s] + \sum_{a_i \in \bar{X}_a} \min [a_i, |X_b|p] \geq \sum_{b_k \in X_b} b_k \quad (6.98)$$

holds for each nonempty subset $X_a \subseteq S_a$, where X_a and X_b are the corresponding subsets of S_a and S_b.

The second condition (6.97) or (6.98) consists of $2^n - 1$ inequalities, n being the number of nonnegative integer pairs in π. These can be reduced to a set of n inequalities for $p = 1$ and $s = 0$, if the elements of π are properly ordered.

COROLLARY 6.4

In a given sequence $\pi = \{[a_i, b_i] \mid i = 1, 2, \ldots, n\}$ of nonnegative integer pairs, alter the indices if necessary so that $b_i \geq b_{i+1}$. Furthermore, if $b_i = b_{i+1}$ then $a_i \geq a_{i+1}$ for $i = 1, 2, \ldots, n - 1$. Then the sequence π is $(1, 0)$ digraphic if and only if

$$\sum_{i=1}^{n} a_i = \sum_{j=1}^{n} b_j \tag{6.99}$$

$$\sum_{i=1}^{n} \min [a_i, n - 1] \geq \sum_{j=1}^{n} b_j \tag{6.100}$$

and

$$\sum_{i=1}^{k} \min [a_i, k - 1] + \sum_{j=k+1}^{n} \min [a_j, k] \geq \sum_{i=1}^{k} b_i \tag{6.101}$$

for $k = 1, 2, \ldots, n - 1$.

Proof. Necessity. The inequalities (6.100) and (6.101) follow directly from (6.98) by taking $X_b = S_b$ and $X_b = \{b_i \mid i = 1, 2, \ldots, k\}$, respectively.

Sufficiency. We show that (6.100) and (6.101) imply (6.98). Observe first that (6.100) implies (6.98) for $X_b = S_b$. Thus, it is sufficient to show that (6.101) implies (6.98) for all nonempty proper subsets $X_b \subseteq S_b$. To this end, let

$$a_t^*(X_a) = |\{a_i \mid a_i \in X_a \quad \text{and} \quad a_i \geq t\}| \tag{6.102}$$

for $t = 1, 2, \ldots$. To simplify the notation, write

$$a_t^*(S_a) = a_t^* \tag{6.103}$$

We retain the functional notation only when proper subsets of S_a are used. Then the left-hand side of (6.98) can be expressed as

$$a_k^*(\bar{X}_a) + \sum_{t=1}^{k-1} a_t^* \tag{6.104}$$

where the second term is defined to be zero for $k = 1$. If we can demonstrate that the right-hand side of the inequality

$$\sum_{t=1}^{k-1} a_t^* \geq \left(\sum_{b_i \in X_b} b_i\right) - a_k^*(\bar{X}_a) \tag{6.105}$$

is maximized over all k-element subsets $X_a \subseteq S_a$ or $X_b \subseteq S_b$ by letting

$$X_b = \{b_i \mid i = 1, 2, \ldots, k\} \tag{6.106}$$

then we need only consider the subsets of (6.106) for $k = 1, 2, \ldots, n$ because (6.98) is equivalent to (6.105). That this is indeed the case is shown below.

Let $\hat{X}_b$ be any k-element proper subset of S_b, that is different from (6.106). Let b_x be an element of $\{b_1, b_2, \ldots, b_k\}$ but not in $\hat{X}_b$, and also let b_y be an element of $\hat{X}_b$ but not in $\{b_1, b_2, \ldots, b_k\}$. By virtue of the ordering of the b_i, it is clear that $x < y$. Consider the set

$$X_b'' = (\hat{X}_b - \{b_y\}) \cup \{b_x\} \tag{6.107}$$

and its corresponding set $X_a'' \subseteq S_a$. It is apparent that $a_k^*(\bar{X}_a'')$ and $a_k^*(\bar{X}_a)$ differ at most by 1 where $\bar{X}_a''$ denotes the complement of X_a'' in S_a. Thus, for $b_x \neq b_y$ we have

$$\left(\sum_{b_i \in X_b''} b_i\right) - a_k^*(\bar{X}_a'') \geq \left(\sum_{b_i \in \hat{X}_b} b_i\right) - a_k^*(\bar{X}_a) \tag{6.108}$$

since

$$\sum_{b_i \in X_b''} b_i > \sum_{b_i \in \hat{X}_b} b_i \tag{6.109}$$

For $b_x = b_y$, (6.109) is satisfied with the equality sign. By our ordering of the a_i, $a_x \geq a_y$, it follows that

$$a_k^*(\bar{X}_a'') \leq a_k^*(\bar{X}_a) \tag{6.110}$$

As a result, (6.108) remains valid for $b_x = b_y$. Since X_b'' has one more element in common with $\{b_1, b_2, \ldots, b_k\}$ than $\hat{X}_b$, we conclude that the set $\{b_1, b_2, \ldots, b_k\}$ can be obtained from $\hat{X}_b$ by the repeated application of this process. Thus, from (6.101)

$$\sum_{t=1}^{k-1} a_t^* \geq \sum_{i=1}^{k} b_i - a_k^*(\{a_j \mid j = k+1, \ldots, n\})$$

$$\geq \left(\sum_{b_i \in \hat{X}_b} b_i \right) - a_k^*(\bar{X}_a) \tag{6.111}$$

for all nonempty proper k-element subsets $\hat{X}_b \subseteq S_b$. Hence we obtain the desired result. This completes the proof of the corollary.

Following a similar argument, a generalized version of the above result may be stated.

COROLLARY 6.5

In a given sequence of nonnegative integer pairs $\{[a_i, b_i] \mid i = 1, 2, \ldots, n\}$ if the indices of a_i and b_i can be altered such that $a_i \geq a_{i+1}$ and $b_i \geq b_{i+1}$ for $i = 1, 2, \ldots, n-1$, $n \geq 2$, then the sequence is (p, s) digraphic, $p \geq s$, if and only if

$$\sum_{i=1}^{n} a_i = \sum_{j=1}^{n} b_j \tag{6.112}$$

$$\sum_{i=1}^{n} \min [a_i, (n-1)p + s] \geq \sum_{j=1}^{n} b_j \tag{6.113}$$

$$\sum_{i=1}^{k} \min [a_i, (k-1)p + s] + \sum_{t=k+1}^{n} \min [a_t, kp] \geq \sum_{j=1}^{k} b_j \tag{6.114}$$

for $k = 1, 2, \ldots, n-1$.

Before we consider other special cases, we illustrate the above results by the following examples.

Example 6.5

We wish to determine whether the following sequence of four-tuples of nonnegative integers is $(2, 1)$ digraphic:

$$\pi' = \{(3, 4, 3, 4), (2, 3, 3, 4), (3, 4, 3, 4)\} \tag{6.115}$$

From Theorem 6.5, we can make the following identifications:

$$p = 2 \tag{6.116a}$$

$$s = 1 \tag{6.116b}$$

$$S_a = \{a_1, a_2, a_3\} = \{3, 2, 3\} \tag{6.117a}$$

$$S_{a'} = \{a'_1, a'_2, a'_3\} = \{4, 3, 4\} \tag{6.117b}$$

$$S_b = \{b_1, b_2, b_3\} = \{3, 3, 3\} \tag{6.117c}$$

$$S_{b'} = \{b'_1, b'_2, b'_3\} = \{4, 4, 4\} \tag{6.117d}$$

For the single element subsets $X_a \subseteq S_a$ and $X_b \subseteq S_b$, (6.95) becomes

$$\min [b'_1, s] + \min [b'_2, p] + \min [b'_3, p]$$
$$= \min [4, 1] + \min [4, 2] + \min [4, 2] = 5 \geqq a_1 = 3 \tag{6.118a}$$
$$\min [b'_2, 1] + \min [b'_1, 2] + \min [b'_3, 2]$$
$$= 5 \geqq a_2 = 2 \tag{6.118b}$$
$$\min [b'_3, 1] + \min [b'_1, 2] + \min [b'_2, 2]$$
$$= 5 \geqq a_3 = 3 \tag{6.118c}$$
$$\min [a'_1, s] + \min [a'_2, p] + \min [a'_3, p]$$
$$= \min [4, 1] + \min [3, 2] + \min [4, 2]$$
$$= 5 \geqq b_1 = 3 \tag{6.119a}$$
$$\min [a'_2, 1] + \min [a'_1, 2] + \min [a'_3, 2]$$
$$= 5 \geqq b_2 = 3 \tag{6.119b}$$
$$\min [a'_3, 1] + \min [a'_1, 2] + \min [a'_2, 2]$$
$$= 5 \geqq b_3 = 3 \tag{6.119c}$$

For the two-element subsets $X_a \subseteq S_a$ and $X_b \subseteq S_b$, (6.95) becomes

$$\min [b'_1, p + s] + \min [b'_2, p + s] + \min [b'_3, 2p]$$
$$= \min [4, 3] + \min [4, 3] + \min [4, 4]$$
$$= 10 \geqq a_1 + a_2 = 5 \tag{6.120a}$$
$$\min [b'_1, 3] + \min [b'_3, 3] + \min [b'_2, 4]$$
$$= 10 \geqq a_1 + a_3 = 6 \tag{6.120b}$$

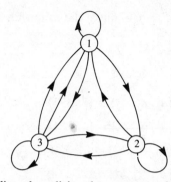

Fig. 6.15. A $(2, 1)$-digraph realizing the sequence of four-tuples of (6.115).

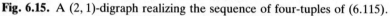

$$\min [b_2', 3] + \min [b_3', 3] + \min [b_1', 4]$$
$$= 10 \geqq a_2 + a_3 = 5 \tag{6.120c}$$

$$\min [a_1', p + s] + \min [a_2', p + s] + \min [a_3', 2p]$$
$$= \min [4, 3] + \min [3, 3] + \min [4, 4]$$
$$= 10 \geqq b_1 + b_2 = 6 \tag{6.121a}$$

$$\min [a_1', 3] + \min [a_3', 3] + \min [a_2', 4]$$
$$= 9 \geqq b_1 + b_3 = 6 \tag{6.121b}$$

$$\min [a_2', 3] + \min [a_3', 3] + \min [a_1', 4]$$
$$= 10 \geqq b_2 + b_3 = 6 \tag{6.121c}$$

Finally, for the sets S_a and S_b themselves, we obtain

$$\min [b_1', 2p + s] + \min [b_2', 2p + s] + \min [b_3', 2p + s]$$
$$= \min [4, 5] + \min [4, 5] + \min [4, 5]$$
$$= 12 \geqq a_1 + a_2 + a_3 = 8 \tag{6.122a}$$

$$\min [a_1', 2p + s] + \min [a_2', 2p + s] + \min [a_3', 2p + s]$$
$$= \min [4, 5] + \min [3, 5] + \min [4, 5]$$
$$= 11 \geqq b_1 + b_2 + b_3 = 9 \tag{6.122b}$$

Thus, all the conditions are satisfied, and the sequence π' is $(2, 1)$ digraphic. One such realization is shown in Fig. 6.15.

Example 6.6

Determine whether the following sequence of nonnegative integer pairs is

(2, 1) digraphic:

$$\pi = \{[a_i, b_i] \mid i = 1, 2, 3, 4\} = \{[3, 1], [2, 5], [4, 1], [0, 2]\} \quad (6.123)$$

From Corollary 6.3, we can make the following identifications:

$$p = 2 \qquad\qquad\qquad\qquad\qquad (6.124a)$$

$$s = 1 \qquad\qquad\qquad\qquad\qquad (6.124b)$$

$$S_a = \{a_1, a_2, a_3, a_4\} = \{3, 2, 4, 0\} \qquad\qquad (6.125a)$$

$$S_b = \{b_1, b_2, b_3, b_4\} = \{1, 5, 1, 2\} \qquad\qquad (6.125b)$$

Condition (6.96) is satisfied because

$$\sum_{i=1}^{4} a_i = 3 + 2 + 4 + 0 = 9 = \sum_{j=1}^{4} b_j = 1 + 5 + 1 + 2 \qquad (6.126)$$

Condition (6.97) consists of 15 ($= 2^4 - 1$) inequalities, as follows:

$$\min [b_1, s] + \min [b_2, p] + \min [b_3, p] + \min [b_4, p]$$
$$= \min [1, 1] + \min [5, 2] + \min [1, 2] + \min [2, 2]$$
$$= 1 + 2 + 1 + 2 = 6 \geq a_1 = 3 \qquad\qquad (6.127a)$$

$$\min [b_2, 1] + \min [b_1, 2] + \min [b_3, 2] + \min [b_4, 2]$$
$$= 1 + 1 + 1 + 2 = 5 \geq a_2 = 2 \qquad\qquad (6.127b)$$

$$\min [b_3, 1] + \min [b_1, 2] + \min [b_2, 2] + \min [b_4, 2]$$
$$= 1 + 1 + 2 + 2 = 6 \geq a_3 = 4 \qquad\qquad (6.127c)$$

$$\min [b_4, 1] + \min [b_1, 2] + \min [b_2, 2] + \min [b_3, 2]$$
$$= 1 + 1 + 2 + 1 = 5 \geq a_4 = 0 \qquad\qquad (6.127d)$$

$$\min [b_1, p + s] + \min [b_2, p + s] + \min [b_3, 2p] + \min [b_4, 2p]$$
$$= \min [1, 3] + \min [5, 3] + \min [1, 4] + \min [2, 4]$$
$$= 1 + 3 + 1 + 2 = 7 \geq a_1 + a_2 = 3 + 2 = 5 \qquad (6.128a)$$

$$\min [b_1, 3] + \min [b_3, 3] + \min [b_2, 4] + \min [b_4, 4]$$
$$= 1 + 1 + 4 + 2 = 8 \geq a_1 + a_3 = 7 \qquad\qquad (6.128b)$$

$$\min [b_1, 3] + \min [b_4, 3] + \min [b_2, 4] + \min [b_3, 4]$$
$$= 1 + 2 + 4 + 1 = 8 \geq a_1 + a_4 = 3 \qquad\qquad (6.128c)$$

$$\min [b_2, 3] + \min [b_3, 3] + \min [b_1, 4] + \min [b_4, 4]$$
$$= 3 + 1 + 1 + 2 = 7 \geq a_2 + a_3 = 6 \qquad\qquad (6.128d)$$

$$\min [b_2, 3] + \min [b_4, 3] + \min [b_1, 4] + \min [b_3, 4]$$

$$= 3 + 2 + 1 + 1 = 7 \geqq a_2 + a_4 = 2 \tag{6.128e}$$

$$\min [b_3, 3] + \min [b_4, 3] + \min [b_1, 4] + \min [b_2, 4]$$

$$= 1 + 2 + 1 + 4 = 8 \geqq a_3 + a_4 = 4 \tag{6.128f}$$

$$\min [b_1, 2p + s] + \min [b_2, 2p + s] + \min [b_3, 2p + s] + \min [b_4, 3p]$$

$$= \min [1, 5] + \min [5, 5] + \min [1, 5] + \min [2, 6]$$

$$= 9 \geqq a_1 + a_2 + a_3 = 3 + 2 + 4 = 9 \tag{6.129a}$$

$$\min [b_1, 5] + \min [b_2, 5] + \min [b_4, 5] + \min [b_3, 6]$$

$$= 9 \geqq a_1 + a_2 + a_4 = 5 \tag{6.129b}$$

$$\min [b_1, 5] + \min [b_3, 5] + \min [b_4, 5] + \min [b_2, 6]$$

$$= 9 \geqq a_1 + a_3 + a_4 = 7 \tag{6.129c}$$

$$\min [b_2, 5] + \min [b_3, 5] + \min [b_4, 5] + \min [b_1, 6]$$

$$= 9 \geqq a_2 + a_3 + a_4 = 6 \tag{6.129d}$$

$$\min [b_1, 3p + s] + \min [b_2, 3p + s] + \min [b_3, 3p + s] + \min [b_4, 3p + s]$$

$$= \min [1, 7] + \min [5, 7] + \min [1, 7] + \min [2, 7]$$

$$= 9 \geqq a_1 + a_2 + a_3 + a_4 = 9 \tag{6.130}$$

Thus, all the conditions are satisfied, and the sequence π of (6.123) is $(2, 1)$ digraphic. A realization of the sequence π is shown in Fig. 6.16.

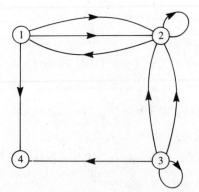

Fig. 6.16. A $(2, 1)$-digraph realizing the sequence of nonnegative integer pairs of (6.123).

Example 6.7

Test to see if the following sequence is $(1, 0)$ digraphic:

$$\{[2, 3], [2, 2], [4, 0], [1, 4], [3, 3]\} \tag{6.131}$$

To apply Corollary 6.4, we first alter the indices of the elements of (6.131) to yield a properly ordered sequence

$$\pi = \{[a_1, b_1], [a_2, b_2], [a_3, b_3], [a_4, b_4], [a_5, b_5]\}$$
$$= \{[1, 4], [3, 3], [2, 3], [2, 2], [4, 0]\} \tag{6.132}$$

Substituting these in (6.99)–(6.101) gives

$$a_1 + a_2 + a_3 + a_4 + a_5 = 1 + 3 + 2 + 2 + 4 = 12$$
$$= b_1 + b_2 + b_3 + b_4 + b_5 = 4 + 3 + 3 + 2 + 0 \tag{6.133}$$

$$\min [a_1, 4] + \min [a_2, 4] + \min [a_3, 4] + \min [a_4, 4] + \min [a_5, 4]$$
$$= 1 + 3 + 2 + 2 + 4 = 12$$
$$\geqq b_1 + b_2 + b_3 + b_4 + b_5 = 12 \tag{6.134}$$

$$\min [a_1, 0] + \min [a_2, 1] + \min [a_3, 1] + \min [a_4, 1] + \min [a_5, 1]$$
$$= 0 + 1 + 1 + 1 + 1 = 4 \geqq b_1 = 4 \tag{6.135a}$$

$$\min [a_1, 1] + \min [a_2, 1] + \min [a_3, 2] + \min [a_4, 2] + \min [a_5, 2]$$
$$= 1 + 1 + 2 + 2 + 2 = 8 \geqq b_1 + b_2 = 7 \tag{6.135b}$$

$$\min [a_1, 2] + \min [a_2, 2] + \min [a_3, 2] + \min [a_4, 3] + \min [a_5, 3]$$
$$= 1 + 2 + 2 + 2 + 3 = 10 \geqq b_1 + b_2 + b_3 = 10 \tag{6.135c}$$

$$\min [a_1, 3] + \min [a_2, 3] + \min [a_3, 3] + \min [a_4, 3] + \min [a_5, 4]$$
$$= 1 + 3 + 2 + 2 + 4 = 12 \geqq b_1 + b_2 + b_3 + b_4 = 12 \tag{6.135d}$$

Thus, the sequence π is $(1, 0)$ digraphic. One such realization is presented in Fig. 6.17.

Observe that if we use Corollary 6.3 to test the realizability of the sequence π, we need to check $31 \ (= 2^5 - 1)$ inequalities. Corollary 6.4 requires only 5, a reduction by a factor of more than 6. The price we paid in achieving this is the proper ordering of the elements of π.

We shall now proceed to consider other special cases. The reason for doing this is that the conditions obtained for these special cases are much the simplest, and they are sufficiently important to be considered explicitly.

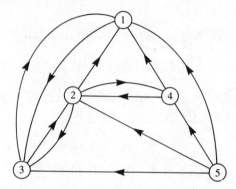

Fig. 6.17. A $(1,0)$-digraph realizing the sequence of nonnegative integer pairs of (6.131).

However, before we do this we define the dual sequence of a sequence of nonnegative integers.

DEFINITION 6.7

Dual Sequence. Let $\{a_i\}$ be a sequence of nonnegative integers. The *dual sequence* of $\{a_i\}$ is the sequence $\{a_i^*\}$, the ith element a_i^* of which denotes the number of the a_j in $\{a_i\}$ greater than or equal to the integer i.

There is a simple pictorial representation of the number a_i^*: Let each integer a_j be represented by a row of a_j dots, and arrange these rows in a vertical array so that a_{j+1} lies under a_j. Then the number a_i^* is simply the number of dots in the ith column of the array. As an example, let

$$a_1 = 5, \quad a_2 = 4, \quad a_3 = 4, \quad a_4 = 5, \quad a_5 = 1 \tag{6.136}$$

The array corresponding to these integers is shown below:

$$
\begin{array}{c c c c c c c c}
 & a_1^* & a_2^* & a_3^* & a_4^* & a_5^* & a_6^* & a_7^* \\
a_1 & \cdot & \cdot & \cdot & \cdot & \cdot & & \\
a_2 & \cdot & \cdot & \cdot & \cdot & & & \\
a_3 & \cdot & \cdot & \cdot & \cdot & & & \\
a_4 & \cdot & \cdot & \cdot & \cdot & \cdot & & \\
a_5 & \cdot & & & & & &
\end{array}
\tag{6.137}
$$

Thus, we have

$$a_1^* = 5, \quad a_2^* = 4, \quad a_3^* = 4, \quad a_4^* = 4, \quad a_5^* = 2 \qquad (6.138a)$$

$$a_k^* = 0, \quad k \geq 6 \qquad (6.138b)$$

They correspond to the numbers of dots in the columns of the array. Evidently, they are independent of the ordering of the elements of $\{a_i\}$. As a matter of fact, if for a given sequence $\{a_i\}$ we define

$$\{a_i\}^* = \{a_j^* \mid j = 1, 2, \ldots\} \qquad (6.139)$$

then it is clear that $\{a_i\}^*$ determines $\{a_i\}$ since the integer a_i occurs exactly $a_x^* - a_{x+1}^*$, $x = a_i$, times in $\{a_i\}$.

The sequence $\{a_i\}^*$ is the dual sequence of $\{a_i\}$. In fact, the correspondence between $\{a_i\}$ and $\{a_i\}^*$ is completely dual in the following sense:

$$\{\{a_i\}^*\}^* = \{a_i\} \qquad (6.140)$$

In other words, the dual of a dual sequence is the sequence itself. The validity of (6.140) is quite obvious in view of the pictorial representation discussed in (6.137).

We remark that two sequences can be brought to the same length by adding an appropriate number of zeros if necessary. Consider, for example, the sequence

$$\{a_i\} = \{5, 4, 4, 5, 1\} \qquad (6.141)$$

Its dual sequence is given by

$$\{a_i\}^* = \{5, 4, 4, 4, 2, 0, 0\} \qquad (6.142)$$

The original sequence $\{a_i\}$ can be brought to the same length as its dual by the insertion of two zeros:

$$\{a_i\} = \{5, 4, 4, 5, 1, 0, 0\} \qquad (6.143)$$

After this digression into a discussion of the dual sequence, let us return to consider special cases of Corollary 6.3. One of the special cases was considered by Berge (1962) by putting $p = s$ in (6.98), resulting in

$$\sum_{i=1}^{n} \min [a_i, |X_b| p] \geq \sum_{b_k \in X_b} b_k \qquad (6.144)$$

for each $X_b \subseteq S_b$. If the b_i are ordered so that $b_i \geq b_{i+1}$ for $i =$

$1, 2, \ldots, n-1$, then the inequality (6.144) is satisfied if and only if

$$\sum_{i=1}^{n} \min \left[a_i, kp\right] \geq \sum_{j=1}^{k} b_j \tag{6.145}$$

for $k = 1, 2, \ldots, n$. This establishes the following result.

COROLLARY 6.6

Consider a sequence $\{[a_i, b_i]\}$ of n nonnegative integer pairs in which, by altering the indices if necessary, $b_i \geq b_{i+1}$ for $i = 1, 2, \ldots, n-1$, $n \geq 2$. Then the sequence is (p, p) digraphic if and only if

$$\sum_{i=1}^{n} a_i = \sum_{j=1}^{n} b_j \tag{6.146}$$

$$\sum_{i=1}^{n} \min \left[a_i, kp\right] \geq \sum_{j=1}^{k} b_j, \qquad k = 1, 2, \ldots, n \tag{6.147}$$

In the case where $s = p = 1$, Corollary 6.6 can be further simplified. It is possible to reformulate the result so that it can be tested more rapidly. This result was first established by Ryser (1957) and Gale (1957) in an attempt to obtain the existence conditions of a matrix of zeros and ones having prescribed row and column sums. This equivalent matrix problem will be treated in a later section.

COROLLARY 6.7

In a given sequence $\{[a_i, b_i]\}$ of n nonnegative integer pairs, alter the indices of the b_i so that $b_i \geq b_{i+1}$ for $i = 1, 2, \ldots, n-1$, $n \geq 2$. The necessary and sufficient conditions for the sequence to be $(1, 1)$ digraphic are that

$$\sum_{i=1}^{n} a_i = \sum_{j=1}^{n} b_j \tag{6.148}$$

$$\sum_{i=1}^{k} a_i^* \geq \sum_{j=1}^{k} b_j \tag{6.149}$$

for all integers k, where $\{a_i^*\}$ is the dual sequence of $\{a_i\}$, and the sequences $\{b_i\}$ and $\{a_i^*\}$ are assumed to have been brought to the same length by the insertion of an appropriate number of zeros if necessary.

Proof. From Corollary 6.6, it is sufficient to show that

$$\sum_{i=1}^{n} \min [a_i, k] = \sum_{j=1}^{k} a_j^* \tag{6.150}$$

for all k. We prove this by induction over k. For $k = 1$, we have

$$\sum_{i=1}^{n} \min [a_i, 1] = a_1^* \tag{6.151}$$

from the definition of a_i^*. Assume that (6.150) is true for any k or less. We show that it is also true for $k + 1$. Since

$$\min [a_i, k + 1] = \min [a_i, k], \qquad a_i \leq k \tag{6.152a}$$
$$\min [a_i, k + 1] = \min [a_i, k] + 1, \qquad a_i \geq k + 1 \tag{6.152b}$$

it follows that

$$\sum_{i=1}^{n} \min [a_i, k + 1] = a_{k+1}^* + \sum_{i=1}^{n} \min [a_i, k]$$

$$= a_{k+1}^* + \sum_{j=1}^{k} a_j^* \tag{6.153}$$

The second line follows from the induction hypothesis. So the corollary is proved.

In words, Corollary 6.7 states that a sequence is $(1, 1)$ digraphic if and only if the sum of the a_i is equal to that of the b_i and the partial sums of the b_i are dominated by the corresponding partial sums of the a_i^*.

Recall that in Corollary 6.3 condition (6.97) or (6.98) consists of $2^n - 1$ inequalities. These can be reduced to n inequalities for $p = 1$ and $s = 0$ if the elements of the sequence are properly ordered. In the following, we show that conditions (6.100) and (6.101) can be combined and simplified in terms of the modified dual sequence of $\{a_i\}$.

DEFINITION 6.8

Modified Dual Sequence. Let $\{a_i\}$ be a sequence of nonnegative integers. The *modified dual sequence* of $\{a_i\}$ is the sequence $\{a_i''\}$, the kth element a_k'' of which is defined by the number

$$a_k'' = |I_k| + |J_k| \tag{6.154}$$

where

$$I_k = \{i \mid i < k, a_i \ge k - 1\} \qquad (6.155a)$$

$$J_k = \{i \mid i > k, a_i \ge k\} \qquad (6.155b)$$

Like the number a_k^*, the number a_k'' also has a simple pictorial representation, again in terms of rows of dots, except that this time no dots are placed on the main diagonal of the array. For example, the array corresponding to the sequence

$$\{a_i\} = \{4, 4, 3, 5, 2\} \qquad (6.156)$$

is shown below:

	a_1''	a_2''	a_3''	a_4''	a_5''	a_6''
a_1		.	.	.	.	
a_2	.		.	.	.	
a_3	.	.		.		
a_4	.	.	.		.	.
a_5	.	.				

$$(6.157)$$

Then the number a_k'' is the number of dots in the kth column of the above diagonally restricted array of dots. Thus, we have

$$a_1'' = 4, \quad a_2'' = 4, \quad a_3'' = 3, \quad a_4'' = 3, \quad a_5'' = 3, \quad a_6'' = 1 \qquad (6.158)$$

giving the modified dual sequence of $\{a_i\}$ as

$$\{a_i''\} = \{4, 4, 3, 3, 3, 1\} \qquad (6.159)$$

Using this we see immediately that the left-hand sides of (6.100) and (6.101) can be expressed as

$$\sum_{i=1}^{n} \min[a_i, n-1] = \sum_{i=1}^{n} a_i'' \qquad (6.160a)$$

$$\sum_{i=1}^{k} \min[a_i, k-1] + \sum_{j=k+1}^{n} \min[a_j, k] = \sum_{i=1}^{k} a_i'' \qquad (6.160b)$$

respectively. Thus, conditions (6.100) and (6.101) are simply that the partial sums of the sequence $\{b_i\}$ be dominated by the corresponding partial sums of the modified dual sequence of $\{a_i\}$. This result was first pointed out by Fulkerson (1960) in connection with his study of the existence of a square matrix of zeros and ones having prescribed row sums and column sums with zero trace. We summarize the above result as a corollary.

COROLLARY 6.8

Consider a sequence $\{[a_i, b_i]\}$ of n nonnegative integer pairs in which, by altering the indices if necessary, $b_i \geq b_{i+1}$ and, furthermore, if $b_i = b_{i+1}$ then $a_i \geq a_{i+1}$ for $i = 1, 2, \ldots, n-1$, $n \geq 2$. The sequence is $(1,0)$ digraphic if and only if

$$\sum_{i=1}^{n} a_i = \sum_{j=1}^{n} b_j \tag{6.161}$$

$$\sum_{i=1}^{k} a_i'' \geq \sum_{j=1}^{k} b_j, \qquad k = 1, 2, \ldots, n \tag{6.162}$$

We illustrate the above results by the following examples.

Example 6.8

Test the sequence (6.123) to see if it is $(1, 1)$ digraphic. In order to apply Corollary 6.7, it is necessary that we alter the indices of b_i so that $b_i \geq b_{i+1}$ for $i = 1, 2, 3, 4$. A new sequence is given as

$$\pi = \{[a_i, b_i] \mid i = 1, 2, 3, 4\} = \{[2, 5], [0, 2], [4, 1], [3, 1]\} \tag{6.163}$$

The dual sequence of the sequence

$$\{a_i\} = \{a_1, a_2, a_3, a_4\} = \{2, 0, 4, 3\} \tag{6.164}$$

is given by

$$\{a_i\}^* = \{a_i^*\} = \{a_1^*, a_2^*, a_3^*, a_4^*\} = \{3, 3, 2, 1\} \tag{6.165}$$

where a_k^* is the number of dots in the kth column of the following array:

$$
\begin{array}{cccc}
a_1^* & a_2^* & a_3^* & a_4^* \\
a_1 & \cdot & \cdot & \\
a_2 & & & \\
a_3 & \cdot & \cdot & \cdot & \cdot \\
a_4 & \cdot & \cdot & \cdot
\end{array}
\tag{6.166}
$$

Using these, conditions (6.148) and (6.149) become

$$a_1 + a_2 + a_3 + a_4 = 2 + 0 + 4 + 3 = 9$$

$$= b_1 + b_2 + b_3 + b_4 = 5 + 2 + 1 + 1 \qquad (6.167)$$

$$a_1^* = 3 \ngeq b_1 = 5 \qquad (6.168a)$$

$$a_1^* + a_2^* = 3 + 3 = 6 \ngeq b_1 + b_2 = 5 + 2 = 7 \qquad (6.168b)$$

$$a_1^* + a_2^* + a_3^* = 3 + 3 + 2 = 8$$

$$\geqq b_1 + b_2 + b_3 = 5 + 2 + 1 = 8 \qquad (6.168c)$$

$$a_1^* + a_2^* + a_3^* + a_4^* = 9 \geqq b_1 + b_2 + b_3 + b_4 = 9 \qquad (6.168d)$$

Since not all the inequalities are satisfied, the sequence π is not $(1, 1)$ digraphic.

Instead of looking for a $(1, 1)$-digraph, suppose that we wish to know if the sequence π is $(2, 2)$ digraphic. To this end, we appeal to Corollary 6.6, and obtain from (6.147)

$$\min [a_1, 2] + \min [a_2, 2] + \min [a_3, 2] + \min [a_4, 2]$$

$$= 2 + 0 + 2 + 2 = 6 \geqq b_1 = 5 \qquad (6.169a)$$

$$\min [2, 4] + \min [0, 4] + \min [4, 4] + \min [3, 4]$$

$$= 9 \geqq b_1 + b_2 = 5 + 2 = 7 \qquad (6.169b)$$

$$\min [2, 6] + \min [0, 6] + \min [4, 6] + \min [3, 6]$$

$$= 9 \geqq b_1 + b_2 + b_3 = 5 + 2 + 1 = 8 \qquad (6.169c)$$

$$\min [2, 8] + \min [0, 8] + \min [4, 8] + \min [3, 8]$$

$$= 9 \geqq b_1 + b_2 + b_3 + b_4 = 5 + 2 + 1 + 1 = 9 \qquad (6.169d)$$

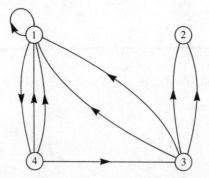

Fig. 6.18. A 2-digraph realizing the sequence of nonnegative integer pairs of (6.163).

showing that the sequence π is $(2, 2)$ digraphic. One such realization is presented in Fig. 6.18.

Example 6.9

Test to see if the following sequence of nonnegative integer pairs is $(1, 0)$ digraphic:

$$\pi = \{[a_i, b_i]\} = \{[3, 3], [1, 3], [0, 3], [4, 1], [2, 1], [2, 1]\} \quad (6.170)$$

Then we have

$$\{a_i\} = \{3, 1, 0, 4, 2, 2\} \quad (6.171)$$

$$\{b_i\} = \{3, 3, 3, 1, 1, 1\} \quad (6.172)$$

The modified dual sequence of $\{a_i\}$ is found to be

$$\{a_i\}'' = \{a_i''\} = \{4, 4, 2, 1, 1, 0\} \quad (6.173)$$

where a_k'' is the number of dots in the kth column of the following array:

$$
\begin{array}{ccccccc}
 & a_1'' & a_2'' & a_3'' & a_4'' & a_5'' & a_6'' \\
a_1 & \cdot & \cdot & \cdot & & & \\
a_2 & \cdot & & & & & \\
a_3 & & & & & & \\
a_4 & \cdot & \cdot & \cdot & & \cdot & \\
a_5 & \cdot & \cdot & & & & \\
a_6 & \cdot & \cdot & & & &
\end{array}
\quad (6.174)
$$

Since the elements of the sequence π are properly ordered so that $b_i \geq b_{i+1}$ and, furthermore, if $b_i = b_{i+1}$ then $a_i \geq a_{i+1}$ for $i = 1, 2, 3, 4, 5$, we can apply the conditions of Corollary 6.8 directly and obtain

$$a_1 + a_2 + a_3 + a_4 + a_5 + a_6 = 12$$

$$= b_1 + b_2 + b_3 + b_4 + b_5 + b_6 \quad (6.175)$$

$$a_1'' = 4 \geq b_1 = 3 \quad (6.176a)$$

$$a_1'' + a_2'' = 4 + 4 = 8 \geq b_1 + b_2 = 3 + 3 = 6 \quad (6.176b)$$

$$a_1'' + a_2'' + a_3'' = 4 + 4 + 2 = 10$$

$$\geq b_1 + b_2 + b_3 = 3 + 3 + 3 = 9 \quad (6.176c)$$

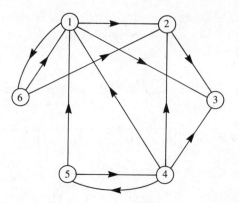

Fig. 6.19. A $(1,0)$-digraph realizing the sequence of nonnegative integer pairs of (6.170).

$$a_1'' + a_2'' + a_3'' + a_4'' = 4 + 4 + 2 + 1 = 11$$

$$\geqq b_1 + b_2 + b_3 + b_4 = 3 + 3 + 3 + 1 = 10 \qquad (6.176d)$$

$$a_1'' + a_2'' + a_3'' + a_4'' + a_5'' = 4 + 4 + 2 + 1 + 1 = 12$$

$$\geqq b_1 + b_2 + b_3 + b_4 + b_5 = 3 + 3 + 3 + 1 + 1 = 11 \qquad (6.176e)$$

$$a_1'' + a_2'' + a_3'' + a_4'' + a_5'' + a_6'' = 4 + 4 + 2 + 1 + 1 + 0 = 12$$

$$\geqq b_1 + b_2 + b_3 + b_4 + b_5 + b_6 = 3 + 3 + 3 + 1 + 1 + 1 = 12 \quad (6.176f)$$

Thus, according to Corollary 6.8, the sequence π is $(1,0)$ digraphic, a realization of which is presented in Fig. 6.19.

6.3 THE SUBGRAPH PROBLEM OF A GRAPH

In Section 6.1, we considered the criterion for the existence of a (p, s) subgraph with prescribed outgoing and incoming degrees in a given directed graph. In the present section, we consider a similar problem for a class of graphs. In order to deduce similar results from those obtained earlier for the directed graphs, we introduce the notion of a symmetric (p, s)-digraph.

DEFINITION 6.9

Symmetric (p, s)-Digraph. A (p, s)-digraph $G(V, E)$ is said to be *symmetric* if for each arc $(i, j) \in E$, the arc (j, i) is also in E such that $|(i, j)| = |(j, i)|$ for $i \neq j$ and $|(i, i)| = 2e$ for $i = j$, where e is a nonnegative integer.

DEFINITION 6.10

Symmetric (p, s) Subgraph. A *symmetric* (p, s) *subgraph* of a directed graph is a subgraph which is also a symmetric (p, s)-digraph.

Since an undirected graph may be transformed into a symmetric directed graph by representing each undirected edge by a pair of directed edges with opposite directions, and vice versa, it is convenient to use a simpler term.

DEFINITION 6.11

(p, s)-**Graph.** A symmetric $(p, 2s)$-digraph is called a (p, s)-*graph*. A (p, p)-graph is simply called a *p-graph* and a (∞, ∞)-graph is also referred to as a *graph*.

The directed graph of Fig. 6.20 is a symmetric $(2, 4)$-digraph, and can be converted to a $(2, 2)$-graph or 2-graph as shown in Fig. 6.21. The immediate problem is to find necessary and sufficient conditions for the existence of a symmetric (p, s) subgraph with prescribed outgoing and incoming degrees in a given directed graph.

Let $G(V, E)$ be a given directed graph and let $G_s(V, E_s)$ be a maximal spanning symmetric subgraph of G. Associate with each $x \in V$ two nonnegative integers $a(x)$ and $a'(x)$ satisfying

$$0 \leqq a(x) \leqq a'(x), \qquad x \in V \tag{6.177}$$

Then G has a symmetric (p, s) subgraph H whose outgoing and incoming degrees $d_H^+(x)$ and $d_H^-(x)$ satisfy

$$a(x) \leqq d_H^+(x) \leqq a'(x), \quad a(x) \leqq d_H^-(x) \leqq a'(x), \quad x \in V \tag{6.178}$$

if and only if H is a subgraph of a maximal spanning symmetric subgraph of G. Thus, it is sufficient to consider only symmetric directed graphs or simply graphs.

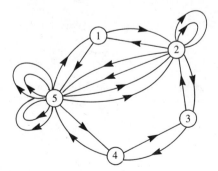

Fig. 6.20. A symmetric $(2, 4)$-digraph used to convert to a 2-graph.

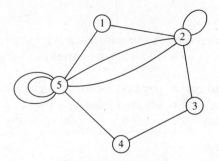

Fig. 6.21. A 2-graph.

DEFINITION 6.12

d-**Invariant.** Two (p, s) subgraphs or (p, s)-digraphs are said to be *d-invariant* if they possess the same sequence of degree pairs of their nodes.

The term *d-invariance* stands for degree invariance. One of the implications of the *d*-invariance is that if two labeled (p, s)-digraphs are not *d*-invariant, then there does not exist a one-to-one correspondence between their node sets such that the corresponding nodes have the same degree pair. The two labeled directed graphs of Fig. 6.22 are *d*-invariant because they possess the same degree-pair sequence $\{[1, 1], [2, 2], [1, 1], [2, 2], [2, 2]\}$ even though they have different labels.

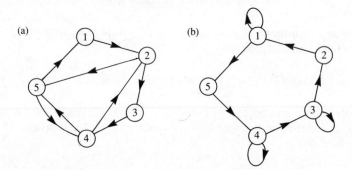

Fig. 6.22. Two labeled *d*-invariant directed graphs.

DEFINITION 6.13

Elementary (p, s) *d*-Invariant Transformation. In a directed graph $G(V, E)$, if there are two arcs (i_1, i_2) and (j_1, j_2), $i_1 \neq j_1$ and $i_2 \neq j_2$, such that

$$|(i_1, j_2)| < p, \qquad i_1 \neq j_2 \qquad\qquad (6.179a)$$

$$|(i_1, j_2)| < s, \qquad i_1 = j_2 \qquad\qquad (6.179b)$$

Fig. 6.23. An elementary (p, s) d-invariant transformation.

$$|(j_1, i_2)| < p, \qquad j_1 \neq i_2 \qquad\qquad (6.179c)$$

$$|(j_1, i_2)| < s, \qquad j_1 = i_2 \qquad\qquad (6.179d)$$

then the operation of replacing the arcs (i_1, i_2) and (j_1, j_2) by the arcs (i_1, j_2) and (j_1, i_2) is called an *elementary (p, s) d-invariant transformation* of G. An elementary (∞, ∞) d-invariant transformation is simply referred to as an *elementary d-invariant transformation*.

The operation is depicted in Fig. 6.23. Clearly, this kind of operation will result in a d-invariant (p, s)-digraph. Two d-invariant $(1, 0)$-digraphs G_1 and G_2 are shown in Fig. 6.24. It is easy to verify that if we replace the arcs $(1, 2)$ and $(5, 3)$ in G_1 by $(1, 3)$ and $(5, 2)$, we obtain G_2. In other words, G_2 can be obtained from G_1 by an elementary $(1, 0)$ d-invariant transformation. It was shown by Chen (1971) that any two d-invariant (p, s)-digraphs are transformable from each other by a finite sequence of elementary (p, s) d-invariant transformations, a proof of which will be given in Section 6.7.

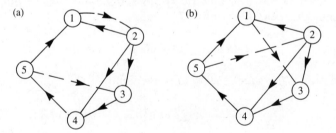

Fig. 6.24. Two d-invariant $(1, 0)$-digraphs: (a) G_1 and (b) G_2.

THEOREM 6.6

For a given (p, s)-digraph G, let $\{G\}$ be the set of all (p, s)-digraphs that are d-invariant from G. Then any two (p, s)-digraphs of $\{G\}$ are transformable from each other by a finite sequence of elementary (p, s) d-invariant transformations.

We now proceed to the derivation of the necessary and sufficient conditions for the existence of a symmetric $(p, 0)$ subgraph with preassigned outgoing and incoming degrees for a class of directed graphs possessing the odd-circuit condition.

DEFINITION 6.14

Odd-Circuit Condition. A directed graph is said to satisfy the *odd-circuit condition* if it has the property that any two of its directed circuits of odd length either have a node in common, or there exists an arc connecting these directed circuits.

The directed graph of Fig. 6.24(a) satisfies the odd-circuit condition, because the only two odd directed circuits $(3, 4)(4, 5)(5, 3)$ and $(1, 2)(2, 3)(3, 4)(4, 5)(5, 1)$ have at least a node in common. On the other hand, the directed graph of Fig. 6.22(b) does not satisfy the odd-circuit condition because there is no arc connecting the two odd directed circuits $(1, 1)$ and $(4, 4)$ directly. We remark that directed bipartite graphs and the complete directed graph all satisfy the odd-circuit condition.

THEOREM 6.7

Let $G(V, E)$ be a symmetric directed graph without self-loops satisfying the odd-circuit condition. Associate with each $x \in V$ a nonnegative integer $a(x)$. Then G has a symmetric $(p, 0)$ subgraph H whose outgoing and incoming degrees $d_H^+(x)$ and $d_H^-(x)$ satisfy

$$d_H^+(x) = d_H^-(x) = a(x), \qquad x \in V \qquad (6.180)$$

if and only if the sum of all $a(x)$ is even and

$$\sum_{y \in \gamma(X)} \min\left\{a(y), \sum_{x \in X} \min\left[|(x, y)|, p\right]\right\} \geq a(X) \qquad (6.181)$$

for all subsets $X \subseteq V$, where $\gamma(X)$ denotes the set of terminal nodes of the arcs of G having their initial nodes in X.

Proof. Let

$$d_H^+(x) = d_H^-(x) = d_H(x) \qquad (6.182)$$

If H is symmetric, it contains an even number of arcs. This number is equal to the sum of all $d_H(x)$ and the sum of all $a(x)$ must, therefore, be even.

The necessity of (6.181) follows directly from Theorem 6.2 by setting $a(x) = b(x)$ for each $x \in V$ and $s = 0$ and by observing that

$$\min\left[|(x, y)|, (1 - \delta_{xy})p\right] = \min\left[|(x, y)|, p\right] \qquad (6.183)$$

To prove sufficiency, we appeal to Theorem 6.2 and observe that there exists a $(p, 0)$ subgraph K whose outgoing and incoming degrees $d_K^+(x)$ and $d_K^-(x)$ satisfy

$$d_K^+(x) = d_K^-(x) = a(x) \qquad (6.184)$$

Thus, K is the arc-disjoint union of directed circuits. Let K_s be a maximal symmetric subgraph of K. If $K - K_s = \varnothing$, the empty graph, the proof is completed. Assume that $K - K_s \neq \varnothing$. Three cases are distinguished.

Case 1

In $K - K_s$, there is a directed circuit

$$(i_1, i_2)(i_2, i_3)\ldots(i_{2m-1}, i_{2m})(i_{2m}, i_1) \qquad (6.185)$$

of length $2m$. Then a series of elementary d-invariant transformations would transform (6.185) to

$$(i_2, i_3)(i_3, i_2), (i_4, i_5)(i_5, i_4), \ldots, (i_{2m}, i_1)(i_1, i_{2m}) \qquad (6.186)$$

which is symmetric and is a $(p, 0)$ subgraph of G.

Case 2

In $K - K_s$, there are two directed circuits of odd length having a common node i_1. Without loss of generality, let the two directed circuits be

$$(i_1, i_2)(i_2, i_3)\ldots(i_{2m-1}, i_1) \qquad (6.187a)$$

$$(i_1, j_2)(j_2, j_3)\ldots(j_{2q-1}, i_1) \qquad (6.187b)$$

Then a series of elementary d-invariant transformations would transform (6.187) to a symmetric $(p, 0)$ subgraph of G, as follows:

$$(i_2, i_3)(i_3, i_2), (i_4, i_5)(i_5, i_4), \ldots, (i_{2m-2}, i_{2m-1})(i_{2m-1}, i_{2m-2}) \qquad (6.188a)$$

$$(i_1, j_2)(j_2, i_1), (j_3, j_4)(j_4, j_3), \ldots, (j_{2q-1}, i_1)(i_1, j_{2q-1}) \qquad (6.188b)$$

Case 3

In $K - K_s$, there are two node-disjoint directed circuits of odd length, which can be expressed as

$$(i_1, i_2)(i_2, i_3) \ldots (i_{2m-1}, i_1) \tag{6.189a}$$

$$(j_1, j_2)(j_2, j_3) \ldots (j_{2q-1}, j_1) \tag{6.189b}$$

By assumption, there is an arc connecting the two directed circuits in G. Without loss of generality, let this arc be (i_1, j_1). If (i_1, j_1) is not in K_s, then a series of elementary d-invariant transformations would transform (6.189) to a symmetric $(p, 0)$ subgraph of G, as follows:

$$(i_2, i_3)(i_3, i_2), (i_4, i_5)(i_5, i_4), \ldots, (i_{2m-2}, i_{2m-1})(i_{2m-1}, i_{2m-2}),$$

$$(i_1, j_1)(j_1, i_1), (j_2, j_3)(j_3, j_2), (j_4, j_5)(j_5, j_4), \ldots,$$

$$(j_{2q-2}, j_{2q-1})(j_{2q-1}, j_{2q-2}) \tag{6.190}$$

If (i_1, j_1) is in K_s, then consider the subgraph composed of the arcs of (6.189) and (i_1, j_1) and (j_1, i_1). This subgraph can be transformed by a series of elementary d-invariant transformations to yield a symmetric $(p, 0)$ subgraph of G of the form:

$$(i_1, i_2)(i_2, i_1), (i_3, i_4)(i_4, i_3), \ldots, (i_{2m-1}, i_1)(i_1, i_{2m-1}),$$

$$(j_1, j_2)(j_2, j_1), (j_3, j_4)(j_4, j_3), \ldots, (j_{2q-1}, j_1)(j_1, j_{2q-1}) \tag{6.191}$$

By repeated application of the above three types of transformations and by noting that since the sum of all $d_K^+(x) = a(x)$ is even, the number of directed circuits of odd length must be even, we conclude that K can be transformed into a symmetric $(p, 0)$ subgraph of G by a finite sequence of elementary d-invariant transformations. This completes the proof of the theorem.

A different version of the theorem can be stated equivalently in terms of a graph without self-loops. As in Definition 6.14, we say that a graph satisfies the *odd-circuit condition* if it possesses the property that any two of its circuits of odd length either have a node in common, or are connected by an edge.

THEOREM 6.8

Let $G(V, E)$ be a graph without self-loops satisfying the odd-circuit condition. Associate with each $x \in V$ a nonnegative integer $a(x)$. Then G

has a $(p, 0)$ subgraph H whose degrees $d_H(x)$ satisfy

$$d_H(x) = a(x), \qquad x \in V \tag{6.192}$$

if and only if the sum of all $a(x)$ is even and, for all subsets $X \subseteq V$,

$$\sum_{y \in V} \min \left\{ a(y), \sum_{x \in X} \min \left[|(x, y)|, p \right] \right\} \geq a(X) \tag{6.193}$$

To obtain the necessary and sufficient conditions for the existence of a subgraph with prescribed degrees in a given graph, we set $p = \infty$ and obtain the following corollary.

COROLLARY 6.9

Let $G(V, E)$ be a graph without self-loops satisfying the odd-circuit condition. Associate with each $x \in V$ a nonnegative integer $a(x)$. Then G has a subgraph H whose degrees $d_H(x)$ satisfy

$$d_H(x) = a(x), \qquad x \in V \tag{6.194}$$

if and only if the sum of all $a(x)$ is even and

$$\sum_{y \in V} \min \left[a(y), |(X, y)| \right] \geq a(X) \tag{6.195}$$

for all subsets $X \subseteq V$.

We illustrate the above results by the following example.

Example 6.10

We wish to determine if the graph $G(V, E)$ of Fig. 6.25 possesses a $(1, 0)$

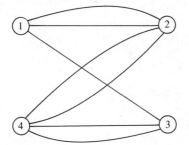

Fig. 6.25. A $(2, 0)$-graph used to illustrate the subgraph problem.

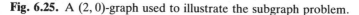

subgraph H whose degrees $d_H(x)$ satisfy

$$d_H(1) = a(1) = 2, \qquad d_H(2) = a(2) = 2$$
$$d_H(3) = a(3) = 1, \qquad d_H(4) = a(4) = 1 \qquad (6.196)$$

According to Theorem 6.8, the problem is solvable if and only if (6.193) holds for each $X \subseteq V = \{1, 2, 3, 4\}$, as follows:

$\min \{a(1), \min [|(1, 1)|, 1]\} + \min \{a(2), \min [|(1, 2)|, 1]\}$

$\quad + \min \{a(3), \min [|(1, 3)|, 1]\} + \min \{a(4), \min [|(1, 4)|, 1]\}$

$\quad = \min [2, 0] + \min [2, 1] + \min [1, 1] + \min [1, 0]$

$\quad = 0 + 1 + 1 + 0 = 2 \geqq a(1) = 2 \qquad (6.197a)$

$\min [2, 1] + \min [2, 0] + \min [1, 0] + \min [1, 1]$

$\quad = 1 + 0 + 0 + 1 = 2 \geqq a(2) = 2 \qquad (6.197b)$

$\min [2, 1] + \min [2, 0] + \min [1, 0] + \min [1, 1]$

$\quad = 1 + 0 + 0 + 1 = 2 \geqq a(3) = 1 \qquad (6.197c)$

$\min [2, 0] + \min [2, 1] + \min [1, 1] + \min [1, 0]$

$\quad = 0 + 1 + 1 + 0 = 2 \geqq a(4) = 1 \qquad (6.197d)$

$\min \{2, \min [|(1, 1)|, 1] + \min [|(2, 1)|, 1]\} + \min \{2, \min [|(1, 2)|, 1]$

$\quad + \min [|(2, 2)|, 1]\} + \min \{1, \min [|(1, 3)|, 1] + \min [|(2, 3)|, 1]\}$

$\quad + \min \{1, \min [|(1, 4)|, 1] + \min [|(2, 4)|, 1]\}$

$\quad = 1 + 1 + 1 + 1 = 4 \geqq a(\{1, 2\}) = 2 + 2 = 4 \qquad (6.198a)$

$\min [2, 1] + \min [2, 1] + \min [1, 1] + \min [1, 1]$

$\quad = 4 \geqq a(\{1, 3\}) = 3 \qquad (6.198b)$

$\min [2, 0] + \min [2, 2] + \min [1, 2] + \min [1, 0]$

$\quad = 3 \geqq a(\{1, 4\}) = 3 \qquad (6.198c)$

$\min [2, 2] + \min [2, 0] + \min [1, 0] + \min [1, 2]$

$\quad = 3 \geqq a(\{2, 3\}) = 3 \qquad (6.198d)$

$\min [2, 1] + \min [2, 1] + \min [1, 1] + \min [1, 1]$

$\quad = 4 \geqq a(\{2, 4\}) = 3 \qquad (6.198e)$

$\min [2, 1] + \min [2, 1] + \min [1, 1] + \min [1, 1]$

$\quad = 4 \geqq a(\{3, 4\}) = 2 \qquad (6.198f)$

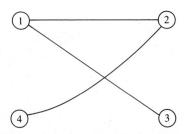

Fig. 6.26. A $(1, 0)$ subgraph of the graph of Fig. 6.25, whose degrees satisfy the requirements (6.196).

$$\min [2, 2] + \min [2, 1] + \min [1, 1] + \min [1, 2]$$
$$= 5 \geq a(\{1, 2, 3\}) = 2 + 2 + 1 = 5 \qquad (6.199a)$$

$$\min [2, 1] + \min [2, 2] + \min [1, 2] + \min [1, 1]$$
$$= 5 \geq a(\{1, 2, 4\}) = 5 \qquad (6.199b)$$

$$\min [2, 1] + \min [2, 2] + \min [1, 2] + \min [1, 1]$$
$$= 5 \geq a(\{1, 3, 4\}) = 4 \qquad (6.199c)$$

$$\min [2, 2] + \min [2, 1] + \min [1, 1] + \min [1, 2]$$
$$= 5 \geq a(\{2, 3, 4\}) = 4 \qquad (6.199d)$$

$$\min [2, 2] + \min [2, 2] + \min [1, 2] + \min [1, 2]$$
$$= 6 \geq a(\{1, 2, 3, 4\}) = 2 + 2 + 1 + 1 = 6 \qquad (6.200)$$

Thus, all the conditions are satisfied, and the graph G possesses such a $(1, 0)$ subgraph. One of these subgraphs is presented in Fig. 6.26.

6.4 GRAPHICAL SEQUENCES

In the present section, we consider the realizability of a sequence of nonnegative integers as the degree sequence of a (p, s)-graph.

DEFINITION 6.15
Graphical Sequence. A sequence of n nonnegative integers

$$\pi = \{a_i \mid i = 1, 2, \ldots, n\} \qquad (6.201)$$

is said to be (p, s) *graphical* if there exists a (p, s)-graph having π as the sequence of the degrees of its nodes, and such a graph is called a *realization* of the sequence.

The sequence $\pi = \{3, 4, 3, 4\}$, for example, is $(2, 0)$ graphical because it can be realized as the degree sequence of the graph shown in Fig. 6.25. However, it is not $(1, 0)$ graphical because in a four-node $(1, 0)$-graph, the maximum degree of a node cannot exceed $3\ (= n - 1)$.

THEOREM 6.9

A sequence $\{a_i\}$ of n nonnegative integers is $(p, 0)$ graphical if and only if the sum of all a_i is even, and

$$\sum_{a_i \in \bar{X}_a} \min [a_i, |X_a| p] + \sum_{a_j \in X_a} \min [a_j, (|X_a| - 1)p] \geq \sum_{a_k \in X_a} a_k \quad (6.202)$$

holds for each nonempty subset $X_a \subseteq \{a_i\}$, where $\bar{X}_a$ denotes the complement of X_a in $\{a_i\}$.

Proof. Let $G(V, E)$ be the n-node graph such that for each pair of distinct nodes there are p and only p edges connecting between them and there are no self-loops. This graph clearly satisfies the odd-circuit condition, and, furthermore, each of its subgraphs is a $(p, 0)$ graph. Using this graph $G(V, E)$ in Corollary 6.9, the left-hand side of (6.195) becomes

$$\sum_{y \in \bar{X}} \min [a(y), |(X, y)|] + \sum_{y \in X} \min [a(y), |(X, y)|]$$

$$= \sum_{a_i \in \bar{X}_a} \min [a_i, |X_a| p] + \sum_{a_j \in X_a} \min [a_j, (|X_a| - 1)p] \quad (6.203)$$

where $a_y \in X_a$ if and only if $y \in X$. The theorem follows.

Condition (6.202) consists of $2^n - 1$ inequalities. These can be reduced to a set of n inequalities if the elements of $\{a_i\}$ are properly ordered.

THEOREM 6.10

The necessary and sufficient conditions for a sequence

$$\pi = \{a_i\}, \quad a_i \geq a_{i+1} \quad \text{for} \quad i = 1, 2, \ldots, n-1 \quad (6.204)$$

to be $(p, 0)$ graphical are that the sum of all a_i be even and

$$\sum_{j=1}^{k} \min [a_j, (k-1)p] + \sum_{i=k+1}^{n} \min [a_i, kp] \geq \sum_{j=1}^{k} a_j \quad (6.205a)$$

for $k = 1, 2, \ldots, n-1$ and

$$\sum_{i=1}^{n} \min [a_i, (n-1)p] \geq \sum_{j=1}^{n} a_j \qquad (6.205b)$$

The proof of the theorem is similar to that of Corollary 6.4, and is omitted. As before, conditions (6.205) can be expressed in terms of the modified dual sequence of $\{a_i\}$ for the $(1, 0)$-graphs. We show that the sequence π is $(1, 0)$ graphical if and only if the partial sums of π are dominated by those of its modified dual sequence.

COROLLARY 6.10

The necessary and sufficient conditions for a sequence of n nonnegative integers

$$\pi = \{a_i\}, \quad a_i \geq a_{i+1} \quad \text{for} \quad i = 1, 2, \ldots, n-1 \qquad (6.206)$$

to be $(1, 0)$ graphical are that the sum of all a_i be even, and any one of the following three conditions is satisfied:

$$\sum_{i=1}^{k} a_i'' \geq \sum_{i=1}^{k} a_i \qquad (6.207)$$

for $k = 1, 2, \ldots, n$, where $\{a_i''\}$ is the modified dual sequence of $\{a_i\}$;

$$x(x-1) + \sum_{i=x+1}^{n} \min [a_i, x] \geq \sum_{j=1}^{x} a_j \qquad (6.208)$$

for $x = 1, 2, \ldots, n-1$; or

$$k(x-1) + \sum_{i=x+1}^{n} a_i \geq \sum_{j=1}^{k} a_j \qquad (6.209)$$

for all k, x in $1 \leq k \leq x \leq n$, the first summation being zero for $x = n$.

Proof. Observe that for $p = 1$ the left-hand side of (6.205) can be written as

$$\sum_{i=1}^{k} a_i'' = \sum_{i=1}^{k} \min [a_i, k-1] + \sum_{j=k+1}^{n} \min [a_j, k] \qquad (6.210a)$$

for $k < n$ and

$$\sum_{i=1}^{k} a_i'' = \sum_{i=1}^{k} \min [a_i, k - 1] \qquad (6.210b)$$

for $k = n$. Condition (6.207) follows.

To show that condition (6.208) is necessary, we demonstrate that (6.207) implies (6.208). To this end, two cases are distinguished.

Case 1

$a_k \geq k - 1$. Then $a_q \geq k - 1$, $q \leq k$, and the right-hand side of (6.210a) and left-hand side of (6.208) are identical with $k = x$ for all x. Thus, (6.208) follows from (6.207) and (6.210a).

Case 2

$a_k < k - 1$. Then

$$k(k - 1) > \sum_{i=1}^{k} \min [a_i, k - 1] \qquad (6.211)$$

which in conjunction with (6.207) would imply (6.208).

Thus, conditions (6.208) are necessary. To prove sufficiency, we show that if (6.208) is satisfied for all x, then (6.207) is satisfied for all k. To facilitate our discussion, two cases are again distinguished.

Case 1

$a_k \geq k - 1$. Then the left-hand side of (6.208) and the right-hand side of (6.210a) become identical with $x = k$ for all $k < n$. Thus, (6.207) is satisfied for all $k < n$. To show that it is also satisfied for $k = n$, we consider (6.208) with $x = n - 1$, which yields

$$(n - 1)^2 \geq \sum_{j=1}^{n-1} a_j \qquad (6.212)$$

For the above inequality to hold, it is necessary that $a_n \leq n - 1$. Now consider (6.210b), which, under the assumed constraint, can be written as

$$\sum_{i=1}^{n} a_i'' = n(n - 1) = (n - 1)^2 + (n - 1)$$

$$\geq (n - 1)^2 + a_n \geq \sum_{j=1}^{n} a_j \qquad (6.213)$$

The last inequality follows from (6.212). Hence, (6.207) is satisfied for all k.

Case 2

$a_k < k - 1 > 0$. Let y be the largest index such that $a_y \geq k - 1$. Then $a_q < k - 1$, $y < q \leq n$, and $y \leq k - 1$. Consider (6.210a) which can be rewritten as

$$\sum_{i=1}^{k} a_i'' = \sum_{i=1}^{y} \min[a_i, k-1] + \sum_{i=y+1}^{k} \min[a_i, k-1] + \sum_{j=k+1}^{n} \min[a_j, k]$$

$$= y(k-1) + \sum_{i=y+1}^{k} a_i + \sum_{j=k+1}^{n} a_j$$

$$= y(y-1) + y(k-y) + \sum_{j=k+1}^{n} a_j + \sum_{i=y+1}^{k} a_i \tag{6.214a}$$

$$\sum_{i=1}^{k} a_i'' \geq y(y-1) + \sum_{i=y+1}^{k} \min[a_i, y] + \sum_{j=k+1}^{n} \min[a_j, y] + \sum_{i=y+1}^{k} a_i$$

$$= y(y-1) + \sum_{i=y+1}^{n} \min[a_i, y] + \sum_{i=y+1}^{k} a_i$$

$$\geq \sum_{j=1}^{y} a_j + \sum_{i=y+1}^{k} a_i = \sum_{j=1}^{k} a_j \tag{6.214b}$$

The last inequality follows from (6.208) by letting $x = y$. Thus, (6.207) holds for all $k < n$. For $k = n$, we consider (6.210b), which is the same as (6.214) except that all the terms containing $\sum_{j=k+1}^{n}$ are replaced by zeros. Note that in (6.214) we define $\sum_{j=1}^{y} \min[a_j, k-1] = 0$ for $y = 0$. So conditions (6.208) and (6.207) are equivalent.

Finally, we show that conditions (6.209) are both necessary and sufficient. For $a_k \leq k$, (6.208) is identical to (6.209) for $k = x$. For $a_k > k$, (6.210) is reduced to

$$\sum_{i=1}^{k} a_i'' = k(y-1) + \sum_{j=y+1}^{n} a_j \geq \sum_{i=1}^{k} a_i \tag{6.215}$$

for some y, $k \leq y \leq n$, where $\sum_{j=y+1}^{n} a_j = 0$ for $y = n$. The last inequality follows from (6.209) for $x = y$. This proves sufficiency. For necessity, we need only to prove the situation where $k < x$. It is sufficient to show that (6.208) implies (6.209). To this end, consider the left-hand side of (6.209) which can be expressed as

$$k(x-1) + \sum_{i=x+1}^{n} a_i = k(k-1) + k(x-k) + \sum_{i=x+1}^{n} a_i$$

$$\geq k(k-1) + \sum_{i=k+1}^{x} \min[a_i, k] + \sum_{i=x+1}^{n} \min[a_i, k]$$

$$= k(k-1) + \sum_{i=k+1}^{n} \min[a_i, k] \geq \sum_{j=1}^{k} a_j \qquad (6.216)$$

The last inequality follows from (6.208) with x being replaced by k. This completes the proof of the theorem.

We remark that, unlike the conditions stated in (6.207) and (6.208), which consist of n and $n-1$ inequalities, respectively, conditions (6.209) involve a set of $\frac{1}{2}n(n+1)$ inequalities and are thus of limited practical value. Condition (6.207) was first given by Chen (1973), (6.208) by Fulkerson, Hoffman and McAndrew (1965), and (6.209) by Erdös and Gallai (1960).

We illustrate the above results by the following examples.

Example 6.11

Determine whether the sequence

$$\pi = \{a_i\} = \{6, 5, 4, 4, 3, 3, 3\} \qquad (6.217)$$

is $(1, 0)$ graphical. Since the elements of the sequence π are already arranged in non-increasing order, we can apply Corollary 6.10 directly. The sum of all a_i is even because

$$\sum_{i=1}^{7} a_i = 6+5+4+4+3+3+3 = 28 \qquad (6.218)$$

To apply (6.207), we first compute the modified dual sequence of π and obtain

$$\{a_i''\} = \{6, 6, 6, 3, 4, 2, 1\} \qquad (6.219)$$

Conditions (6.207) become

$$6 \geq 6 \qquad (6.220a)$$

$$6+6 = 12 \geq 6+5 = 11 \qquad (6.220b)$$

$$6+6+6 = 18 \geq 6+5+4 = 15 \qquad (6.220c)$$

$$6 + 6 + 6 + 3 = 21 \geqq 6 + 5 + 4 + 4 = 19 \qquad (6.220d)$$

$$6 + 6 + 6 + 3 + 4 = 25 \geqq 6 + 5 + 4 + 4 + 3 = 22 \qquad (6.220e)$$

$$6 + 6 + 6 + 3 + 4 + 2 = 27 \geqq 6 + 5 + 4 + 4 + 3 + 3 = 25 \qquad (6.220f)$$

$$6 + 6 + 6 + 3 + 4 + 2 + 1 = 28 \geqq 6 + 5 + 4 + 4 + 3 + 3 + 3 = 28 \qquad (6.220g)$$

Thus, the sequence π is $(1, 0)$ graphical. A realization of π is shown in Fig. 6.27.

Alternatively, we can use (6.208) and obtain

$$0 + \min [5, 1] + \min [4, 1] + \min [4, 1] + \min [3, 1]$$
$$+ \min [3, 1] + \min [3, 1]$$
$$= 0 + 1 + 1 + 1 + 1 + 1 + 1 = 6 \geqq 6 \qquad (6.221a)$$

$$2 + 2 + 2 + 2 + 2 + 2 = 12 \geqq 6 + 5 = 11 \qquad (6.221b)$$

$$6 + 3 + 3 + 3 + 3 = 18 \geqq 6 + 5 + 4 = 15 \qquad (6.221c)$$

$$12 + 3 + 3 + 3 = 21 \geqq 6 + 5 + 4 + 4 = 19 \qquad (6.221d)$$

$$20 + 3 + 3 = 26 \geqq 6 + 5 + 4 + 4 + 3 = 22 \qquad (6.221e)$$

$$30 + 3 = 33 \geqq 6 + 5 + 4 + 4 + 3 + 3 = 25 \qquad (6.221f)$$

confirming that the sequence π is $(1, 0)$ graphical.

Observe that (6.207) consists of 7 inequalities, whereas (6.208) involves only 6. If, on the other hand, conditions (6.209) are used for testing, we need to check 28 inequalities.

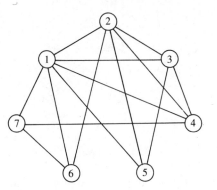

Fig. 6.27. A $(1, 0)$-graph realizing the sequence of nonnegative integers of (6.217).

Example 6.12

Test to see if the sequence

$$\pi = \{a_i\} = \{5, 4, 4, 3, 2\} \tag{6.222}$$

is $(2, 0)$ graphical. Since the integers in π have already been arranged in non-increasing order, we can apply Theorem 6.10 directly. The sum of all a_i is even:

$$\sum_{i=1}^{5} a_i = 5 + 4 + 4 + 3 + 2 = 18 \tag{6.223}$$

Conditions (6.205) become

$$\min [5, 0] + \min [4, 2] + \min [4, 2] + \min [3, 2] + \min [2, 2]$$
$$= 0 + 2 + 2 + 2 + 2 = 8 \geqq 5 \tag{6.224a}$$
$$\min [5, 2] + \min [4, 2] + \min [4, 4] + \min [3, 4] + \min [2, 4]$$
$$= 2 + 2 + 4 + 3 + 2 = 13 \geqq 5 + 4 = 9 \tag{6.224b}$$
$$\min [5, 4] + \min [4, 4] + \min [4, 4] + \min [3, 6] + \min [2, 6]$$
$$= 4 + 4 + 4 + 3 + 2 = 17 \geqq 5 + 4 + 4 = 13 \tag{6.224c}$$
$$\min [5, 6] + \min [4, 6] + \min [4, 6] + \min [3, 6] + \min [2, 8]$$
$$= 5 + 4 + 4 + 3 + 2 = 18 \geqq 5 + 4 + 4 + 3 = 16 \tag{6.224d}$$
$$\min [5, 8] + \min [4, 8] + \min [4, 8] + \min [3, 8] + \min [2, 8]$$
$$= 5 + 4 + 4 + 3 + 2 = 18 \geqq 5 + 4 + 4 + 3 + 2 = 18 \tag{6.224e}$$

Thus, the sequence π is $(2, 0)$ graphical, a realization of which is shown in Fig. 6.28.

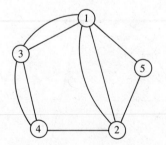

Fig. 6.28. A $(2, 0)$-graph realizing the sequence of nonnegative integers of (6.222).

6.5   THE (p, s)-MATRIX

In Section 6.2, we presented the necessary and sufficient conditions for the existence of a (p, s)-digraph with prescribed incoming and outgoing degrees. In the present section, we demonstrate that the existence of a (p, s)-digraph also establishes the existence of a class of matrices known as the (p, s)-matrices.

DEFINITION 6.16

(p, s)**-Matrix.** For given nonnegative integers p and s, a square matrix of nonnegative integers is called a (p, s)-*matrix* if and only if all of its off-diagonal elements are bounded above by p and all of its diagonal elements are bounded above by s. A (p, p)-matrix is also referred to as a *p-matrix*.

For a given (p, s)-matrix M of order n, let the sum of the elements of its row i be denoted by a_i and let the sum of the elements of its column j be b_j for $i, j = 1, 2, \ldots, n$. Then the sum of the elements of M is given by

$$\sum_{i=1}^{n} a_i = \sum_{j=1}^{n} b_j \tag{6.225}$$

Our problem is to establish arithmetic conditions that are necessary and sufficient for the existence of a (p, s)-matrix having prescribed row sums a_i and column sums b_j. The problem can be interpreted in terms of the existence of a (p, s)-digraph with prescribed degree pairs $[a_i, b_i]$ of its nodes: Let

$$M = [m_{ij}] \tag{6.226}$$

Then the *associated* (p, s)-*digraph* $G(V, E)$ of M is an n-node directed graph such that if $m_{ij} \neq 0$ there are m_{ij} parallel arcs from node i to node j for $i, j = 1, 2, \ldots, n$. Conversely, for a given n-node (p, s)-digraph $G(V, E)$, the *associated* (p, s)-*matrix* is a square matrix M such that if there are m_{ij} parallel arcs from node i to node j, then its ith row and jth column element is m_{ij}. Thus, there exists a one-to-one correspondence between these two different representations.

As an illustration, consider the $(1, 0)$-digraph G_1 of Fig. 6.24(a). The associated $(1, 0)$-matrix is found to be

$$
M_1 = \begin{array}{c} \\ 1 \\ 3 \\ 1 \\ 1 \\ 2 \end{array}
\begin{array}{c}
\begin{array}{ccccc} 2 & 1 & 2 & 2 & 1 \end{array} \\
\left[\begin{array}{ccccc}
0 & 1 & 0 & 0 & 0 \\
1 & 0 & 1 & 1 & 0 \\
0 & 0 & 0 & 1 & 0 \\
0 & 0 & 0 & 0 & 1 \\
1 & 0 & 1 & 0 & 0
\end{array}\right]
\end{array}
\tag{6.227}
$$

For the $(1, 0)$-digraph G_2 of Fig. 6.24(b), its associated $(1, 0)$-matrix is given by

$$
M_2 = \begin{array}{c} \\ 1 \\ 3 \\ 1 \\ 1 \\ 2 \end{array}
\begin{array}{c}
\begin{array}{ccccc} 2 & 1 & 2 & 2 & 1 \end{array} \\
\left[\begin{array}{ccccc}
0 & 0 & 1 & 0 & 0 \\
1 & 0 & 1 & 1 & 0 \\
0 & 0 & 0 & 1 & 0 \\
0 & 0 & 0 & 0 & 1 \\
1 & 1 & 0 & 0 & 0
\end{array}\right]
\end{array}
\tag{6.228}
$$

Consequently, all the results obtained for the (p, s)-digraphs can be carried over for the (p, s)-matrices. It is hardly necessary to repeat the same results all over again. However, we shall point out the corresponding operation for a (p, s)-matrix of an elementary (p, s) d-invariant transformation for a (p, s)-digraph.

Consider the 2×2 submatrix of M of the type

$$
H_1 = \begin{bmatrix} a & b \\ c & d \end{bmatrix} \quad \text{and} \quad H_2 = \begin{bmatrix} b & a \\ d & c \end{bmatrix}
\tag{6.229}
$$

where $\min(a, d) \neq 0$, and $b, c < p$ if b or c is an off-diagonal element of M and $b, c < s$ if b or c is a diagonal element of M. Let

$$
H_3 = \begin{bmatrix} a - 1 & b + 1 \\ c + 1 & d - 1 \end{bmatrix} \quad \text{and} \quad H_4 = \begin{bmatrix} b + 1 & a - 1 \\ d - 1 & c + 1 \end{bmatrix}
\tag{6.230}
$$

A (p, s)-*interchange* is defined as a transformation of the elements of M that changes a specified submatrix of type H_1 into H_3, or else a submatrix of type H_2 into H_4, and leaves all other elements of M unaltered. Suppose that we apply a finite number of (p, s)-interchanges to M. Then by the nature of the operation, the resulting matrix has the same row sums and the same column sums. As a consequence of Theorem 6.6, if $\{M\}$ is the set of all

(p, s)-matrices having the same row and column sums as those of M, then every element of $\{M\}$ can be obtained from any other one by a finite sequence of (p, s)-interchanges.

For example, the two $(1, 0)$-matrices M_1 and M_2 of (6.227) and (6.228) have the same row sums and column sums. If in M_1 we replace the submatrix $M_1(15; 23)$ consisting of the rows 1 and 5 and columns 2 and 3 by the corresponding submatrix $M_2(15; 23)$ in M_2, we transform M_1 into M_2 by a $(1, 0)$-interchange.

We remark that since any matrix can be made square by the addition of a sufficient number of zero rows or columns, the above results can easily be extended to the non-square matrices. However, since this extension only complicates the matter and does not provide any additional information, for our purposes we shall only consider the square matrices except for a few cases where the general situation can be presented concisely.

We restate Theorem 6.5 as follows.

THEOREM 6.11

Given a sequence of n nonnegative integer four-tuples

$$\pi' = \{(a_i, a_i', b_i, b_i') \mid a_i \leqq a_i', b_i \leqq b_i', i = 1, 2, \ldots, n\} \qquad (6.231)$$

there is an $n \times n$ (p, s)-matrix $M = [m_{ij}]$ satisfying

$$a_i \leqq \sum_{j=1}^{n} m_{ij} \leqq a_i', \qquad i = 1, 2, \ldots, n \qquad (6.232a)$$

$$b_j \leqq \sum_{i=1}^{n} m_{ij} \leqq b_j', \qquad j = 1, 2, \ldots, n \qquad (6.232b)$$

if and only if conditions (6.95) hold.

In the special situation where $a_i = 0$ and $b_i' = \infty$, we obtain a result of Gale (1957) and Ryser (1957).

COROLLARY 6.11

Let $\{a_i \mid i = 1, 2, \ldots, m\}$ and $\{b_j \mid j = 1, 2, \ldots, n\}$ be two sequences of nonnegative integers, where $b_j \geqq b_{j+1}$ for $j = 1, 2, \ldots, n - 1$. Then there is an $m \times n$ matrix $W = [w_{ij}]$ composed of zeros and ones satisfying

$$\sum_{j=1}^{n} w_{ij} \leqq a_i, \qquad i = 1, 2, \ldots, m \qquad (6.233a)$$

$$\sum_{i=1}^{m} w_{ij} \geqq b_j, \qquad j = 1, 2, \ldots, n \tag{6.233b}$$

if and only if

$$\sum_{j=1}^{k} a_j^* \geqq \sum_{j=1}^{k} b_j, \qquad k = 1, 2, \ldots, n \tag{6.234}$$

where $\{a_i^*\} = \{a_i\}^*$, the dual sequence of $\{a_i\}$.

Proof. To facilitate our discussion, two cases are distinguished.

Case 1

$m \leqq n$. The a_i sequence can be brought to the same length as the b_j sequence by the insertion of $n - m$ zeros. Let the resulting sequence be again denoted by $\{a_i\}$. Appealing to Theorem 6.11 by first setting $a_i = 0$ and $b_j' = \infty$ in (6.232) and (6.95) and then by replacing a_i' in the resulting (6.232a) and (6.95b) by a_i, we see that condition (6.95a) is trivially satisfied and condition (6.95b) becomes

$$\sum_{i=1}^{n} \min [a_i, |X_b|] \geqq \sum_{b_j \in X_b} b_j \tag{6.235}$$

with $p = s = 1$ for each $X_b \subseteq \{b_j\}$. Observe that the right-hand side of the inequality (6.235) is maximized over all k-element subsets $X_b \subseteq \{b_j\}$ by choosing the subset $\{b_1, b_2, \ldots, b_k\}$, where $k = |X_b|$:

$$\sum_{i=1}^{n} \min [a_i, k] \geqq \sum_{j=1}^{k} b_j \geqq \sum_{b_t \in X_b} b_t \tag{6.236}$$

or, in terms of the dual sequence,

$$\sum_{i=1}^{k} a_i^* = \sum_{i=1}^{n} \min [a_i, k] \geqq \sum_{j=1}^{k} b_j, \qquad k = 1, 2, \ldots, n \tag{6.237}$$

Case 2

$m > n$. The proof can be carried out in a similar manner after bringing the b_j sequence to the same length as the a_i sequence, and is omitted. This completes the proof of the corollary.

In the case that the sum of a_i equals that of b_i, the problem becomes that of filling an $m \times n$ matrix with zeros and ones so that the ith row sum is a_i, and the jth column sum is b_j.

COROLLARY 6.12

There is an $m \times n$ matrix composed of zeros and ones with prescribed row sums a_i $(i = 1, 2, \ldots, m)$ and column sums b_j $(j = 1, 2, \ldots, n)$ with $b_1 \geqq b_2 \geqq \cdots \geqq b_n$ if and only if

$$\sum_{i=1}^{m} a_i = \sum_{j=1}^{n} b_j \tag{6.238}$$

$$\sum_{j=1}^{k} a_j^* \geqq \sum_{j=1}^{k} b_j, \qquad k = 1, 2, \ldots, n \tag{6.239}$$

where $\{a_i^*\} = \{a_i\}^*$.

We illustrate the above results by the following examples.

Example 6.13

There are five families having 3, 3, 2, 2 and 1 members to be seated at three tables having 5, 4 and 4 seats. The problem is to make a seat assignment so that no two members of the same family are seated at the same table.

The problem is feasible if the following two sequences

$$\{a_i\} = \{5, 4, 4\} \tag{6.240a}$$

$$\{b_i\} = \{3, 3, 2, 2, 1\} \tag{6.240b}$$

satisfy conditions (6.234). The dual sequence of $\{a_i\}$ is found to be

$$\{a_i^*\} = \{a_i\}^* = \{3, 3, 3, 3, 1\} \tag{6.241}$$

giving from (6.234)

$$3 \geqq 3 \tag{6.242a}$$

$$3 + 3 = 6 \geqq 3 + 3 = 6 \tag{6.242b}$$

$$3 + 3 + 3 = 9 \geqq 3 + 3 + 2 = 8 \tag{6.242c}$$

$$3 + 3 + 3 + 3 = 12 \geqq 3 + 3 + 2 + 2 = 10 \tag{6.242d}$$

$$3 + 3 + 3 + 3 + 1 = 13 \geqq 3 + 3 + 2 + 2 + 1 = 11 \tag{6.242e}$$

Thus, the problem is feasible and a seat assignment is given by

$$
\begin{array}{cccccc}
& 3 & 3 & 2 & 2 & 1 \\
5 & \begin{bmatrix} 1 & 1 & 1 & 0 & 1 \\
4 & 1 & 1 & 0 & 1 & 0 \\
4 & 1 & 1 & 1 & 1 & 0 \end{bmatrix}
\end{array}
\tag{6.243}
$$

Example 6.14

Determine whether there is a 4×5 matrix of zeros and ones with preassigned row sums 3, 1, 2 and 3 and column sums 2, 1, 2, 2, and 2.

According to Corollary 6.12, the problem is feasible if and only if conditions (6.238) and (6.239) hold. In order to apply (6.239), we rearrange the column sums in a monotonously decreasing order as

$$
\{b_j\} = \{2, 2, 2, 2, 1\} \tag{6.244}
$$

giving from (6.238)

$$
3 + 1 + 2 + 3 = 9 = 2 + 2 + 2 + 2 + 1 \tag{6.245}
$$

and from (6.239)

$$
4 \geqq 2 \tag{6.246a}
$$

$$
4 + 3 = 7 \geqq 2 + 2 = 4 \tag{6.246b}
$$

$$
4 + 3 + 2 = 9 \geqq 2 + 2 + 2 = 6 \tag{6.246c}
$$

$$
4 + 3 + 2 + 0 = 9 \geqq 2 + 2 + 2 + 2 = 8 \tag{6.246d}
$$

$$
4 + 3 + 2 + 0 + 0 = 9 \geqq 2 + 2 + 2 + 2 + 1 = 9 \tag{6.246e}
$$

where

$$
\{a_i^*\} = \{a_i\}^* = \{4, 3, 2, 0, 0\} \tag{6.247}
$$

Thus, the problem is solvable, a solution of which is given by

$$
\begin{array}{cccccc}
& 2 & 2 & 2 & 2 & 1 \\
3 & \begin{bmatrix} 1 & 0 & 1 & 1 & 0 \\
1 & 0 & 0 & 0 & 1 & 0 \\
2 & 0 & 1 & 0 & 0 & 1 \\
3 & 1 & 1 & 1 & 0 & 0 \end{bmatrix}
\end{array}
\tag{6.248}
$$

COROLLARY 6.13

Let $\{a_i \mid i = 1, 2, \ldots, m\}$ be a sequence of nonnegative integers and let b be a given nonnegative integer. Then there is an $m \times n$ matrix $W = [w_{ij}]$ composed of zeros and ones satisfying

$$\sum_{j=1}^{n} w_{ij} \leq a_i, \qquad i = 1, 2, \ldots, m \tag{6.249a}$$

$$\sum_{i=1}^{m} w_{ij} \geq b, \qquad j = 1, 2, \ldots, n \tag{6.249b}$$

if and only if

$$\sum_{j=1}^{n} a_j^* \geq nb \tag{6.250}$$

Proof. If we set $b_j = b$ for all j in Corollary 6.11, (6.233) reduces to (6.249), and (6.234) becomes

$$\sum_{j=1}^{k} a_j^* \geq kb, \qquad k = 1, 2, \ldots, n \tag{6.251}$$

For $k = n$, (6.251) is the same as (6.250). Thus, it is sufficient to show that (6.251) holds for $k = 1, 2, \ldots, n - 1$. Since the dual sequence $\{a_j^*\}$ is monotonously decreasing, we have

$$(n - k) \sum_{j=1}^{k} a_j^* \geq (n - k)ka_k^* \geq k(n - k)a_{k+1}^*$$

$$\geq k \sum_{j=k+1}^{n} a_j^* \tag{6.252}$$

which can be written as

$$n \sum_{j=1}^{k} a_j^* \geq k \sum_{j=1}^{n} a_j^* \geq knb \tag{6.253}$$

The last inequality follows from (6.250) by assumption. Thus, (6.251) holds for $k = 1, 2, \ldots, n - 1$, and the proof is completed.

COROLLARY 6.14

Let $\{b_j \mid j = 1, 2, \ldots, n\}$ be a sequence of nonnegative integers and let a be a given nonnegative integer. Then there is an $m \times n$ matrix $W = [w_{ij}]$ composed of zeros and ones satisfying

$$\sum_{j=1}^{n} w_{ij} \leqq a, \qquad i = 1, 2, \ldots, m \tag{6.254a}$$

$$\sum_{i=1}^{m} w_{ij} \geqq b_j, \qquad j = 1, 2, \ldots, n \tag{6.254b}$$

if and only if

$$b_j \leqq m \tag{6.255a}$$

$$\sum_{j=1}^{n} b_j \leqq ma \tag{6.255b}$$

Proof. We show that if $a_i = a$ for all i, (6.255) imply (6.234) for all k. If $k \leqq a$, then from (6.255a)

$$\sum_{j=1}^{k} b_j \leqq mk = m \min [a, k] \tag{6.256a}$$

and if $k > a$, then from (6.255b)

$$\sum_{j=1}^{k} b_j \leqq \sum_{j=1}^{n} b_j \leqq ma = m \min [a, k] \tag{6.256b}$$

Since

$$m \min [a, k] = \sum_{i=1}^{m} \min [a, k] = \sum_{j=1}^{k} a_j^* \tag{6.257}$$

inequalities (6.256) can be combined to yield

$$\sum_{j=1}^{k} a_j^* \geqq \sum_{j=1}^{k} b_j, \qquad k = 1, 2, \ldots, n \tag{6.258}$$

This completes the proof of the corollary.

We illustrate the above results by the following examples.

Example 6.15

Determine whether there is a 4×5 matrix of zeros and ones with row sums bounded above by 3, 1, 2, and 3 and each column sum bounded below by 2.

Appealing to Corollary 6.13, we can make the following identifications:

$$m = 4, \qquad n = 5, \qquad b = 2 \tag{6.259a}$$

$$\{a_i\} = \{3, 1, 2, 3\} \tag{6.259b}$$

the dual sequence of which is found to be

$$\{a_i^*\} = \{a_i\}^* = \{4, 3, 2, 0, 0\} \tag{6.260}$$

Since (6.250)

$$4 + 3 + 2 + 0 + 0 = 9 \nleqq 5 \times 2 = 10 \tag{6.261}$$

is not satisfied, the problem is infeasible and no such matrix exists.

Example 6.16

Test to see if there is a 3×5 matrix of zeros and ones with each row sum bounded above by 4 and the column sums bounded below by 3, 3, 2, 2, and 2.

According to Corollary 6.14, the problem is feasible if and only if inequalities (6.255) are satisfied:

$$b_j \leq m = 3, \qquad j = 1, 2, 3, 4, 5 \tag{6.262a}$$

$$\sum_{j=1}^{5} b_j = 3 + 3 + 2 + 2 + 2 = 12 \leq ma = 3 \times 4 = 12 \tag{6.262b}$$

Thus, the problem is solvable, and a solution is given by

$$
\begin{array}{c}
\;\; 3 \;\; 3 \;\; 2 \;\; 2 \;\; 2 \\
\begin{array}{c} 4 \\ 4 \\ 4 \end{array}
\begin{bmatrix}
1 & 1 & 1 & 0 & 1 \\
1 & 1 & 0 & 1 & 1 \\
1 & 1 & 1 & 1 & 0
\end{bmatrix}
\end{array}
\tag{6.263}
$$

Observe that in the present case since the sum of $a_i = a$ equals that of b_j, the problem becomes that of filling a 3×5 matrix with zeros and ones with prescribed row sums and column sums, as exhibited in (6.263).

Before we proceed to the consideration of other special cases, we remark that a square matrix of zeros and ones is a 1-matrix, which is different from a $(1, 0)$-matrix. A $(1, 0)$-matrix is a square 1-matrix with zero trace, the sum of its diagonal elements being zero.

THEOREM 6.12

Let $\{a_i \mid a_i \geqq a_{i+1}\}$ and $\{b_j \mid b_j \geqq b_{j+1}\}$ be two sequences of n nonnegative integers. There is a $(1, 0)$-matrix $W = [w_{ij}]$ of order n satisying

$$\sum_{j=1}^{n} w_{ij} \leqq a_i, \qquad \sum_{j=1}^{n} w_{ji} \geqq b_i \tag{6.264}$$

for $i = 1, 2, \ldots, n$ if and only if

$$\sum_{i=1}^{k} a_i'' \geqq \sum_{i=1}^{k} b_i, \qquad k = 1, 2, \ldots, n \tag{6.265}$$

where $\{a_i''\} = \{a_i\}''$ is the modified dual sequence of $\{a_i\}$.

Proof. We appeal to Theorem 6.11 by first setting $a_i = 0$, $b_j' = \infty$, $p = 1$ and $s = 0$ in (6.232) and (6.95), and then by replacing a_i' in the resulting (6.232a) and (6.95b) by a_i, we see that condition (6.95a) is trivially satisfied and condition (6.95b) becomes

$$\sum_{a_j \in X_a} \min\,[a_j, |X_b| - 1] + \sum_{a_i \in \bar{X}_a} \min\,[a_i, |X_b|] \geqq \sum_{b_t \in X_b} b_t \tag{6.266}$$

where X_a and X_b are the corresponding subsets of $\{a_i\}$ and $\{b_j\}$, respectively, and $\bar{X}_a = \{a_i\} - X_a$. Using the symbol $a_t^*(X_a)$ defined in (6.102), the left-hand side of (6.266) can be expressed as

$$a_k^*(\bar{X}_a) + \sum_{t=1}^{k-1} a_t^* \tag{6.267}$$

for $k = |X_b|$, where the second term is zero for $k = 1$. Equation (6.266) becomes

$$\sum_{t=1}^{k-1} a_t^* \geqq \left(\sum_{b_t \in X_b} b_t \right) - a_k^*(\bar{X}_a) \tag{6.268}$$

Since $\{a_i\}$ and $\{b_j\}$ are monotonously decreasing sequences, the right-hand side of (6.268) is maximized by selecting $X_b = \{b_1, b_2, \ldots, b_k\}$. Thus,

(6.266) may be replaced by the n inequalities

$$\sum_{t=1}^{k-1} a_t^* + a_k^*(\{a_{k+1}, a_{k+2}, \ldots, a_n\}) \geq \sum_{t=1}^{k} b_t, \qquad k = 1, 2, \ldots, n$$

$$(6.269)$$

Since

$$\sum_{t=1}^{k-1} a_t^* + a_k^*(\{a_{k+1}, a_{k+2}, \ldots, a_n\}) = \sum_{i=1}^{k} a_i'' \qquad (6.270)$$

inequalities (6.265) follow. This completes the proof of the theorem.

Particular cases under which an ordering of the elements of the sequences $\{a_i\}$ and $\{b_j\}$ exists are those where $b_i = b$ for all i or $a_i = a$ for all i, as in Corollaries 6.13 and 6.14. In words, Theorem 6.12 states that a $(1, 0)$-matrix satisfying (6.264) exists if and only if the partial sums of the b_j sequence are dominated by those of the modified dual sequence of the a_i sequence.

COROLLARY 6.15

Let $\{a_i \mid a_i \geq a_{i+1}\}$ be a sequence of n nonnegative integers, and let b be a given nonnegative integer. Then there is a $(1, 0)$-matrix $W = [w_{ij}]$ of order n satisfying

$$\sum_{j=1}^{n} w_{ij} \leq a_i, \qquad \sum_{j=1}^{n} w_{ji} \geq b \qquad (6.271)$$

for $i = 1, 2, \ldots, n$ if and only if

$$\sum_{i=1}^{n} a_i'' \geq nb \qquad (6.272)$$

where $\{a_i''\}$ is the modified dual sequence of $\{a_i\}$.

Proof. Recall that the dual sequence $\{a_i^*\}$ of $\{a_i\}$ is monotone, but the modified dual sequence $\{a_i''\}$ is not necessarily monotone. However, it is straightforward to show that the monotonicity of the sequence $\{a_i\}$ implies that either the sequence $\{a_i''\}$ is monotone, or else it has at most one point of unit increase; that is, either

$$a_1'' \geq a_2'' \geq \cdots \geq a_n'' \qquad (6.273a)$$

or, for some $t = 1, 2, \ldots, n - 1$,

$$a_1'' \geq a_2'' \geq \cdots \geq a_t'', \qquad a_{t+1}'' = a_t'' + 1 \geq a_{t+2}'' \geq \cdots \geq a_n'' \qquad (6.273b)$$

To complete the proof, we need to show that (6.272) and (6.273) imply (6.265) or

$$\sum_{i=1}^{k} a_i'' \geq kb, \qquad k = 1, 2, \ldots, n \qquad (6.274)$$

We establish this by induction over n. For $n = 1$, (6.272) and (6.274) are identical. Assume that (6.272) implies (6.274) for any $n - 1$ or less. We show that the proposition is also true for any n. If $a_n'' > b$, then by (6.273) we have $a_i'' \geq b$ for all i, and (6.274) follows. If, on the other hand, $a_n'' \leq b$, then in order for (6.272) to hold, it is necessary that

$$\sum_{i=1}^{n-1} a_i'' \geq (n - 1)b \qquad (6.275)$$

By induction hypothesis, we have

$$\sum_{i=1}^{k} a_i'' \geq kb, \qquad k = 1, 2, \ldots, n - 1 \qquad (6.276)$$

This together with (6.272) gives (6.274), and the proof is completed.

COROLLARY 6.16

Let $\{b_j \mid b_j \geq b_{j+1}\}$ be a sequence of n nonnegative integers and let a be a given nonnegative integer. Then there is a $(1, 0)$-matrix $W = [w_{ij}]$ of order n satisfying

$$\sum_{j=1}^{n} w_{ij} \leq a, \qquad \sum_{j=1}^{n} w_{ji} \geq b_i \qquad (6.277)$$

for $i = 1, 2, \ldots, n$ if and only if

$$b_i \leq n - 1 \qquad (6.278a)$$

$$\sum_{j=1}^{n} b_j \leq na \qquad (6.278b)$$

Proof. We show that (6.278) implies

$$\sum_{j=1}^{k} a_j'' \geq \sum_{j=1}^{k} b_j, \qquad k = 1, 2, \ldots, n \qquad (6.279)$$

To facilitate our discussion, two cases are distinguished. If $k \leq a$, then

$$a_j'' = n - 1, \qquad j \leq k \qquad (6.280)$$

giving

$$\sum_{j=1}^{k} a_j'' = k(n-1) \geq \sum_{j=1}^{k} b_j \qquad (6.281)$$

If, on the other hand, $k > a$, then

$$a_j'' = \begin{cases} n-1, & j \leq a \\ a, & j = a+1 \\ 0, & j > a+1 \end{cases} \qquad (6.282)$$

obtaining

$$\sum_{j=1}^{k} a_j'' = na \geq \sum_{j=1}^{n} b_j \geq \sum_{j=1}^{k} b_j \qquad (6.283)$$

This completes the proof of the corollary.

We illustrate the above results by the following examples.

Example 6.17

Given two sequences $\{3, 3, 4, 2, 2\}$ and $\{3, 3, 3, 3, 2\}$ of nonnegative integers, determine whether there is a $(1, 0)$-matrix whose row sums and column sums are bounded above and below by the elements of the two sequences, respectively.

In order to apply Theorem 6.12, we interchange the first and third elements of the two sequences simultaneously, and obtain

$$\{a_i\} = \{4, 3, 3, 2, 2\} \qquad (6.284a)$$
$$\{b_j\} = \{3, 3, 3, 3, 2\} \qquad (6.284b)$$

The modified dual sequence of $\{a_i\}$ is found to be

$$\{a_i''\} = \{4, 4, 2, 3, 1\} \qquad (6.285)$$

which is not necessarily monotone, as we observed in (6.273). The problem is solvable since from (6.265)

$$4 \geqq 3 \tag{6.286a}$$

$$4 + 4 = 8 \geqq 3 + 3 = 6 \tag{6.286b}$$

$$4 + 4 + 2 = 10 \geqq 3 + 3 + 3 = 9 \tag{6.286c}$$

$$4 + 4 + 2 + 3 = 13 \geqq 3 + 3 + 3 + 3 = 12 \tag{6.286d}$$

$$4 + 4 + 2 + 3 + 1 = 14 \geqq 3 + 3 + 3 + 3 + 2 = 14 \tag{6.286e}$$

A desired $(1, 0)$-matrix is given by

$$
\begin{array}{c}
\begin{array}{ccccc} 3 & 3 & 3 & 3 & 2 \end{array} \\
\begin{array}{c} 4 \\ 3 \\ 3 \\ 2 \\ 2 \end{array}
\left[
\begin{array}{ccccc}
0 & 1 & 1 & 1 & 1 \\
1 & 0 & 0 & 1 & 1 \\
1 & 1 & 0 & 1 & 0 \\
0 & 1 & 1 & 0 & 0 \\
1 & 0 & 1 & 0 & 0
\end{array}
\right]
\end{array}
\tag{6.287}
$$

Since the sum of a_i equals that of b_j, the $(1, 0)$-matrix yields the prescribed row sums and column sums.

Example 6.18

We wish to know if there is a $(1, 0)$-matrix, whose row sums are bounded above by 4, 3, 3, 2, 2 and each column sum is bounded below by 3.

According to Corollary 6.15, the problem is solvable if and only if inequality (6.272) holds:

$$\sum_{i=1}^{5} a_i'' = 4 + 4 + 2 + 3 + 1 = 14 \not\geqq 5 \times 3 = 15 \tag{6.288}$$

where $\{a_i\} = \{4, 3, 3, 2, 2\}$ and $\{a_i''\} = \{4, 4, 2, 3, 1\}$. Since (6.272) does not hold, no such $(1, 0)$-matrix exists.

Recall that Theorem 6.5 was deduced from Theorem 6.1, which in turn was derived from Theorem 5.5. A counterpart to Corollary 5.1 can now be stated explicitly for the existence of a nonnegative matrix whose row and column sums lie between designated limits, and, furthermore, whose elements are bounded above by specified numbers.

THEOREM 6.13

Let $0 \le a_i \le a_i'$, $i = 1, 2, \ldots, m$; $0 \le b_j \le b_j'$, $j = 1, 2, \ldots, n$; and $c_{ij} \ge 0$ be given constants. If there are $m \times n$ matrices

$$F_\alpha = [f_{ij\alpha}] \quad \text{and} \quad F_\beta = [f_{ij\beta}] \tag{6.289}$$

satisfying

$$\sum_{j=1}^n f_{ij\alpha} \ge a_i, \quad \sum_{i=1}^m f_{ij\alpha} \le b_j', \quad 0 \le f_{ij\alpha} \le c_{ij} \tag{6.290a}$$

$$\sum_{j=1}^n f_{ij\beta} \le a_i', \quad \sum_{i=1}^m f_{ij\beta} \ge b_j, \quad 0 \le f_{ij\beta} \le c_{ij} \tag{6.290b}$$

then there is an $m \times n$ matrix $F = [f_{ij}]$ satisfying

$$a_i \le \sum_{j=1}^n f_{ij} \le a_i', \quad b_j \le \sum_{i=1}^m f_{ij} \le b_j', \quad 0 \le f_{ij} \le c_{ij} \tag{6.291}$$

In words, the theorem states that if there is a matrix meeting the lower bound requirements for the row sums and the upper bound requirements for the column sums, and if there is a matrix satisfying the upper bound requirements for the row sums and the lower bound requirements for the column sums, and, furthermore, if their elements are bounded above by specified numbers, then there is a matrix, whose row and column sums lie between designated limits and whose elements are bounded above by the specified numbers.

6.6   REALIZATION OF THE 1-MATRIX AND THE (1, 0)-MATRIX

In this section, we present a simple, direct n-stage algorithm for the construction of a 1-matrix satisfying the row and column constraints (6.233) in the case where the problem is feasible. The algorithm was first given by Gale (1957).

Let $\{a_i \,|\, i = 1, 2, \ldots, m\}$ and $\{b_j \,|\, j = 1, 2, \ldots, n\}$ be two sequences of nonnegative integers, where $b_1 \ge b_2 \ge \cdots \ge b_n$. Suppose that the conditions

$$\sum_{j=1}^k a_j^* \ge \sum_{j=1}^k b_j, \quad k = 1, 2, \ldots, n \tag{6.292}$$

are satisfied. The following algorithm either constructs a solution or shows that the problem is infeasible.

The 1-matrix algorithm

Select any column p and assign b_p ones to the rows a_{i_t} $(t = 1, 2, \ldots, b_p)$ having the largest row sum bounds. Repeat the procedure in the reduced problem by taking $\hat{a}_i$ $(i = 1, 2, \ldots, m)$ and $\hat{b}_j$ $(j = 1, 2, \ldots, n - 1)$ to be the new upper and lower bounds on row and column sums, so that

$$\hat{a}_i = \begin{cases} a_i - 1, & i \in \{i_1, i_2, \ldots, i_{b_p}\} \\ a_i, & \text{otherwise} \end{cases} \tag{6.293a}$$

$$\hat{b}_j = \begin{cases} b_j, & j = 1, 2, \ldots, p - 1 \\ b_{j+1}, & j = p, p + 1, \ldots, n - 1 \end{cases} \tag{6.293b}$$

To verify, we appeal to Corollary 6.11. The reduced problem is feasible if and only if

$$\sum_{j=1}^{k} \hat{a}_j^* \geq \sum_{j=1}^{k} \hat{b}_j, \qquad k = 1, 2, \ldots, n - 1 \tag{6.294}$$

where $\{\hat{a}_j^*\} = \{\hat{a}_j\}^*$ is the dual sequence of $\{\hat{a}_j\}$. Using the symbol defined in (6.102), the left-hand side of (6.294) can be rewritten as

$$\sum_{j=1}^{k} \hat{a}_j^* = a_{k+1}^*(I) - b_p + \sum_{j=1}^{k} a_j^* \tag{6.295}$$

where $I = \{a_{i_1}, a_{i_2}, \ldots, a_{i_{b_p}}\}$. As a result, the feasibility conditions (6.294) for the reduced problem become

$$a_{k+1}^*(I) + \sum_{j=1}^{k} a_j^* \geq b_p + \sum_{j=1}^{k} b_j, \qquad k = 1, 2, \ldots, p - 1 \tag{6.296a}$$

$$a_{k+1}^*(I) + \sum_{j=1}^{k} a_j^* \geq \sum_{j=1}^{k+1} b_j, \qquad k = p, p + 1, \ldots, n - 1 \tag{6.296b}$$

Since by choice a_{i_t} $(t = 1, 2, \ldots, b_p)$ correspond to the b_p largest a_i, we have

$$a_{k+1}^*(I) = \min\left[b_p, a_{k+1}^*\right] \tag{6.297}$$

showing that conditions (6.296) always hold under the constraints (6.292); for if $k < p$ and $\min\left[b_p, a_{k+1}^*\right] = b_p$, (6.296a) becomes

$$\sum_{j=1}^{k} a_j^* \geq \sum_{j=1}^{k} b_j \tag{6.298}$$

and if $k < p$ and min $[b_p, a_{k+1}^*] = a_{k+1}^*$, (6.296a) can be written as

$$\sum_{j=1}^{k+1} a_j^* \geq b_p + \sum_{j=1}^{k} b_j \tag{6.299}$$

which is valid since from (6.292)

$$\sum_{j=1}^{k+1} a_j^* \geq b_{k+1} + \sum_{j=1}^{k} b_j \geq b_p + \sum_{j=1}^{k} b_j \tag{6.300}$$

The last inequality follows from the fact that for $b_1 \geq b_2 \geq \cdots \geq b_n$, $b_{k+1} \geq b_p$ for $p \geq k + 1$. If, on the other hand, $k \geq p$ and min $[b_p, a_{k+1}^*] = b_p$, (6.296b) reduces to

$$\sum_{j=1}^{k} a_j^* \geq \sum_{\substack{j=1 \\ j \neq p}}^{k+1} b_j \tag{6.301}$$

which is again valid since from (6.292)

$$\sum_{j=1}^{k} a_j^* \geq \sum_{j=1}^{k} b_j = b_p + \sum_{\substack{j=1 \\ j \neq p}}^{k} b_j \geq b_{k+1} + \sum_{\substack{j=1 \\ j \neq p}}^{k} b_j \tag{6.302}$$

and if $k \geq p$ and min $[b_p, a_{k+1}^*] = a_{k+1}^*$, (6.296b) becomes

$$\sum_{j=1}^{k+1} a_j^* \geq \sum_{j=1}^{k+1} b_j \tag{6.303}$$

Thus, the algorithm constructs a desired 1-matrix.

Example 6.19

Suppose that we wish to construct a 1-matrix W, whose row sums are bounded above by 4, 3, 2, 2, 1 and whose column sums are bounded below by 4, 3, 3, 2. Thus we have

$$\{a_i\} = \{4, 3, 2, 2, 1\} \tag{6.304a}$$

$$\{b_j\} = \{4, 3, 3, 2\} \tag{6.304b}$$

$$\{a_i^*\} = \{5, 4, 2, 1\} \tag{6.304c}$$

where $m = 5$ and $n = 4$. The problem is feasible since from (6.234)

$$5 \geqq 4 \qquad (6.305a)$$

$$5 + 4 = 9 \geqq 4 + 3 = 7 \qquad (6.305b)$$

$$5 + 4 + 2 = 11 \geqq 4 + 3 + 3 = 10 \qquad (6.305c)$$

$$5 + 4 + 2 + 1 = 12 \geqq 4 + 3 + 3 + 2 = 12 \qquad (6.305d)$$

For $b_1 = 4$, the transpose of the first column of W is found to be

$$[1 \quad 1 \quad 1 \quad 1 \quad 0] \qquad (6.306)$$

Next, consider the reduced problem having the sequences

$$\{a_i\} = [3, 2, 1, 1, 1] \qquad (6.307a)$$

$$\{b_j\} = \{3, 3, 2\} \qquad (6.307b)$$

For $b_1 = 3$, the transpose of the second column of W is given by

$$[1 \quad 1 \quad 1 \quad 0 \quad 0] \qquad (6.308)$$

Now, consider the new sequences $\{2, 1, 0, 1, 1\}$ and $\{3, 2\}$ for the reduced problem. The transpose of the third column of W becomes

$$[1 \quad 1 \quad 0 \quad 1 \quad 0] \qquad (6.309)$$

The next sequences are $\{1, 0, 0, 0, 1\}$ and $\{2\}$. They generate the transpose of the last column of W as

$$[1 \quad 0 \quad 0 \quad 0 \quad 1] \qquad (6.310)$$

The desired matrix becomes

$$W = \begin{array}{c} \\ 4 \\ 3 \\ 2 \\ 2 \\ 1 \end{array} \begin{array}{cccc} 4 & 3 & 3 & 2 \\ \begin{bmatrix} 1 & 1 & 1 & 1 \\ 1 & 1 & 1 & 0 \\ 1 & 1 & 0 & 0 \\ 1 & 0 & 1 & 0 \\ 0 & 0 & 0 & 1 \end{bmatrix} \end{array} \qquad (6.311)$$

We remark that since the sum of the elements of the a_i sequence equals that of the b_j sequence, the problem becomes that of filling a 5×4

matrix with zeros and ones so that the ith row sum is a_i and the jth column sum is b_j.

Instead of looking for a 1-matrix, suppose that we wish to construct a symmetric $(1, 0)$-matrix having prescribed row and column sums. This problem is equivalent to the realization of a $(1, 0)$-graph having preassigned degrees of its nodes. A direct n-stage algorithm for its construction is available, and was first described by Havel (1955) and Hakimi (1962).

THEOREM 6.14

Let $\{a_i\}$ be a sequence of n nonnegative integers, where $a_1 \geq a_2 \geq \cdots \geq a_n$ and $n \geq 2$. Then there is a symmetric $(1, 0)$-matrix, the ith row or column sum of which is a_i, if and only if $n - 1 \geq a_1$ and the reduced sequence

$$\{a_2 - 1, a_3 - 1, \ldots, a_{a_1+1} - 1, a_{a_1+2}, \ldots, a_n\} \qquad (6.312)$$

is feasible, i.e. there is a symmetric $(1, 0)$-matrix, whose row sums or column sums are prescribed as in (6.312).

Observe that if there is a symmetric $(1, 0)$-matrix W of order n, there are at most $n - 1$ ones in any row or column and a_1 cannot exceed $n - 1$. Thus, by deleting the row and column corresponding to a_1, the row sums and the column sums of the resulting matrix are those given in (6.312). By reversing the process, an iterative algorithm is obtained. Theorem 6.14 also establishes the existence of a $(1, 0)$-graph with prescribed degrees of its nodes. A formal proof of Theorem 6.14 can be found in Hakimi (1962) or Chen (1976); only an informal justification was described above.

Example 6.20

Determine if there is a symmetric $(1, 0)$-matrix of order 5 having prescribed row and column sums 4, 4, 3, 3, and 2.

According to Theorem 6.14, the problem is feasible if and only if the reduced sequence

$$\{4 - 1, 3 - 1, 3 - 1, 2 - 1\} = \{3, 2, 2, 1\} \qquad (6.313)$$

is realizable. Applying Theorem 6.14 once more shows that the sequence (6.313) is realizable if and only if the new reduced sequence

$$\{2 - 1, 2 - 1, 1 - 1\} = \{1, 1, 0\} \qquad (6.314)$$

is realizable. A symmetric $(1, 0)$-matrix satisfying (6.314) can easily be

constructed and is given by .

$$\begin{bmatrix} 0 & 1 & 0 \\ 1 & 0 & 0 \\ 0 & 0 & 0 \end{bmatrix} \qquad (6.315)$$

To realize (6.313), we insert a row [0 1 1 1] and a corresponding column to the matrix of (6.315) and obtain

$$\begin{bmatrix} 0 & 1 & 1 & 1 \\ 1 & 0 & 1 & 0 \\ 1 & 1 & 0 & 0 \\ 1 & 0 & 0 & 0 \end{bmatrix} \qquad (6.316)$$

Finally, to construct a desired matrix, we insert a row [0 1 1 1 1] and a corresponding column to the matrix of (6.316) to yield

$$\begin{bmatrix} 0 & 1 & 1 & 1 & 1 \\ 1 & 0 & 1 & 1 & 1 \\ 1 & 1 & 0 & 1 & 0 \\ 1 & 1 & 1 & 0 & 0 \\ 1 & 1 & 0 & 0 & 0 \end{bmatrix} \qquad (6.317)$$

The associated (1, 0)-graph of the matrix of (6.317) is shown in Fig. 6.29. Thus, the algorithm can also be used to construct a (1, 0)-graph with prescribed degrees of its nodes if the problem is feasible.

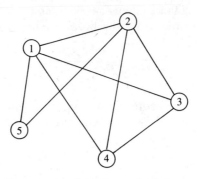

Fig. 6.29. The associated (1, 0)-graph of the matrix (6.317).

6.7 MINIMAL TRANSFORMATIONS

In Section 6.3, we indicated that any two (p, s)-digraphs having the same degree pairs are transformable into each other by a finite sequence of elementary (p, s) d-invariant transformations. Similar results can be stated for the (p, s)-matrices having the same row sums and column sums. In the present section, we shall determine the minimal number of such transformations or interchanges required to transform one into the other.

Let G_1 and G_2 be two (p, s)-digraphs in the set $\{G\}$ of all (p, s)-digraphs that are d-invariant from a given (p, s)-digraph G. We denote by $G_1 \oplus G_2$ the n-node directed graph obtained from G_1 and G_2 such that the arc (i, j) is in $G_1 \oplus G_2$ if and only if (i, j) is either in G_1 or in G_2 but not in both, where n is the number of nodes of G. We assume that the arcs of $G_1 \oplus G_2$ are properly distinguished or labeled so that we can distinguish the arcs of G_1 from those of G_2. Accordingly, we shall write $(i, j)_1$ if (i, j) is an arc in $G_1 \oplus G_2$ but not in G_2, and write $(i, j)_2$ if (i, j) is an arc in $G_1 \oplus G_2$ but not in G_1.

DEFINITION 6.17

Alternating Edge Train. An *alternating edge train* in $G_1 \oplus G_2$ is an edge train in which the arcs along the edge train belong alternately to G_1 and G_2 and in which if we reverse the directions of those arcs in G_1 (or G_2) we obtain a directed arc train.

Thus, a closed alternating edge train and, in particular, an alternating circuit can be meaningfully defined only when it is of even length. As an example, consider the $(2, 0)$-digraphs G_1 and G_2 of Figs. 6.30 and 6.31, respectively. The directed graph $G_1 \oplus G_2$ is shown in Fig. 6.32 with the arcs of G_1 being denoted by the solid lines and the arcs of G_2 denoted by the

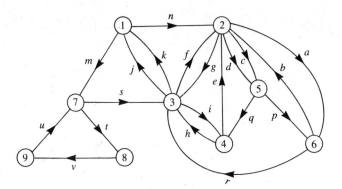

Fig. 6.30. A $(2, 0)$-digraph G_1.

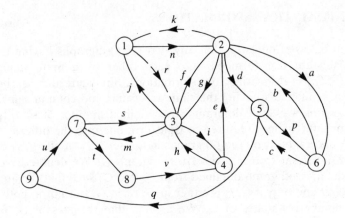

Fig. 6.31. A $(2, 0)$-digraph G_2.

dashed lines. Two closed alternating edge trains of $G_1 \oplus G_2$ are given by

$$(1, 7)(3, 7)(3, 1)(2, 1)(2, 5)(6, 5)(6, 3)(1, 3) \qquad (6.318a)$$

$$(5, 9)(8, 9)(8, 4)(5, 4) \qquad (6.318b)$$

However, the closed edge train

$$(3, 7)(6, 3)(6, 5)(2, 5)(2, 1)(1, 7) \qquad (6.319)$$

is not a closed alternating edge train because if we replace the arcs $(6, 3)$, $(2, 5)$ and $(1, 7)$ by the arcs $(3, 6)$, $(5, 2)$ and $(7, 1)$, respectively, in the edge train, the resulting graph is not a directed arc train.

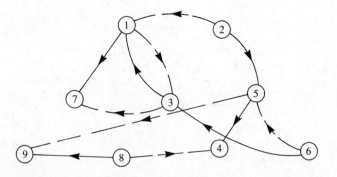

Fig. 6.32. The ring sum $G_1 \oplus G_2$ of the $(2, 0)$-digraphs G_1 and G_2.

DEFINITION 6.18

Distance. The *distance* between two n-node (p, s)-digraphs G_1 and G_2 in $\{G\}$ is defined to be the number

$$\frac{1}{2}\left[\sum_{i=1}^{n}\sum_{j=1}^{n}\left| |(i, j)_1| - |(i, j)_2| \right|\right] \tag{6.320}$$

where $(i, j)_1$ and $(i, j)_2$ denote the arcs from node i to node j in G_1 and G_2, respectively.

In words, the distance between the two digraphs G_1 and G_2 is the number of arcs in one but not in the other. For example, the distance between the two $(2, 0)$-digraphs G_1 and G_2 of Figs. 6.30 and 6.31 is 6, the number of arcs in G_1 not belonging to G_2, or vice versa.

We remark that in all the discussion in this section, we have implicitly assumed that all the elements in $\{G\}$ are labeled (p, s)-digraphs. We consider two (p, s)-digraphs G_1 and G_2 of $\{G\}$ as being identical when they are isomorphic, and they are denoted by $G_1 = G_2$. Thus, if $G_1 = G_2$, $G_1 \oplus G_2$ need not be null. For example, consider the two directed circuits

$$L_1 = (1, 2)(2, 3)(3, 4)(4, 1) \tag{6.321a}$$

$$L_2 = (1, 4)(4, 3)(3, 2)(2, 1) \tag{6.321b}$$

Clearly, $L_1 = L_2$ and L_1 and L_2 are d-invariant $(1, 0)$-digraphs. However, $L_1 \oplus L_2$ is not the null graph. This brings out an important point in that two elements of $\{G\}$ are transformable into each other by a finite sequence of elementary (p, s) d-invariant transformations only within isomorphism. Two isomorphic (p, s)-digraphs may not be transformable into each other by these transformations. Two directed circuits of length 3, oriented in the opposite directions, are two such $(1, 0)$-digraphs, one of which cannot be transformed into the other by a finite sequence of elementary $(1, 0)$ d-invariant transformations. Another such example is shown in Fig. 6.33, where the two $(1, 0)$-digraphs are isomorphic. Thus, we have to define precisely what we mean by the minimal number of such transformations required to transform elements of $\{G\}$ into each other.

Let G_α and G_β be two elements of $\{G\}$. The minimal number of elementary (p, s) d-invariant transformations required to transform G_α into G_β is defined as the minimal number of elementary (p, s) d-invariant transformations which, when they are applied to G_α, will result in a (p, s)-digraph G'_α such that $G'_\alpha \oplus G_\beta = \varnothing$, the null graph. In the following, we shall determine the minimal number of such transformations. The main difficulty in establishing the lower bound is that the application of one such

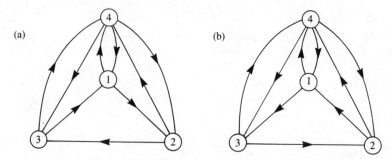

Fig. 6.33. Two $(1, 0)$-digraphs which cannot be transformed into each other by any finite sequence of elementary $(1, 0)$ d-invariant transformations.

transformation may result in a (p, s)-digraph that contains arcs neither in G_α nor in G_β.

LEMMA 6.1

If $G_\alpha \oplus G_\beta$ is not null, then $G_\alpha \oplus G_\beta$ can be decomposed into an arc-disjoint union of closed alternating edge trains of even length greater than 3.

Proof. Without loss of generality, let $(i_1, i_2)_\alpha$ be an arc of $G_\alpha \oplus G_\beta$ in G_α. Since the incoming degree of i_2 is the same in both G_α and G_β, there is a node i_3, $i_3 \neq i_1$, such that $(i_3, i_2)_\beta$ is an arc of $G_\alpha \oplus G_\beta$ in G_β. The same argument can now be applied to i_3 and generates an arc $(i_3, i_4)_\alpha$ of $G_\alpha \oplus G_\beta$ in G_α. Since $G_\alpha \oplus G_\beta$ contains a finite number of arcs, the process can be repeated indefinitely only by returning to the arc $(i_1, i_2)_\alpha$. Thus, for some positive integer k, $k \geq 2$, there exists a sequence of nodes

$$i_1, i_2, \ldots, i_{2k-1}, i_{2k}, i_1 \qquad (6.322a)$$

such that

$$L_1 = (i_1, i_2)_\alpha (i_3, i_2)_\beta (i_3, i_4)_\alpha \ldots (i_{2k-1}, i_{2k})_\alpha (i_1, i_{2k})_\beta \qquad (6.322b)$$

is a closed alternating edge train L_1 in $G_\alpha \oplus G_\beta$. Note that not all the nodes in $(6.322a)$ are necessarily distinct. If $(G_\alpha \oplus G_\beta) - L_1$ is not null, the same argument may be employed to generate a closed alternating edge train of length ≥ 4 because $(G_\alpha \oplus G_\beta) - L_1$ possesses the same property as that of $G_\alpha \oplus G_\beta$. By repeated application of this procedure, we see that $G_\alpha \oplus G_\beta$ can be decomposed into an arc-disjoint union of closed alternating edge trains of even length ≥ 4. This completes the proof of the lemma.

LEMMA 6.2

Let L be a closed alternating edge train of length $2k$, $k \geq 2$, in $G_\alpha \oplus G_\beta$. If $s \neq 0$, then there exists a sequence of $(k-1)$ elementary (p, s) d-invariant transformations involving the arcs of L only which will transform G_α into G_γ so that the distance between G_β and G_γ is k shorter than that between G_β and G_α.

Proof. Clearly, $p \neq 0$; for otherwise $G_\alpha \oplus G_\beta$ is null. Without loss of generality, let us assume that L is of the type

$$L = (i_1, i_2)_\alpha (i_3, i_2)_\beta \ldots (i_{2k-1}, i_{2k})_\alpha (i_1, i_{2k})_\beta \qquad (6.323)$$

We shall prove the lemma by induction over k. For $k = 2$ we have

$$(i_1, i_2)_\alpha (i_3, i_2)_\beta (i_3, i_4)_\alpha (i_1, i_4)_\beta \qquad (6.324)$$

Hence, an elementary (p, s) d-invariant transformation of replacing the arcs (i_1, i_2) and (i_3, i_4) of G_α by the arcs (i_3, i_2) and (i_1, i_4) would result in a (p, s)-digraph in $\{G\}$ which is of distance two closer to G_β than G_α. Thus, there exists such a transformation. Assume that the assertion is true for any L which is of length $2q$, $q < k$. We show that it is also true for k, $k \geq 3$. To facilitate our discussion, two cases are distinguished.

Case 1

In G_α, $|(i_1, i_4)| < p$ for $i_1 \neq i_4$ or $|(i_1, i_4)| < s$ for $i_1 = i_4$. Then the operation of replacing the arcs (i_1, i_2) and (i_3, i_4) in G_α by the arcs (i_3, i_2) and (i_1, i_4) is an elementary (p, s) d-invariant transformation and would result in a (p, s)-digraph G'_α that is of distance at least one closer to G_β than G_α. Consider the closed alternating edge train

$$L' = (i_1, i_4)_\alpha (i_5, i_4)_\beta \ldots (i_{2k-1}, i_{2k})_\alpha (i_1, i_{2k})_\beta \qquad (6.325)$$

in $G'_\alpha \oplus G_\beta$ where the index α now indicates the arcs of G'_α in $G'_\alpha \oplus G_\beta$. Since L' is of length $2(k-1)$, by induction hypothesis there is a sequence of $(k-2)$ elementary (p, s) d-invariant transformations involving the arcs of L' only which will transform G'_α into G_γ. Thus, G_α can be transformed into G_γ by a sequence of $(k-1)$ elementary (p, s) d-invariant transformations involving the arcs of L only.

Case 2

In G_α, $|(i_1, i_4)| = p$ for $i_1 \neq i_4$ or $|(i_1, i_4)| = s$ for $i_1 = i_4$. If $(i_1, i_4)_\alpha$ is in $G_\alpha \oplus G_\beta$, then L' in (6.325) is a closed alternating edge train in $G_\alpha \oplus G_\beta$, which is of length $(2k-2)$. By induction hypothesis, there is a sequence of $(k - 2)$ elementary (p, s) d-invariant transformations involving the arcs of L' only which will transform G_α into G_α'' such that the distance between G_α'' and G_β is $(k - 1)$ shorter than that between G_α and G_β. Since (i_1, i_4) is not in G_α'', an elementary (p, s) d-invariant transformation of replacing the arcs (i_3, i_4) and (i_1, i_2) in G_α'' by the arcs (i_3, i_2) and (i_1, i_4) will transform G_α'' into G_γ, which is k closer to G_β than G_α. If $(i_1, i_4)_\alpha$ is not in $G_\alpha \oplus G_\beta$, then (i_1, i_4) must be in both G_α and G_β. Let G^* be the directed graph obtained from $G_\alpha \oplus G_\beta$ by adding the arcs $(i_1, i_4)_\alpha$ and $(i_1, i_4)_\beta$. Then L' in (6.325) is again a closed alternating edge train in G^*. Thus, by induction hypothesis, there is a sequence of $(k - 2)$ elementary (p, s) d-invariant transformations involving the arcs of L' only which will transform G_α into $G_{\alpha 1}$ such that the distance between $G_{\alpha 1}$ and G_β is $(k - 2)$ shorter than that between G_α and G_β. Since (i_1, i_4) is not in $G_{\alpha 1}$, an elementary (p, s) d-invariant transformation of replacing the arcs (i_1, i_2) and (i_3, i_4) in $G_{\alpha 1}$ by the arcs (i_1, i_4) and (i_3, i_2) will transform $G_{\alpha 1}$ into G_γ, which is k closer to G_β than G_α. Note that the last transformation will shorten the distance between $G_{\alpha 1}$ and G_β by 2. This concludes the proof of the lemma.

LEMMA 6.3

In $G_\alpha \oplus G_\beta$ let L be a closed alternating edge train of length $2k$, $k \geqq 2$, based on at least four distinct nodes. Then there is sequence of $(k - 1)$ elementary (p, s) d-invariant transformations involving the arcs of L only which will transform G_α into G_γ such that the distance between G_β and G_γ is k shorter than that between G_β and G_α.

Proof. Without loss of generality, assume that the nodes i_1, i_2, i_3 and i_4 are distinct nodes of L. Following a similar argument as given in the proof of Lemma 6.2, we arrive at the desired result.

With these preliminaries, we now state the main result of this section.

THEOREM 6.15

Let G_α and G_β be two d-invariant (p, s)-digraphs with $s \neq 0$. Then G_α can be transformed into G_β by a sequence of

$$\tfrac{1}{2} E(G_\alpha \oplus G_\beta) - C(G_\alpha \oplus G_\beta) \tag{6.326}$$

and no fewer elementary (p, s) d-invariant transformations, where $E(G_\alpha \oplus G_\beta)$ denotes the number of arcs in $G_\alpha \oplus G_\beta$, and $C(G_\alpha \oplus G_\beta)$ is the maximum number of arc-disjoint closed alternating edge trains in $G_\alpha \oplus G_\beta$.

Proof. Assume that $G_\alpha \oplus G_\beta \neq \emptyset$; for if not we are finished. From Lemma 6.1, $G_\alpha \oplus G_\beta$ can be decomposed into an arc-disjoint union of a maximum number of closed alternating edge trains L_x, $x = 1, 2, \ldots, C(G_\alpha \oplus G_\beta)$, of length $2k_x$, $k_x \geq 2$. By Lemma 6.2, G_α can be transformed into G_β by a sequence of

$$\sum_{x=1}^{C} (k_x - 1) = \tfrac{1}{2} \sum_{x=1}^{C} 2k_x - \sum_{x=1}^{C} 1$$

$$= \tfrac{1}{2} E(G_\alpha \oplus G_\beta) - C(G_\alpha \oplus G_\beta) \qquad (6.327)$$

where $C = C(G_\alpha \oplus G_\beta)$, elementary (p, s) d-invariant transformations. Thus, the existence of such a sequence is assured.

To show that no fewer than this number is possible, we must prove that the number of transformations in any sequence which transforms G_α into G_β is no less than that given in (6.326). From Theorem 6.6 and Lemmas 6.1–6.3, we see that there is a minimal sequence of (p, s)-digraphs $G_0, G_1, \ldots, G_k$ in $\{G\}$ such that $G_\alpha \oplus G_0 = \emptyset$, $G_\beta \oplus G_k = \emptyset$ and $G_i \oplus G_{i-1}$ is a closed alternating edge train of length 4 for $i = 1, 2, \ldots, k$, each of which corresponds to an elementary (p, s) d-invariant transformation. Now, we shall establish the lower bound by induction over k. For $k = 1$, we have

$$\tfrac{1}{2} E(G_\alpha \oplus G_\beta) - C(G_\alpha \oplus G_\beta) = 2 - 1 = 1 \qquad (6.328)$$

Thus, (6.327) is a lower bound for $k = 1$. Assume that the assertion is true for any $k - 1$, $k \geq 2$. We show that it is also true for any k.

It can be shown that

$$G_\alpha \oplus G_\beta = \bigoplus_{i=1}^{k} (G_i \oplus G_{i-1}) \qquad (6.329)$$

Let $q(G_i \oplus G_{i-1})$ be the number of arcs of $G_i \oplus G_{i-1}$ which are also contained in $G_\alpha \oplus G_\beta$. Then there is a $G_i \oplus G_{i-1}$ for which $q(G_i \oplus G_{i-1}) \geq 3$; for otherwise we would have

$$E(G_\alpha \oplus G_\beta) \leq \sum_{i=1}^{k} q(G_i \oplus G_{i-1}) \leq 2k \qquad (6.330)$$

which, in conjunction with (6.327), would imply that k is not the minimal number of transformations required to transform G_α into G_β, a contradiction. To facilitate our discussion, two cases are distinguished.

Case 1

There exists a $G_j \oplus G_{j-1}$, $1 \leq j \leq k$, for which $q(G_j \oplus G_{j-1}) = 4$. Let

$$G_j \oplus G_{j-1} = (i_1, i_2)_\alpha (i_3, i_2)_\beta (i_3, i_4)_\alpha (i_1, i_4)_\beta \qquad (6.331)$$

Let

$$G'_\alpha = G_\alpha - (i_1, i_2)(i_3, i_4) \qquad (6.332a)$$

$$G'_\beta = G_\beta - (i_3, i_2)(i_1, i_4) \qquad (6.332b)$$

Then G'_α and G'_β are d-invariant (p, s)-digraphs, and

$$G'_\alpha \oplus G'_\beta = \bigoplus_{\substack{i=1 \\ i \neq j}}^{k} (G_i \oplus G_{i-1}) \qquad (6.333)$$

Since G'_α can be transformed into G'_β by a sequence of $(k-1)$ elementary (p, s) d-invariant transformations, by induction hypothesis we have

$$k - 1 \geq \tfrac{1}{2} E(G'_\alpha \oplus G'_\beta) - C(G'_\alpha \oplus G'_\beta) \qquad (6.334)$$

because the right-hand side of (6.334) is the minimal number of transformations required from G'_α to G'_β. Since $G_\alpha \oplus G_\beta$ is the arc-disjoint union of $G'_\alpha \oplus G'_\beta$ and $G_j \oplus G_{j-1}$, it follows that

$$C(G_\alpha \oplus G_\beta) \geq C(G'_\alpha \oplus G'_\beta) + 1 \qquad (6.335a)$$

$$E(G_\alpha \oplus G_\beta) = E(G'_\alpha \oplus G'_\beta) + 4 \qquad (6.335b)$$

Combining (6.334) and (6.335) yields

$$k \geq \tfrac{1}{2} E(G_\alpha \oplus G_\beta) - C(G'_\alpha \oplus G'_\beta) - 1$$
$$\geq \tfrac{1}{2} E(G_\alpha \oplus G_\beta) - C(G_\alpha \oplus G_\beta) \qquad (6.336)$$

Case 2

There exists a $G_j \oplus G_{j-1}$, $1 \leq j \leq k$, for which $q(G_j \oplus G_{j-1}) = 3$. Without loss of generality, we may assume that

$$G_j \oplus G_{j-1} = (i_1, i_2)_\alpha (i_3, i_2)_\beta (i_3, i_4)_\alpha (i_1, i_4) \qquad (6.337)$$

where (i_1, i_4) is an arc which is not contained in $G_\alpha \oplus G_\beta$. Two subcases are considered. *Subcase 1.* (i_1, i_4) is in both G_α and G_β. Again we form

G'_α and G'_β as in (6.332). Then we have (6.333). Let

$$G'_\alpha \oplus G'_\beta = \bigoplus_{x=1}^{C'} L_x \qquad (6.338)$$

be a decomposition of $G'_\alpha \oplus G'_\beta$ into an arc-disjoint union of a maximum number of closed alternating edge trains L_x, where $C' = C(G'_\alpha \oplus G'_\beta)$. We remark that L_x should be formally defined as a spanning subgraph of $G'_\alpha \oplus G'_\beta$ containing a closed alternating edge train, but the present usage is sufficient for our purposes. Let L_i be the closed alternating edge train in (6.338) which contains the arc $(i_1, i_4)_\alpha$. Then $L_i \oplus (G_j \oplus G_{j-1})$ is also a closed alternating edge train. Since

$$G_\alpha \oplus G_\beta = L_i \oplus (G_j \oplus G_{j-1}) \oplus \bigoplus_{\substack{x=1 \\ x \neq i}}^{C'} L_x \qquad (6.339)$$

it follows that

$$C(G_\alpha \oplus G_\beta) \geq C(G'_\alpha \oplus G'_\beta) \qquad (6.340)$$

Also we have

$$E(G_\alpha \oplus G_\beta) = E(G'_\alpha \oplus G'_\beta) + 2 \qquad (6.341)$$

Since from (6.333) G'_α can be transformed into G'_β by a sequence of $(k-1)$ elementary (p, s) d-invariant transformations, by induction hypothesis we have (6.334). Combining (6.334), (6.340) and (6.341) shows that (6.336) remains valid in this case. *Subcase 2.* (i_1, i_4) is neither in G_α nor in G_β. Let

$$G'_\alpha = G_\alpha \cup (i_1, i_4) - (i_1, i_2)(i_3, i_4) \qquad (6.342a)$$

$$G'_\beta = G_\beta - (i_3, i_2) \qquad (6.342b)$$

Clearly, G'_α and G'_β are d-invariant (p, s)-digraphs, and we have (6.333) and (6.334). Following an argument similar to that of Subcase 1, we obtain (6.340) and (6.341) and finally (6.336). Thus, (6.326) is also a lower bound required to transform G_α and G_β into each other. This completes the proof of the theorem.

We illustrate the above results by the following example.

Example 6.21

Consider the two $(2, 1)$-digraphs G_α and G_β of Figs. 6.30 and 6.31, respectively. We wish to determine the minimal number of $(2, 1)$

d-invariant transformations required to transform G_α into G_β or vice versa.

To this end, we first construct the directed graph $G_\alpha \oplus G_\beta$ and the result is shown in Fig. 6.32. Since $G_\alpha \oplus G_\beta$ can at most be decomposed into two closed alternating edge trains

$$L_1 = (1, 7)(3, 7)(3, 1)(2, 1)(2, 5)(6, 5)(6, 3)(1, 3) \qquad (6.343a)$$

$$L_2 = (5, 9)(8, 9)(8, 4)(5, 4) \qquad (6.343b)$$

we obtain

$$E(G_\alpha \oplus G_\beta) = 12, \qquad C(G_\alpha \oplus G_\beta) = 2 \qquad (6.344)$$

From Theorem 6.15, we conclude that G_α and G_β can be transformed into each other by a sequence of $\frac{1}{2} \times 12 - 2 = 4$ elementary $(2, 1)$ d-invariant transformations and no fewer than four such transformations are possible. One such sequence is shown below:

$(1, 7)$ and $(6, 3)$ by $(1, 3)$ and $(6, 7)$

$(3, 1)$ and $(6, 7)$ by $(3, 7)$ and $(6, 1)$

$(2, 5)$ and $(6, 1)$ by $(2, 1)$ and $(6, 5)$

$(5, 4)$ and $(8, 9)$ by $(5, 9)$ and $(8, 4)$

In fact, G_α and G_β are also the $(2, 0)$-digraphs. As a result, one can be transformed into the other by four elementary $(2, 0)$ d-invariant transformations.

As mentioned in Section 6.5, the existence of a (p, s)-digraph also establishes the existence of a class of matrices called the (p, s)-matrices. Two (p, s)-matrices are said to be *equivalent* if and only if they have the same row and column sums. Then we have the following corollary.

COROLLARY 6.17

Let $\{M\}$ be the set of (p, s)-matrices that are equivalent to a given (p, s)-matrix M. Then any two elements M_α and M_β of $\{M\}$ can be transformed into each other by a sequence of

$$\tfrac{1}{2}E(M_\alpha - M_\beta) - C(M_\alpha - M_\beta) \qquad (6.345)$$

and no fewer (p, s)-interchanges $[(p, 1)$-interchanges if $s = 0]$, where

$E(M_\alpha - M_\beta)$ denotes the sum of the absolute values of the integers in $M_\alpha - M_\beta$, and $C(M_\alpha - M_\beta)$ is the maximum number of closed alternating edge trains in $G_\alpha \oplus G_\beta$, G_α and G_β being the associated (p, s)-digraphs of M_α and M_β, respectively.

Clearly, the discussion on (p, s)-matrices can easily be extended to any matrix of bounded nonnegative integers with prescribed row and column sums by the addition of an appropriate number of rows or columns consisting only of zeros. For $p = s = 1$, (6.345) gives the minimal number of interchanges required to transform equivalent matrices of ones and zeros into each other, as given by Ryser (1957).

Finally, for (p, s)-graphs, Theorem 6.15 becomes Corollary 6.18.

COROLLARY 6.18

Let $\{G\}$ be the set of (p, s)-graphs that are d-invariant from a given (p, s)-graph G. Then any two elements G_α and G_β of $\{G\}$ can be transformed into each other by a sequence of

$$\tfrac{1}{2}E(G_\alpha \oplus G_\beta) - C(G_\alpha \oplus G_\beta) \qquad (6.346)$$

and no fewer elementary (p, s) d-invariant transformations.

We remark that in Corollary 6.18, the requirement that s be nonzero has been dropped. In Figs. 6.30 and 6.31 if we remove all the orientations or directions of the edges, we obtain two $(2, 0)$-graphs G_α and G_β. The corresponding $G_\alpha \oplus G_\beta$ is shown in Fig. 6.32, again with all orientations removed. Thus, from Corollary 6.18 we conclude that G_α and G_β can be transformed into each other by a sequence of four elementary $(2, 0)$ d-invariant transformations and no fewer than four are possible.

Before we conclude this chapter, we justify an earlier assertion (Theorem 6.6) that any two (p, s)-digraphs G_1 and G_2 of $\{G\}$ can be transformed into each other by a finite sequence of elementary (p, s) d-invariant transformations.

Let $\{G_1\}$ be the set of all (p, s)-digraphs into which G_1 is transformable by finite sequences of elementary (p, s) d-invariant transformations, and let $\{G_2\}$ be the corresponding set arising from G_2. Let G_1' and G_2' be the elements of $\{G_1\}$ and $\{G_2\}$, respectively, such that the distance between them is the minimum distance between the (p, s)-digraphs in $\{G_1\}$ and $\{G_2\}$. If G_1' and G_2' are of zero distance or if $G_1' = G_2'$, we are finished. If $p = 0$ then all the elements of $\{G\}$ are isomorphic. So let us assume that $p \neq 0$, $G_1 \neq G_2$ and G_1 and G_2 contain no isolated nodes and are of positive distance.

Since $G'_1 \oplus G'_2 \neq \emptyset$, there is a closed alternating edge train L of length $2k$, $k \geqq 2$. If $s \neq 0$ or if L is based on at least four distinct nodes, then by Lemmas 6.2 and 6.3 there is a (p, s)-digraph G''_1 in $\{G_1\}$ which is closer to G'_2 than G'_1, violating our assumption on the minimality of the distance between G'_1 and G'_2. Thus, $s = 0$ and any closed alternating edge train L of $G'_1 \oplus G'_2$ is based on exactly three distinct nodes. In other words, $G'_1 \oplus G'_2$ consists of a set of node-disjoint closed alternating edge trains, each of which is based on exactly three distinct nodes. Without loss of generality, let L be one such edge train based on the distinct nodes i_1, i_2 and i_3. Thus, L is composed of at least two directed circuits of length 3 oriented in opposite directions. If in G'_1 or G'_2 there exists a node j, which is distinct from i_x ($x = 1, 2, 3$), such that, say, (i_1, j) or (j, i_1) is in G'_1 or G'_2 and $|(i_y, j)| < p$ or $|(j, i_y)| < p$ for $y = 2$ or 3, then an elementary $(p, 0)$ d-invariant transformation involving the nodes i_1, i_2, i_3 and j would yield a $(p, 0)$-digraph G_3 in $\{G_1\}$ or $\{G_2\}$ such that the distance between G_3 and G'_2 or G_3 and G'_1 is the same as that between G'_1 and G'_2. Furthermore, in $G_3 \oplus G'_2$ or $G_3 \oplus G'_1$ there exists a closed alternating edge train based on at least four distinct nodes, so that by Lemma 6.3 our assumption on the minimality of the distance between G'_1 and G'_2 is violated. Thus, in G'_1 or G'_2 either $|(i_x, j)| = p$ or $|(j, i_x)| = p$ or no such node j exists. In either case, G'_1 and G'_2 would be isomorphic, again a contradiction. So the assertion is justified.

As a result, for any G_α and G_β in $\{G\}$ there is a sequence of (p, s)-digraphs $G_x, x = 1, 2, \ldots, k$, in $\{G\}$, such that

$$G_\alpha = G_1, G_2, \ldots, G_k = G_\beta \tag{6.347}$$

in which G_i and G_{i+1} are related by an elementary (p, s) d-invariant transformation for $i = 1, 2, \ldots, k-1$.

6.8 SUMMARY AND SUGGESTED READING

We began this chapter by considering the subgraph problem of a directed graph. We applied the flow theorems to generalize Ore's results by presenting criteria for the existence of (p, s) subgraphs with preassigned bounds for their outgoing and incoming degrees. A special case of the problem is to find the necessary and sufficient conditions for the existence of a directed graph with prescribed outgoing and incoming degrees. In general, these conditions consists of $2^n - 1$ inequalities, n being the number of nodes of the directed graphs. However, they can be reduced to a set of n inequalities if the elements are properly ordered. In the cases of 1-digraphs and $(1, 0)$-digraphs, the conditions can be stated in terms of the dual sequence and the modified dual sequence. More specifically, a sequence of nonnegative integer pairs $[a_i, b_i]$ with monotone b_i is $(1, 1)$ digraphic if and only if the sum of a_i equals that of b_i and the partial sums of the b_i sequence are dominated by the corresponding partial sums of the dual sequence of the a_i sequence. Likewise, with proper ordering of the elements of a_i and b_i, the sequence is $(1, 0)$ digraphic if and only if the sum of a_i equals that of b_i and the partial sums of the b_i sequence are dominated by the corresponding partial sums of the modified dual sequence of the a_i sequence.

By introducing the notions of a symmetric (p, s)-digraph and an elementary (p, s) d-invariant transformation, we showed that the criteria for the existence of a (p, s) subgraph with prescribed outgoing and incoming degrees in a given graph satisfying the odd-circuit condition can be deduced from those for the directed graphs. In particular, we discussed the realizability conditions of a sequence of n nonnegative integers to be the degree sequence of a $(p, 0)$-graph. As in the case for directed graphs, these conditions consist of $2^n - 1$ inequalities. They can be reduced to a set of n inequalities if the sequence is monotone. We showed that a monotone sequence is $(1, 0)$ graphical if and only if the partial sums of the sequence are dominated by those of its modified dual sequence.

The existence of a (p, s)-digraph having prescribed bounds for its outgoing and incoming degrees also establishes the existence of a class of matrices known as the (p, s)-matrices. We demonstrated that arithmetic conditions for the existence of such a (p, s)-matrix can be deduced from those for directed graphs. In the case where the sum of the lower bounds equals that of the upper bounds, the problem becomes one of filling a matrix with the prescribed row sums and column sums. We also gave a more general theorem which states that if there is a matrix meeting the lower bound requirements for the row sums and the upper bound requirements for the column sums, and if there is a matrix satisfying the upper bounds for the row sums and the lower bounds for the column sums, then there is a matrix whose row and column sums lie between the designated limits. In addition, all elements are bounded above by specified numbers.

Simple direct n-stage algorithms were presented for the construction of the 1-matrix and the $(1, 0)$-matrix having preassigned bounds for their row sums and column sums. In the case where the sum of the lower bounds equals that of the upper bounds, the algorithms construct a desired matrix having prescribed row sums and column sums.

Finally, we showed that any two (p, s)-digraphs having the same degree pairs are transformable into each other by a finite sequence of elementary (p, s) d-invariant transformations. Similar results can be stated for (p, s)-matrices having the same row sums and column sums using the (p, s)-interchanges. Formulas for determining the minimal number of such transformations or interchanges required to convert one into the other were given.

For further study on the various aspects of the problems discussed in this chapter, the reader is referred to the original papers of Gale (1957), Ryser (1957), Fulkerson (1960) and Chen (1966, 1971, 1973, 1980). For other standard books on the subject matters, we refer to Ford and Fulkerson (1962) and Chen (1976).

REFERENCES

Bauer, D. (1980), "Line-graphical degree sequences," *J. Graph Theory*, vol. 4, pp. 219–232.

Berge, C. (1962), *Theory of Graphs and its Applications*, London, England: Methuen.

Chen, W. K. (1966), "On the realization of a (p, s)-digraph with prescribed degrees," *J. Franklin Inst.*, vol. 281, pp. 406–422.

Chen, W. K. (1971), "On d-invariant transformations of (p, s)-digraphs," *J. Franklin Inst.*, vol. 291, pp. 89–100.

Chen, W. K. (1973), "On equivalence of realizability conditions of a degree sequence," *IEEE Trans. Circuit Theory*, vol. CT-20, pp. 260–262.

Chen, W. K. (1976), *Applied Graph Theory: Graphs and Electrical Networks*, Amsterdam, The Netherlands: North-Holland, 2nd revised edition.

Chen, W. K. (1980), "Subgraphs and their degree sequences of a digraph," *J. Franklin Inst.*, vol. 310, pp. 349–363.

Eggleton, R. B. and Holton, D. A. (1979), "Graphic sequences," in *Combinatorial Mathematics IV*, Lecture Notes in Mathematics, vol. 748, pp. 1–10, New York: Springer.

Erdös, P. and Gallai, T. (1960), "Gráfok elöirt fokú pontokkal," *Mat. Lapok*, vol. 11, pp. 264–274.

Ford, L. R. Jr and Fulkerson, D. R. (1962), *Flows in Networks*, Princeton, N.J.: Princeton University Press.

Fulkerson, D. R. (1959), "A network-flow feasibility theorem and combinatorial applications," *Can. J. Math.*, vol. 11, pp. 440–451.

Fulkerson, D. R. (1960), "Zero–one matrices with zero trace," *Pacific J. Math.*, vol. 10, pp. 831–836.

Fulkerson, D. R., Hoffman, A. J. and McAndrew, M. H. (1965), "Some properties of graphs with multiple edges," *Can. J. Math.*, vol. 17, pp. 166–177.

Fulkerson, D. R. and Ryser, H. J. (1961), "Widths and heights of (0, 1)-matrices," *Can. J. Math.*, vol. 13, pp. 239–255.

Gale, D. (1957), "A theorem on flows in networks," *Pacific J. Math.*, vol. 7, pp. 1073–1082.

Gallai, T. (1950), "On factorization of graphs," *Acta Math. Acad. Sci. Hungar.*, vol. 1, pp. 133–153.

Haber, R. M. (1960), "Term rank of 0, 1 matrices," *Rend. Sem. Mat. Univ. Padova*, vol. 30, pp. 24–51.

Hakimi, S. L. (1962), "On realizability of a set of integers as degrees of the vertices of a linear graph I," *J. Soc. Indust. Appl. Math.*, vol. 10, pp. 496–506.

Hakimi, S. L. and Schmeichel, E. F. (1978), "Graphs and their degree sequences: A survey," in *Theory and Applications of Graphs*, Lecture Notes in Mathematics, vol. 642, pp. 225–235, New York: Springer.

Hall, P., (1935), "On representatives of subsets," *J. Lond. Math. Soc.*, vol. 10, pp. 26–30.

Havel, V. (1955), "Poznámka o existenci konečných grafù," *Časopis Pěst. Mat.*, vol. 80, pp. 477–480.

König, D. (1950), *Theorie der endlichen und unendlichen Graphen*, New York: Chelsea.

Lan, J. L. and Chen, W. K. (1985), "On f-factors of a graph," *J. Franklin Inst.*, vol. 320, pp. 55–62.

Lovász, L. (1970), "Subgraphs with prescribed valencies," *J. Combinatorial Theory, Series B*, vol. 8, pp. 391–416.

Lovász, L. (1974), "Valencies of graphs with 1-factors," *Periodica Math. Hungar.*, vol. 5, pp. 149–151.

Mahmoodian, E. (1977), "On factors of a graph," *Can. J. Math.*, vol. 29, pp. 438–440.

Ore, O. (1956*a*), "Studies in directed graphs I," *Ann. Math.*, vol. 63, pp. 383–406.

Ore, O. (1956*b*), "Studies in directed graphs II," *Ann. Math.*, vol. 64, pp. 142–153.

Ore, O. (1957), "Graphs and subgraphs I," *Trans. Amer. Math. Soc.*, vol. 84, pp. 109–136.

Ore, O. (1958*a*), "Conditions for subgraphs of directed graphs," *J. de Math.*, vol. 37, pp. 321–328.

Ore, O. (1958*b*), "Studies in directed graphs III," *Ann. Math.*, vol. 68, pp. 526–549.

Ore, O. (1959), "Graphs and subgraphs II," *Trans. Amer. Math. Soc.*, vol. 93, pp. 185–204.

Rado, R. (1949), "Factorization of even graphs," *Quart. J. Math.*, vol. 20, pp. 95–104.

Ryser, H. J. (1957), "Combinatorial properties of matrices of zeros and ones," *Can. J. Math.*, vol. 9, pp. 371–377.

Ryser, H. J. (1958), "The term rank of a matrix," *Can. J. Math.*, vol. 10, pp. 57–65.

Ryser, H. J. (1960*a*), "Traces of matrices of zeros and ones," *Can. J. Math.*, vol. 12, pp. 463–476.

Ryser, H. J. (1960*b*), "Matrices of zeros and ones," *Bull. Amer. Math. Soc.*, vol. 66, pp. 442–464.

Senior, J. K. (1951), "Partitions and their representative graphs," *Amer. J. Math.*, vol. 73, pp. 663–689.

Tutte, W. T. (1947), "The factorization of linear graphs," *J. Lond. Math. Soc.*, vol. 22, pp. 107–111.

Tutte, W. T. (1952), "The factors of graphs," *Can. J. Math.*, vol. 4, pp. 314–328.

Tutte, W. T. (1953), "The 1-factors of oriented graphs," *Proc. Amer. Math. Soc.*, vol. 4, pp. 922–931.

Tutte, W. T. (1954), "A short proof of the factor theorem for finite graphs," *Can. J. Math.*, vol. 6, pp. 347–352.

Tutte, W. T. (1974), "Spanning subgraphs with specified valencies," *Discrete Math.*, vol. 9, pp. 97–108.

INDEX

(1,0)-matrix, realization, 463, 467
0-cell, 1
0-simplex, 1
1-matrix, realization, 463, 464
1-matrix algorithm, 464
1-simplex, 1
2-isomorphic graph, 48
2-isomorphism, 48

Abstract directed graph, 74
Abstract graph, 1
Acyclic directed graph, 92
Adjacent node, 3
Advance of preflow, 224, 225
Algebra of the residue class modulo 2, 52
   addition, 52
   multiplication, 52
Algorithm:
   blocking flow, 205
   Borůvka, 254, 255
   Dijkstra, 103
   Dinic, 220
   Edmonds–Karp, 216
   feasible circulation, 357, 358
   Floyd–Warshall, 146
   Ford–Fulkerson, 130, 184
   Ford–Moore-Bellman, 113
   Gomory–Hu, 280
   Karzanov, 223, 225
   Kruskal, 259
   matrix, 139

   maximum tree, 252
   minimum tree, 252
   MPM, 205, 206
   1-matrix, 464
   Prim, 261, 262
   proof of Gomory-Hu, 290
   round robin, 266
   shortest directed path, 103, 113, 122, 130, 139, 146
   variants of the Ford–Fulkerson, 215, 216, 220, 221
   Yen, 122
Alternating edge train, 469
Arc, 1, 74, 387
   basic, 146
   circuit, 77
   closed, 224
   directed, 75
   flow in net with lower bound on, 366
   flowless, 179
   forward, 179
   length, 100
   noncircuit, 77
   open, 224
   oriented, 75
   outgoing, 75
   parallel, 75, 387
   reverse, 179
   saturated, 179
   special, 193
   useful, 197

Arc capacity, 167, 390
  irrational, 192
  residual, 192
Arc flow, 168
Arc length, 100, 216
Arc sequence, 77
  directed, 78
  length, 77
Arc train, 77
  directed, 78
Articulation point, 15
Associated (p,s)-digraph, 449
Associated (p,s)-matrix, 449
Associated undirected graph, 76
Augmentation routine, 185
Augmenting path, flow, 180

Backward process, 144
Balanced node, 224
Balance of preflow, 224, 225
Basic arc, 146
Basis circuit matrix, 61, 83
Basis cut matrix, 66, 87
Basis incidence matrix, 55, 82
Bipartite graph, 14, 17
  complete, 25
  directed, 92
Block, 16, 77, 123
Blocked node, 226
Blocking flow, 201
Blocking flow algorithm, 205
Blue rule, 252
Bordering node, 261
Borůvka algorithm, 254, 255
Branch, 1, 55, 77, 241
Breadth-first search, 216

Capacitated net:
  feasible flow in node-and-arc, 372
  flow in node-and-arc, 231
Capacity, 167, 173, 373, 390
  arc, 167, 390
  irrational arc, 192
  node, 231, 373
  residual, 192
  terminal, 266
Capacity function, 168, 329, 390
Capacity of a generalized disconnecting set, 373
Capacity matrix, terminal, 266, 267
Chord, 58, 77, 242
Circuit, 7, 8, 77
  directed, 79, 99
  f-, 59, 83, 242
  fundamental, 59, 83, 242

length, 7
length of a directed, 99
negative directed, 99
orientation of an f-, 83
oriented, 82
Circuit arc, 77
Circuit-edge incidence matrix, 58
Circuit matrix, 57, 58, 83, 93
  basis, 61, 83
  complete, 61
  f-, 59, 83
  fundamental, 59, 83
Circuit rank, 8
Circulation, feasible, 345, 384
Circulation algorithm, feasible, 357, 358
Circulation theorem, 345, 384
Closed arc, 224
Closed directed-arc sequence, 78
Closed edge sequence, 7
Coincident orientation, 82, 85
Color invariance, 253
Combinatorial dual graph, 38
Common edge, 248
Communication net, 240
  directed, 308
  oriented, 308
  synthesis of an optimum undirected, 293
Complementary subgraph, 4, 75
Complete bipartite graph, 25
  order, 25
Complete circuit matrix, 61
Complete directed graph, 92
  order, 92
Complete graph, 25
  order, 25
Complete incidence matrix, 55
Component, 8, 77
  exterior, 29
  interior, 30
  strong, 80
  strongly connected, 80
Condensed net, 276
Conditional distance, 131
Connected directed graph, 77
Connected graph, 8
Connection, 1, 7, 77
Connection matrix, 140
Connectivity, 9
Conservation equation, 168
Constraint:
  feasible, 319, 383
  infeasible, 319, 383
Contraction, graph, 35
Corresponding subsets, 414

Cotree, 58, 77, 242
Cut, 64, 171
  incidence, 64
  minimum s-t, 173
  oriented, 85
  s-t, 170, 172
    capacity, 173
Cut-edge incidence matrix, 65
Cut matrix, 63, 65, 86
  basis, 66, 87
Cut orientation, 85
Cutpoint, 15, 77
Cutset, 63, 64, 170
  f-, 67, 87
  fundamental, 67, 87
  minimum s-t, 173
  s-t, 171
    capacity, 173
Cutset matrix:
  f-, 67, 87
  fundamental, 67, 87
Cut-tree, 281
Cycle, 8
Cycle rank, 9
Cyclomatic number, 9

Decomposition, 16, 153
Degree, 9, 387
  incoming, 387
  negative, 387
  outgoing, 387
  positive, 387
Degree pair, 387
Demand, 319, 373
Demand function, 319, 329, 373
Depth-first search, 220
Difference, symmetric, 10, 11
Difference of sets, 10, 11
Digraph, 74
  p-, 389
  (p,s)-, 388
Digraphic realization, 413, 414, 441
Digraphic sequence, 413
  (p,s), 413, 414
Dijkstra algorithm, 103
Dinic algorithm, 220
d-invariance, 434
Directed arc, 75
Directed-arc sequence, 78
  closed, 78
  length, 78
  open, 78
Directed-arc train, 78
Directed bipartite graph, 92

Directed circuit, 79, 99
  length, 79, 99
  length of a negative, 99
  negative, 99
Directed communication net, 308
Directed edge, 74, 75
Directed edge train:
  length, 99
  shortest, 99
Directed graph, 74, 93, 386, 387
  abstract, 74
  acyclic, 92
  bipartite, 92
  complete, 92
  connected, 77
  isomorphic, 77
  matrix associated with, 81
  nonseparable, 77
  planar, 77
  regular, 408
  separable, 77
  strongly connected, 79
  subgraph problem, 386
  symmetric, 91
Directed network, 99
Directed path, 78, 373
  length, 78, 100
  multiterminal shortest, 139
  shortest, 99, 100
Directed path algorithm, shortest, 103
Directed path between node sets, 373
Disconnecting set, generalized, 373
Distance, conditional, 131
Distance matrix, 140
Distance of nodes, 100, 244, 471
Distance of (p,s)-digraphs, 471
Distance of trees, 244
Dominant flow net, 303
Dominant flow realization, 303
Dominant requirement, 296
Dominant requirement tree, 294
Dual:
  combinatorial, 38
  geometric, 36
Dual graph, 36, 47
  combinatorial, 38
  geometric, 36
Dual sequence, 424
  modified, 427
Duality, 47

Edge, 1
  common, 248
  directed, 74

Edge (*Continued*)
  parallel, 2
  removal, 10
  shorting an, 13
  subdivision, 26
  successive, 7
Edge-disjoint subgraph, 3
Edge incidence, 75
Edge length, 246, 247
Edge removal, 10
Edge sequence, 6
  closed, 7
  endpoints, 7
  initial node, 7
  internal nodes, 7
  length, 6
  open, 7
  terminal node, 7
Edge subdivision, 26
Edge train, 7
  alternating, 469
  length of a directed, 99
  shortest directed, 99
Edmonds–Karp algorithm, 216
Element, 1
Elementary *d*-invariant transformation, 435
Elementary (*p,s*) *d*-invariant transformation,
    434, 435
  minimum number, 471
Elementary tree transformation, 245
Endpoint, 2, 7, 74
Enumeration of shortest directed paths, 153
Equivalency, flow, 270
Equivalent net, flow, 270
Equivalent (*p-s*) matrices, 478
Euler formula, 20
Extended supply–demand theorem, 335, 336,
    339
Exterior of a circuit, 29
Exterior component, 29

f-circuit, 59, 83, 242
  orientation, 82, 83
f-circuit matrix, 59, 83
f-cutset, 67, 87
f-cutset matrix, 67, 87
Feasibility theorem, 318
Feasible circulation, 345, 384
Feasible circulation algorithm, 357, 358
Feasible constraint, 319, 383
Feasible flow, 366
Feasible flow in node-and-arc capacitated net,
    372
Feasible flow pattern, 168, 318

Feasible net, 293
Finite graph, 2
First Betti number, 9
Flow, 167, 168
  blocking, 201
  feasible, 366
  maximum, 168, 177
  minimum, 369
Flow algorithm, blocking, 205
Flow augmenting path, 180
Flow conservation equation, 168
Flow equivalency, 270
Flow equivalent net, 270
Flow-equivalent tree, synthesis, 275
Flow function, 168
Flowless arc, 179
Flow net, dominant, 303
Flow in net with lower bound on arc, 366
Flow in node-and-arc capacitated net, 231
  feasible, 372
Flow pattern, 168
  feasible, 168, 318
  value, 168
Flow potential, 206
Flow problem, simultaneous maximum, 240
Flow realization, dominant, 303
Flow in undirected and mixed net, 229
Flow value, 168
Floyd–Warshall algorithm, 146
Forbidden subgraph, 26
Ford–Fulkerson algorithm, 130, 184
  variants, 215, 216, 220, 221
Ford–Moore–Bellman algorithm, 113
Forest, 241, 243
Forward arc, 179
Forward process, 143
Four-tuple net representation, 413
Function:
  capacity, 168, 329, 390
  demand, 319, 329, 373
  flow, 168
  length, 100, 246
  requirement, 293
  supply, 319, 329, 373
Fundamental circuit, 59, 83, 242
Fundamental circuit matrix, 59, 83
Fundamental cutset, 67, 87
Fundamental cutset matrix, 67, 87

Generalized disconnecting set, 373
  capacity, 373
Geometric diagram, 1
Geometric dual graph, 36
Geometric graph, 2

Gomory–Hu algorithm, 280
  proof, 290
Gomory–Hu realization procedure, 297
Graph, 1, 6, 433
  abstract, 1
  abstract directed, 74
  acyclic directed, 92
  associated undirected, 76
  bipartite, 14, 17
  complete, 25
  complete bipartite, 25
  complete directed, 92
  connected, 8
  directed, 74, 93, 386, 387
  directed bipartite, 92
  dual, 36
  finite, 2
  geometric, 2
  geometric dual, 36
  homeomorphic, 28
  infinite, 2
  intersection, 11
  isomorphic, 4, 77
  labeled, 6
  linear, 1
  matrix associated with, 52
  matrix associated with a directed, 81
  nonseparable, 14, 15, 77
  null, 3
  operation on, 10
  p-, 433
  (p,s)-, 433
  Petersen, 34
  planar, 18, 77, 93
  requirement, 293
  separable, 15, 77
  subgraph problem, 432
  subgraph problem of a directed, 386
  sum, 11
  symmetric directed, 91
  2-isomorphic, 48
  weighted, 6
Graph contraction, 35
Graph decomposition, 16, 153
Graphical sequence, 441
  (p,s), 441
Graph isomorphism, 4, 77
Graph operation, 10
  triple, 147
Greedy method, 252

Height of a layered net, 201
Homeomorphic graph, 28
Homeomorphism, 28

Incidence, 1, 75
Incidence cut, 64
Incidence matrix, 53, 81
  basis, 55, 82
  circuit-edge, 58
  complete, 55
  cut-edge, 65
  node-edge, 53
Incoming degree, 387
Induced subgraph, 14
Infeasible constraint, 319, 383
Infinite graph, 2
In-flow potential, 206
Initial node, 7, 74, 78, 387
Inner piece, 30
Integrity theorem, 191, 192
Interchange, (p,s)-, 450
Interior of a circuit, 30
Interior component, 30
Intermediate node, 168
Internal node, 7
Interrelations of graph matrices, 70, 89
Intersection graph, 11
Intersection of sets, 10, 11
Into matching, 411
Invariance, color, 253
Irrational arc capacity, 192
Isolated node, 3, 243
Isomorphic graph, 4, 77
Isomorphism, 4, 77

Junction, 1

Karzanov algorithm, 223, 225
Kruskal algorithm, 259

Label:
  permanent, 103
  temporary, 103
Labeled graph, 6
Labeled node, 103, 184, 357
Labeling routine, 185
Labeling rules, 367
Layer, 197
  unbalanced, 224
Layered net, 197
Layered residue net, 217
Length, 99, 100, 246, 247
Length of an arc, 100
Length of an arc sequence, 77
Length of a circuit, 7
Length of a directed-arc sequence, 78
Length of a directed circuit, 79, 99
Length of a directed edge train, 99

Length of a directed path, 78, 100, 216
Length of an edge, 246
Length of an edge sequence, 6
Length function, 100, 264
Length of a path, 7, 216
Length of a tree, 247
Line, 1
Linear graph, 1
Linear tree, 279
Link, 58, 242
Loop, 8

Major submatrix, 56
Mapping, 18
Matching in a directed graph, 411
Matrices, interrelationships among graph, 70, 89
Matrix:
  basis circuit, 61, 83
  basis cut, 66, 87
  basis incidence, 55, 82
  circuit, 57, 58, 83, 93
  circuit-edge incidence, 58
  complete circuit, 61
  complete incidence, 55
  connection, 140
  cut, 63, 65, 86
  cut-edge incidence, 65
  distance, 140
  f-circuit, 59, 83
  f-cutset, 67, 87
  fundamental circuit, 59, 83
  fundamental cutset, 67, 87
  incidence, 53, 81
  interrelationships among graph, 70, 89
  node-edge incidence, 53
  node-to-datum path, 71, 72, 89
  p-, 449
  (p,s), 449
  principally partitionable, 271
  requirement, 293
  semi-principally partitionable, 309
  terminal capacity, 266, 267
Matrix algorithm, 139
Matrix associated with a directed graph, 81
Matrix associated with a graph, 52
Max-flow min-cut theorem, 177, 178
Maximum flow, 168, 177
Maximum flow problem, simultaneous, 240
Maximum tree, 246, 247
Maximum tree algorithm, 252
Mesh, 19
  outside, 23
Minaddition operation, 140
Minimal property, 171

Minimal transformation, 469, 471
Minimum flow, 369
Minimum s-t cut, 173
Minimum s-t cutset, 173
Minimum tree, 240, 246, 247
Minimum tree algorithm, 252
Mixed and undirected net, flow in, 229
Modified dual sequence, 427
MPM algorithm, 205, 206
Multiterminal shortest directed path, 139

Negative degree, 387
Negative directed circuit, 99
Neighboring node, 3
Net, 99
  capacitated, 167
  communication, 240
  condensed, 276
  directed communication, 308
  dominant flow, 303
  feasible, 293
  feasible flow in node-and-arc capacitated, 372
  flow equivalent, 270
  flow in node-and-arc capacitated, 231
  flow in undirected and mixed, 229
  layered, 197
  layered residue, 217
  oriented communication, 308
  residue, 216
  synthesis of an optimum undirected
    communication, 293
  undirected, 246
Net with lower bound on arc, flow in, 366
Network:
  capacitated, 167
  directed, 99
n-factor, 408
Node, 1, 74
  adjacent, 3
  balanced, 224
  blocked, 226
  bordering, 261
  initial, 7, 74, 78, 387
  intermediate, 168
  internal, 7
  isolated, 3, 243
  labeled, 103, 184, 357
  neighboring, 3
  reference, 55, 82
  removal, 10
  scanned, 184, 357
  sink, 168
  source, 102, 168
  terminal, 7, 74, 78, 387

unbalanced, 224
unlabeled, 184, 357
unscanned, 184, 357
Node-and-arc capacitated net:
  feasible flow in, 372
  flow in, 231
Node capacity, 231, 373
Node degree, 9
Node-disjoint subgraphs, 3
Node-edge incidence matrix, 53
Node label, 103
Node removal, 10
Node-to-datum path matrix, 71, 72, 89
Noncircuit arc, 77
Nonseparable directed graph, 77
Nonseparable graph, 14, 15, 77
Null graph, 3
Nullity, 8, 75

Odd-circuit condition, 436, 438
Onto matching, 411
Open arc, 224
Open directed-arc sequence, 78
Open edge sequence, 7
Operation on graph, 10
Opposite orientations, 82, 85
Optimum undirected communication net, synthesis, 293
Ordered pair, 74
Orientation of a cut, 85
Orientation of an f-circuit, 83
Oriented arc, 75
Oriented circuit, 82
Oriented communication net, 308
Oriented cut, 85
Outer piece, 29
Out-flow potential, 206
Outgoing arc, 75
Outgoing degree, 387
Outside mesh, 23
Outside region, 19

(p,s)-digraph, 388
  associated, 449
(p,s) digraphic realization, 414
(p,s) digraphic sequence, 413, 414
(p,s) digraphs, distance, 471
(p,s)-graph, 433
(p,s) graphical realization, 441
(p,s) graphical sequence, 441
(p,s)-interchange, 450
(p,s)-matrix, 449
  associated, 449
  equivalent, 478

(p,s) subgraph, symmetric, 433
Parallel arc, 75, 387
Parallel edge, 2
Partition:
  principal, 271
  semi-principal, 309
Path, 7, 77
  directed, 78, 373
  flow augmenting, 180
  multiterminal shortest directed, 139
  shortest directed, 100
Path of arc length, 216
Path length, 7, 216
  directed, 78, 216
Path matrix, node-to-datum, 71, 72, 89
p-digraph, 389
Petersen graph, 34
p-graph, 433
Phase, 201, 217
Piece:
  inner, 30
  outer, 29
Planar graph, 18, 77, 93
  circuit matrix, 93
p-matrix, 449
Point, 1
  articulation, 15
Positive degree, 387
Potential:
  flow, 206
  in-flow, 206
  out-flow, 206
Preflow, 224
  advance, 224, 225
  balance, 224, 225
Prim algorithm, 261, 262
Principally partitionable matrix, 271
Principal partition, 271
Process:
  backward, 144
  forward, 143
Proof of the Gomory–Hu algorithm, 290
Proper subgraph, 2
  symmetric, 432

Quadruplet net representation, 168
Queue, 225
Quintuplet net representation, 345, 373

Rank, 8, 75
  circuit, 8
  cycle, 9

Realization:
  dominant flow, 303
  (p,s) digraphic, 414
  (p,s) graphical, 441
Realization of the 1-matrix, 463, 464
Realization of the (1,0)-matrix, 463, 467
Red rule, 253
Reference node, 55, 82
Region, 19
  outside, 19
Regular directed graph, 408
  degree, 408
Removal of an edge, 10
Removal of a node, 10
Requirement:
  dominant, 296
  uniform, 297
Requirement function, 293
Requirement graph, 293
Requirement matrix, 293
Requirement subtree, synthesis of a uniform, 299
Requirement tree:
  dominant, 294
  synthesis of a uniform, 299
Residual capacity, 192
Residue class modulo 2 algebra, 52
  addition, 52
  multiplication, 52
Residue net, 216
  layered, 217
Resultant main submatrix, 272, 309
Reverse arc, 179
Ring sum, 10, 11
Round robin algorithm, 266
Rule:
  blue, 252
  red, 253

Saturated arc, 179
Scanned node, 184, 357
Search:
  breadth-first, 216
  depth-first, 220
Sectional subgraph, 14, 75
Self-dual, 38
Self-loop, 2, 75, 389
Semi-principally partionable matrix, 309
Semi-principal partition, 309
Separable directed graph, 77
Separable graph, 15, 77
  decomposition of, 16
Separation, u-v, 30
Sequence:

digraphic, 413
dual, 424
graphical, 441
modified dual, 427
(p,s) digraphic, 413, 414
(p,s) graphical, 441
Set difference, 10, 11
Set intersection, 10, 11
Set ring sum, 10, 11
Set union, 10, 11
Shortest directed edge train, 99
Shortest directed path, 100
  multiterminal, 139
Shortest directed path algorithm, 103, 113, 122, 130, 139, 146
Shortest directed-path enumeration by decomposition, 153
Shorting an edge, 13
Simultaneous maximum flow problem, 240
Sink node, 168
Source node, 102, 168
Spanning subgraph, 3
Spanning tree, 241
Special arc, 193
Stack, 225
s-t cut, 170, 172, 173
  capacity, 172
  minimum, 173
s-t cutset, 170, 171, 173
  capacity, 173
  minimum, 173
Strong component, 80
Strongly connected component, 80
Strongly-connected directed graph, 79
Subdivision of an edge, 26
Subgraph, 2, 75
  complementary, 4, 75
  edge-disjoint, 3
  forbidden, 26
  induced, 14
  node-disjoint, 3
  proper, 2
  sectional, 14, 75
  spanning, 3
  symmetric (p,s), 433
Subgraph problem of a directed graph, 386
Subgraph problem of a graph, 432
Submatrix:
  major, 56
  resultant main, 272, 309
Subsets, corresponding, 414
Subtree, 241, 243
  synthesis of a uniform requirement, 299
Successive edge, 7

Sum graph, 11
Supply, 319, 373
Supply–demand theorem, 318
  extended, 335, 336, 339
  symmetric, 335, 336, 340, 384
Supply function, 319, 329, 373
Symmetric difference, 11
Symmetric directed graph, 91
Symmetric (p,s)-digraph, 432
Symmetric (p,s) subgraph, 433
Symmetric supply–demand theorem, 335, 336, 340, 384
Synthesis of a flow-equivalent tree, 275
Synthesis of an optimum undirected communication net, 293
Synthesis of a uniform requirement subtree, 299
Synthesis of a uniform requirement tree, 299

Terminal capacity, 266
Terminal capacity matrix, 266, 267
Terminal node, 7, 74, 78, 387
Terminating node, 75
Theorem:
  circulation, 345, 384
  extended supply–demand, 335, 336, 339
  feasibility, 318
  integrity, 191, 192
  max-flow min-cut, 177, 178
  supply–demand, 318
  symmetric supply–demand, 335, 336, 340, 384
Transformation:
  elementary d-invariant, 435
  elementary (p,s) d-invariant, 434, 435
  elementary tree, 245
  minimal, 469, 471
Tree, 55, 77, 241
  dominant requirement, 294

linear, 279
maximum, 246, 247
minimum, 240, 246, 247
spanning, 241
synthesis of a flow-equivalent, 275
synthesis of a uniform requirement, 299
Tree algorithm:
  maximum, 252
  minimum, 252
Tree length, 247
Tree transformation, elementary, 245
Triple operation, 147
Triplet net representation, 100

Unbalanced layer, 224
Unbalanced node, 224, 357
Undirected communication net, synthesis of an optimum, 293
Undirected graph, associated, 76
Undirected and mixed net, flow in, 229
Undirected net, 246
Uniform requirement, 297
Uniform requirement subtree, synthesis, 299
Uniform requirement tree, synthesis, 299
Unlabeled node, 184, 357
Unordered pair, 1
Unscanned node, 184, 357
Useful arc, 197
u-v separation, 30

Variants of the Ford–Fulkerson algorithm, 215, 216, 220, 221
Vertex, 1

Weighted graph, 6
Window, 19

Yen algorithm, 122